TRUMP AGAINST THE WORLD:
FOREIGN POLICY BULLY
RUSSIAN COLLUSION

TRUMP AGAINST THE WORLD:
FOREIGN POLICY BULLY
RUSSIAN COLLUSION

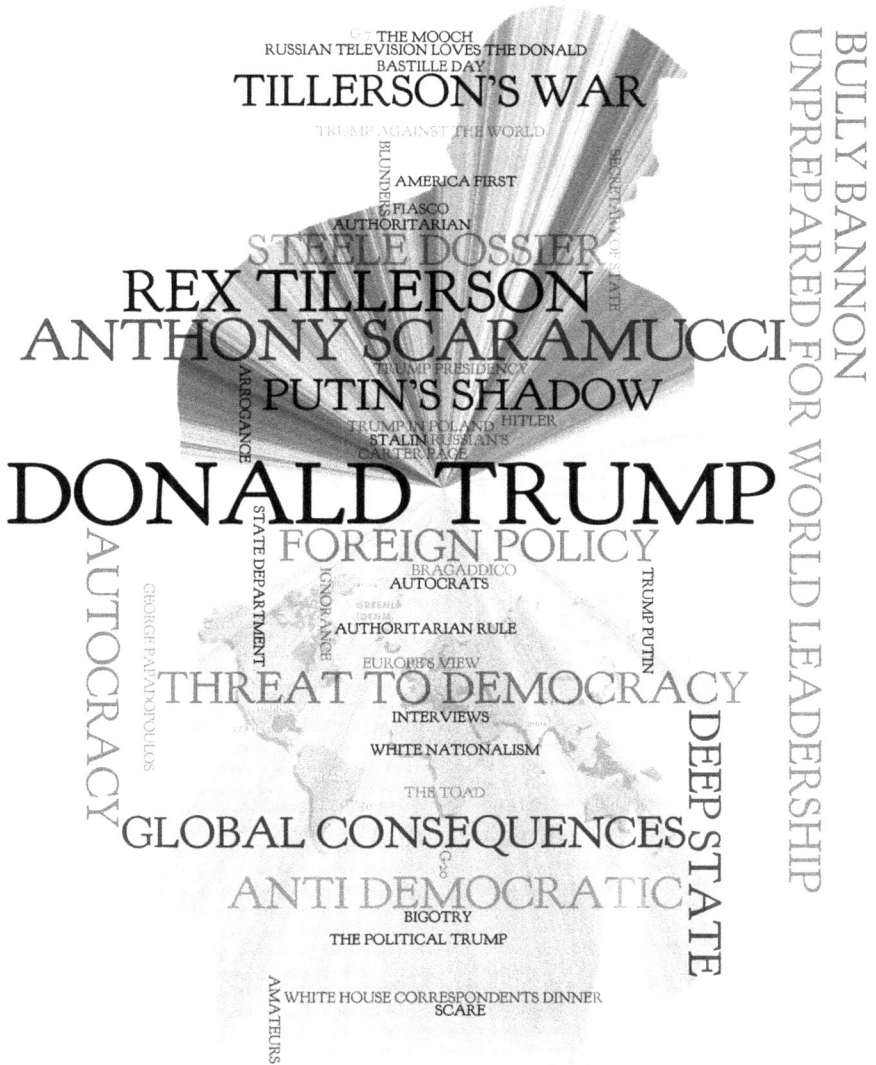

THE MOOCH
RUSSIAN TELEVISION LOVES THE DONALD
BASTILLE DAY

TILLERSON'S WAR

TRUMP AGAINST THE WORLD

BLUNDERS

AMERICA FIRST

FIASCO
AUTHORITARIAN

STEELE DOSSIER

REX TILLERSON

ANTHONY SCARAMUCCI

TRUMP PRESIDENCY

PUTIN'S SHADOW

ARROGANCE

TRUMP IN POLAND   HITLER
STALIN RUSSIAN'S
CARTER PAGE

DONALD TRUMP

STATE DEPARTMENT

FOREIGN POLICY

BRAGADDICO
AUTOCRATS

IGNORANCE

AUTHORITARIAN RULE

EUROPE'S VIEW

THREAT TO DEMOCRACY

INTERVIEWS

WHITE NATIONALISM

THE TOAD

GLOBAL CONSEQUENCES

ANTI DEMOCRATIC

BIGOTRY
THE POLITICAL TRUMP

WHITE HOUSE CORRESPONDENTS DINNER
SCARE

AMATEURS

AUTOCRACY

GEORGH PAPADOPOULOS

TRUMP PUTIN

DEEP STATE

BULLY BANNON
UNPREPARED FOR WORLD LEADERSHIP

ROCK N ROLL BOOKS BY HOWARD A. DEWITT

Searching For Sugar Man II: Rodriguez, Coming From Reality, Heroes & Villains (2017)

Searching For Sugar Man: Sixto Rodriguez' Mythical Climb To Rock N Roll Fame and Fortune (2015)

Van Morrison: Them and the Bang Era, 1945-1968 (2005)

Stranger In Town: The Musical Life of Del Shannon (with D. DeWitt (2001)

Sun Elvis: Presley In The 1950s (1993)

Paul McCartney: From Liverpool To Let It Be (1992)

Beatle Poems (1987)

The Beatles: Untold Tales (1985, 2nd edition 2001)

Chuck Berry: Rock 'N' Roll Music (1981, 2nd edition1985)

Van Morrison: The Mystic's Music (1983)

Jailhouse Rock: The Bootleg Records of Elvis Presley (with Lee Cotton) (1983)

HISTORY AND POLITICS

Sicily's Secrets: The Mafia, Pizza & Hating Rome (2017)

Meeting Hitler: A Tragicomedy (2016)

Obama's Detractors: In The Right Wing Nut House (2012)

The Road to Baghdad (2003)

A Blow To America's Heart: September 11, 2001, The View From England (2002)

Jose Rizal: Philippine Nationalist As Political Scientist (1997)

The Fragmented Dream: Multicultural California (1996)

The California Dream (1996)

Readings In California Civilization (1981, 4th edition revised 2004)

Violence In The Fields: California Filipino Farm Labor Unionization (1980)

California Civilization: An Interpretation (1979)

Anti Filipino Movements in California: A History, Bibliography and Study Guide (1976)

Images of Ethnic and Radical Violence in California Politics, 1917-1930: A Survey (1975)

NOVELS

Stone Murder: A Rock 'N' Roll Mystery (2012)

Salvador Dali Murder (2014)

SPORTS BOOKS

The Phoenix Suns: The View From Section 101 (2013)

Horizon Books
P. O. Box 4342
Scottsdale, AZ 85261-4342

E Mail: Howard217@aol.com

First Published 2018

ISBN-10: 069213932X
ISBN-13: 978-0-692-13932-5 (Horizon Books)
Library of Congress Control Number: 2018956079
CreateSpace Independent Publishing Platform
North Charleston, South Carolina

TRUMP AGAINST THE WORLD:
FOREIGN POLICY BULLY
RUSSIAN COLLUSION

By Howard A. Dewitt

HORIZON BOOKS
PO BOX 4342
SCOTTSDALE, AZ 85261

TABLE OF CONTENTS

INTRODUCTION

"The president's willingness to attack judges and federal investigators on Twitter, even if it raises the prospect of deepening his legal trouble."

TIMOTHY L. O'BRIEN

"We learn from history that we do not learn from history."

FRIEDRICH HEGEL

"My drawing is the direct and purest translation of my emotion."

HENRY MATISSE

"President Trump is not the first person at the highest level of government to own great quantities or real estate with the risk of massive conflict of interest."

PETER SCHWEIZER

"Trump is morally unfit to be president."

JAMES COMEY

Donald J. Trump sat in his private bedroom at his Mar-a-Logo estate with a massive cheeseburger on a small table with an enormous canopied bed with an ostentatious bedspread in a room that is a paean to bad taste. It was Sunday night. He was getting ready to watch Anderson Cooper's 60 Minutes interview with porn star Stormy Daniels. He looked at the silver domed warmer holding the cheeseburger. Nothing was better for the Donald than hanging out with his best friend—himself.

The television sets in his bedroom are Trump's only means of communication with the outside world. He is an outlier living with well-educated, cultured billionaires who resent his presence in Palm

Beach, Florida. He could care less. He is the president of the United State. Even he has trouble believing it.

How do the denizens of Palm Beach view Trump's Mar-a-Logo compound? In the 1990s when Trump purchased the property, the town council placed restrictions on Trump's weekend residence. He attacked the Palm Beach town council labeling them bigots. He instructed his lawyer to send every member of the town council two movies **A Gentleman's Agreement** and **Guess Who's Coming To Dinner**. Both movies deal with prejudice and racism. The irony of Trump calling out others for bigotry and racism infuriated everyone. The Palm Beach town council was angry. It was typical Trump. He would not abide by local government ordinances. His failure to follow Palm Beach's rules of conduct was a personality trait defining his entitled life.

Trump's continual differences with Palm Beach government provide insight into a difficult personality with an out of control ego. Locals refer to Trump as the "look at me ego." Trump got most of the restrictions lifted attacking the town council and accusing them of racism. The notion of Trump as an aggrieved party caused uproarious laughter at upscale cocktail parties. "It's all about the Trumpster," Laurel Baker said. She is the Executive Director of the Palm Beach Chamber of Commerce. She has remarked locals do not consider him "one of their own."

It is in this atmosphere the president may have watched a porn actress Stormy Daniels describe meeting him dressed in his pajamas for a private dinner. She alleged they had sex. His spokespeople said: "No." The Stormy Daniels story sadly defines American politics.

HOW STORMY DANIELS DEFINES AMERICAN POLITICS

On Sunday, March 25, 2018 porn actress Stormy Daniels appeared on 60 Minutes interviewed by Anderson Cooper. It was a show watched by more than twenty million Americans. It was a much ballyhooed ratings blockbuster for CBS. The actual content did little, if anything, to change the direction of American politics. Stormy whose real name is Stephanie Gregory Clifford is a thirty-nine year old porn icon on the downside of her career. She is married with two children. She is an equestrian performer owning two horses. Her net worth is estimated at more than three million dollars. She lives on a toney Texas ranch with her latest husband from the porn industry. She is bright. She is business minded. She is not a lunatic. Why the lawsuit? That is the million-dollar question.

Daniels claims she wants her life back. She wants to speak her mind. Her lawyer is not some fly by night hustler operating out of his car. Michael Avenatti is a brilliant litigator who has won more multi-million-dollar law suits than almost any legal beagle. Why is he taking the case? That is another unanswerable question. Did Trump have sex with Stormy Daniels? Was she paid for her silence a few days before the election? Was Trump behind paying the hush money?

Trump initially said: "No." His lawyer paid the money. Then Rudy Giuliani arrived as a White House attorney. He said Trump knew about the $130,000 payment. The next day Giuliani backtracked and said Michael Cohen paid the money because he was Trump's fixer. That was his job. Then the story changed again. It was revealed Trump began paying Cohen $35,000 a month for his legal work. He didn't specify the legal work. Daniels attorney wanted to find out the truth. Michael Avenatti was all over the media pointing out Cohen paid two more women hush money over sex with Donald J. Trump.

Then President Trump filed required paperwork on his spending for 2017, and there was the $130,000 payment for Daniels's hush money. The Office of Government Ethics, a U. S. federal agency created after the Watergate scandal, requires an annual accounting of Trump's personal finances. The report disclosed payments of between $100,001 and $250,000 to Michael Cohen for legal work. The conflicting accounts of the hush money were compounded by Giuliani's continual press gaffes.

As Avenatti filed a motion in federal court in California to depose Trump and his attorney Michael Cohen, the high stakes in the Stormy Daniels saga evolved. The questions Avenatti asked were: "Was Trump involved in the $130,000 hush payment?" Did any of this violate campaign finance law? Did Trump consent to the agreement?

Trump defenders said he would not be required to testify. The Daniels legal team disagreed. Avenatti cited a 1997 Supreme Court case involving President Bill Clinton. In the court's ruling they said a sitting president has no immunity from civil litigation. That sent

Trump scurrying to find new lawyers. Most top criminal defense lawyers declined to join his defense team.

"We expect to be placing the President and his fixer under oath in the coming months," Avenatti said. That comment is one Trump has not addressed. His attorney's allegedly threatened Daniels. Avenatti on CNN and MSNBC described an incident of an unknown person verbally threatening Daniels in a Las Vegas parking lot. **The New York Times**, in an op-ed editorial, weighed in with a column "All The President's Thugs." They retold the story of when she was threatened in Las Vegas by an unknown person who said: "That's a beautiful little girl. It'd be a shame if something happened to her mom." In fairness to Trump and his lawyers, this claim is unsubstantiated.

What is substantiated is there is a pattern of intimidation, threats and alleged collusion with mobsters within the Trump organization. Much of what has been written about Trump since his presidency is vile, bitter and hateful. The comments on his personal life, his programs and his leadership are not positive ones. He has not been treated fairly by CNN and MSNBC. Much of that is his fault. He continually attacks those who write critically about him. He refuses criticism. He also has a documented history of bullying. It goes back more than thirty years.

In 1982 Anthony Gliedman, a New York City Housing Commissioner, refused a twenty million dollar tax abatement request for the Trump Tower. The Donald threatened to fight back. He did. Gliedman said he was threatened by a Trump associate. Then in a strange twist he went to work at Trump Tower. This is a lifelong pattern where Trump puts someone out of business, destroys a public service career or ruins a reputation, and then he hires that person to work for the Trump organization.

In July 2015 the **Daily Beast** reported a book on Trump alleged that he raped his first wife during the divorce. The source for this story was Ivana Trump. This salacious revelation prompted Trump's lawyers to remark to the **Daily Beast** editor: "I will take you for every penny you still don't have." Later Michael Cohen said: "I will mess you up...." Stormy Daniels is not the first person to be threatened by someone within the Trump sphere.

Those who write about Trump are bullied, sued and defamed in the press. In the 1993 book **Lost Tycoon: The Many Lives of Donald J. Trump**, the allegation he raped Ivana caused Trump to file a lawsuit. The result? Harry Hurt III sold more books. The first printing of 30,000 sold out immediately. Trump held a grudge against Hurt's tell all book that became a bestseller. It was twenty-four years after Hurt's book was published when Trump found out he was playing golf at his West Palm Beach golf course with billionaire industrialist David Koch. Trump had Hurt kicked off the course. As Trump and Hurt met for a brief moment, the Donald said the author had written "shit about him." Hurt responded: "It was all true." Trump retorted. "Not the way you wrote it." This is an insight into the control mania that is central to Trump's unregulated personality.

BuzzFeed News in 2017 reported investors who lost a billion dollars in a Trump Casino received a phone call from a man calling himself Carmine. He said: "If you keep messing with Mr. Trump, we know where you live and we're going to your house...." The call was reported to the FBI. They traced it to a phone booth across from the Ed Sullivan Theater. That night Trump was a guest on the Late Night With David Letterman Show.

When Michael Wolff's **Fire And Fury: Inside The Trump White House** hit the number one slot on the **New York Times** best seller list, Trump not only disputed it, he attempted to prevent its publication. He wasn't successful.

STORMY DANIELS ATTORNEY'S EXPLAINS HER CASE
Michael Avenatti explained Stormy Daniels's case in a thirty-one-page document. It can be found on drop box. Here is the link:

https://www.dropbox.com/s/yqnwbycsnsamf6b/Memo%20of%20Points%20and%20Authorities.pdf?dl=0

This brief has a simple explanation. Trump paid Daniels hush money. He attempted to disengage from the lawsuit. His attorney said he paid the $130,000 hush money. Daniels was allegedly threatened, intimidated and made to believe her civil rights didn't exist. After all she was a porn star. But Daniels is a smart, resilient woman. Avenatti is an attack dog lawyer with a mild, controlled media friendly personality. Trump's in your face barrister attempted to intimidate Avenatti, who simply laughed at the Trump legal team.

Michael Avenatti made Trump's legal team look like amateurs. When they suggested Stormy Daniels could not be libeled because she is an adult film actress, Avenatti responded: "This is the demeaning approach to women that people should be outraged by." The case blew up when Cohen said Trump was unaware of the payment. Later the president recanted. In the aftermath of the Stormy Daniels case the president's attorney, Michael Cohen came under federal investigation. One of the supreme ironies of this incident is a porn star caused the president and his attorney problems. The subsequent bullying was the means of obscuring the real issue. The bullying began with Trump's inauguration. It has never ended. This is a new dimension in presidential power.

THE BULLY IS INAUUGURATED: TRUMP IS CONFUSED ABOUT BEING THE PRESIDENT

At Noon on January 20, 2017 Donald J. Trump placed his hand upon a Bible and swore he would to the best of his ability, preserve, protect and defend the United States. His Make America Great Again slogan and other comments radiated from his smiling face. He had other promises. He remarked he would "unite the country." He vowed to control Muslim extremists. He said of Muslim radicalism: "We will eradicate them completely from the fact of the earth….From this day forward, it's going to be America first." As Trump was inaugurated, the question of who advised him, how he viewed government, and the expectations for his presidency were serious concerns. He was on the lips of every American. In the conduct of foreign policy, he turned into an outlier and a bully. He was a president who had little, if any, respect for the established world order.

As Trump basked in the glow of his victory, Roger Ailes, who was recently forced out of Fox News, gloated. He created Trump's candidacy. Fox, under Ailes leadership, formed the conservative mold of disgruntled senior citizens, right wing Christians, blue collar workers and those who hated big government into a Trump coalition. In the background the outright racists who silently thought "there's a Negro in the White House" supported Trump. It was a sad time in

America. Bigots, racists, pro-gun nuts, anti-government zealots, white supremacists and Christian fundamentalists seized the Republican Party and the White House. Roger Ailes couldn't believe Donald J. Trump was the President of the United States. Ailes considered Trump "a fucking fool."

What were Trump's qualifications for the presidency? None! He seized the moment. He talked of "draining the swamp," building a wall to keep Mexican immigrants out and having Mexico pay for it. It was bluster. It was braggadocio. It was effective. American voters were sick of traditional politicians.

QUESTIONS OF MONUMENTAL IGNORANCE:
THE CRITICS COME OUT

"Donald J. Trump is a man of monumental ignorance," Peter Wehner commented on January10, 2018 on CNN. One wonders if Wehner is a left wing critic? No! He was a George W. Bush speechwriter, and he is a conservative Republican. Wehner is a Senior Fellow at the Ethics and Public Policy Centre and the director of the Faith Angle Forum. He is one of America's most respected conservatives. He was upset Trump was elected. The reason was a simple one. The Donald didn't understand government. Wehner saw trouble ahead.

Others have emphasized Trump's lack of qualifications. This is what elected him. Voters were tired of traditional politics. There was a revolution brewing. What is the general consensus, after a year in office? It is Trump is the most ill-suited, ill-prepared president in American history. Why? When Michael Wolff's explosive book arrived to sell a million copies in its first four days, Wolff described the Trump presidency as "an idiot surrounded by clowns." That sounded harsh until noted Trump biographer, Michael D'Antonio weighed in with an op-ed piece praising **Fire And Fury: Inside The Trump White House**. He labeled it a first rate depiction of how the Trumpettes are destroying the base of American democracy. This book, unlike Wolff's, combines domestic with foreign policy to suggest the dangers of Trump's presidency.

He vowed to end traditional diplomacy. He criticized the ideas behind the institutions of post-WWII American foreign policy. His lack of understanding concerning our role in world affairs is monumental. Since the end of World War II, the U. S. world strategy focused on creating a stable international order. This is what Trump will replace with a business model in the White House.

Now America is the Art of the Deal. Every country pursues its own interests! To hell with world security! Making America Great Again is little more than taking advantage of world trade. Trump says he is dedicated to maintaining respect through world economic domination.

TRUMP'S ROAD TO THE PRESIDENCY AND HIS THOUGHTS ON FOREIGN POLICY

As he assumed the presidency, Donald J. Trump ignored the advice of friendly, non-partisan foreign policy think tanks. He brushes off conservative Republican attempts to educate him on foreign affairs. He told adoring crowds: "I know things the Generals don't know." Trump sold the American public on the idea of Making America Great Again. He vows to do this by leaving Europe. He is also opting out of Far Eastern and Mexican trade agreements. He is promoting a bullying, robust nationalism backed by a rebuilt military machine. As he demonstrated in media fights with the North Korean dictator with bad hair, Kim Jong Un, he would blow the "rocket man" out of the water. His supporters cheered this bellicose, irresponsible foreign policy. They support U. S. isolation from Europe.

He argued: "a small handful of special global interests rigged the system." To combat what he saw as the failure of professionals in the State Department, Trump appointed well-known generals, Wall Street financiers and CEO's to run the government. The CEO in charge of American foreign policy, Rex Tillerson, ran Exxon, and he was close to Vladimir Putin. He made Exxon billions in oil deals with Russia. This is his singular qualification for running the State Department.

When he traveled to Europe for the G-7 and G-20 Summits in the summer of 2017, Trump insulted Germany, he disparaged the European Union, and he declared there was a new American foreign policy. He complained the Iran nuclear deal was a disastrous one. He seldom listened to or acknowledged his Secretary of State, Rex Tillerson.

THE TRUMP DOCTRINE: WHY IS IT DANGEROUS?

Bob Corker, the Senate Foreign Relations Committee Chairman, expressed his fear Trump was leading the nation toward World War III. The Trump Doctrine in foreign policy has three elements. 1.) He baits adversaries like North Korea and ISIS. 2.) He rattles allies with threats to withdraw aid, trade and military support. 3.) He lectures Congress. He will do as he pleases in foreign affairs. America First has evolved into America Alone. We have left our position of world leadership. We are now a nation of businessman looking to make money. When Trump left for his first Asian tour there were thirty-nine CEO's on Air Force One. The only deals made were private ones by American business.

The Trump Doctrine has a domestic side. He favors an economic nationalism to foster jobs at home. That is any trade policy adversely impacting U. S. jobs is threatened with tariffs or other protectionist trade policies. The withdrawal from the Trans Pacific Partnership was due to Trump's belief it took jobs away from Americans. One of the dangers of the Trump Doctrine is during his first year in office many foreign policy decisions were based on personal relationships not strategic international interests.

Another danger to the Trump Doctrine is the president selected inexperienced foreign policy officials, notably Secretary of State Rex Tillerson, and Trump's son-in-law Jared Kushner, to conduct a foreign policy they often didn't understand.

The president's well-publicized nepotism, his outright disdain for established political norms, his dislike of democratic institutions and his attacks on the media make the Trump Doctrine a radical departure. It is also a dangerous step in threatening traditional governmental practices. Democracy is in peril. Under the Trump Doctrine, American foreign policy no longer has a reputation for world leadership. The image of the U. S. leading the way in the fight against hunger, over population, disease, humanitarian concerns, women's rights, agricultural reform and a host of other issues has given way to greedy American businessmen lining their pockets in the name of a new nationalism. It will take decades for our traditional allies to recover from the Trump Doctrine.

THE DANGER TRUMP'S IGNORANCE PRESENTS
TO AMERICAN FOREIGN POLICY

The strong stand Trump evidences concerning foreign policy is a ruse to attack the intelligence community. The Trump administration from day one made it a priority to weaken federal intelligence agencies. International intelligence is an independent source of facts useful in formulating foreign policy. The State Department often produces intelligence contrary to Trump's thinking. On North Korea he has asked intelligence experts to stop forwarding informational packets. That is dangerous to world security. The president wants the State Department obedient to the White House. He can't understand why the FBI is not a presidential ally. Trump's ignorance of basic governmental institutions is a key to his lack of enlightened leadership.

Max Boot, a perennial conservative, who advised three Republican presidents, maintains a file on his computer labeled "Trump Stupidity File." It is next to his "Trump Lies" file. Boot told **The New Yorker's** Robin Wright after six months as president "Trump has an appalling ignorance of the current world, of history, of previous American engagements, of what former Presidents thought and did." He said this is a recipe for disaster. Boot is not alone in his criticism. "The President has little understanding of the context-of what's happening in the world-and even less interest in hearing the people who want to deliver it," Michael Hayden, a Four Star General and former director of the CIA and NSC remarked to **The New Yorker**.

What is it that Trump does not understand? First, the Russians are not our friends. Second, don't alienate the European's who are our friends. Third, the President must avoid travel to countries that curtail individual freedom. Poland, the Philippines and Saudi Arabia are nations controlled by brutal regimes. He has repeatedly praised these nations. Public protests are not allowed. In these states Trump praised the leaders and the system. He has no knowledge of world civil rights abuses. Fourth, China can't fix North Korea's nuclear problems. Fifth, the demand for concessions from the Iran Nuclear deal is a non-achievable goal. Sixth, pulling out of innovative trade deals, like the Trans-Pacific Partnership, increases China's economic might and heightens its global influence. All of this is to America's disadvantage. Seventh, put the Russian election meddling on the front burner, recognize it and cooperate with Mueller's investigative team.

The real question is how to prevent Trump's blunders and his lack of knowledge from derailing American foreign policy. One critic described Trump as "lazy and stupid." This is not true. He is not stupid. Lazy! Yes. He knows very little about American history. When he said Andrew Jackson was upset about the Civil War, he didn't realize Jackson died sixteen years before the Civil War. When he talked of Judges signing legislation he didn't realize this was not the case. He is unaware there are three branches of government. He talks of doing what he pleases with the Justice Department. His lazy, imperious attitude on matters of government displays his sheer ignorance concerning the process of governing. George Will, the conservative Republican columnist, left the Republican Party due to Trump's arrogance, abuse of power and what Will describes as Trump's "dangerous inability to think and speak clearly."

TRUMP'S BLUNDERS: WHAT DO THEY MEAN?

Donald J. Trump came to the presidency without a basic knowledge of American history. He has had snippets or clips concerning foreign policy in his speeches. These examples highlight his lack of in-depth information. He has also shown an unwillingness to acquaint his administration with basic diplomatic principals. Here is a list of Trump's foreign policy blunders.

First, he said Germany owed "vast sums" to the United States for NATO defense. It doesn't. No NATO member pays the U. S.

Second, during an interview with the **Wall Street Journal** in April 2017 he said Korea "actually used to be a part of China." Not true!

Third, he landed in Israel and said he had just come from the capital of the Middle East. He arrived from Saudi Arabia and he couldn't answer simple questions on the region.

Fourth, during his trip to France in July 2017, he confused Napoleon Bonaparte with Napoleon III who was France's first popularly elected president.

Fifth, when British Prime Minister Theresa May visited the White House, Trump's staff spelled her name Teresa May. Who is Teresa May? She is a soft porn actress who starred in "Leather Lust."

Sixth, in July 2017 Trump called Xi Jinping "the President of the Republic of China." This is the name for the other Chinese government on Taiwan rather than the leader of the People's Republic of China on the Communist mainland.

Seventh, Trump said Shinzo Abe was the President of Japan. He is the nation's prime minister.

Eighth, the president called the Prime Minister of Canada "Joe." His name is Justin Trudeau.

Ninth, he has embraced and supported the dictator led governments of Egypt and Turkey. He is friendly with governments who downplay democracy notably Poland, the Philippines and Russia.

Tenth, he made confrontational phone calls to the president of Mexico and the Prime Minister of Australia.

Eleventh, he promised, while campaigning, to bomb the oil fields in Iraq that ISIS controlled when in fact these oil fields are in Syria.

Twelfth, on the Iranian deal, Trump said the U. S. would have to come to the aid of Iran and fight Israel in the event of war. When he appeared on Morning Joe in September, 2015, Trump said: "You know, there is a clause in there that people are not even talking about, that we are essentially supposed to come to their defense, the Iranian's defense, and if Israel attacks, you know, where are we?" There was no such clause. Trump simply made this fact up.

Thirteenth, while appearing on Meet the Press with Chuck Todd, Trump said he didn't care whether or not the Ukraine enters NATO. Ukraine was already a member of NATO.

Fourteenth, Trump said ninety-nine percent of Egyptians wanted to break their countries treaty with Israel. FactChck.org. reported it was fifty-four percent.

Fifteenth, Trump didn't know the difference between Hamas and Hezbollah. He was asked by talk radio host Hugh Hewitt to identify the leaders of the militant groups. Trump said he couldn't, he said when he became president he would learn. He hasn't.

Sixteenth, he embraced a Philippine dictator who randomly killed drug dealers, drug users and others without due process. He then called the Philippine President by his first name while toasting him.

Joe McLaughlin, who worked for seven presidents at the CIA, remarked: "Trump thinks having a piece of chocolate cake at Mar-a-Lago bought him a relationship with Xi Jinping. He came in as the least prepared President we've had on foreign policy. Our leadership in the world is slipping away," McLaughlin continued. "Trump is an arrogant amateur disparaging foreign policy professionals."

President Trump sent his son-in-law, Jared Kushner, a real estate developer, to broker Middle East peace. In April 2017 he landed in Iraq to help plan policy against ISIS. Trump refuses to rely on American intelligence agencies. He is systematically dismantling the State Department.

Eliot A. Cohen, a conservative Republican, who worked with Condoleezza Rice at the State Department, said of Trump: "This is a man who is idiotic and bigoted and ignorant of the law."

IS TRUMP THE FIRST MAFIA PRESIDENT? BUSINESS PLUTOCRATS IN THE WHITE HOUSE

It was cold and windy on Tuesday, November 8, 2016 when late night television pundits announced Donald J. Trump was the president of the United States. The notion that America elected a president much like the Mafia influenced Italian Prime Minister, Silvio Berlusconi, brought shock and awe to the world. The journalist who made this comparison, Jeff Greenfield, compared Trump to Berlusconi because white nationalists, mobsters who sold cement in New York and various other criminal business interests supported the Donald. He may have been joking. Then again Greenfield is a respected journalist. He is not "fake news."

The Trump-Berlusconi comparison, according to Greenfield, shows they share similar traits. Both are successful entrepreneurs. Their business deals mix real estate with the entertainment industry. Both are rich enough to finance their own campaigns. Both are excellent communicators. Both have egos making them insufferable. Both consider lower taxes, economic competition and shrinking government as the core of their political beliefs. Both single out journalists, political radicals, the free press, immigrants and liberals for criticism. Both harshly criticize professional politicians. They also disdain established political organizations. They are populists. They are determined to bring politics back to the people. They personalize politics. They talk tough. They cajole and threaten.

The comparison between Trump and Berlusconi misses some key components. American democracy is stronger than the Italian version. Berlusconi controlled the press. Trump is trying but failing to alter press freedoms. Berlusconi, like Trump, pursued a contrarian foreign policy angering and alienating much of Europe. The U. S. Constitution differs from its Italian counterpart. The checks and balances in the American system work to thwart autocratic power. So far!

In November, 2017 Trump's former campaign manager, Paul Manafort, was accused of money laundering by Special Prosecutor Robert Mueller. He was charged, arrested and prepared for trial. He wasn't a Mafia enforcer. He did look like an extra in the Godfather. His clothing bill for one recent year was almost $900,000. It costs a lot of money to do business in the Ukraine with Russian interests. Manafort may have looked like he walked off the lot of Francis Ford Copolla's **The Godfather,** he was simply a prosperous businessman charged with money laundering. Why is this important? As this book demonstrates, candidate Trump and later President Trump made one disastrous foreign policy decision after another. The people he brought into government were arrogant amateurs with little knowledge of administrative functioning. There was a mantra to end all government regulation.

NBC NEWS PRESENTS TOP NINE TRUMP LIES: JANE C. TIMM'S BIGGEST DONALD WHOPPERS OF 2017

The inability of Trump to tell fact from fiction intrigued the media during his first year in the presidency. Here is NBC News Top Nine list of Trump lies.

1.) "More people watched the Trump inauguration than any previous inaugural event." On January 26, 2017, six days after Trump was sworn into office, he said: "The overall audience was, I think, the biggest ever to watch an inauguration address, which was a great thing." The overwhelming evidence indicates President Barack Obama's 2009 inaugural witnessed the largest crowd. Photos from the U. S. Parks Department verified this fact. The Trump administration disciplined those in the Parks Department who provided the press with these photos. The truth is 720,000 people attended the Trump event, whereas 1.8 million witnessed President Obama's 2009 inaugural speech. Press Secretary Sean Spicer said seventeen million people watched the inaugural on live streaming devices. He said this made them a part of the crowd. This was the beginning of the Trumpites fake news syndrome that is still with us.

2.) "Hillary Clinton won the popular vote because of fraud." There is no evidence millions of fraudulent votes were cast. Trump continues to allege three million votes were illegal. Even Trump's lawyers wrote in a court filing: "All available evidence suggests that the 2016 general election was not tainted by fraud...."

3.) "When I looked at the information, I said, I don't think he (General Michael Flynn) did anything wrong. If anything, he did something right." This February 16, 2017 quote ended with Trump stating: "The thing is, he didn't tell our vice president properly." This sounds like the statement of a professional weasel, Mr. President. When Acting Attorney General Sally Yates informed Trump General Flynn subjected himself to Russian blackmail with his alleged lies and deception, Trump took immediate action. He fired Yates. Flynn pleaded guilty to a felony. He cooperated with special counsel Robert Mueller. This is a telling point. Yates challenged Trump's authority. She called attention to his lack of detail. She made it clear he had not mastered the nuances of being president. This led to her firing. He is first and foremost an authoritarian.

4.) "We've got to keep our country safe. You look at what's happening in Germany, you look what's happening last night in Sweden. Sweden! Who would believe it?" This Trump quote is a strange one. Nothing happened in Sweden. Trump criticized Europe's refugee policy to defend his travel ban. He invented a terrorist attack in Sweden to make his point. The Swedish newspaper, Aftonbladet, said the only problems were a drunken driver and a famous singer he was having trouble preparing for a concert.

5.) "Terrible! Just found out that Obama had me 'wire tapped' in Trump Tower just before the victory. Nothing found. This is McCarthyism." This is a March 4, 2017 tweet at 4:35 AM. But it didn't end there. Raging twenty-seven minutes later Trump tweeted: "How low has President Obama gone to tap my phones during the very sacred election process. This is Nixon/Watergate. Bad (or sick) guy." A Fox and Friends commentator, former Judge Andrew Napolitano, was the source of this bogus fact. Fox TV News suspended him for a few days. Then he was back with his anti-Obama tirades. The Director of National Intelligence, James Clapper, remarked to NBC News "there was no such wiretap actively mounted against the president, the president-elect at the time, or as a candidate, or against his campaign." The Justice Department and the FBI investigated the charges. They found no evidence of wiretaps. Since that time Trump has mounted a campaign to disparage everyone who disagreed with his lies.

6.) "You know, this Russian thing with Trump and Russia is a made up story. It's an excuse by the Democrats for having lost an election that they should have won." Trump made this statement to NBC News' Lester Holt on May 11, 2017. Russian interference is real. The Mueller investigation has linked five Trump insiders to illegal activity and collusion with Russia. Including Russians, there have been nineteen Mueller indictments for interfering in the 2016 election. Not only is Mueller investigating, the House and Senate Intelligence Committee's also have concluded Russian interference was real.

7.) "There were people in that rally and I looked the night before, if you look, there were people protesting very quietly in the taking down of the statue of Robert E. Lee. I'm sure in that group there were some bad ones. The following day it looked like they had some rough, bad people-Neo Nazis, white nationalists, whatever you want to call them. But you had a lot of people in that group that were there to innocently protest, and very legally protest because I don't know if you know, they had a permit. The other group didn't have a permit." This is a Trump comment from August 15, 2017 as he defends Nazis and white nationalists. Both groups had permits. Trump couldn't distinguish the Nazi protesters. He refused to comment on a Nazi slogan: "Jews will not replace us."

8.) "We pay more tax than anybody in the world. We're going to reduce taxes." This August 10, 2017 Trump statement is false. We do not pay more taxes than our international peers.

9.) "Tax reform is going to cost me a fortune –this thing, believe me, believe me, this is not good for me." Trump made this statement in Missouri on November 29, 2017 and it is completely inaccurate. An NBC News analysis of the House tax plan said the president would save twenty million in taxes. His family would save more than one billion dollars.

Trump quickly displayed a short temper, a penchant for grandiose statements (some label them lies) on television, and he retreats to his private residence to watch Fox News or scream CNN and MSNBC are practicing "fake news." He was as one White House staffer remarked: "a temperamental toddler." His Secretary of State Rex Tillerson called Trump "a fucking moron." When questioned about the statement Tillerson neither confirmed nor denied it. Draw your own conclusions. By December 2017 Trump was working on a plan to send Tillerson back to his Texas horse farm. A few months later, he was fired.

WHAT DOES TRUMP AGAINST THE WORLD DEMONSTRATE?

Europeans who value the NATO alliance with the U. S., particularly Article 5, which makes collective defense a centerpiece of the NATO treaty, have worked diligently since 1949 to maintain peace and prosperity. The U. S. helped introduce a European system of defense where all nations come together to protect each other. This has created a spirit of solidarity within NATO. Trump threatened this alliance by stating he wasn't sure if the U. S. would continue to honor Article 5. This is the collective security defense pledge to counter hostile forces. The idea of the European Union depending upon the American military to protect its sovereignty was something Trump wouldn't tolerate. He had no idea of the level of U. S. involvement in European affairs since the conclusion of World War II. When NATO was established, it was the lynchpin to save Europe from the Soviet Union's bellicose military aggression. Trump never studied the Cold War. He knew little, if anything, of U. S. involvement in Europe's affairs. Where did Trump stand on these matters? He called Europeans "free loading allies." He said he was tired of the U. S. supporting NATO troops while European Union countries couldn't or wouldn't pay their fair share of defense costs. Rather than holding diplomatic discussions, Trump berated, humiliated and threatened long-standing allies.

German newspapers skewered Trump. **Der Spiegel** had a cartoon of Trump with a sword in his left hand and the severed head of the Statue of Liberty in his right hand. European Union countries worried "America First" meant isolation, a decline in trade and less support from the U. S. in times of international crisis.

Trump's initial interaction in Europe came in the summer of 2017 when the G-7 and G-20 Summits met to discuss political, economic and military issues. These summits defined Trump's foreign policy for Europeans and the world.

How Trump interacted with European leaders in the summer of 2017 at the G-7 and G-20 Summits is consistent with his foreign policy views.

What is the significance of the G-7 and G-20 Summits? These were international conferences held in Hamburg, Germany and Taormina, Sicily in the summer of 2017 where President Trump talked of European security, world trade, immigration, NATO issues and a host of other topics. These summits introduced the American president to the world of international diplomacy. No one knew what to expect. Trump said "America First." He let Europe know they would go it alone. The G-7 and G-20 were an early indication American foreign policy would have an economic not a diplomatic direction.

These international meetings, along with Trump's visits to Warsaw and Paris, point to his lack of knowledge concerning foreign affairs. There was also no clear definition of the direction of American foreign policy. He had no idea about America's leadership or its place in the international order. Historically, Trump knew little, if anything, about the role of the U. S. stabilizing the world militarily and economically. He was too busy eating a cheeseburger in his bedroom and watching Fox News.

His unwillingness to educate himself on U. S. diplomacy, his lack of foresight and his indiscretion in appointing individuals to State Department and other foreign advisory positions doomed his European policies. During his first year in office, his administration weakened American foreign policy. There were also internal scandals, firings, resignations and an atmosphere that Michael Wolff characterized as "children" running the White House. Wolff's **Fire And Fury: Inside The Trump White House** described confusion, back stabbing, amateurs in charge and the result was a chaotic mess. Organizational structure was not a key. As a result foreign policy trips, like the G-7 and G-20, had no real agenda. Trump announced the U. S. would go it alone. The reason is he didn't have a foreign policy. He didn't trust the State Department professionals. There were other problems as early appointees were not properly vetted. The Trump administration made a joke out of security clearances by ignoring the basic rules. When the FBI completed these security applications there were problems. The earliest was the National Security Adviser General Michael Flynn. He lied to the FBI. He failed to register as a foreign agent while working for another country. He acted like he was above the law. He wasn't.

As General Flynn pleaded guilty to lying to the FBI, he unwittingly highlighted one of the conundrums of the Trump presidency. Flynn was one of many amateurs operating without restraint. When outgoing President Barack Obama met with Trump, he urged him not to bring Flynn into his administration. The Donald ignored Obama's advice. By December 2017 Robert Mueller indicted two Trump insiders Flynn and George Papadopoulos for lying to the FBI. They took plea agreements. The guilty pleas placed the two Trump transition team members into a position where they agreed to cooperate with the Special Prosecutor.

When Flynn marched into the courtroom, a person hollered: "You are a traitor to your country." Flynn didn't flinch or acknowledge the voice. After he pleaded guilty, he basically said he didn't do anything wrong. He continued to tell people he was a patriot. He lacked repentance.

What did General Flynn lie about? It was about a conversation he had with the Russian Ambassador in December 2016. Sean Spicer, the press secretary to be, said that Flynn made a courtesy call to the Russian Ambassador. Not true! Flynn lied about discussing lifting Russian sanctions. Why? Only Flynn can tell us! Perhaps because he knew Trump would appoint him National Security Adviser.

He was the National Security Adviser for twenty-five days. He was operating on his own without loyalty to President Trump. He did more to hurt Trump than to help him. President Barack Obama fired Flynn when he worked in his administration. Obama warned Trump to be wary of the cowboy General. Obama said he did as he pleased. He did so without regard to presidential policy.

In the aftermath of Flynn's guilty plea the **Wall Street Journal** on May 7, 2018 reflected on the scenario editorializing "it is a dubious practice for a prosecutor to force a cooperating witness to plead guilty to a crime he didn't commit." The **WSJ** claimed that when FBI agents interviewed Flynn they reported he had not lied. The **Journal** concluded: "The FBI has a conflict of interest in overseeing redactions given that the behavior of its leaders and agents are in question." The question is: Why does the **Wall Street Journal** headline of Flynn: "He pleaded guilty to a crime FBI agents said he didn't commit." Maybe! Maybe not!

GENERAL FLYNN AND PRESIDENT TRUMP

The Logan Act is a 1799 law that states unauthorized persons who negotiate with foreign governments have committed a felony. It was the wedge Robert Mueller used in talking with Flynn's attorneys. He was not charged with violating the law. Only two people have been charged with violating the Logan Act. In the late 1990s it was amended making a $5000 fine the maximum penalty for this felony. The Logan Act was held over Flynn's head. He pleaded guilty to the lesser charge of lying to the FBI. The notion is the plea deal Flynn took was to protect his son. But how does one know Flynn will tell the truth? He will because Mueller has the answers to the questions.

Flynn's lawyers arrived. They had a list of what his client knows and what he will say. The Mueller Committee has plenty of evidence. In March 2017 Trump, in a tweet, called the charges against Flynn a "witch hunt." How does Flynn fit into the Trump campaign? He was the one leading Trump rally's screaming "Lock Her Up" in reference to Hillary Clinton. Now he is in danger of being locked up.

There is no evidence Flynn colluded with the Russian's to alter the electoral process. There is evidence he talked of limiting Russian sanctions. He worked for a foreign government for large sums of cash without registering as working with a foreign government as American law requires. He was allegedly involved in a plot to kidnap an Egyptian businessman and send him home to face trial. Some of these charges are substantiated and others are rumors. There is no doubt there were discussions with various Russian leaders. What those talks produced is known only to Mueller's investigation. The Mueller findings have not been released. The question Flynn's behavior raised was potential Russian collusion from Trump insiders.

RUSSIAN ROULETTE AND GENERAL FLYNN

The questions of General Flynn's role in Russia's hacking of the 2016 election and his alleged negotiations with top Russian officials are murky. The best explanation of Flynn is in Michael Isikoff and David Corn's **Russian Roulette: The Inside Story of Putin's War On America And The Election of Donald Trump**. The veteran Washington D. C. insider journalists interviewed Flynn on July 18, 2016 during the opening day of the Republican National Convention. Isikoff asked Flynn about his dealings with Russia. Isikoff grilled the general on a December 2015 trip to Russia for the tenth anniversary of RT. This state controlled television network is little more than a Kremlin propaganda outlet. Isikoff suggested Flynn had close ties to Russian intelligence. The general was enraged with the question. The general was there to promote a book he had written **The Field of Fight: How We Can Win The Global War Against Radical Islam And Its Allies**. Flynn e-mailed Isikoff that he was not close to the Kremlin. Flynn e-mailed Isikoff: "Did you really read my book and see how much I took Russia to task?" The smoking gun in the **Russian Roulette** book is Flynn's attempts to "reset relations with Moscow." (p. 285) The reason for suspicion of collusion is Trump and some of his followers made contact with Russia prior to his inauguration. A month before his inaugural Flynn and others were cozying up to the

Kremlin. There are two ways of looking at this scenario. The Trumpsters were rank amateurs or they were colluding. Either way it was suspicious behavior.

How do we know about Flynn and other top Trump aides and future Cabinet members talked to the Kremlin? President Barack Obama's Justice Department, with the help of Susan Rice, released information on Trump officials who were talking to the Russians. These officials were reading intelligence reports that were shared with Trump prior to his inauguration.

To Trump supporters this was President Obama spying on the new president. President Trump charged Barack Obama wiretapped his phone during the 2016 election. James Clapper has repeatedly said there is no evidence for this charge. To the Obama administration, Trump supporters were too close to the Kremlin. Isikoff and Corn quoted an Obama aide: "Were the incoming national security adviser and Trump's son-in-law in the bag with the Russians?" (p. 286) Then ten days after the election Republican Senator John McCain found out about the Steele Dossier. The question of Russian collusion was in the air before Trump's inaugural.

The persistence of Russia's interference in the 2016 election and alleged collusion with the Kremlin prompted Robert Mueller in May 2017 to be named Special Counsel for the Russia investigation. From that day the question of collusion persisted with President Trump weekly claiming "no collusion." The Republican Party and Trump supporters charged Mueller was attempting to bring down the president. This led conservative Republican members of the House of Representatives to demand an investigation of the Justice Department, the FBI and the so-called deep state. This behavior was an attempt to divert the public from legitimate questions of Russian collusion.

Trump has denied collusion with Russia, while stating his admiration for Vladimir Putin. The president has attempted to slow down or shut down the Russian investigation. He continues to call it a witch-hunt. He also said after a year there were no charges of collusion or any other points of law being violated. If Trump is guilty of anything, it is employing rank amateurs in the White House.

During the summer of 2017, Trump lobbied senior Senate Republicans, including the Chairperson of the Senate Select Intelligence Committee, to curtail the investigation into Russia's interference in the 2016 election. Trump's requests were highly unusual. They highlight his lack of knowledge of how government functions. Senator Richard Burr of North Carolina told **The New York Times** the President said: "I hope you can conclude this as quickly as possible."

LOBBYING TO END THE RUSSIAN INVESTIGATION

The New York Times reported the President repeatedly asked Senate Majority Leader Mitch McConnell to conclude the Senate portion of the Russian investigation. In August 2017, Republican Senator Thom Tillis of North Carolina introduced a bipartisan bill, limiting the president's ability to dismiss the special prosecutor. This bill would protect Robert Mueller. His investigative team faces partisan opposition from hard-core Republican Trump supporters. This is the most intense attack on the Justice Department and the FBI since Senator Joe McCarthy of Wisconsin terrorized America with his Red Scare.

Senator Thom Tillis, a first term North Carolina Republican, was criticized for his proposed bill that shielded Robert Mueller from being fired. Tillis's bill did not have enough votes to pass. He was bailed out when Trump said he didn't have plans to fire Mueller. Senator Tillis commented Special Counsel Mueller was a career professional. He had the support from both sides of the aisle. That wasn't true. Congressional Republicans did everything they could to impugn Mueller's investigation. That is until he proved Russian interference in the electoral process. Then he began indicting Trump insiders. The president calls the investigation a "witch hunt."

Trump ignores or downplays General Michael Flynn lied to the FBI and to Vice President Mike Pence. The president has never mentioned Flynn worked for the Turkish government without registering as a foreign agent as required by U. S. law.

Flynn registered retroactively as an agent working with a foreign government. It was too late. This late registration highlighted his unwillingness to follow the rules, the protocol and the legal requirements for working in the international community. Flynn said the decision to cooperate was made to honor his family and his country. It was an indictment of his arrogance and lack of contrition. Flynn's guilty plea means he is now a convicted felon. If he could, he would still scream: "Lock her up." Somehow the irony of the moment escapes General Michael Flynn. No one has ever accused him of being a rocket scientist.

TRUMP'S VIEW OF THE RUSSIAN INVESTIGATION

The Russian investigation indicated President Trump had no idea Congress took a negative, often combative, view of Russia. Nor did the president care what Congress thought of Putin and the new Russia. All Trump saw was an authoritarian leader he admired. Those close to him say he emulates Putin.

As a rank amateur entering the Oval Office, Trump posited his hope for better relations with Russia. He continually claimed Russia did not interfere in our election. Why is this important? It is the first step in dooming the fabric and future of American democracy.

Another troubling aspect of the Trump presidency is his chagrin over signing an August 2, 2017 bill imposing further sanctions on Moscow. He was visibly uncomfortable wielding the pen to these sanctions. Trump criticized Congress for the sanctions. He didn't recognize the separation of powers inherent in American Constitutional Democracy. He has no idea how government works. Trump is lazy. He refuses to read the materials necessary to mastering the presidential office.

When Congress voted for renewed Russian sanctions in early 2018, Trump ignored their demands. He failed to impose new penalties on Russia. Eventually, if reluctantly, he imposed these mandated sanctions. When a bipartisan Congressional agreement was sent to Trump, he not only refused to impose another round of sanctions, he ignored Congress.

Donald J. Trump: "Since the first day I took office, all you hear is the phony Democrat excuse for losing the election-Russia, Russia, Russia." Rather than learn about how government operates, Trump dooms the future of American democracy. Trump is obsessed with the Russian inquiry. Does this have the potential to doom the future of American democracy?

HOW TRUMP DOOMED THE FUTURE
OF AMERICAN DEMOCRACY

Donald J. Trump and his supporters are a danger to the future of American democracy. He was elected with rumors of Russian interference. He brought amateurs into Washington. They are in the process of dismantling government. Trump called it "draining the swamp." They also continue to demonize Hillary Clinton.

The most egregious example of buying into Trump's attacks on "Crooked Hillary" came when FBI Director, James Comey, announced he was re-investigating Hillary Clinton's e-mails for criminal activity eleven days before the election. This event prompted Trump's victory.

The FBI almost single-handedly defeated Clinton. On July 5, 2015 the Bureau received a referral from the inspector general of the Intelligence Community concerning Hillary Clinton's mishandling of classified information on her personal e-mail. In these e-mails, she discussed classified material without proper security. The controversy over the e-mails was clouded by Republican charges of malfeasance and Democratic claims former Secretary of State Colin Powell used his personal e-mail for business.

What was the purpose of the FBI investigation? Did Clinton mishandle classified information? The answer was: "Yes." Clinton and her aides talked about Top Secret or classified materials without proper security. FBI Director James Comey wrote in **A Higher Loyalty: Truth, Lies And Leadership** of Clinton's misuse of her e-mails: "There were thirty-six e-mail chains about topics that could cause 'serious' damage to national security...." (p. 163) What does this mean? Comey investigated whether or not her actions were criminal or merely sloppy. The FBI found it was simply computer illiteracy or ignorance of computer security. The notion a hacker might compromise national security materials meant computer amateurs were running Clinton's part of the State Department.

The blowback from the conservative press, the Trump campaign's demand to "jail her" and Fox TV continually labeling her a criminal ended Clinton's bid for the presidency.

Comey defended his actions to investigate Clinton once again less than two weeks before the election costing her the White House. The irony is the FBI had anecdotal proof Russia wanted Donald J. Trump as president. The FBI materials on Russian collusion were in the background. No one believed it. The preposterous thought of hackers working in the Kremlin was too ridiculous for comment. Trump's victory was an equally unthinkable conclusion.

James Comey: "I have seen and read reports Hillary Clinton blames me…for her surprising election defeat." (p. 204) Comey's defense was his wife and daughters voted Hillary. They also walked in the Women's March. This lame excuse hides one key fact. Comey could have investigated using the cover of "top secret." By giving the press the story of a potentially "Crooked Hillary," Comey unwittingly fed into Trump's outrageous charges.

OTHER FACTORS IN TRUMP'S VICTORY
AND RUSSIA WON'T GO AWAY

There were other factors. The state of Virginia was found to have eliminated a large number of African American voters. The alt-white, led by Steve Bannon, aided by an allegedly racist news organization, known as Breitbart, conspired to defeat Hillary Clinton. In Phoenix, Arizona the Secretary of State, Helen Purcell, didn't properly staff voter locations in heavily populated Latino and African American areas causing low voter turnout. This was another factor helping Trump march into the White House. These examples are just a few of the strange occurrences leading to what is the implausible presidency of Donald J. Trump.

When General Michael Flynn campaigned for Trump he had no idea he would be indicted for violating the Foreign Agents Registration Act or for lying to the FBI. He was only indicted on one of these charges, lying to the FBI. His guilty plea made him a felon. The other Trump team members indicted, Paul Manafort, Rick Gates and George Papadopoulos, were like cartoon characters. Manafort looked, acted, walked and dressed like he had watched the

Godfather. Papadopoulos was a low level twit who rolled over so fast for the Mueller team he must have had skies on his testimony. No matter how anyone defends Trump, there were a number of Trump insiders charged with crimes by the Special Prosecutor Robert Mueller. Papadopoulos and Flynn took plea deals. That is they admitted they were guilty of crimes. Manafort is ready to go to trial. His assistant Rick Gates faced serious charges. He also took a plea deal. These events, President Trump charged early on, resulted from a corrupt, overzealous and out of control dishonest media, the crooked FBI, and the deep state. Trump continues to argue there is a media-Democratic Party conspiracy to get rid of him. For the president, Comey's investigation of collusion with Russia was the last straw. He tweeted or shouted daily. "No collusion." Trump showing his lack of understanding of the role of the DOJ, lamented his Attorney General, Jeff Sessions, recused himself from the Russia investigation. This was unacceptable. The president said he would never have appointed him had he known about recusing. He implied the Attorney General's job was to protect the president. He couldn't understand why his Attorney General was not there to protect him. The press asked: "To protect the Donald from what?"

President Trump fired FBI Director Comey calling him "a loose cannon" and "a nut job." It was a surrealistic moment. He didn't realize the FBI was independent of the president. The DOJ is also independent of the Chief Executive. Trump failed to understand this basic point of American government. The Trump administration constantly challenges those who criticize his actions. It is fake news! It is a conspiracy. There is never a talking point. There is never debate. There are no facts. This is how oligarch's and totalitarian's work in the political arena.

After Comey was fired the Acting Attorney General, Rod J. Rosenstein, on May 17, 2017 appointed Mueller to conduct a thorough and impartial investigation of the Russian government's attempts to influence the 2016 election. It was Mueller acting as the Special Prosecutor that led to over 400,000 documents being reviewed by Christmas 2017. Did these documents prove that a few in Trump's inner-circle were working with Russian interests? Yes! Only the Mueller investigative team knows the depth of their collusion. The press concentrated on Jared Kushner.

By March 2018 Kushner's overseas business interests caused red flags to erupt. His top-secret security clearance was never completed. Chief of Staff General John Kelly downgraded Jared's top-secret security clearance to simply secret security. Press reports contend foreign governments tried to manipulate him. There was also the question of investment funds for his businesses. He allegedly secured preferential loan treatment while he was on government business. Conflict of interest was a key question. After he was stripped of his interim security clearance, Kushner updated his financial disclosure statement. There is no evidence of financial wrongdoing. Trump and his inner circle made a joke out of the security clearance protocol. The **London Independent** concluded: "The President and those working for him believe the rules don't apply to them." The **Independent** wrote: "White House Communications Director Hope Hicks admitted to House investigators that she lies for the President."

When the **London Independent** wrote Hope Hicks lies for the president, the **New York Times** was their source. Hicks said Trump often told outright falsehoods, which required her to tell "white lies." This comment came after Hicks went through eight hours of private testimony before the House Intelligence Committee. She refused to testify about the president's first year in office, as did Stephen K. Bannon. Democratic Representative Adam B. Schiff of California accused the Trump administration of stonewalling the Russian collusion investigation. Schiff said of Bannon and Hicks failure to answer questions: "an overly broad claim of privilege that I don't think any court of law would sustain. This is not executive privilege, it is executive stonewalling."

As the House Intelligence Committee's top Democrat, Schiff has been a thorn in Trump's side. He used Hicks testimony to charge there was a lack of transparency in the Oval Office. The persistent questions concerning Russia prompted changes.

On March 1, 2018 Kushner's top security clearance was downgraded. The reason? A **Washington Post** article alleged four countries were working Kushner's lack of experience in fiscal areas and his financial trouble as a building he owned in New York was a year away from a huge payment. There was no indication of impropriety from Kushner. The criticism centered upon worries about potential conflicts of interest. There is no question Kushner is not qualified to work in foreign policy. He doesn't have the requisite training. Trump is ignoring nepotism rules. This does very little, if anything, to advance the interests of American foreign policy.

Trump was angry American intelligence put together a dossier charging China, Israel, Mexico and the United Arab Emirates had conversations on how to manipulate Kushner. This is the problem when amateurs govern America. Or when a contrarian, outlier ascends to the Oval House.

TRUMP'S REFUSAL TO ACT PRESIDENTAL: A CONTRARIAN OUTLIER

When he was the square jawed, defiant Republican nominee, who only months earlier had bragged of grabbing a woman's pussy, he held rally's promising to Make America Great Again. He was elected the President of the United States. The Pussy Grabber in Chief as President. Had I woken up to a bad movie? No, as President Barack Obama said: "Trump won. Accept it." I did! Reluctantly!

I viewed Trump's election as an impossibility. Times were changing. The rise of a vicious often-violent white majority wreaked havoc on what most of us thought was a multi-cultural political system. The old racism resurfaced under the Donald.

A window into Trump's policies were provided when he traveled to Europe in the summer of 2017 to participate into two international summits bringing together Europe's most prominent economic partners, military alliances and political allies. He proved he had little, if any, knowledge of foreign policy. He had even less interest in educating his administration in world affairs. He had his view-America First.

When Trump interacted with Germany's Angela Merkel and France's Emmanuel Macron, he made his message clear. The United States would leave the climate control agreement, and Germany would have to alter its trade policies and pay for its share of NATO defenses. He described France as a second rate power. The French patched it up by inviting the American president to celebrate Bastille

Day. Along the way Trump praised Russia leader Vladimir Putin while continually shaking his hand at the G-20 when television cameras showed the two comrades. It was not just a change in American foreign policy. It was a revolution.

The Trump administration altered how foreign policy is conducted. Billionaire businessmen from oil rich states dominated the President's Cabinet, others were members of Wall Street's mega wealthy financial firms, and there were a group of right wing Southern conservatives who despise government regulation. They were all entitled, anti-government amateurs. What does this have to do with foreign policy? Plenty! The majority of those in Trump's inner circle want the U. S. out of world affairs. Isolation was the mantra in Trump's foreign policy.

The 2017 European Summits demonstrate how and why Trump represents a new vision in American foreign policy. There is a tendency to disparage him. That is a mistake. He is a bright person. He knows how to use social media. He is a deal maker. While his knowledge of history and foreign policy is at best minimal, he does have the executive power. That power over the next four or eight years will do a great deal of international damage. The threat of nuclear war hangs over our heads. He represents a newly emerging conservative white majority threatening to take American political history backward into the dark recesses of racial repression, international bullying and a Make America Great Again mentality with a nuclear arsenal promoting world disunity. This is a recipe for disaster.

In the summer of 2017 Trump traveled to two European summits. He was a guest of the French government during the July 14 Bastille Day celebration. He also delivered a speech in Poland with the reactionary and less than democratic Polish president smiling by his side. These foreign adventures defined the Trump administration in world affairs. He was now a major world leader. He was recognized and feted in many countries.

There were two economic summits held in Europe in the summer of 2017. He was featured at these events. The 43rd G-7-Summit held on May 26-27, 2017 in the resort town of Taormina in Sicily, Italy brought seven nations together. There were many issues. The key ones were finding a means to conclude the Syrian crisis, helping to empower the UN Mission in Libya and combating ISIS. This was followed by a July 7-8, 2017 G-20 Summit held in Hamburg, Germany. This meeting had an extended agenda with a wide variety of subjects considered.

Trump was the most important figure in the G-7 and G-20 Summits bringing Europeans closer to cooperating with one another and ignoring the U. S. One must look at the long list of disagreements President Trump fostered with other nations to understand the turbulent nature of these summits. German Chancellor Angela Merkel said the G-20 should focus on climate change, free trade and guaranteeing total press freedom. These issues are ones the American president differs with from Merkel and her cohorts. From the beginning it was Trump versus the world. This is hardly what one expects from a worldwide summit or historically from an American president. But, as a political outsider, Trump revels in being a contrarian.

The key issues during the G-7 and G-20 Summits evolved around climate change and trade policies. The era of cooperating with Europe was over. Trump sought a better deal in separate treaties. No one understood Trump. He was truly a man of mystery. The European Union didn't realize he is a political amateur in over his head.

Trump's policies were out of step with the rest of the world. For his supporters, it was an indication of Making America Great Again by using the diplomacy that is and remains isolationist minded. Trump's critics were surprised by what seemed to be small triumphs in trade agreements and a budding friendship with Vladimir Putin.

The G-7 and G-20 Summits caused some to ponder the future of such meetings. Was the U. S. out of step? The question was raised continually concerning world cooperation. For decades the U. S. has been the world leader. Trump single-handedly ended the direction of American diplomacy since 1945. Why? He doesn't understand the Cold War, the need for European unity and how the Trans Pacific Partnership controlled China economically.

The two European summits are an indication of the future of American foreign policy. The embryo American policy is one standing apart from world affairs. The pros and the career officers in the State Department have been disrespected, shunted to the side, forced to retire, eliminated from the serious issues and this has resulted in a disastrous direction for Trump's foreign policy.

There is a diplomatic community with rules and customs. When President Trump had his daughter, Ivanka, sit at his G-20 seat, there was a storm of criticism. Trump defended his action. He said Chancellor Merkel approved. There was no word from Merkel. The problem for Trump at the G-7 and at the G-20 is he was isolated due to a group of advisers who appeared more at home in a county fair pie eating contest than on the stage of an international diplomatic summit.

Trump's disrespect for the media created other problems. His daily tweets argue he is a victim of "fake news." He said repeatedly CNN, MSNBC, the **New York Times** and the **Washington Post** practice character assassination. Fact checking is not a Trump forte. His followers blindly accept his bold faced lies.

While this book was in progress the question of Russian collusion with the Trump campaign exploded daily. For months there was no smoking gun, no evidence Trump was colluding with Russian interests. The president appeared free of undue Russian influences. Then all hell broke loose. Four members of Trump's inner circle were indicted and two took plea deals.

Donald Trump Jr. admitted meeting with a gorgeous female lawyer, obviously under official Russian supervision. She claimed to have scandalous revelations on Hillary Clinton. It turns out she had no such information. Her behavior made Donald Jr. look like a rank amateur.

In July 2017 the news exploded with Russian election interference. The **New York Times**, the **Washington Post**, MSNBC and CNN reported in depth their concerns. They questioned Trump's ability to master the presidency. Since he ascended to the Oval Office there has been a disregard for decency and political restraint. His blatant nepotism placed too many family members into the White House. His ties to old school billionaires formed the base of his Cabinet. By thumbing his nose at the political establishment, the Donald announced a new sheriff was in town. He relishes in the role of disruptor. He is now the disruptor in chief. His followers ignore his overt misogyny. They cheer his brash, often racist, remarks. They savor his every word.

But cracks in his supporters began appearing in the summer of 2017 when Trump criticized Attorney General Jeff Sessions for recusing himself in the Russian investigation. Once again the Donald has no understanding of how government works. Why did Sessions recuse himself? The answer is a simple one. He had conflicts of interest.

The Trump approach to international bullying harkened back to the gunboat diplomacy favored by President Theodore Roosevelt. This approach suggests Trump lacks the sophistication, the training and the understanding to maintain effective foreign policy. As his presidency evolved into eighteen months of chaos, confusion and controversy one thing was clear. Trump acted with willful arrogance at times and strategic ignorance at other times.

We are living in historically difficult times. The rise of intolerant nationalists, the abrasive, violent right wing, the loss of faith in democratic institutions, the rise of strong, authoritarian leaders, the aggressive nature of the Christian right bringing religion into the White House, the demonizing of the gay community, the racism inherent in urban America, the thrust against multiculturalism, the hostility of the Me Too movement, the disrespect for all Muslims regardless of their place in the U.S. and the threat to take away children from illegal immigrants caught entering the United States is a thumbnail sketch of Donald J. Trump's America. It is not a pretty picture.

The number of pro and anti-Trump books is a cottage industry. Regnery Publishing is the right wing nut house of corporate publishers and the five major U. S. publishers turn out a wide variety of books. There is one author who is outside the box. Timothy Snyder's **The Road To Unfreedom: Russia, Europe, America** is the only book which labels the first years of Trump's presidency "a gathering storm." An esteemed Yale University Professor with a specialty in Ukraine politics, Snyder warns us our freedoms are slowly, but surely, being eroded. There is no sugar coating the dangers of Trump's presidency. The Donald is uneducated, irresponsible, entitled, he doesn't accept opposition viewpoints, he is angry, nasty, vile and he cuts a path of personal destruction through his enemies.

Trump's inability to recognize conventional diplomacy, his unwillingness to engage in mutual respect, and attacking institutions like the FBI and the Justice Department is unacceptable. But that is the Donald. The intolerance for those who disagree is what is bringing American democracy into a crisis.

The emphasis on power and virility is Donald J. Trump's appeal to the authoritarian voter, the old folks eating their oatmeal in front of Fox TV News and those who want to bring back a white America.

Is there a Russian connection in America? Yes. Is there a Russian connection to Donald J. Trump? No. Not as this book goes to press. Other authors see it differently. Professor Timothy Snyder has no trouble-concluding Trump is "the Russia candidate." In 2013 Russia's foreign minister wrote a foreign policy document to bring his nation back to international prominence. In that program, Snyder tells us, there was an attempt to compromise and perhaps blackmail Donald J. Trump. When the Steele Dossier suggested Russia collusion in American politics and then the Mueller investigation confirmed it, the right wing went after those alleging Russian collusion. That is where we are in the present day. Snyder's work appears more credible and stronger with each passing day.

The turmoil surrounding America's political quagmire threatens our future liberties. The future is a dangerous one. It is necessary for every American to speak his or her mind about the changes in the political scene. The comment: "Hey, how about that economy" hides the dangers to our individual liberties. By draining the swamp Trump has filled it with pompous alligators that have little understanding of the average person and his or her needs.

"Dignified theatricality is an essential element of power," John Meacham wrote in **The Soul of America: The Battle For Our Better Angels**. (p. 38) He also mentions character matters and this suggests why Trump's presidential legacy will be less than a successful one. As Meacham points out: "What counts is not just the character of the individual at the top, but the character of the country...." (p. 40)

Trump may be a reflection of the division in the citizens' view of the battle for "the soul of American democracy."

PROLOGUE

"Many of the tools of modern life are increasingly
priced beyond most people's reach."

EDWARD LUCE

"Democracy is not the multiplication of ignorant opinions."

BEATRICE WEBB

"Fiction is art and art is the triumph over chaos (no less)
and we can accomplish this only by the most vigilant
exercise of choice, but in a world that changes more
swiftly than we can perceive there is always the danger
that our powers of selection will be mistaken and that
the vision we serve will come to nothing."

JOHN CHEEVER

"It is thus a primary tradition to consider history when our political
order seems imperiled."

TIMOTHY SNYDER

"What a fucking idiot."

RUPERT MURDOCH, DECEMBER 2016, COMMENTING AFTER
A PHONE CONVERSATION WITH PRESIDENT-ELECT TRUMP.

Why write a book about Donald J. Trump's blunders or successes in foreign policy? One reason is Western liberal democracy is under attack. It is not dead. It is on life support. President Trump hopes to kill it off. He and his cohorts represent the greatest danger to democracy since Adolf Hitler. No, I do not compare Trump to Hitler. When I talk to his supporters there is a messianic feel they have brought him to the presidency. Trump represents the last burst of America's white majority. They believe President Obama was soft on ISIS, the U. S. was losing its cultural heritage and the old days of maintaining a world order through diplomacy was no longer possible. Trump's supporters believe the U.S. is under siege. Muslims, African Americans, welfare cheats, Latinos, Communists, Socialists, NFL players who won't stand for the National Anthem, college protesters and those who don't believe in God are the target of Trump's supporters. The result is a white rage, combined with blue-collar job concerns, thereby electing Trump president.

Trump's election is not the last dying breath of the white majority. It is happening all over the world. Marine Le Pen lost the French election, but she challenged French domestic liberalism. Trump and his followers supported her. There have been at least two-dozen democracies that have failed in the last two decades. One only has to look at what has happened in Russia, Hungary, Egypt and Turkey to see how these nations failed in democratic experiments. Democracy is threatened in the U. S. by a president who doesn't understand the rules of politics.

The threat of Western liberalism began before Trump's ascension to the presidency. The decline of the middle class is only one symptom of the divide between Americans. The cost of college is freezing out future qualified students. The dysfunction in politics creates a polarization leading to a roller coaster economy. The economic elites continue to control Wall Street. The drug crisis highlights our health systems failures, the decline of blue-collar jobs and the rancorous class differences fueled the name-calling campaign-electing Trump.

What is it that holds liberal democracies together? The glue is economic growth, a strong job market, education open to everyone, a wide variety of economic-social-intellectual ideas and unfettered equal opportunity. The tools to success are increasingly priced beyond many people's reach. In 2017 it took the average blue collar worker twice as many hours a month working to pay rent in a big city as it did in 1950. The cost of a college education and health care are virtually out of the reach for the middle and lower class. The middle class is in rapid decline. We are evolving into two classes making way for demagogues like Donald J. Trump.

There is another factor. The West is now in decline. Since 1970 Asia's per capita income has increased fivefold. The U. S. average per capita income has stagnated. What is happening? China's economy now dominates Far Eastern affairs. That is the challenge for President Donald J. Trump and his advisers. Xi Jinping, China's Communist leader, can depend upon heavy foreign investment, the support of multinational companies that relocated to China and a system of world trade making the Chinese the dominant player, along with the U. S., in world economic affairs. China's economy surpassed the U. S.'s in 2014.

THE PROBLEMS ALTERING AMERICAN DEMOCRACY

The decline of recent liberalism began with George W. Bush. When he took office in January 2001, he instituted a tax cut. He fought two wars on a credit card. The result was middle class income was lower when he left office. The U. S. median income is lower today than it was in 2000. Who has benefitted from this decline? The uber rich and the world's top one percent earners, who have seen their incomes jump by two thirds since 2000. There has not been a trickle down of funds. The top one percent dominates almost sixteen percent of the global economy.

A few years ago a **New Yorker** cartoon caught the essence of the change in the world economy when it showed a Chinese mother waging her finger at her daughter and telling her: "Eat your rice Han Ling, don't you know there are children in West Virginia who are starving?" This **New Yorker** cartoon was neither funny nor accurate. It told a story that resonated with Trump's supporters. It highlighted hostility to China's growing dominance in world economic affairs. This cartoon also shows our continued preoccupation with declining wages, increased living costs and a loss of prestigious in world affairs. These are some of the reasons Donald J. Trump was elected.

When Trump announced his tax cut there were big gifts for the rich. He said he would increase defense spending and repair the infrastructure. Trump never said how. There were unprecedented cuts in social service programs. Mick Mulvaney, Trump's budget director, laid it out with over $600 billion cut in Medicaid over the next decade, reductions of $193 billion in food stamps, cuts in student loans of $142 billion over ten years and decreases in federal worker retirement programs of $63 billion. The people who brought Trump into office will lose more than those who voted against him. That is the supreme irony of Trump's policies.

Rising income inequality is another problem. What does rising inequality lead to in a democratic society? Generally, there is pressure to ensure government financed social services. The issues of health care, pension protection, worker rights, gender equality, equal opportunity, education funding and a myriad number of plans to guarantee a living standard for all citizens. The gap between pay for executives and the average worker has widened dramatically since 1970.

ELECTION NIGHT: AN UNPRECEDENTED SURPRISE

Election night saw Americans sitting around waiting for the first female president. As the vote was counted Hillary Clinton tallied 65,844,610 votes and Donald J. Trump garnered 63,979,636 votes. But Trump won the election. It was narrow victories in Wisconsin, Michigan and Pennsylvania that carried Trump to the White House. If 77,000 votes were altered in the three states there would have been a Clinton presidency.

President Barack Obama was shocked as was the nation. There was one important conclusion. Despite the rancor, periodic violence, the bad taste during the campaign and the shouts and intimidation from both sides the electoral process worked. There was no disruption and minimal chaos.

When the 2016 election results were analyzed, there were some interesting conclusions. The four-hundred-ninety-three wealthiest counties in the U. S., all of them urban, voted for Hillary Clinton.

The rest of the 2623 counties, most of them suburban or small town, went solidly for Trump. There were other anomalies. When fifty-three percent of the female vote cast their ballot for Trump, there was little concern in the Democratic Party. Clinton supporters believed the female vote would be overwhelmingly Democratic. It wasn't. This suggests how out of touch Hillary Clinton was with the electorate.

The small margin of victory prompted analysis. Clinton's decision not to campaign late in small electoral states was a mistake. The Comey investigation, Russian hacks, WikiLeaks and Putin's meddling favoring Trump were other factors. But they were not the decisive ones. Hillary Clinton was not acceptable to conservatives, religious right advocates opposed to many of her policies, and the notion that the swamp had to be drained hurt her candidacy.

On election night Democratic strategists and the Clinton's sat in silence looking at the Television screens. The Democratic victory party never took place. The irony was Trump expected to lose. He rented a small reception area.

In Moscow there was a party in a bar in downtown Moscow. At the end of it a life-sized photos of Trump stood next to a photo of Vladimir Putin. People were chanting "Trump, Trump, Trump." Dmitry Drobnitsky, a pro-Kremlin writer, observed Russia now had a place alongside America as a world leader. Liberal democracy was in a perilous position.

In Moscow, Alexi Zhuravlvov, a Russian legislator representing the right wing Rodin Party, said: "This is the reset of the Western world." Then Zhuravlvov walked over to the Russian Duma where they were applauding Trump's victory. Russian influenced Trump's election. It would be some time before the Mueller investigation confirmed the level and intensity of the Kremlin's electoral interference.

As CNN, MSNBC, ABC, CBS and NBC attempted to explain how and why Trump was elected, there was egg on the media's face. Few saw Trump's unprecedented election.

THE GROUNDSWELL OF SUPPORT FROM THE WEST FOR TRUMP

In the American West there was a groundswell revolt-supporting Trump. The small towns, the outlying areas were in economic depression and often in a depressed state, and they voted Trump. In Payson, Arizona while I was working on this book about Trump in a Starbuck's a local came up to me. He smiled. He told me: "We are spending Trump bucks." When I asked him about Russian collusion, lying about his policies and attacking the media he said: "The media presents fake news and assholes like you can't change my opinion." I said: "Can I gave you some facts?" He said: "Do you think I'm stupid?" The divide in American politics is enormous. There is no coming together on facts, opinions or America's direction.

What we see happening in America is the divide between the rich and the middle class. The lower middle class lives into quasi-poverty. Trump tells them he is producing jobs and looking after their welfare.

What are the changes eroding the middle class dream? Why is it so difficult financially for many Americans? San Francisco has a housing market where eight out of every ten homes is a million dollar or more property. Young people, immigrants without large sums of money, and the increasingly downsized middle class now move to Phoenix, Sacramento, Boise, Reno, Tucson, Albuquerque and Las Vegas for affordability. This further accentuates the differences between the rich, the growing poor and the shrinking middle class.

Why is this important? What does it have to do with the Trump presidency? Plenty! Trump and his billionaire advisers are taking advantage of social class and economic differences to wipe out government regulation. Look what has happened in America. We are calling each other names in the interest of politics. We are divided. We are angry. We have the perfect political climate for Donald J. Trump to abrogate our rights, alter our political institutions, erode the role of the courts, ignore advice from Congress, attack the independence of state voting and lower standards for freedom of the press. Trump believes most other cherished institutions need to be dramatically altered or perhaps eliminated. Reform is not a Trump mantra. He believes in altering the structure of government. This is

1

the behavior of a politician without understanding and insight. It is also the first step toward a dramatic loss of freedom.

THE MORNING AFTER THE ELECTION

When President Barack Obama walked into the Oval Office the day after Trump's election, he told the staff to hold their heads high. He also began the peaceful and respectful transition to the Republican Party. There were two months left in the Obama presidency.

As President Obama prepared for private life he invited president-elect Trump to the White House. The reason was to show the peaceful transition implicit in the American system of government. The question of Russian collusion continued to rear its ugly head.

Michael Isikoff and David Corn in **Russia Roulette: The Inside Story of Putin's War On American And The Election of Donald Trump**, point out "there was contacts between the Kremlin and the Trump team during the campaign." (p. 278) This may have been social, it may have been for business reasons. Isikoff and Corn suggest, without proof of complicit behavior that Trump colluded with the Kremlin.

The National Security Agency Chief Admiral Michael Rodgers speaking at a conference a few days after the election created controversy when he stated the question of Russian interference was not a fake one. They had an impact on the 2016 election. Rodgers' statement initiated the confrontation between the intelligence community and President Trump. It has continued for more than a year and a half.

The Trump administration since that day has not owned up to Russian interference in the 2016 election. Trump said he received a marvelous letter of congratulations from Russia President Vladimir Putin. He was looking forward to a good relationship with Russia.

HERE IS WHAT YOU NEED TO KNOW TO UNDERSTAND TRUMP

In order to understand how and why Trump operates, it is necessary to examine his political thinking. One of the definitional points of Trump's political approach is his slogan "America First." He hopes to hold our interests above everyone else's. The choice of America First brought back memories of bigots, anti-Semites, pro-Hitler Americans and others who didn't want us to interfere in World War II. America First represented a group of 1930s bigots hollering: "Better Hitler than Blum." This was a reference to Leon Blum, a Jewish Socialist, important to French politics. Racist anti-Semitic patriots like Charles Lindbergh and Henry Ford said it was just fine for Nazi Germany to seize France. In the 2000 presidential campaign Christian activist Pat Robertson campaigned arguing Hitler would have never arrived in America with his hordes of goose-stepping soldiers. What does this have to do with Donald J. Trump? Plenty! Long before he ran for the presidency, Trump courted the disaffected white voter. This is the voting bloc who don't often participate in elections. The promise of jobs brought out these normally disinclined voters to the polls in record numbers.

He consistently displays a lack of knowledge concerning culture, economics and the history of other countries. At times the president is virtually schizophrenic in condemning China as a "money manipulator." Then he praises the Chinese leadership. Inconsistency is a hallmark of Trump's foreign policy. No one in China's political hierarchy knows what he expects. Trump has threatened China when a sane approach would be as Sun Tzu or Carl von Clausewitz observed: "put yourself in your opponent's shoes." Trump has little understanding of China's history. Every time he meets with a foreign leader he remarks it was a great meeting. They are best friends. Somewhere in Communist China there are howls of laughter. His approach to China makes little sense. One day he is friendly to China. The next day he is a virulent critic. Some Americans see this as negotiating genius. The Chinese view it as the actions of a confused and ill-prepared leader.

Trump's biggest blunder was to drop out of the Trans-Pacific Partnership which includes Japan, South Korea, Vietnam, Australia and six other countries but not China. Why is this a mistake? It forces these nations to deal in matters of trade with China. That is not to their advantage. This makes China pre-eminent in Far Eastern trade. He also infuriated China by being unaware of the one China policy. When he talked with Taiwan he called them China. Not acceptable! The only China is the mainland People's Republic, according to a long-standing agreement with the U. S. Trump knows nothing of history. In spite of the evidence Trump calls himself "a stable genius." The future of U. S.-China relations is uncertain. The trade war has begun. Don't expect the Donald to know its direction.

The dysfunction in the White House during Trump's first year led to the resignation of his press secretary, Sean Spicer, the Chief of Staff, Reince Priebus, and the wholesale firing of key people who run the White House's daily life. This led the press to conclude children were running the American government.

The problem the Donald had in the first year of his presidency was the Donald. He wouldn't abide by conventional political rules. He wouldn't accept advice from government professionals. He discouraged his people from airing their differences publicly. His family was not ready for prime time. His daughter, Ivanka, and his son-in-law, Jared Kushner, are rank amateurs who don't understand the governmental structure. When Anthony Scaramucci was hired to run the communications end of the White House, it was because he was nice to Kushner. He said he would protect him. Or as Ivanka said: "Jared would get good press." No wonder Steve Bannon said she was "dumb as a rock." The rigors of Washington politics and their outsider mantra led to one mistake after another. They all seemed to have a grudge. It was a volatile, explosive atmosphere dividing the nation. The question of Russian collusion continually reared its ugly head.

"Did Trump collude with Russia." He said: "No." His supporters said "No." Fox TV News said "No." The Mueller investigation continued. The ever-present soap opera is a daily news event. After four Trump insiders were indicted, the question of Russian collusion intensified.

DID TRUMP'S FOREIGN POLICY HAVE COHERENCE?

Trump arrived at the Oval House with no experience in foreign affairs. He hadn't served in the military. He appeared to have a sword rattling view of the world. No one gave Trump a chance in foreign policy. Yet, since 1980, during a celebrity interview with Rona Barrett, he displayed an interest in and clear concept of foreign policy. Trump would change his positions on issues, often abruptly, but he generally argued his American First philosophy since 1980. It is authoritarian with high-ranking, military men, Southerners, billionaires, religious zealots and those suspicious of government in key positions. They are America First zealots.

To dismiss Trump's presidency is a mistake. He will have a lasting impact upon the future of the American political system. The problem is one of personality, lack of maturity, erratic decision-making, excessive ego and disorganization by amateurs in the White House. He is a populist disrespected by the experts.

WILL THE U. S. SURVIVE A TRUMP PRESIDENCY?

After a year in office the **Atlantic** concluded: "Trump's bizarre behavior has coarsened politics and induced a harmful norm.... These changes will be hard to undo." The end result is freedom of speech, press rights and religious freedoms are in peril. As is the future of our democracy!

What were Trump's initial steps towards authoritarianism? The courts struck down his proposed ban on immigration from seven Muslim majority countries. Why? They violated constitutional principles including religious freedom. He acted like he wanted to fire the Judges. His public comments illustrate he has no idea the judicial system reviews the actions of the two other branches of government. The courts stepped in to curb's Trump's excesses. His lack of understanding concerning the judicial system is embarrassing. His occasional press conferences continue to highlight his malfeasance in office. What do I mean by malfeasance? Trump's attacks on a judge who stayed the immigration ban tells one all they need to know about the new administration's respect for judicial integrity. He has none. As Roger Cohen observed in the **New York Times**: "Trump is more comfortable in a universe where morality ceases to exist."

When a Federal District Court Judge, James Robart, issued his ruling in Seattle, halting the Trump immigration order, the president shot back with defiance. He called Robart: "This so-called judge." He said it was an outrageous judicial decision. It was Trump's demeaning, insulting language and his rank hostility to anyone who disagreed with him that brought the controversy to a head. To understand Trump in foreign policy, it is necessary to examine what he brings to the presidency.

During his first year in office the courts repeatedly struck down President Trump's policies. His attempt to have the Deferred Action and Childhood Protection (DACA) withdrawn was another legal blow following the court decisions preventing his Muslim ban. On January 10, 2018 in San Francisco U. S. District Judge, William Alsup, ruled the Trump administration cannot end the DACA program until the court case brought by the University of California system against the Department of Homeland Security is resolved.

When Attorney General Jeff Sessions argued DACA was an Obama-era program that was unconstitutional, Judge Alsup told Sessions his interpretation was a misreading of the law. That sounds better than calling Sessions judicially challenged or for that matter a moron. That sounds better than suggesting Sessions has exceeded his educational level. Or his intellectual potential.

THE TRUMP APPOINTEES AND WHAT THEY BRING TO THE TABLE

As a talent scout for those qualified to serve in foreign affairs, Trump has an abysmal record. He selects right wing zealots, inept pathetically loyal followers and his unqualified millionaire-billionaire friends to hold key government positions. They are supporters who handle positions they were appointed to with little, if any, qualification. They lack the knowledge to serve in a government capacity. Some are complete dopes. Former Texas Governor Rick Perry has the glossy slick backed hair and the looks of a movie star politician. Brains? You decide! One qualification for high-level political life Perry has hidden. He was a cheerleader as an undergraduate at Texas A and M. Trump loves cheerleaders. He also loves people who know nothing about energy. He also loves people with good hair.

As Secretary of Energy Perry is an unmitigated disaster. He courts the press with stupid comments and ill-defined policies. On a trip to African in the Fall of 2017, he said one of the strangest things ever uttered by a politician. He was attending a meeting of "Africa Oil Week" held in South Africa. He said if we provide electricity to small

African villages, it would act as a hindrance to sexual assault. It would also reduce abortion. It would end large families. Were the lights on in Perry's head? While not directly engaged in mainstream foreign affairs, Perry is an embarrassment to American governmental interests. But Perry does have good hair.

Sam Clovis is one of the worst examples of a top government nominee. He was nominated as chief scientist in the Department of Agriculture. He had no science background. He was a conservative Iowa radio talk show host. He was a political science professor. He withdrew his nomination because he was associated with foreign policy advisor George Papadopoulos in the attempt to establish the relationship between the Trump campaign and Russian officials. Clovis not only didn't hold the advanced degree in science and medicine that is the general requirement for this appointive position, he is contemptuous of those who do. He sees science as the work of the devil. He sees God, his Christian faith and his opposition to Darwinian thought as key qualifications to be the nation's chief scientist. I can hardly wait for his first scientific report. This suggests Trump does not appoint people to important positions due to their expertise. It is as a result of their loyalty and a deep pocketbook. He has appointed to foreign affairs positions people who lack training, expertise and a worldview.

Not only is Sam Clovis an enigma, he has a strange background. He earned a doctorate in public administration from the University of Alabama. He has never had experience in the science field. Why then his interest in science? He is a fundamental Christian protecting the world from science. He came into the public eye in 2010 as a Rush Limbaugh style right wing radio talk show host in Sioux City, Iowa. By 2016 he was chairman of the Rick Perry for President organization in Iowa. He criticized Trump, but he did a turnabout and became a Trump supporter as well as co-chairman of the Trump campaign. When he was nominated by Trump as the U. S. Department of Agriculture Chief Scientist there was disbelief. Clovis withdrew his name from consideration. The reason? He was tied to a former campaign adviser, George Papadopoulos, who pleaded guilty to lying to the FBI about his Russian connections. Clovis recommended Papadopoulos to Trump's foreign policy advisory board. Steve Bannon said of Papadopoulos: "How the fuck did he get on the foreign policy advisory team."

The Department of Agriculture pointed out Trump attempted to politicize science. Fortunately, he nominated a fool as the Chief Scientist. The damage the Trump administration is inflicting on government is incalculable. There is universal scientific ignorance from Trump's appointees concerning the Department of Agriculture. The reason? It is simple! Trump's supporters fear science. They fail to understand how the federal bureaucracy functions. They respond to federal programs by implementing fiscal cuts. When the Trump administration left the Trans-Pacific Partnership it cost American farmers an estimated $4.4 billion a year in foreign sales proving Trump neither understood the Department of Agriculture nor world trade. Department of Agriculture employees still fear a Sam Clovis clone could be foisted on the staff.

DONALD J. TRUMP IS NUTS AND I'M NOT FEELING SO GOOD MYSELF

The question of Donald J. Trump's mental stability was debated from the day he was elected president. Professor Bandy X. Lee's book, **The Dangerous Case of Donald Trump: 27 Psychiatrists and Mental Health Experts Assess A President** did little to settle the debate. Dr. Lee is a specialist in erratic decision-making, violence and narcissism. The Donald should be worried. She has the goods on his behavior. He has not proven to be unstable. Just unpredictable! Just a childlike personality! These things are not against the law. If they were, he would be in Guantanamo.

The problem is no one can figure out Trump's next tweet, next policy or next statement of America's world intent. The Lee book concludes he is mentally unsound. He is a narcissistic personality. He is excessively ego driven. Sounds like the type of person you would want with his finger on the nuclear button. Why does it take twenty-seven psychiatrists to analyze if the newly elected president is a danger to democracy? After reading the book, I was not feeling so good myself. Maybe Donald J. Trump is nuts. Then again! There is no proof, only anecdotal evidence.

The concept of truth is the first thing the psychiatrists concentrate upon as Trump had trouble telling truth from fiction. The doctor's analyzed narcissism, unbridled hedonism and a lack of responsibility. Trump excelled in all areas. But does this make him unfit for the presidency? Franklin D. Roosevelt, John F. Kennedy and Bill Clinton were examples of effective president's with these traits.

One of the curious conclusions by the psychiatrists is Trump has a desire to engage in war with the rest of the world. The twenty-seven psychiatrists had a panoply of other Trump deficiencies. Trump's followers organize into groups of narcissistic clones that never question his policies or his motives.

The question of Trump's volatile mental health brings the Twenty-Fifth Amendment to the U. S. Constitution into focus. In 1994, President Jimmy Carter observed that there were few restraints on an unbalanced President except for the 25th Amendment, which allows for the removal of the president if the Vice President and a majority of the Cabinet inform the Congress that he is "unable to discharge the powers and duties of his office." That is not likely to take place under a Trump presidency. A more likely scenario is the Republican Party, along with Paul Ryan and Mitch McConnell, will reconsider their allegiance to a man who never should have been the party's nominee, let alone the president. He never should have been elected president. He is the president! We are stuck with him. This is why I am not feeling so good.

IT SURE LOOKS LIKE COLLUSION BETWEEN
RUSSIA AND TRUMP'S SUPPORTERS

This book began as a study of Trump's interaction with Europe in the 2017 summer. The G-7 and G-20 Summits, as well as the trips to Warsaw and Paris, are the focus of what was to be a small monograph. Then Robert Mueller III was appointed the Special Prosecutor to investigate Russian interference in the 2016 presidential election. Suddenly everything I was writing about was in the center of the Russian investigation. Was President Trump involved? There is not a definitive answer.

Trump's campaign associates had business connections to people in the Russian government or entrepreneurs close to Vladimir Putin's inner circle. Many Trump supporters knew the Russian's hacked Hillary Clinton's e-mails. They lied about this bit of information when questioned by the FBI.

When Donald Trump Jr. was offered negative information on Clinton, he agreed to listen. He held a meeting with Russian operatives. During the campaign the candidate, Donald J. Trump, publicly asked Russia to hack into Clinton's computers and release her e-mails. The Russians hacked into Democratic strategist John Podesta's private e-mails. The DNC's e-mails contained information that harmed Clinton's candidacy. Podesta was Hillary's campaign manager. The resulting controversy was another factor in her defeat. She didn't look presidential using a private server for government e-mails. General Flynn opened up every campaign rally he attended leading the audience in chants of "lock her up." Now he is the one threatened with being locked up.

After entering the White House Trump fired FBI director James Comey. By the end of the year he was attacking the FBI suggesting the bureau was "a mess." The acting FBI Deputy Director, Andrew McCabe, decided to retire in 2018 due to the constant attacks from Trump. Then Trump's Attorney General fired him. This took away his pension. The President continually accused the FBI of not fulfilling its mandate. That mandate, according to Trump, is to investigate and jail Clinton. She has committed no crime. Trump says she is guilty. She should be jailed. Trump's over the top rhetoric and use of innuendo is tragic.

Senator Charles Grassley, an Iowa Republican, called for Acting FBI Director McCabe's firing. Grassley said: "He ought to go for reasons of being involved in some of the things that took place in the previous administration. We want to make sure that there's not undue political influence within the FBI." Then an internal investigation questioned McCabe's veracity. He was accused of lying in an internal investigation. McCabe denies the charges but this cast a pale over the FBI's influence. Trump charged they were after him, as he screamed "no collusion" hundreds of times.

This is of course a smoke screen to take attention away from possible collusion within the Trump inner circle with Russian interests. As Mueller quietly investigated the House Intelligence

Committee concluded its probe into Russian influences with a partisan conclusion. There was no evidence of collusion involving the Trump campaign. The vote was along party lines. Democrats disagreed.

The Senate Judiciary Committee, which Grassley chairs, is particularly vehement the FBI needs a complete reorganization. The Senate, along a party line Republican vote, argued the FBI, the State Department, the CIA, the National Security Administration and the Justice Department need to be reorganized, perhaps even reformed, and like the House-Senate Republicans they deflected from Trump that his cronies contacted with and had support from the Kremlin. Congressional Republicans are certain there is a deep state conspiracy to undermine President Trump.

The Special Prosecutor, Robert Mueller, quietly investigates behind the scenes. The Trump camp is nervous. On October 30, 2017 at 7:28 AM Trump tweeted: "Also, there is no collusion." He was angry. He was depressed. He acted like a bully. He was!

There are facts Trump's minions and the Donald cannot erase. There are eight points that are etched in stone. President Trump has not been tied to Russian collusion. Those around him are a different story.

Here are eight damning facts tying Trump's supporters to Russia.

1.) U. S. intelligence agencies verified Russian hacking of Hillary Clinton's e-mails. The sequential release of these document to Trump's supporters helped derail her presidential candidacy. The e-mail issue is in part Clinton's fault. She ignored government security protocols. The result was her e-mails were scattered across her personal unsecured servers, her personal assistants laptops, a convicted pedophile's laptop and who knows how any other cell phones. One government official said this was an irresponsible act.

2.) After the Clinton's e-mails were hacked, George Papadopoulos, a foreign policy adviser, was told by a London professor, with ties to the Kremlin, what was going on to ensure Trump's victory. Then Papadopoulos began drinking in a London wine bar and an Australian diplomat informed the CIA that Papadopoulos said there was a Russian plot to influence the 2016 presidential election. The FBI questioned him. Papadopoulos lied to the FBI. He was indicted. He pleaded guilty to a felony. He provided Mueller's team with inside information on the Russian collusion question.

3.) Paul Manafort, Trump's campaign manager, was paid by a Russian linked political party in Ukraine, and the Mueller investigation concluded more than $75 million flowed through offshore accounts. The Special Prosecutor alleged $18 million was laundered. Manafort pleaded not guilty. He opted for a trial. He was placed under house arrest. Manafort's lawyers deny these figures. Trump instructed his Press Secretary, Sean Spicer, to describe Manafort as an insignificant figure. Spicer's exact words at a press conference were: "Manafort played a very limited role for a very brief period of time." This is, of course, a bold faced lie. But, then again, during Christmas 2017 Spicer described Charles Dickens' **A Christmas Carol** as a book containing songs to celebrate the holidays. Thank God for Sarah Huckabee Sanders.

After he was charged with the initial crimes by Mueller's investigation, Manafort was not contrite. He continued to say he was innocent. He ignored his bail restrictions. He made a video stating his innocence in direct violation of his bail agreement. The court stepped in and clamped down.

Then on February 22, 2018 Mueller indicted Manafort with new charges. He is, of course, innocent until proven guilty. The second set of charges against Manafort cast aspersions on President Trump's colleagues. The Howdy Dowdy bad haired, cheap suit spokesman for Trump, Press Secretary Sean Spicer, called Manafort a minor character. Spicer should be ashamed of himself. He is a liar. Manafort was Trump's campaign manager.

What were the new charges against Manafort. First, twenty counts of income tax evasion. Second, Manafort faced three counts of failure to file reports of foreign bank and financial accounts. Third, nine charges of bank fraud conspiracy involving million dollar loans were filed. The charges said Manafort hid some of this while he was Trump's campaign chairman. It wasn't just money Manafort is charged with mishandling. He was talking to the Russians allegedly about lifting sanctions. Is this a crime? Who knows! That notion is being adjudicated.

Paul Manafort was for a time the chief political strategist for the president of the Ukraine, Viktor Yanukovych, that is until the president fled in disgrace to Moscow. In the Ukraine Manafort allegedly made millions working with oil executives, as well as other foreign business interests, Cold War spymasters and those manipulating the Ukraine economy allegedly helped Manafort's bank account flourish. He placed much of that money in tax havens in Cyprus, the Grenadines and other tax haven areas. Mueller charged him with tax avoidance and a host of other crimes in an eighteen-count indictment.

When a revolution took place in the Ukraine in 2014, Manafort's Sugar Daddy president left the country. Suddenly at age sixty-six Paul Manafort experienced a tight cash flow. His daughter Jessica was about to get married, and his money problems derailed her wedding plans. Manafort texted his daughter suggesting she scale back the menu to hot dogs. He was in financial trouble by early 2015.

What was the reason for Manafort's fall in the Ukraine? He profited from the rampant corruption, outside influences and a lack of the rule of law. When President Yanukovych fled to Russia fearful of his life, Manafort left his business interests behind. Rick Gates, Manafort's aide, told the **Atlantic** "You have to understand, we've been working in Ukraine a long time, and Paul has a whole separate shadow government structure ... In every ministry he has a guy." That comment tells one all they need to know about Manafort's ethics and integrity.

The FBI was onto Manafort long before Trump announced his presidential candidacy. A Russian oligarch threatened Manafort. Oleg Degipaska invested $18.9 million in a Ukrainian company, and he wanted to know where Manafort placed his money. Degipaska wanted his money back, and there were rumored physical threats. Russian oligarchs do not take lightly to losing millions.

The hostility to Manafort in the Ukraine led the "hacktivist collective" to hack his texts from 2012 through 2016 with six million words collected. His daughter's phone was also hacked. The material was sent to **Politico**, the **New York Times** and perhaps to the **Atlantic**.

The texts show a loving husband and father. Manafort indulged his daughter who said on a friend's podcast: "I only go to luxury restaurants." He also nursed his wife back to health from a horseback accident that nearly killed her in 1997. Then, the **Atlantic** reported, Manafort had a series of extramarital affairs leading to couples therapy. He arrived in Arizona for rehab for unannounced reasons. Rumor has it he allegedly was in the same facility Harvey Weinstein was treated.

After these personal problems, Manafort was back in Washington in 2016 looking to recoup his fortune. He began his career in the nation's capital as a lobbyist and political consultant. He officially joined the Trump campaign on March 28, 2016. He worked as campaign chair without a salary, but, according to the Mueller investigation, he allegedly applied for loans using fraudulent documents. Hence, the second set of charges filed against him in late February 2018. He hurt Trump's campaign. The evidence is the president had little, if any, knowledge of Manafort's activity.

4.) In June 2016, Donald Trump Jr., Jared Kushner and Paul Manafort met with Russian operatives who said they had dirt on Hillary Clinton. Rob Goldstone, a London based publicist, was the catalyst to this meeting. Goldstone had known Trump for years. Donald Jr. was also a friend. When he heard of the information compromising Clinton's campaign, Trump Jr. wrote a Russian prosecutor had "offered to provide the Trump campaign with some official documents and information that would incriminate Hillary and her dealings with Russia and would be very useful." The meeting took place in June 9, 2016 and the subsequent publicity prompted the Trump campaign to alter the intent, the message and the importance of the meeting. There is no denying that political advertisements stating: "Hillary is a Satan, and her crimes and lies had proved just how evil she is," were of Russian origin. A Russian posted in stilted language a number of anti-Hillary posts.

The June meeting between Trump Jr. and others didn't yield incriminating information on Hillary Clinton. Trump won the election. But the Russians persisted. Recently released documents by the Senate Judiciary Committee show Russian operatives requested a second meeting with Donald Jr. Rob Goldstone said a second meeting would help the Kremlin explain why the Magnitsky Act, which froze the bank accounts of Russian officials for human rights abuses, was a mistake. In other words Kremlin insiders proposed an investigation into why and how the act was passed. Donald Jr. was told the Magnitsky Act angered Vladimir Putin. The second meeting never took place but the Senate documents clearly indicate the level of cooperation between those in the Trump inner circle and Kremlin operatives. Goldstone forwarded a three-page document to Trump insiders requesting a presidential viewing to determine if the Magnitsky Act violated American law.

Although the June meeting with the Russian insiders didn't yield incriminating information, it indicated ties to the Kremlin. The Senate documents quote Jared Kushner asking why the American contingent was wasting its time talking about the Magnitsky Act. The Senate documents, released by Democratic California Senator Dianne Feinstein, show that a Russian operative, Aras Agalarov, a Russian real estate developer, acted independently of the Russian government when he visited Trump Tower and he may have acted without Kremlin approval in setting up the meeting between Donald Jr. and others. The Senate Committee did not find any legal problems, but the level of cooperation between Trump campaign insiders and Kremlin operatives was obvious. What was also obvious is no one broke the law. Ethics and integrity are another problem. The Trump campaign didn't appear ethical or filled with integrity minded individuals. But that is not against the law.

5.) Donald Trump in July 2016 requested Russia to find and release any and all Clinton e-mails. This request mentioned 33,000 e-mails Clinton deleted as insignificant. Trump's advisers cast this as a vicious plot by Clinton to get rid of compromising materials. Trump in a press conference said: "Russia, if you're listening, I hope you're able to find the 30,000 e-mails that are missing. I think you will probably be rewarded mightily by our press." It appears George Papadopoulos allegedly was the source for this comment.

6.) Russia released e-mails that helped Trump. They also planted fake news. They employed anti-Hillary Clinton social media advertisements. They organized anti-Clinton meetings to discredit her candidacy. They hacked into the election systems in twenty-one states. Russian operatives did their best to discredit Bernie Sanders' campaign. The Mueller indictment of thirteen Russian nationals who organized the anti-Clinton events during the 2016 campaign proved Kremlin interference. The thirty-seven-page indictment charging thirteen Russians with attempting to sabotage the 2016 election was filled with specific examples of how and where Russia interfered. The Russians stole the identities of U. S. citizens. They posed as political activists. Trump's defenders called these indictments much ado about nothing.

7.) When FBI Director James Comey was fired, it was because he would not go easy on General Michael Flynn. He would not stop the investigation into Russia's role in the 2016 election.

8.) Jeff Sessions, the Attorney General, recused himself from the investigation of collusion with Russian influences. He also forgot, when testifying before Congress, that he had met and talked with Russian officials.

What does all this mean? It means Mueller's investigation was getting too close to the president. By Christmas 2017 Republicans were attacking Mueller's credibility. Fox TV News nightly argued the Special Prosecutor's team was filled with Clinton supporters.

"I had nothing to do with Russia," Trump remarked to reporters. He then headed off to an FBI graduation ceremony.

The question of collusion, the role of amateurs Trump appointed to his Cabinet and inner circle and the lack of understanding of how government functions made Trump's first year a roller coaster ride into oblivion.

CAN TRUMP GOVERN: YES AND NO!

Whether you like it or not, Trump can govern. He hasn't mastered the office but he is showing signs of developing the subtle nuances to effectively govern. That means he is pushing his agenda, his policies and reshaping American institutions.

The notion that Trump is an uneducated blowhard, accidentally elected president is a major story. Why was he elected? It was due to discontent with American politics. His road to the White house, his detractors scream, is due to Russian collusion. They claim his success in the 2016 election was due to well-planned Kremlinology to alter the fabric of American democracy. The villainous Vladimir Putin placed Trump in the presidency. This explanation is typical of the fractured political atmosphere. It is not close to the truth.

Equally fictional is those who defend Trump as a brilliant businessman restructuring government. The Donald's supporters holler "fake news," and this prevents him from governing. Why? It prevents a bi-partisan coalition. They believe the deep state will take him down. They scream "No collusion." Christian conservatives believe God sent Trump to break down the barriers between Christian values and secular government.

What is the truth? Did Trump collude? Does the media make up stories to hinder his politics? Is there a deep state conspiracy? Did Russia get Trump elected? Did President Barack Obama, as Trump charged, spy on the Donald? Is Hillary Clinton a criminal? The answer to these questions is a resounding: "No." We are waiting for Robert Mueller III's investigation to fill in the blanks.

The problem is the Democratic candidate, Hillary Clinton. She is portrayed as boring, pompous; the captive of Wall Street, non-trustworthy because of the Clinton Foundation and the press said repeatedly she was convinced she had won the presidency. This was a roadmap for failure. The Republican standard bearer, Donald J. Trump, was a name calling, woman grabbing, pompous, entitled narcissist. His calling card was "Draining The Swamp" and "Making America Great Again." This sounded much better for America's future.

Trump's victory should embarrass his supporters. He is a bully. They love it. This book analyzes his bully personality at the G-7 and G-20 Summits and contrasts his European bullying with his attack on American democratic institutions. Trump's lack of veracity was shown when the Access Hollywood tape where he talking of "grabbing a woman's pussy" and then a year later he denied it. Maybe it was a Saturday Night Live skit with Alec Baldwin. It wasn't. No one seemed to notice. Trump was elected president.

We are living a nightmare. The Democrats are unable to field candidates attractive to voters. The FBI, the CIA and National intelligence advisers didn't recognize the level of Russian electoral interference until a few weeks before Trump's inaugural.

If there is a villain in this book it is the FBI. It is not a corrupt organization. It is an honest, hardworking arm of the U. S. government. It is efficient. But decision-making is a problem. The investigation into Hillary Clinton's private e-mail server may have cost her the election.

There is a vulgarity to American politics. This will not end soon. The racial hostility to an African American president is another strain of the electoral mess creating the 45th President Donald J. Trump. The number of issues surrounding foreign policy, domestic political change and ties to Russian collusion run through the following narrative.

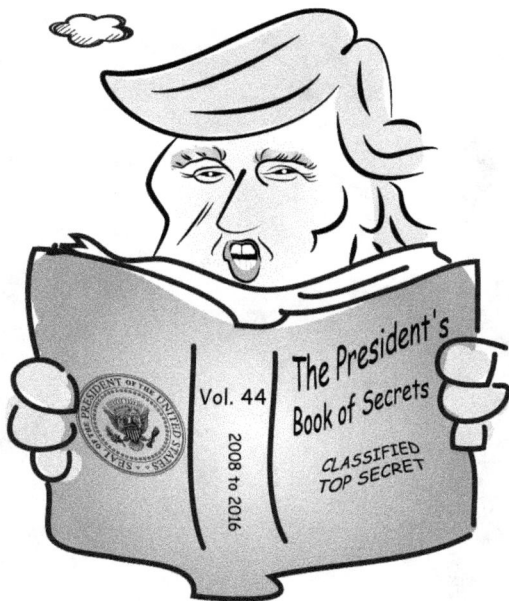

ONE

HOW PRESIDENT BARACK OBAMA CREATED THE POLITICAL TRUMP: THE WHITE HOUSE CORRESPONDENTS' DINNER

"Tonight for the first time, I am releasing
my official birth video."

PRESIDENT BARACK OBAMA AT THE 2011
WHITE HOUSE CORRESPONDENTS' DINNER.

"Donald Trump has been saying he will run for
president as a Republican-which is surprising,
since I just assumed he was running as a joke."

MIKE MEYERS

"He played a game with reality."

AUTHOR MICHAEL WOLFF ON TRUMP

In 2011 Donald J. Trump attended the annual White House Correspondents' dinner. The Donald sauntered in with his beautiful wife Melania. She looked radiant. He looked like her father. His hair

1

glistened under the lights in colors of orange, blonde and gray. The Donald's custom suit jacket was buttoned to hide a rapidly expanding waistline. At six feet four and two hundred fifty pounds, he towered over a crowd of elite journalists, connected celebrities and political donors eager to hoist drinks in a mirthful night of merrymaking. At the time Trump was remembered as the decade long star of the TV hit "Celebrity Apprentice."

Trump took his seat. He was the leading birther. He funded a movement determined to prove President Barack Obama was not an American. The lie that Trump sold was Obama was a Muslim born outside the United States. President Obama got his pound of salt that evening. He spent five minutes roasting Trump. The Donald privately bristled with anger.

In six years Trump would be the president of the United States. Many observers believe the roasting he received from President Barack Obama, the disrespect from the media and movie stars, and the humiliation that went with the dinner began Trump's determined march to the White House. When asked if the dinner influenced his decision to run for the presidency, Trump said emphatically: "No." When asked if he was humiliated by President Obama's barbs that night. He repeatedly said, "No." The evening was one of fun and frivolity. Trump's answers were disingenuous. He was angry. He vowed to get even. He did!

The Correspondents' Dinner is a time to bring the press and the White House together for a fun night before the press continues its daily battle covering politics. That night created the public-political Donald J. Trump. President Barack Obama abused him verbally. He was ridiculed for his birther activity. He was shown to be the vain, petty, egotistical and bullying opportunist that would be inaugurated in January 2017, as the 45th President of the United States. This was considered far-fetched in 2011.

President Obama was angry at Trump. After having been attacked for allegedly being born in Indonesia, Obama responded three days before the Correspondents' Dinner by releasing his birth certificate. Despite this release, Trump's supporters, the Tea Party and right wing Republicans continued to fan the flames that perhaps Barack Obama was a "secret Muslim." The president was angry.

2

OBAMA HUMILIATES TRUMP CREATING
THE POLITICAL DONALD

As Trump sat down for the 2011 dinner, he was at the peak of his birther campaign. What was the birther campaign? It was a Trump organized plan to humiliate President Barack Obama. The idea of an African American in the White House infuriated the Donald. One can say he was possessed with destroying him. That night at the White House Correspondents' dinner President Obama picked the Donald to pieces in a scathing indictment of his lack of character. In the process the president exposed Trump's fragile ego and naked ambition.

When the dinner commenced, President Obama released his Hawaii birth certificate. Trump continued to falsely claim the president was born in Indonesia. The lies, duplicity and outright character assassination Trump spewed didn't bother people. It was simply the Donald being the Donald. He was like a spoiled teddy bear, although an angry one.

When Trump told reporters he dispatched eleven private detectives to Hawaii to prove Obama wasn't a citizen, there was allegedly was not an ounce of truth in this testosterone-laced statement. There is no proof Trump spent a penny. It was all hype.

When President Obama spoke he zeroed in on Trump. "We all know about your credentials and breadth of experience," Obama continued. "For example-no, seriously-just recently, in an episode of Celebrity Apprentice…."-There was laughter at the mere mention of the program's name. Then Obama said the program was no longer impressive. "You fired Gary Busey. And these are the kinds of decisions that would keep me up at night," Trump concluded. The raucous laughter bounced off the red faced Trump. He silently fumed. The Donald was publicly humiliated. He sat stone-faced. It looked like steam was coming out of his ears.

Those close to Trump remarked he is thin-skinned and vengeful. That was the night Trump decided to pursue a presidential run. The hatred Obama instilled in Trump during that dinner fueled his run for the presidency. The roast's ritual was something the thin skinned, egomaniacal Trump didn't understand. Obama shamed him. He would get his revenge. Roxanne Roberts, a Washington Post reporter,

3

sat directly behind Trump at the dinner. She observed: "Trump was so humiliated by the experience…that he triggered some deep, previously hidden yearning for revenge." The New York Times agreed: "That evening of public abasement, rather than sending Mr. Trump away, accelerated his ferocious efforts to gain stature in the political world."

There were many barbed comments from President Obama. What was the one comment that sent Trump running for the White House? It was the following remark: "Now, I know that he's taken some flack lately, but no one is better suited to put this birth certificate matter to rest than the Donald," President Obama continued. "And that's because he can finally get back to focusing on the issues that matter-like, did we fake the moon landing? What really happened in Roswell? And where are Biggie and Tupac?" Trump bristled with indignation. He was being disrespected. He couldn't stand it.

It wasn't just Obama who disrespected Trump. Mike Meyers, the Saturday Night Live veteran, joked: "Donald Trump has been saying he will run for president as a Republican-which is surprising, since I just assumed he was running as a joke." Meyers wasn't through with the jokes, when he did everything but call Trump a racist. Donald Trump said recently he's got a great relationship with "the blacks." Unless the Blacks are a family of white people, I bet he's mistaken, Meyers concluded to raucous applause. Trump sat scowling. The irony of this 2011 roast is Trump was the honored guest of the Washington Post.

Trump may have wondered what he was doing at the dinner when comedian Gilbert Gottfried said: "What's the difference between a wet raccoon and Donald J. Trump's hair? A wet raccoon doesn't have seven billion fucking dollars in the bank." Everyone laughed. Trump sat stone-faced.

The next morning Trump was furious. The press described him as "humiliated." This led to the birth of his notion of "fake news." The Donald said he was baffled by the press reports. The press wouldn't leave the story alone. A sensationalist minded London newspaper, the Sun, picked up the story, as American's voted arguing the 2011 Correspondents' Dinner was a "public humiliation of Donald Trump." Emma Lake, a London Sun's reporter, described the event

4

as "the moment Trump decided to run for president." Maybe! Maybe not! Since 2000 Trump had issued trial balloons for a presidential run. He decided President Obama was unbeatable in 2012. The following election was one he eyed as early as 2011. Only Trump knows if the White House Correspondents' Dinner was the turning point. The London based Daily Mail echoed the Sun's story. Nikki Schwab observed: "Obama's mockery of the billionaire at the 2011 White House Correspondents' Dinner…motivated the businessman to run for president." Maybe the British press is right. Roger Stone, one of Trump's close associates, said: "I think that is the night he resolved to run for president."

After he entered the White House, Trump's minions talked of boycotting future White House Correspondents' Dinners. They didn't need to worry. Trump refused to attend these events once he entered the White House; he saved his comedy for governing America.

On April 29, 2017 the White House Correspondents' Dinner took place on the One Hundredth Day of the Trump presidency. The president was invited. His aides, Kellyanne Conway and Hope Hicks, didn't know how to approach Trump about the invitation. Would he attend? The answer was a resounding "No." He didn't have a sense of humor. He doesn't make jokes. He was prone to violent, vocal outbursts. Finally, the two Trump aides approached the president stating the Correspondents' Dinner reeked of favoritism for the Democrats. Trump agreed. They told him how unfairly the media treated him. Trump smiled. They had no trouble selling the president on the idea the media was out to get him. He agreed. He would ignore most, if not all, press requests. Fake news was everywhere.

TWO

AUTOCRACY, AN AUTHORITARIAN AND TRUMP'S THREAT TO DEMOCRACY

> "Trump stoops ever lower in his plundering of truth and thought."
>
> ROGER COHEN, NEW YORK TIMES

> "Trump is stealing a page out of Richard Nixon's playbook once again. When you get criticized by the press for a book that attacks you, you attack back with ferocity. It's a misuse of presidential powers."
>
> DOUGLAS BRINKLEY

> "Mr. Trump hereby demands that you immediately cease and desist from any further publication, release or dissemination of this book...that you issue a full apology...as to all statements made about him in the book."
>
> TRUMP'S LAWYER TO HENRY HOLT AND COMPANY, PUBLISHER ON MICHAEL WOLFF'S BOOK.

> "A writer who needled the elite enrages the president."
>
> NEW YORK TIMES COMMENTING ON MICHAEL WOLFF, FIRE AND FURY: INSIDE THE TRUMP WHITE HOUSE

To compare Donald J. Trump to Adolf Hitler is to miss the point. Trump is not Stalin, Castro, Hitler or Mussolini. He is the elected

6

leader of the world's most stable democracy. When he insults, disparages, bullies or attempts to destroy an opponent, he is met with heavy criticism from the Democratic Party, a free press and a world spotlight decrying his boorish, impulsive, arrogant and insipid behavior. Trump would love to rule by decree. Fortunately, he can't. He is attempting a coup of sorts. It is a legal coup where he alters institutions fundamental from a free, functioning democratic society into an authoritarian based democracy.

FIRE AND FURY EXPLAINS TRUMP'S AUTHORITARIANISM

The authoritarian nature of Trump's presidency is seen in his inability to recognize the First Amendment. When Michael Wolff's Fire And Fire: Inside The Trump White House was leaked to the press, prior to its publication, the full fury of the White House was directed at the author and his publisher, Henry Holt and Company. The president's demand to rescind publication and apologize for criticizing him led to huge sales. The book quickly sold a million copies the four days prior to its official release. One of Wolff's major premises is President Trump suffers from a narcissist personality disorder.

Wolff is not the first writer to describe the president's inability to accept legitimate criticism. His delusional relationship with the truth provides a window into how he views the First Amendment. He has few concerns for press freedoms. Freedom of the press is what the Trump administration hopes to curtail. His inability to distinguish legitimate protest from legally attempting to circumvent the First Amendment tells one all they need to know about his lack of education on governmental matters.

As Wolff made the rounds of the television talk shows, he was a master at selling Fire And Fury. His invective reached new heights in the weeks after his books release. This spurred sales to record highs. The tales were tantalizing and seductive. He hinted that at the moment he was making media appearances Trump was having an affair. The media quickly selected U. N ambassador Nikki Haley as the president's femme fatale. According to White House sources this was a rumor Trump loved. There was no way to verify it. It is patently untrue.

7

WHY IS IT NO MAJOR LEGISLATION
PASSED UNTIL THE TAX CUT?

As of December 1, 2017, Trump's Republican followers failed to pass any major legislation. That is until the tax cut. America was at a standstill. The legislative process was stalled. It was at this point Trump's authoritarian instincts and autocratic impulses intensified. He recommended the United States bring back torture because "it works." This statement, reported by the New York Times, angered Trump. He was outraged his comments were reported, fact checked and criticized.

Why is Donald Trump a threat to democracy? He is in the process of systematically eroding it. There are many examples of his attack on the democratic process. Trump's remarked all National Football League players who don't stand for the National Anthem should be fired. Trump's rabid mob screamed the NFL players were disrespecting the flag. The majority of the players are African American. They have said repeatedly this is not about the flag. It is about conditions in America for black people. This is what the pro-Trump people have ignored. Trump's supporters never mention the player's comments.

The irony is the outrage over the NFL didn't begin when San Francisco 49er quarterback Colin Kaepernick refused to stand for the national anthem. It was August 2016 when Kaepernick made his protest. It was more than a year later that Trump went on a tirade against the NFL players supporting the San Francisco quarterback. When Trump weighed in on the issue, his support base erupted. His demagogic comments set off a firestorm of NFL criticism.

Those supporting Trump on the national anthem controversy argued as one commentator said: "The African American NFL players hi-jacked an American sacred ceremony and turned it into a selfish 'what about me' campaign. The National Anthem is strictly about patriotism." The NFL's African American players said they respected the ceremony, it was a protest to equalize opportunity for young African American's in education, the job market and maintaining equal rights in the wake of the Ferguson and other incidents of police brutality.

The Trump presidency is a serious threat to American democracy. The bulwark against authoritarian rule remains in the press, in the courts, in the continual rule of law, in the presence of ethics oversight in government, in the guarantee of voting rights and in maintaining election integrity. His constant prodding for restrictions on the free press and his egregious tweets tell us he doesn't understand these concepts. Or perhaps he does and wants to take them away.

IS THE AUTOCRAT WINNING IN AMERICA AND THE WORLD?

Is Trump reducing democracy? This question was asked repeatedly when Donald J. Trump assumed the presidency. It appears so! We are headed for an autocracy. What is an autocrat? He is a person much like Donald J. Trump. The definition of an autocrat is a leader who will dilute constitutional privileges. Trump says this is for the greater good of the people. That is nonsense.

How authoritarian is Donald J. Trump? He is the ultimate authoritarian. Trump plays to public opinion by creating what he terms "bad guys." He goaded FBI Director James Comey into opening an investigation of Hillary Clinton less than a month before the voters went to the polls. Comey did nothing wrong. What he did was to listen to the campaign managers of an autocrat—Donald J. Trump who was expected to lose the election. In an effort to display fairness, Comey investigated Hillary Clinton. He found no evidence of criminal intent. But clearly in the weeks before the election this hurt her chances of an electoral victory.

The Washington Post argued Comey did not cost Clinton the election. He may have tipped the scales slightly toward Trump. Why did Hillary lose? It was a combination of four factors. First, Clinton underperformed in swing states. She seldom campaigned in these states. Second, the Democratic Party looked to be the captive of Wall Street. The old hard line labor union and working person coalition was in tatters. Third, Trump won by less than one percent in Michigan, Pennsylvania and Wisconsin. In these states Comey's letter was decisive. Fourth, the hostility to President Obama's policies often disguised the racism inherent in opposition to the first African American Chief Executive. White power, dissatisfaction with government bureaucracy, and the alt-right swung the election to Trump.

"When a person is an autocrat they do not delve deeply into issues. They have little concern with in-depth knowledge. They are like cheerleaders. They want to make you feel good. Trump is an unabashed autocrat," Edward Luce wrote in The Retreat of Western Liberalism. What did he mean? Why did he come to this conclusion?

Luce did not expect Trump to win the presidency. "It was obvious Hillary Clinton could only win the presidency by default," Luce wrote. He pointed out Democrat's had "tone-deafness towards the middle class…." This cost Clinton the electoral victory.

WHERE LIBERALS FAILED AND WHY:
HILLARY WAS NOT A SURE WINNER

In 2014, Luce wrote Hillary was a sure winner. He concluded there were not enough registered Republican voters to elect their candidate. Where did Luce and other liberals go wrong? They didn't anticipate the shift in nationalism and the decline of western liberalism. The data gurus insisted Clinton would poll more votes than Trump. She did! They didn't analyze the Electoral College. They had no idea of the degree of hostility in the Mountain States in parts of the mid-West and the South to Clinton's candidacy.

There was a groupthink mentality to Hillary's supporters. They thumbed their nose at Trump. They labeled his followers as "disreputable." The disreputable faction brought him to the White House. Hillary's supporters acted like they won the election. They didn't.

The infighting over appointments, spoils and power within Clinton's campaign caused her defeat. Rather than working diligently for the Democratic candidate many of Hillary's supporters pursued personal policies. Trump said she was the tool of Wall Street. It looked like it. The Democrats were not able to effectively counter his comments. The idea she committed crimes raising money for the Clinton Foundation took on a life of its own. When Hillary failed to deny the story, it turned into a fact. Trump's supporters argued she should be jailed. The argument after leaving the Secretary of State position was she made too much money. By not challenging Trump's outrageous attacks, credence was given to fictional facts. This is the direction and message that brought Trump to the White House.

Hillary's image as a criminal who should be in jail was never challenged. Trump's magnetic personality, over the top rallies in areas where he was popular and the cheering crowds endorsing his demand to "Build a wall and Mexico will pay for it," or the popular rally slogan "Jail her" helped to bring an autocratic charlatan to the White House. Trump's campaign altered the fundamental fabric of American democracy. Is it permanent? Only time will tell.

The Democratic Party detached itself from the middle class. They incurred a defeat. The churches, town halls and trade union headquarters were visited by Trump. These interests were the former bastions of the Democratic Party. They slowly morphed into Trump supporters.

Hillary's campaign was soft. She chided Trump for his slogan: "Making America Great Again." Most Americans laughed at her slogan "Our Families, Our Future" or "Next Begins With You." Trump sounded like a strong leader. Hillary came off as boring. Clinton was out of touch with those who would have cast their ballot for her. On taxes, student loans, foreign policy and most other issues she had little impact.

During the course of writing this book I began with the premise Trump's foreign policy was a disaster. Or at best ill thought out! I was wrong. Donald J. Trump's foreign policy in his first year did have moments of success. His policies were in line with what he had said and advocated since he first talked to celebrity gossip columnist Rona Barrett about foreign policy in 1980. This doesn't mean Trump's foreign policy was generally well thought out. It wasn't. It was consistent with how he viewed the world. Few took Trump seriously in matters of foreign policy. This was a mistake. He has shown himself to be shrewd in foreign affairs despite erratic behavior that frightens our long-term allies. He befuddles some nations. When Trump traveled to Europe he sought out the dictatorial Polish president, he praised Vladimir Putin and he came off as a leader who favored tyrants, dictators and those hostile to democracy. Trump's first significant European speech was a forerunner of his future foreign policy.

When he delivered a July 6, 2017 speech in Warsaw Poland, Trump outlined his intellectual or thematic approach to foreign policy. No one listened. No one cared. The press should have spent more time on the speech. It articulated everything Donald J. Trump meant and intended in foreign policy. Why is this speech important? It is because President Trump said the survival of the West depended upon the "community of nations" who will "share a common way of life." This was a warning a new foreign policy was in place. Military might was now a focus. He ended his speech stating the U. S. would be in the forefront of the "defense of civilization itself." He set a moral tone pointing out he would not tolerate Syria gassing citizens. He opposed the dictator Bashar al Assad. By setting this moral humanitarian tone the president declared his sympathy for the victims. He was a tough foreign policy president and Trump reminded Bashar al Assad he would pay the price for using chemical weapons on his people. A portion of the press was shocked. Most of the American press didn't report the positive reaction to Trump's new policies. In the U. K. Professor Stephen Wertheim, a historian at King's College, University of Cambridge, was one of the first academics to praise Trump while pointing out President George W. Bush waged a disastrous war in Iraq. President Barack Obama drew a red line. He didn't enforce his threat. Then President Donald J. Trump came along with a foreign policy rooted in a stronger militarist path. Right or wrong it is the direction America is headed to in the world arena. Trump set a red line. He would enforce it. Professor Wertheim gave Trump high foreign policy ratings. This was a complete turnaround from six months earlier when Wertheim stated: "The problem is, Trump isn't an isolationist. He is a militarist, something far worse. And calling Trump, as isolationist isn't an effective critique." Professor Wertheim is typical of U. K. historians, he isn't sure if Trump was positive or negative. So Wertheim concluded he embraced a little success with a bit of failure. "Trump's foreign policy critics are failing to counter Trump and build a better foreign policy," Wertheim tweeted on March 9, 2018.

How does one view President Trump? His display of vulgarity is constant. His elements of racism evolve daily. How he promotes his brand of authoritarianism is a problem. His disastrous Cabinet appointments of rich white, male, billionaires caused ethics' probes. There were constant complaints of overspending by Cabinet members, there were favors for lobbyists and government policy increasingly catered to big business. There is criticism for excessive spending and favoritism toward conservative, pro-Trump employees. They lack foreign policy expertise. The Trump cabinet is made up of ultra conservatives out of touch with the political mainstream. His personal presidential style tends toward cronyism. His language is limited using phrases like "I call them losers, losers." He preaches authoritarian concepts.

The risk Trump poses to our political system is enormous. How could someone so unfit, so unqualified and so intellectually deficient be elected president? He represents the new breed of voters. Those who sit in front of Fox TV News, those who have never read a book, a magazine or a newspaper, those who act on Trump's tweets or public statements, and those who fear the encroachment of Communism, Socialism, Big Government, the transgender people and welfare folks. They argue the U. S. is headed toward a constitutional crisis. It is! One of Trump's making!

TRUMP'S WORLD VIEW: IS IT DANGEROUS?

By examining Trump's behavior at the G-7 and G-20 Summits, his tweets and his statements on America's role in world affairs, it was possible to see the first signs of his worldview.

He has threatened to destroy North Korea, blamed both sides in the Charlottesville racial protests, never criticized the Nazis in Charlottesville and he has for all practical purposes withdrawn from Europe. He fired key Cabinet members for disagreeing with him. He fired his alt-right political strategist Stephen G. Bannon for receiving too much media attention. He replaced his blustering, inept Howdy Dowdy look alike press secretary in an ill-fitting suit, Sean Spicer, with a Southern belle who can do the job in an ill-fitting dress and enough Southern charm to make us want Tammy Faye Baker back. He pardoned Sheriff Joe Arpaio for continually violating immigrant rights and being convicted of a federal crime. The Donald doesn't think so. He informed a crowd of raving right wing Phoenix conservatives: "I have a feeling Sheriff Joe is going to be alright." I think what the president meant is Sheriff Arpaio is "alt-right." Everyone else realizes Sheriff Joe thumbed his nose at federal law. The crisis in America is Trump pardoned Arpaio a convicted felon. The Maricopa County Sheriff then announced he was running to represent Arizona in the U. S. Senate.

Trump's pardon of Sheriff Arpaio unleashed a storm of criticism. Tom Bossert, the head of Homelands Security, defended Arpaio's pardon, he said: "All presidents end up with some controversial pardons." Bossert continued stating the media was unfair "to characterize Trump as not caring about the rule of law." Trump gave his law and order base a gift in pardoning Sheriff Joe.

E. J. DIONNE TELLS US WHAT HAPPENED TO AMERICAN POLITICS: HOW DOES THIS IMPACT FOREIGN POLICY

What has happened to American politics? Fox TV News has turned coffee shop philosophers into political scientists. Bipartisan politics is dead. There is a never-ending attack on the press and the term "fake news" is now a major threat to the First Amendment. As Trump moved to the nomination and was elected president, he took over a Republican Party riddled with dissension, fuzzy politics and a host of issues threatening the fabric of American democracy. Facts, evidence and science are suspect. Truth and trust have passed into the night. Coffee shop philosophers tell you Hillary Clinton sold our uranium in a corrupt deal with Russia. They claim she embraces the "New Politics of Extremism." They feel she should be prosecuted, put in jail, and they talk about the money machine that is the Clinton Foundation. The radical arguments of the Republican Party are taken as mainstream news.

E. J. Dionne, Jr., Norman Ornstein and Thomas E. Mann's One Nation After Trump: A Guide To the Perplexed, And The Not Yet Deported is a book by three left of center analysts who charge "the Republican Party has become an insurgent outlier-ideologically extreme." Republican's ignore or denigrate facts. Radical conservatives have taken control of the Republican Party. When Arizona Republican Senator Jeff Flake announced he would not seek re-election, he pointed to GOP extremism. He lamented the failure to recognize traditional American political institutions.

Who are Dionne, Jr., Ornstein and Mann? They are a team of distinguished journalists and professors who have researched and written about elections for decades. Dionne is a senior research fellow at a number of academic research facilities. He is also a featured columnist with the Washington Post. Dionne is a best-selling author. Ornstein and Mann are well-known academics. Ornstein is a political science professor. His research centers on elections and their impact upon American democracy. Why does this team exist?

E. J. Dionne is a respected, best-selling journalist with a wide readership. He writes a twice-weekly column for the Washington Post. He is also a government professor at Georgetown University and a senior fellow at the Brookings Institute. He partnered with the two brilliant academic political scientists to produce a popular book with important conclusions. They have analyzed the dangers of the Republican attack on governmental institutions. What are the GOP's successes? They have struck down, in partnership with President Trump, safeguards in health, the environment, education and the fiscal safety net for the rapidly shrinking middle class. By advocating a Bill of Rights for Workers the authors provide a plan for 2018 and beyond. Dionne and his fellow scholars lay out the reasons for Trump's election.

RACISM, VULGARITY AND TRUMP

The main argument Dionne presents is Trump's racism, vulgar attacks, cronyism and worshipful praise for America's long time authoritarian enemies suggests a presidency devoid of historical knowledge. Trump intensified the war on the media Richard M. Nixon began in the early 1970s. The Washington Post pressed Nixon for his refusal to release the Pentagon Papers. Later Nixon covered up the burglary of the Democratic National Committee. In both cases the Post revealed the duplicity, dishonesty and law-breaking attitude of the Nixon presidency. It demonstrated the role of the free press. The Watergate burglary forced Nixon out of office. He was impeached. He resigned before he was tried and convicted of covering up a burglary. It was Nixon's criminal behavior, and his penchant for cronyism that almost altered the constitutional principles of our country. Does this sound familiar?

15

There is a parallel in Trump's presidency. The disregard for rules was shown when EPA head Scott Pruitt demanded a twenty person security detail, a bulletproof desk, flew first class and rented a high end apartment for fifty dollars a night from an individual in the energy business. When confronted with Secretary Pruitt's wasteful spending, Trumps said: "He was doing a good job."

Republican leaders refuse to distance themselves from Trump's egregious behavior. He is making the GOP over in his image. How could someone so unfit, so unqualified be elected? The answer is a simple one. Social scientists tell us fears of immigrants, fears of Muslim radicalism, fears of declining religious freedoms, fears of excessive gun control, fears of job loss, fears of diminishing white rights and fears of a multiethnic culture drove Trump's victory.

There is another important line of thinking. The promise to "Make America Great Again." This phrase resonated with the Donald's supporters. It sealed Trump's electoral victory. Dionne writes: "Trump clearly appealed to two broad overlapping streams of discontent-immigration and race."

But to assume racists and bigots elected Trump is to miss what happened in 2016. The lack of job growth, manufacturing outsourcing, hostility to Obamacare, the place of the U. S. in world trade, failed military affairs and the divisions in the Democratic Party led by an unpopular, underwhelming candidate with a lack of credibility accelerated Trump's road to the White House.

AMERICA'S FUTURE: BLEAK OR BRIGHT?

What do Dionne Jr., Ornstein and Mann see in America's future? They are concerned about the continual attacks on democracy. Liberal democracy, a free and open society, and the First Amendment are in danger. When NFL players knelt for the national anthem it ignited a debate over the First Amendment right to protest. When Nazis showed up in Virginia to demonstrate against African Americans, Trump said both sides were at fault for the riots. Trump would not condemn the Nazis. He lacks the political background to understand his faux pas.

There is no question liberal democracy is threatened. When Trump arrived in Europe during his three trips to the G-7, the G-20 and later to celebrate France's Bastille Day, he encouraged Poland's President Andrzej Duda to strip Polish courts of much of its power. This is a window into Trump's thinking. He believes the courts have too much influence. He doesn't understand the separation of governmental powers.

Trump's attacks on the judiciary are part of his larger war on the courts. Why is there a war on liberal democracies? The answer is a simple one. Trust and tradition are no longer a part of the public consciousness.

The resistance to an amateur bully in the White House is necessary to the future of American democracy. In One Nation After Trump, Dionne, Orenstein and Mann question if the reactionary, right wing, racist rants supporting "Making America Great Again" is a danger to democracy. Only time can tell!

THE NEED FOR BI-PARTISAN CONTROLS ON TRUMP AND THE RUSSIAN QUESTION PERSISTS

The need for bipartisan solutions is the only way to end the political pit of despair that America has descended into since Trump's election. The dysfunctional direction of our politics continues with a Special Prosecutor indicting Trump's campaign cronies.

Trump failed to achieve many campaign goals in his first year in the presidency. The long awaited repeal of Obamacare is still an issue. The Republican Party unraveled. Congress with Republican majorities failed to pass key legislation. In sharp contrast the Democrats were no better. They lacked leadership. They continued to promote ill-defined policies. They had no idea how to remedy political factionalism.

Why is democracy in peril? Since his election, Trump refuses to acknowledge Russian interference. He has disparaged and attacked the U. S. State Department. He systematically eviscerates its budget. He ignores their high level research. He minimizes their role in the governmental process.

In the months after the G-7 and the G-20 Summit's Trump criticized American intelligence agencies, as well as attacking former FBI Director James Comey, former CIA Director James Brennan and former Director of National Intelligence Director James Clapper. To divert attention away from those in his inner circle who may have colluded with or were zealous in their support of Russia and Vladimir Putin, President Trump calls his critics "political hacks."

Donald. J. Trump: "I believe that (Putin) feels that he and Russia did not meddle in the election." Then to further obfuscate matters he said he stood by the American intelligence community. This is typical of his mental contradictions. He changes his policies daily. A morning tweet announces the next shift in policy.

John Brennan: "He was referring to us as political hacks because he was trying to delegitimize the intelligence community assessment that was done." Brennan pointed out assessments written by professional, career intelligence officers create valuable foreign policy intelligence. Neither Trump's intellect nor his ego understood intelligence briefings. The lack of professionalism from Trump is unforgivable. The State Department staff is largely a non-partisan group of career civil servants with in-depth foreign policy expertise. The Trump administration neither recognizes nor uses this research arm.

Former CIA Director John Brennan appeared on CNN's "State of the Union." Jake Tapper asked him about Russia's cyber threat. "It's puzzling as to why Mr. Trump does not acknowledge that and embrace it, and also push back hard against Mr. Putin," Brennan remarked. Brennan said that there was clear evidence Russia meddled in the election. Trump said: "No."

Trump can be played by anyone who appeals to an ego knowing no bounds. Former Director of National Intelligence, James Clapper, said it was "naïve" for Trump to think Russia could be an ally. Once again the president's lack of knowledge dooms his policies.

Clapper was astonished that two months of in-depth intelligence reports were ignored by Trump. These reports contain factual based information proving Russia's extensive use of Facebook and Twitter to create fake accounts, to buy ads, to spread fake news, and to disseminate disinformation in the 2016 election.

An example of Trump's attack on fake news is a February 17, 2017 tweet: "The Fake News Media (failing @nytimes, @NBCNews, @ABC, @CBS, @CNN) is not my enemy, it is the enemy of the American people!" Later in the month, speaking to the Conservative Political

Action Committee, Trump doubled down on the fake media. He charged they misquoted, they misrepresented, they misread and they reported stories bearing little resemblance to reality. It wasn't just the major news outlets the president criticized. He went after all other aspects of government. He targeted the FBI, the CIA, the NSA and the State Department among others. His criticism was unjustified, He never let up in his demeaning behavior.

Trump's criticism of former FBI Director James Comey was over the top. He said Comey was "a liar" and "a leaker." He intimated Vladimir Putin had more credibility than Comey. What did Trump miss concerning the men he labeled as "hacks?" Clapper served in the military for thirty-five years. He flew in excess of seventy combat missions over Vietnam. Clapper, like Arizona Republican Senator John McCain, put his life at risk for the country's national security. Trump had three deferments thereby avoiding Vietnam.

James Clapper summed up Trump's naiveté about the international political arena. Clapper said: "The threat posed by Russia…is manifest and obvious. To try to paint it in any other way is, I think, astounding, and in fact, poses a peril to this country." John Brennan also weighed in on Trump's lack of expertise in foreign affairs. Brennan said: "Giving Putin a pass" invites other countries to sway Trump. The right wing Polish government and the president of the Philippines worked Trump with massive welcoming ceremonies. If you appeal to the Donald's ego, he is your best friend. Trump's sin is one of excessive narcissism. He fails to criticize other countries for gross violations of human rights, shutting down the press and indiscriminately jailing opponents. One has the impression Trump is jealous of Poland and the Philippine where they jail political opponents. He would love to jail the "Fake News" opposition. The First Amendment is clearly the enemy.

James Clapper: "I do think both the Chinese and the Russians think they can play him." A year later when it was revealed the FBI spied on the Trump campaign, Clapper said it was a "good thing" for the country due to Trump's lack of experience in international affairs, his unwillingness to educate himself on foreign policy and his brutal, often dehumanizing, comments on foreign leaders. In conversation with CNN's Don Lemon, Clapper said; "If there was someone that was observing that sort of thing. That's a good thing because the Russians pose a threat to the very basis of our political system."

The fallout from the charge that an FBI insider infiltrated the Trump campaign was instant. Trump called it bigger that Watergate. What is not reported? As early as January 3, 2018 Trump insiders contacted the FBI fearing compromising materials from the Kremlin. The FBI insider investigation did help to indict George Papadopoulos, Paul Manafort, Richard Gates III and General Michael Flynn. Had there not been an FBI agent inside the Trump campaign these charges would not have been filed. At this writing three have taken a plea deal.

Trump's new attack dog, Rudy Giuliani, left his bowl of oatmeal and his Fox TV News channel to babble through an explanation on the imbedded FBI agent. "For a long time we've been told that there was some kind of infiltration," Giuliani paused adjusted his dentures and continued. "I don't know for sure, nor does the president, if there really was one."

The next day Trump screamed and hollered the FBI invaded his privacy and tried to elect Hillary.

WHY TRUMP IS A DANGER TO DEMOCRACY
AND WORLD STABILITY

In May 2017 Trump's campaign insiders were accused of colluding with Russian interests. Trump's inner-circle said they had nothing to hide. They continued to react with outright rage and pent up hostility! They screamed no collusion on a daily basis. The Mueller investigation had shown this is not true. By April 2018 there were five major indictments of Trump insiders.

The Atlantic reported Donald J. Trump Jr. began contacts with Wikileaks to obtain stolen e-mails to help his father's election efforts. Donald Jr.'s alleged relationship with Wikileaks continued for nine months. Why is this important? The evidence is clear that Wikileaks was in Trump's corner. Russian interests directed the WikiLeaks campaign to bring about a Trump Presidency. The evidence is unclear as to the degree of Russia's influence. There is concrete evidence they hacked into sensitive areas influencing the election.

Did this work? Yes. The damage? No one knows. The Mueller investigation shows us Russian agents organized anti-Clinton rallies during the 2016 election.

MANAFORT, THE TRUMP CAMPAIGN AND MUELLER

Trump's campaign manager, Paul Manafort, was charged with laundering money. Where did the money originate? He already obtained the funds from Russian interests.

There is no evidence Trump knew about Manafort's suspicious business deals. The FBI and Mueller monitored his activity. Michael Isikoff and Davie Corn's number one New York Times bestseller, Russia Roulette argues Manafort was in business with Russian billionaire Oleg Deripaska, and one of their deals left Manafort in debt to the oligarch. They claim Manafort joined Trump's campaign to provide influence to Russian's investing in America. It was Deripaska who set Manafort on the path to riches and influence in Ukraine, Isikoff and Corn observed. (p. 97) They detail how Manafort helped Viktor Yanukovych win the Ukraine presidency in 2010. They describe how things quickly went south and the Ukraine political situation changed. There were complaints to the FBI when Manafort attempted to gain support in Washington D. C. for Yanukovych's Ukraine policies. The notion Manafort was acting as an unregistered foreign agent caught the FBI's attention.

By 2014 Yanukovych was recognized as a Russian puppet. Vladimir Putin was pulling the strings. Yanukovych fled to Russia. Manafort allegedly began experiencing financial problems. There is no evidence Trump was aware of Manafort's alleged financial problems.

There is a sense to entitlement from one close Trump adviser. As Special Prosecutor Robert Mueller demonstrated, George Papadopoulos told Trump insiders he could arrange a Trump-Putin meeting. Papadopoulos plead guilty to lying to the FBI. There were other charges that went away for his cooperation. Papadopoulos is credited with the information that made the Mueller probe necessary. He rolled over to become a cooperating witness with Mueller's investigation. For a coffee boy, he caused a lot of damage.

The Mueller investigation is a window into the corruption Trump brought to 1600 Pennsylvania Avenue. Special Prosecutor Mueller represents a system built to investigate a divisive demagogue. The checks and balances in the American system angers Trump.

THE DIVIDE IN AMERICAN POLITICS BRINGING TRUMP TO POWER AND THE AUTHORITARIAN VOTER

How did Trump become president? In 2009 two political scientists, M. J. Hetherington and J. D. Weiler, examined the division between the right and the left leading to stringent polarization. Out of this polarization the authoritarian voter emerged to bring Trump to the presidency. This clash quickly turned into one where the liberal left supports the rights and protection of minority viewpoints, as well as a well-funded welfare system. The right looks for authoritarian leadership. This is to cut waste in government, to curtail excessive foreign policy aid, to reduce the welfare state, to protect gun rights and to control an oppressive, exceptionally bureaucratic, government. Those who support authoritarian views are less likely to be concerned with the democratic process. This person is known as the authoritarian voter. This is part of what brought Trump to the presidency.

What drives the authoritarian voter? They are concerned with internal and external threats to the U. S. Trump told the authoritarian voter the internal threat could be the National Football League's players. If the players do not stand at attention during the national anthem, they should be punished. The external threat could be ISIS or North Korea and the authoritarian voter wants immediate military action. The praise for Donald J. Trump is overwhelming for his tough language and authoritarian policies.

Trump's election is due to the authoritarian response to the us versus them in his campaign rhetoric. On June 15, 2015 Trump announced his plan to run for president. His initial message appealed to the authoritarian voter. He emphasized our "enemies are getting stronger…and we, as a country, are getting weaker." Then Trump turned on the other candidates running for the Republican nomination. He belittled them for various weaknesses. This led to a partisan, authoritarian polarization in the Republican Party. This was the reason for sporadic violence at Trump rallies. Trump highlights the real and imagined threats to America. His supporters continue to rally around his message with a loyalty previously unknown.

Not only does Trump's strongman message resonate with white voters, it appeals to a large number of voters who don't regularly go to the polls. These voters think in terms of black and white issues. They fear everyone from Latinos to Muslims.

In December 2015 the fear of terrorism reached its highest point since 9-11. Trump played on these fears. The threats, real and imagined, led to an increase in support for Trump's demagogic message. Trump is the angry voice appealing to white bigots, blue collar workers, stringent nationalists and those who are opposed to abortion, welfare, public education, immigrants and special government programs for the less fortunate.

What is the role of the authoritarian voter? They follow Trump due to the fear of marginalizing America in world politics. They also want a "White America!" From Mexicans to Muslims, Trump said we are under attack by people who fail to share our values. He promised to "drain the swamp." He talked of putting "Crooked Hillary" in jail. He vowed to have Mexico pay for a border wall. It was over the top rhetoric. It lacked reality. It worked. He became president. The authoritarian voter triumphed.

Authoritarian voters threaten democracy. They blindly follow a leader. They don't consider policies and agendas. They are dogmatic. They refuse to answer questions in political debate. They reward Trump for attacking and abusing the political system. He does this with the cheers and the complicity of his authoritarian followers. They scream "fake news." They want everyone to have the same concept of patriotism. They worship the rich. They disparage the poor.

The continual threats from the president initiates a bullying effect allowing his supporters to fragment democracy. At his rallies violence is encouraged. It is a frightening time. Trump's bigoted and irresponsible behavior led to unbridled violence. The cries of throw out the protesters and beat them up resonates during many of Trump's rallies.

HOW DID THE AUTHORITARIAN
VOTER EMERGE AND WHY?

The authoritarian voter erupted in 2008 when the Republican Party realized Muslim immigrants, increased Mexican workers coming legally and illegally into the U. S., and then the downturn in the economy caused a voter to emerge who wanted a strong man. Mitt Romney in 2012 was not that Republican strong man. Donald Trump was in 2016.

Fox TV News, conservative over the top writers, like Bill O'Reilly, authoring history books with a present day message the world is out to destroy conservatives prompts Trump's supporters to stand solidly behind him. It is the educated immigrant who is feared. The rise of foreign engineers, doctors, lawyers and liberal business people set the stage for an at times violent white reaction. This took place in 2016 when Trump brilliantly adopted the phrase "Make America Great Again" to promote his vision.

The sporadic violence in Phoenix, New York, Los Angeles and a host of other cities indicated the tension within the U. S., and the manner in which the authoritarian voter exploited it. Some of the violence was at Trump rallies while other sparks of violence resulted from anti-Trump demonstrations.

The Huffington Post headlined a story in March 2016: "Donald Trump Encourages Violence At His Rallies. His Fans Are Listening." The accompanying story said that a thirty-one year old Arab-American lady, Yasmeen Alamiri, was called a terrorist at a Trump rally. The irony is Alamiri is a working reporter for Facebook. While Trump had nothing to do with the slur, his posture, speech and body language endorsed attacking this reporter. "I'm a foreign policy reporter. My family lives in Iraq … For me to be scared says a lot," Alamiri said. This same pattern occurred throughout Trump's campaign as the authoritarian voter brought him to the presidency.

THE AUTHORITARIAN VOTER: THE ROLE AND TRUMP

The authoritarian voter argues a lack of respect; a crumbling world order, opposition to excessive foreign aid, a weak court system and entitlements for people who don't deserve financial aid is the road to ruin.

Trump's leadership style is simple. He emanates power. He punishes those who oppose his policies. Trump said a strong leader combats fear with force. He does so with humiliation, innuendo, sarcasm and bad manners. The political scientists who study authoritarian behavior were shocked at Trump's excesses and successes. After the Iowa Republican Caucus in 2016, which is the first important Republican political event on the road to the nomination, selected political scientists talked to voters. They discovered why he came out of nowhere to finish second in this prestigious caucus. He had a three-pronged message. First, bring back jobs. Second, drain the swamp of burdensome government regulations and lazy bureaucrats. Third, combat the flood of immigrants and destroy Muslim radicalism. It was a simple message. It worked.

RACISM MOTIVATED TRUMP VOTERS
MORE THAN AUTHORITARIANISM

The Trump supporter in large numbers is a low-income, high school educated voter who feels disrespected. This was true especially in the Midwest, the South and Mountain States. There is a perennial feeling of being excluded in presidential elections. Trump campaigned to these voters. A large number of Trump supporters are authoritarian voters. This is a person who fears social change and worries about loss of status. If minorities, women or immigrants appear to be rising in American the authoritarian voter follows an authoritarian figure like Trump.

Analyzing racial attitudes is difficult. When Trump made overt racial comments, there was little electoral penalty. He reflected the incipient racism burning in America. The Washington Post published a survey in which questions were asked on race and class. This led to the conclusion race, not economics, not immigration, not world conflicts, elected Trump.

Professor Michael Tesler argues race was more important in 2016 voting than candidates or partisan issues. Tesler observed white support for the Republican presidential nominee increased due to fears of a vibrant, aggressive black culture, the me-too movement and political correctness. Party and ideology were not as significant. A fear of white discrimination was an issue driving Trump voters. The conclusion is racial attitudes drove the 2016 vote. Hostility to Obama was not always shown in overt racist behavior. There was a quiet racism reflected in the reaction to Obama's policies, thereby obscuring the racial divide.

As Hillary Clinton moved to the left on racial issues large numbers of Democrats fled to vote for Trump. They were attracted to Trump's rhetoric and viewpoint on race. Clinton had no race specific policies. Trump appealed to white identity and those with racial resentment.

The belief President Obama favored African Americans was strong amongst Trump's supporters. People with racial antagonism could disguise it by criticizing the Obama administration's policies. The real reason was silent racism. To confront Trump, Democrats need to confront racism.

The Washington Post studied the results of the 2016 election for a year and concluded forty-one percent of white millennia's that voted for Trump did so due to fears of "white vulnerability." The argument the economy, the cost of education and too much government were reasons for Trump's election fails to meet tests from political scientists. They concluded race was the key issue. This information came from voter profiles analyzed for over a year in all parts of the country. When Trump insulted a Mexican judge, he also called Mexican immigrants criminals. He vowed to be tough on crime. His supporters, according to fact-based interviews, celebrated his incipient racism. His comments were racially insensitive. Race and racial resentment drove Trump's victory.

TRUMP: BAD BEHAVIOR AND AN AUTHORITARIAN NORM

Trump's election brought the GOP into a mainstream political position to destroy previously accepted concepts, traditions and assumptions of government. Trump changed how a president acts. The excuse for this was "drain the swamp." He made fun of a handicapped reporter. He disparaged a Gold Star family. He embraced religious discrimination. He backed an alleged pedophile for a vacant Alabama Senate seat. He continued his assault on anyone who disagrees with him.

No one is immune from Trump's wrath. House Speaker Paul Ryan, Senate Majority Leader Mitch McConnell, as well as Democratic leaders Chuck Schumer and Nancy Pelosi are ridiculed daily. His attacks on the Republican Party worked. They have crumpled rather than oppose his inane policies. They have shown little interest for investigating Russian interference in the 2016 election and Trump's inner circles connection to it.

When Trump refused to release his tax returns, his followers praised him. He said he couldn't do it. He was under audit. This wasn't true. He didn't divest himself completely from his business interests. His family runs these concerns. Donald Jr. and Eric Trump are the key CEO's. They are also integral to the White House. Trump doesn't understand government. He laughs at the rules. The checks and balances inherent in our governmental system is a foreign language to Trump. He lacks the education and knowledge to understand American politics.

He brought in special advisers, like Carl Icahn, who do little more than put forth plans to boost Wall Street profits. His Cabinet appointments are primarily rich billionaire, white men. Betsy DeVos in the Department of Education is the exception. She opposes public education. She is also a billionaire. His Cabinet selections are people like Oklahoma's Attorney General Scott Pruitt who heads the EPA. For years Pruitt has advocated abolishing the EPA. The entire Cabinet lacks governmental experience. They are hostile to federal regulation. They talk openly of dismantling key agencies. To understand the dysfunction of Trump's White House it is necessary to analyze a chief spokesperson, Kellyanne Conway. She is known affectionately as the "wicked witch of the White House."

KELLYANNE CONWAY: THE WICKED
WITCH OF THE WHITE HOUSE

"Kellyanne Conway lies like a fat kid likes cake," Rick Wilson, former Rudy Giuliani campaign adviser

Trump needs loyal supporters to carry out his road show. Kellyanne Conway is what some reporter's dub: "The Wicked Witch of The White House." She supports, explains and doubles down on

Trump's lies, authoritarian threats, lack of knowledge and dubious explanations.

Conway has attacked the FBI, the Washington Post, the New York Times, CNN, MSNBC and the Democratic Party for their egregious treatment of the president. When Michael Flynn took a plea agreement for lying to the FBI, the rumor was Trump knew about Flynn's illegal actions long before his plea agreement. Conway said he didn't. She was with him most of the time to prove it. Her support rang hollow. She said there was no attempt by the president to obstruct justice. In December 2017 there was a tweet that appeared to incriminate Trump. But his lawyer, John Dowd, said he wrote it. No one knew the real story. It was a convoluted mess. Conway helps to perpetuate the mess that comes daily out of the White House.

How Kellyanne Conway survived in the Trump White House is a testimony to her grit, her high level intelligence, her elusive relationship with the truth and her brutal means of diminishing others to move Trump's brand forward. She is the Donald's ultimate bulldog. She hates many people in Trump's inner circle. At the top of her hate list stands Reince Priebus. She views him as a hack sent over by the Republican National Committee. She despises him. She is right. Why? He wasn't tough enough, according to Conway, and he wasn't nice to Jared Kushner. She thought of how much she liked Trump's son-in-law. He is a brilliant tough guy, according to Conway. She began to slowly, but surely, poison those close to Trump concerning Priebus's loyalty, reliability and expertise. By the time Trump fired him the president had paranoid conspiracies. He believed Priebus was out to get him. He also had the same thoughts about the Republican Party. He may have been right.

STEVE BANNON: DID HE ELECT TRUMP?
"Nothing makes us more unreasonable than fear." EDMUND BURKE

Steve Bannon used fear as the motivating factor guiding Donald J. Trump's election and his road to the presidency. Then Bannon told the press he elected the Donald. Bannon was described as the brain in the Trump campaign. This wasn't true. Bannon was little more than a cranky voice, a low level political philosopher, he has little, if any, knowledge of past American history. He appealed to a racist, bigoted, disrespected voting bloc. After sitting for a year in the White House and watching Bannon's act, Michael Wolff found little to recommend the president's so-called brain.

When Michael Wolff's book came out he said Bannon had little, if anything, to do with his ascension to the presidency, or the policies of the first year of his administration. Bannon, like Trump, is a threat to liberal democracy. Whether or not he is the supreme intellectual the press depicts is open to question. He is a bright individual. He has a mind to match those who hope for a redefinition of democracy. In his early sixties, Bannon is overweight, badly dressed, he wears two shirts, but he does have good hair. When he speaks he puckers his lips like he is sucking on a lemon. He is an overwrought baron in bad clothes.

In 2013 radical historian-turned right wing apologist, Ronald Radosh, interviewed Bannon in his multi-million dollar townhouse on Capitol Hill. It is a rental. For all his reported genius and high-end thoughts, Bannon is not a rich man. He has the couth of a polar bear walking on Miami Beach. His home does have a gold throne displayed prominently. It once belonged to Saddam Hussein. There is a picture of his daughter, Maureen, holding a machine gun sitting on Hussein's throne.

As they talked Bannon told Radosh he was a Leninist. Bannon clarified his statement. Like Lenin, he told Radosh, he wanted to destroy the state. Radosh posted his interview on a website The Daily Beast. Few people paid attention to it. They should have as it was a sounding board for the end of traditional American democracy. One of Bannon's friend remarked: "He is in love with war, it's poetry to him." Steve has spent his life studying war. His untidy townhouse is filled with books on war from the Greek and Roman times to the present. Sun Tzu's book The Art of War is Steve's favorite. Trump found all this out about Bannon and promoted him to campaign manager, as well as chief White House political strategist. Bannon would wear his welcome out with Trump in less than a year. He would teach the president to intimidate and threaten democracy. Bannon was the intellectual factotum to a president with few intellectual concerns.

29

WHAT DOES TRUMP'S INTIMIDATION
DUE TO DEMOCRACY?

By employing intimidation Trump alters the facts. He tells plausible lies. He distorts the democratic process. He often speaks of the "so-called" judges, he praises Vladimir Putin as a strong leader. He believes Turkey's Recep Tayyip leadership is a positive influence. One can see Trump's admiration for these strong men. He also praises Egypt's Abdel Fattah el-Sisi who jails his political opponents.

The contempt for rules and norms threatens the fabric of American democracy. Trump has made the onerous claim he has virtually absolute power to decide all issues. He sees himself as "the law." But what law has he violated? He appears to have run astray of the foreign emoluments clause, which states in Article I, section 9 of the Constitution the president cannot profit from foreign government economic contacts. The argument is he received foreign money after moving into the White House. This has not been proven. Trump's business holdings around the world appear to some critics to fit into the foreign emoluments clause. So far there is no word on an investigation into the violation of this clause.

FOX TV NEWS WAR ON THE MUELLER INVESTIGATION

Fox TV News has a series of talking heads acting as propagandists for the Trump administration. Sean Hannity is the head propagandist. He is Charlie McCarthy to Donald J. Trump's Edgar Bergen. The presence of right wing political propaganda is an excellent reference point for those on the responsible right, the middle and the not so far left. Trump talks of "fake news." There is no greater example of irresponsible news than Fox. The seasoned and articulate talking heads Jeanine Pirro, Laura Ingraham, Michelle Malkin and Chris Wallace are credible journalists whose pro-Trump slant bastardizes the news. Their message is seldom credible. They work for a propaganda machine intent upon a Limbaugh America. They practice obfuscation. They employ innuendo. They make charges lacking in fact. When the president speaks they refuse to fact check his egregious comments.

The decline of democracy, Trump's autocratic rule and the marginalizing of American institutions is the role Fox TV News plays to the hilt.

As President Trump watches television from four to eight hours a day, he becomes enraged at every channel except Fox TV News. This is the scenario defining Trump's autocratic behavior. Trump's supporters want Robert Mueller investigated. The reason? They argue he is inherently biased. They talk of the deep state, the corrupt FBI and the need for transparency. Ironically, they never apply this standard to Trump. The reality is Mueller, a lifelong Republican, is an independent investigator. He is searching for evidence the president or those in his inner circle have violated the law. At this writing five in the inner circle have been charged and three have accepted plea agreements. There is evidence those close to the president are involved in business deals, if not collusion, with the Kremlin. Is Trump involved? Not while this book was in progress.

Fox TV News is sullying Mueller's investigative team daily. They argue the former FBI head is biased while distorting the facts. The irony of Fox TV News charging factual distortion is unbelievable. As Special Counsel, Robert Mueller, was seven months into his investigation, he was getting closer and closer to Trump's inner circle. Then the attacks on his credibility escalated. Fox calls the Mueller investigation "illegitimate and corrupt."

Gregg Jarrett, a legal analyst, appears regularly on the Sean Hannity show casting doubts on Mueller's integrity. Jarrett said: "Mueller's stooges literally are doing everything within their power, and then some, to try and remove President Trump from office." Laura Ingraham said: "What a total travesty! They should all step aside."

JUDGE JEANINE ON FOX GOES ON UNHINGED, ATTACKS ON MUELLER AND COMEY: SHE CALLS COMEY A POLITICAL WHORE

"Justice With Judge Jeanine" set the standard for irresponsible coverage. She is a savvy former prosecutor with a theatrical appearance. Judge Jeanine is a well thought out and a highly professional newsperson. That makes her dangerous. She has the appearance of authority.

In these divisive times, Judge Pirro made a frightening comment: "It (the FBI) needs to be cleansed of individuals who should not just be fired but who need to be taken out in handcuffs." This comment comes right out of the "Lock Her Up" chants with General Flynn leading the charge against Hillary Clinton. To Trump supporters the idea of neutralizing the FBI is an important one.

Pirro begins her conspiratorial examination of FBI malfeasance charging James Comey is: "so, political, so, corrupt." Other Trump supporters charge Andrew McCabe, the FBI's Deputy Director, is a Clinton supporter. There is also concern from Trumpites that when Peter Strzok was removed from the investigative team it was due to his pro-Hillary, anti-Trump bias. It was! Mueller demonstrated his professionalism by removing him from the investigation. No impropriety on Strzok's part in terms of influencing the investigation was proven.

Judge Jeanine continues to attack Mueller. She said: "He can't come up with a piece of evidence." She argues the investigation is bogus. She said the Mueller investigation must come to an end. People allegedly heard her say "witch hunt." That was the Christmas 2017 message the Trump camp sent to Mueller's investigative team. Judge Jeanine allegedly is seen regularly having dinner with President Trump when he is in New York.

As a paid talking head and no longer a Judge, Pirro irresponsibly charged Robert Mueller and James Comey were "trying to cover their butts." She has urged Trump to fire Mueller. She said: "There is a cleansing needed in… our FBI...handcuffs for Andrew McCabe." Pirro remarks almost nightly on Fox TV News "the FBI is corrupt." She also attacked Comey as a "political whore." She doesn't appreciate the irony of her statements.

Judge Pirro is typical of Trump supporters. She abuses her platform. She bullies her detractors. She supports half-baked arguments. She throws out conspiracy theories. Her defiance of government institutions is continual. She is the number one Trump apologist after the insufferable Sean Hannity. The reason for Mueller's investigation is not to remove Trump from office. It is to assess, evaluate and collect data on Russia's attempts to interfere in the 2016 election. This will allow the president to gauge the level of increased national security protection.

Trump's supporters are upset. The Mueller investigation is too close to the White House. The question remains: "Why did Trump select so many advisers who talked to or had business deals with Russia?" Do they want to protect an inexperienced president who refuses to act presidential or lead the nation with equanimity? That is what Mueller is investigating.

Fox TV News and its minions, like Judge Jeanine Pirro, create a web of conspiracy playing out daily to national audiences. People forget the Trump administration appointed Mueller. He is a Republican. He was originally appointed by President George W. Bush to head the FBI. Deputy Attorney General Rod Rosenstein named him Special Counsel, after Attorney General Jeff Sessions recused himself. They are all Republicans. The Republicans who attack Special Counsel Robert Muller scream: "fake news." This enables the president to erode our rights.

INCREASED ATTACKS ON MUELLER BY REPUBLICAN APOLOGISTS FOR TRUMP'S INNER CIRCLE

The pro-Trump crowd points to Mueller team members who supported Hillary Clinton for president, and donated money to the Democratic Party. They claim they are part of the deep state. Republicans charge the FBI and Mueller are working together to take down the president. By late December 2017 Trump supporters called for a conclusion to Mueller's investigation. Mueller responded by indicting thirteen Russians and the Kremlin backed businesses for interfering in the presidential election.

In the weeks before Christmas 2017 Republican lawmakers ratcheted up their demands for an investigation into the FBI. Rod Rosenstein responded the special counsel's investigation needed to be completed. Rosenstein defended the non-partisan nature of Mueller's investigation. "The special counsel is conducting himself consistently with our understanding of the scope of the investigation," Rosenstein concluded.

Donald J. Trump took to twitter on December 12, 2017 weighing in on the Mueller probe. Trump tweeted: "Despite thousands of hours wasted and many millions of dollars spent, the Democrats have been unable to show any collusion with Russia, so now they are moving to the false accusations and fabricated stories of women who I don't know and/or have never met. FAKE NEWS!" The House and Senate have Republican majorities. Mueller is a Republican. Maybe there are phantom Democrats going after the Donald.

Those opposing the Mueller investigation argue FBI lawyer Lisa Page, as well as senior FBI agent Peter Strzok, sent private text messages labeling Trump an "idiot." The Republican members of the House Judiciary Committee argued this proves the political nature of the Mueller investigation. It proves nothing more than bad judgment.

Mueller removed Strzok from the investigation when he learned of the text. FBI and Special Counsel rules allow for personal opinions, as long as it does not influence their work. First Amendment freedoms are something Trump's supporters fail to understand.

This controversy prompted Trump to comment the FBI's reputation is in "tatters." Rosenstein responded: "I don't know exactly what the president meant by that. The special counsel investigation is not a witch hunt."

Sometimes stupidity on both sides of the political aisle makes history. When the Congressional Republican leadership attempted to intimidate and derail the Mueller investigation, they made asinine charges and stupid mistakes. But fear not the Democrats were even more marginal in their use of intelligence. The GOP fantasy that an FBI conspiracy exists to bring down President Trump is matched by a lack of realism within the Democratic Party. No one looks like a rocket scientist in this scenario.

THE GOP FANTASY INVESTIGATION OF MUELLER: DOES STUPIDITY ON BOTH SIDES MAKE HISTORY?

In order to cover Trump's boorish behavior, his use of words like "shithole" to describe African countries, and his battle with the truth, the Republican leadership continues its attack on Special Counsel

Robert Mueller. The outcry concerning Mueller's integrity resonated on Fox TV News. They attempted to destroy him. Judge Jeanine wanted select members of the FBI sent to a gulag for re-education. She provided the fiery rhetoric arguing the FBI destroyed American freedoms. The opposite is true. To the Trumpites the goal is to change the argument. Attack the messenger. Confuse the issues. It works. This is why Congressional Republicans are a threat to the future of American justice. They have joined Trump in muddying the waters of the administration's Russian collusion. The Steele Dossier was attacked. The former British MI6 agent, who produced it, was vilified. Deflection by Trump's supporters worked to cast doubt on a British patriot, Christopher Steele, attempting to warn the FBI and CIA of internal meddling by Russian agents.

What is the Republican rationale? They argue Hillary Clinton's campaign hired Fusion GPS to collect anti-Trump misinformation. The result is Fusion hired Christopher Steele, a former MI6 British agent, who compiled a thirty-five-page dossier on Trump. The Democratic National Committee funded it. Steele delivered the document. The DNC lost interest. He was concerned about Russian interference in the 2016 presidential election. Steele went to the FBI and shared his information.

What did the Steele Dossier allege? The major charge was Trump and his followers cooperated with Russia in what Steele said was an "extensive conspiracy" to elect Donald J. Trump. There is no verification for this statement.

Congressional Republican leaders looked at this scenario. They concluded the FBI was dirty. They looked around and found evidence to support their theory. One FBI agent, a married one, had an affair with a female FBI agent and the operative wisdom was they were conspiring against Trump when not between the sheets. It appears they spent so much time between the sheets there wasn't much material. Mueller reassigned the agent, Peter Strzok, when he found out about the affair. The e-mails demonstrated nothing more than a lack of good judgment. Those e-mails were leaked to the press. Strzok's wife also worked for Fusion. This is the company that compiled the Steele Dossier. This set off alarms within the Congressional Republican leadership. Did this behavior break any laws? No! Was there unethical behavior? Yes! Did any of this impact the investigation? No! Were Strzok and others involved using their constitutionally guaranteed rights? Yes! Did Robert Mueller replace Strzok after the e-mail became public? Yes! The investigation of Mueller is unwarranted. It is the Republican way of deflecting from the collusion that those close to Trump have exhibited. Collusion is not a crime. But it leads down a dark path to possible charges. That is why Mueller's investigation must remain on track.

TRASHING CIVIL SERVICE AND DESTROYING
REGULATION VIA HIS CABINET

By destabilizing the civil service, appointing people hostile to federal regulation, and eliminating federal government authority business regulations slowed. By reducing the role of the CIA, the FBI and NSA the oversight for domestic and foreign crimes is reduced. National Security is imperiled. Businessmen and bankers run the country. This is exactly Trump's strategy. The Republican establishment believes all government agencies need to be downsized. Or better yet made inoperable. Donald Trump is destroying the government infrastructure. His Cabinet's job is to destroy government regulation while lining the pockets of the top one percent.

Trump's Cabinet is an all-star roster of appointments that have said they will downsize or virtually end the functions of their organization. When Scott Pruitt was confirmed to head the EPA, he had been a committed opponent of EPA's policies. When Trump announced Pruitt's selection, the president remarked the EPA's "totalitarian tactics" and "onslaught of regulations" would end. When Trump said fossil fuel would Make America Great Again, he made it clear new pipelines would be built regardless of environmental concerns. He said he would cancel U. S. participation in the Paris Climate Accord. Tom Price, the Georgia Congressman, came in to head Health and Human Services, and he had a mandate to repeal the Affordable Care Act. Price seldom called it ACA. He referred to it as Obamacare. Price acted like it was a disease. It turns out Price made dubious decisions. He spent federal funds inappropriately. He had little, if any, medical expertise. He resigned in September 2017 over the inappropriate use of private charter planes. After eight months as HHS Secretary Price failed to replace Obamacare or for that matter accomplish anything else. Appoint a clown. Expect a circus. Betsy DeVos, the billionaire Secretary of Education, increased government support for charter schools while cutting aid to public education. In Latino and African American neighborhoods funding was cut to a bare minimum. DeVos is a longtime supporter of programs to defund public education. Andrew Puzde, the head of the Labor Department, is a fast food chain entrepreneur who believes in a low minimum wage. Ben Carson, who is an esteemed African American physician, headed Housing and Urban Development. He is a long time anti-welfare conservative. Carson reduced funds for subsidized Section 8 public housing, limited government growth in supporting affordable housing and his wife purchased a $130,000 dining table for his office. Trump's appointments appealed to comedians.

There was a wonderful Saturday Night Live skit in which Trump (Alec Baldwin) is shown appointing Walter White, the meth head from "Breaking Bad," to head the DEA. This was a joke but an analysis of Trump's early campaign choices made it clear they were appointed to end government regulation, and to water down checks and balances. The notion of federal power to regulate state malfeasance has faded.

The worst Trump Cabinet appointment is former Texas Governor Rick Perry. The lights are on but no one is home. The former governor has demonstrated time and time again he has no energy plan. How could he screw up an agency? He isn't that smart. From day one Perry had no idea what the Energy Secretary did or why the Cabinet position existed. He was perfect for the job.

Perry was so inept he told the press the Energy Secretary's job was to act as a world ambassador for Texas oil and gas. His education didn't inform him there were forty-nine other states. When the press asked him about his responsibilities as Energy Secretary, he didn't answer. He had no idea.

What is the role of the Department of Energy? Its thirty billion dollar budget is largely dedicated to maintaining, refurbishing and safely monitoring the nation's nuclear stockpile. The agency also oversees national laboratories that produce top-level scientific materials. Perry vowed to downgrade or perhaps even eliminate the Energy Department. This is a part of Trump's plan to destabilize traditional democratic institutions. Corporate regulation is needed to guard against business malfeasance.

Sean Hannity of Fox News is the factotum for criticizing the "deep state." As the Mueller team indicted people in Trump's inner circle, Hannity stated on his Fox TV show: "All of this is happening because of the deep state. It's now the deep state gone rouge." After Hannity has dinner in Trump Tower, which he does frequently, he goes on Fox News to inform his listeners Trump is protecting America. The truth is Trump and his minions are destabilizing democracy. In the process Trump is being challenged for ignoring regulations, skirting laws, failing to fill civil service positions, ignoring presidential appointments, and he is cutting back on budgetary items necessary to functioning institutions. If he is criticized he screams "fake news."

TRUMP'S PLAN TO DESTABILIZE DEMOCRACY

The Trump plan is to admit nothing. His supporters deny all charges, they insult, they demean others and they go on the offensive. It is working. He has convinced the fanatical right wing the FBI needs its agents sent off to jail. He says the civil servants should be replaced, as they are agents of the "deep state." The Russian ex-KGB strong man, Vladimir Putin, also praises Trump. He has fits of rage in the Oval House. His minions agree with his every outrageous statement.

The threat Trump poses to democracy is real. America believes it is not subject to authoritarian rule. That is not the case. Trump promotes violence at his rallies. He shouts: "get them out of here." He advocated jailing his opponent as strains of "lock her up" wafted through the rafters of his campaign events. No one believed this egregious behavior could elect a president. It did. Now the tough part comes. That is to maintain the traditional freedom of a liberal democracy as liberalism sinks into the abyss. Trump is the nuclear nightmare waiting to happen.

From the moment the Trump administration took over there was a plan to destabilize democracy. It is working. But how? It is simple. The first step is through Executive Orders replacing as much of President Obama's legacy through presidential decrees. The next step is to systematically dismantle the civil service. Then reduce the funds for government. This destroys long-standing policies and abrogates laws protecting citizens. It is a concerted campaign. It provides a new type of government. One that is business oriented.

HOW GREAT IS TRUMP'S POLITICAL IGNORANCE? GREAT!

How great is Trump's ignorance? When Roger Ailes of Fox News suggested John Boehner as his Chief of Staff, Trump said: "Who's that?" He had never heard of the politician who had stepped down only a year earlier as the Speaker of the House. Trump has no interest in politics.

During his first year in the presidency there was one gaffe after another. Some gaffes were due to a lack of knowledge; others were the result of misinformation and incipient racism. In mid-January 2018 Max Boot, writing in Foreign Policy, observed of Trump's early policies: "It was a Category 5 blizzard of ignorance, crudeness and recklessness." Boot and others believe Trump is in the business of creating his own brand of democracy. That version is one, which will alter and perhaps even destroy traditional democratic values.

In his first year in office, Trump followed the pattern of Hugo Chavez in Venezuela, Alberto Fujimori of Peru and Tayyip Erdogan in Turkey. The first step in ending democracy is to muzzle the press. When Trump called the media "the enemy of the people," he began a media war. This created his "fake news" caveat. His followers endorse "fake news" daily in defense of the Donald.

Lack of knowledge drives Trump. He has requested the FBI, the CIA and the National Security Agency to pledge their loyalty to him. When he invited FBI Director, James Comey, for a private dinner, the president requested a pledge of loyalty. Had Trump had any idea how the American political system works, he would have realized the FBI's independent nature. When Comey refused to drop the investigation into General Michael Flynn's collusion with Russia, Trump fired him.

THE 2016 ELECTION WAS A CROSSROADS
AND THE FRIGHTENING EARLY DAYS

From the moment the Trump administration took over there was a plan to destabilize democracy is working. But how? It was simple. The first step was through Executive Orders replacing as much of President Obama's legacy through presidential decrees. The next step was to systematically dismantle the civil service. Then reduce the funds for government. This would destroy long-standing policies and abrogate laws protecting citizens. It was a concerted campaign. It provides a new type of government. One that is business oriented.

The frightening nature of Trump's White House early days was in the emergence of the petulant man-child. He was agitated. He was hostile. He was unsure of himself. He didn't have a plan to govern. Democracy is threatened. Trump doesn't know how to govern. He can't accept criticism.

Trump is lazy and ignorant. This is a trait that those in his social circle accept. He is a bully appealing to and elected by bullies. A telling point on Trump's lack of awareness of simple government facts took place in the early days of the campaign when Sam Nunberg attempted to explain the U. S. Constitution. It didn't work. Trump told him to stop. He was bored. Trump doesn't read. He retreats many nights to his Trump Tower bedroom with a cheeseburger and three TV's with cable news. He calls friends and screams "fake news."

(Credit: Bill Leak / Australian editorial cartoonist)

In the aftermath of Nunberg's story concerning Trump's lack of intellectual curiosity, he struck back at the political consultant.

Nunberg told CNN in early January Trump was a fool. There were rumblings of a lawsuit. The First Amendment is something Trump doesn't understand. Since July 2016 Trump and Nunberg have been at odds. As a Senior Trump consultant, Nunberg charged the presidential candidate misused campaign funds, he didn't understand American politics and he was personally difficult. Nunberg also alleged Trump set up fake business entities to maneuver his financing around campaign law.

When Nunberg was fired from the Trump campaign it was for allegedly racially insulting remarks. He insulted Al Sharpton and made egregious comments about President Barack Obama. As a political consultant he was a disaster. He arranged for McCay Coppins of Buzzfeed to write a Trump profile. When it appeared it was a hit piece-stating Trump was "a man startled by his suddenly fading relevance and consumed by a desperate need to get it back." When the Buzzfeed article appeared Trump was furious. Nunberg was fired on August 2, 2105. Then Trump sued Nunberg accusing him of violating a confidentiality agreement. He sought ten million dollars in damages. It was settled out of court.

What was the reason for Trump suing Nunberg? He found out his former campaign adviser leaked a story of a dispute between former campaign manager Corey Lewandowski and Trump factotum Hope Hicks. Whatever the reason the dysfunction in the White House and the pettiness of President Trump was there for the world to see in its splendorous and odious form.

TRUMP AND THE OFFICE OF GOVERNMENTAL ETHICS

Trump blistered the Office of Government Ethics. This is an independent watchdog agency. The agency investigates ethical violations. When they investigated those close to the president the stench of corruption was all over the Trump administration. Why did Trump take issue with the Office of Government Ethics? The answer is the director, Walter Schaub, found inconsistencies in applications for security clearances, a lack of veracity in answering questions and an inclination to ignore ethics rules. It was a rocky relationship between the Office of Government Ethics and Trump's appointees.

Walter Schaub, the Director of the Office of Government Ethics, was threatened with a personal investigation when he criticized Trump's unwillingness to divest his business assets, which were in conflict with the presidency. The chair of the House Oversight Committee, Jason Chaffetz, a Utah Republican, hinted Schaub might be investigated. The Trump White House continually harassed Schaub. He resigned. There was no wrongdoing on Schaub's part. It was Trump's bullying act. The fierce, often unfair, comments from his minions drove Schaub out of the government arena.

Libel laws are another Trump concern. During the 2016 campaign the Donald threatened Jeff Bezos, the owner of Amazon and the Washington Post, with antitrust action. He has continued the threats during his presidency. Trump said of Bezos on the campaign trail: "If I become president, oh do they have problems."

When Trump set up the Presidential Advisory Committee on Election Integrity, chaired by Vice President Mike Pence, he established a presidential commission to challenge the voter registrations of Latinos, African Americans and other minorities. The president worked toward a lily white Republican Party. The reason for the Executive Order and the Commission was Trump's ego. He made the baseless claim he won the popular vote. He said there were three to five million Clinton votes because of voter fraud. This wasn't true.

Kris Kobach, of Kansas, took over running the Commission. He systematically advocated policies and programs challenging ethnic voters. Academic studies have shown voter fraud is minimal. It hasn't impacted elections. The hue and cry over the tactics of Kobach and the Commission led to a flurry of critical comments. Trump disbanded the commission. Why? It was an exercise in voter intimidation. It was also unconstitutional.

Why is Kris Kobach important in this scenario? Harvard Professors Steven Levitsky and Daniel Ziblatt describe Kobach as "America's premier advocate of voter suppression." Their book, How Democracies Die, describes the plan the Trump administration employs to trample traditional democracy.

What Trump didn't realize is the National Voter Registration Act has information his administration desired on voting lists. The Department of Homeland Security has immigrant-voting databases. The other simple part of this equation is state governments have the right not to share voting information with Washington. States' rights still exist. When the Trump administration requested voting lists and social security numbers from the states none cooperated totally. The Mississippi Secretary of State, Delbert Hosemann, told Trump to "go jump in the Gulf of Mexico." There are two things Trump and his followers don't understand. First, the difference between state and federal power is one of separation of powers. Second, rights guaranteed under the First Amendment cannot be abridged.

FIRE AND FURY: TRUMP ATTEMPTS TO
SHUT DOWN THE FIRST AMENDMENT

Michael Wolff is an eloquent writer, and the author of the New York Times best seller Fire And Fury: Inside The Trump White House. He is a former magazine editor, a man about New York having dinner with his wife or mistress, and he is one of only a few journalists thrown out of most major restaurants for inappropriate behavior. Then he had a high profile divorce when he cheated on his wife and rubbed it in her face. She divorced him in this headline grabbing marital dispute. His mother in law sued him alleging he stole property. The point is Wolff was hardly an unknown writer. He had a Kitty Kelly reputation. He also had a desk in the White House. He had a blue pass to go where he pleased. The New York Times described Wolff as "a prime piranha" in Manhattan's media circus. He is the Rona Barrett and Kitty Kelly of biography. He wears expensive London cut suits. He sports three hundred dollar Charvet ties. He has never met a young lady under thirty he didn't like at least for that night.

His writing is filled with nasty metaphors and flowery phrases. His book is devoid of supporting facts. When his biography of Rupert Murdoch appeared in 2008, the media mogul did a Donald. Murdoch hated the book. Don't expect hard facts, analysis or anything more than tasty gossip. When Trump read the book or had it read to him, he had a fit. How was Wolff able to wrangle a blue pass giving him unfettered access to the White House? This remains a mystery? Or perhaps it is an insight into the Donald's ever expanding ego. His lack of judgment is another question.

How accurate is Wolff's portrayal of Trump's first year in the White House? It is full of new information thanks to Steve Bannon. His interviews, the comments of underlings and leaked information from insiders, with a disdain for the egomaniacal Donald, make up the books core. Verified? No! Fun to read! Yes! Wolff is not a fiction writer. He deals in cold hard analysis. He is credible no matter what Trump screams. Likeable? I will get back to you on that question.

Wolff on camera is a pretentious little dwarf with a baldhead, a sneering smile and a tendency to smirk like he knows everything. His friends describe him as a pompous jackass. It is only fitting he wrote the widely publicized book on Trump's first year in the White House. One jackass it surely qualified to write about another jackass.

Michael Wolff: "My credibility is being questioned...." That is an understatement. He made this comment on MSNBC. Wolff said of Trump: "They all say he is like a child, a moron, an idiot, I will quote Steve Brannon. 'Trump demands total loyalty."

Among his revelations are noxious comments that can't be verified. Wolff writes Trump rarely sees his wife and son. He is semiliterate. He doesn't read. Others dismiss him as a fool (here Wolff cites Rupert Murdoch as his source). He has little, if any, understanding of how government functions. He is psychologically unbalanced, Wolff concluded. He wrote Ivanka is "dumb as a rock." He says Donald Jr. colluded with Russia. Trump is easily bored suggesting an attention span disorder. Wolf explains how he went about writing Fire And Fury: Inside The Trump White House. How he separated fact from fiction is an intriguing apology for a lack of in-depth outside research. Wolff said he sat in the White House. He listened and wrote with verve and fervor. There must be supporting materials. Wolff defends his book. "Many of the accounts of what has happened in the Trump White House are in conflict with one another; many, in Trumpian fashion, are baldly untrue. Those conflicts, and that looseness with the truth, if not with reality itself, are an elemental thread of the book. Sometimes I have let the players offer their versions, in turn allowing the reader to judge them. In other instances I have, through a consistency in accounts and through sources I have come to trust, settled on a version of events I believe to be true." Wolff concluded.

There are simple facts Wolff gets wrong. When he said Trump didn't know John Boehner, this was contradicted by the fact they played golf together. He described CNN reporting on Trump's exotic sexual adventures. It was BuzzFeed that broke this story. Many of the sources have said they were misquoted. Steve Bannon has never recanted his quotes. Others see Wolff's book as accurate. Janice Min, who worked with Wolff at the Hollywood Reporter, said she witnessed a conversation between Roger Ailes and Steve Bannon with Wolff standing nearby taking notes. He reported with great accuracy.

There is one smoking gun suggesting Wolff is close to President Trump. Before he ran for the presidency, Trump was a reality television star. He made a number of failed TV pilots. In one of Trump's reality TV projects, "Trump Town Girls," Wolff appeared in a cameo role selling real estate to beauty contestants. Those close to Trump said early on he secured the Donald's trust. He was running around the White House with a blue pass. He had free run of the place.

Graydon Carter, Wolff's former editor at Vanity Fair, said: "The mystery is why the White House allowed him in the front door." Could it be lack of judgment? Had they been friends since "Trump Town Girls?" Callum Borchers, in the Washington Post, pointed out that the book was probably not vetted. Borchers asks: "Did it get past a fact checker?" The answer is: "No."

The Borchers article points out Wolff confused lobbyist Mike Berman with Washington Post reporters Mark Berman. He misquoted CNN stating they published details of the Steele Dossier when in fact they summarized the document. He said Rupert Murdoch called Trump "an idiot" when in fact the Australian media mogul called him "a moron." Wolff said Wilbur Ross was Trump choice for labor secretary. He was actually picked to head the commerce department. Wolff talks about Jared Kushner and Ivanka Trump and it appears they were not interviewed. Wolff refuses to talk about his sources. The lack of evidence prompted Trump's minions to scream fake news. But Wolff's book is a good one. It is an honest depiction of White House slowly descending into volcanic destruction.

Credit: (Anthony F. Branco / Cartoonist for legalinsurrection.com)

TRUMP'S MINIONS SCREAMING FAKE NEWS

The Trump minions appear dutifully on Fox TV New screaming: "fake news." They continually question Wolff's accuracy. Fox News described Wolff's book as a "sensational piece of hit journalism." The end result is the accurate insights and the in-depth information floating around the White House is placed between the pages of a fascinating treatise. The portrait of an unbalanced president is questionable. Wolff may have a point. His book is a searing look into the daily life of the most dysfunctional president to occupy the White House. Wolff is a diligent researcher. He is an excellent writer. Facts? Forget it! He is a chameleon who blends into the wall. Think Mr. Peepers as Wally Cox played him.

What is the point of discussing Wolff's book? No president in American history has attempted to prevent a critical book from being released. The Donald demanded that it not be released. This guaranteed a million dollar book. His authoritarian nature, his disregard for constitutional principles and his reckless attempts to use the Justice Department for personal protection highlights a president who arrived in office as an outlier. Now he is headed to outlaw territory. Some of his minions are headed down a criminal path. If he avoids the criminal path, he will continue to erode personal liberties, attack the basic institutions of government and threaten those who criticize him.

Trump's cry of "fake news" emboldens despots around the world. Jeff Flake, Arizona Republican Senator on January 17th 2018 stood up in the U. S. Senate remarking: "Use of the term fake news to undermine journalism seems to have inspired dictators and authoritarians." Is Trump a despot? Yes, says Brian Klaas, in a widely debated book analyzing the horrific changes in American politics.

TRUMP AS THE DESPOT'S APPRENTICE

The best description of the megalomania that is Donald Trump is Brian Klaas's The Despot's Apprentice: Donald Trump's Attack On Democracy, published in 2017. This book is an in-depth description of what makes a tyrant successful. Klaas, a professor at the London School of Economics, analyzes the fascination Trump has with strong leaders in Russia, Turkey, China and Poland. How he attempts to emulate them is frightening.

Brian Klaas: "Last year, despite having an unprepared, uninformed, reckless conspiracy theorists in the White House, there was no global conflagration. American democracy was threatened, but not destroyed."

The dangers of Trump's presidency in 2018 were two-fold. First: Nuclear war was a real possibility. There were continued problems with Syria, defeating ISIS and acting on the Iran nuclear deal. Second, Trump's daily tweets threaten democracy. He castigates any criticism in the press as "fake news." Continually, he has called for jailing Hillary Clinton. He also suggested former FBI Director James Comey should be locked up. He said the Justice Department is part of a "deep state" plot. Trump sees conspiracies everywhere. To the Donald the major ones are in government. Trump's authoritarian instincts make it difficult for him to consider a wide range of solutions to governmental problems. He is tearing down the checks and balances in the American system. He said he could do what he wanted with the Justice Department. He ignored the rule of law. When he tweeted: "My button is bigger than your button" to the North Korean dictator, Kim Jong Un, it was a challenge for a fight. Trump's childish tweet was a warning sign. His supporters cheered. That should frighten all Americans.

BOWING AND SCRAPING TO THE
GREAT DONALD: WOLFF'S SHADOW

One of the themes of MSNBC and CNN's coverage of the presidency is the "bowing and scraping" to President Trump. There is no doubt the two news channels are tough critics. At other times they are overly critical but never blatantly unfair. They point out Trump's lies, his tendency to take credit for any and all international events, and his continual insults. To anyone and everyone who dares to contradict the Donald there is a price to pay.

Jake Tapper interviewed Trump speechwriter and Senior Policy Adviser, Stephen Miller, in the days after the Wolff book exploded as a best seller. The veracity of Wolff's arguments dominated talk news. Was he accurate? Was he truthful? CNN and MSNBC found nuggets of truth beneath his more salacious and least defensible reportage. Fox News treated Wolff's book like a fictional tome. In an effort to provide conservative balance Jake Tapper's State of The Union invited Stephen Miller to appear on his program. Miller praised Trump who was watching the program. Miller refused to answer Tapper's questions, as he bowed and scrapped to Trump's ego. Miller's ego enforced stupidity prompted the CNN anchor to remark: "I think I have wasted enough of our viewer's time." As Tapper went into a commercial, he charged Miller was "a factotum" for Trump. He was also the Donald's shadow.

The media battle between Miller and CNN was round two as Tapper had clashed with other Trump insiders over immigration policy. Then Miller attacked CNN's Jim Acosta. Trump watched the January 7, 2018 Tapper interview tweeting: "Jake Tapper of Fake News CNN just got destroyed in this interview with Stephen

Miller….Watch the hatred and unfairness of this CNN flunky." Not really!

Trump's presidential tweets are another insight into his lack of respect for the democratic process. The idea traditional government serving the people is one of Trump's more dangerous autocratic thoughts. Combine Trump's distaste for career civil servants providing support services for Americans who govern, with the President's hatred for the media, and you have a recipe for destroying governmental institutions.

TRUMP JUST DOESN'T GET IT

President Trump, after a year in office, just doesn't get it. After the publication of Michael Wolff's Fire And Fury: Inside The Trump White House, he wondered why he couldn't stop publication of this critical book. He has no concept of the First Amendment. When his lawyers told him about the concept of prior restraint, he thought it was a new burger at McDonald's. Sarah Huckabee Sanders walked out on stage at a press conference, she said the president was still deciding whether or not to sue. Henry Holt moved the publication date up four days. They should have sent a bottle of champagne and a basket of fruit to celebrate one million books sold four days prior to the books formal release.

Sarah Huckabee Sanders in a black dress and a frown couldn't wait to get off stage. She had to defend the Donald. She did. She was brilliant. One wonders did the pizza get cold back stage? Sanders said Wolff's book was "tabloid trash." She was just warming up calling it "false and fraudulent." When a reporter asked her about "prior restraint," she looked like she had been asked the code for a nuclear weapon. She is not as inept as Sean Spicer. But no one is as inept as Sean Spicer. That is unless he is on a Hollywood movie awards show. As the Donald was criticized for not having an iota of knowledge about the First Amendment, he proved his lack of forbearance on libel law as well. He vowed to rewrite libel laws.

HOW TRUMP RE-DEFINES DEMOCRACY AND THE LEFT

Trump wants to redefine American democracy. Fortunately, he does not have the political skill, the intellect or the institutional expertise

49

to destroy the courts, minimize the media, place Congress on the sidelines and force the Attorney General to investigate the FBI. Trump is a bully leading an attack on American institutions. When it is about American democracy, Trump just doesn't get it. He had no idea concerning democracy.

How does the left prevent Trump from subverting democracy? As the right wing cheers on the president's gross violations of every major aspect of government, Democratic Party opposition is ineffective. If that changes Trump will be in trouble. As establishment politicians attempt a return to normal political patterns the outrageous behavior of Trump and his minions challenge traditional politics.

Fred Hiatt, writing in the Washington Post, observed we are in a contest "between our free and open societies and closed and repressive systems." When H. R. McMaster left his position, as the National Security Adviser, he said: "It is time we expose those who glamorize and apologize in the service of communist, authoritarian and repressive governments." That said it all. McMaster directly confronted Trump congratulating Vladimir Putin's sham presidential election. We are in a fight to preserve liberal democracy. Donald Trump and those who serve him are a threat to that democracy.

As McMaster concluded: "We are presently engaged in competitions with repressive and authoritarian systems to defend our way of life." At a time when democratic nations look to the U. S. for leadership, Trump colludes with dictators, praises strong men and brings warmongers into the Cabinet.

The appeal to white nationalism and the rise of the alt-right suggests race is a key to the Trump presidency. He is a demagogue encouraging racial controversy. He has failed to refute racially hostile attitudes. Whether or not Trump is a racist is of little concern. He attracts and never declines the support of racially hostile coalitions.

JAMES COMEY ON TRUMP AND AMERICAN DEMOCRACY

"I was surprised," James Comey said to George Stephanopoulos of Trump's election. It was mid-April, 2018 and Comey's book, A Higher Loyalty, was ready for release. When Comey met for the first time with President elect Trump, he was nervous. Why? He discussed with Trump the allegations in the Steele Dossier Trump consorted with prostitutes in Moscow. Once he discussed this subject with Trump, the president-elect was convinced Comey was out to get him.

After this meeting, Comey concluded: "The truth did not have value for Trump." In Comey's book the phrase "unethical and untethered to truth," caught the critic's attention. George Stephanopoulos asked him, if Hillary Clinton should be charged with crimes and if the FBI gave her a pass. Comey said: "No." The hundreds of thousands of e-mails Clinton had on her private server were deleted and the FBI investigated these e-mails to find out if there was a crime. There was none.

After the Clinton investigation failed to find a law she or a member of her campaign had violated, Comey cleared her shortly before the election. The cloud over Clinton's ethics and integrity cost her the election. Comey defended his action. He said if he didn't investigate the Clinton emails scandal, her election would be tainted.

A short time after Trump's inaugural, he invited Comey to dinner. They talked with Trump saying he never assaulted women, he didn't make fun of a physically handicapped reporter and then Trump abruptly said he needed loyalty. Comey said he would provide honest loyalty. Comey was uneasy. He told Stephanopoulos he made a mistake. Comey concluded Trump was a liar, a manipulator and an ego-based politician. Privately, Comey concluded Trump acted like a character in the Godfather.

Comey charged a "culture of lies" seeped in and began destroying the Trump administration's credibility. Trump realized this was Comey's conclusion. Comey said Trump asked him to drop the General Michael Flynn investigation

Comey testified that before the Senate Select Intelligence Committee. He refused to say that Trump was not under investigation in the Russian collusion investigation. Trump had enough. He fired Comey. It was May 9, 2017. Comey was in Los Angeles. He looked up into a TV screen and found out he was fired.

The president began attacking Comey on twitter and the question of Russian collusion continued by appointed Special Counsel Robert Mueller. Trump increasingly attacked the rule of law, there was a move by conservative, right wing Republicans to demean the Mueller inquiry.

Comey said: "Trump is morally unfit to be president." Comey continued: "values matter. This president does not reflect the values of this country."

THREE

DONALD TRUMP: THE QUESTION OF RACE ON FOREIGN POLICY?

"The principle of democracy, to its core,
is about equality and inclusion."

BRIAN KLAAS

"Trump called Kaepernick 'a son of a bitch' and called on anyone
who kneeled during the national anthem to be fired."

BRIAN KLAAS

"Donald Trump arrived in the wake of …an entire nigger presidency
with nigger health care, nigger climate accords, and nigger justice
reform, all of which could be targeted for destruction….Trump truly is
something new-the first president whose entire political existence hinges
on the fact of a black president."

TA-NEHISI COATES, THE ATLANTIC, OCTOBER 2017

"Donald Trump is emotionally and intellectually
unqualified to be president."

CHRIS WHIPPLE, AUTHOR OF THE GATE KEEPER

When he campaigned for the presidency in 2016, Trump reached out to African American voters. His cry was: "What do you have to lose?" The answer was their civil rights, constitutionally guaranteed freedom, integrity, independence, jobs, equal opportunity and dignity. His brazen statement indicated he didn't understand the basic questions surrounding race. In his foreign policy he called

African nations "shit holes." His defenders said he meant Third World countries. He said Mexico sent us "criminals, rapists and drug dealers." He wondered why we didn't have more Norwegians. This is full blown racism. The racist tirades continued. While running for the presidency, Trump attacked a Mexican-American judge born in Indiana. He spoke with outright racism of Muslims. He attacked a Gold Star family showing no respect for the death of their son serving in a military capacity. From the summer of 2016, when he was first labeled an alleged racist, until the end of the first year of his presidency, Trump commented: "I am the least racist person that you've ever encountered." When accusations of racism surfaced, Trump responded telling the **Washington Post** he received Don King's endorsement. This ridiculous statement speaks for itself.

At the end of his first year as president, Trump commented he didn't want immigrants. He said if you allowed Africans to immigrate they would never want to "go back to their huts." Naturally, Trump denied saying these things. Senators Lindsey Graham, a South Carolina conservative Republican, and Dick Durbin, an Illinois liberal Democrat, were at the meeting where Trump used the term "shit hole." He also condemned Haiti. Senator Durbin said Trump made comments "which were hate-filled, vile and racist." This is a sad time in American racial history. It is not surprising Trump denies, deflects and screams, "fake news." He has a long history of racial insensitivity. He also has a longer history of lies.

In the aftermath of Trump's "shit hole" comment, Democratic Senator Corey Booker of New Jersey, at a Senate oversight hearing on immigration, criticized the Homeland Security Secretary for not remembering whether or not Trump used the words "shit hole" or "shit house." Booker seethed with anger. He suggested Kirstjen Nielsen had heard the word. She said she didn't remember it. Her qualifications to head DHS were called into question. She said she didn't know that Norway was a white country. Unless she is an illiterate moron, this is a barefaced lie. Then again, this is about not contradicting the Donald. Previously, the president said he would like more immigrants from Norway. Since Norway is a predominantly white country many interpreted this as racist. With a last name, Nielsen, one would think the DHS secretary might have a clue. She didn't. This tells one all they need to know about the expertise of Trump's appointments. It also tells one all they need to know about the administration's relationship to the truth.

"When ignorance and bigotry is allied with power it is a dangerous force in our country. Your silence and your amnesia is complicity," Senator Booker said to Nielsen. She sighed. She laughed. She did a great job of not remembering what went on in her meeting with President Trump. She was recently appointed to head DHS. Amnesia is important to remaining in Trump's inner circle. That may be as important as her high level qualifications. She is a highly qualified Homeland Security expert in the private sector with a University of Virginia law degree. She is also a conservative Republican who supported Trump's candidacy while massaging his ego. Integrity? You decide!

TRUMP FAILS TO RENT TO BLACKS AND ACCUSES THEM OF CRIMINALITY

In business early on in his career, Trump was involved in a major federal discrimination lawsuit. In 1973 the **New York Times** headlined: "Major Landlord Accused of Anti-Black Bias In The City." Guess who! The federal government sued Trump, and his father, Fred, over discriminatory rental practices. The suit was over alleged apartment discrimination. The Trump Empire allegedly did not rent to African Americans. When he asked in 2016: "What do you have to lose?" Most African Americans might have responded: "Housing."

The Trump's settled the case. He has not admitted wrongdoing. This pattern of denial remains a centerpiece of Trump's presidency. Deny! Deny! Deny! Race was a Trump obsession. In 1989 a full-page ad was taken out in the **New York Times** demanding the Central Park Five receive the death penalty. This widely publicized case was one where the five defendants were charged with a vicious rape and brutal assault. The twenty eight year old victim was a lawyer. Her brutal death brought gasps from New York newspaper readers. The youngest defendant was fifteen. It looked like an open and shut case against teenagers on a criminal rampage.

The story of vicious black youths beating up a defenseless white woman was a sensational one. There were four African American young men arrested. The other one was Hispanic. The police brought the five in for a lengthy, threatening interrogation. The young men were interrogated for long hours without food or drink. There was no attorney present. Their stories did little, if anything, to verify this violent crime. During the interrogations two of the defendants confessed they viciously stabbed the young woman. A psychologist concluded stress and psychological abuse led to the confessions. There were no stab marks on her body. When DNA tests were taken all of the Central Park 5 were cleared of the crime. Trump refused to recant his demand for the death penalty. He told the press none of the young men "were angels."

The crime was the young men were convicted and spent from seven to thirteen years behind bars for a crime they didn't commit. The real criminal, Matias Reyes, was caught. He confessed to the brutal murder. The groundswell of publicity that helped to overturn their convictions was due to the press. The DNA evidence was absolute. The young men were not involved. The police came under attack for their methods.

The New York Police Department and the District Attorney admitted the five young men had been wrongfully accused, convicted and imprisoned. In October 2016 when Trump was asked about the case, he refused to apologize. He continued to argue they were guilty. He was wrong. He wouldn't admit it. The precedent was set for the future of his presidency.

QUESTIONS OF RACE AND BIRTHERS

What about the question of race? In Atlantic City Trump was fined $200,000 by the state gambling commission. The fine was due to a policy where Trump allowed his casino to hire white only dealers for select tables. In 2005, when the Apprentice floated the idea of having white versus black contestants, Trump believed this was a brilliant idea. Color was an obsession with the Donald.

In 2011 Trump met with a birther conspiracy guru, Joseph Farah, concerning President Barack Obama's birth certificate. Farah is a conspiracy advocate. He published a six part series arguing that soybeans cause homosexuality. This post on his conspiracy site WorldNetDaily.com should have told Trump all he needed to know about this so-called research specialist. Farah is the rocket scientist who deduced President Obama was born in Indonesia. Trump bought the argument. He spent half a decade promoting the birther conspiracy.

The birther theory was a hoax. The press picked it up. They couldn't get enough of an American president born in Indonesia. Richard Corsi perpetuated this hoax in **Obama Nation: Leftist Politics And The Cult of Personality**. It was released in 2008, to question his American citizenship. If you are not a citizen, you can't run for president. Corsi likes to put PHD after his name but this doesn't' disguise shoddy scholarship, poor writing, misrepresentation of fact and outright ignorance concerning American politics and history. Here is the surprise. Corsi has a Harvard PHD in political science. Despite its loose relationship with the facts and truth, Corsi's book reached number six on the **New York Times** best seller list. Corsi sued **Esquire** when they published a satirical article claiming Corsi's book had been recalled. They alleged it was a form of creative fiction. Corsi sued for $285 million in damages. The U. S. District Court dismissed the suit stating the First Amendment protects satire.

Corsi's book was embraced by the radical right wing. There is a belief in the Trump camp of a "deep state" conspiracy. This is the theory there are people within the federal government conspiring against conservatives. A group known as "Obama For America" released a lengthy list of Corsi's factual errors, erroneous interpretations and alleged lies. Both the left and the right discredited the book.

THE HUFFINGTON POST'S 13 TRUMP RACIST STATEMENTS

In 2016, as Trump become a viable presidential candidate, the **Huffington Post** listed thirteen examples of what Lydia O'Connor and Daniel Marans labeled Trump's racist attitudes. As the Republican presidential front-runner, the operative wisdom was he would not be elected. The **Huffington Post** emphasized he had a long history of racially insensitive statements. The **Huffington Post** concluded Trump was an established racist. His most insulting early tirade was against Muslim Gold Star parent Khizr Khan who spoke out concerning Trump's bigoted rhetoric. His son, the late Army

Captain Humayun Khan, gave his life in Afghanistan defending America. "Let me ask you, have you ever even read the U. S. Constitution," Khan bellowed defiantly at Trump during the Democratic National Convention. Khan's wife, Ghazala Khan, stood next to him in a Muslim headscarf. She looked sad. She didn't speak. Trump answered: "If you look at his wife, she was standing there. She had nothing to say. She probably, maybe she wasn't allowed to have anything to say. You tell me," Trump smirked. He intimated the Muslim faith kept her from speaking.

Gonzalo Curiel, the federal judge, who presided over a class action suit against the for profit Trump University was attacked by the president. Trump said: "He's a Mexican….He is giving us very unfair rulings…." Curiel in fact is an American citizen born in Indiana. He also was a prosecutor in the 1990s. He successful targeted Mexican drug cartels bringing them to justice.

On Trump's racist diatribes, House Speaker Paul Ryan said: "Claiming a person can't do their job because of race is sort of like the textbook definition of a racist comment." Speaker Ryan quickly forgot this statement.

Trump told John O'Donnell, a former president of Trump Plaza Hotel and Casino, "I've got black accountants at Trump Castle and Trump Plaza. Black guys counting my money! I hate it," Trump continued: "The only kind of people I want counting my money are short guys that wear yarmulkes every day."

O'Donnell's book on working for Trump, published in 1991, recalls him remarking of an African American employee: "I think the guy is lazy. And it's probably not his fault because laziness is a trait in blacks. It really is, I believe that. It not anything they can control." The O'Donnell book **Trumped: The Inside Story of the Real Donald Trump-His Cunning Rise And Spectacular Fall** was the observations of a man who worked for Trump for three years. In fairness to Trump, O'Donnell was a bitter employee. He quit. O'Donnell couldn't stand Trump's management style. In a fit of rage, O'Donnell went to work for Trump's competition-Merv Griffin Resorts Casino Hotel.

When Trump heard O'Donnell was writing a book, he attempted to intimidate him. He took legal action. Why did Trump attempt to kill the O'Donnell book? When it came out O'Donnell said Trump's business decisions were not solid ones. He described the Donald as "ignorant of Casino operations." He didn't recognize basic business facts, according to O'Donnell, and the result was bankruptcy. Trump disputed this opinion and took legal action.

O'Donnell said a catalogue of fears focused Trump's thinking. There were Trump phobias. The Donald feared disease and going bald. O'Donnell pointed to his crude language. He said the Donald was cheap. Trump denied the book's allegations. "Nobody has had worse things written about them than me," Trump said with a copy of the book on his desk.

Trump described O'Donnell as a "disgruntled employee." He was for good reason. Trump berated O'Donnell. He criticized his management style. He blamed his bankruptcy on O'Donnell's lack of skill. Trump called him: "A fucking loser." Whether or not Trump is a racist is a matter of opinion. One thing is clear, he has not been kind to the minority community.

Trump has never condemned white supremacists. David Duke was a Donald supporter. White supremacists, neo-Nazis, the alt-right and those who promote the future power of white Europeans were in Trump's corner. The leader of the Virginia KKK told a local reporter "a lot of Klan members like Donald Trump…." The spokesperson for the Klan could not be identified. He was in costume.

Trump denied these racist allegations. The **Washington Post**'s Dana Milbank concluded: "Donald Trump is a bigot and a racist." **The Washington Post** on December 1, 2015 in an op-ed warning to readers. Milbank pointed to the demagogic tendencies in Trump's message. The hateful comments infusing Trump's march to the presidency didn't derail his candidacy. He is also given a pass for funding and championing the birther movement. He praised Phoenix Sheriff Joe Arpaio for willfully violating federal law. When the sheriff was convicted of ignoring and violating federal law, Trump quickly pardoned him. He falsely claimed thousands of Muslims celebrated the 9/11 attacks.

Trump made fun of Serge Kovaleski, a **Washington Post** journalist, who has a chronic condition limiting his mobility As Kovaleski twitched with spasms and his body twisted out of control, Trump mimicked his body language. It was a cruel and callous attack on a disabled person displaying little in the way of empathy. It was televised. Trump couldn't lie about it. He did. Some months later he said he hadn't made fun of Kovaleski. One of four thousand and one lies, according to FactCheck.org., and this says all one needs to know about Trump's lack of humility and humanity.

Trump's detractors do him a disservice by suggesting the majority are bigots or racists. This is not true. He appeals what is true is there is no attempt to isolate the bigots and racists. The Colin Kaepernick issue turned the bigots into an army criticizing the San Francisco 49er quarterback in the name of Making America Great Again. Pure racism!

COLIN KAEPERNICK IS A CIVIL RIGHTS HERO BUT A VILLAIN TO TRUMP

Trump systematically exploits race. He demonizes racial groups. He appeals to intolerant white supporters. In the latter months of 2016, San Francisco Quarterback Colin Kaepernick began sitting during the National Anthem. He said he did so to protest police killings of young African American men. By not kneeling the 49ers cut its quarterback. No NFL team signed him. They all say it has to do with his playing ability. Trump sent his message. The president's minions say they support the First Amendment but not for an African American quarterback. He speaks his mind. Detroit Piston basketball coach, Stan Van Gundy, called the protesters "heroes." The NFL in May 2018 made it mandatory for players to stand during the National Anthem. Even Roger Godell and the NFL succumbed to Trump's wishes. Democracy is in peril.

In a September 2017 rally in Alabama, Trump brought up the Kaepernick incident. It hadn't faded. Bigots, racists and those who demand fealty for athletes to the owners and the fans cheered Trump's attack on the National Football League. The new slavery was back. Colin Kaepernick was the poster person for this idiocy. Trump screamed: "fire him." At his rallies this statement brought out raucous cheers.

The players stated time and time again their protest was about better jobs for young African Americans. They also discussed oversight in law enforcement. Trump's supporters were unaware of these conditions. They didn't care. A white America was what the bigots that hollered about the NFL protests desired. Trump's minions stormed the coffee shops, the bars, the country clubs and the town halls screaming about the menace of disrespectful African American millionaire football players.

Trump's rhetoric concerning African Americans, who he said disrespected the flag, was pure racism. To a man the NFL footballers said they respected the flag. Their protest was about lack of funding for African American schools, a higher level of political violence against the black community, the excessive incarceration rates for young African American males, which was almost double that of their white counterparts, and there were few educational, rehabilitation, job training and advanced college degrees for black youth. The level of white anger toward the NFL protesters was Trump's means of driving a wedge through American society and demeaning the African American community.

IGNORANCE OF HISTORY: TRUMP AND HIS MINIONS

"He doesn't seem to know the difference between criticism and racism,"

JOYCE BEHAR ON TRUMP

Historical ignorance in the White House is catastrophic. The president, as well as his key advisers, have little idea or understanding of American history. Does one need working knowledge of history? Why is this important? Trump and his Cabinet members need to employ historical examples to make informed decisions. Invariably, they confuse the facts, distort reality and wind up espousing racist arguments.

General John F. Kelly, Trump's Chief of Staff, remarked: "The lack of an ability to compromise led to the Civil War." This comment would lead one to believe he was talking about slavery, which was the cause of the Civil War. He wasn't. Kelly continued: "There were men and women of good faith on both sides...including the honorable Robert E. Lee." The press erupted with virulent criticism. "Kelly's understanding of American history and the Civil War is piss-poor and willfully ignorant," a **Salon** editorial stated. The danger is Trump and his minions create alternate facts while distorting history. The real past in lost in a morass of confusion and truculent ignorance.

When historians compared the Donald to Andrew Jackson, he was impressed. He had a picture of Jackson hung in the Oval Office. Trump had no idea Jackson was a slave owner. He didn't know Jackson forced Native Americans from their homes to remove them to remote locations in the American West. This was known as the Trail of Tears. Trump became so infatuated with Old Hickory he paid a visit to Jackson's Tennessee home and to his grave. Trump then said his campaign was like Jackson's in 1828. "And he had a very, very mean and nasty campaign....Because they said this was the meanest and nastiest," Trump remarked.

IMMIGRATION AND TRUMP'S POOR JUDGEMENT

Poor judgment, insensitivity, a lack of understanding of issues, boorish behavior and demeaning statements define Trump's foreign policy. As immigration was debated on Capitol Hill in mid-January 2018, the president rejected a GOP lawmakers deal on immigration. The Dreamers were left out in the cold. Rather than deal with DACA, Trump blamed the Democrats and demanded a border wall for the dreamer's protection. It was a moral issue. Trump lacks an ounce of moral fiber.

"This is like throwing gasoline to the fire," Representative Adriano Espaillat, a Democrat from New York and a Dominican Republic immigrant, said in response to Trump's remark. What set off Trump? It was when one of the Democrats at a White House meeting mentioned a "diverse visa lottery" that Trump erupted. He hates diversity.

"Why do we need more Haitians?" Trump asked. He also said a proposed DACA law was a "big step backwards." He believes immigrants will take over America. The morning after uttering this outrageous comment, Trump denied making it. He tried to spin the story.

Donald J. Trump: "Never said anything derogatory about Haitians other than Haiti is, obviously, a very poor and troubled country.

Never said 'take them out.' Made up by Demos. I have a wonderful relationship with Haitians. Probably should record future meetings-unfortunately, no trust." This 6:48 AM January 12, 2018 tweet is typical of Trump. Lie! Deny! Spin! Confuse! Distort! Obfuscate! The irony of this statement is the White House spokesperson, Rah Shah, did not deny Trump said: "shithole countries." He couldn't deny it. There were too many witnesses. Illinois Democratic Senator Dick Durbin said he had not read a single news report stating that the term "shithole" was falsely reported. Too many witnesses listened to the Donald. But he did deny it. That is the Donald.

Trump is racially insensitive. He makes disparaging, hurtful, off the cuff remarks appealing to his white power base. On January 12, 2018 when Trump stated he had not said "shithole," right wing German racists celebrated Herman Goering's birthday. One remarked it was Goering who invented the term "fake news." I reminded that German, it is President Donald Trump who is taking down the media with a "fake news" mantra. How many American's support the concept of "fake news?" A Monmouth University poll concludes sixty percent of America believes fake news dominates the media. Trump's persistent attacks are working and democracy is in peril.

Much like a carnival huckster, Trump is convincing a segment of the American public that the threats to the nation requires restraint from the press. He also believes it is necessary for the Mueller investigation to end. Trump says it is wasting money while failing to prove collusion. Trump describes the Mueller team as nothing more than the deep state attempting to take down the Trump presidency. The President continually complains President Obama is leading this effort. Nothing could be further from the truth. The undercurrent of racism in the White House and the unwillingness of the president to condemn white nationalists is a dangerous trend in the Oval Office. This is the road to altering the basic democratic process. The unwillingness to recognize racial prejudice in the White House is a serious problem.

The dangers of racial insensitivity in the Trump inner circle are a constant problem. After President Trump mentioned the Holocaust Remembrance Day, he didn't make references to Jews. His press secretary took over the podium telling the press that Hitler did not kill "his own people." Spicer ignored German Jews killed in the Holocaust. No one was sure if it was insensitivity or lack of knowledge. Or perhaps sheer stupidity.

The most damning racial insults were reserved for President Barack Obama. Trump called his presidency "an aberration." RT, Russian Television, continued to broadcast President Obama was not an American. Trump smiled. His fiction was RT fact. Trump did everything in his power to turn whites against blacks. He did so with the Colin Kaepernick incident, he defended Nazi demonstrators in Charlottesville, Virginia, and he urged the police to have less rather than more restraint. He called black athletes "sons of bitches" and he referred to Senator Elizabeth Warren of Massachusetts as "Pocahontas." He questioned her Native American roots. She shot backed labeling him a bigot and racist.

The Charlottesville incident is particularly troubling. Trump would not condemn Nazi agitators and white supremacists. Extremism, racism, nativism and isolationism define Trump's agenda. The politics of fear drives Trump's message. Those supporting him see conspiracies around every corner. Trump's tweets embolden, enrage and push forward a racist, nationalistic agenda. Whitey is back! Civil rights and decency in the political arena no longer exists.

When hurricanes struck Texas and Florida, Trump was pro-active in bringing government aide to these ravaged states. When Puerto Rico was ravaged a contract to bring electricity back was awarded to a Montana firm that had trouble completing the power repairs in a timely fashion. Was race the reason? No one knows! There is no indication of racism. Puerto Rican's don't agree.

Racism is an attitude. Racism is a mentality. Racism is disparaging all Muslims as being Jihadists. Racism is pigeon holing a race. Racism is holding a press conference on NPR, as Chief of Staff John Kelly did, suggesting that a lack of education for newly arrived immigrants made them unsuitable for entry to the U. S. Kelly was unaware his great-great-grandfather was a wagon driver who immigrated with limited English skills. He had little knowledge of America. He did just fine. Now General Kelly would deny that opportunity to immigrants.

Trump is not a racist or bigot. He has ideas heading in that direction. As he said: "I am the least racist person you will ever meet." Kanye West agrees. The rest of us are still making up our mind. Moral leadership and values are not a part of the Trump presidency.

FOUR

IS TRUMP HITLER AND STALIN? NO! HE IS ANTI-DEMOCRATIC

"If you tell a big enough lie and tell it frequently enough, it will be believed."

ADOLF HITLER

"Ideas are more powerful than guns. We would not let our enemies have guns, why should we let them have ideas?"

JOSEF STALIN

"It's not just what they did to us. It's our leader's sympathy with a dictator."

BRET STEPHENS, NEW YORK TIMES ON TRUMP.

"Our foreign policy depends…on what the president sees on Fox TV News in the morning and what gets his attention and obsession…."

TOM NILES, FORMER AMBASSADOR TO CANADA.

There is no way to minimize the dangers President Donald J. Trump presents to the American way of life. His view to Make America Great Again is ending bipartisan political discussion. His threats to the media could alter the fiber and fabric of the Bill of Rights. He is a bully. He is a misogynist. He makes the rules. He enforces the rules. He refuses criticism. Trump is slowly but surely eroding democracy.

What does democracy depend upon? It is constitutional protections. As Robert Mueller investigates corruption in Trump's inner-circle, the president criticizes the Special Counsel and his team. Periodically, he demands an end to the Russian investigation. A liberal democracy allows a strong person to challenge institutions. Trump is not Hitler or Stalin. He has a working knowledge of democracy. The President's tweets, his press conferences, his rallies, his off the cuff remarks do at times threaten traditional democratic institutions. In matters of foreign affairs, he seems lost.

In the 2016 campaign there were one hundred and thirty six academics that put out a paper "Scholars and Writers For America." To a person they supported Trump's election. They issued a "Statement of Unity." Who were these scholars? Most of them were connected to the Claremont Institute. This academic think tank is known as the home of Trumpism. Steve Bannon and Michael Anton are two intellectuals advising Trump with ties to the Claremont Institute. They advocate tearing down and rebuilding American democracy.

When Bannon convinced Trump to withdraw from the Paris Climate Accord, it was a window into his depraved intellectual nature. He believes international cooperation is tantamount to surrender. When the press exposes Trump's deceitful lies, he goes on a twitter rampage. His outrageous claim Ted Cruz's father played a role in the Kennedy assassination, his notion President Barack Obama was born in Kenya or Indonesia, and his claim thousands of New Jersey Muslims celebrated 9/11 speaks to Trump's lack of humanity. These claims also speak to Trump's casual relationship with the truth.

MICHAEL ANTON: A NATIONAL SECURITY COUNCIL ATTACK DOG

Michael Anton is not a familiar figure in America politics. He is equally as dangerous as Bannon. Why? Anton sits on the National Security Council. He is by default the intellectual in the inner-circle. Now that Bannon has been exiled, Anton's role is to defend white populism, insular nationalism and to help raise fears of Muslims, Latinos, a wide range of immigrants, and those who fail to embrace Trump's view of the American way.

He is in charge of strategic communications for the NSC. He is also a brilliant attack dog supporting Trump's viewpoint. Those who follow the Donald hang on Anton's every word. His attacks on Hillary Clinton contain elements of pure poetry. That is if you love the words of an alleged fascist philosopher. "A Hillary Clinton presidency is Russian Roulette with a semi-automatic," Anton continued. "With Trump, at least you can spin the cylinder and take your chances." This type of writing is fluid, florid and intellectual. Those who fear Anton compare him to the Nazi political theorist Carl Schmitt. This may seem extreme, but there is a tendency in Anton's writings drifting toward authoritarian rule. Anton sees authoritarian rule as the only means of maintaining order in America.

What makes Michael Anton dangerous? He controls communication from the White House regarding foreign policy. He began working for President George W. Bush in 2008, he wrote anonymous op-ed editorials and other stories supporting Trump's presidential bid. His pseudonym, Publius Decius Mus, during the 2016 presidential campaign, made thoughtful intellectual arguments for Trump's election. Anton claims to have originated the term "Trumpism." Humility is not one of his virtues. Anton provided the punchy slogans "America First" and "Make America Great Again." He suggests Trump was blocking Middle East immigrants. He wrote "politically correct McCarthyism" was ending the American way. Anton criticized gender issues involving elective bathrooms. He said Iranian supporters were sycophants. He was critical of Black Lives Matter. He was critical of progressive academics. America could survive, Anton lectures, only if a strong leader reshaped democracy.

Like Trump, Anton attempts unsuccessfully to rewrite history. He rejects multiculturalism. He opposes any and all immigration. The America First Committee in the 1930s which was racist, bigoted, anti-Catholic, anti-Jewish and pro-Hitler, Anton says has received incorrect interpretations. This conclusion ignores the basic historical facts. There are facts Trump ignores. Those who follow him display an aggressive bigotry when questioned about obvious facts. Pure and simple Anton is a "white nationalist."

Michael Anton: "If I am a nationalist, I am an American nationalist. I am also an American patriot, and I don't see the difference."

The difference is Anton, like Trump, hopes to muzzle the press while making America white again. Anton is one of the defenders of the Uncle Remus stories published in 1881 with a doll made of tar that sticks to Br-er Rabbit. It is considered one of the most racially intolerant images in American history. Anton's view is there should not be a racial connotation to any of the Uncle Remus stories. This is sheer ignorance. Anton says "racial connotations" are due to white liberals.

Anton is America's leading authoritarian intellectual. He is a former Bush speechwriter. He is consumed with food and dress. He is a quirky person with a penchant for defending authoritarian leaders.

Anton defines Trump's future political direction. He provided justification for some of the most divisive positions. He wrote the children of immigrants were "ringers to form a permanent electoral majority" for the Democratic Party. Anton argues the white Republican voter is the only legitimate individual vote. He says people of color taint the Democratic Party. Anton is a white supremacist cast in an intellectual persona.

Anton is not a typical Trump adviser. He is well educated. He is thoughtful. He writes with the poet's pen. He is a curious figure in the White House. **The Atlantic** described him as: "A thoroughly educated dandy, his writings are at the core of an effort to construct an intellectual framework around the movement that elected a president that has shown no inclination to read and who speaks in a pretentious New York vernacular." He is white nationalist. Steve Bannon continued: "I'm a huge admirer. I think Michael is one of the most significant intellects in this nationalist movement."

Rosie Gray observed in **The Atlantic**, that Anton is "tainted by a residue of prejudice." Anton represents the Claremont Institute's conservative view that if Hillary Clinton won the president the nation was headed for disaster. The Claremont Institute has no affiliation with Claremont College. What Anton attempts is to link the Claremont Institute with the politically liberal and academically sound Claremont College, this is typical right wing deception, Anton would have the reader believe the prestigious Claremont College approves or perhaps finances the Claremont Institute. The truth is the Claremont Institute is little more than a think tank controlled by right wing conservatives with the notion of erasing President Barack Obama's legacy and maintaining a conservative agenda to support Trump's politics.

Like others in the Trump administration, Anton left the National Security Council when John Bolton was appointed to work on foreign policy. He is going to work for the conservative Christian Hillsdale College, which espouses a philosophy of limited constitutional based government. Hillsdale College is a responsible critic of the administrative arm of the federal government. The unchecked power and growth of administrative federal agencies is one of Hillsdale's main points of contention. Those at Hillsdale College believe excessive federal regulation is a danger undermining the original intent of the U. S Constitution. Hillsdale College is a responsible conservative educational institution. This is the atmosphere Anton is escaping to in another phase of his life. Hillsdale College has nine alumni working in the Trump White House.

THE NEED FOR A FREE PRESS: WHY TRUMP DOESN'T WANT IT

The need for a free press is an essential ingredient to American democracy. Trump has attacked, minimized, ridiculed, disparaged and attempted to reduce the media's influence. This is the result of his belief in "fake news." He is attempting to control investigative journalism. Trump isn't aware of the historic role of a free press in an open democracy. It is essential to maintaining freedom. Madeleine Albright's **Fascism: A Warning** concludes Trump's political instincts make him "the first anti-democratic president in modern U.S. history." (p. 246)

By playing to his peanut gallery with the notion you can't trust the press, Trump is doing what Hitler and Stalin did in Germany and Russia. He is slowly taking away basic rights essential to an open democracy. During his first five months in office, Trump held one official press conference. He attacked media personalities, notably Megyn Kelly, Mika Brzezinski and Joe Scarborough. He made references to their sex, body descriptions, and he talked of women bleeding you know where. Whether this was about Brezezinski's face-lift or a female time of the month is not known. The Trump minions laughed at this insensitive remark. He has encouraged violence, intimidation and outright disrespect for the press.

His staffers shield him from criticism. Sean Spicer, the former press secretary, is a cartoon character. He has had trouble explaining Trump's policies. His replacement Sarah Huckabee Sanders is much better as the press secretary. She has no idea about Trump's programs nor does she seem to care. Spicer was in over his head. Sanders is an effective spokesperson without a message. Professor Daniel W. Drezner, of Tufts University, said it best of Sanders: "Sanders possess a unique talent that, heretofore, has not been considered a talent. She can deaden a room." **Politico** called her "the face of the most duplicitous press operation in White House history."

HOW TRUMP HIJACKED THE PRESIDENCY:
OLD WHITE GUYS

Trump's election represented the rise of discontented white voters, the shift of women to the Republican Party, the revolt from the states' rights advocates, those angry about affirmative action, those hostile to feminist concerns, anti-labor union forces and special programs for the disadvantaged. This voter realignment caused a shift to the Republican Party electing Trump.

The president tweets daily attacking anyone and everyone. When he holds a Cabinet meeting they grovel at his feet. They tell him how much they enjoy working with him. Trump is still running a corporation with an iron hand. However, that corporation is the U. S. government. He has no concern with checks and balances. His followers revel in his actions. They view him as tough and decisive. When a protester is thrown out of one of his rallies there are cheers and often fists are thrown at people employing legitimate First Amendment protest rights. He does his best to incite violence.

A DIVIDED AMERICA AND LESSONS FROM THE PAST

The U. S. is divided bitterly, angrily and maybe irrevocably. Once he ascended to the Oval Office, Trump suddenly became a historian, albeit one with no knowledge of the discipline. When Trump said Jackson "was really angry that he saw what was happening in regard to the Civil War," to a **Washington Examiner** reporter there was a stunned silence. The Civil War broke out in 1861. Jackson passed away sixteen years earlier. When informed of his error, Trump simply said he would have been upset had he lived. For Trump's brain dead followers, they defended him.

How have historians reacted to Trump's histrionics? By examining what Trump said it is obvious he was talking without an ounce of knowledge about American history. Trump said: "Why was there the Civil War? Why could that one not have been worked out?" Trump fails to understand the issues of slavery, sectionalism, political party differences, the rise of the American West, the emergence of the Republican Party, and the rise of a strong federal government. These forces were factors in the Civil War's outbreak.

Trump continued to bastardize history. "I mean, had Andrew Jackson been a little later you wouldn't have had the Civil War....he had a big heart. He was really angry that he saw what was happening with regard to the Civil War, he said 'there's no reason for this." The bozos that follow Trump agreed. There is no such history. The Donald distorted Jackson's presidency. He never apologized for his egregious use of history. Trump invents history. Sad! Some call it lies.

When CNN asked a group of eminent historians to analyze Trump's statements, they exposed his inability to understand the fundamentals of American history. Why is this important? It suggests why Trump is having difficulty in foreign policy.

Professor Amy S. Greenberg, the Erwin Erie Sparks Professor of History at Penn State University and the author of four books said: "A fourth grader could have answered the Civil War questions." Another historian, David Reynolds, a Distinguished Professor at the City University of New York and the author of fifteen books, said Trump would defend Jackson's right to own slaves. He would also support the expansion of slavery into the American West.

There is another danger from the Trump presidency. We are so divided as a nation that partisan hostility promotes racial hatred. That said, how do these attitudes impact a book on Trump's foreign policy? The mania to eradicate any traces of President Barack

Obama's legacy is Trump's priority. This leaves Trump no choice but to pursue policies that will take the U. S. out of the mainstream of European and Asian politics.

When President Barack Obama left office the European Union had a 64 percent level of confidence in American government, according to the Pew Center. By the time Trump was in office for a year there was a twenty-two percent confidence level from the EU. The forty-two percent drop in European confidence was for one reason. No one could figure out Trump's policies. His increasingly hostile American foreign policy had neither a direction nor a discernible philosophy.

There is uncertainty concerning the Russian influence. One conclusion is the Russian's wanted Trump in office. He never disavowed Russian support. Trump desperately wants to be friends with Putin. Every foreign dignitary, whether a President or Prime Minister, leaves an Oval Office meeting with Trump, as the president states, they are now best friends. Somehow Angela Merkel missed this distinction.

In the aftermath of the 2016 election, the **London Guardian** weighed in on the incoming Chief Executive. The **Guardian's** comments were points of wisdom. The **Guardian** said the U. S. Constitution "does not demand that our speech be civil." This is an essential point of American government. The Constitution allows for uncivil speech. Trump's presidency is the purveyor of fringe groups, lunatics and those who disrespect the American way of life. No one expected a president to tweet or speak in uncivil tones. It is a daily exercise for Trump. The **Guardian** concludes: "American democracy finds itself in peril."

The question of presidential lies is another insight in Trump's experiment in government. Trump has to cover his lies. He does by attacking the media. The notion the mainstream media engages primarily in "fake news" threatens the concept of free speech. The idea that unreliable reporting dominates the news and erodes major media credibility is seen on Fox TV News and Breitbart. The notion CNN is the enemy placed the channel on full alert. The irony is their reporting is at times overly fair to Trump. When there was a June 2017 news story that didn't pan out, three CNN staffers resigned. **The**

New York Times and **Washington Post** are similarly maligned. The First Amendment covers the libelous nature of Trump's speech. He abuses it to a great degree. He doesn't recognize the rights of others. When former FBI Director James Comey told the press President Trump had little interest in the Russian hacking of our presidential election, his comment was dismissed. When Comey appeared before the Senate Select Intelligence Committee, he shared notes he made after half a dozen meetings with Trump. Not once did the president demonstrate any interest or concern over Russian hacking. Comey found this mystifying. Trump never acknowledged Russia's criminal tampering. Nor did he seem to care about it.

Since James Comey's firing the attacks from Trump have never abated. They are filled with charges that bear no resemblance to reality. Because he feared Trump's vindictive nature, Comey made notes of their conversations. From January to July 2017 Trump tweeted and stated Comey leaked classified information in memos that recounted their conversations. Fox TV News picked up these bogus allegations. They questioned Comey's integrity. Trump continued the vicious early morning tweets. These missives have no credibility. They do have a large audience. The general public believes it.

The truth concerning Comey's memos is quite different. These memos contain classified material and unclassified information. No evidence has emerged he allowed classified information to be released. Comey wrote seven memos, four of which contained classified material. These memos were not leaked. There is only one of the seven memos Comey made public. It did not contain classified material. Trump was aware of this fact. It didn't deter the president from a scurrilous attack on Comey's integrity and stating he leaked classified materials. Pure lies!

The controversy over Comey's firing poses another question. Did Trump obstruct justice? There is no evidence as of this writing. The Special Counsel Robert Mueller was by July 2018 looking into Trump's erratic and unexplainable behavior. The press, as well as Michael Wolff's explosive reporting, described a White House in disarray. It was a dysfunctional government with children in charge.

In addition to organizational difficulties the president was a loose cannon barely able to control his emotions.

In Trump's third day in office the tirades began. He charged: "Between three million and five million illegal votes caused me to lose the popular vote." This was a bare faced lie. It got worse. He established a commission to prove his erroneous contention. When Trump requested from every state voter rolls, social security numbers, professions, any arrest warrants and other personal information in violation of every right American's cherish, the states uniformly said: "No. Trump has no idea about States' rights."

THE REAL RUSSIAN SCANDAL: SURVIVING TRUMP

During his first year in the White House rumors of the president's involvement with Russia swirled around indictments of his inner circle. Trump acted like those indicted were, as he put it, "the coffee boys." The truth is more damning. Paul Manafort was his campaign chairman, General Michael Flynn was the nation's National Security Adviser and there were two coffee boy types. George Papadopoulos, a foreign affairs specialist and Rick Gates, a high-level campaign aide. They were not "coffee boys." They were trusted campaign workers and members of the transition team. Both pleaded guilty and took deals with Mueller due to their contacts with Russia. Their guilty pleas make them convicted felons. It also requires they share their criminal acts in copious detail with Mueller's investigative team. They are all Trump insiders. The Russian scandal is one Trump doesn't recognize. He fails to see the malevolence that is part and parcel of Vladimir Putin's soul. He is a cunning devil-playing Trump like Charlie Daniels plays his fiddle.

One of the earliest indicted Trump insiders was his campaign champion General Michael Flynn. "Lock her up," General Flynn hollered at Trump rallies in reference to Hillary Clinton. Now he is in danger of being locked up. Or is he? This self-proclaimed patriot took a plea deal. Proving he is a liar and a coward. The general didn't register as a foreign agent. He lied to the FBI about his contacts with important politically connected Russians. He admitted all this. He took a plea deal.

This was one of the earliest indications of Russian intrigue from Trump insiders. They ignored the law. Those like Flynn allegedly believed they were above the law. In 2016, , Flynn's book **The Field of Fight: How We Can Win The Global War Against Radicals And Its Allies** came out with arguments Trump embraced. Flynn's book is full of "alternative facts." It is bigoted not only toward Muslims, the Islamic religion and people of color, it also advocates a close relationship with Russia. Flynn put his feelings for cooperation with Putin throughout the book. Trump usurped them.

Flynn and Trump have gone out of their way to appease Putin. Perhaps they have a broader diplomatic agenda. When Attorney General Jeff Sessions told Congress the administration had not done enough to dissuade Russian election meddling, Trump threw a fit. When Congress increased sanctions on Russia, the president and Flynn took umbrage at this policy. The idea of finding a common ground with Russia is one Trump embraces. Why? The president is infatuated with authoritarian personalities. He is susceptible to flattery from dictators. He is a capitalist who has little interest in American foreign policy.

The continual harangues from Trump suggest he believes he is the victim of "fake news." This is the first step to dismantling the First Amendment. The good news is the American media is independent. They can fight back. Trump's ridiculous daily accusations are a staple of his politics. His minions follow every morning tweet. They place his ridiculous comments on a platform of sainthood connected to political wisdom. Why does Trump need the term "fake news?" It is due to his inability to separate fact from fiction. It is dangerous in a democracy not to have free and open debate.

TRUMP'S ATTACK ON THE NEWS: WHEN REAL NEWS TAKES PLACE HE CALLS IT "FAKE NEWS"

At the conclusion of his first year in office, Trump accelerated his "fake news" claims. "Why isn't the Senate Intel Committee looking into the Fake News Networks in OUR country to see why so much of our news is just made up-FAKE," Trump tweeted on October 5, 2017. This Trump tweet came as his inner circle was investigated and indicted for alleged Russian collusion. Much of the verified material on Russian collusion comes from the media. No wonder he wants them investigated and silenced. This tweet also came a day after Secretary of State Rex Tillerson called Trump "a moron."

When Trump's appointees are attacked, he strikes back with a vengeance. In late June 2017 CNN reported a White House Communications appointee, Anthony Scaramucci, might be connected to the Russian Direct Investment Fund. CNN withdrew the story. CNN claimed it did not meet their editorial standards. What this means is a second source is needed to corroborate. This source was not available. CNN apologized and Scaramucci dropped his threat to sue. Trump spent days talking about CNN's fake news.

When Trump's first year in office came to a close, he made up a Fake News Awards ceremony. The president announced CNN was the winner in four of seven fake news categories. **The New York Times** was second with ABC News, **Time**, the **Washington Post** and **Newsweek** receiving honorable mention. The difference between Trump and the media is when they get it wrong they withdraw the story. They apologize. Trump will create an even bigger lie and recount an even taller tale.

The Trump administration presented the Fake News Awards on the Republican National Committee's website. Ethics professionals commented this website is partially funded by taxpayer resources. They wondered! Is this ethical? The Trump administration never addressed this issue.

Donald J. Trump: "Despite some very corrupt and dishonest media coverage, there are many great reporters I respect and lots of GOOD News for the American people to be proud of!" This January 17, 2018 Trump tweet at 6:05 PM was an indication of his continual war on the media. He has threatened to go after licenses as the FCC has discretionary power over all media outlets. The war is on. Trump wants to destroy press freedoms.

Republican Senator Jeff Flake of Arizona, a staunch conservative, answered Trump: "When a figure in power reflexively calls any press that doesn't suit him 'fake news,' it is that person who should be the figure of suspicion, not the press."

TRUMP WANTS TO DESTROY THE PRESS

He labels journalists "the enemies of the American people." At a campaign rally in Texas in February 2016 Trump told his audience if he were elected president he would promote legal changes to end critical reporting. "I am going to open up our libel laws, so when they write purposely negative and horrible and false articles, we can sue them and win lots of money," Trump told his Texas audience. They cheered.

Things got worse. Trump took a page out of Vladimir Putin's authoritarian handbook. He threatened media tax changes. This was another means in controlling the press. He implied he would tax the media disproportionately. When he was asked about Jeff Bezos and Amazon, he remarked they would have problems if he were elected president. No Chief Executive in modern times has threatened a business. There were also fiscal threats he would take to the courts. The Donald threatened lawsuits that he said would bankrupt newspapers. This threat came at a time the press was squeaking by financially. Trump's attacks upon the **New York Times** were relentless. The good news is profits have increased dramatically for the **New York Times**, the **Washington Post** and the major TV news outlets. Contrary to Trump's claims of declining readers and listeners the circus in Washington has fiscally empowered the media.

Many of Trump's supporters, whether they are in the crowd or in his inner-circle, have physically threatened the press. Corey Lewandowski, Trump's campaign manager, was arrested in Florida. He was charged with assault. The arrest was due to an altercation with Michelle Fields, a reporter with the alt-right Breitbart, which supported Trump. He physically attacked her.

When Fields attempted to ask Trump a question, Lewandowski almost threw her to the ground. She went to the police and reported the incident Her report detailed Lewandowski's physically threatening behavior. Throughout the campaign physical threats were a part of the Trump strategy. The reporter's police report was disputed. Lewandowski said she lied. There was a video. It was by two Fox TV News reporters who proved Lewandowski lied about the incident.

The Jupiter, Florida police arrested Lewandowski. He was charged with battery. This wasn't the end of Lewandowski's behavior. He was arrogant and imperious in dealing with reporters, workers in the campaign and with many of Trump's key supporters. He did as much to hurt Trump's campaign as to help it. After Trump fired him, Joy Villa, a Trump supporter, called the police and accused the former campaign manager of sexual assault. Villa alleged Lewandowski "struck her extremely hard on the buttocks." Villa wore a "Make America Great Again" dress and she told the press she was a singer and potential congressional candidate. Villa seemed more interested in the press than pressing charges. She was seen at the Grammys wearing a dress with Trump's campaign slogan. She also said she was releasing a July 4 song on her label entitled "Make America Great Again." Trump was often hurt more by his followers than his critics. When Carter Page was described as "wackadoodle," that appellation could be used on many other Trumpsters.

In late May 2017 there were two publicized attacks in a few days on reporters. Montana voted Trump by more than twenty points. Montana Republican Congressional candidate Greg Gianforte slammed a British reporter to the ground. The reason? Gianforte didn't like the way the Brit asked a question about healthcare reform. After the attack the reporter, Ben Jacobs, bewildered by the physical attack, complained to authorities.

What was Gianforte's motivation? He was running in a Montana special election for Congress. His right wing politics prompted him to view the media as an opponent. After all Trump inferred the media was the enemy. Gianforte, a multimillionaire tech entrepreneur, misled the police about the assault. He told local Montana police the "liberal media…is trying to make a story…." When he was told there was a video of his assault, he became contrite and apologized. There was a frightening visual image to the assault. The gigantic in-shape Gianforte grabbed the reporter's wrist and they both fell to the ground at a Republican campaign volunteers BBQ. Everyone thought it was funny except the diminutive British reporter. He was scared to death by the physical assault.

Gianforte allegedly continued to lie about the incident. When it was over a spokesperson told the AP: "No one was misled and anyone who says otherwise is mistaken," Sergeant Scott Secor of the Gallatin County Sheriff's Office reported. The police Sergeant said: "Gianforte felt threatened by the reporter's questions." The Gallatin County Sheriff's report allegedly condoned Gianforte's attack. The video proved it was an assault. Gianforte acted like a cowboy who would kick your ass. He did! Just ask Ben Jacobs.

When the investigation concluded, there were more than one hundred pages of documents, photos and audiotapes. One of Gianforte's campaign volunteers said he saw the candidate strike the British reporter with a closed fist.

Greg Gianforte pleaded guilty of assaulting Ben Jacobs. He paid a $385 fine. He was sentenced to forty hours of community service and twenty hours of anger management counseling. A civil settlement was worked out. The Montana Congressman donated $50,000 to the Committee To Protect Journalists. He also wrote an apology letter. Gianforte told friends he was outraged his mug shot appeared in the press. This is what Trump supporters are like. They will lie. They will distort. They will distract. They will kick your ass. They will scream the liberal left is destroying America. In the irony of all ironies, Gianforte didn't explain that Fox News reporters witnessed the assault and reported it to the police. What is apparent is Gianforte is an obnoxious bully. He is also a Congressman from Montana.

There were other violent incidents associated with Trump. In Portland, Oregon an American Nazi attacked two women on a train. When two people came to their defense they were stabbed to death. In Washington State a white man ran over two Native Americans as he shouted racial slurs. Racial tension in the classroom was obvious. While Trump wasn't personally responsible for all of these incidents, many suggest the white nationalist mood intensified these violent acts. At some schools students hollered "Trump" to minority students in racial antagonism.

KEEPING THE PRESS OUT: TRUMP'S DUPLICITY

The level of Trump's totalitarian tendencies is demonstrated when he periodically bans the American press from the White House. On May 10, 2017 Trump met with Russian Ambassador Sergey Kislyak and the Russian foreign minister, Sergey Lavrov. The American press was not invited. The state controlled Russian media, TASS, was in full attendance. After the meeting an embarrassing photo of Trump laughing with the two Russians appeared in the world press. Lavrov and Kislyak allegedly were involved in the hacking of the 2016 election. Trump just didn't get it. The Russians were playing him.

When Secretary of State Rex Tillerson met with the Saudi Arabian Prime Minister, Adel bin Ahmed Al-Jubeir, only the foreign media was invited. American journalists received the information on this meeting from transcripts provided by Saudi state television. The irony is the most powerful democracy in the world had its media access restricted, and the information on the Saudi visit came from a totalitarian state controlled Saudi media. Trump didn't realize the extent of restrictions on the Saudi Arabian press. There is no media freedom in the Saudi kingdom. Trump's minions have no respect for the First Amendment. The idea of an official government controlled Trump news channel is a chilling comment on the administration's view of the news.

TRUMP'S CONTINUED FOX NEWS LOVE AFFAIR

To return his love for Fox and Friends, Trump has tweeted more than four hundred times suggesting Fox is the "real news." He gives exclusive interviews to Fox. On Fox, Trump talks continually about "fake news." The anchors agree. The president will go on a tirade about the "deep state." How does Trump define the "deep state?" Trump argues the "deep state," which he defines as the Justice Department, the FBI and the National Intelligence agencies are conspiring to force him out of office. It was Trump's oldest son, Donald Jr., who stood on stage at Hofstra University on September 26, 2016 arguing the media, federal government employees and hidden liberal forces were conspiring to defeat his father's bid for the presidency. In December 2017, after a year of Trump's presidency, his son continued his tirade.

Donald J. Trump Jr. said the "deep state" conspiracy theorists argue cadres of tenured government officials are placing roadblocks in Trump's policy and legislative agenda. Donald Jr. points to leaks emanating from the U. S. intelligence community as proof of "deep state" covert activity. On July 7, 2017, Donald Jr. tweeted: "If there was ever confirmation that the Deep State is real, illegal & endangers national security, it's this. Their interests above all else...." Then Donald Jr. refers to a Drudge Report that argues there have been unprecedented leaks from the State Department. The implication is clear. There was a conspiracy to make Trump's presidency a difficult one. There is no evidence of the deep state except in the mind of Trump whackos and the president. Trump's supporters remark the deep state is real. You can't see it. But you know it is there.

Fox News is the media apparatus Trump uses to combat his persistent fears of the mainstream media. When Roger Ailes, the deposed head of Fox News, was told of Trump's presidential victory, he was flummoxed. Then he suggested the conservative Fox TV message created the fan base accelerating Trump's path to the White House. He realized Trump's election was as much due to Fox TV News as to what was wrong with America. Much of what benefitted Trump came from Fox TV News demanding Trump drain the swamp. Ailes gave credence to the conspiracy theories Trump embraced.

TRUMP DESCRIBES THE ISSUES AND THE MEDIA

On June 25, 2017 a Fox TV News talking head, Peter Hegseth, asked Trump what was his most significant opponent? Trump said fake news, the deep state leaks, the Democratic Party and those who conspired to thwart his policies. Hegseth's questions gave credence to Trump's conspiracy theories. Fox TV News continually defends him. They distort events and play loose with the facts. Lou Dobbs declared Trump's critics were attempting to "carry out a coup d'état against him." Dobbs dangerously and inappropriately equated democratic dissent with the military overthrow of a democratically elected leader. This outrageous statement is typical of Fox TV News.

Who is Peter Hegseth? He is a former military officer. He is an executive director of Vets For Freedom. Not surprisingly, in mid-March 2018 Hegseth, a Veteran's affairs advocate was a constant critic of Veteran's Cabinet Secretary David Shulkin. What did Hegseth possess that made him a strong critic of how Secretary Shulkin carried out his duties.

Hegseth had a platform. It was on Fox TV News where he spun tales of how the Vets needed a voice. He was that voice. He is a good looking, media savvy, young guy with an entitled education. He has also been a leading voice for Making Trump Great Again. His political message is to the responsible right. He is impressive. He is articulate. He is a conservative voice with a political future. Who is he and how did he get to the White House?

He is a Princeton educated right wing conservative who backed Marco Rubio and then Ted Cruz in the 2016 election. He is an advocate of traditional family values. He is happily married to his second wife, Samantha, after divorcing his first wife Meredith Schwarz over his alleged infidelity. He had a baby with Samantha before their marriage. But, hey, he is a family values guy, a church going Christian and a staunch Trump attack dog. What more can you ask for?

Hegseth was a co-host of Fox And Friends and his work on Veteran's affairs caught Trump's attention. He is an Iraqi war veteran who has worked over the years with a number of politically significant veterans groups. The Koch brothers funded much of his work for better veteran benefits and services. This led to dinner with President Trump at the White House, and he dramatically increased his support for Trump's policies.

The extent of Hegseth's support for Trump was evident when Fox Business Network anchor, Dagen McDowell, criticized Trump for factional splits in the Republican party. She said: "The problem is President Trump, when he was running for the nomination, he gobbled up Republicans right and left like M & M's. Little Marco, Lyin' Ted and Low-energy Jeb. He decimated, I mean he destroyed, the party and they resent it." Hegseth quickly went on the defensive. He argued that Republican Senators Susan Collins and Lisa Murkowski "run against Obamacare and then they vote with Democrats." Raising his voice, Hegseth almost shouted: "He is a little different, he's outside the box, he speaks differently, they can't get behind him." Hegseth is an example of the fanatical follower who doesn't allow criticism. Dagen McDowell was silent. After all she is a woman. This is Fox TV News.

On Fox TV News and other media outlets Hegseth is one of the attacks dogs supporting Making America Great Again. The **Washington Post** describes his voice as that supporting the Veterans Affairs agenda. Not surprisingly He joined Fox News in 2014, at times he is a co-host on Fox And Friends. He also worked on The Kelly File. He is an articulate, good-looking guy telling you that Hillary is evil, the deep state is real and the FBI is corrupt. I like that from a family values guy.

It is reporters like Peter Hegseth who tell the old folks drooling and eating their oatmeal in front of Fox TV News how to think. Hegseth's message is to Make America Great Again, retire Nancy Pelosi, place Hillary Clinton in jail and make sure that never again there is "a Negro president." This is the state of Fox News and their support for the Donald. On his twitter account Hegseth is dressed in his military uniform, he is a distinguished veteran of the Iraq and Afghanistan wars, and he stands in front of a tank. He looks like he is ready to kill. He is!

Hegseth on his twitter account didn't display a deep understanding of the Bill of Rights: "The reality is the Second Amendment's not about hunting, it not about self-defense only, it's about free people and chocks on a tyrannical government." After Hegseth tweeted this on March 25, 2018 I felt safe. Then he let go with another tweet. "After watching the anti-NRA crap yesterday, only one thing felt appropriate." Hegseth ended his observation with the statement: "NRA Thank you." Once again I feel really safe. A member of Fox TV News in full uniform in front of a tank makes me proud to be an American.

THE PARANOIA FROM BELIEVING IN THE DEEP STATE

Lou Dobbs's paranoia on Fox Business concerning the "deep state" is his favorite fantasy. It is reflected among Trump supporters. As Dobbs looks into the Fox TV Business camera, he eloquently explains the deep state prevents Trump from governing. David Remnick, writing in the **Washington Post**, said the problem was not the deep state. He said it was the president. "The problem is a shallow man-an untruthful, vain, vindictive, alarmingly erratic president," Remnick continued, "is hampering government."

In July 2017 Trump News was inaugurated with the first show called "Real News of The Week." This maniacal attempt to control the news is typical of his totalitarian mind. The risk of losing the independent political press is a possibility under Trump's presidency. If millions of people begin to receive their news from Trump TV, the free press ceases to exist.

In a democracy information is the key to freedom. An informed citizenry creates an intelligent voting public. Without debate, reliable information and constant questioning, a democracy becomes a hollow shell ruled by an authoritarian.

What we have in the White House is a president who believes, as George Orwell wrote, "lies sound truthful." Trump describes the work of Special Counsel Robert Mueller as "a coup." In the darkest days of our democracy, Trump has gloated and ridiculed the rule of law. He is a charlatan selling gibberish to a gullible public. He urges American's to vote an alleged child predator into the U. S. Senate. He has issued public statements prompting Polifact to analyze his facts. Polifact concluded four of every hundred Trump facts were verifiable truth. The enemy is Trump not the truth.

PROFESSOR DANIEL DREZNER'S VIEW
ABOUT THE SYRIAN THREAT

After sixteen months in the presidency, Professor Daniel Drezner, of the Fletcher School of Law and Diplomacy at Tufts University, observed of Trump's tweets on Syria, when he wrote they have "all the panache of a fourth grader who has been denied a third helping of dessert." The basis for this conclusion is Trump's April 11, 2018 that U. S. missiles: "will be coming, nice and new and smart!" Drezner criticized Trump "for telegraphing an explicit threat."

It is obvious Trump operates impulsively. He lacks in-depth knowledge. He is not interested in educating himself. He suffers what political science professors label "audience cost." This is a term in international relations theory describing the penalty a leader faces from escalating a crisis without a plan or a solution.

Just a few weeks before threatening Syria, Trump said the U. S. would leave Syria. This erratic and mindless policy does little, if anything, to foster confidence in American foreign policy. Just a few days before threatening Russia for its support of Syria, the president talked of working with the Kremlin. The contradictions and confusion in his foreign policy is astounding.

Polarization is the other problem with Trump's foreign policy. The country is so divided it is difficult to achieve a consensus on foreign policy. This means decisions will be debated but seldom with agreement. The president exacerbates the arguments by refusing to negotiate, consider other ideas and not feel he is a genius. Ego not intellect is driving Trump's concept of foreign policy. He will do it his way. This is not the policy of a rational leader in a democracy.

Trump is incorrectly labeled a populist. This is a bastardization of the term. A populist increases economic opportunity for the less fortunate. He is promising greater economic rewards and the tax cut did that for the top one percent. Crumbs were thrown to the working class as a bully in the White House continued to threaten Hillary Clinton while stating former president Barack Obama was "a sick guy" for spying on him. There was no evidence to support this contention.

FIVE

TRUMP: HISTORY, IGNORANCE, BIGOTRY AND BRAGGADOCIO

"You know, people don't understand. I went to an Ivy League college. I did very well. I'm a very intelligent person."

DONALD J. TRUMP

"It used to be cars were made in Flint and you couldn't drink the water in Mexico. Now cars are made in Mexico and you can't drink the water in Flint."

DONALD J. TRUMP

"Foreign policy by twitter is a dangerous game. We do not want to turn Syria into a game of chicken given limited U. S. options...."

RICHARD HAASS

"He has trusted a moron with his inner most secrets."

MICHAEL AVENATTI IN CONVERSATION WITH BILL MAHER ABOUT MICHAEL COHEN'S RELATIONSHIP WITH PRESIDENT TRUMP

There is no way to minimize the danger President Donald J. Trump presents to the American way of life. His actions attacking anyone who disagrees with his policies, his view to Make America Great Again by ending bipartisan political agreements, and his continued misogynist behavior bodes ill for the future. He makes the rules. He enforces the rules. He has no respect for a free press. What this means is he is a hero in many countries with totalitarian regimes or with heads of state compromising democracy.

The need for a free press is essential to American democracy. The Trump administration has attacked, minimized, ridiculed, disparaged and worked to diminish the media. He has said repeatedly the media must play a less significant role in American politics. This is the result of Trump's view of the press is he believes that "fake news" is attacking him.

TRUMP: HISTORY, IGNORANCE, BIGOTRY AND BRAGGADOCIO

"Donald Trump's ignorance of government policy, both foreign and domestic is breathtaking," Eugene Robinson remarked. This was a conclusion reached by a **Washington Post** opinion writer in March 2016. Does it sound harsh? It does! Upon further examination it also sounds like the truth. This conclusion was drawn after Trump sat down for an hour talk with the **Washington Post** opinion board. They asked questions. He answered questions. The transcript of this meeting provided frightening insights into his lack of knowledge and fitness for the presidency.

During questions involving race, Trump was a weasel. He wouldn't answer. Why? He had no knowledge of the key racial concerns. When the editorial board asked him questions concerning race and bigotry, he talked around the issues. Here is an example of the **Post** asking: "Do blacks and white receive disparate treatment?"

Donald J. Trump: "I've read where there are and I've read where there aren't. I mean, I've read both. And, you know, I have no opinion on that. Because frankly, what I'm saying is you know we have to create incentives for people to go back and to reinvigorate the areas and to put people to work. And you know we have lost millions and millions of jobs to China and other countries. And they've been taken out of this country, and when I say millions, you know it's, it's tremendous. I've seen 5 million jobs, I've seen numbers that range from 6 million to, to smaller numbers. But it's many millions of jobs, and it's to countries all over. Mexico is really becoming the new China. And I have great issue with that."

This was a typical campaign answer. David Cay Johnston, Trump's most perceptive biographer, wrote in the **London Guardian** "Trump's ignorance is becoming more evident with each passing day." Johnston is concerned Trump hopes to fulfill his campaign promises, which includes nuclear war.

"He acts like a classic con artist," Johnston continues, "all bluster and vagaries." It is Trump's attempts to recall history that frightens everyone. When he met with African American leaders the Donald said Frederick Douglass was "an example of somebody's who's done an amazing job and is being recognized more and more." Trump didn't realize Douglass had been dead for one hundred and twenty two years or that he was an abolitionist. The president didn't seem to know what an abolitionist was or why black leaders would discuss this subject. "Trump's own words show he is utterly unprepared for the job of city council member," Johnson continues. "He possesses the nuclear launch codes. Ignorance is not bliss, but death and disaster waiting for the right mix of circumstances."

The Washington Post headlined in an opinion piece: "Donald Trump Is A Bigot and A Racist." This seemed harsh. That is until columnist Dana Milbank laid out the argument. The president criticized African Americans, immigrants, Latinos, Asians, women, Muslims and the disabled. Does that make him a racist or a bigot? Let's say for argument purposes Trump is not a racist. Let's also stipulate not all his followers are bigots. What is apparent is some of Trump s' supporters tend to be nationalistically white, less educated, and a portion are middle to upper class often making large sums of money. This is despite a lack of formal education. They are people searching for an authority figure. They describe themselves as independents. They are authoritarian voters. A look at their voting record shows they invariably vote Republican. They have had eight years of President Barack Obama. This hardened their conservative views. They look to a strong authoritarian figure to bring America back to world prominence. The irony is the U. S. leads the world in promoting democracy, fair trade and equalizing the world's economic gap. In sharp contrast, Trump and his followers look for America to be open for business but without involving our country in regulating clean air, promoting weaponry controls and fighting third world poverty and diseases. Trump's foreign policy abandons the humanitarian side of American foreign policy. To label Trump a bigot or racist, as the **Washington Post** did, is to miss the larger question. That is the insatiable attraction of a vibrant economy and a prosperous lifestyle. This is important to a segment of American voters prompting them to overlook humanitarian concerns. It appears many American voters are attracted to this platform. They ignore the subtle nuance of a democratic, humanitarian governmental structure.

On the campaign trail in late September 2016, Trump sent people scurrying for their dictionaries when he said: "I wrote 'The Art of The Deal.' I say that not in a braggadocios way." What the word means is arrogant. Trump displayed a great deal of arrogance and condescension during the campaign. He didn't write **The Art Of The Deal**. It was ghost written by Tony Schwartz. Trump probably hasn't read it.

WHAT DID A YEAR OF TRUMP BRING?

The Trump presidency, during its first year, challenged every aspect of American government spending. To augment increased defense spending there were heavy cuts in numerous governmental departments. In order to provide a down payment on the border wall, Trump held up a bill on the dreamers. To increase charter school vouchers, Betsy DeVos eviscerated public school funding. Other proposals cut deeply into the Environmental Protection Agency. The Agriculture Department and the State Department's government oversight programs are vanishing as are their budgets.

Funding for the arts and grants for professorial and public intellectual pursuits were defunded. There is an attack on anything intellectual or science based. Trump's budget cuts included nine hundred million dollars from the Energy Department's Office of Science. The Trump administration defunded public television, and the National Endowment For The Humanities. Special programs for women, minorities and the underemployed were put on hold. The fourteen percent cut in the Department of Education goes even deeper as key federal funds were taken away from the public schools and provided to white dominated charter schools. The cuts in education most deeply influence the quality of education for Latinos, African American's and schools with a decided minority population. It is the new racism. Hold back the money. End quality education. Support the charter schools.

There is a consistency to Trump's policies. The **Washington Post** charged Trump is tough. He is racist. He is bigoted. Here is the contradiction. Trump sees himself as liberal on issues of race. He is appealing to a nationalistic base frustrated with world affairs. He is tired of affirmative action. He is sick of government regulation.

WHY TRUMP IS A DEMAGOGUE

Why is Donald Trump an effective demagogue? The answer is a simple one. Demagogues arouse passion. They have pat answers to complex questions. They appeal to uber nationalism. Trump displays the ideals of white power. This view dominates his political philosophy. Trump became a wrecking ball to the old political order. He used fear on the campaign trail. He said a border wall would keep drug crazed Mexican criminals out of the U. S. Trump talked of bombing ISIS into submission.

When former FBI Director James Comey informed the press President Trump had little interest in the Russian hacking of our presidential election, his comment was dismissed. When Comey appeared before the Senate Select Intelligence Committee, he brought notes he made after half a dozen Trump meetings. Not once did the president demonstrate any interest or concern over Russian hacking in the 2016 presidential election. Comey found this mystifying.

Since James Comey's firing, Trump's attacks intensified. They are filled with charges that bear no resemblance to reality. Because he feared Trump's vindictive nature, Comey made notes of their conversations. From January to July 2017 Trump tweeted stating Comey leaked classified information. Fox TV News picked up this bogus allegation. Trump continued the early morning tweets. They had credibility with the general public who listened to Fox TV News.

The truth about Comey's memos is quite different. Some contained classified material and others were not classified. No evidence has emerged he allowed unclassified information to be

91

released. Comey wrote seven memos, four of which contained classified material. None of those memos has gone out to the general public. There is only one of the seven memos Comey made public. It did not contain classified material.

WHO IS DONALD J. TRUMP AND WHAT DOES HE BRING TO THE PRESIDENCY IN FOREIGN POLICY?

When Donald J. Trump won the 2016 presidential election most people had no idea what he stood for in foreign affairs. This book analyzes foreign policy against the window of domestic politics. Those who have written about Trump do so in a partisan manner. It is either love or hate him. His business successes are well known. His well-publicized three marriages. His career as a TV celebrity and producer on the top rated Apprentice show alerted many to his business brilliance. His populist message resonated with voters as did his business acumen.

Many ignored Trump's early statements on American foreign policy. His first serious interview was an October 6, 1980 with NBC's Rona Barrett. She was a credible celebrity journalist. Her subjects were actors with facelifts who slept around and the gossipmongers that controlled the press. She was not a news journalist. Trump was a wealthy playboy with a stable of girlfriends, hotels and lackeys who hung on his every word. Trump made some serious comments on foreign policy. No one took him seriously.

What did Trump emphasize in his first statement on foreign policy in the Rona Barrett interview? He talked of life being "a battle to win." He went on to say America should work toward "greatness." He lamented the lack of political leadership. He said there was no one looking to Make America Great Again. His slogans, his ideas and his demeanor in foreign policy were established that day in 1980. Trump told Barrett "I feel that this country with the proper leadership can go on to become what it once was….and certainly hope, that it does go on to be what it should be." Then thirty-seven years later, Trump was in charge of American foreign policy. He is described as an "unconventional president in foreign policy."

Fareed Zakaria, in an op-ed piece in **The Washington Post,** commented "President Trump's bizarre foreign policy moves, we are often told he is 'unconventional' and that this could well be an asset." Zakaria goes on to suggest the president is one who "doesn't follow standard operating procedure on almost anything…." Zakaria asks: "How do American institutions survive an assault by the president?"

What does it mean Trump doesn't weigh his words carefully when dealing with other countries? Most presidents are diplomatic in dealing with friends and foes. In sharp contrast, Trump insults friends and foes. His policy in foreign affairs is not consistent. It is often puzzling. During the campaign he exorcized Saudi Arabia for killing gays and making women slaves. After he was elected Trump's first trip abroad was to Saudi Arabia where he dressed like a clown and did a dance with a sword. How do you spell inconsistent? The imprecise rhetoric and boastful threats highlight Trump against the world.

The fit of temper Trump throws in the Oval Office is well documented. The Donald is precise and will explode if a task is not properly carried out. "When he's really mad, he screaming at you," Steve Bannon said. He is usually watching Fox TV News when he erupts.

When Trump complains about leaks in the press, he never suggests he is a leaker. The most significant leaker is Kellyanne Conway. But Trump regularly phones Maggie Haberman of the **New York Times** and Philip Rucker of the **Washington Post**. Their stories usually list a senior White House official as a source. Haberman's stories are invariably negative. The team at Morning Joe was for a time friendly with Trump and then he called Joe Scarborough names and insulted Mika.

Insulting behavior, boorish incidents and inane comments can also be attributed to other Trump insiders. When Sarah Huckabee Sanders took over Spicer's duties she tweeted a photo of a chocolate pecan pie she had baked on the family farm. April Ryan of American Urban Radio Networks called it a "fake pie." It is not just Trump who has behavior that needs explaining, it is many of the people working in the White House.

SIX

WHAT PRESIDENT TRUMP BRINGS TO FOREIGN POLICY: HIS INTERVIEWS 1980 THROUGH 2014

**"A madman and his legislative minions
are holding America hostage."**

CHARLES M. BLOW, THE NEW YORK TIMES

"I know things the generals don't know."

DONALD TRUMP

"Americanism not globalism will be our credo."

DONALD TRUMP

**"Most of the power of authoritarianism is freely given.
In times like these, individuals think ahead about what
a more repressive government will want, and then offer themselves
without being asked. A citizen who adapts
in this way is teaching power what it can do."**

TIMOTHY SNYDER

There is a surprising consistency to Trump's views on foreign policy from 1980 through 2014. Few people paid attention to his comments. In this period he wasn't considered a serious presidential contender. There was very little press on how he viewed the world. This chapter analyzes the thirty-five years of Trump interviews highlight his foreign policy philosophy. The surprise is he is consistent in his views. In decision-making he is erratic and shifts his opinions from day-to-day, but there is a coherent underlying theme to Trump's foreign affairs message.

TRUMP'S FOREIGN POLICY VIEW:
HIS LACK OF KNOWLEDGE

When he became President Trump, he made it clear he had little concern with advancing human rights and promoting democracy abroad. He reinforced his feelings when he said people from "shit hole" nations were not welcome in the U.S. He said immigrants who came from Africa would never return to their "mud huts" once they settled in America. Trump's out front racism and his America First devotees cheered his continued bigotry. This bully, who places democracy in peril, frightened the rest of the world. Trump's narrow nationalistic view isolated America from world affairs.

Trump has not read, considered in depth, or examined the course of American foreign policy. The contradiction is he established clear views on foreign policy solely from his business experiences outside the U. S. He felt disrespected in world finance. He took the personal sleights and made them a part of his foreign policy philosophy. Bluster and bravado characterize his aggressive American First nationalistic foreign policy. There were glaring contradictions in his conduct of foreign affairs. These contradictions result from lack of knowledge, as well as from an unwillingness to abide by internationally accepted protocol. The gaps between rhetoric and policy became a hallmark of Trump's foreign policy.

Once he became president, there was a mercurial nature to Trump's vision of American foreign policy. Hal Brands, the Henry A. Kissinger Distinguished Professor of Global Affairs at Johns Hopkins University's School of Advanced International Studies, wrote in **Foreign Policy**, "Trump Doesn't Believe In His Own Foreign Policy. Does That Matter?" This article reflected on Trump's foreign policy after a year of his administration's role in world affairs.

Brands concluded there was a "vast distance between the president and his policies." He suggests Trump talks about policy as his administration veers into another direction. The president displayed his loathsome feelings for NATO and his complete disregard for Section 5 in the NATO defense agreement while in

Europe at the G-7 Summit. After showing contempt for international cooperation at the G-7 and G-20 Summits in 2017 there was a slow, but subtle, change in the president's demeanor. In time, Trump's administration embraced NATO supported mutual defense agreements. No one in Europe could figure him out. He repudiated Section 5 and the weeks later embraced the concept after some reflection. Europeans realized inconsistencies were Trump's hallmark.

In December 2017 the Trump administration released a National Security Strategy paper. Many Trump insiders said he had not read it nor did he understand it. He is lazy and generally unfamiliar with past foreign policy.

As he mounts his incendiary tweets, his outrageous comments to the press and his praise for world authoritarian leaders, Trump diminishes the presidency. His comments are continually damaging to statecraft. The volatile, continually unpredictable, nature of Trump's policy does not bode well for the future. America's role and power in the world rests on predictability. In the past promoting democracy and protecting our allies is the design of American foreign policy. That is no longer guaranteed under the Trump administration.

There are a number of important media interviews with Donald J. Trump from 1980 through 2014. By examining these encounters with the press, one can see Trump has a consistent, coherent foreign policy philosophy. The press did not pay attention to these early interviews. The formation of Trump's foreign policy can be seen in this thirty-five year window into his policies visa via these interviews.

THE FIRST MAJOR TRUMP FOREIGN POLICY INTERVIEW

As a television host Rona Barrett was viewed as a gossip-entertainment media figure. Hard news was not her forte. But NBC gave Barrett's production company a deal for a special program "Rona Barrett Looks At The Super Rich." "I've always felt money, power and sex is all that anybody really cares about...." Barrett said. She called the Trump organization. He readily agreed to the interview. It was his first major network interview where he discussed politics. He was handsome. He was in the mid-thirties. He was perfect as a symbol of sex, power and money. The 1980 Rona Barrett interview is one Trump's critics have ignored.

The Barrett interview was the first one to demonstrate his fixation on Middle Eastern oil. The Iranian Revolution of 1979, and the Iran-Iraq War prompted Trump to become wary of Middle Eastern nations, particularly Saudi Arabia. He feared the U. S. could eventually run out of oil. He was hostile to OPEC influencing prices. Trump believed American intervention in the Middle East would make the U. S. an oil rich nation.

He noted inflation and unemployment was a problem. His comments were a virtual echo of what he said in 2016. He was critical of Iran. The Iranian hostage crisis, under President Jimmy Carter, was troublesome. He saw in it America's decline. He also employed faulty historical analogies.

"Abraham Lincoln would probably not be electable today because of television," Trump told Barrett. He said he knew people who would make excellent presidents. "None of them would run," Trump stated. He called "media scrutiny" a "national tragedy."

The answers he gave to Barrett's questions were ones he reiterated in the 2016 election. Trump said: "Isn't it terrible how bad this country really is at this time when it could still be great." When Barrett asked Trump if he wanted to be president? He said: "No!" That wasn't the case. He began a decades long obsession with the Oval Office. The press wasn't paying attention in the 1980s. He had to secure press coverage where and when he could. This led to a 1990 **Playboy** interview. Before the 1990 **Playboy** piece, he didn't have much of a media presence. **Playboy** caught the attention of the mainstream media. They helped Trump develop his earliest political platform. The irony of Trump going mainstream because of **Playboy** was not lost on his critics.

Not surprisingly, the 1990 **Playboy** interview had a second life. When Prime Minister Shinzo Abe and German Chancellor Angela Merkel prepared to meet with Trump, they read the **Playboy** interview. Why? The material in this piece was the usual self-congratulatory statement from Trump. He talked of unfair trade agreements. He complained of a lack of international respect for the U. S. He said the U. S. should end funding for some foreign policy ventures. It was an eerie interview as twenty-six years later he remained committed to those points. "I'd throw a tax on every Mercedes-Benz rolling into the country and on all Japanese products and we'd have wonderful allies again," Trump commented to **Playboy**. Of Japan, Trump said: "They are openly screwing us." He also told **Playboy**: "I have a far greater ego than you will ever understand." These comments helped foreign dignitaries understand Trump. Long before he was a household political name, he had presidential aspirations.

In 1988, Trump told Oprah Winfrey that he had no plans to run for the presidency. "I probably wouldn't do it," Trump responded to Winfrey's question of a potential presidential run. But a few months after the Oprah appearance, Trump attended his first Republican convention watching George H. W. Bush accept the party's nomination.

THE REAL TRUMP: THE 1990 PLAYBOY INTERVIEW

The March 1990 **Playboy** interview is a window into his political mind. Glenn Plaskin asked some serious and thoughtful questions. No one was paying attention. As the Trump interview began, **Playboy** placed an ad for Trojan condoms at the beginning of the article suggesting they were not taking Trump's remarks seriously. They asked softball questions. The Donald was surprisingly forthcoming. Trump said America needed a strong world leader. He said he supported President George H.W. Bush, but he believed the Republican's should look to business people. "I think if we had people from the business community-the Carl Icahns, the Ross Perots-negotiating some of our foreign policy, we'd have respect around the world," Trump concluded. Trump believed "very strongly in extreme military strength." In addition to comments on foreign policy, Trump had some interesting thoughts on his appeal to voters.

Trump said: "The working guy would elect me. He likes me. When I walk down the street, the cabbies start yelling out their windows." In 1990 this sounded pompous. In 2016 the blue-collar voter brought him to the presidency.

His definition of presidential power and the question of presidential leadership was explained when he criticized President

98

Jimmy Carter for weakness in dealing with Iran. "Some of our presidents have been incredible jerk-offs. We gotta be tough," Trump said.

On politics and the press, Trump said: "When somebody tries to sucker-punch me, when they're after my ass, I push back a hell of a lot harder than I was pushed in the first place." The use of slurs in the campaign such as "Little Marco" for Senator Marco Rubio of Florida or "Lying Ted" to describe Senator Ted Cruz of Texas suggests his gutter campaign. These types of comments were all over the 1990 **Playboy** interview. Trump may have had a good education. It certainly didn't show any in-depth political knowledge.

Many of the Trump comments to Plaskin illustrate his egomaniacal view of a potential candidacy. He said he was more special than his critics realized. He saw foreign policy as the road to the presidency.

During the 1990s Trump emerged as a quiet critic of American foreign policy. By the end of the decade, he had a new theme. He charged China was taking advantage of its trade relationship with the U. S. By 1999 Trump continued this theme blaming China for U. S. fiscal difficulties.

THE LARRY KING SHOW AND TRUMP'S FIRST
MAJOR FORIGN POLICY STATEMENTS

During early October 1999, Trump appeared on CNN's Larry King Show. For a decade Trump advocated increased business expertise in world affairs. He had a mania for unfairness, disrespect and not being number one. Unfortunately, Trump combined these beliefs with a demagogic approach to world affairs. This set the stage for a decade of contradictory statements on foreign policy.

During the 1990s Trump criticized Germany, Saudi Arabia and Japan for trade policies detrimental to the U. S. He said American allies needed to pay their fair share for military protection. This is a message he carried into the 2016 election. In the King interview, Trump observed NATO had too little ground and air power to make a difference in world affairs. It was clear Trump was not in favor of funding NATO.

In 2000 Trump's book **The America We Deserve**, he concluded NATO worked things out in Kosovo. This shift in his position is not surprising. Trump will do that what he needs to align his policies with prevailing political attitudes. Trump's book, ghost written by Dave Shiflett, sums up his America First argument and the direction he would take in foreign policy if elected president. It helped his drive to the presidency.

The Larry King interview should not have been ignored. Trump said: "I am going to form a presidential exploratory committee, I might as well announce that on your show...we are going to take a very good, strong look at it." Trump backed away from a political run as he said: "I have a lot to lose, Larry." Trump began working with political consultants. He would spend the next decade and a half forming his political persona and analyzing why and how people voted.

In 2000 Trump flirted with the idea of running for the presidency as the Reform Party candidate. He realized he could not win. When Michael Wolff's tell all book came out, he said Trump expected to lose the 2016 election. This observation is untrue. The Donald never expects to lose. What happened in 2000 is he began plotting his run for the presidency. He would announce he was running for president when he could win. He did. In 2015, as he witnessed what he believed was the negative reaction to Barack Obama's presidency, he entered the Republican Party. How did Trump view the world in 2000? He had a view surprisingly in tune with a large segment of the voting public.

THE WORLD CHANGES IN 2000: WHERE IS TRUMP?

By 2000, Trump had a defined worldview. He wondered! Was it in our best interests to protect our allies in Asia and Europe? The spending for foreign affairs, Trump emphasized, was counterproductive. He said they were not paying their fair share of the cost. This is one of the longest running themes to Trump's foreign policy.

The essence of Trump's foreign policy philosophy by 2000 was the U. S. didn't make enough money in trade to justify the cost of a military presence around the world. Trump said America had bad trade deals with Europe. The U. S. had alliances with over sixty countries. American military bases were located in sixty-five nations. How did this impact Trump's thoughts when he became president? In two ways, he vowed to rebuild the military and allow commanders in the field greater latitude in decision-making. He would also cut back on foreign aid. Trump began paying closer attention to foreign policy when President George W. Bush went to war in Iraq.

Mark K. Updegrove's **The Last Republicans: Inside the Extraordinary Relationship Between George H. W. Bush and George W. Bush** concludes Trump's comments were that of "an arrogant bully." President George H. W. Bush called Trump "a blowhard." George W. Bush said: "Trump doesn't know what it means to be president." The Trump White House fired back stating neither Bush left a positive legacy. Trump said he opposed the Iraq War because of George W's lack of skill. Not surprisingly, Trump forgot he told Howard Stern in a 2002 interview he supported the invasion of Iraq. In answering the two Bush's, Trump said: "I was totally against the Iraq war." This wasn't true. To understand the vacillation in Trump's foreign policy it is necessary to examine what he thought and said during and after the Iraq war. Trump changed his position repeatedly. He demonstrated he was a shrewd judge of political opinion, as he was always with the majority. He was on his way to become a professional politician. The Iraqi War is the first lesson in how well Trump adapted his policies to public opinion.

WHERE WAS TRUMP DURING THE IRAQ WAR?
THE APPRENTICE GOT IN THE WAY

When George W. Bush fought the Iraq war on a credit card, Trump supported it. He wasn't a vocal supporter. He remained on the sidelines. Why? He is a calculating politician. He was waiting for the fallout from the war. Then he would state his opinions. Trump did have some thoughts on the vicissitudes of war. There are a number of things that are clear. Trump displayed compassion for Iraqi civilian victims. He praised America's military role. One of the missing ingredients in those who study Trump's foreign policy is his sense of compassion for war's victims. He has strong compassion.

Trump's comments on politics were ignored until 2016. Why? He was a reality television star with a program known as "The Apprentice." He had opinions on foreign policy, because of his celebrity. They were increasingly ignored. Much of what he said concerning foreign affairs remains a permanent part of Trump's policy program.

As the Bush administration began fighting the war on terror, Trump was increasingly occupied with economic concerns and the rise of China in the world economy. In the year after 9-11 Trump appeared on The Howard Stern Show on WXRK in New York, he remarked he supported invading Iraq. It was like many of Trump's positions. He was vacillating on foreign policy. He didn't understand foreign policy. This led him to contradict and deny his own statements. The Howard Stern Show is not known for politics. Trump was able to squeeze in some of his ideas on America's foreign policy. Trump's most interesting comment to Stern was: "We have an idea who the enemy is and a lot of times politicians don't wanna tell you that." The Donald believed in conspiracies.

The Howard Stern interview highlighted Trump's thoughts on foreign policy. By February 2016 Trump morphed into a politician who was against the Iraqi war. His 2002 Stern appearance contradicted this claim. This is pure Trump. He will either lie or not readily recall earlier comments.

Neil Cavuto of Fox News was Trump's favorite newsperson. On January 28, 2003 appearing on Fox TV News, he criticized what he termed the "telegraphing" of military plans. "Whatever happened to the days of Douglas MacArthur?" Trump asked. What this meant he never explained.

Trump told Cavuto: "When I watch Dan Rather explaining how we are going to be attacking, where we are going to attack, what routes we're taking, what kind of planes we're using, how to stop them, how to stop us, it is a little bit disconcerting. I've never seen this, where newscasters are telling you how-telling the enemy how we're going about it….It is ridiculous."

This comment suggests the continued maturation of Trump's mania to control the press. He wants to shape what is written about him. He forces his views on the media. He labels anyone who disagrees with him "a loser." This behavior is constant. How many times has he said: "I call them losers, Losers."

On March 21, 2003 Trump returned to Fox's "Your World With Neil Cavuto." He was a guest invited to discuss the invasion of Iraq. As Trump sat down with Cavuto, the day after U. S. troops invaded Iraq, he criticized the French, who aligned with Germany, to oppose the U. S. invasion of Iraq. The French President, Jacques Chirac, argued the UN Security Council should make the decision on whether to use military force in Iraq to control Muslim extremism. Trump said this was nonsense.

Trump was ambivalent about the U. S. invasion of Iraq. He was angry because America was disrespected. He suggested military might produced international respect. The genesis of "Making America Great Again" flowed from this appearance with Cavuto. "There are a lot of countries right now that aren't too fond of us," Trump remarked to Cavuto.

During this interview, Trump displayed little, if any, enthusiasm for the Iraq war. He was formulating his foreign policy. Much of what the future president believed centered around weaponry. "The main thing is to get the war over with and just make it a tremendously successful campaign and it will be very interesting to see what kind of weapons they find," Trump said.

Neil Cavuto is one of Fox TV News's best journalists. He asks Trump hard questions. His "Your World" program is not filled with the usual Fox right wing message. In May 2018 Cavuto called Trump out for conflicting stories and false statements. Cavuto said the Stormy Daniels payment story was convoluted. He charged Trump with exaggerating illegal voting during the 2016 election. **Esquire** praised Cavuto for his remark when Cavuto said: "You didn't know about the $130,000 payment to a porn star until you did, the time you said the Russians didn't interfere in the 2016 election, until a lot of Republicans had to remind you they did….You claimed your tax plan was the biggest in U. S. history, when it wasn't." Cavuto was the first Fox TV News talking head to point out Trump's duplicity. But he did so in 2018 when the president's distortions, misuse of facts and outright lies brought him to the presidency. At least Cavuto recognized Trump's duplicity. But this is 2018 criticism, in 2004 in the midst of George W. Bush's presidency, Trump was talking foreign policy to an unsuspecting Cavuto.

TRUMP EXPLAINING FOREIGN POLICY 2004 ONWARD
For the next six months, Trump didn't appear on television discussing foreign policy. He was formulating his ideas. On the second anniversary of 9-11, he was a guest on MSNBC's "Scarborough Country." He told Joe Scarborough he "would not necessarily have invaded Iraq." The Iraq war was not going well as the rise of Muslim radicalism, and the resurgence of the Taliban prompted Trump to observe: "It wasn't a mistake to fight terrorism and fight it hard, and I guess maybe if I had to do it, I would have fought terrorism but not necessarily Iraq."

As the 2004 presidential election was in its early stages, Trump was upset about Republican Middle Eastern policy, and the prospects of another Bush presidency. He appeared on Wolf Blitzer's CNN program Late Edition on March 21, 2004. This mainstream media platform set the stage for his politics going national. Trump mentioned he was "more of a Democrat." The reason for this statement was his belief the United States, as he told Blitzer, "is not a popular country right now...."

In October 2004 **Playboy** interviewed Trump. Once again the subject was American foreign policy. Trump had an increasingly liberal view of recent foreign policy. He lamented the loss of innocent lives in Iraq. He remarked: "Iraqi children being killed and maimed, walking around with no legs and no arms" saddened Trump. This compassionate tone was real. Surprisingly, he said John Kerry was doing a great job as Secretary of State. He talked of Kerry for President. Trump said he was "a great guy, a very smart guy." Then he told **Playboy,** he was concerned about weapons of mass destruction. There were too many of them. They were dangerous. The **Playboy** interview was the last one for the next twenty-six months.

As Trump leaned increasingly left a liberal British weekly, the **Observer**, interviewed him for the January 7, 2007 issue. He talked of what he would do if the was president. He said he would "try and solve the problems in the Middle East." He had no plan. He emphasized as a deal maker he could end differences in the Middle East.

The **London Guardian** described Trump as "America's most flamboyant tycoon, as likely to be featured in the gossip columns as the business pages." In early January 2007 **Guardian** reporter Gaby Wood was led back to Trump's private office on the 26th floor of Trump Tower. Sitting down in front of the Donald, Wood noted his desk was so lavish, so large and so devoid of papers one wondered if it was actually a prop and not a business desk. The Donald greeted the **Guardian** reporter. He hollered for a biography. "Today, I'm in all the papers. You saw the amount of press? It was beyond belief." Wood was speechless.

When Wood asked Trump about his presidential aspirations, he had some thoughts. "I'd try and solve the problems in the Middle East-that could be solved. It's sad what's happening, but let's go on to another subject." In 2007 Trump wanted to discuss his hotels, his television show and his books. The **Guardian** interview highlighted his concern with foreign policy. He did tell Wood he owns eighteen million square feet of Manhattan. This was his concern not politics.

LARRY KING AND TRUMP'S RISING POLITICAL STAR AND ON TO DAVID LETTERMAN 2010

By April 2009, Trump was a rising star amongst business conservatives. The press talked at length about President Obama's support for bailing out the banks. Trump discussed market stabilization and the need for the national government to temporarily take over the banks.

As Trump appeared on CNN's Larry King Show, he was asked what he thought of President Barack Obama. Trump replied: he "really liked him." In matters of foreign policy, Trump remarked Iran needed "policing."

These comments came at a time the U. S. celebrated the first few months of Barack Obama's presidency. Although Trump supported John McCain's Republican candidacy, he remarked President Obama "is a wonderful personality, a good speaker, somebody that people trust." He paused and looked at Larry King continuing: "He's trying to rebuild our reputation throughout the world." Trump believed the

Bush years were ones of failure. "The new President is really doing a nice job in terms of representation of this country," Trump concluded.

In a surprisingly liberal comment, Trump said: "We're fighting a war in Iraq and yet we are not taking care of New Orleans." This was the genesis of his American First agenda. The oil rich Middle East countries and OPEC were criticized by Trump for raising oil prices to the detriment of the world economy. When King pressed him for further comments on President Obama, Trump said: "I really like him. I think that he's working very hard...." He paused and continued: "The previous administration was a total disaster, a total catastrophe...." Trump would change his view as he considered a serious run for the presidency.

On March 11, 2010, the first sign Trump was unhappy with the Obama administration came when he appeared on the Late Show With David Letterman. For a year he pondered a presidential run. He had feelers out to the Republican Party. He realized an independent or third party candidacy was a sure loser. He also increasingly identified China as the cause of American economic problems. He had harsh words for China undercutting the U. S. in the world market. He looked out at the audience. He made the case his business expertise made him qualified for the presidency.

THE JOY BEHAR INTERVIEW BEGINS
TRUMP'S WAR ON FAKE NEWS

By 2010 Trump believed he had foreign policy expertise. He told Joy Behar business expertise made him a prime presidential candidate. On December 8, 2010 he appeared on CNN's Joy Behar Show criticizing money spent for the Iraq War. "I don't want to build roads in Iraq. I want to build roads in New Jersey," Trump said. He was hitting a note with American voters. He needed the media to get his message out. He hated Joy Behar. He would tolerate her for TV face time.

In the Joy Behar interview, Trump was obsessed with America's lack of respect. He remarked President Obama was a failure. He said the outsourcing of jobs had a dramatic impact upon the decline of blue collar and construction jobs. He continued to complain about

106

OPEC. He remarked to Behar: "Eleven guys sitting round a table and just dictating the price of oil was objectionable.".

The Behar appearance was a major turning point. The problem is they hated each other. She was an unrequited liberal. He was morphing into an authoritarian conservative. She was a firebrand. She made fun of his hair. She didn't show him the respect he believed he deserved. This was the beginning of a media war with Behar. It eventually blossomed into an all-out assault on the press.

Donald Trump: "I thought George W. Bush was a disaster. I thought he didn't do a good job….He had an opportunity after the World Trade Center to really, make this country into a popular place…..And we had a chance to really translate that into something good. And he just blew it."

This was the turning point in Trump's evolving political philosophy. He identified his politics as that of a tough America First type demanding respect in world political affairs and leverage in the changing world economy.

From 2010 until his election, Trump fought with Behar. She said he wore a wig. She called him names. He sent her a letter demanding an apology. "I hope Donald will come on the show, I won't try to pull his hair, I know it's really a wig," she said. Trump was furious. She called Trump's bid for the presidency "a stunt." Melania appeared on HLN's Behar show in 2011 defending her husband's presidential run. They talked of the Donald's obsession with finding President Obama's birth certificate. Trump realized his fight with Behar attracted political supporters. By 2017 Behar remarked Melania treated the president like he had "the zika virus." Joy Behar on "The View" became one of Trump's strongest critics. When General Michael Flynn pleaded guilty, she was gleeful. She also said the future held new Trump scandals.

TRUMP DISRESPECTING SENATOR GILLIBRAND

At the conclusion of Trump's first year in office, Behar appeared on The View with a panel debating his tweet concerning Senator Kirsten Gillibrand. Trump tweeted: "Lightweight Senator Kirsten Gillibrand, a total flunky for Charles E. Schumer and someone who would come to my office 'begging' for campaign contributions not so long ago (and would do anything for them), is now in the ring fighting against Trump…." This tweet from Trump was sent from his account @realDonaldTrump December 12, 2017. The implication was clear. It was sexist. He said it was no more than a tweet. Sarah Huckabee Sanders said: "There's no way this is sexist at all." This incendiary statement came from Trump's press secretary who didn't have her children until she was almost thirty. That makes her a specialist on sexual innuendos.

What was the basis of Trump's outrageous attacks on New York Democratic Senator Kirsten Gillibrand? She opposed his every policy. She would not vote for anything the president supported. He took it personally. It was about his inability to think, formulate policy and govern that prompted her staunch opposition to his presidency.

She voted no on every Trump appointment. That is until Nikki Haley became U. S. Ambassador to the U. N. Gillibrand voted for her. Why does Gillibrand hate Trump? She views his tweets as "sexist." She says he is personally demeaning. She was outraged at his attempt to muzzle her comments. "It was certainly just a sexist smear intended to silence me," Gillibrand commented in an angry tweet. She is one of a number of rising Democratic feminist voices calling the president out for unacceptable behavior. In December 2017 Gillibrand told CNN Trump should resign over allegations of sexual assault. But in 2011 as he considered a run for the presidency, this was in the future.

TRUMP FINDS HIS CONSERVATIVE AUDIENCE, 2011

By 2011 the Trump message evolved. He spent the next five years polishing it. What was the message? It was a simple one. China takes advantage in selling manufactured goods to the U. S. Mexico took away jobs through NAFTA. He vowed to end these practices. OPEC makes the gasoline prices prohibitive. Immigrants are living on welfare. The U. S. funded NATO without taking their fiscal obligations seriously. The European Union took too much of American money in trade and this was, said Trump, keeping the stagnant European economy afloat. These Trump talking points shaped his political persona.

Everywhere Trump spoke he was obsessed with respect. "The United States has become a whipping post for the rest of the world. The world is treating us without respect," Trump remarked on February 10, 2011 to the Conservative Political Action Committee Conference. He went on to talk about the need for quality leadership. The conservative crowd cheered loudly. He found his audience. Trump became more mendacious exaggerating one point after another to the adoring crowd. The big lie worked. He was ready for a presidential run.

Donald Trump: "I deal with people from China with people from Mexico. They cannot believe what they are getting away with. I have said on numerous occasions that countries like China, like India, South Korea, Mexico and the OPEC nations view our leaders as weak and ineffective and have repeatedly taken advantage of them.…"

The mainstream press ignored Trump's comments. His argument China manipulated U.S. currency brought fiscal conservatives into his impending campaign. It was his get tough talk about how to deal with terrorist tactics that convinced many in the Bible Belt to support him. He also attracted those with Christian leanings much to the surprise of the left. The right wing nationalists believed he was an electable presidential candidate. The press treated Trump like he was a joke. In retrospect, this was a mistake.

The media was a factor in Trump's early political days. On March 28, 2011, he was a guest on CNN's "Piers Morgan Tonight." He discussed how our NATO allies needed to pay their fair share for the cost of containing terrorism. With the economy struggling, the housing market at rock bottom and joblessness at a record high, Trump's message of world disrespect and fiscal impropriety resonated.

On Piers Morgan Tonight, Trump set a tone for his foreign policy. The critics ignored his message. The voters didn't. His earliest supporters rallied around his cry to end the rule of Libya's Moammar Gaddafi. The **Washington Post** and **New York Times** reported Trump attempted to make business deals with Libya. He failed. He was angry. In mid-March 2011 NATO intervened, Trump said NATO prevented him from making a series of excellent business deals. He seethed over government restrictions on private enterprise capitalism. He vowed to end that as president.

The **Washington Post** reported Trump made a business deal for Gaddafi to set up a tent on his New York estate. The deal fell through. Trump said it still made him "a lot of money." The idea of making millions for allowing the Libyan dictator to literally camp on Trump's estates sounded like fake news. It wasn't. In 2011 Libya was open for American business interests.

TRUMP'S BREAK THROUGH ON FOX NEWS WITH O'REILLY

On March 30, 2011 Trump appeared on the The O'Reilly Factor. It was a love fest. The issue of illegal immigration had O'Reilly interrupting and dominating the conversation. When Trump called for military control at the Mexican border, O'Reilly found his candidate to oppose President Barack Obama. When he was questioned about immigration, Trump developed one of the issues important to his presidential victory.

Donald J. Trump: "Mexican immigrants are selling drugs all over the place. They are killing people all over the place."

The conservative Christian right found their candidate. The protection of evangelical civil liberties and religious freedoms were primary reasons the evangelicals supported Trump. The left was shocked evangelicals supported Trump with all of his baggage. The left didn't seem to mind the baggage attendant to the Clinton legacy. Conservatives said they would rather have a sinner in the White House who protected their freedom than a potential jailbird elected president. Christians feared liberal Democracy would force them to compromise their religious principles.

Trump was just warming up. Muslims, the Qur'an and jihadists were the next targets. He said those who read the Qur'an preached hatred. The message was clear. He would be the strong executive protecting America from immigrant hordes. He was so popular with the conservative audience Fox draws, he came back to the O'Reilly show the next night.

The March 31, 2011 interview on The O'Reilly Factor accelerated Trump's candidacy. He knew enough to lay low until 2016. But the planning for a presidential run surfaced in 2011. The two nights with

Bill O'Reilly had a major news network following him blindly. Responsible journalism ended. The second night on O'Reilly's show, he trotted out the same old arguments he espoused since 1980. But his audience was growing and so were his potential voters.

The second night on O'Reilly the name-calling, the salty language, the insults and the lack of verifiable facts established the Trump message. He described President Obama as "our weak president that kisses everybody's ass." That comment had O'Reilly leaping out of his seat. He demanded Trump appear on the show for a third night. The Donald smiled, blushed and agreed. O'Reilly anointed him.

On April 1, 2011 some of the Fox News staff on The O'Reilly Factor joked Trump was part of the April fool's message of a Trump presidency. They were wrong. He emerged as a serious presidential candidate. The liberal press continued to treat him with disrespect. The third night with O'Reilly saw Trump concentrate upon criticizing Pakistan for aiding the Taliban.

Donald J. Trump: "This is the first run on your show," Trump told O'Reilly. That comment continued Fox TV News's love affair with Trump. They couldn't get enough of his political pronouncements. The rest of the mainstream media ignored him. Or did they?

GOOD MORNING AMERICA: EXPLANING FOREIGN POLICY

On March 17, 2011 Trump appeared on ABC's Good Morning America, he told Ashleigh Banfield: "If I ever got the nomination, if I ever decide to run, you may go back and interview people…." What is the point of this remark? It is simple. Trump knew he had baggage. He was explaining away his egregious behavior and his well-publicized trysts with the ladies. More significantly, he was planning a presidential run. No one paid attention. There wasn't anyone in the media or political establishment who thought a Trump run for the presidency was anything more than a pipedream. Or perhaps a publicity stunt. It wasn't. He was planning. In this 2011 interview, Trump said he would spend $600 million of his personal fortune to become president.

During the Good Morning America interview with Ashleigh Banfield, Trump said he would cure the unrest in the Middle East. He promised to take out the Somalia pirates. Trump said: "I don't get

111

along with rich people. I get along with the middle class and the poor people better than I get along with the rich people." There was never a challenge to Trump's statement nor was there a follow up question. What he said went unchallenged.

Donald J. Trump: "I am very, very disturbed by what's happening in this country. I love this country very much. And over the years a lot of people have asked me whether or not I was going to run…but when I see the kind of things that our representatives are allowing to happen to this country it just bothers me so much." Banfield had neither a follow up question nor a reaction. She looked happy to have the star of the hit TV show, "The Apprentice" on the air.

The Good Morning American appearance defined Trump's attitudes on foreign policy. He believed America spent too much money protecting other countries. He mentioned money spent on South Korea as a waste. "We've never been so weak. We've never been so vulnerable," Trump concluded.

The Good Morning America interview highlighted his toughness on foreign policy. Trump said Libyan leader Muammar Gaddafi's brutal use of force against civilians and rebels should be handled with a "surgical strike." This opinion reflects his attitude in 2017 on Syria's Bashar al-Assad. There is a continuity in Trump's foreign policy that is traced to his first serious interview with Rona Barrett in 1980

The turning point in Trump's media presence occurred on April 18, 2011. George Stephanopoulos interviewed him on ABC News. This long interview was due to Trump announcing a run for the 2012 presidency. He backed off.

TRUMP'S 2012-2014 INTERVIEWS: SETTING
THE STAGE FOR A PRESIDENTIAL RUN

In 2012 there were fewer interviews. Why? Trump hired political consultants, statisticians, and collectors of data to analyze if a presidential run was feasible. It was! He carefully began crafting his political person for the 2016 presidential run. On January 4, 2014 Trump appeared with Piers Morgan on CNN. This is the first time the "Make America Great Again" slogan caught the media's attention. His outsized ego was evident as Morgan found him mirthful rather than truthful. Trump was angry. He said Morgan's lack of respect enraged him. "I have millions of people that want me to run. They want me to run as an independent," Trump said. He told Morgan that people in Texas were forming a political party called "Make America Great." He said he would if he could change the party name to "Make American Great Again."

In 2013 Trump carefully selected his major interview spots to discuss foreign policy. He appeared only on CNN and MSNBC. He spent much of the year analyzing world affairs. Although Trump talked about foreign affairs since he appeared with Rona Barrett in 1980, he realized he was on a bigger stage. He couldn't get away with his off the cuff remarks. He vowed to look for a devil. He found one in Syria.

The issue of Bashar al Assad and Syria's thumbing their nose at President Barack Obama's so-called red line infuriated Trump. When President Obama stated there was a red line on the use of chemical weapons, Assad ignored it. He crossed the red line. Trump was furious. He told Piers Morgan on September 13, 2013 there needed to be toughness in American foreign policy. In four years Trump showed his toughness and changed the direction of foreign policy.

Trump said there needed to be a compromise or to mediate Assad's use of chemical weapons. The next time Trump appeared on Piers Morgan Live on CNN on October 10, 2013, he continued his familiar message attacking those who were taking economic advantage of the U. S. He complained China and OPEC were the chief perpetrators. China received the brunt of Trump's criticism. He screamed they were manipulating their currency. When he became president he ignored this issue.

When he concluded this interview with Piers Morgan, Trump said that until the U. S. had the right leadership its prominence in world affairs would continue to decline. "You have to take jobs away from other countries, China, India, all of these countries, they're taking our jobs…." Trump continued. "We've made it so good for Mexico, what they're doing to us is unbelievable." Those comments rang true with a white declining middle class without jobs as blue-collar workers faced fading wages.

On November 9, 2013 Trump appeared on MSNBC for an interview with Thomas Roberts. At the time Trump was in Moscow for the Miss Universe Pageant. He talked positively of Putin. He said he had a "relationship" with the Russian leader. He praised his leadership. Trump said Putin has "eaten our president's lunch" in Syria. The irony is in the 2016 presidential campaign Trump denied meeting Putin.

Back in the U. S. on December 11, 2013 Trump appeared again on CNN's Piers Morgan Live on CNN. Nothing new came from this appearance. He skewered China for economic reasons.

The only major Trump interview worth discussing the following year was his March 6, 2014 speech to CSPAN. This is the Conservative Political Action Conference. This speech reaffirmed his determination to run for president as a Republican. His attitude on foreign affairs continued to evolve. As Russia invaded and occupied the Crimea, taking over a portion of the Ukraine, Trump did not condemn it. He continued to praise President Putin. Then strangely Trump talked about the marvelous reception he received in Moscow in 2013. He condemned President Obama's "lack of leadership." He said the president did not stand up to Russia. China's economic malfeasance and the lack of respect for America prompted Trump to criticize the Chinese for taking advantage of our trade practices, stealing our intellectual property and being a money manipulator. This was the same tried and true theme he had enunciated since 2011. Suddenly everything was President Obama's fault. Trump's audience built as a result of these arguments.

THE EARLY RUSSIA CONNECTION: MISS UNIVERSE AND THE STEELE DOSSIER

In 2013 when Trump visited Moscow for the Miss Universe contest, the Kremlin rolled out the red carpet. The pageant's inaugural evening was a memorable one with the NBC Peacock in a black and white logo hung over the said. When asked why NBC's colors were not the usual rainbow, a Russian spokesman said the colorized version of the NBC Peacock would give publicity to gay pride.

After Miss Venezuela was crowned Miss Universe, Trump met a thirty year old model, Kata Sarka, who had once been Miss Hungary. The **London Daily Mail** reported he gave the young lady his business card; his hotel room number and he invited her to America. This incident was reported in the Steele Dossier. Why is the important? The Steele Dossier claims this is one of many incidents the Russians documented in a portfolio meant to compromise, intimidate or blackmail Trump the businessman. When it became a possibility that he might be elected the American president the Kremlin's data collectors were giddy.

One statement in the Steele Dossier received inordinate publicity. This infuriated Trump. When FBI Director James Comey told Trump of the material, alleging he watched prostitutes urinate on each other, in a private meeting in January 2017, two weeks prior to his inaugural, he vowed to make Comey swear his loyalty to the president's administration. When he couldn't convince Comey to swear fealty, he was fired. Trump denied all allegations in the Steele Dossier.

At the Miss Universe event Trump talked at length with Russia's largest banker, Herman Gref, and he talked at length with other Russian oligarchs. These conversations don't prove collusion or any other crime. What is obvious is Trump had a presence in Moscow. He had connections to Kremlin influences. He had a relationship with Gref the Chief Executive of Sberbank, Russia's largest bank and a fiscal institution close to Vladimir Putin. Was it criminal? No! Do these circumstances counter Trump's assertions about his Russian presence? Yes!

Politico argues Trump's love affair with Russia and Putin didn't mature until 2013. They argue Putin wins in the world diplomatic community with his ability to convince Trump that he is nothing more than a concerned world leader. When Trump attended the Miss Universe pageant it was all about being treated well. He was! Russia won!

Donald J. Trump: "We have so many problems and we have so little leadership….And it's all about leadership. I was in Moscow a couple of months ago, I own the Miss Universe Pageant and they treated me so great."

The statements on foreign policy from 1980 to 2014 demonstrate he held consistent views. He would alter these opinions for voter approval. While running for the presidency his views focused on regaining American respect. He hoped to take the U. S. out of trade deals, climate agreements, cut back the State Department and lecture the world that American foreign policy was heading into an isolationist direction.

Trump's foreign policy interviews from 1980 through 2014 suggest a dual edged sword defining the Donald. He had a black and white view of the world. When he became president he diminished, ignored and belittled his Secretary of State, Rex Tillerson. There was a confused coherence in the White House. This frustrated our allies, as well as the Secretary of State, and the foreign policy community when it came to implementing policy. To understand Trump's foreign policy it is necessary to analyze why and how Trump was unprepared for world leadership.

SEVEN

AMERICAN FOREIGN POLICY: TRUMP UNPREPARED FOR WORLD LEADERSHIP AND THE BULLY BANNON

"We must remind ourselves that Trump's very presence in the White House defiles it and the institution of the presidency."

CHARLES M. BLOW, THE NEW YORK TIMES

"Donald Trump is New York. Glitz, greed, glamour and an ambition so colossal that it will probably not rest until he rules the word-which one day he just might."

POLLY TOYNBEE, 1988, LONDON GUARDIAN, MAY 26, 1988

"He is one great big example of exploiting public for private gain. Of course, it's a scandal."

KATHLEEN CLARK, LAW PROFESSOR WASHINGTON UNIVERSITY

"We're living through a chaos presidency. It's destabilizing the country, and it's hurting our foreign and military policy."

NICHOLAS BURNS, UNDER SECRETARY OF STATE, UNDER PRESIDENT GEORGE W. BUSH, PROFESSOR HARVARD KENNEDY SCHOOL

To many observers Trump is little more than P. T. Barnum blustering about Making America Great Again. His grandiose statements are meant to startle. His publicity stunts cause a reaction. His showmanship for the cameras caught the world's eye. He comes off as a bully. He is a prevaricator of facts. He is mercurial. He is unpredictable. Or is he? He does have a world-view. It is an insular one. Respect! Deal making! Independence from world affairs! These are some of Trump's views on foreign affairs. What does this mean?

His defenders argue his personality guarantees success. He will cajole. He will berate. He will use threatening language. Then he will make a new deal. The art of the deal is his presidency. Along the way he demonstrates he is unprepared for world leadership. For a time his bully in residence, Steve Bannon, provided foreign policy advice that hurt rather than helped the president.

Donald J. Trump is not just unprepared for world leadership. He has done little to educate himself on world affairs. He has repeatedly remarked he is "a very stable genius." In a series of over the top tweets, Trump wrote: "Now that Russian collusion, after one year of intense study, has proven to be a total hoax on the American public, the Democrats and their lapdogs, the Fake News Mainstream Media, are taking out the old Ronald Reagan playbook and screaming mental stability and playbook." This statement, reported by Emma Stefansk in a January 2018 article in **Vanity Fair** in which she went on to question Trump's leadership style, as well as his sanity. Stefansk asserted that his narcissism, his inability to focus on a subject, his erratic decision-making, his continual change of policy and his personal attacks suggest a psychological disorder. This may seem extreme. Michael Wolff's book came to the same conclusion. Wolff observed: "100 percent of the people around (Trump), senior advisers, family members, every single one of them, questions his intelligence and fitness for office."

Thomas Wright, a fellow at the Brookings Institute, warns those who do not take Trump seriously in foreign policy are unaware of his strengths. Wright argues: "Trump's statements over three decades shows that he has a remarkable coherent and consistent worldview that makes a great leap backward in history, embracing antiquated notions of power that haven't been prevalent since prior to World War II."

TRUMP'S POLICIES AND OPPOSITION
TO HIS ERRATIC LEADERSHIP

Trump is withdrawing the U. S. from a leadership role in world affairs. He is in the long tradition of isolationist minded U. S.

Senators who worked to remain out of World War II. Trump had a helter skelter foreign policy. It changes from day to day. Secretary of State Rex Tillerson had an aide who daily made a chart of Trump's early morning tweet. U. S. foreign policy has been running day to day on presidential tweets. Then Tillerson was fired. So was the aide.

Trump's detractors have a different view of his foreign policy. The **Washington Post** headlined: "Trump's Incoherent, Inconsistent, Incomprehensible Foreign Policy," poses a danger to America in the world. This April 28, 2016 op-ed piece by the **Post's** editorial board concluded: "It's a good bet that the United States under a President Trump would be…to the peril of itself and the rest of the world." Trump was elected. He began his vendetta against the **Post**.

Others critics see a brilliance in Trump's foreign policy. Stephen Sestanovich, writing in the **Atlantic,** defended what he labeled: "The Brilliant Incoherence of Trump's Foreign Policy**."** This May 2017 article differed from other critics as Sestanovich said Trump was keeping world leaders on edge and making excellent foreign policy decisions. Whether or not the so-called incoherence and the lack of philosophy exist, the point is Trump has some foreign policy triumphs.

THE EARLIEST SIGN OF TRUMP'S SUSPICION THAT FOREIGN POLICY ADVISERS WERE "BULLSHIT"

On January 6, 2017 President-elect Donald J. Trump walked into his Trump Tower office. It was the day he started defining the future of American foreign policy. That afternoon the heads of the FBI, the CIA and the National Security adviser, as well as a host of security specialists, arrived to brief Trump. He was in a foul mood.

When the meeting began the president-elect was told the intelligence community had substantial intelligence from multiple sources Russia had hacked into the 2016 election. They described a mass covert operation to disrupt the American political system. Did this material send Trump into a rage? It did. Because American defense interests concluded Vladimir Putin might have helped him win the presidency. He had one word for this intelligence briefing— "bullshit."

As Trump sat listening to America's defense specialists, he viewed them as purveyors of the "deep state." His close adviser, Steve Bannon, reinforced this conclusion.

What is the "deep state?" It is a group of people within government agencies or the military believed to be involved in the control of or secret manipulation of government. President Trump charges the FBI, the State Department, the CIA and other intelligence agencies have deep state ties preventing him from effectively governing. He labels anyone who opposes him or can't get along with him as deep state supporters.

The Director of National Intelligence, James Clapper, struck Trump as a Hillary Clinton supporter. He saw the CIA Director, John Brennan, as weak on Iran. The National Security Agency head, Admiral Mike Rogers, was a career military figure. Trump believed he was too kind to America's enemies. After they made their argument on how Putin's Russia attacked our political institutions. The group left. The FBI Director James Comey remained to discuss a sensitive document. It was the Steele Dossier. Trump believes they are part of the deep state.

The two-page summary of the Steele Dossier alleged there was collusion between Russia and the Trump electoral team. It was presented by Comey in ominous detail. The president-elect could barely contain his anger. He vowed to fire Comey, if he didn't defend the president. At that moment, Trump decided to ignore professional national security specialists. They were all part of the deep state. Trump saw this conspiracy as one dedicated to ruining his presidency.

Comey told Trump he was not under investigation. The president-elect asked Comey why he came forth with this information? Comey said the press had the material. He did not want Trump to be blind-sided by this information.

After Comey left Trump Tower, the president-elect turned to an aide and screamed: "It's bullshit." He made the decision to do everything in his power to downgrade, personally attack and expose the deep state conspiracy. Comey was done. That is unless he swore loyalty to the president. Trump told his aides it was his administration against the world. They had to be tough or the intelligence community and the State Department would them down.

As he prepared for the inauguration, Trump told his close aides the deep state was attempting to destroy him. His first year in office was one of rage, rash decisions, continual turnover of personnel and in the process Trump isolated the U. S. from the world.

His early morning tweets, his raging at the "fake news," his preference for Fox TV News, his frequent dinners with Sean Hannity who daily praises him on his Fox TV show, and the fawning, almost worshipful, attitudes of acolytes like Hope Hicks, Sarah Huckabee Sanders, Jared and Ivanka Kushner and dozens of other boot licking sycophants place Trump as far from reality as possible.

Vladimir Putin was directing a cyberwar on the U. S. but Trump refused to accept this fact. He feared it would invalidate his election. Since the 1980s, he has been fascinated with Putin. He did everything in his power to become his friend. During the first year of his presidency the Donald refused to criticize Russia and Putin. Finally, in March 2018, he made his initial critical remarks on Russia. Why? That is a story the ongoing Mueller investigation is attempting to answer. In the midst of this chaos Donald J. Trump mapped out his national security strategy.

TRUMP'S NATIONAL SECURITY STRATEGY

Once he assumed the presidency, Trump's national security strategy de-emphasized America's role in world affairs. The U. S. is no longer the "indispensable leader of the free world." Trump's staff entitled a National Security Strategy (NSS) paper "A Competitive World." This fifty-six-page NSS document views the world as "a dangerous place." Trump said a more aggressive world position leads to greater economic rewards. This means business is the key to American foreign policy. Humanitarian concerns are not in the mix. Domestic priorities, economic prosperity and cutting back on foreign aid are the keys to unlocking Trump's vision of American foreign policy.

The debate over Trump's diplomacy prompted Thomas Wright in **Politico** to define his American foreign policy in copious detail. He had three beliefs: he is against trade, he wants to end traditional alliances, and he continually praises strongmen abroad. In his first year in office Trump emphasized these points. The White House had hats made up with the insignia: "Make Alliances Even Greater."

When 122 Republican conservative national security professionals signed a letter-opposing Trump as president in March 2016, he made sure few of these professionals as possible remained in his administration. He said he knew more about foreign policy than the professionals.

Why did 122 conservative foreign policy experts oppose a Trump presidency? There are many reasons. They are hostile to Trump's hateful, anti-Muslim rhetoric cutting off attempts for peace with the Muslim world. His admiration of Vladimir Putin was criticized. They opposed his recommendation to use torture. The foreign policy professionals pointed to his vacillating opinions on foreign affairs. What does Trump think about American foreign policy?

TRUMP ON FOREIGN POLICY

During the 2016 campaign Trump was asked who advised him on foreign policy. He responded: "I'm speaking with myself, number one, because I have a very good brain and I know a lot of things." This March 16, 2016 statement on Morning Joe brought disbelief. As Trump conducted his campaign for the presidency, he was an isolationist. His America First policy radiated a go to hell to the world message. He was a foreign policy bully appealing to world dictators. He initially stated those views to Rona Barrett on a 1980 prime time television special everyone ignored. He tapped into a white nationalist pride where talking tough brought respect and votes. It was a mantra for his supporters. Trump took American foreign policy to a new low. Humanitarian concerns were secondary.

The press was puzzled by the lack of expertise from his foreign policy team. There were six foreign policy amateurs selected to advise him on foreign policy. The two most interesting early appointees were retired Lt. General Keith Kellogg and retired General Joseph Schmitz who had problems in the military after allegations of misconduct. Schmitz resigned from Trump's foreign policy team after accusations of anti-Semitism surfaced. General Kellogg took over acting National Security Adviser for one week for General Flynn when allegations of fiscal impropriety and lying to Vice President

122

Mike Pence prompted Trump to fire him. Kellogg also did not continue as the NSC adviser to the president. But on April 23, 2018 Vice President Pence announced the appointment of Lieutenant General (Ret) Joseph Keith Kellogg, Jr. as National Security Adviser to the Vice President. H. R. McMaster was selected for the position.

The rest of the team was inexperienced and not qualified. Walid Phares was an anti-Muslim activist with ties to right wing Christian militia groups during the Lebanese civil war. George Papadopoulos was an amateur who pleaded guilty to lying to the FBI. The Mueller team left other counts against him off the table. Carter Page was a foreign policy dunce that the Russians disavowed as did Trump. They were weak on foreign affairs expertise. They were a group of amateurs, wannabes and star seekers. They had no idea or training how to conduct foreign policy. This is exactly what Trump wanted. He was so sure of his intellect on matters of foreign affairs, he said he only wanted a weekly update. On December 11, 2016 when he appeared on Fox TV News, Trump made it clear his was the only opinion that mattered. He belittled the foreign policy professionals. He suggested they were the reason for world problems. He arrogantly said he would fix it.

When asked about the international diplomatic order, he had no idea what the question meant. He told reporters he would get back to them. There were some hints as to what he thought. During the campaign, he said the United Nations was "not a friend to freedom."

Trump depended upon the advice of the former Ambassador to the U. N. John Bolton. He is a right wing fanatic, hating Muslims, and disparaging African nations. Like most of the Republican alt-right, he thinks climate change is an atheist's plot. With his white moustache, fierce demeanor and over the top comments Bolton is a mini-Donald. He is also an advocate of nuclear strikes. He wasn't initially in the White House. When Bolton was appointed as the National Security Adviser in April 2018, Trump had assembled a NSC in which nominally the Secretary of Defense James Mattis was the only moderate voice.

TRUMP'S PRE-PRESIDENTIAL VIEWS ON FOREIGN POLICY

Trump's views on foreign policy were not those of the Republican establishment. He not only differed from establishment Republicans, he rejected everything their foreign policy experts advocated. He was interested in only one goal. That was establishing the "greatness" of the U. S. in world trade affairs. Forget diplomacy! He had no interest. He disavowed coalition building. He had little concern for the safety of other countries. Being great economically, militarily and politically was his goal. He was telling the rest of the world to go to hell.

How did Trump arrive at his final foreign policy position? It was simple! He viewed President George W. Bush, as an interventionist. Trump said he was a president who couldn't complete the rebuilding of Afghanistan and Iraq. He viewed President Barack Obama as the ultimate compromiser. He believed President Obama was a weak man with Muslim sympathies. In making these judgments, he knew nothing about world history. He had even less knowledge of how diplomacy was conducted. He ridiculed past diplomatic efforts.

Trump did have a foreign policy vision. It was economic! He was much like the nineteenth century imperialists. He would find a way to economically exploit other nations. The profits would rebuild the American infrastructure. This was the direction Trump took during his campaign. He continued this policy in the first year of his presidency. He advocated what some called "national capitalism."

NATIONAL CAPITALISM IS THE NEW MERCANTILISM

What is national capitalism? Trump defined it as the power of American construction and manufacturing rather than banking and finance to control the world marketplace. His "national capitalism" can work. The idea of exporting American technology, the power of construction companies and trade in goods brings more jobs, revives manufacturing and leads to new markets. The problem is labor costs. Can American business compete with our wages? This is a question to be answered.

Trump is a mercantilist. This is an economic theory owing more to the sixteenth to eighteenth century than to the present day. Mercantilism was a theory and system of accumulating national wealth through established colonies, a strong merchant marine while developing industry to achieve a favorable balance of trade with colonies providing the raw materials. Trump probably has never heard of mercantilism. He is practicing this archaic policy.

The New York Times recognized Trump broke with two hundred years of sound economics in foreign policy. Trump doesn't realize mercantilism will weaken America. How? While mercantilism historically benefits government officials and big business, it hurts all other classes. Most notably the working class suffers lower wages, a declining living standard and soaring prices on consumer goods. Mercantilism looks to eliminate competition. To do this tariffs, quotas or bans on imports protects American manufacturing. It sounds good. Is there fall out? You bet! The collusion between the rich and government officials provides less democracy and less economic mobility. The immediate impact is higher prices to consumers. The ordinary people without political connections lose in this system.

Trump has discussed raising tariffs as much as thirty-five percent on imports until China, as Trump says, "plays ball." But he waffles on this commitment. The fact mercantilism has long been excluded from mainstream economics is another reason Trump supports the theory. He is after all an outlier.

TRUMP THE CANDIDATE AND FOREIGN POLICY

In the 2016 presidential campaign, no previous candidate had used such unorthodox methods. His daily tweets were followed by millions. His television appearances were much like the reality TV show he starred on. He insulted everyone. The press couldn't get enough footage to feature him on prime time. The radio gurus, left and right, talked daily about his candidacy. Did anyone in 2015, when he began his campaign, think he could win the presidency? The answer is uniformly: "No." There were only a few supporters like Alabama Senator Jeff Sessions. Now Trump calls him: "The failed Attorney General."

In 2015-2016, Trump laid out his version of a coherent and well-defined foreign policy. He had thought long and hard about America's role in world affairs. He said his coherent views would go a long way to delivering a presidential victory. One critic of the idea

Trump had "coherent views" during the 2016 campaign suggested he was a disruptor and destroyer. He would alter the basic structure of American foreign policy. "I would like some other word other than disruptor," a retired General added. There are ten key points to Trump's foreign policy. These points are beguiling intriguing and frightening. He defines his version as a coherent policy. The ten points Trump articulated resonated with voters. Whether it works is another question.

First, he identified the problem. It was China's unfair trade policies, their thirty-five percent tariff on American imports and their manipulation of the currency. He said these factors made it difficult for the U. S. to achieve fair trade. He would rectify that problem.

Second, Trump decries the U. S. being taken advantage of in military armaments. He said the U. S. funds the majority of the money for Article 5, which guarantees NATO's mutual military alliance. "This is unacceptable," Trump commented. It was unfair to the American taxpayer. The military protection provided the world by the U, S., according to Trump, is a bad financial deal. He demanded a two and a half percent increase for defense spending from each NATO nation.

Third, unequivocally Trump does not see Russia or Putin as the enemy. He has repeatedly said: "What is wrong with Putin and Trump liking each other?" What this demonstrates is his lack of historical knowledge, his refusal to accept State Department briefings or advice, his inability or unwillingness to recognize Russia's world aggression, and he has shown no interest or knowledge of the history of the Cold War.

Fourth, in matters of foreign policy, Trump labels his views as that of a realist. What is a realist? It is a view suggesting strength. Trump emphasizes doing business in Russia makes America a stronger country. Recently, political scientists and historians have criticized the realist tag as being unrealistic. Robert Kaplan, writing in the **Washington Post**, argued Trump was not a realist. He picked up the term. He uses it without understanding its implications.

Fifth, in military matters, Trump says he is a hawk. His early military spending pronouncements and the people appointed to key military positions support this view.

Sixth, until he was elected president, Trump had little, if any, interest in nuclear proliferation. That changed after he was inaugurated. North Korea's aggressive nuclear program and the specter of Iran's nuclear treaty obligations turned his attention to non-proliferation. He says if North Korea doesn't dismantle its nuclear programs there will be consequences. He appears to have little concern with the negative aspects of a nuclear action. He loves to say: "locked and loaded." This testosterone-based remark frightens world leaders. On Fox TV News one retired general talked of eliminating North Korea with nuclear weapons. In early August 2017 National Security Adviser H. R. McMaster appeared on Fox TV News remarking: "It's impossible to overstate the danger associated with a rogue, brutal regime." This comment from McMaster indicated the possibility of a war. Look at all the generals in the Trump administration. This suggests war is a real possibility. Donald J. Trump's judgment will decide that issue. Generals are not supposed to make policy. After six months into his presidency, Trump relinquished a small bit of decision making to the generals. It is Trump's responsibility, as Commander in Chief, to make these decisions.

Seventh, there is a humanitarian side to Trump's foreign policy. He urged intervention into Libya and Syria on humanitarian grounds. Bashar al Assad turned chemical weapons on his own people, Trump responded twice with force. He also issued a red line. He told Syria not to cross it. As of the writing of this book they haven't crossed the line. He has shown a great deal of compassion for Iraqi and Syrian victims of war. His public statements of compassion for the victims of war is little more than a publicity stunt as he was opposed to resettling refugees.

Eighth, Trump displayed concern in 2015-2016 when a portion of the Iraqi civilian population was killed by the American invasion. He is not a fan of collateral damage. On the campaign trail he was critical of foreigners, this obscured the compassionate side of his personality. That compassion is not matched with a plan or a program to help those who suffer the brutality of collateral damage. His unwillingness to support DACA suggests his public statements on refugees are little more than press fluff.

Ninth, Trump favors the use of airpower, military drones and technology for combat. He is against boots on the ground.

Tenth, there are many issues including trade, domestic security and fighting terrorism that are hallmarks of Trump's foreign policy. He sees radical Islam and the threat of cheap Mexican labor as key problems. His administration successfully reduced ISIS influences.

In the irony of all ironies, Donald J. Trump traveled to Europe for the first time as President in May 2017 as former president Barack Obama also returned to Europe for the first time since leaving the White House. The European press criticized Trump for his foreign policy. They labeled it populist, ultra nationalistic and out of step with the European community. Obama received a hero's welcome.

From the time he was elected, Europe's view of Trump was negative. As he traveled to the continent, the Pew Research Center reported nine per cent of Europeans had confidence in him. Europeans remarked they would like a rational, sophisticated and educated president. Europeans described Obama as "a healer." The European press labeled Trump "an outlier." The Donald revels in that description. It is his badge of honor.

TRUMP'S IMAGE AT THE 2017
G-7 AND LATER AT THE G-20

The G-7 Summit was held in the beautiful Sicily city of Taormina on May 26-27, 2017. It was the first time Europe's politicians were able to talk with President Trump. Then the G-20 was held in Hamburg, Germany on July 7-8. The two international summits were Trump's baptism into world diplomacy.

The image of Trump's first foreign policy trip was not a positive one. He demonstrated little sophistication as a diplomat. His role at the G-7 and later the G-20 was as an outlier. It was Trump against the world. His personal demeanor was as a tough, no nonsense, negotiator. It was the Art of The Deal in international affairs.

As members of the G-7 convened from May 26-28, 2017 in the hillside town of Taormina, Sicily, there was uncertainty about the American president. European nations had no idea concerning the direction of U. S. foreign policy. The purpose of the G-7 was to bring leaders from the U. S., the U. K., France, Italy, Germany, Canada and

Japan to talk of trade, world problems and the future of international stability.

The image Donald J. Trump projected, attending the G-7, set the tone for his rocky reception from our European allies. He did everything he could to embarrass, harass, insult and demean international agreements. He did it with a smile. He displayed a sense of entitlement. It was truly an embarrassing moment in American diplomatic history.

When the G-7 concluded there were concerns from German Chancellor Angela Merkel. She found it difficult to negotiate, talk or deal with Trump. Angela Merkel said he was a bully without diplomatic skills. The truth is somewhere in the middle.

Trump didn't understand the purpose of the G-7. Free trade and climate change were the key subjects. Trump let the G-7 know the U. S. would leave the Paris Climate Accord. On matters of trade the president said it was every nation for itself. The strong survive, Trump said time and time again, with good trade deals. The weak, he emphasized, were left out of the world economic order.

During the first week of July 2017 in Hamburg Germany the twelfth meeting of the G-20 took place to discuss world economic growth, international trade and financial market regulations. The G-20 presents a comprehensive program on migration, changing occupations, health issues, Women's Economic Empowerment and how to develop and implement aid programs throughout the world. Nothing is legally binding at the G-20. It is an exercise in international cooperation. It is an attempt to bring jobs, trade, issues of poverty, health care and world economic stability into a friendly framework. The G-20 works to involve less developed nations in world trade. It is a friendly meeting with little discord. That is until President Trump puffed his chest out. He let world leaders know there was a new sheriff in town.

The purpose of the G-20 is to promote cooperative international trade. Trump said: "No." The U. S. was open for business. He viewed global economic growth as unfair to the American economy. He also opposed any form of financial market regulation. To Trump it was the strong nations against the weak. He remarked those who survived in a world competition deserved the financial rewards.

As the G-20 Summit commenced, President Donald J. Trump had the opportunity to begin a dialogue concerning key issues ranging from climate control, to financial regulation, and finally to immigration. Since 1999 the G-20 has met in cabinet-room style talks with the leaders of the world providing cooperation on a wide variety of issues.

Trump brought a selfish, insular attitude. His "Make America Great Again" program was his defined direction. He implied the world could be damned. He cajoles. He insults. He berates. His demands in daily messages make the American presidency look like the captive of an adolescent. He will stretch the truth. He will make remarks that are less than credible. If he is attacked, he will scream: "Fake News."

He also ignores international agreements. The U. S. withdrawal from the Paris Climate Accord wasn't due to any other reason than it is a means of getting rid of another Obama policy. When asked why the U. S. left the climate agreement, Trump said unconvincingly it was a bad deal. He also commented he had a plan. He never detailed that plan. He will withdraw from an agreement. Then he will announce it can be renegotiated. In the case of free trade agreements, he continually states they are "a bad deal". German Chancellor Angela Merkel remarked: "The world is less united. The discord is obvious and it would be dishonest to paper over the conflict."

The petty nature of German Chancellor Angela Merkel was shown at the G-20 when there was no hotel for President Trump. The Four Seasons was full but King Salman of Saudi Arabia and his large entourage stayed at the Four Seasons and two other high end hotels. No other Hamburg hotel had room for Trump. That seems an impossibility. Secretary of State Rex Tillerson had to say in a sanitarium outside of Bonn. Vladimir Putin was at the Park Hyatt and Chancellor Merkel stayed at the Atlantic Kempinski with delegates from India and Canada. Trump never complained about this obvious oversight. German officials found him a suburban private residence for his stay. The pettiness of Merkel and the German government was never mentioned as President Trump took the high road.

ON TO PARIS FOR BASTILLE DAY AND
RUSSIA COLLUSON HEATS UP

As he prepared to fly to Paris for Bastille Day on July 14, 2017, Trump tried to minimize the Russia collusion investigation. As charges of Russian meddling in the U. S. election took on credence, Trump went on the offensive. He criticized former President Barack Obama for being weak and ineffective. He said his Democratic challenger, Hillary Clinton, should have been locked up for her crimes. He never defined the crimes.

When Republican Arizona Senator John McCain was asked about Trump's foreign policy, he replied leadership under President Barack Obama was much greater. He made this remark on the eve of the G-20 Summit. McCain commented under Trump's leadership the western alliance was divided and weakened. With Trump's belated support for NATO's mutual defense commitment, he made it clear Europe could not count permanently on the U. S. in military matters. The depth and commitment of the U. S. to Europe is at best tenuous. McCain pointed out Europeans had no idea about Trump's policies. The EU shouldn't have been surprised. Trump had no idea about his policies let alone the EU's. "The U. S. was no longer a friendly world leader," Angela Merkel observed.

The **London Guardian** said the G-20 Summit should be renamed the "G-19." The reason? Nicola Slawson wrote: "Nineteen of the 20 leaders were able to agree on all points made in the joint declaration (known as the communiqué) with the exception of Donald Trump who could not agree on climate change." He loved causing discord and dissent.

Newsweek observed: "Trump wrapped up his time at the Group of 20 Summit Saturday in Hamburg, Germany, his second overseas trip since moving into the White House, and it certainly made for a jam packed couple of days rife with some accomplishments and some head scratching moments."

What did Trump not accomplish at the G-20? **Newsweek** said he accepted the explanation of Vladimir Putin and Russian Foreign Minister Sergey Lavrov claiming U. S. intelligence exaggerated Russian hacking in the 2016 election. **Newsweek** pointed out Trump believed a Russian version of hacking that "was not accurate."

There were some Trump successes at the G-20. He said the U. S. would provide six hundred and thirty nine million dollars to the United Nations World Food Program to help those starving in Somalia, South Sudan, Nigeria and Yemen. He also supported a plan to ensure the growth of women entrepreneurs by pledging fifty million dollars to a recently established World Bank program.

TRUMP VERSUS THE WORLD: MACRON BRINGS TRUMP BACK INTO THE EUROPEAN FOLD

As the G-20 wound down Trump versus the world was the theme. He intrigued the European press. He basked in the publicity. He said free trade deals that allow goods to come through borders without import taxes or regulatory hurdles have hurt American companies and workers. "America First," Trump said, is the future. Previously, at the G-7 Summit, Trump received an invitation from French President Emmanuel Macron to be a guest of the government during the Bastille Day celebration. Macron appealed to Trump's ego to win some concessions. He planned a celebration that brought the two countries back into a strong friendship. Trump was only too happy to leave Washington. The investigation of his inner circle's collusion with Russia during the 2016 was on the front page of every newspaper.

After attending to business for a few days in the Oval House, Trump boarded Air Force One for Paris. As a guest of the French government, the president was wined, dined and feted. The European and U. K. newspapers argued the U. S. abandoned the E. U. The **London Guardian** was typical of the press coverage when they concluded Trump was insensitive to Europe. When the American president said: "Paris is no longer Paris," the **Guardian** said this was only one of Trump's mistakes. The press concluded Europe would have to go it alone. Angela Merkel, the German Chancellor, picked up this theme.

French President Emmanuel Macron was the winner in this turf battle. While he told **Le Soir** and other Paris newspapers he disagreed with Trump on climate change, they had common ground in fighting terrorism and reaffirmed the historic U. S. relations with France. The result! Trump downplayed climate change differences.

When the two leaders visited Napoleon's tomb they left to have serious discussions on Syria and counter terrorism. Macron single-handedly brought Trump back into the European orbit.

What did Trump take away from the Bastille Day celebration? He spent twenty-four hours in Paris. He was a guest of honor at the historic military complex at Les Invalids, built by the Sun King Louis XIV. As Trump inspected French troops walking side by side with President Macron he was smitten with the military ceremony. He attended a French army reception recognizing the military.

Macron hosted a dinner at the Eiffel Tower with famed chef Alain Ducaisse displaying the best of French cuisine. As Trump walked with Macron, he lamented the lack of recognition for the American military. During his visit the American president had numerous questions for Macron concerning Napoleon and French history. One can only speculate on what Macron said about this French hero. On the way home for the Bastille Day celebration, Trump talked of his hopes for an American military celebration. It was eight months after the Bastille Day celebration that Trump asked his staff to plan military parade in Washington D. C.

Trump's visit to Paris had positive results. They talked for more than an hour at the Elysee-Palace. Christopher Castaner, a French minister, said it was an attempt to bring Trump "back into the inner circle." Macron told the press he believed Trump was backed into a corner. He wanted to show France's love for America.

When he returned home Trump told his advisers Macron's military pomp and ceremony reflected France's prestige and leadership. The American President said he would do the same for the U. S. He began planning a military parade only to find a hostile reception from Congress and the military.

Chris Uhlmann, the political editor of the government funded Australian Broadcast Corporation, observed President Trump left the G-20 Summit "isolated and friendless." He further charged the American president "has no desire and no capacity to lead the world." On Australian television, Uhlmann concluded Trump was "the biggest threat to the values of the West." The journalist was horrified at Trump's war on the press, his insistence the judiciary be controlled and his disdain for independent government agencies.

"Mr. Trump is a man who craves power because it burnishes his celebrity," Uhlmann said. This judgment may seem harsh. It was heard time and time again on Australian television, the radio and in the print media.

Chris Uhlmann: "He is a man who barks out bile in 140 characters, who wastes his precious days as president at war with the west's institutions like the judiciary, independent government agencies and the press." The conclusion, said Uhlmann, suggests the U. S. position in world affairs had reached a new low. He observed when Ivanka Trump took her father's seat at the G-20 Summit the American president displayed his lack of diplomatic knowledge. He also exhibited his disdain for his G-20 colleagues. Uhlmann said Trump wasn't smart enough to realize he committed a major faux pas.

Foreign Policy echoed another message. This prestigious monthly said Trump wasn't the problem-"it's the Donald Trump in all of us." What did they mean? James Traub argues the U. S. is going through a period of redefining its place in world affairs. It is also attempting to come to grips with the divisions in American society. Democracy and foreign policy, Traub maintains, is being brutalized by racist, rank amateurs who have taken over the federal government.

Traub argues there is a precipitous cultural decline. He employs a parallel with the Roman Empire. It is Trump's self-aggrandizing personality, and his continual self-interest that bothers Traub. While writing for the **Business Insider**, Traub argues a right-wing conspiracy has morphed American voters into a reactionary force. He wonders if democracy will survive? There is no question President Trump is redefining America's role in Europe.

HOW TRUMP IS REDEFINING THE U. S. IN EUROPE

Donald J. Trump is a smart man. He is also a better politician than people suspect. He controls the political debate. His snarky tweets and disingenuous press comments occupy the media giving him center stage. He has never been pinned down for an early solution to a problem. Trump is a constantly evolving commentator on matters of foreign policy. He is always looking to negotiate a deal. Even when there is not a deal, he will give his opinion, change it a day later and blow up the conversation. He is the ultimate contrarian. His European policy appeals to the ultra-national right. He is courting those who oppose liberalism, a free press and a global economy.

When he spoke in Warsaw, prior to the G-20 Summit, he appealed to Poland's sense of survival nationalism. He bellowed: "The fundamental question of our time is whether the West has the will to survive." That simple sentence sent a clarion call to local nationalists. It was aimed at the right in Germany. They oppose Chancellor Angela Merkel. It caused Marine Le Pen's French supporters to react positively to Trump's proposed European policies. Trump courted the resurgent German right without realizing it was a strange mixture of alt-right conservatives, and those with Nazi style sympathies. He had no clue!

The media accused Trump of blowing up post World War II alliances. He reaffirmed U. S. support for some allies, notably Poland, while connecting with ultra-nationalists in the European Union. He is hostile to the liberal democratic order. He views it as a bastion of welfare state politicians. Trump argued Europe feeds off the largesse of tax dollars. What does this have to do with U. S. influence in Europe? Plenty! It prevents the Secretary of State from carrying out a coherent foreign policy.

THE QUESTION OF RACE AND CLASS IN AMERICAN FOREIGN POLICY: WHY STEVE BANNON IS DANGEROUS

The major criticism of Trump's foreign policy involves race and class. His Cabinet, his key advisers, his policy gurus and his family represent a white, elite, upper class persona. This doesn't mean they are racist. Elitism rules his advisers. Trump has, fired, downgraded, disrespected and ignored career State Department employees. This diminishes American foreign policy. There is little substantive information for the president to digest. He prefers it that way.

Steve Bannon is a bully. He comes into a segment of society and explodes it. The result is disrupting the civilized nature of American society. He wants to change the world. He abhors rules. He single-handedly talks of altering the status quo. Bannon's idea of getting rid of the swamp is to destroy the government infrastructure. He advocates no regulations, no rules and nothing more than business success. Bannon's influence is much less than the critics acknowledge. He was anointed the intellectual who brought Trump to the presidency. This is an oxymoron. The disruptive rallies, the idea of getting rid of the judges, ignoring the rules of civilized society and crowning the elites is the work of an amateur in politics. He is a delusional philosopher. He is disguised as a political consultant. He has little respect for the American political system. He has no respect for other opinions.

Steve Bannon plays the racial card constantly in his role as the self-proclaimed White House intellectual. He teamed with the president to attack political correctness. They demand an alt-white civilization. They believe all Muslims are placing the west under siege. To survive, Bannon tells us, we need to embrace our Christian identity. This sounds like incipient racism. Bannon represents an evangelical political notion of reshaping the world in Christian values. These values, as well as the controls from outside forces, are attempting to make U. S. government a neglectful one in terms of civil liberties.

Since the Marshall Plan rescued Europe from economic disaster after World War II, there has been an economic liberalism helping the European Union achieve unbridled prosperity. In Bannon's view it is time for this to end. The rise of terrorism and immigration issues, says Bannon, must end liberalism.

Even more dangerous is Bannon's view that a free press is taking the U. S. down the road to oblivion. The press, in Bannon's opinion, abuses its powers, invents the news and fosters a liberal agenda. He remarks these are reasons to suppress the media. It is for America's own good. Trump is the agent of press suppression.

BANNON AND TRUMP: THE WOLFF OBSERVATIONS

When Michael Wolff's **Fire And Fury: Inside The Trump White House** appeared it sold a million copies four day before its official release. The reason? It was due to Steve Bannon's insider comments. He was Wolff's main source. Not surprisingly, Wolff devotes five of the chapters to his influence. Trump fired him. Why? He criticized Jared and Ivanka labeling them Jarvanka. To understand the juvenile nature of President Trump and the egomaniacal pronouncements, it is necessary to examine his tweets, his rumored rants in the Oval

Office and the constant change in the inner staff. Wolff described in copious detail how and why the White House is the most dysfunctional in American history.

Trump's initial respect for Bannon was shown when he became the first senior staffer to be sworn in. That respect soon faded. Then a strange thing happened. Bannon wanted an office. Not just any office. He quickly found a small, descript, ill equipped office across from the palatial digs occupied by the Chief of Staff Reince Priebus. Bannon was sending a message. He would control the Chief of Staff. Priebus and Bannon fought constantly. Trump fired them. Both talked in depth to Michael Wolff.

Bannon's quirky nature was demonstrated when he outfitted his office without a sitting space. He didn't want to talk to anyone. Staffers were afraid of Bannon. He was like a toy Emperor with bad hair in smelly clothes marching around giving orders. He had no concern for others. He was after all a self-styled genius. His personality underwent a dramatic change. His White House office reflected his personality. Emperor Steve didn't talk to anyone. This included Jared Kushner and Ivanka Trump. They would in less than a year convince President Trump to fire him. The genius's days were numbered. The only person who didn't know it was the genius.

Why did Trump hire Bannon? He never held an appointed or elected political position. His first formal appearance in the political arena came when he was sixty-three years old. He joined the Trump presidential campaign as the campaign manager working with Kellyanne Conway. He despised her. His title: "Chief Strategist." Roger Stone, Trump's close adviser, laughed at Bannon's theoretical intellectual superiority. He thought it was a case of delusional leadership and Trump's lack of judgment. It was!

What did Trump miss in anointing Bannon? His former careers were short-lived. They were also not particularly successful ones. He spun them as success tales. He left a naval career after seven years. Why? It has never been explained. He worked in the movie business. He formed Bannon And Company. He was a minor player in Hollywood. Michael Wolff describes Bannon: "A type. Alcohol. Bad marriages. Cash-strapped in a business where the measure of success is excesses of riches." (p. 55) Who then is the real Bannon?

The real Bannon is a press whore. He recognized through the alt-right Breitbart website the road to taking his version of fake news to the bank. **The New Yorker** asked how a person who was suddenly one of the most important media figures in American politics didn't have a footprint in the past? He had more failures than successes. The list included business, the movies, his personal life and his military career. His intellectual credentials were at best shaky ones. He was like a ghost pressing through alternate lives. None of which bore fruit. No books! No articles! Nothing! How did he sell his "Trump brain" story. He is a disingenuous personality. He does have enough verbal horseshit to sink a boat.

Michael Wolff zeroes in on Bannon's personality or his lack of it. He describes Bannon as playing "a contrarian's game." (p. 57). Bannon's Irish Catholic background led to three volatile marriages with this second wife providing tabloid tales with a police report alleging physical abuse. Mary Louis Picard presented her abuse allegations in divorce papers. Picard alleged Bannon was anti-Semitic. She claimed he opposed their daughters attending a private school because if created a situation she said in Court papers where Bannon "didn't want the girls going to school with Jews." His establishment careers led to one failure after another. He was an angry man. There was little that was successful about Bannon. He came on board to direct the Trump campaign. He was an arrogant bully. He had a penchant for destroying people and institutions. The Donald loved him. At least until he used the term "Jarvanka," then he was fired.

To those around him, Bannon is not friendly, nor is he a good guy. He hates meetings. He refuses to debate. When Trump says: "I call them losers, losers." He might be describing Bannon. He is a classic loser. As Michael Wolf wrote of Bannon: "He's mean, dishonest, and incapable of caring about people." (p. 57) But Bannon is a real hustler.

When he discovered the contrarian, alt-right Breitbart Internet outlet, he found his home. He quickly hooked up with a wealthy father and daughter, Bob and Rebekah Mercer, who provided the funds for Bannon's political forays. They are right wing zealots who envision America's decline. They make the Koch brothers look like liberals. Bannon convinced them he could bring back conservative political ideals. The Mercer's believe in anti-Muslim laws. They support pro-Christian schools, a stronger death penalty, minimizing civil rights laws, the return of the gold standard, home schooling and small government. Bannon played into their disparaging ideas. They showered him with money for Breitbart. The alleged goal was to bring white people to power.

Bob Mercer is a strange person. He has a baby grand piano on his yacht. He often plays it while ignoring his fellow party folks. In 2012 Mercer's daughter realized with the death of Andrew Breitbart, Bannon could take over the news outlet. The Mercer's funded Breitbart. They insisted on Bannon's leadership. It was not a popular decision.

Michael Wolff described Rebekah Mercer: "She's nuts…nuts…full fledged…like whoa, ideologically, there is no conversation with her." (p. 59)

Breitbart rented Bannon its sumptuous Capitol Hill townhouse. He was one of a number of new and influential conservatives sniffing around Washington politics. To make a case for his intellect, Bannon printed out articles on his exploits and provided them to Trump. Exactly when he did this remains a mystery. Trump doesn't read. The operative wisdom is in early 2016 Bannon made his pitch to Trump for his leadership on the campaign. The Republican National Committee sent Corey Lewandowski to run the presidential campaign. Lewandowski is a rank amateur, and an arrogant asshole. He acted like he knew it all when he met with the press. He fit perfectly. Then Trump came to believe Lewandowski was a spy for the RNC. He was gone. Bannon came in to run a successful campaign for the presidency.

It was August 15, 2016 when Bannon planted himself in Trump Tower. He virtually slept in his office. With his rumbled clothes, his hair flying in the breeze and the smell of someone with poor hygiene, Bannon devoted his time to winning over women, the religious right and corporate donors. He did!

BANNON'S VIEW OF GOVERNMENT: SHOCK
AND AWE, THE DONALD LOVES IT

Bannon influenced Trump's view of government. He believed in what he termed "shock and awe." Dominate never negotiate. Never reveal your views. Distort! Confuse! Threaten! Alter the facts! These devices account for much of Trump's presidential demeanor. Bannon hates bureaucrats. Trump is dismissing bureaucrats.

In America there is no King. You cannot rule by royal order. You have restraints on your power. Congress and the Courts are a check and balance in the American system. Trump believes he can rule by decree. Trump used the Executive Order to undo many of Obama's policies.

What is an Executive Order? It is a presidential directive issued by the President that manages the operations of the federal government and has the force of law. Executive orders are subject to judicial review and they give the president a means of ending a previous president's policies. Trump used the Executive Order to end many of President Barack Obama's accomplishments. Was this due to Trump's belief they were bad laws or policies? Or was it due to his hatred for President Obama? These questions are still being debated. There are no answers.

"Never has there been a president-with few exceptions, in the case of FDR he had a major Depression to manage, who's passed more legislation, who's done more things than what we've done," Trump said. This is Steve Bannon talking not Donald J. Trump. It appears Trump believes Executive Orders are laws. Trump and Bannon agree the bureaucracy must be stripped down to bring governmental change. Bannon explained how to govern. Attack the opposition. Lie if cornered. Never be pinned down on issues.

AMATEURS, ARROGANCE AND AUDACITY:
THE GERMAN EXAMPLE

One of the problems of the Trump presidency is a group of amateurs are running American foreign policy. Trump has reduced much of the professional career State Department staff. This has hurt the U. S. in its relationship with Germany and England. He has little in the way of competent advice on the historical connection between American,

British and German interests. It is this lack of historical knowledge, as well as an unwillingness to change his Neanderthal America First policies, that has all but ended our amicable relationship with Germany.

David Frum, a former George W. Bush speechwriter, observed in **The Atlantic** Trump "is doing damage to the deepest and most broadly agreed foreign-policy interests of the United States." The president vows to end trade imbalances.

Germany has a huge trade surplus. At the G-7 Summit in Sicily, Trump said of Germany: "They're very bad on trade...." In the next breath, he said he didn't have a problem with it. What did Trump mean? He suggested Germany imported millions of cars into the U. S. in a special trade agreement. "We'll stop that," Trump said. It was a simple message from the president. The American automobile industry was hurting due to the low cost and quality of imported automobiles. Germany's global exports are worth more than $270 billion more than its imports. In sharp contrast the U. S.'s global trade deficit is unacceptable to Trump. The president criticized BMW for building a plant in Mexico to assemble the BMW 3 series sedan. "If they think they're going to build a plant to sell cars into the U. S. without a 35% tax, it's not gonna happen," Trump said.

Trump made it clear. A tariff on imported goods was essential to the recovery of the American economy. Trump remarked traditional diplomacy was at an end. This prompted many analysts to state the U. S. was a "country in disarray."

RICHARD HAASS: A COUNTRY IN DISARRAY OR IS IT JUST THE TRUMP ADMINISTRATION?

Richard Haass's **A World In Disarray** ends with a chapter: "A Country In Disarray." As Haass demonstrates the "old order has crumbled." It is economic concerns among the blue-collar worker, the union worker, those who fear of loss of jobs due to globalization, the fear of free trade and increased immigration that is ruining American society. The cost of doing business outside the United States is now an unpopular choice. This is the reason U. S. Treasury Secretary Steven Mnuchin is working toward establishing a weaker dollar. It will accelerate world trade. Shortly after Mnuchin's remarks the U. S.

slapped stiff import tariffs on washing machines and solar panels as a means of protecting American jobs.

The shock of Donald Trump's presidency prompted conservative pundit Karl Rove to label him outrageous. Another conservative, Ken Starr, echoed similar comments. Trump's presidency has made the U. S. insignificant in world affairs or at best less significant than in the past. Germany is the European leader. Europe has re-established a unity that makes the European Union stronger. Russian influences continue to increase.

What do the professors and key journalists think? Princeton University Professor Julian Zelizer argues the Republican Party protects Trump's inane and bizarre tweets, as well as his egregious comments on domestic and foreign affairs. He calls the Donald's policies bankrupt. **The Wall Street Journal** went further accusing Trump of being lazy. They editorialized he failed to educate himself on diplomacy.

ONCE AGAIN MAUREEN DOWD IS ON
TRUMP'S CASE: HE IS A BULLY

Trump's detractors include **New York Times'** columnist Maureen Dowd. She observed in the **Times**: "his own sadistic assault on Jeff Session," tells one all they need to know about Trump's lack of humanity. She was just warming up. She berated him for encouraging "police brutality." The President did this in a speech before an assembled law enforcement audience. Her thesis is Trump is the penultimate bully. On of Trump's aides, Katrina Pierson, commented of Trump: "People have to get comfortable being uncomfortable." Consider the following list of personal slights by President Trump. They highlight his bullying and lack of candor.

Before he fired Reince Priebus they were at a meeting with a fly buzzing around the room. Trump stopped and told Priebus he had the job of killing the fly. Priebus was scheduled to travel on Air Force One, with Trump on the day he was fired. He was informed riding in a car to board Air Force One, he no longer worked for the White House. His limousine arrived as the message was delivered. He sat on the runway and watched the president and his close aides lifted off in

Air Force One. Why did Trump behave this way? Was it cruelty? Was it inept government? Who knows! It is Donald J. Trump.

A Trump staffer explained it. "Priebus is a Washington insider, a close friend and supporter of Paul Ryan, he is calm, relaxed, and never critical and he is a team player who doesn't criticize." This comment may or may not be true. Why get rid of Priebus? Only Trump can answer that question. Perhaps he fired the former RNC official because of advice from Anthony Scaramucci.

Scaramucci charged Priebus was "a leaker," an RNC spy and mentally unstable. What could Trump do? He believed the mooch. You had to get a guy like that out of the White House. Am I talking about Priebus or Scaramucci? It turns out I am talking about both of them. It appears Scaramucci was brought in to get rid of Priebus. He did! Then the mooch was fired.

There are other reasons. Trump hated Priebus. He never forgave his Chief of Staff for urging him to leave the presidential race after the Billy Bush "Access Hollywood" tape. This is where Trump, as Kinky Friedman might say, was talking about grabbing a beaver. To the Donald, Priebus never showed the unrestrained loyalty the mooch and others of his ilk did during times of crisis.

MARTIN AMIS ON TRUMP: THE EUROPEAN VIEW

Martin Amis is a best-selling British author. **Esquire** commissioned him to analyze the Trump presidency. It is not flattering. "No shame, no honor, no conscience, no knowledge, no curiosity, no decorum, no wit and no nous," Amis continued. "By watching Trump rallies on TV, the crowd had mastered a quartet of trisyllabic chants: BUILD THAT WALL, LOCK HER UP, WE LOVE TRUMP, MAKE AMERICA GREAT." Amis is a journalist. How accurate is his description? That depends if you are a follower hanging on the Donald's every word, or if you are a critic, a liberal Democrat or a human being.

In his criticism of Trump, Amis is straight on pointing out globalism and multiculturalism will soon be much like a Sears' store. That is one that is out of business. Amis hits it on the head when he points out Trump fired Paul Manafort and brought in Steve Bannon and Kellyanne Conway to run what was a failed campaign. They combined to bring him victory. How? Insults! Innuendo! Fear mongering! Threats! These are the tactics of the Trump White House. He is draining the swamp appointing rank amateurs with a personal agenda. The swamp is being filled with redneck, billionaire alligators.

Trump became the "Falstaff in flip-flops." The Donald screamed he was being marginalized, disrespected and ignored. Lacking moral credulity, the Mensa moron, as Amis described him, led the war for the alt-right, the bigots who wanted a white America, and the growing force of voters demanding governmental change. Trump enabled the Christian right. The raging white nationalists coalesced into critics of Hillary Clinton as they chanted: "Lock her up." This set the stage for Trump's electoral victory. This win resulted from a coup of previously ignored or forgotten voters. They marched behind Trump like unwitting storm troopers. Whatever he said they repeated it like ventriloquists.

President Barack Obama was the force unifying Trump's minions. The backlash from alt-right conservatives and racists who quietly organized against Clinton was an indication of changing attitudes. Race was the key issue. Followed by Democratic corruption, which the Trump team repeatedly screamed about in an election where some American's wanted Hillary jailed. Trump's supporters screamed: "Help there is a Negro in the White House."

The blind white nationalism supporting Trump was demonstrated in a campaign rally in Youngstown Ohio in which the Donald screamed: "Is there any place that's more fun, more exciting than a Trump rally." Amis concludes: "Trump is a category one mistake made by the American people." Or is he? My guess is Trump represents a segment of people supporting a new white, bigoted, racist American nationalism. Ask a Trump supporter if the Donald lies. They will say: "It doesn't matter." That is the crux of the new America.

TRUMP IGNORES TRUTH AND THE RISE OF ALTERNATE FACTS

Trump lacks ethics, integrity, honesty, knowledge and perspective. These are not impeachable offenses. It is not against the law to be an egomaniacal jackass. His war on the press led to alternate facts.

Anything critical of the Donald he labels "fake news." He attacks information professionals. Those who verify facts are ridiculed. His initial attacks began a few hours after he was inaugurated. Since that time he has demonstrated a casual relationship with the truth.

The argument over whether or not Trump had the largest inaugural audience is a meaningless one. But he continues to challenge visual images showing his small audience. Public transportation to the inaugural was the lowest since the 1960s. He said he had the largest inaugural crowd. The evidence didn't prevent Trump from challenging the press. Not surprisingly, Trump sent Press Secretary Sean Spicer to spin the tale of "the biggest inaugural in history." This set the tone for a lie a day. "We had the biggest audience in the history of inaugural speeches," Trump said. That was a frightening comment. He was either delusional or selling the big lie. The worst was yet to come.

The tone of the Trump presidency was set the day after the inauguration. Sean Spicer waddled out as press secretary and defended the Donald's inane and ridiculous remarks. Spicer's press conferences made him a revered Saturday Night Live character. He was a joke representing a clown. America elected a clown. They were now living in a circus. But make no mistake. Television was the catalyst to Trump's ascension to the Oval Office.

HOW TV ELECTED TRUMP AND HIS CASUAL
RELATIONSHIP WITH THE TRUTH

The media helped to elect Trump, particularly television. How did this happen? A tracking firm MediaQuant estimated Trump received $1.89 billion worth of free media during the nominating process. This was six times the coverage Ted Cruz garnered. Ironically, Cruz was the number two presidential front-runner in free media coverage. In sharp contrast, Hillary Clinton garnered $746 million in free publicity. Media executives were praiseworthy of the Donald. He brought in ratings, advertisers and excitement. Leslie Moonves, the Board President of CBS News, said of Trump: "He's damn good for CBS."

The major media outlets treated Hillary with a combination of disrespect, disbelief, disingenuous coverage and skepticism. Trump's supporters hollered: "Lock her up." This reinforced the notion she was unfit for the presidency. Her speaking fees, the money raised by the Clinton Foundation and the perception she was a cold, calculating liberal bitch was reinforced by Trump's constant campaign attacks. Drain the swamp was an effective campaign slogan. The media ignored it. That was a mistake.

Since the major news outlets viewed Trump as a cartoon character, they were inordinately fair to him. They didn't feel it was necessary to criticize his inane stupidity, his lack of knowledge and his folly in policy. He would never be elected president. When Trump talked of building a fence to keep Mexicans out David Lettermen said: "He should build the fence around that thing on the top of his head." It was a comedy show. No one took Trump seriously. That turned out to be an enormous mistake.

Was Trump treated fairly by the media early in the campaign? He was! His chief adviser, Steve Bannon, realized the more you accused the media of bias the less likely they were to criticize. This caused the media to downplay Trump's scandals. When eleven women accused the Donald of sexual impropriety the story vanished. The media was too busy combating "alternative facts." The Trump attack on the First Amendment obscured the issues.

"To abandon facts is to abandon freedom," Thomas Snyder remarked. Snyder, a Yale Professor of History, has some good advice. He cautioned, as Trump attacked institutions, i. e. the press, the courts, Congress, state governments, that citizens must defend these instruments of government from his authoritarian attacks. There must be a return to professional ethics. Trump used key words "terrorism" and "extremism" to make legislative changes.

The irony is the free press helped elect Trump. The media also accelerated Clinton's defeat Hillary by spending too much time on her e-mails and not concentrating on the issues. **The New York Times** and **Washington Post** in attempting to be fair were not tough enough on Trump's transgressions. After the election they attacked him. To the Donald's followers these stories became "fake news."

Why didn't multiple allegations of groping women, and the Billy Bush "Access Hollywood" interview, where Trump talked of groping women, have consequences? There was seldom mention of his two

146

failed marriages. The press stayed away from these issues. The Republican campaign excelled in the defining cry of "Crooked Hillary" and "Lock Her Up." They never stopped attacking Hillary's credibility.

The press didn't analyze in depth or chart Trump's scandalous behavior until virtually inauguration day. The **Atlantic's** David Graham authored "The Many Scandal of Donald Trump: A Cheat Sheet." It was January 2017 and few paid attention to this warning. He was days from inauguration. The allegations against Trump seemed preposterous and insignificant. He was president of the United States. It was time to give him respect. Summer Zervos, a former Apprentice contestant, sued accusing Trump of sexual assault or misconduct prior to the election. No one seemed to care. Trump denied her claims. The suit was dismissed.

The other charges against Trump, even Frum's article admits, seemed preposterous. There were tales of Russian oligarchs influencing his finances. This couldn't be true. Then his lawyer, Michael Cohen, had his home raided, his office raided and his hotel room searched. A short time later he was shown smoking cigars with people allegedly identified as Russian mobsters. Cohen seemed to be waving his middle finger at the Mueller investigation, the FBI and the Stormy Daniels case. His defenders screamed "client privilege" is not honored. Michael Avenatti, Stormy Daniels attorney, said on CNN "the morons" who defend Cohen are unaware that his relationship with Trump's businesses is only a small part of Mueller's investigation. He is allegedly being investigated for money laundering. The Trump scandals are not going away. They are everywhere.

Michael Avenatti is an American hero. He outed Cohen for what may turn out to be influence peddling. As the book goes to press, Cohen is not guilty of a crime. He approached many large-scale corporate interests for lobbying contracts. Whether or not the president's fixer could provide an entre to Trump was not known. But a number of Fortune 500 companies hired him as a consultant. Why? You would have to ask the corporations. Avenatti was all over CNN and MSNBC alleging Cohen was "selling access" to the White House. That question is still being debated.

THE LESSONS FROM THE CONSERVATIVE
WAR ON THE MEDIA

There are lessons from the conservative's war on the media. Conservatives depend upon Fox TV News, the **Wall Street Journal** and Breitbart. There was also a host of best-selling anti-Hillary books. This helped get out the message! There was a united right wing media pillaring Clinton and the Democrats.

In sharp contrast liberals didn't match the conservative zeal to twist the television news. Since conservatives list Fox TV News as their media choice, they follow it religiously. In the liberal camp MSNBC, CNN and National Public Television offer a wide range of programs. The difference is the conservative message is united and strong in tone. The liberal media has more debate and uncertainty. The conservative movement has a disdain for real news. Hence, Trump's ability to sell the concept "fake news." As conservatives cut themselves off from mainstream media, they fragment political discussion.

In the middle of April 2018 an unlikely Trump supporter called for an end to the war on the media. Anthony Scaramucci appeared on Sirius XM's Dean Obeidallah's show stating: "I wish the president and his communications teams would end the war on the media." The mooch is great with the press. He did Trump a great deal of good with his comments. Scaramucci: "Get him out there. He's got to explain his agenda to the moderates, he's got to explain his agenda to the independents, and he'll win reelection resoundingly." It sounded like the mooch was auditioning for another White House position.

Scaramucci made a good point. Since taking office Trump sat down for interviews with Fox News or Fox Business New almost thirty times. He loves to sit down with Judge Jeanine Pirro. She is like a truck driver on steroids defending the Donald. One wonders about Scaramucci. As he looked back on his White House days, he said: "Whatever happened, happened. But it was the best eleven days in my life experience as it related to employment in public service," he remarked to John Catsimatidis on the "Cats Roundtable" radio show on Salem Radio in October 2017. The mooch is back in the news whenever he can find an outlet.

NEGATIVITY LEADS TRUMP TO
1600 PENNSYLVANIA AVENUE

Negativity brought Trump to the White House. He convinced the nation Obamacare failed, Muslims were coming into the U. S., and charging Mexican immigrants were criminals and drug dealers. He summed it up with the charge the economy was in shambles. By draining the swamp, Trump told his followers, prosperity would increase and America's greatness and the threat from outside would end. This is exactly the message many Americans wanted to hear.

Both candidates were viewed in a negative light. For the voters, almost three million more preferred Clinton. Neither was considered an ideal candidate. The long and steady conservative campaign against the media brought out voters who seldom went to the polls. They were overwhelmingly Trump supporters. He sold the big lie. Drain the swamp! Get rid of the professional politicians. These phrases were ones he used to bring the right wing Republican message to power. The result is an embarrassing president in foreign policy.

WHY IS TRUMP AN EMBARRASSMENT
IN FOREIGN POLICY?

After his 2017 summer trip to Warsaw, Polish protesters demanded a "White Europe" as they marched through Warsaw's streets. His continual embrace of Russian president Vladimir Putin and his never ceasing criticism of the "fake news" placed democracy in peril. On Russian interference, Trump said Putin denied it. "Every time he sees me he says," Trump continued. "I didn't do that, and I really believe that when he tells me that, he means it." This suggests the amateur nature of Trump's foreign policy. He has never read, studied or understood the nature of U. S.-Russian relations since the Cold War.

Trump not only admires Putin, he is doing his best to emulate him. When he beat Japanese Prime Minister Shinzo Abe at golf, Trump brought up the large sums of money the U. S. spends on military defenses in Japan and the money made by the Japanese exporting goods to the U. S. Earlier Trump criticized Japanese trade policies. Now he embraces them. This is another window into the dysfunctional White House. When the Japanese visited the White House, they worked Trump. Then came the Chinese.

Chinese President Xi Jinping played Trump like a fiddle. The Donald called these meetings "tremendous." He said his attitude toward Xi was "an incredible warm one." Liu Xiaobo, a Nobel Peace Prize recipient, died in a Chinese prison in July. Trump ignored this obvious human rights issue.

On the question of intellectual property (IP) rights, the Chinese have a long-standing reputation for ignoring patent and other IP rights. "Who can blame a country for being able to take advantage of another country for benefit of their citizens," Trump continued. "I give them great credit."

TRUMP'S TWEETS, INSULTS AND EGREGIOUS BEHAVIOR

A lack of judgment, an inability to recognize the truth and a fascination with insults was the early pattern in Trump's presidency. He made one ridiculous decision after another. His erratic behavior served to steer attention away from political arguments.

Trump was the first president to employ tweets as a political device. The results are not pleasant ones. The level of tweet insults brought the president's mental stability into question. His tweets displayed his belief in conspiracies.

On March 4, 2017 he tweeted: "Terrible! Just found out that Obama had my 'wires tapped' in Trump Tower just before the victory. Nothing found. This is McCarthyism." This 6:35 A. M. tweet was the first in a number of new lows as Trump heightened personal attacks against former President Barack Obama. There was no evidence to support his attacks. It was the first step in accusing President Barack Obama and former Secretary of State Hillary Clinton of abusing the law.

It wasn't just politicians Trump attacked. He sent out a tweet that Arnold Schwarzenegger ruined his former number one TV show "The Apprentice." Many of these tweets were hastily written. There is little thought in them. Trump is an undisciplined, insecure person who doesn't read. He doesn't analyze political issues. He is like a parrot.

150

One of Trump's strangest character traits is confidence. He says he can master any field. "I am a very stable genius," Trump said. He looked upon international diplomacy as a job requiring little, if any, training. He isolated the U. S. from world affairs, he offended German Chancellor, Angela Merkel, he infuriated Theresa May in Great Britain and he greeted France's first lady with insulting remarks about her physical appearance.

IF TRUMP IS PREPARED FOR FOREIGN POLICY
DINA H. POWELL IS THE REASON

Dina H. Powell was an adviser in Trump's foreign policy circle. She seldom makes the news. She was a Deputy National Security Adviser until mid-December 2017. Then in mid-February 2018 the Harvard Kennedy School of Diplomacy named Powell a Senior Fellow. Since many of Trump's appointees appear to be ill prepared, personally egomaniacal and spout out thoughtless statements, Powell is a strong and reasoned voice in a fractured foreign policy group. She is well educated. She is competent. She is thoughtful. She is loyal. She told Trump honestly what she believed was important for the future of foreign policy. Stephen Miller made it so uncomfortable for her. After all she is a woman with a brain. She disagreed with him. She resigned. She is an experienced internationalist in an inner circle of isolationists and political amateurs. She threatens them. Why did she leave the White House? This has never been explained. She was an honest critic of Miller's international view. This appears to be the reason she is no longer in the White House.

Who is Dina H. Powell? She is a forty-four year old former Goldman Sachs executive who moved over to direct the Goldman Sachs Foundation. She served for a time in the George W. Bush administration as an Assistant Secretary of State. She worked closely with other nations on the For Educational and Cultural Affairs Committee. The reason for her emergence is she worked under Secretary of State Condoleezza Rice. There was no one in the Trump inner circle who knew more about national moods in countries around the world than Powell.

During Trump's first year in office, Powell sat next to the president as he attempted to broker a peace between the Palestinians and Israel. She traveled to Asia with him. Powell is a New Yorker. She is also a long-time friend of Ivanka Trump and Jared Kushner. She is not a hard liner like Bannon or Miller. She is the sane and rational antidote to the hard line nationalism of some Trump advisers.

Entering the Trump administration, Powell had no relationship with the president. She was hired for her expertise. Powell was one of the key architects of Trump's first foreign policy strategy. She was also instrumental in the red carpet treatment the president received in Saudi Arabia and Israel. She is a logistics and planning genius.

After leaving the White House, Powell continued to assist the administration in working on an Israel-Palestinian peace accord. She drafted the Trump administration's proposal on nuclear proliferation in the Middle East. She is an Egyptian–born Coptic Christian who grew up in Texas. This helped her frame the issues and point out the needs in the Middle East. She has Arabic language skills, which have proven useful in negotiating with Saudi and Egyptian officials.

She lives in New York. She left a full time position after one year in the White House to spend time with her family. She will continue as a part-time foreign policy adviser. Her knowledge of Arab-Israeli differences, and her centrist policies are a welcome addition to a White House's fractured foreign policy team.

When she entered the White House, Ivanka Trump was impressed with her work at Goldman Sachs with the 100,000 Women program. This is a five-year program to provide business and management education to underserved female entrepreneurs. The progressive intellectual approach Powell demonstrated in the White House made her a valuable addition to the foreign policy team.

WHY POWELL IS NOT TOUCHED BY
THE RUSSIAN INVESTIGATION

Powell is the only person among Trump's senior advisers not touched by the internal in fighting or the Russia collusion probe. She was also the co-author with H. R. McMaster of important position papers Trump used in foreign affairs. In the Middle East and Asia, Powell provided the information-allowing Trump to navigate difficult diplomatic waters. She is a globalist who tempered Steve Bannon's untenable foreign policy direction and steered Trump into a more centrist direction.

She was able to influence Ivanka Trump and Jared Kushner convincing them that Kushner's star would eventually prevail as a foreign policy advocate. She continues as an informal adviser to Ivanka Trump. She will continue to advise Trump on Middle East matters. As a person with ties to the Washington establishment, Powell opens communication doors with Congress and the media.

WHY TRUMP LACKS FOREIGN POLICY CREDIBILITY

The first year of Trump's presidency resulted in the majority of America's former key allies, among them, Australia, France, Germany, Japan, Jordan, Mexico, South Korea and the United Kingdom questioning Trump's foreign policy credibility. **The New York Times** pointed out he said something that was untrue each day for the first forty days of his embryonic presidency. So why should anyone believe him?

He has flip-flopped on most foreign policy decisions. He traveled to Europe declaring NATO was dead. Then three months leader he embraced NATO.

Consistency is a virtue in foreign policy. Trump lacks this quality. When a leader follows through on a policy, he has credibility. Trump talks. He didn't act in his first year in office. If that changes his credibility increases.

Trump had some successes during his first year in office. He bombed Syria twice after Assad used chemical weapons on civilians. He stepped up America's presence in Afghanistan. He pressured North Korea to limit its nuclear program. He reduced ISIS's presence. He urged a two state solution for the Israeli-Palestinian conflict while relocating the American Embassy to Jerusalem.

He also made disastrous diplomatic moves. He talked with Tsai Ing-wen, the president of Taiwan. This was considered forbidden as the U. S. recognized mainland China as the only China. Since 1979 the U.S. has not had diplomatic relations with Taiwan. Then Trump said he was considering abandoning the "one China" policy. In February 2017 he flip-flopped and recognized the "one China" concept.

When Trump threatened a trade war with China, he labeled them a "currency manipulator." He changed his attitude when he came into office. The list of inconsistencies in foreign policy continues. His idea of ending our commitment to nuclear nonproliferation is one where he argues Japan and South Korea should develop nuclear weapons. Then he backtracked on this suggestion.

The North Korea situation is frightening. Trump initially said Kim Jong Un was "a smart cookie." He would be willing to "meet with him." Trump also said Kim was "Little Rocket Man." He followed with a threat to "totally destroy" North Korea. The president said the military was "locked and loaded." Which of these points is the really Donald J. Trump? Who knows!

By April 2018 a proposed summit with Trump and Kim Jung Un was in the works. He received high marks for bringing the Korean dictator to the negotiating table. Some say it was a brilliant move. It was! The meeting set at a neutral site, Singapore, on June 12 2018 in what was a great moment of triumph for Trump in foreign affairs. Then abruptly Trump announced the Summit was cancelled. A day later, the president said it might happen. Then slowly the wheels turned with both sides meeting to iron out details.

Is Trump's foreign policy brilliant? Or is this simply erratic behavior? Trump undermined Secretary of State Rex Tillerson, and he has dismantled the research in the State Department. He has ignored filling important ambassador positions. The consensus is he is downgrading American foreign policy. He is not experienced in world affairs. Tillerson was fired. Now Mike Pompeo is running the show.

The good news is Trump has some experienced foreign policy advisers. General H. R. McMaster, the National Security Adviser, was a top-flight mind. He was fired. Uber warmonger John Bolton has replaced him. General James Mattis provides the Secretary of Defense's office with an experienced and even-handed style of leadership. Chief of Staff John Kelly has cleaned up internal problems.

The problem is not completely Trump's advisers. It is the president's unwillingness to educate himself on the needs of the world and America's role. His reputation in the world is a tarnished one. There is a feeling he has abandoned Europe and the Far East for an insular nationalism predicated on world trade with the advantages solely to American business.

HOW TRUMP'S TWEETS DESTROY
AMERICAN FOREIGN POLICY

After a year of Trump's foreign policy most countries view American policy as one of confusion, disorder and self-interest. Why? The answer may surprise you. Trump's tweets are read daily throughout the world. When North and South Korea met to discuss the Olympics, border security and bringing families together the Donald tweeted he was the instigator for this historical meeting. He took credit. He didn't deserve it. When Iranian's protested their increasingly militant religious government taking rights away from the average citizen, Trump said the U. S. stood behind the Iranian people. By default he said he was the beacon or symbol that allowed Iranian's to protest.

What happened during Trump's first year representing the U.S. in foreign affairs? He set a direction and policy different from traditional foreign policy. He is also a president who issues threats. The threat to withdraw military support for NATO was one of Trump's early foreign policy talking points. The threat to go to nuclear war with North Korea, the threat to end military of financial aid to numerous nations and the demands to renegotiate trade agreements highlight his helter skelter approach to foreign policy. In some respects, this has worked.

Trump doesn't realize his tweets cause not only diplomatic problems, they cast America in a negative light. Traditional diplomacy is anathema to Trump. As the so-called dealmaker, Trump should embrace this principal. He doesn't. It is about ego, self-gratification and his appearance on the world media stage. His personality makes it impossible for President Trump to lead the way in the international arena.

Richard Haass, president of the Council of Foreign Relations, commented to the **New York Times** words matter and Trump's continual insulting and abrasive tweets do little to promote a successful American foreign policy.

Secretary of State Rex Tillerson said his department handles and marginalizes Trump's unexpected tweets. "I take what the president tweets out as his form of communicating, and I build it into my strategies and my tactics," Tillerson said. What this means is he has to overcome the damage the president does daily with inane tweets. There was little cooperation between the president and Tillerson. The president who from time to time disparages him, contradicts him and appears not to value him. Then he abruptly fired him.

What Trump doesn't realize is good judgment is a hallmark of successful diplomacy. Common sense is another factor, as well as historical knowledge in world diplomacy. Trump fails in this regard. Threats are another problem. When you work with foreign countries threats cause them to back off breaking down diplomacy. In the United Nations General Assembly American Ambassador Nikki Haley threatened to cut off aid to any country that opposed the relocation of the American Embassy from Tel Aviv to Jerusalem. President Trump dictated this position. This is only one of many ways the president is alienating the world. He doesn't care. It is about him. His power. His prestige. His programs. His incoherent policies dictate a leader who is clueless about the world.

When he was elected President one of Trump's first phone calls was to the Pakistani Prime Minister Nawaz Sharif. After they talked Trump said Nawaz was "a terrific guy." The new president had no idea Pakistan provided little more than one supply road and a small air space for the U.S. to enter Afghanistan. It is the country harboring terrorists while hiding Osama bin Laden in plain sight. But Trump wasn't done with his praise. He told Sharif: "Please convey to the Pakistani people that they are amazing and all Pakistanis I have known are exceptional people." The lack of sincerity in this statement speaks for itself. Trump loves authoritarian countries. He praises repressive dictators.

Trump is constant with his tweets. He gets up early and sets the news agenda for the day. Pierre Vimont, a former French Ambassador to the U. S., said Trump's tweets creates confusion. European political analysts have no idea about the direction of American foreign policy. This prompted German Chancellor Angela Merkel to recommend Europe "go it alone."

President Emmanuel Macron of France criticized American foreign policy as one appearing to take the world to war. Macron worries Iran, North Korea and Iraq could form an "axis of evil" making war a distinct possibility. The Donald doesn't have a clue. He is too busy telling the world he knows more than the generals.

EIGHT

REX TILLERSON: THE MOST UNPREPARED SECRETARY OF STATE, A GOOD MAN WITH NO POLICY IS GONE

"Tillerson did not use the word
'moron' to describe the president."

HEATHER NAUERT

"People have the power, to dream, to rule,
to wrestle the world from fools."

PATTI SMITH

"Everything Trump touches dies."

RICK WILLIAMS, REPUBLICAN STRATEGIST

"With an isolated leader, a demoralized diplomatic corps and
a president dismantling international relations one tweet
at a time, American foreign policy is adrift in the world."

JASON ZENGERLE, THE NEW YORK TIMES

When President Trump decided to fire Rex Tillerson in mid-March 2018 there was confusion in the State Department. The uncertain leadership from the Oval Office and a foreign policy that drifted without direction caused concern. While in Africa on a diplomatic mission, Tillerson found out he was fired via a Trump tweet. The administration tried to spin it. General John Kelly said he left Tillerson a message he was being replaced. The White House said Tillerson probably didn't pick up his messages. Tillerson was angry. In his farewell remarks, he didn't mention Trump. Tillerson was not an effective Secretary of State. When the U. S. withdrew from the Paris Climate Accord, Tillerson dissented. He also urged the president to remain with the Iran nuclear deal. He believed diplomacy could solve the North Korean nuclear controversy. Trump disagreed. He fired him.

Tillerson's lack of credibility made it imperative to fire him. His inability to do the job was directly related to his relationship with Trump. He was never a friend. They didn't have the same philosophy. Foreign leaders give Tillerson no credibility. Why? Because he was consistently over ruled by the president. He was personally unfriendly. He wouldn't address State Department employees. He didn't know the inner workings at Foggy Bottom. He had no idea about the State Department budget. He became angry when people asked him questions. He was in over his head.

At Foggy Bottom he was instructed to restructure the State Department. The resignation of seasoned Foreign Service professionals was one result of his failed attempts to alter State's philosophy. He has no legacy. This was due to a lack of management skills and a diffident personality.

Tillerson had no interest in sitting for policy briefings. British and French diplomats complained he didn't return phone calls. The Secretary of State is entrusted with setting up strategic dialogues with other nations. Tillerson failed to observe this time honored tradition. He never discussed diplomacy with Congress. He failed to bring in high-level bureaucrats for their advice. His didn't staff his office with care or insight.

Fiscally speaking Tillerson was an unmitigated disaster. He left a legacy of twelve million dollars paid out in private consulting fees. He hired approximately ninety consultants to revamp State. The result? There were numerous power point presentations. There were no real changes. How was the twelve million spent? No one knows! What we do know is the consultants charged three hundred dollars an hour.

He wasn't a hawk. Mike Pompeo and John Bolton fit Trump's foreign policy agenda. The **New York Magazine** stated Tillerson was leaving a mess behind as he exited into private life.

The man who labeled Trump as an "effing moron" did not get along with McMaster, Mattis and Kelly despite erroneous press comments he did. The leaks in the State Department, the lack of cooperation with Tillerson and the downsizing of the workload make State as duplicitous as Tillerson in the failures of American diplomacy.

Tillerson shrunk the number of junior diplomats. This caused morale to sink to a new low. He was officious, cold and seldom friendly. Gina Abercrombie-Winstanley, a senior ambassador, left during Tillerson's tenure remarking he was ineffective. He also lacked humanity and humility. He had no sense of the U.S. world mission. When he came into State no one knew who he was or why Trump selected him.

WHO IS REX TILLERSON?

There is no doubt Rex Tillerson is an excellent, multi-million dollar businessman. As the Chief Executive Officer of Exxon Mobil from 2006 to 2016 he presided over record profits and helped explain negligent oil spills. He was promoted from his position as an engineer to the pinnacle of his company. It was the only business he worked for after earning a bachelor's degree in civil engineering from the University of Texas. He is independent minded. He is a person of high ethics. There has never been a hint of scandal in his life. He is also not acquainted with the political world. He is not a people person. He views dissenting opinions as insubordination.

Tillerson was a high-powered businessman whose opinions were seldom challenged. He was the CEO you worshipped not consulted. This worshipful background made the transition into public life a difficult one.

Although not a politician, Tillerson conducted business deals in Russia for Exxon with President Vladimir Putin. Tillerson's business career prior to becoming Secretary of State made him a Russian oil specialist. This is the reason Trump selected him as the Secretary of State. This should have been a red flag to the U. S Senate when they confirmed Tillerson. He had a down-home, good old boy persona that hid his brash egotistical side. He wasn't used to taking advice from peons.

But Tillerson had a calling card. He was a friend with Vladimir Putin. Trump genuflected about meeting Putin. It had been his goal in life since visiting Russia for a beauty pageant. When Tillerson said Ayn Rand's **Atlas Shrugged** was his favorite book he displayed his ruthless business side. He has a faith in unrestricted free enterprise and early on this appealed to Trump.

He also served as a director of a U.S.-Russia oil company Exxon Neftegas. In July 2017 the U. S. Treasury Department issued a negative assessment of Tillerson's former employer. A government release charged: "Exxon Mobil demonstrated reckless disregard for the U. S. sanctions program. Exxon Mobil caused significant harm to the Ukraine-related sanctions program." This release raised questions of Tillerson's effectiveness within the State Department. He has shown integrity. He is a hard working diplomat in a dysfunctional White House. But could he manage the State Department? The answer was a resounding: "No."

From the first day he stepped into the State Department he was out of step. He didn't understand the policies, the protocol and the ways of Washington. He was lost in simple matters.

WHY AND HOW TILLERSON FAILED AT STATE

As late as July 2017, the Trump administration had not put forth nominations for the assistant secretary for the Eurasian and East Asian affairs, or for the Near Eastern and African affairs offices. Such traditional diplomatic positions, despite being ceremonial, are important in conducting foreign policy. The Trump administration believes the Chief of Protocol, the Chief Counselor and the top terrorism and nonproliferation positions are unimportant. Trump does not want to staff the U. S. State Department. Why? He is the diplomatic head. He doesn't need specialists. He distrusts academics. He abhors professional civil servants. By dismantling the State Department, he can bring forth his America First policy.

As a media shy politician, Tillerson is ill at ease with the press. He is also a Secretary of State Trump actively sabotaged. A good example is the attempts to bring North Korea to the negotiating table to modify the rogue nation's nuclear weapons program. With his gratuitous tweets and public threats, Trump has placed Kim Jong Un into an angry, confrontational position. Trump refuses to allow Tillerson to appear as a strong, independent force in world affairs. Only the president can have this persona. Trump says he is a better negotiator than Tillerson.

Then after he fired Tillerson, Trump sent future Secretary of State Mike Pompeo secretly to North Korea. This was the genesis of the movement to denuclearize Kim Jong Un's regime. It was a brilliant move on Trump's part. Pompeo handled the job discreetly with skill and this helped the coming confirmation hearing where he was easily confirmed. A meeting with Kim Jong Un was finalized. It was a moment or triumph for Trump's foreign policy.

TILLERSON'S RUSSIAN TIES: WHAT DO THEY MEAN?

It was Tillerson's Russian ties that attracted Trump. The business partnership between Russia's state owned oil company, Rosneft, and Exxon is Tillerson's greatest accomplishment. He has spent more time with Vladimir Putin than any American. When he was ready to retire from Exxon, Tillerson had more than 100 million dollars in various compensation packages. He had deferred stock worth $180 million. He reached an agreement with Exxon to sever all ties with the company. They bought out his future stock options. This agreement ended any apparent conflict of interest. This paved the way for his appointment.

It was influential Russians who admired Tillerson. Igor Sechin, the Executive Chairman of Rosneft, the Russian State oil country who some feel is the second most powerful Russian after Putin, endorsed Tillerson's appointment. Exxon purchased a house next to Sechin's. Tillerson spent a great deal of time with his Russian counterpart while living there.

In August 2011, Putin met with Tillerson and Sechin. They signed an agreement to drill in Russian oil fields in the Arctic Ocean. This agreement netted almost three hundred million dollars. Exxon and Rosneft benefitted from this agreement. Rosneft was granted a thirty percent ownership in Exxon Oil Russia due to this production deal.

WHAT IS TILLLERSON'S ROLE AT STATE?

At the State Department there were those who wondered about him. What was Tillerson's role? In March 2017, with Trump in office for two months, there was no consensus about the new Secretary of State's role. In normal times, the State Department is the most visible part of the Executive Office. The Secretary of State's power comes from the Constitution with the support of the President and the advice and consent of Congress. The State Department is replete with domestic career research-management officials, excellent research and career foreign diplomats. The amount of expert information, the knowledge of other countries, and the generally smooth diplomacy makes the Secretary of State a power in world affairs. Tillerson was unable to maximize the State Department assets. Why? He didn't understand the subtle nuances of diplomatic culture.

When Rex Tillerson was sworn in as Secretary of State there were wholesale changes. He seldom read the career employees intelligence reports. He downsized the State department. He refused to spend money allocated by Congress for diplomatic missions. When he recommended Elliott Abrams for the number two position at State, Trump vetoed it. The operative wisdom is the Secretary of State picks his team. Not in the Trump administration.

Often when Trump met with foreign leaders, Tillerson was not present. When Trump entertained Japanese Prime Minister Shinzo Abe in January 2017, after a North Korea missile launch, Trump neglected to include Tillerson or for that matter inform him what took place. The earliest sign of their differences became public when Trump imposed deep budget cuts for diplomacy and foreign aid. The president did so without consulting Tillerson.

The ways of the State Department escaped Secretary of State Tillerson. He did nothing to remedy his ignorance. He didn't make his voice heard as Trump blundered along in foreign policy. He was suspicious of career foreign service officers. The leaks from the State Department were numerous. Tillerson does not meet with reporters, nor did he return their phone calls. For a time, he ended departmental press briefings. Moral was in tatters.

By Christmas 2017, there was little appreciation for Secretary Tillerson. The **New York Times** said he "made war on diplomacy."

Jason Zengerle's profile of Tillerson headlined: "Rex Tillerson Is Running The State Department Into The Ground." Academics, investigative journalists and serious foreign policy scholars gave Tillerson low marks. The knock is on his leadership skills. He is aloof. He is isolated. He is ineffective. He also is charged with gutting the State Department. He reduced the workload. The result was to lay off employees. He cut the budget as well as minimizing the paper work. This is Trump's means of destroying the administrative state.

Tillerson has his defenders. They claim he made contributions to American foreign policy. They argue he is working for an egomaniacal president who thinks he knows everything about world affairs. Despite the criticism here are some of Tillerson's changes in the foreign policy establishment that make sense. There were four key areas where Tillerson attempted reform.

First, he reorganized the State Department to make it more efficient. Critics see this as an attempt to destroy State. That may not be the case. He recognizes that a third of ambassador positions are awarded to unqualified amateurs that contribute financially to the party. Tillerson attempted to reform this practice. It didn't work.

Second, the career path for most employees is slow and not well defined. Tillerson addressed this issue. Trump vetoed it.

Third, Tillerson attempted to streamline information coming out of the State Department. He failed miserably. He repeatedly said this is not a vendetta. Tillerson believes less information is a bonus to those serving in the State Department.

Fourth, he urged President Trump to appoint ambassadors to countries that have vacancies and to fill key positions. At this writing there are thirty-seven important diplomatic positions that Trump has not filled. There were limited successes for Tillerson. By maintaining diplomatic relations with countries Trump criticizes in his daily tweets, Tillerson has attempted to smooth over hurt feelings. In the case of the United Kingdom, Trump has insulted the prime minister, condemned the country for its immigration policy and informed Prime Minister Theresa May he would not visit until the English were receptive to his political message. Trump told May he would arrive only if he was feted and banqueted. In a December 19, 2017 phone conversation May made it clear she opposed what she called Trump's

"Islamaphobia." She also told him his decision to relocate the U. S. Embassy in Jerusalem was a mistake. The President responded by cancelling a planned U. K. visit.

WHY TILLERSON FAILED: TWEETS, THE PROFESSORS, AND NO POLICIES

Trump's tweets and mercurial comments have systematically negated Tillerson's potential diplomatic successes. A good example of Trump's amateur meddling in foreign policy came when Tillerson traveled to China to persuade President Xi Jinping to tighten economic pressures on North Korea to bring them to the negotiating table.

In mid-March 2017, Tillerson and Xi Jinping met in the Great Hall of The People in Beijing for a public display of diplomatic cooperation. Jinping said he was happy that "China U. S. relations can only be defined by cooperation and friendship."

In the midst of these negotiations, Trump tweeted: "While I greatly appreciate the efforts of President Xi & China to help with North Korea, it has not worked out." This tweet caused doubt among Chinese diplomats and cast aspersions on Tillerson's efforts.

In the midst of this meeting, Trump tweeted: "China has done little to help on North Korea." Strangely, these actions by the president may have pushed North and South Korea toward a détente.

Tillerson may be the only Cabinet member to voice opposition to many of Trump's policies. He doesn't back down on his opinions. He often told the president he needed more information on a particular foreign policy issue. This enraged the egomaniacal Trump.

They are both strong personalities. Tillerson also has said the president "speaks for himself." That says it all. Tillerson doesn't agree with Trump's foreign policy. He actively opposed Trump's amateur meddling in foreign affairs. Since November 2017 they have clashed, and by early March 2018 the president decided to bring Mike Pompeo in from the CIA.

On March 13, 2018 Tillerson was fired. Trump did not speak to him prior to sending the Secretary of State into retirement. A tweet told him he was fired. A senior administration official told the **Washington Post** and CNN that White House Chief of Staff John

Kelly called Tillerson on Friday night and told him he would be replaced. This was not true. Tillerson found out like everyone else when Trump tweeted just before nine in the morning on Tuesday, March 13 that Mike Pompeo would replace him as Secretary of State.

Why was Tillerson fired? Why was Kelly spinning the tall tale that the Secretary of State knew about it? The answer is a simple one. On Monday March 12, Tillerson backed the British government's charge Russia was the perpetrator of a nerve-agent attack on United Kingdom soil. The day before he was fired, Tillerson had no idea he was soon to be gone. The story he had been fired on March 9 was one that General Kelly spun. It was untrue.

The reaction to Tillerson's firing was immediate. Professor Paul Musgrave of the University of Massachusetts concluded: "Tillerson would be at the bottom or near the bottom of the list of secretaries of state, not just in the post-Second World War world but in the record of U. S. secretaries of state." After a year in office he left without a single accomplishment.

He was gone for urging Trump to take a tougher stand on Russia. Other reasons include his lack of interest in working with State Department employees. He was wary of the media. He often couldn't explain his policies. The applications for employment at the State Department declined by fifty per cent.

Professor Elizabeth Saunders, of George Washington University, said of Tillerson: "He weakened State for a generation." Trump said of Tillerson he had "totally establishment views of foreign policy." This is one reason Tillerson was invisible in the White House. Then after Tillerson called Trump "a fucking moron" his days were numbered.

DANIEL DREZNER'S REASONED CRITIQUE
OF FAILED FOREIGN POLICY

The most reasoned and intelligent analysis of Tillerson's foreign policy failings came from the facile pen of Professor Daniel Drezner, at the Fletcher School of Law and Diplomacy, at Tufts. Drezner is not a Tillerson fan. He is even less of a Trump acolyte. He gave Tillerson high marks for controlling the president's instincts, ignorance and impulsive actions. He worked well with Defense Secretary James

Mattis. But in the end Tillerson did not reform the State Department, he virtually destroyed it.

Drezner pointed out Tillerson's credibility was zero. His influences were minimal. Trump continually undermined him. If a foreign head of government met with the Secretary of State an agreement, a policy or an understanding could vanish the next day. To Drezner's way of thinking, Tillerson was so incompetent "I called for him to resign in August." The number of well thought of career foreign officers who left Foggy Bottom tells one all they need to know about Tillerson's incompetence. He didn't have a management team. The State Department struggled without direction. Why? The President has a questionable grasp on policy and how government functions. Tillerson was imperious, lazy, entitled, and he paid little attention to detail.

Foreign diplomats complain Tillerson didn't return phone calls. He failed to set up meetings. He didn't have constructive foreign policy dialogue. Tempering the Donald was a role in which Tillerson failed. He is judged harshly for his transgressions.

Drezner's criticism comes from leaks in the State Department, as well as formal briefings. He is a professor with a unique view into the corruption running rampant in the Trump administration. As a columnist for the **Washington Post,** Drezner has his ear to the political gossip frequenting the Oval Office and in the halls of Congress.

As a national security analyst for the **Washington Post**, Drezner often gives Trump credit for significant foreign policy accomplishments. He praised Trump's campaign to bring North Korea to the negotiating table. What Drezner fears is that renegotiating trade deals with South Korea and Japan may harm our relationship with those close allies.

The **Washington Post** was not surprised when unidentified U. S. State Department officials announced the president operates largely on impulse, he has little patience, and by June 2018 there were no signs of constraint from his advisers. The **Post** and Drezner point out the Secretary of Defense Mattis, Security of State Pompeo and Chief of Staff Kelly attempt to moderate the president without success. The bottom line is Trump' erratic behavior does little, if anything, to advance American foreign policy. Drezner sees a bully in the White House with empty threats, an empty mind and an empty policy.

The danger Trump presents to American democracy is real. Drezner writes: "Trump has bastardized the term 'deep state' so much that even its progenitor, Mike Lofgren, wishes he would stop." When John Bolton arrived as the National Security Adviser the scales tipped into a War Cabinet.

Trump's "deep state paranoia" bodes ill for the future. He is systematically dismantling American government. As Drezner and Comey point out, Trump is not the problem it is the electorate. Following his irrational and ill-informed leadership places the nation in peril. Trump's tactics to bypass the bureaucracy, ignore the specialists and failing to cooperate with Congress, while dismantling the courts, is one of many indications of his unfitness for the presidency.

THOSE WHO HAD THE PRESIDENT'S EAR: IT HURT TILLERSON

Jared Kushner and Steve Bannon had Trump's ear during the president's first year. They urged the president to fire Tillerson. Why? They claimed he didn't understand the important issues, and he was not promoting Kushner's image in foreign policy. Michael Wolff came to the same conclusion. Much of what caused others problems was Jared Kushner's role as a de facto foreign policy adviser. If you crossed Jared or disrespected him you were fired.

In the day-to-day operation of the State Department, Tillerson was an abject failure. Of his one hundred fifty-three political appointees, Tillerson had only sixty-four confirmed. Was it laziness or incompetence? It didn't matter. Either way it sullied his reputation. When Trump overruled Tillerson at a meeting, Rex would say: "It's your deal." Trump was outraged. Tillerson had every intention of staying on as the Secretary of State. He was so outraged with the Trump tweet firing him, in his farewell remarks he didn't thank the president.

As Tillerson left the State Department, **Foreign Policy** described him as "a dead man walking for months." As he exited Tillerson defended his fourteen months running the State Department claiming his successes were placing maximum pressure on North Korea to get Kim Jong Un to the negotiating table. He said his honesty set a new standard in diplomacy. His farewell statement left a great deal to be desired. "Much work remains to respond to the troubling behavior and actions on the part of the Russian government," Tillerson concluded. He sent a direct message to Trump to get tough on the Kremlin and Vladimir Putin.

MICHAEL WOLFF ON TILLERSON

Michael Wolff spent almost a year hanging out the Trump White House. He had an opportunity to watch every member of the administration. He concluded they all thought the Republican mantra would work despite Trump. By year's end, Wolf said, "there was not literally one member of the senior staff who could any longer be confident of that premise." (p. 304)

After Secretary of State Tillerson called Trump "a moron," it appeared his fate was sealed. It was October 2017 and no one disrespected the president. But Tillerson remained on the job. Wolff wrote Steve Mnuchin and Reince Priebus called Trump "an idiot" and Gary Cohen said: "He was dumb as shit." (p. 304) The **Washington Post's** Jennifer Rubin reported on May 1, 2018 Chief of Staff John Kelly called Trump "an idiot." He denied it. She said she had four sources.

Why did Tillerson survive? The answer is a simple one. Donald J. Trump doesn't run the Oval Office. The three generals Mattis, McMasters, and Kelly respected Tillerson. Soon McMaster and Tillerson were gone. Trump does run the White House. Chief of Staff Kelly survived Trump's daily tirades. Kelly was told about the president's brilliance in foreign affairs daily and usually by Trump. This guaranteed another five months on the job. Kelly was concerned about Trump's ability to lead, according to Wolff, and he didn't think the Donald was qualified to be a dogcatcher.

Jennifer Rubin, writing in **The Washington Post**, said Chief of Staff John Kelly was attempting to bring discipline to the White House. He was so frustrated by Trump's unwillingness to accept advice that NBC news reported, citing multiple sources, that Kelly frequently calls

President Trump "an idiot." Kelly denied calling Trump "an idiot." He said it is "total BS."

Kelly made these comments to members of Congress, according to Rubin. She stood by her story. She said Kelly complained constantly for one reason about Trump. The reason? Trump's lack of knowledge concerning policy and government made Kelly a quiet but volatile critic.

What is it that bothers Kelly? When he served as Homeland Security secretary, he had an excellent grasp of and suggestions for immigration policy. Whether or not he called Trump "an idiot" is debatable. What is not debatable is he influences Trump's hard line stance on immigration. According to two White House officials, Jennifer Rubin reported, Kelly said "Trump doesn't even understand what DACA is."

MICHAEL WOLF WEIGHS IN ON GOVERNMENT SHADOWS

Wolff concluded Tillerson could work in the government's shadow. He was surprisingly good at his job. Wolff wrote: "Jared Kushner was the driver of the Trump doctrine." Without access to Russian sources, Wolff claimed, Putin had no interest in a Trump friendship. How does this relate to Tillerson? It appears the Secretary of State remained on the job for as long as he did as a conduit to the Kremlin.

The most terrifying point in Wolff's book is Trump is prepared to go to war. The president, Woolf believes, has a sense of history. He wants to go down at the Chief Executive who saved the world through war. Wolff defends his observations, his book and his means of reporting by suggesting he was in the middle of the story. That is Wolff tells the reader he sees things others miss from his small White House desk. He does this through insightful interviews.

Wolff's sin is allowing people to spin tall tales. He doesn't have a second source. He doesn't corroborate these stories. Super wealthy narcissists dominate Wolff's reporting. One thing is clear. Policy concerns, mismanagement, operational dysfunction and a fear of the "deep state" are aspects of the Trump administration that are real. Russian collusion is another story Wolff alludes to Russian collusion without substance, facts or conclusions. But his book does raise questions. Answers? Never!

FIONA HILL: A TRUMP APPOINTEE WHO IS ANTI-PUTIN

In the early Trump administration the National Security Adviser, H. R. McMaster, had a less than friendly view of Putin and the Russian oilmen. This was one reason Trump fired him. He was also not a Tillerson fan. They fought and shouted as each other inside the Oval Office. The White House did have one Russia specialist who helped to identify Putin's policies and analyze Russia's impact upon America. Her name is Fiona Hill. She was outside the media's radar.

Who is Fiona Hill? Why is she important? Hill is the president's senior director for European and Russian affairs. She is a career academic. She earned a PHD from Harvard and as the director of the Brookings Institute; she published a seminal book **Mr. Putin: Operative in the Kremlin**. Hill's hiring indicated the Trump administration attempted to understand Putin. She is also a liberal scholar. She was hired largely on the basis of an op-ed piece detailing how and why Putin might want to interfere in the U. S. presidential election. Her July 2016 article caught the attention of Trump's struggling foreign policy team. A year later Trump brought her into the White House. It was on the recommendation of General Keith Kellogg. Why was she in the Oval Office?

The reason is Hill dissected Putin's mind. She told Trump he would see America as weak if there weren't sanctions. The Russian government expected travel bans, the expulsion of diplomats and increased sanctions. Hill said he should point out to the press he was tough on the Kremlin by imposing the penalties. Hill said the Russians would not hold it again him. They expected sanctions. Trump listened to her. Putin was all about ego strength and cunning, said Hill. She is a strong anti-Putin voice in the Trump White House. She is a confidential adviser to the president who helped Trump navigate the difficult waters surrounding his relationship with Putin.

When he talked with Putin, Trump attempted to bring Russia into the U. S.'s sphere of diplomacy. The President proposed a joint team of American and Russian specialists to investigate future cyber crimes. As Luke Harding pointed out, this was "like inviting a burglar into your house." After Trump's advisers told him he would be duped he dropped the attempts at the cyber crime agreement.

Fiona Hill's role in the White House remains a mysterious but important one. Did she educate Trump on Putin? Did she help with the Russian collusion investigation? No one knows the degree of her influence. She is truly a mysterious figure.

HOW TRUMP DISRESPECTED TILLERSON AT DAVOS

In late January 2018 Trump traveled to Davos, Switzerland to attend the World Economic Forum. Past presidents have not attended, as it is about business greed and not issues of world economic equality. It is about private enterprise opening its doors to align with major governments. This is why American presidents have not attended the World Economic Forum.

For Trump it was all about ego. His planned appearance, as he entered the second of year of the presidency, is one Trump relished. Why? People who have ignored him will be paid back. Those who have not invited him to conferences, including this one, will have to listen to the Donald drone on about American business.

European business executives played to the president's massive ego. When he was introduced at Davos a brass band sitting near the stage began playing. As he met with a multitude of European business executives, President Trump beamed like an overweight Panda. He was in his element. Making money through a big business-government connection not the interests of the people was his theme.

One of Trump's aides told him he was the most adored, celebrated, respected and banqueted World Economic Summit leader since Angelina Jolie's appearance. Then he looked perplexed. Why was she an honored guest? Trump's preparation for Davos was limited. Secretary Tillerson looked relieved to have avoided the mainstream circus Trump brought to Davos. Elect a clown. Expect a circus.

During the Davos meeting, Trump hosted a dinner for some of the world's business tycoons. Tillerson was on the select guest list. When he arrived there was not a seat for him at the dinner table. In what was the ultimate humiliation, the Secretary of State stood on the side as Trump talked American foreign policy and Tillerson ate from a paper plate standing up.

Trump ignored Tillerson telling world business leaders the U. S. was "open for business" with reservations. European businesses represented at the dinner included Adidas, Siemens and Nestle. The cold, calculating cruelty Trump exhibits continued as he treated Tillerson like "a coffee boy." Trump didn't realize this was George Papadopoulos's job.

When the Davos conference began, Trump's speech defined his America First theme. As an independent businessman, Trump was never invited to the World Economic Conference. He was incensed. He mentioned it numerous times. The mooch was invited. That frustrated Trump.

At Davos Trump joked privately he would order his coffee boy Secretary of State to Africa to apologize for disrespecting African nations. This was an indication Tillerson was about to be fired. In a letter to African leaders, the president announced he would send Secretary Tillerson on an extended visit to the continent. In Trump's letter he said he "deeply respects" the African people. But he had other business that was more important.

WHY AND HOW THE STATE DEPARMENT IS IN DECLINE: DEMOCRACY IN PERIL

Trump controls the U. S. State Department with an iron hand. He doesn't tolerate differing opinions or dissent. He views career diplomats as disingenuous. He has disrespected the professionalism of the State Department, and he continually diminished his Secretary of State. Trump disrespected State and Tillerson never stood up to the bully.

There have been key people who have left government service due to Trump's disrespect. Elizabeth Shackelford, a career political officer based in Nairobi, sent a November 7, 2017 letter to Tillerson complaining about the "stinging disrespect" for State employees, and how it was systematically dismantling the experienced staff. "The cost of this is visible every day in Mission Somalia, my current post, where State's diplomatic influence, on the country and within our own interagency, is waning," Shackelford wrote.

Shackelford complained Secretary Tillerson instructed employees not to consider "advancing human rights across the globe…." When she inquired why employees should ignore human rights, Tillerson said it was bad for business. As the Trump administration ignored human rights violations in the Philippines, Turkey and Russia there was concern traditional American rights were under attack. Shackelford left the State Department with the warning President Trump shows no respect for democratic institutions.

The sad part of the Tillerson State Department is he refused to release the human rights report that every Secretary places into the public domain. Like Trump, Tillerson's approach to foreign policy is business oriented. It was also disingenuous.

How badly did Tillerson destroy the State Department? He gutted it. He has refused to spend the sixty million dollars appropriated by Congress for programs to counter Islamic and Russian propaganda. When **Politico** asked why Tillerson didn't spend money to combat Russian media? R. C. Hammond, explained: "Money is unwelcome because any extra funding for programs to counter Russian media influence would anger Moscow." This Tillerson assistant is typical of those surrounding the Secretary of State. They want to keep Russia happy.

When Tillerson met with former Secretary of State Coneleezza Rice he said: "I don't even have a twitter account that I can follow what he is tweeting, so my staff usually has to print out his tweets and hand them to me." One wonders what Secretary Rice thought of White House security, protocol and intelligence gathering?

There are more troubling concerns. Trump told Tillerson to "lay off" negotiations with North Korea. Trump said: "We'll do what has to be done." When Trump traveled to Saudi Arabia, he didn't consult the Secretary of State. Tillerson is clearly frustrated, he told Condoleezza Rice: "I am probably going to go to my grave and never have a social-media account."

WHAT DOES TILLERSON'S FIRING TELL US ABOUT THE STATE DEPARTMENT AND TRUMP?

Rex Tillerson's firing is another indication Trump can't govern. Tillerson was never on the same page with Trump. The **London**

Guardian described Tillerson as "hapless, hopeless and tragic." As Tillerson spoke of leaving State his press conference was a dispirited one. He didn't criticize and he didn't thank Trump. After the press conference all of Tillerson's duties were turned over to deputy secretary John Sullivan until the formal end of Tillerson's State tenure at midnight March 31, 2018. Then Mike Pompeo came on board.

Not only was Tillerson an abject failure, when he listed his accomplishments, they appeared mundane and inconsequential. He said: "We exceeded the expectations of almost everyone" in reference to North Korea. Not true! There was little progress with Kim Jong Un's rouge dictatorship until Trump personally took charge.

It was on the question of Russia that Tillerson got himself into hot water with Trump. "Russia must assess carefully as to how its actions are in the best interest of the Russian people and of the world more broadly," Tillerson continued. "Their current trajectory is likely to lead to greater isolation on their part...." This comment doomed Tillerson with Trump. He fired him.

The reaction to Tillerson's firing left U. S. diplomacy in temporary turmoil. As Mike Pompeo left the CIA and career employee, Gina Haspel, took over the agency, the pundits commented the State Department would benefit from new leadership. Pompeo was close to Trump on all issues. The initial problem was human rights groups. They pointed to Pompeo and Haspel as Trump insiders favoring torture, nuclear escalation and a lack of transparency.

Tillerson's comment on the president's handling of the North Korea problem precipitated his firing. "We're a long way from negotiations," Tillerson continued. "We just need to be very clear-eyed and realistic about it...." Tillerson went on to say this was impossible. A month after this statement Trump agreed to meet with Kim Jong Un.

Trump had some unexpected allies and defenders in firing Tillerson. **The Washington Post** agreed the Secretary was ineffective. Why? Tillerson had his own agenda. He was not the president's man. He was a distant and diffident figure in the White House. He called the president "a fucking moron." **The Washington Post's** Marc A.

Thiessen editorialized Tillerson was "insubordinate." That did it. Trump fired him.

THE NEW YORK TIMES WEIGHS IN ON
DANGERS TO NATIONAL SECURITY

Tillerson disagreed with every one of Trump's positions on international affairs. He stood up to the president. He attempted to explain his positions on maintaining the Iran agreement. He urged the president not to implement tariffs. He supported the Paris Climate Accord. He believed diplomacy with North Korea was possible. He supported NATO. He was tough on Russia. He urged cooperation with the EU and the U. K. He embodied Theodore Roosevelt's "Walk Softly But Carry A Big Stick." From his first day in office, Tillerson was minimized, ignored, vilified and eventually sent out to pasture. He will not go down as being as effective as Henry Kissinger or Dean Acheson. Tillerson reached out to talk to Kissinger, he read about Dean Acheson and George W. Marshall. It wasn't that Tillerson didn't work hard. He did! The problem is President Trump didn't have a foreign policy. Tillerson never formed an alternative.

Jared Kushner's meddling was another problem. The attempts to tear down State by Steve Bannon and the intrigue from a host of boot lickers close to Trump were forces decimating State. It was an impossible situation. Tillerson did his best. It wasn't good enough. He had little control and less influence.

In an editorial **The New York Times** observed: "There's nothing about President Trump's shake up of his national security team to reassure a world that is growing ever more anxious about the chaotic, hard-line leadership." The **Times** suggested Trump was "hawkish and confrontational." The editorial described the president as "a hot headed president uninterested in diplomacy." America's allies came to the same conclusion in the summer of 2017. He took America out of a leadership position in world affairs. As the G-7 and G-20 Summits convened there was a distant ad unfriendly American foreign policy. Europe was no longer in the midst of American diplomacy.

WHO NEEDS A SECRETARY OF STATE?

After President Trump fired Secretary of State Rex Tillerson, the **Wall Street Journal** charged, in an op-editorial, that the Democrats "new standard seems to be that any nominee who agrees with the elected president is disqualified." The **WSJ** doesn't recognize there is a threat of the end of traditional diplomacy.

Senator Tim Kaine, a Democrat from Virginia and Hillary's running mate, said: "I don't want a Secretary of State who is going to exacerbate President Trump's tendencies to oppose diplomacy." The **WSJ** commented Kaine is still sore over losing the election. Kaine does have a point. Trump is seeking to end long standing diplomatic rules. There are other issues.

Mike Pompeo has a long history of making disparaging remarks concerning Muslims. He is neither a racist nor a bigot but as California Democratic Senator Dianne Feinstein made clear Muslims and the LGBT have suffered from Pompeo's remarks. Pompeo is well qualified. He has the experience to become an excellent Secretary of State. He also has the personality.

As he exited the State Department, Tillerson told Ronan Farrow he may have been too inexperienced to head American foreign policy. He didn't have the foresight to run the State Department. He was, like Trump, unwilling to educate himself on foreign affairs. He was not only unprepared to act as the Secretary of State, he wasn't interested.

MIKE POMPEO TAKES OVER A DYSFUNCTIONAL STATE DEPARTMENT: FOUR THINGS THAT ARE WRONG AND WHY

After the U. S. Senate confirmed Mike Pompeo as Secretary of state by a 57-42 vote the problems in the State Department were revealed. There were four areas of concern.

First, Pompeo needed to fill important positions. A diplomatic mission cannot be achieved without diplomats. Pompeo discovered there was no permanent undersecretary for arms control and international security affairs. Why is this position important? In order to negotiate with North Korea and Kim Jong Un there needed to be a timetable for controlling missile tests and nuclear proliferation. The lack of a permanent assistant secretary for East Asian and Pacific

177

Affairs left little reliable intelligence information on how to deal with Asian diplomats. The lack of ambassadors in South Korea, Germany and Australia hurt Pompeo's early diplomatic efforts.

Second, Tillerson had no clear lines of communication to foreign diplomats. He couldn't work with the president. Pompeo appears to be able to overcome these obstacles.

Third, those who have resigned, transferred, were fired or retired decimated the State Department's experienced work force. The level of expertise has declined rapidly. When John Feeley, resigned at the U. S. Ambassador to Panama, he stated he quit because of Trump. "As a junior foreign service officer, I signed an oath to serve faithfully the president and his administration in an apolitical fashion, even when I might not agree with certain policies," Feeley continued. "My instructors made clear that if I believed I could not do that, I would be honor bound to resign. That time has come."

Fourth, the influence and interference of Trump family members, notably Jared Kushner and Ivanka Trump as de facto state secretaries have torn the department apart. Kushner fought with Tillerson. Kushner developed a Middle East peace plan where he didn't have the courtesy to consult Tillerson. They clashed repeatedly over Israel. The notion of rank amateurs making governmental policy is an impossible one Tillerson's time at State was doomed from his first day at work.

THE FALLOUT FROM TILLERSON'S DEPARTURE

Once Tillerson was fired the changes continued in the State Department. When reporters asked Undersecretary of State Steve Goldstein about Tillerson's firing, he put out a memo stating of Tillerson: "The Secretary had every intention of remaining because of the tangible progress made on critical national security issues," Goldstein continued: "The Secretary did not speak to the President this morning and is unaware of the reason he was fired, but he is grateful for the opportunity to serve." Trump read the press release and fired Goldstein.

A Trump insider, Heather Nauert, formerly of Fox News, was named to replace Goldstein. As Tillerson and Goldstein left State, eight of the nine top posts at the State Department, President Trump announced, will not be filled. A State Department official speaking to **Foreign Policy** observed: "I think the record will show it wasn't Rex who got himself fired. It was the echelon of inept and obstructionist staff he came with who got him fired." A South American diplomat told **Foreign Policy:** "My personal view as an observer is that this change shows the administration is still in search of a grand strategy….We wonder if this change can bring about a new perspective. Given the new Secretary's background, though, it highly doubtful." This comment says it all about the U. S. foreign policy image and Trump's America First strategy.

NINE

THE TOAD SERVING TRUMP: THE GEORGE PAPADOPOULOS FIASCO, BLUNDERS IN FOREIGN POLICY BEFORE THE TRUMP PRESIDENCY

"Trump campaign officials told the Daily Beast that Papadopoulos was never a key player....They saw him as a grifter...a wannabe, a kid and a con man."

LACHLAN MARKEY, ASAWIN SUEBSAENG, SAM STEIN

He's an "excellent guy."

DONALD J. TRUMP, WASHINGTON POST, MARCH 2016

"He's a hapless wannabe."

A BEN CARSON COMMITTEE AIDE.

On July 27, 2016 a Trump foreign policy adviser stepped off a flight from Germany at Dulles airport outside of Washington. The FBI was waiting to arrest him. Why had the FBI arrested George Papadopoulos at seven in the evening after a long flight from Germany? It was to impress upon the twenty-nine year old Trump foreign policy adviser, he was in serious trouble for his duplicitous behavior. He was charged with lying to the FBI. He pleaded guilty. He was in handcuffs. He was charged with a felony. He shot off his big mouth in a London bar. This was his undoing. An Australian diplomat informed American authorities Papadopoulos was bragging about setting up a Donald J. Trump and Vladimir Putin meeting. This alerted the FBI to possible collusion from Trump insiders. It was the reason for the appointment of Robert Mueller to investigate Russian influences upon the electoral process. Papadopoulos didn't realize his level of duplicity.

When Papadopoulos struck a plea deal with Special Counsel Mueller, it was over lying about his contacts with Kremlin connected Russians. When the documents on Papadopoulos's political intrigue became public, these sources showed he was an amateur who attempted to set up a Trump-Putin meeting during the early part of the 2016 campaign. How much Trump knew of the efforts is unknown. What court papers show is a Trump campaign supervisor, who was not named, encouraged the young Chicago based Greek-American to travel to Russia to talk with governmental officials. The subject? It was about a potential Trump-Putin meeting. "Through his false statements and omissions, defendant…impeded the FBI's ongoing investigation," Mueller's team commented. Court documents reveal Papadopoulos lied about his relationship with a Russian professor, Joseph Mifsud, and the result of these lies was a guilty plea. The October 5, 2017 guilty plea made the other charges go away. When the press asked Papadopoulos for an explanation. He said: "No comment."

The George Papadopoulos story is like a fictional tale of a Greek James Bond with a delusional hope for fame and fortune. The tragedy is he tried to help the Donald become president. The result was his action brought an investigation bringing down a number of Trump insiders.

WHO IS THIS COFFEE BOY?

He told the ladies he was Trump's main man. He was like a Saturday Night Live character. The seriousness of the issue didn't immediately dawn on Papadopoulos. He attempted to secure Russian help to elect Trump. The allegations were Papadopoulos was a direct link to Vladimir Putin and Russian collusion. He bragged of being able to arrange a meeting between the Donald and Putin. This loud-mouthed fool became a household word. The little weasel immediately cooperated with Mueller. He was a foreign policy adviser to the Trump campaign. The president described him as "a coffee boy." He is an arrogant former C student in political science who somehow was on Trump's initial foreign policy advisory committee. He had little, if any, background in foreign policy. He became the first person to admit to a crime as a Trump insider.

Papadopoulos didn't realize he sent e-mails that raised concerns about national security, alleged collusion with Russian agents, and in the process he may have violated American law concerning his alleged attempts to secure information from a foreign nation to help Trump become president. He is innocent of everything except lying to the FBI. The other charges were dropped. When his indictment became public, there was no question as to this coffee boy's duplicitous behavior. He was an amateur in international politics. His actions harmed rather than helped Donald J. Trump.

The National Security meeting in early 2016, with George Papadopoulos attending, was no more than a photo op for the **New York Times**. A picture of Trump's advisory team appeared in the newspaper. Papadopoulos sat three chairs down from Trump. There wasn't a story about what they accomplished. Why? Because there was nothing of substance discussed. There were no women appointed to this make shift panel of advisers who had no idea about what Trump had in mind about the direction of American foreign policy.

HOW DID THE TOAD GET ON THE LIST?

The mystery surrounding Papadopoulos is an unanswerable one. How did he angle an appointment to Trump's fledgling foreign policy advisory committee? He was like most of Trump's early foreign policy advisers. None of them had a scintilla of experience.

Diplomacy was not their forte. There were a number of foreign policy advisers with suspicious backgrounds. Walid Paris, a Fox TV News counterterrorism analyst, had a suspect background. He was a close adviser to a Lebanese Christian warlord accused of operating hit squads against Shia Muslims. Joseph Schmitz was a former Pentagon Inspector General. He was essentially a pencil pusher. He left government employment to work for Blackwater the controversial security firm whose employees were charged with gunning down unarmed Iraqi civilians in 2008 at a Baghdad traffic circle.

When Steve Bannon looked over the list of foreign policy advisers, he said: "These people are a bunch of clowns." When he came to Papadopoulos name, Bannon blurted out: "How the fuck did he get on the list?"

Bannon realized Russian intelligent agents were playing Papadopoulos. On March 24, 2016, three days after Trump praised Papadopoulos to the Washington Post editorial board, the amateur politico was in London where History Professor Joseph Mifsud talked with him about the election. Then he met Olga Vinograda or Ola Polonskaya whichever name she gave to the press. They made Papadopoulos look like a fool introducing her as Putin's niece. Papadopoulos was elated. He envisioned a high-level job in the White House. It was lunch with Olga and Mifsud that prompted Papadopoulos to e-mail Sam Clovis and other Trump campaign officials with the promise of dirt on Hillary Clinton.

While in London, Papadopoulos met with Stefan A. Halper, an emeritus professor at the University of Cambridge, who was also an FBI informant. Halper had talked with Carter Page about the Trump campaign, and he informed the FBI of Papadopoulos's plans to secure damaging information on Hillary Clinton. He proved to be inept. He had no impact on Trump and the campaign. His impact was to provide the rat6ionalle for appointing Special Counsel Robert Mueller.

THE TOAD WHO PROMPTED THE MUELLER INVESTIGATION: HOW DOES ONE EXPLAIN PAPADOPOULOS?

If there is one thing we can thank Donald J. Trump for it is poor judgment. He brings people into his inner circle that has no business in government. How does one explain George Papadopoulos? He was appointed to Trump's foreign policy advisory team with little or no experience in international affairs. That is if you don't include drinking beer and shooting off your big mouth in a London pub. Papadopoulos single-handedly created the appointment of the Special Prosecutor Robert Mueller with his revelation to the FBI that Russia interfered in the 2016 election. The investigation surrounding Russian interference was the result of his loose talk in a London wine bar. One of the byproducts of Papadopoulos's inane comments begs the question of the Trump administration's alleged collusion with Russia. Is it a moot point? Talks of a Trump-Putin meeting was just talk. How did Papadopoulos achieve this seemingly impossible feat? An Australian diplomat reported him to the FBI. Jail was the next step. The story sounds like something out of a James Bond movie. That is if Woody Allen was cast as James Bond.

In March 2016 Papadopoulos was drinking in a London wine bar. He was full of himself. Bragging! Story telling! Ego statements! This is the little weasel's mantra. The New York Times reported George accidentally started the Russia investigation after talking too much to a high level Australian diplomat, Alexander Downer, during a night of marathon drinking. At first Downer didn't believe this wanker who said he was a member of the Trump foreign policy advisory team. Downer laughed. He couldn't be a part of Trump's inner circle. He was!

Who is Alexander Downer? He is a former foreign affairs minister and an Australian conservative politician. He was in office for eleven years as the Aussie's longest serving foreign affairs minister. He loves to drink in London's posh Kensington Wine Rooms. It was at one of these drinking sessions that Downer is famous for that he ran into George Papadopoulos. The Kensington Wine Rooms is a noted pick up place for the lonely.

While in London, Papadopoulos told people there was a dossier of compromising material on Hillary Clinton. This material was contained in thousands of hacked e-mails. For some unexplainable reason, he shared this information with Downer. Papadopoulos also said the Trump election team was working with the Russian's to elect the Donald. Papadopoulos allegedly remarked Russia was a key player in the election. Why did he make such outrageous statements? Ego driven importance! Or perhaps it is inexperience in governmental affairs. Or perhaps it is sheer ignorance. Who knows!

Alexander Downer ignored the American's comments. Then in July 2016 WikiLeaks started publishing hacked e-mails from the Democratic National Committee. Downer contacted the FBI explaining what Papadopoulos had told him. Downer said of Papadopoulos, he looks like a smiling toad in his stylish business suit and dark sunglasses. He loves the camera shoved in his face.

Trump said Papadopoulos was "an excellent guy." Who is George Papadopoulos? No one knows! He is the unknown loud mouth who prompted the Mueller investigation. CNBC described Papadopoulos as "the first domino in Russia-gate."

WHO IS GEORGE PAPADOPOULOS?

Who is George Papadopoulos? He made the news when the Special Prosecutor, Robert Mueller, turned him into a government witness. He is the first Trump insider to plead guilty and cooperate with Mueller's investigation into Russian influences. For a month, Papadopoulos secretly wore a wire to garner Mueller information. So far the jury is out on what he discovered, if anything.

He finds himself in the midst of a foreign policy scandal. Why did Trump bring him onboard his foreign policy team? He told the Trump campaign he was an oil, gas, energy and foreign policy specialist. Thy believed it.

When Papadopoulos was arrested in July 2016, his guilty plea of lying to the FBI stunned The general public. It surprised Trump's inner circle. While Trump dismissed the young Greek as a low-level volunteer, there is an incriminating picture of a small coterie of foreign policy advisers at a meeting where Papadopoulos is sitting three seats from Trump.

A LOW LEVEL VOLUNTEER BECOMES
A FOREIGN POLICY ADVISER

There is little information on Papadopoulos. When the news broke he was a government witness, the president called him "a low level volunteer" and "proven to be a liar." The truth is more complicated.

He wasn't the unpaid political volunteer Trump described. He was a political wannabe. When news broke he was a government witness wearing a wire the so-called glorified coffee boy became a person of media interest. His background was not remarkable.

One thing is clear. Papadopoulos doesn't have a political philosophy. He is an opportunist and an amateur in foreign policy. The New York Times pointed out the glorified coffee boy didn't have foreign policy credentials. It didn't matter. He never gave up on arranging meetings with the Russians. He did a lot of harm to the Trump campaign.

He did have some successes. Papadopoulos claimed he arranged a meeting between Trump and President Abdel Fatah el-Sisi of Egypt. There is no evidence to support this boast. It is another example of how tall tales cast a shadow over Trump's presidency. There was no need to worry about the Democrats and Mueller going after Trump. His insipid and ill-equipped followers hurt him with their amateur attempts at diplomacy.

None of this seemed remotely possible when he was in college. Papadopoulos was not a scholar. He was an average student. It is hard to imagine this rank amateur with average grades becoming a centerpiece in American politics. But mediocrity prevails and Papadopoulos is the King of Mediocrity.

WHAT COLLEGE DID OR DIDN'T DO FOR PAPADOPOULOS

While in college at Chicago's DePaul University, Professor Richard Farkas, whose specialty is Russia, didn't remember Papadopoulos. He checked a past class roster. By all accounts the young Greek was a forgettable student with a mediocre academic record. Although he took many courses in Russian history and politics, no faculty member recalled him. He claims to have a master's degree from University College London. The school and politics faculty would not confirm this for me. His school associates described him, as a right leaning young man with infectious enthusiasm and a burning desire to achieve political importance. Trump campaign officials described Papadopoulos as "a wannabe." He attended DC Young Republican events. No one remembered him.

How could this inept, ill informed, barely qualified, academically mediocre young man get on the Trump foreign policy advisory committee? The answer is Sam Clovis. Paul Manafort is another person allegedly favoring Papadopoulos's expertise. Perhaps Ivanka and Jared Kushner loved his act. There has to be some explanation for this smiling wanker.

WILL PAPADOPOULOS BECOME A TRIVIAL PURSUIT CARD?

After graduating from DePaul, with a degree in political science, Papadopoulos told anyone who would listen he speaks Greek, Arabic and French. He began working as an unpaid intern at the Hudson Institute in 2011. What is the Hudson Institute? It is a right wing, non-profit think tank based in New York. It analyzes military strategy and futurist programs. The institute promotes a world economy with the U. S. in the driver's seat.

From 2011 to 2015 Papadopoulos re-invented his curriculum vita. He became in his own mind an energy consultant. It worked. He caught the attention of Sam Clovis. He was one of Trump's close advisers. Clovis examined Papadopoulos's qualifications. He was impressed. The Greek kid wore nice suits. He was personable. He carried an expensive briefcase. He could talk a mile a minute about the amount of money America could make from world energy. He learned all this at the Hudson Institute, which provided his entry into American politics. Papadopoulos' story is of a person lacking qualifications, being a rank amateur and succeeding in politics. That is until the FBI investigation turned him into a witness against Trump.

THE HUDSON INSTITUTE PROVIDED
THE ENTRY LEVEL TO POLITICS

What did Papadopoulos learn at the Hudson Institute? After spending time studying and working at the Hudson Institute, Papadopoulos called himself an: "Oil, gas and policy consultant." He was thirty years old. He didn't possess a graduate degree in science or engineering. His undergraduate political science degree was his claim to scientific expertise. He overstated his education, his qualifications, but his lack of political expertise doomed him. He still lived in the basement of family friends in a Chicago suburb. He purchased expensive dark suits. He carried a finely tooled leather brief case. He told everyone the U. S. government should support Israel, Greece and Cyprus. He walked, talked and acted like an international business specialist and no one caught on to his duplicitous behavior. But Papadopoulos was smart. He used a respected political think tank to curry favors with Trump insiders.

The Hudson Institute was an unwitting catalyst to Papadopoulos' entry into mainstream politics. In November 2015 a terrorist attack in Paris led American presidential candidates to search for foreign policy experts. The Ben Carson campaign hired Papadopoulos. Why? No one knows. Barry Bennett, Carson's campaign manager, looked at Papadopoulos' skimpy resume. He was a stopgap appointment to advise Carson on terrorism. The reason he was selected was the Hudson Institute's reputation and recommendation. Kenneth Weinstein, the Hudson Institute President, gave Papadopoulos a good recommendation. In a few weeks the young Greek was in the middle of the Carson campaign.

How much work did Papadopoulos do for the Carson campaign? "If there was any work output, I never saw it," Bennett said. Jason Osborne, a senior Carson campaign officials, said: "Honestly I only remember his name because it was unique and reminded me of Webster." This was a strange comment as Webster was a 1970s television show.

How was Papadopoulos used by the Trump campaign? It appears he had a plan to extract politically explosive materials on Hillary Clinton. The means for this sounds more like a James Bond movie than realistic foreign policy.

PAPADOPOULOS'S RISE AND FALL

How do you explain George Papadopoulos? He has a drive for fame. He overstates his qualifications. A case study in his personal arrogance took place in a May 2016 Greek visit. He arrived without fanfare or media attention. He said he was on a mission from Donald J. Trump. Only two months earlier Papadopoulos was named to Trump's campaign foreign policy team. The Greeks were so taken with Papadopoulos that he was allowed to judge a local beauty contest.

When the Mueller investigation took place there was concern Papadopoulos used his connections in Greece to contact Russian agents supporting Trump's candidacy. When he visited Greece, Papadopoulos contacted and talked to Greek's foreign minister, its president and a former prime minister. For a young politico this was amazing access. Why? The Mueller investigators believe the young Greek met with pro-Russian Greek politicians perhaps discussing the sanctions and other issues. Vladimir Putin was in Greece at the same time. There is no evidence he met with Papadopoulos. When Marianna Kakaounaki interviewed him for Kathimerini, Papadopoulos claimed he had a blank check for any position in the Trump administration. It was only days after this egregious comment the FBI arrested Papadopoulos. He became a footnote to the collusion investigation between Trump's supporters and Russia. The crazy part is Papadopoulos is the reason Mueller was appointed Special Counsel.

HOW THIS AMATEUR GOT CAUGHT

In February 2016 he was affiliated with the London Centre of International Law Practice. Then he became a shadowy foreign policy presence as Trump marched to the presidency. It was in London Papadopoulos met a Russian described as "the professor" who courted the young man's favor. The Professor offered to provide "dirt" on Hillary Clinton. The professor, Joseph Mifsud, was at the time an adviser to the London Centre of International Law Practice. The young George was easily duped.

Since that time Professor Mifsud has been difficult to find. He is described as having vanished. His bio has been removed from the University of Scotland website. Italian legal authorities can't reach Mifsud who is sought in a case involving financial wrongdoing. He has very few academic publications or qualifications. There are no books of academic expertise. It appears he is a self-styled professor working with the Kremlin. The rumor is Mifsud is close to Russian foreign minister Sergei Lavrov. Mifsud hasn't been seen since

October 2017. He remains the figure who promised Papadopoulos dirt on Hillary Clinton.

If Papadopoulos was an insignificant, low-level employee why is he important? His testimony could implicate Trump insiders in possible Russian collusion. This is one reason the Donald and his supporters are attacking the depth, breadth and scope of the Mueller investigation. Trump's minions argue Mueller's investigation has gone beyond its legal scope.

The press labeled Papadopoulos the John Dean of Trump insiders. It was Dean who testified Richard M. Nixon lied, committed perjury, and covered up the Watergate burglary prompting him to resign. Mueller's investigation has not indicated Trump colluded or covered up anything. The question of the president's lack of judgment persists. Trump's appointees, like Papadopoulos, demonstrate he has not vetted those who support him. Many are just like Papadopoulos. They are rank amateurs without training or qualifications.

The investigation of Russian connection led to criminal charges against former Trump Campaign head Paul Manafort, foreign policy adviser George Papadopoulos and National Security Adviser General Michael Flynn.

Trump's supporters cried "foul." "Why aren't you investigating Hillary Clinton?" This was the cry from the right wing and Fox TV News. Trump is the only president to demand his opponent be jailed. There is no evidence Hillary colluded with the Russians or broke any law.

There is one simple assumption. Why did Putin's minions release her damaging e-mails? It was to help the Trump campaign. They released more than 30,000 e-mails. All of these missives were designed to damage Hillary's candidacy. Trump was elected. Russia helped.

The Papadopoulos scandal is a real one. He was an empty suit working for the Trump campaign. While in London he worked as the director of energy and natural resources, law and security. Or so he said. Rumor has it he was a conduit to American oil interests with intentions to do business with Russia. In mid-March 2016 Professor Mifsud and Papadopoulos established a connection. The idea of allegedly compromising Hillary Clinton's bid for the presidency intrigued Papadopoulos.

Who was Professor Joseph Mifsud? He is a loud, burly man who looks like a Mafia enforcer. He insists he is nothing more than an academic. With his short haircut, jiggling jowls, oversized hand motions and bad suits, he looks like a man who could be working in the Kremlin. He had made it clear he is proud of his high level Moscow connections. Like Papadopoulos, he brags about his qualifications and connections. Mifsud told the London Daily Telegraph he knew nothing about compromising Hillary Clinton e-mails. This so-called academic, who hails from Malta, had his profile removed from the London Centre of International Law Practice's website. That should tell everyone about Mifsud's so-called academic expertise.

THE QUESTION OF PAPADOPOULOS' GUILT

What is Papadopoulos guilty of? At this writing lying to the FBI! What is known is on March 31, 2016, which was the first meeting of the Trump foreign policy advisory group, he informed the Trump campaign he could arrange a meeting between Trump and Putin. The week before the meeting, Trump called Papadopoulos "an excellent guy" and "a good man."

The initial meeting of the Trump foreign policy advisory group was a sorry experience. No one had a clue as to what Trump thought, what he wanted, or how he might proceed in foreign policy. This set the tone for his early presidency. Inconsistency was a continual theme.

At this meeting Papadopoulos stood up, he smiled, he paused, and he said he could arrange a meeting with Putin. There was one sane person in the room. Retired Navy Rear Admiral Charles Kubic said it was not a good idea. He pointed out Russia was under sanctions for their actions in the Ukraine. Despite being told "No" to a meeting, Papadopoulos continued to spin the story. As late as March 15, 2018 he was still telling the press Trump approved of his actions. There is no evidence to back up this claim.

WHAT DID MUELLER'S INVESTIGATION
SHOW ABOUT TRUMP'S FOREIGN POLICY?

The Mueller investigation into Papadopoulos is a significant window into the Trump administration's view of foreign affairs. It demonstrates rogue players can use the U. S. name, the Trump administration and the billionaire acolytes who populate the swamp to delve nefariously into foreign policy.

When the federal indictment against Papadopoulos was released, it centered on false statements and material omissions from his January 27, 2017 FBI interview. The FBI indictment detailed the lengths Papadopoulos went to pursuing information on Clinton that was potentially useful to Trump's presidential campaign. That is not a crime. His crime was lying to the FBI who detailed his every move in London and Italy while meeting with individuals identified as Kremlin insiders. By colluding with individuals close to Russia and providing e-mails the FBI uncovered a disturbing link between an American citizen and Russia's operatives.

A sampling of Papadopoulos's e-mails suggests how he attempted to use information from a foreign power to defeat Hillary Clinton. On April 27, 2016 Papadopoulos e-mailed a high-ranking official in the Trump campaign stating: "Have been receiving a lot of calls over the last months about Putin wanting to host him and the team when the time is right." These e-mails continued. Professor Mifsud also kept in touch. On May 24, 2016 Papadopoulos sent another e-mail: "Russia has been eager to meet Mr. Trump for quite some time and have been reaching out to me to discuss." This was probably a blatant lie. It demonstrates the lengths to which Papadopoulos went to curry favor with Trump campaign officials.

One obvious conclusion from the Papadopoulos investigation is those supporting Trump were eager to collude with the Russians. Anything to get political dirt on Hillary Clinton! As one politico told me: "the gift of dirt on Hillary was an all-consuming passion."

The most damning evidence of Trump's team colluding with Russia came in the meeting attended by Donald J. Trump Jr., Jared Kushner, Paul Manafort and a Russian connected lawyer Natalia Veselnitskaya. This meeting took place after a person described as an intermediary promised Donald Jr. dirt of Hillary. Guess who the intermediary was? None other than George Papadopoulos.

The evidence of collusion comes from the March 31, 2016 campaign consultation in which Papadopoulos said, according to FBI sources: "He would use his Russian contacts to try to set up a deal." When Attorney General Jeff Sessions testified to Mueller's group he said he had no recollection of any contacts with Russia or talks about such future conversations. Sessions was reminded Papadopoulos presented a sworn statement that he discussed some campaign items with Trump and Sessions at the March 31, 2016 meeting. Suddenly Sessions remembered the comment.

WHY DID PAPADOPOULOS TRAVEL TO GREECE?

George Papadopoulos is Greek. It is not surprising he went to Greece as a representative of the Trump administration. That is how he described his mission. Trump knew nothing of it. He was a low level volunteer. He presented himself to the Greek President and Foreign Minister as a senior campaign official. He was personable to get this far on gall and cunning.

He spoke with two Greek reporters about his career, his role in the 2016 campaign and his friendship with his good buddy Donald J. Trump. The article, reported in a Greek newspaper, was ignored until Papadopoulos rolled over for the Mueller team like a dog getting a gourmet biscuit.

The delusional, self-promoting young Greek, told the reporters he was called personally by Trump. They discussed foreign policy on more than one occasion. As Papadopoulos told the Greek reporters of his connection to the Trump campaign, the FBI walked his Chicago neighborhood interviewing friends. The friends said he was a self-promoter, a C student and he knew as much about foreign affairs as Don Rickles did about being subtle.

During his interview with the Greek reporters, Papadopoulos made the claim the future President promised him a "blank check" to select a senior administrative position. In defense of Trump, it appears Papadopoulos had no personal contact with the candidate. He was placed on the foreign affairs advisory board to beef it up. No one listened to him. No one cared about his opinions.

Papadopoulos's duplicity was shown in a text message to a Greek newspaper. He texted: "Everyone knows I helped him get elected now I want to help him with the presidency." Trump called him what he is "a coffee boy."

When he became a person of interest in the federal investigation alleging ties between the Trump campaign and Russia's interference in the presidential election, Papadopoulos was caught attempting to set up a meeting with key Russian politicians and select members of the Trump administration.

The Mueller investigation presented documents to a U. S. court proving Papadopoulos' involvement with Russian officials in violation of federal law. Whether Trump knew about this is unclear. What is clear is amateurs were giving advice to the future president on matters of foreign policy.

Most of Trump's advisers are ass kissers and sycophants. No one was better at it than Papadopoulos.

What is George Papadopoulos' role in the tale of Russian collusion? It is about cooperating with Mueller's investigation. Since July 2, 2017, when he was arrested by the FBI the Chicago native has cooperated with the FBI. On October 5, 2017 Papadopoulos pleaded guilty in the U. S. District Court for the District of Columbia to making false statements to FBI agents related to contacts he had with high level Russian government agents. Because of the plea deal, Papadopoulos was not sentenced. What does this mean? It suggests he has inside information on other Trump officials who colluded with Russian agents to influence the 2016 election.

Some have compared Papadopoulos to John Dean who brought down President Richard M. Nixon with his revelations of Nixon's criminal behavior. That may be an observation that gives Papadopoulos too much credit. Time will tell.

PAPADOPOULOS BECOMES PART OF THE RIGHT WING NUT HOUSE BOOK COTTAGE INDUSTRY IN RUSSIAN COLLUSION AND OTHER DARK TALES OF CONSPIRACY

The cottage industry in books on Trump insiders who colluded with, talked to or somehow wallowed in the mess that is Russian collusion shows signs of being a major publishing event. These books uniformly tell one the deep state is working to take down the Donald. The idea that the FBI, the Justice Department and the State Department is filled with professionals doing their best is to take down the Trump presidency is sheer nonsense. It is about destroying the Special Counsel Robert M. Mueller. The danger is these books present an alternative view of history that is apart from reality. It is a dangerous time in American intellectual thought. Bullies, distort and confuse American history.

As this book was a month from going into production a lawyer, Stephen Roh, prepared for the June 2018 release of The Faking Of Russia-Gate: The Papadopoulos Case is an attempt to cash in on the story of a foreign policy amateur caught in a web of international intrigue.

What does Roh's book contain? The Atlantic's Natasha Bertrand weighed in on the major questions. She claims Mueller was interested in finding out whether the Trump campaign knew in advance Russian planned to hack into the U. S. election and interfere in other ways.

Russia hacked into the Democratic National Committee and would later break into Clinton campaign chairperson John Podesta's inbox. Did Professor Joseph Mifsud know in advance that Russia sought to defeat Hillary Clinton? That is apparently one of Roh's contentions. Who is Stephen Roh? He is a German multimillionaire with alleged ties to the Kremlin.

Here is where things appear to be complicated. Roh hired professor Joseph Mifsud in 2015 as a "business-development consultant." He is Mifsud's "partner and best friend," according to Bertrand in the Atlantic as she observes: "Papadopoulos's wife, Simona Mangiante, worked for Mifsud briefly." It gets even stranger. Roh's wife, Olga Roh, is a Russian fashion designer. She has appeared on the British reality show "Meet The Russians."

Why is Roh writing the book? It appears he arrived in New York and Mueller's investigative team pulled him aside at the airport in October 2017. He said, he was "fished from the passport control" at JFK Airport. He was interrogated for hours by a Mueller team from Mueller investigating what Roh called "Russia-Gate." His book, co-written with Thierry Pastor, alleges that his family was "observed,

195

followed and taped, in every moment and every place in New York" by the FBI. He also charged his family was assigned "special rooms at the hotel."

Roh's book is an interesting one. He claims Professor Joseph Mifsud is a mystery figure "deeply imbedded in the network of Western Intelligence Services." It gets even weirder. The book suggests Papadopoulos is a "western spy." He was sent by the FBI to infiltrate the Trump campaign. He concludes there is an FBI, Justice Department conspiracy to end the Trump presidency.

An interview with Joseph Mifsud is a bonus in Roh's generally well written book. Mifsud claims he didn't tell Papadopoulos anything about Hillary Clinton e-mails. He also intimated the Russian collusion investigation was nothing more than a plot of the U. S. deep state.

Roh's book is in line with other Trump defenders, particularly Roger Stone and Nigel Farage, who daily scream "Fake News" and echo the charge there is a FBI, Mueller, Justice Department and deep state conspiracy to destroy Trump's presidency. Another book along this line is Ted Malloch's The Plot To Destroy Trump: How The Deep State Fabricated The Russia Dossier To Subvert the President. He argues the west, not Russia, is attempting to end Trump's presidency.

"From coffee boy to spy," Papadopoulos's wife, Magiante told Bertrand, "he has been upgraded." What is clear is there is a cottage book industry attempting to explain away Russian influences on the 2016 election. Those influences have been explained, and George Papadopoulos got in over his head. He is paying the price. Now Papadopoulos has Rush Limbaugh defending him. "Well, Papadopoulos was entrapped by three people, including the person who is reputed to have been the spy. And very simply here's the Cliff Notes version of what happened. George Papadopoulos, 24-year-old (wrong age Russ) peripheral member of the Trump foreign policy campaign. He was nothing. He was a nobody, which made him a perfect mark. He was a young man who wanted to go places." This is of course complete horseshit. Read my book Russ, get some facts and get it straight. The tragedy is millions of Americans tune into his program and listen to this drivel. The lack of real history, verifiable facts, research and integrity in writing is not part of the pro-Trump cottage book industry. This is a sad comment on a liberal democracy in decline.

PAPADOPOULOS CREATES FBI OPERATION HURRICANE AND THE ROOTS OF THE SPECIAL COUNSEL

George Papadopoulos is the reason for Robert Mueller being appointed Special Counsel in May to investigate possible collusion between the Trump campaign and Russia in the 2016 presidential election. The genesis of the FBI investigation into the Trump campaign came two days after Papadopoulos bragged to Alexander Downer, an Australian diplomat, that he was a Trump insider setting up a meeting between the erstwhile Republican candidate and Vladimir Putin. Stay tuned.

TEN

CARTER PAGE TESTIFYING ABOUT TRUMP'S FOREIGN POLICY, THE STEELE DOSSIER IS REAL AND THE DEEP STATE IS A TRUMP PLOY ON THE ROAD TO AUTHORITARIAN RULE

"I have had extensive experiences in Russia and with Russian people since the final days of the Soviet era in 1991...."

CARTER PAGE TESTIFYING, HOUSE INTELLIGENCE COMMITTEE TRANSCRIPT.

"I had not heard of Carter Page before it came out in the media."

A PROMINENT WESTERN BUSINESSMAN
WORKING IN THE FORMER SOVIET UNION.

"Trump campaign aide Carter Page may have been a Russian agent, Justice Department believed, according to Nunes Memo."

NEWSWEEK, JANUARY 29, 2018

Carter Page became a front-page story when conservative House members and Fox News accused the FBI and the Mueller Investigation of improperly targeting Page and then securing a FISA warrant. The defense of Page's civil liberties has nothing to do with him. The issue was Donald Trump. His supporters called it "a witch hunt" and Trump's detractors labeled it a legitimate investigation.

The word from the Trump camp was Mueller had to be stopped. Suddenly in the House of Representatives there was concern over First Amendment abuses. It reads like a skit from Saturday Night Live.

In 2017 Page was asked by congressional investigators to turn over seven years of records doing business in Russia. When Fox News profiled him, they stated: "Much of Page's early life is relatively unknown." This is untrue. Page has a long and storied career in Russia. He is an Annapolis graduate. He earned a PhD. He has a lengthy business career. What Fox News suggested is Carter Page was a little guy insignificant to Russian collusion. Mueller and the FBI were picking on him. Again not true.

Page's fingerprints are all over the Russian collusion story. At this point he is guilty of nothing more than egotistical behavior. That is not a crime.

But Fox News did get some of the Page story right. He bragged in a 2013 letter he was an "informal adviser" to the Kremlin. This wasn't true. Russian politicians and businessmen couldn't get him out of Moscow quick enough.

Where does Fox News twist the story? They claim the Steele Dossier was the reason for the FISA warrant. Sean Hannity, after he is

199

through with dinner at Trump Tower or in the White House, rushes back to the Fox TV studio to let everyone know how badly Page is being treated. Hannity quotes Republican freedom caucus members and Trump bootlickers, like Devin Nunes, as they scream the fate of civil liberties are in decline. They should scream as they are the ones attacking traditional civil liberties.

For the House Freedom Caucus Carter Page is a gift. The head Freedom Caucus whacko, Representative Mark Meadows, a Republican from North Carolina and a Trump confidant, said he was preparing an impeachment charge against Deputy Attorney General Rod J. Rosenstein for failing to control FBI excesses. Rosenstein laughed. The idea he was failing to enforce the law was a ludicrous right wing plot. Fortunately, the Freedom Caucus consists of only a few dozen conservative Republicans with little or no influence on the House of Representative. The impeachment document was only one page. Maybe when he attended the University of South Florida, where he graduated from in 1981, they didn't teach political writing. Then again when you are a member of the Sigma Chi Fraternity your interests are elsewhere. After college he started Aunt D's, a small restaurants in Highlands, North Carolina, and he was soon on his way to Washington D. C. Meadows should stick to baking pies and forget about politics. Or perhaps he should learn to write more than a one-page impeachment bill. Saturday Night Live is allegedly calling to make a deal.

A KREMLIN INSIDER SAID OF PAGE: BADLY DRESSED, SMILING FOR THE CAMERA

The initial image Carter Page projected was not a positive one. Page is a bright person who loves the camera. He has done more to hurt Trump's presidency than the **New York Times**, the **Washington Post**, CNN, MSNBC and the Mueller investigation combined. Why? He loves the camera. Make no mistake Carter Page is accomplished, interesting, well educated and a strong Trump supporter. He did not come off well in the Russia interference story. He became all things to all people. The right wing defended him. They concluded there should not have been a FISA warrant. The problem with the House Freedom Caucus is the FBI has had Page under surveillance since

2005. Who he talked to and what he did with the Russians is still a sealed document. Only the Mueller team knows this information. One Kremlin insider said: Page was "badly dressed, bald headed and smiling for the camera." He remains in the American mind an enigma.

As the controversy surrounding alleged Trump administration collusion with Russia was raised during the 2016 presidential election, the speculation burned up the media hot line concerning Carter Page. He emerged, according to **Newsweek**, as a self-described Trump foreign policy adviser. Unbeknownst to Trump, the FBI had a lengthy file on Page. They suspected he might be a Russian agent. The Carter Page story is that of a bumbling amateur. If Inspector Closeau had a brother, he would be Carter Page. In the realm of suave, secret agents, Page looks like a clerk in a 7-11 store. He does have a PHD. He was an honor student in college. **Newsweek** described him as an "alleged spy." His entire life could be viewed as an attempt to garner media fame. He is intelligent. He does have limited foreign policy expertise.

Page is an example of Trump's campaign hiring rank amateurs, wannabes, media clowns and poseurs. With his goofy smile, his ill-fitting suit, his French beret tilted to the side of his head, Page doesn't cut an elegant presence. He did drive a flashy, expensive Mercedes. Why is Page important? He is the Republican poster boy for arguing the FBI abused their power with a FISA warrant. The Republican dominated House Intelligence Committee accused the FBI of violating Page's civil rights. Maybe! Maybe not!

By 2018 Page was the right wing poster boy for protecting American Civil Liberties. This partisan attempt by Republican's loyalists was a sham. Page worked with, and he had coalesced with, Russian's since 2006. None of this was illegal as far as we know. The London press alleged he had a handler. There is no evidence to corroborate this statement. He has not been charged with a crime. He is a pro-Russian apologist whose rights were not respected, Page maintains, and like Trump, he claims he is the victim of a "witch-hunt."

An alleged Republican memo to discredit the Mueller investigation argues Deputy Attorney General Rod Rosenstein approved an FBI application to continue surveillance of Page without evidence. This is untrue. The FBI's concern was that Page was a Trump campaign insider who made numerous trips to Russia. He allegedly talked with many of Putin's aides suspected of hacking the 2016 presidential election.

The House Intelligence Committee Chairman, Devin Nunes, a Republican from California, was not protecting Page's civil liberties by attempting to discredit the Mueller investigation. He was trying to shut down those looking into Trump insiders who were doing business with Russia, attempting to find scurrilous information on Hillary Clinton and profiting from business deals with Kremlin insiders. The sanctimonious defenses of Page's civil liberties are surprising, as Nunes initially told David Corn, he was unfamiliar with Carter Page. Nunes had never heard of him. No one asked how Nunes could provide such a strong defense without knowledge of the charges against Page. Or for that matter who he was and why he was connected to the Trump campaign. The implication is clear. Nunes was operating on orders from President Trump or one of his subordinates. Carter Page is a pawn in a larger game.

David Corn, an investigative reporter for **Mother Jones**, interviewed Nunes. "When I asked Nunes whether he agreed with Trump's recent tweet that the 'Russia story' was 'fake news' cooked up by Democrats, he wouldn't provide a straight answer," Corn wrote. The only conclusion is Trump hadn't told Nunes what to say and what to do.

He was after Rod Rosenstein and Robert S. Mueller III. Page was the conduit to telling the world there was no collusion from Trump's camp. This argument changed after Mueller indicted five Trump insiders. Now Nunes argues the Mueller probe should conclude.

House Republican's allege President Barack Obama wiretapped Trump. They also claim former FBI Director James Comey lied about his conversations with Trump. His supporters charge the FBI chief leaked classified information. None of this has been proven. The Trump supporters say it is fact. It isn't.

Carter Page is an inept foreign policy adviser who is a walking cartoon. No one found him credible. No one found him knowledgeable. How did this nebbish get into the middle of the

Russian collusion story? It is a long and convoluted tale. It is one suggesting our government is in a rapid democratic decline.

As the Trump administration's attempts to discredit the Mueller investigation evolved, there was a demand for Rod Rosenstein to be fired. As this book was in its final stages, he was hanging on. Trump has already prompted Deputy FBI Chief, Andrew G. McCabe to retire with his attack on the FBI. After McCabe took sick leave and prepared to retire on March 31, 2018, Attorney General Jeff Sessions fired McCabe twenty-six hours before his pension was guaranteed. Then Trump attacked the FBI, the State Department and the Justice Department. The Justice Department Inspector General concluded McCabe lied while under oath. **Newsweek** speculated on the question of prosecuting McCabe. Hans von Spavkovsky wrote of McCabe: "Will he be prosecuted as Flynn was? It seems as if the FBI and the Justice Department have no choice-unless they believe their colleagues are somehow above the law."

The President tweeted: "The Fake News is beside themselves that McCabe was caught, called out and fired." Trump finished this Tweet calling out James Comey.

When Trump tweeted that McCabe's wife was "a loser" it was because she lost a campaign for state office. He showed he was an unrequited bully. Trump's minions cheer this attempt to prove the "deep state." They continually complain, "key FBI officials are corrupt." He charges daily they are attempting to bring him down.

Page, an oil and gas industry consultant and former investment banker, was a Trump foreign policy adviser caught in a web of intrigue. The irony is he was never brought into the campaign. He neither met nor talked to Trump. He was a mysterious figure. He loved the intrigue. He loved the press. He was an entitled wanker. He created a media persona. How did Page emerge?

THE EMERGENCE OF CARTER PAGE

In March 2016, during an interview with the **Washington Post's** editorial board, Trump revealed a short list of foreign policy advisers. Trump labeled them "excellent people." It was a hastily assembled collection of non-entities with ego driven agendas. The list didn't include a single trained foreign policy scholar. But, as Trump said, he was a different type of candidate. One of the names he mentioned was "Carter Page PHD." The **Washington Post** editorial board sat in stunned silence. They had never heard of him. Another was George Papadopoulos. Who? That was the reaction from the newspaper. Both men garnered excessive press coverage. Both men were rank amateurs. Both men extended the facts, their influence and their expertise beyond limits of credibility. They were unknown nebbish personalities. Many Trump insiders labeled them "amateur fools."

WHY IS CARTER PAGE A MYSTERIOUS FIGURE?

Page was wiretapped by The FBI. Congressional investigators interrogated him over his alleged Russian connections. He said he was an original adviser to the Trump campaign. Few people knew he had never met the president or talked to Trump. The prescient nature Page said he possessed was a figment of his imagination. He loves the limelight. He never stops talking. Despite his education, his financial accomplishments, and his fleeting link to the Trump administration, he remains a mystery.

Like Anthony Scaramucci and George Papadopoulos, Carter Page is a Trump adviser with minimal expertise. He never met a camera he didn't like. Fortunately, nothing of substance came from his pea brain. When he was called before the House Intelligence Committee, he testified about Trump campaign officials who had contacts with Russian representatives. He glowed when a reporter asked him about his campaign role. He said it was confidential. He looked like a giant stork caught in the glow of the media.

Page might have escaped press attention had it not been for the Steele Dossier. When Christopher Steele, a British former MI6 agent, put together a file on American's who colluded with Russia, he identified Page. Steele said at a meeting with a senior Russian government official, Arkady Dvorkovich, in August 2016, he worked with the Kremlin to elect Trump. After this trip, Steele continued, he said Page e-mailed Trump's closest campaign adviser's sensitive Russian government information on Hillary Clinton. Page believed there was the possibility of dark and dirty secrets on Democratic candidate Hillary Clinton. The veracity of this information is murky.

204

When the Steele Dossier surfaced, conservatives attacked it rather than attempting to verify the material. The company conducting the research, Fusion GPS, was subject to legal harassment. Congressional skepticism and personal attacks on the founders, Glenn Simpson and Peter Fritsch, was the Republican Party attempt to cast doubt on the Steele Dossier. It is estimated seventy percent of the material is accurate.

The Steele Dossier wouldn't go away. There was damaging material. The **Wall Street Journal** led the charge the Steele Dossier was not credible. Breitbart, Fox TV News and its Trump sound a like commentator Sean Hannity, complained about "fake news." When the attacks failed to disprove the Steele Dossier, Trump's supporters went after the veracity of Mueller's investigation. There were too many corroborated cases of political malfeasance to ignore the documents.

The House Intelligence Committee issued a report, with only the Republican majority participating; they said there was no collusion from Trump. They failed to mention the indictment of five inner circle Trump supporters. House Republicans were cleaning up the mess Trump's amateurs made during his first year in the Oval Office. Many days after the House Intelligence Committee concluded its hearings, the House Permanent Select Committee on Intelligence ranking member, Devin Nunes, went to the White House to talk to the president about their investigation. Nunes kept Trump abreast of their findings. By mid-March 2018 he said: "There is no one left to indict." He demanded Mueller's investigation end. This took place as the major conservative Trump spewing newspaper, **The Wall Street Journal**, acting like a lackey for the president, charged Fusion GPS was out to destroy Trump. **The Wall Street Journal** scoffed at the notion the Kremlin supported Trump's election.

Glenn Simpson fought the **Wall Street Journal** charges. He said Fusion's charges were credible. The Fusion founder stated he had America's best interests at heart. He worried Donald Trump was attempting to collude with "a notoriously corrupt police state." That may seem like a harsh judgment on Simpson's part. The reason is the attack on the Steele Dossier, whether or not it is completely credible is a moot point. It has an inkling of truth. Simpson took exception to the attacks on Fusion's research. The operative question is: "Does the Steele Dossier provide information on the Trump campaign colluding with Russia?" It does! Otherwise the inner circle indictments would not have occurred.

WHERE DOES THE STEELE DOSSIER FIT
INTO THE RUSSIAN COLLUSION STORY?

When the Steele Dossier was released in early 2017, it appeared to be a blockbuster document. The Democrats claimed it hinted Trump was involved in collusion with the Kremlin to garner the presidency. The Republican's countered with the charge it was opposition research. They said it was filled with innuendo and facts that could not be verified.

More than a year after the Steele Dossier was released, there was still no common agreement on whether it was fact or fiction. But over time solid facts emerged in the it. The **Wall Street Journal** believed the thirty-five-page document "fit the Kremlin playbook." The **Journal** theorized the Steele Dossier was part of a larger plan to disrupt American politics. There were three things the **Journal** called into question. First, Steele did not travel to Russia. He depended upon intermediaries for much of his information. This calls into question, the **Journal** theorized, the entire dossier. Second, the newspaper claimed Russian intelligence used and manipulated Steele. Third, the Kremlin hacked into the Democratic National Committee. They realized Steele was putting together a damaging file on Trump. Consequently, they fed false information into the dossier making it lack credibility.

Those who believed the Steele Dossier fit into the Russian collusion story have a different view. When BuzzFeed published the dossier, they shared potentially damaging political information that all American's had the right to read. The mainstream media disagreed. They refused to publish the Steele Dossier. NBC's Chuck Todd said: "You just published 'fake news," President Trump continued. "BuzzFeed is a failing pile of garbage."

Through the Steele Dossier the Mueller investigation uncovered nuggets of truth. The Russian investigation is not a sideshow. It is a serious investigation of criminal behavior as shown by five indicted

Trumpite's with three of them pleading guilty to felonies. Another defendant, Paul Manafort, wrote an op-ed piece defending his actions in spite of court sanctions against this behavior. He now wears two ankle bracelets. He is charged with felonies in Washington D. C. and Virginia. He faces trials in both judicial districts. The attacks on the Steele Dossier display the arrogance, the petulance and the lack of respect for the law from some of Trump's supporters.

Then in June 2018 Mueller accused Manafort of violating the conditions of his bail. The Special Counsel asked for his bail to be revoked. Former United States Attorney and University of California law professor, Harry Litman, told **Newsweek** that Manafort appeared to be headed for jail for alleged witness tampering. "This is the stupidest thing that a defendant can do, this sort of witness tampering," Litman concluded.

When the FBI investigated they discovered that Manafort attempted to contact witnesses by phone and via WhatsApp, an encrypted messaging program, to induce them to change their testimony.

IF THE STEELE DOSSIER IS REAL: HERE IS WHY

The FBI verified some of the dossier. They used it to obtain two FISA warrants. The BBC claimed the dossier was "a roadmap to the FBI investigation." The BBC reported FBI Director James Comey testified to Congress the Steele Dossier had grains of truth.

The FISA warrant for surveillance on Carter Page is one where the FBI went beyond its mandate, according to the Trump administration, and members of the House Intelligence Committee. Devin Nunes, a Trump ally and defender, is behind a memo that alleges the Justice Department and the FBI treated the president unfairly. They used Carter Page to cast aspersions on the president. The House Intelligence committee concluded in late April 2018 that The Trump campaign used poor judgment in dealing with the Russians. They officially cleared Trump in the probe.

The Republican contention is the Foreign Intelligence Surveillance Court was unduly influenced by false information in the Steele Dossier, and they leaked material on Carter Page damaging his reputation. The FBI cited forty pieces of evidence in its Carter Page

FISA application. Only one of the forty evidentiary pieces was from the Steele Dossier. The FBI believed Page allegedly was working for Russia as early as 2013. The Steele Dossier was not unfair to Trump. Page had been on their radar for years. In June 2013 the FBI interviewed Page. He admitted to providing documents to Victor Podobnyy whom the FBI identified as a Russian spy.

Page seemed proud American intelligence followed his every move. This dunce couldn't get enough attention. Even though that interest might land him in jail. So far he is guilty of nothing more than guile.

When he testified before the House Intelligence Committee, Page stated he had a brief interaction with Russian Deputy Prime Minister Arkady Dvorkovich in July 2016. This activity placed Page again on the FBI radar. They requested a FISA warrant. They had plenty of evidence. It had nothing to do with Trump. It was alleged Page and the Russians wanted Trump as president. That was not against the law. That is unless Page used Russian information to influence the election.

Whether or not the Steele Dossier is credible remains a debatable question. There are some verifiable facts in the document. Both the Democratic and Republican National committees were hacked. There was a voluminous Trump file in the Kremlin, and Dmitry Peskov, Putin's press secretary, maintained it. There were rumors of fiscally compromising material. The problem was a lack of verification. This made the Steele Dossier a starting point for investigating Russian collusion. The House Intelligence Committee held closed-door sessions with Glenn Simpson to verify what they could about the documents veracity.

THE HOUSE INTELLIGENCE COMMITTEE
CLOSED SESSION WITH GLENN SIMPSON

On a brisk Fall day in 2017 Glenn Simpson entered the classified space known as SCIF to testify behind closed doors to the House Intelligence Committee. The SCIF is a Sensitive Compartmental Information Facility. The person testifying sits behind a screen and cell phones and other devices are confiscated. A former federal prosecutor, Republican Representative Trey Gowdy of South

Carolina began asking Simpson the nature of his business. He replied: "It's a commercial research firm." Simpson explained how his firm compiled the Steele Dossier. He was outraged at the criticism of his intelligence gathering. Simpson was a former investigative reporter with the **Wall Street Journal**. He defended his credentials. He believed he was the subject of a witch-hunt and he complained of First Amendment abuses.

He told the House Committee in the fall of 2015 the **Washington Free Beacon**, a privately owned for profit conservative news website, hired Simpson's company, Fusion GPS, to conduct lengthy research on Donald J. Trump. The early results indicated Trump had ties to Russian financiers. Simpson's testimony frightened House investigators.

Glenn Simpson: "As we've got deeper and deeper into understanding, you know, Donald Trump's business career and his history, it gradually reached a point where it seemed like most of the people around Trump had a connection to Russian organized crime or Russia in one way or another."

House members were nervous and flabbergasted. They couldn't believe Simpson's testimony. There was no smoking gun linking Trump to anything criminal. There were, however, too many Russian connections to ignore.

Who was driving the anti-Trump Steele Dossier? Paul Singer, a billionaire, funded the payments for the Steele Dossier that is until March 2016 when he realized Trump might be the 45th president. He ended his financial support. It was at this point that Simpson reached out to Hillary Clinton and the Democratic National Committee for financing to keep the Steele Dossier going. Marc Elias, the Clinton campaign's general counsel, who was a partner at Perkins Cole a Seattle law firm, began funding the continued work on the Steele Dossier.

When was the Steele Dossier compiled? After a great deal of research the first report for what would become the Steele Dossier was finished on June 20, 2016 and when it arrived at Fusion GPS's offices it was an explosive document. The document alleged Trump consorted with prostitutes while in Moscow. Proof for this allegation didn't exist. The dossier claimed Kremlin insiders worked against

Hillary Clinton with the promise that there would be no mention of Russian interference in the Ukraine and sanctions would be weakened or left off the table. Proof! No one knows.

Trump fought back. Press Secretary Sarah Huckabee Sanders said: "The Democrat linked firm, Fusion GPS, actually took money from the Russian government while it created the phony dossier that's been the basis for all the Russia scandal fake news." In early January 2018 Trump doubled down attacking the Steele Dossier, the Clinton campaign and the media for what he termed "fake news."

Donald J. Trump: "Now there has been collusion between Hillary Clinton, the DNC, and the Russians. Unfortunately, you people don't cover that very much. But the only collusion is between Hillary and the Russians, and the DNC and the Russians."

Whom did this scenario frighten? It was Christopher Steele who told anyone who would listen Trump was a danger to American democracy. He claimed Russian meddling was altering the political system. This prompted Steele to share his findings with the FBI. Arizona Republican Senator John McCain telling people he leaked the Steele Dossier. He didn't. But Senator McCain was frightened by it. It's veracity! No one knew!

Donald J. Trump wasn't shy about the Steele Dossier. He tweeted: "fake news-a total political witch hunt." Steve Bannon told the president this was brilliant. Deny! Detract! Destroy the opposition. These were Trump's goals as he intensified the continued mystery over the Steele Dossier.

THE CONTINUED MYSTERY OVER THE STEELE DOSSIER

The Steele Dossier is difficult to verify. There are elements of truth to it. When Buzzfeed became the first news source to publish the thirty five-page document online, there was a media uproar. There was no smoking gun concerning President Trump colluding with Russia. Early on there was no sign of impeachable offenses. Why was there so much concern over and attention paid to the Steele Dossier?

The reason is a simple one. Many of those close to the Trump presidential campaign met with Russian diplomats, politicians and business people. Is this illegal? No! But the possibility of collusion is rampant. It is illegal if a member of the Trump presidential team was able to obtain information from a foreign government, i. e. Russia that could be used to influence the 2016 election. Yes! That has not been proven.

The appointment of Special Counsel Robert Mueller was a byproduct of the Steele Dossier. The dossier, compiled by Christopher Steele a former British MI6 intelligence officer, pointed to possible collusion between Trump insiders and the Russians.

In London, Christopher Steele operates a private intelligence organization for corporate interests. This for profit company sniffs around the political arena. His company, Orbis Business Intelligence Ltd., was hired by the Republican Party and later by the Democratic National Committee to gather compromising material useful in the U. S. 2016 presidential election. That material centered in Russia. This is where Steele had been an MI6 spy. He was now a private businessman in the intelligence-gathering field. His office in London is sparsely furnished and not impressive. There are Russian dolls and other souvenirs from Moscow. For a price he will put together a file on any subject. This led to the thirty-five page Steele Dossier. This was a document detrimental to Trump's campaign. It contained non-substantiated allegations. These charges became fodder for the press. It eventually helped to create the Special Prosecutor. Robert M. Mueller III. Russian collusion with the Trump campaign was not solely due to the Steele Dossier. But the document was a contributing factor.

What was Steele's assignment? He was asked to uncover the Kremlin's dark and dirty secrets about Donald J. Trump. Steele's findings were sensational. The problem was verification. Fact or fiction? No one knew. The findings were outrageous. Trump was posited as the Kremlin's candidate. There was no proof. He was said to be a friend of Vladimir Putin. Arizona Republican Senator John McCain weighed in calling Putin "a murderer and a thug."

THE STEELE DOSSIER CONFUSES
CLAIMS OF RUSSIAN COLLUSION

Former intelligence officials urged caution when reading the document. Why then the concern with the Steele Dossier? The reason is the U. S's top intelligence official's briefed candidates

Hillary Clinton and Donald Trump a week prior to the election. There was no agreement concerning the document's findings. There were select elements of truth in the Steele Dossier. Some observers disputed all parts of it. There was no common agreement except from London where the Steele Dossier was viewed as accurate. The English also argued Steele was a British patriot attempting to educate the FBI on the dangers of Russian interference. Former MI6 agents took a dim view of the manner as conservative American political activists crucified the Steele Dossier.

One analyst, former Moscow **Los Angeles Times** correspondent, Robert Gillette, said the U. S. Director of Intelligence concluded Vladimir Putin and Russian cyber hackers conducted a campaign to elect Trump. A concerted Russian hacking team went after Clinton posting fake news, purchasing derogatory Facebook ads and releasing private e-mails making her look like the captive of Wall Street. The media and the Republican Party attacked the Steele Dossier. It was all about protecting President Trump.

Newsweek published thirteen things that didn't make sense about the Steele Dossier. Trump called the document "fake news." Trump doubled down on the intelligence community charging them with hostility to his administration. He continues to attack what he labels as an out of step and out of date intelligence community.

TRUMP'S SUPPORTERS: USING THE DEEP STATE
TO CONFUSE THE MUELLER INVESTIGATION

President Trump and Steve Bannon have made charges the deep state exists. They claim it resides in the FBI, the CIA, the State Department and the Justice Department. Trump argues there are also hundreds of unseen federal employees making up a pool of specialists dedicated to destroying his presidency. Trump said the deep state is "an entrenched bureaucracy." At the conclusion of his first year in office, Trump remarked the Department of Justice was the deep state. Why? Because Attorney General Jeff Sessions hadn't prosecuted Hilary Clinton's longtime aide Huma Abedin for her handling of Clinton's classified and sensitive e-mails. Trump supporters charged Abedin covered up Clinton's crimes. They scream they both should be jailed. Why did the president level this charge? How does it support his conspiratorial notion of Abedin's alleged criminal activity? Why does Trump want Abedin prosecuted? There are no answers to these questions. Clinton and Abedin are guilty of being Trump critics and liberal Democrats.

The president believes Abedin deleted e-mails sent to Hillary Clinton when she worked as an aide to the Secretary of State and later when Clinton was a presidential candidate. The Justice Department investigated. They found no evidence of criminal wrongdoing. Trump's supporters said Abedin's family had connections to the radical Muslim Brotherhood. This turned out to be an outrageous claim.

Trump and his minions scream the deep state is attacking his presidency. **The Nation** weighed in with an examination of this issue. Greg Grandin wrote: "The deep state apparently has Trump in its sights," at least according to former NSA intelligence analyst John Schindler, who tweeted "Donald Trump will die in jail" to a friend in 'the intelligence community'. **The Nation** pointed out the term the deep state is "used to suggest dishonorable individuals are subverting the virtuous state." **The Nation** concluded there is not a deep state.

The liberal newsmagazine argued this political debate bordered on the ridiculous. Trump has fought back. He is systematically decimating the work force in the Department of State. He seldom talks to high-level employees. He views some state officials as the enemy. The idea that elite employees control content in the State Department prompts Trump to not read or use their reports. The conspiratorial suspicion that goes with his belief in the deep state isolates Trump's Cabinet from civil service employees and their expertise. The key information necessary to good government is not digested by the Trump administration.

There is a battle between Trump and the bureaucracy. This is one of many reasons for the dysfunction and fragmentation of American government. Trump is not backing down on the deep state. He sees the geeky analysts, the career professionals and the nonpartisan agencies, like the Congressional Budget Office, as the enemy.

Why would Trump target the CBO? They disagreed with the president's conclusions, assessments, methods and means of replacing Obamacare. He was incensed. The Trumpites complained.

They found an ally in former House Speaker Newt Gingrich. He remarked to **Media Matters**: "Here's the Congressional Budget Office as part of the deep state doing a hit job on the Senate Republicans." The stupidity of Gingrich's statement is beyond reason. The head of the CBO, Keith Hall, is a conservative Republican who was the Health and Human Services Secretary. Tom Price, helped him secure the job. He is a staunch Trump conservative. But, unlike most Trumpites, Hall follows the constitutional mandate.

By criticizing every institution of government, Trump is slowly destroying the fabric of American democracy. The president believes Robert Mueller is at the top of the "deep state conspiracy." Sean Hannity said the deep state conspiracy is "a clear and present danger to this country and to you." The chilling thought of Trump and Hannity combining to attack an integrity based Special Prosecutor highlights the fragile nature of our democracy.

The notion of Hannity questioning anyone's integrity is a farce. There is no way for him to sink any deeper into the ethical quagmire that his show represents. Hannity's view of Trump and his presidential actions is a perversion of fair and balanced. He is a Trump apologist twisting facts into an innocuous reality show. The tragedy is Fox TV News sells it as hard facts. The Trumpites wallow in its intellectual morass.

THE STEELE DOSSIER AND PAGE: LINKED TOGETHER

The Steele Dossier and Carter Page are linked together. In 2017 the Special Counsel investigation established links between Trump associates, i. e. Page and Russian insiders. One of those officials was Page. The Mueller team investigated whether Russian officials interfered in the presidential election. The end result helped Trump to enter the Oval Office.

On April 18, 2018 the Mueller investigation uncovered an alleged trip by Trump attorney Michael Cohen to clean up some of the mess Carter Page caused meeting with Russian operatives. Sonam Sheth, writing in the **Stamford Advocate**, observed of the Steele Dossier: "Cohen's visit to Prague was made to 'clean up the mess' resulting from the revelations about Page's Moscow trip and Manafort...." This meant that Page, like Papadopoulos, caused Trump's campaign more harm than anyone associated with the campaign.

Who said he was a Trump team member? He was named in the Steele Dossier. According to the Steele Dossier, the real purpose of Page's trip to Moscow was to meet with Kremlin officials. The Steele Dossier said meetings with Igor Sechin, a former spy who had close connections to Putin, was planned. This hinted at espionage. There is no evidence Carter Page entered into espionage. There is no evidence he has breached the law.

The meeting with Sechin tells one a great deal about Page's search for fame. Sechin has been at the center of Russian espionage for more than three decades. He is one of Putin's closest advisers. He began his career in the KGB. When Putin was elected president, Sechin became his chief deputy. He was promoted to Executive Secretary of the Russian government oil company Rosneft.

The Steele Dossier charged Page met in a secret meeting with Sechin. Steele didn't provide information on what took place. The alleged rumor it was probably about lifting or reducing sanctions.

Michael Isikoff and David Corn: "Page and Sechin supposedly discussed a possible deal about the lifting of sanctions under a Trump presidency. It was provocative and possibly checkable information that could well be evidence of collusion between the GOP candidate's campaign and the Kremlin." (p. 223)

Who was Page dealing with? Why was the Special Prosecutor interested? Sechin was banned from the U. S. for spy activity. The E. U. sanctioned Rosneft for improper business activity. Sechin and Rosneft were viewed as economic criminals with political connections. They talked at length with Page. That is not a crime. It is suspicious behavior.

In April 2017 **Newsweek's** Mirren Gidda's article "Who is Carter Page And Why Is The FBI Surveilling Him?" claimed Page was the only American the FBI was surveilling for connections to the Russian energy sector. The operative question was: "Why?" **Newsweek** pointed out Page was an elusive and mysterious figure. There was little credible information on him. Who was Carter Page?

WHO IS CARTER PAGE?

When someone asks: "Who is Carter Page?" The answer is invariably: "Who?" Donald Trump said he was an individual who advised him on foreign policy during the early days of the 2016 campaign. Page founded the Global Energy Capital Group. It is a New York investment fund. It is a consulting firm specializing in Russian and Central Asian oil and gas enterprises. He is the only member of Global Energy Capital.

When you walk into Global Energy Capital the office reeks of bad taste and not enough money coming through the door. Page's office is around the corner from Trump Tower. Page told the **New York Times**: "I have frequently dined in Trump Grill, had lunch in Trump Café, had coffee meetings in the Starbuck's at Trump Tower, attended events and spent many hours in campaign headquarters on the fifth floor last year." Page maintains he knew little, if anything, about Russian interference in American politics. Most people believe Page knows very little about intelligent life on planet earth.

The Global Energy Capital offices are a joke. Page shares space with a wedding band that also plays bar mitzvahs. The National Shingles Foundation is also a tenant near Page's firm. It is a strange office with bad taste. A painting of an Orchid is the extent of the office visuals. Maybe his parsimonious attitude is due to his military training.

After he graduated from the United States Naval Academy in 1993, he was in the top ten percent of his class. He caught the attention of a number of important military people for an academic paper he wrote analyzing historical tensions between the President and Congress over questions of national defense. This paper helped him establish credentials in foreign policy.

While a Senior at the Naval Academy, he worked as a researcher for the House Armed Services Committee. He was named a Trident scholar. This is a program for postgraduate education. Page used this program to study in London and Moscow. Then he spent five years in the navy. During his navy days he was flashy. He drove a black Mercedes. He served on loan as a Marine intelligence officer in the Sahara. His friend from the Naval Academy, Richard Guerin, described him as academic. He was! Page received a fellowship from the Council on Foreign Relations. He also had a grant for a master's from Georgetown. His MA in National Security Studies began his interest in spy craft and espionage.

He was obsessed with Russia and the former Soviet Union. It was an academic infatuation. He studied for a time in 1991 as a midshipman in Moscow. He also worked in Russia for three years. He knows Putin's Russia in a business sense. Not many foreign citizens have the inside access that Page did to come to Moscow for business reasons.

While studying at the Naval Academy, Page read deeply about the careers of Secretary of State Dean Acheson and Averill Harriman. They operated in the cloak and dagger Cold War atmosphere with Russia. Page romanticized the Cold War. Rather than studying it, he envisioned himself as the new James Bond. Page saw himself as operating discreetly behind the scenes. He envisioned a place in history for his sage advice. When I contacted his professors they didn't remember him.

His Russian connections began in 1998 when he worked for the Eurasia Group, a strategy-consulting firm. He was not a top-level employee. The Eurasia Group founder, Ian Bremmer, said Page was his "most wackadoodle alumnus." All Page did was talk about his love for Russia. Bremmer sent him packing.

Page left the Navy after completing a MA degree in National Security Studies at Georgetown University. In 2001 he earned an MBA from New York University. He began work on Wall Street as an energy consultant for Merrill Lynch. They sent him to Moscow. It was while working in Russia that Page established a relationship with the Russian firm, Gazprom, whom he advised on transactions in the oil and gas fields near Sakhalin, a remote island on Russia's Pacific Coast. Soon Page purchased large numbers of Gazprom shares. He reportedly made a lot of money.

In 2008, when he founded his investment equity firm, Global Energy Capital LLC, he made a great deal of money. His partner, a former Gazprom manager, Sergei Yatsenko, had contacts in Russian with the business and espionage community. There is no evidence Page or Yatsenko broke the law. There is evidence they loved the business and political end of Moscow. They also praised Vladimir

Putin's leadership. While Obama was president Page was a virulent critic. In a blog post for **Global Policy**, an online journal, Page said Putin wasn't to blame for the 2014 Ukraine conflict. It was Obama. He also opposed U. S. sanctions against Russia. He accused the Obama administration of starting "the crisis in the first place."

Page has an eye for the spotlight. He talks incessantly of being in the company of Trump. No one knew he has never met nor talked with Trump. It was his PHD that brought him into the Trump camp. Even the PHD had a clouded countenance.

He earned a PhD from the University of London's Oriental and African Studies Department. He failed his PHD exam twice. He argued it was due to an inherent anti-Russian bias. It certainly wasn't due to his lack of knowledge. Or was it? When University of London PHD examiners, Peter Duncan and Gregory Andrusz, read Page's doctoral dissertation, they tested him in a face-to-face interview. They found his doctoral dissertation "trite." They told the **London Guardian** it was not easy to read. They used the word "tedious" to describe Page's writing. One wonders if this was a description of his personality. They said Page knew "next to nothing" about the social sciences. Page responded. He talked at length in an interview claiming bias against him. The University of London faculty said he was attempting to appear "well informed." He failed to do so. They failed him. In November 2010, he resubmitted the doctoral dissertation and Andrusz said he made "substantial improvements." It wasn't enough. They failed him once again. In November 2011 on his third exam Page was awarded a PHD. He changed advisers for the third exam. He passed. Should he have passed? Who knows! It is unprecedented to take a third PhD exam but the London educational system is liberal.

His new doctoral dissertation adviser, Professor Shirin Akiner, is a right wing Kremlin apologist who fails to analyze human rights abuses in her scholarly work. Her reputation is at best shoddy. She is a seventy five year old scholar who is described in the press as "a propagandist." How effective was her support for Page? Not very effective! Page has tried without success to find a publisher for his doctoral dissertation. Why? It is a confusing piece of work. It adds little, if anything, to scholarship on the energy industry in Central

Asia. For Trump this didn't matter. He described Page as a quality guy and a good man.

Page's road inside the Trump campaign began when Ed Cox, the chairman of New York's Republican Party, recommended him as a foreign policy adviser. The Trump campaign was aware of his Russian connections. Corey Lewandowski and Sam Clovis met with Page. They approved his entre into Trump's inner circle.

In March 2016 Page joined the Trump campaign team as a foreign policy adviser. Trump said he was "Carter Page PhD." What this meant remains a mystery. Trump met with the **Washington Post** to announce his foreign policy team. He read off five advisers. The second name was Carter Page PHD.

THE FBI INVESTIGATES PAGE'S RUSSIAN ROLE

In July 2016 the FBI obtained a warrant to monitor Page's electronic communication. He had too many visits to Moscow and too many Russian discussions with Trump's inner circle. In time, he would spend more than twenty hours before the House and Senate Select Intelligence Committees, as well as an appearance before Mueller's investigators.

How does Page differ from others in the center of the Russian investigation on interference in the 2016 election? He can't shut up. He loves to talk to reporters. He has not hired a lawyer. Why would he? He knows everything. He is waging his war for transparency. He has told many reporters about his brilliance.

With his head shaved, his eyes bugging out and his suit looking like it came off a Goodwill sale rack, Page is not the typical Trump insider. He is a celebrity wanna be. He works out at Anderson Cooper's gym and one day said: "Hi Anderson." Cooper didn't know him. He had never heard of him. He writes letters to the U. S. Justice Department offering his theories and various ideas on diplomacy. No one answers his letters. These missives boggle the mind of those reading his insipid letters.

What did the FBI find out about Page? They analyzed the large number of academic conferences, the papers Page wrote and the people he met with in his quest to know everything about Russia.

The background to Page's ties to Russian intelligence, according to FBI files, began in 2013. Page met with a Russian intelligence operative, Sergey Kislyak, who identified himself as a United Nations diplomat. This Russian diplomat allegedly tried to recruit Page as a spy. The Russian operative decided against recruiting Page. The FBI tape revealed the Russian agent remarked Page was "an idiot."

The meeting with Kislyak is a suspicious one. The long time Russian ambassador to the United Nations was interested in improving Russian-American relations. Kislyak was interested in Page's oil and gas expertise. Page passed him articles from magazines. Kislyak wondered why? He could buy these magazines on any American newsstand. Page's behavior alerted those interested in Russian collusion. The FBI stepped in and monitored the Page-Kislyak meetings. An FBI file was available. The House Intelligence Committee failed to consult this information.

THE SENATE JUDICIARY COMMITTEE
AND PAGE'S TESTIMONY

The Senate Judiciary Committee, one of three Congressional panels examining Russia's involvement in the 2016 presidential election, in late November 2017, sent a letter to Carter Page, asking for documents. He testified before the Senate Select Intelligence Committee after the Judiciary Committee made this request. What was going on? Senator Dianne Feinstein, the California Democrat, pointed out the Judiciary Committee was interested in contacts with Russia and discussions about the election.

Carter Page responded: "I'll be happy to help with this latest tranche of irrelevant Witch Hunt information." This nasty remark didn't hide Page's concern that members of Trump campaign foreign policy team were under scrutiny. What should have concerned Senator Feinstein and the Judiciary Committee was Page's truculent arrogance and unreasonable attitude. "Tranche," does Page even know the meaning of the word?

How did this Russian brouhaha begin? It is the result of a speech Page made in Moscow in early July 2016. This speech was critical of American foreign policy. In an interview with **USA Today**, Page said he was a Trump campaign National Security Adviser given permission to travel to Moscow. Once there he delivered a blistering attack on American sanctions against Russia. Corey Lewandowski, Trump's campaign manager, said he was not given the campaign's blessing. Page said he was. Is anyone in charge?

At the prestigious New Economic School in Moscow, Page delivered the keynote address to recent graduates. This is an honor accorded to top academics. How did Page do in this speech? He made a fool of himself. His speech was filled with misinformation, hyperbole and statistical examples bearing little resemblance to reality. The flummoxed audience sat in disbelief as this theoretical PHD failed to make sense. It was a low moment in Russian intellectual history. The Trump campaign immediately said Page was "an informal adviser."

The Russian media presented a much different picture. They described him in a fancy brochure stating Page was "a celebrated American economist." The London press accurately portrayed Page. Shaun Walker, writing in the **Guardian**, said Page was "really weird." What is strange is a select few in the Trump camp described Page as their most important Russian expert. He didn't speak fluent Russian. He didn't have deep knowledge of the country. His grasp of the broader scope of Russia, according to Kislyak and others, lacked scholarly recognition.

So far Page is guilty of nothing more than arrogance, ineptitude and an unwillingness to accept Senate and House oversight. The truth is as yet unverified.

The July trip to Moscow remains a mystery. In a five-day trip to Moscow, Page delivered a speech at the New Economic School, and he was fired from the Trump team. The FBI file quoted a high level Russian source that allegedly labeled Page "an idiot." This is unfair. His zest for fame and fortune make him overly zealous. But as Professor Andrusz said, Page was the only PHD candidate who failed twice in his career in over forty years. Page is certainly not "an idiot." He is a smart man with an eye for the media. He has never met a camera or a microphone he didn't love.

PAGE BEFORE THE HOUSE INTELLIGENCE COMMITTEE: SOMEONE HAD INTELLIGENCE, WAS IT PAGE? NO!

When Page testified before the House Intelligence Committee on November 2, 2017, he said Trump campaign officials approved the July 2016 Russia trip. Page said the approval for his trip came from J. D. Gordon. This wasn't true. Who was J. D. Gordon? He was Trump's National Security Adviser at the Republican National Convention. It appears Gordon's alleged role was to guarantee to the Kremlin that candidate Trump would oppose arming the Ukrainian government. Page allegedly talked with Kremlin insiders. He informed them that if Trump became president there would be a rapprochement. The Russian insiders translated that as a lessening of sanctions.

Friendly Russian-American relations, Gordon may have believed, could be fostered by Page's trip. Isikoff and Corn's **Russian Roulette** describes Gordon as "Page's handler." (p. 158)

Long before he testified to the House Intelligence Committee, Page attempted to influence the campaign. In May, 2016 he sent a letter to Gordon demanding high-level campaign access. He also observed Trump should visit Moscow to, as Page intimated, intensify the Russian issue in American politics. He told Gordon a Trump visit to Moscow would give him foreign policy credibility. As Page sent numerous policy papers to the Trump campaign, he was systematically ignored. Frustrated Page flew to Bismarck North Dakota where Trump was delivering an energy speech. He wasn't able to talk to Trump. The campaign realized he was a bit strange. They should have deduced that when he testified to the House Intelligence Committee. It was at this committee hearing that he ranted and raved a bit about his role in the 2016 campaign. Trump had the good sense to ignore this imperious amateur.

J. D. Gordon refused Page's request for permission to travel to Moscow. He received it from campaign chairman Corey Lewandowski. No one seemed to know anything about Page. What did he want to do to help Trump become president? No one could answer that question.

When Page told the House Intelligence Committee he was an official campaign representative to Russia and that the Attorney General Jeff Sessions approved the trip, he was, said Page, a diplomatic envoy. Page stands by his statement Sessions sent him to Moscow.

Attorney General Jeff Sessions didn't remember hearing from Page about such a trip. Why would he tell the Attorney General about a speech in Russia as a private citizen? It didn't make sense. Nothing Page said made sense. The House Intelligence Committee scrutinized him without conclusions concerning his veracity.

The six hours Page spent testifying before the House Intelligence Committee was a window into the hapless amateurs populating Trump's foreign policy. Page's arrogance was demonstrated when he showed up without a lawyer. His testimony saw him veer into tangents. He often worked himself up emotionally stating it was all a witch-hunt. The House backed him into a corner with questions about his e-mails. He took the Fifth Amendment seventeen times. He claimed he didn't have meetings with anyone high up in Russian government. He met with Deputy Prime Minister Arkady Dvorkovich and the House couldn't believe he thought Dvorkovich was not a top level Kremlin official. But there were other important businessmen-politicians with ties to the Kremlin that Page talked with, had dinner with and conducted business.

During his House testimony, Page detailed a meeting with Igor Sechin, the president of the state-controlled Russian oil company Rosneft. This led investigators to conclude why the Steele Dossier identified Page as an accomplice in Russian collusion. They found no crime. He has not been indicted.

Page said he had never met or talked with President Trump. He sounded like the campaign and the president were working in tandem with him. He was delusional. Despite his high level education, the large amounts of money he had made and his self-aggrandizing statements, he is a rank amateur in the world of diplomacy and international politics.

What is demonstrated is the hanky panky by amateurs, like Page, prior to Trump's election hurt him. Collusion has not been proven. Bad judgment in appointments is clearly proven. There is anecdotal evidence of collusion with Russian representatives exploiting his Trump connections. There is no evidence Trump was involved.

Behind closed doors on November 2, 2017 Carter Page testified about Russian interference in the 2016 presidential election. Unwittingly, he provided key insights into Trump's 2017 European visits. What were Page's insights? He said Arkady Dvorkovich supported Trump's bid for the presidency.

Who is Dvorkovich? He is the Deputy Prime Minister of Russia and a close Putin ally. As Page talked to the House Intelligence Committee, he proudly told them he briefly said hello to Dvorkovich. What did this mean? It meant Page made an attempt to demonstrate he was close to key Kremlin figures. Not true!

He claimed Russian leaders were behind Trump's candidacy. When California Representative Adam Schiff, the committee's senior Democrat, asked Page how long he talked to Dvorkovich, Page said less than ten seconds. There was an awkward silence. The committee stared at Page. They thought he had lost his mind. They realized they were dealing with a witness looking for the limelight. He was devoid of key information. Trey Gowdy, the hawkish, pro-Trump South Carolina Republican Congressman, was lost for words. This is a House of Representatives first.

Later, Page changed his story. He said he didn't have a meeting. He simply said hello. This comment piqued everyone's interest. He denied having anything to do with Russia. Everyone shook his or her head. He worked in Russia. He lectured in Russia. He had connections to the oligarchs and other government officials. The Mueller Commission looked at his comments and scratched their heads. As did everyone else!

THE HOUSE INTELLIGENCE COMMITTEE ON PAGE: WHAT THE HELL IS GOING ON?

When the transcript of the House Intelligence Committee was released, it ran to two hundred forty three pages. It was a mishmash of contradictory, confusing and ill thought out ideas. In this document Carter Page discusses a conversation with future Attorney General Jeff Sessions. He claims top Trump officials knew of his Russia connections. They were, according to Page, "eager to hear his thoughts." There is no independent verification of this preposterous claim.

The testimony before Special Counsel Robert Mueller prompted Page to remark he discussed the U. S. election with Russia officials. He said he did so in what he labeled "general terms."

When the FBI applied for the FISA warrant, they suspected Page was a Russian spy. A FISA warrant requires a large file of information on how and why Page might be a Russian spy. What is obvious is he was the most inept alleged spy in the history of modern espionage. Ego! That was the key. Brains! You decide! Conclusion! He wasn't a spy.

The Wall Street Journal challenged the FISA warrants. Had the FBI exceeded its authority? The **Journal** editorialized the FBI misused the FISA provision: "What is FISA for? To serve as a potted plant so the FBI can get whatever warrants it wants." What is important about the **Journal** editorial? It defends the Trump complaint the FBI and those in the "deep state" are out to destroy the president. By attacking the credibility of the FBI, Trump's minions and the **WSJ's** editorial argued the FBI is corrupt. They claim the FBI is the captive of the deep state. This deflects from looking into Trump and his followers concerning the Russian question. The Trumpites are successfully selling this argument to a large segment of the American voting public.

Why did Trump like Page? The reason is a simple one. Page in discussion tells one that Vladimir Putin's politics and sense of leadership is the wave of the future. Page said the U. S. fails in attempts to create democracy outside of the U. S. Trump loved his remarks.

CARTER PAGE ON CARTER PAGE

The transcript from the House Intelligence Committee tells one all they need to know about Carter Page. He begins his statement observing the: "Obama Administration intelligence officials including James Comey seem to be based on inferences drawn from their personal beliefs about Russian President Vladimir Putin's motivation about why they have little or no actual knowledge or understanding." This statement tells one why Page flunked his PHD exam twice, not to mention English syntax. It also suggests why no one would publish his doctoral dissertation. It gets worse.

Page said: "Given the complete disaster that the Clinton/Obama made of U. S.-Russia relations and the related problems they inflicted on private industry across the Russian economy, I had no other financial or real estate holdings related to Russia during the period of the U. S. presidential campaigns other than this miniscule stake of Gazprom's American Depository Receipts." Once the House Intelligence Committee digested Page's statement, they were mute. It didn't make sense. It was poorly written and ill conceived. It didn't fit the facts. The FBI was aware of Page's quirky nature.

In a letter to James Comey on September 25, 2015, Page said he was the focus of "a witch hunt." Page wrote: "I have not met this year with any sanctioned individual in Russia or any other country despite the fact that there are no restrictions on U. S. persons speaking with such individuals." His grandiose and exaggerated importance was displayed when Page wrote to Director Comey: "Having interacted with members of the U. S. intelligence community including the FBI and CIA for many decades, I appreciate the limitations on your staff's time and resources. Since I have not been contacted by any member of your team in recent months, I would eagerly await their call to discuss any final questions…" Page is still waiting for that call.

In his letters, public statements and testimony before the House and Senate, Page was prone to erratic opinions, over the top insults and faulty logic. Facts! He couldn't recognize a fact from a Russian hooker. Then again! A good example is in another letter to Comey, he remarked he was being targeted by government agencies. He said it was for "unjustified civil rights abuses committed again me in 2016…." What these abuses were remain a mystery.

Page saw a conspiracy against him through the Steele Dossier and the Clinton campaign. "Although I stepped away from my role as an informal, unpaid campaign volunteer based on the 2016 Dodgy Dossier, like many millions of Americans I continued my support as a member of the Trump movement…." Huh!

Like many Trump supporters, Page has grandiose feelings about the Republican campaign. "Ours was not a campaign but rather an incredible and great movement, made up of millions of hard working men and women who loved their country and want a better, brighter future for themselves and for their family…." This is the type of delusional statements made by those who follow an autocratic dictator with no policy.

WHAT WE DO AND DON'T KNOW ABOUT CARTER PAGE

After Page spent six plus hours testifying before the House Intelligence Committee, the mystery surrounding what he did and didn't do in Russia came to light. It was clear senior members of Trump's campaign staff were aware of Page's visits to Russia. During his testimony Page urged Trump's campaign staff to send him to Russia to deliver a foreign policy speech. He said the campaign turned a cold shoulder to this doltish idea. Page's testimony indicated he kept the Trump campaign abreast of his Russian activities. He defended himself as a private citizen traveling to Russia to deliver a lecture. He didn't seem to understand he could not be an official of the Trump campaign and a private citizen on the same trip.

His hollow explanations didn't explain his duplicitous behavior. In an e-mail Page sent to Trump campaign officials, he wrote: "Please let me know if you have any reservations or thoughts on how you'd prefer me to focus these remarks." He returned to the U. S. where he met with Sam Clovis. He detailed what he saw in Russia. His pitch was how his insider information might help the Trump campaign. Page's testimony revealed he consulted with high-level Russian officials. Whether that constitutes a criminal offense remains for Mueller to define. He appeared like a person swimming in the muck of self-delusion and amateur political behavior.

THE MORE PAGE TALKS, THE MORE CONFUSED WE ARE

The more Page talks the more convoluted is his role in Russia hacking the 2016 election. The confusion surrounding his thoughts had everyone scratching their head. Page says things that make no sense. "I've learned a lot from the past mistakes of my fellow Annapolis grad, Senator McCain," he told the **New York Times'** Jason Zangerle. The reporter was speechless after this comment.

When asked about his role in the Russian investigation, Page said: "No one is better prepared to have gone through this than me." What is it he has gone through? That question remains lost to history. He thought for a moment and continued. "Not only am I ready for it. I savor it." Page smiled and walked out of the Rockefeller Center to gaze at its famous Christmas tree.

"I like being a shadowy figure," Page said. In Russia Page's nickname was "Stranichka," which means "little Page." This proves the Russian's are a brilliant judge of character and intellect.

THE TRUMP CAMPAIGN AND PAGE: DISAVOWING A FOOL

The Trump campaign quickly ended its relationship with Page prior to the November 2016 election. A Trump lawyer sent Page a letter demanding he disassociate himself from the candidate and the campaign. This stern letter from one of Trump's top lawyers was as much a threat as a warning. Legal action was implied.

The end of Carter Page in the Trump campaign was due to the Steele Dossier. When this document circulated amongst intelligence agencies, amongst select members of the press, amongst a few politicians and amongst Trump's insider the full extent of Page's lack of expertise was evident.

Yahoo News was a cause of concern for the Trump campaign. Yahoo reported Page met twice with Russian officials. This piqued the intelligence community's interest. In December 2016, Page returned to Russia and held court with Moscow reporters. He told them how and why Trump was elected president. In New York Trump and his advisers had a fit. This absolute fool was a continual embarrassment.

Don McGahn, Trump's campaign lawyer, was given the task of finally getting rid of Carter Page. McGahn wrote Page: "You never met Mr. Trump nor did you ever advise Mr. Trump about anything." This strongly worded letter had little impact upon Page. He continued to act like he had elected the president. To emphasize his point, McGahn wrote: "You are thus not an adviser to Mr. Trump in any sense of the word." Either Page couldn't read or he didn't understand. The White House didn't want him near the Oval Office, the front lawn or the park across the street. But Dr. Page continued to act like a tenured professor with deep knowledge.

CARTER PAGE: AND VITOR PODOBNYY: I THINK HE'S AN IDIOT, IS THERE EVIDENCE OF RUSSIAN COLLUSION?

In 2013 Victor Podobnyy was a spy working for Russian intelligence. His career was neither glamorous nor exceptionally fruitful. He was dispatched to New York where he was attached to the Russian delegation to the United Nations. Podobnyy's real job was with the Russian intelligence agency, the SVR. He was a spy with a diplomatic cover.

Podobnyy was an inept spy as well as an egomaniac. He drank too much. He talked about his clandestine activity to young women. It didn't take long for the FBI to identify him as a spy. The SVR had a New York office and Podobnyy hung out there complaining about the lack of James Bond adventures. Soon he would meet Carter Page.

The SVR has a New York bank as cover for their covert activities. The SVR's bank, VEB, was a front for Russian intelligence. A VEB employee, Yevgeny Burakov, was arrested in January 2015 for gathering "economic intelligence." Russian intelligence was a comedy act. The various agents would meet outdoors. They would have a signal with a fake umbrella or a funny hat or some other device for a meeting. The FBI was with them every step of the way.

One of Podobnyy's assignments was to recruit unsuspecting Americans to spy. They suspected the Kremlin could use Carter Page for nefarious purposes. The Russian's placed Page under surveillance. He didn't have a plush office in New York. He rented a small space at 590 Madison Avenue. This small office was linked to Trump Tower via a glass atrium walkway. It was in this neighborhood that Podobnyy met Carter Page.

When he met Page, Podobnyy said he was not the brightest person. He labeled this energy consultant dull. The Russian spy would stand in front of Niketown and watch Page come and go. There was no sign of anyone following him or being interested in his whereabouts.

In reports to Moscow, Podobnyy used the code name Male-1. He told his Russian superiors no one had heard of this non-descript person. Moscow asked for more details. If this person was dull, bland and not very smart what was the point of recruiting him? The description of Page provided to Russian intelligence said he was bald, in his mid -forties, lean, not particularly well dressed, and he always seemed to be in a hurry. He rode a Cannondale mountain bike awkwardly. When he is nervous he grins. He was also litigious minded. Page loved to sue those critical of him.

Page says he is innocent of any wrongdoing. He called the Russian probe a witch-hunt. There are other strange actions suggesting the screws in his head need tightening. He filed a libel suit against Yahoo's corporate parent and the Broadcasting Board of Governors for defaming him on European radio. He also sued the Huffington Post for a story stating he was under investigation for meeting Russian officials who meddled in the election. They operate Radio Free Europe. He took exception to their reportage. The basis of Page's suit was their reporting on his July 2016 Moscow trip. Like Trump, he hates criticism.

When reporters asked Page about his Yahoo lawsuit against Yahoo, he said: "The real investigation, I think, is going to be the discovery process in my lawsuit." He smiled for the cameras and continued: "The information that will come out of this may be far more revealing than these other investigations." This grandiose statement suggests Page was not aware of the seriousness of the Russian investigation.

When he talked with the **New York Times'** Jason Zangerle, he said he was the person that could bring the U. S. and Russia together. Delusional! No! It is simply Carter Page. He makes no sense. Here is a quote he gave while tugging on his Wal-Mart suit and his Kmart tie: "The bigger motivation is to prevent the legacy of ashes, the next Iraq, the next Libya, the next Vietnam, which are all minuscule compared to the level of potential conflict between the two countries." I think the best description of Carter Page comes from Victor Podobnyy: "I think he's an idiot." Well said! Victor you have a way of putting all this in perspective. When he was in a New York meeting, Podobnyy remarked of Page: "You get the documents from him and tell him to go fuck himself." I believe Carter Page when he says he doesn't get respect. The two professors in London who flunked Page on his PHD exam should be given the Nobel Peace Prize.

THE RUMORS ABOUT PAGE: IS TRUTH POSSIBLE?

There is no evidence Carter Page has broken the law. There are the seventeen times he took the Fifth Amendment testifying to the House Intelligence Committee. He has denied collusion with Russia. The Steele Dossier claims Page was the go between in a proposed deal where Russia urged the U. S., if Trump was elected, to drop sanctions. In return, Kremlin intelligence would provide the Trump campaign with damaging information on Hillary Clinton. This is rumor not fact.

American intelligence was bothered by Page's numerous contacts with senior Russian officials. The FBI was concerned. Could Page be a Russian agent? He wasn't. In the summer of 2016 the FBI bugged his phone. This led to a FISA warrant. This is the toughest test for law enforcement. In order to secure a FISA warrant the FBI presented extensive documentation of Page's continual meetings with Russian officials. The FISA warrant is argued before a secret panel. It is a cloak and dagger operation. The FBI said they believed Page was acting as a Russia agent. The Judge took the FBI's material under advisement. They agreed and the FISA warrant was issued. There was nothing found after the FISA warrant was issued for ninety days and then it was renewed.

The fallout from Page's Moscow speech radiated during the course of the Trump campaign. Why? When the prestigious Moscow New Economic School invited Page to speak they had no idea about his expertise. Page's speech "The Evolution Of The World Economy: Trends And Potential" not only bored students, it made little sense. His theme was Russia and China achieved success in Central Asia. A secondary theme was the U. S. was not as successful in world markets as it should be due to a lack of business leadership. Page's speech appealed to the Kremlin. It was also an open invitation to support Trump's presidential bid.

On July 7, 2016 Page walked out onto the stage of the New Economic School, he proceeded to attack American policy toward Russia. Page said Igor Sechin, the Chairman of Rosneft, had done more to advance U. S.-Russian relations than anyone. Then he praised Putin's leadership. For two hours Page drowned on about economic relations as the students fell asleep.

Page was a detriment to Trump. Could he be as inept as people reported? Yes! According to the **Washington Post**, Page attended three dinners and wrote policy memos. This is fake news. There is no record of Page in Trump's campaign. In fact, there are no indications he met, talked with or had any dealings with President Trump.

There were rumors of Page's duplicity. Senate Minority leader Harry Reid, a Nevada Democrat, wrote a memo to James Comey identifying activity between Russian and American sources that were suspected of illegal activity. Yahoo News described Page as a mysterious figure. He was a public figure. He acted like a spy. He loved the limelight. They couldn't shut him up. Page met with what the FBI described as "sanctioned individuals."

In December 2016 Page made what was probably his last significant trip to Moscow. To his surprise no one in the government would talk to him. Donald J. Trump was elected the U. S. president, Vladimir Putin sold 19.5 percent of the stock in the state owned oil company Rosneft, and there were rumors of pay-offs to foreign associates. None of this had anything to do with Page. The FBI and the House Intelligence Committee thought otherwise.

While in Russia for six days, Page couldn't keep quiet. The Trump campaign sent him another threatening letter to "cease and desist" in describing himself as a campaign associate. Putin directed Russian officials to ignore the imperious American.

When Page spoke to the Russian press in December 2016, he said he was in Moscow to speak with "business leaders and thought leaders." No one had an idea what this comment meant. He continued to badger the press even though they ignored him. An avid reader of British newspapers, Page took to sending long, oblique and rambling letters to the press. He said he was "a peace seeker." No one knew what he meant. These grandiose statements tell one more about the rambling mind and incoherent thoughts that define Carter Page.

An e-mail to the **London Guardian** provided insights into Page's concerns. Luke Harding, a **Guardian** reporter, quoted the e-mail in which Page said President Barack Obama persecuted a Russian diplomat. Not surprisingly, that diplomat, Victor Podobnyy, was one of Page's alleged conduits to the Kremlin inner circle. Page attempted to re-enter the Kremlin's political family. It didn't work. Why? Podobnyy said of Page in a report: "I think he's an idiot." This was an unfair observation. Page is a respected oil and gas expert, and he was at one time a Trident scholar. But he couldn't stay away from the media. He resurfaced when **Business Insider** reporter, Natasha Bertrand, described Page's testimony before the House Intelligence Committee as verifying many aspects of the Steele Dossier.

SUMMING UP CARTER PAGE: IS IT POSSIBLE?

When the House Intelligence Committee released the transcript of their interrogation of Carter Page in November 2017 there were some surprises. He said the Steele Dossier was accurate. He also remarked Sam Clovis asked him to sign a non-disclosure agreement while working with the Trump campaign. Page said he discussed his Moscow trip with Clovis prior to and after he returned to the U. S. It appeared Page was searching for information on Hillary Clinton that Trump's campaign could use during the election.

Adam Schiff, a California Democrat, read an e-mail to Page he wrote on July 8, 2016 to Trump campaign adviser J. D. Gordon in which Page claimed to have "incredible insights and outreach…from a few Russia legislators and senior members of the presidential administration here." What did this mean? Page couldn't explain either the "insights" or the "outreach."

The Steele Dossier answered the question. Christopher Steele said an "official close to Kremlin Presidential Administration Head, S. Ivanov, confided to a compatriot that a senior colleague in the Internal Political Department of the PA met secretly with Page." The Steele Dossier identified Page as a major player in collusion with Russia. Page denied the charges. These allegations remain unproven.

In his congressional testimony, Page denied meeting with senior Russian officials. He maintained his innocence. He describes himself as a peaceful patriot. Despite the controversy over his House Intelligence Committee testimony, Page sat down with **Business Insider** for a lengthy interview. He said his mission was to clear his name. He didn't. Much of what he said cast a shadowy presence around his role in Russia visa via the Trump campaign.

The question from the Page mess is did he attempt to discuss or negotiate lifting American sanctions on Russia? The answer appears to be "No." Congressman Schiff asked: "Did you ever express support for the idea of lifting U. S. sanctions on Russia with Mr. Baranove?" Page responded: "Not directly."

Who is Andrey Baranov? He is the head of investor relations for Rosneft and at the time the Russian oil company was subject to sanctions. Page allegedly didn't disclose he had a decade long friendship with Baranov. Why is this important? Page's close relationship with Russian's suspected of interfering in the U. S. electoral process caught the FBI's attention.

Michael Isikoff and David Corn observed of Page: "He boasted to the campaign that he had been in contact with top Russian officials during his trip." (p. 160) This is not a crime. It is one of many reasons the FBI opened a file on him while investigating Russian collusion.

The truth is more complicated. Carter Page did meet with Russian officials. Did he discuss sensitive issues? Was he thrown out of the Russian inner circle? Was he fired by the Trump administration? Was he forthright with Congress? Who knows!

CARTER PAGE WILL NOT GO AWAY

In late January 2018 Carter Page filed a Freedom of Information act request to find out what FBI surveillance collected on him. He was allegedly contacting George Clooney to play Page in the movie: "The Dr. PHD Spy Who Came In From The Cold." What Page should have worried about was a classified memo prepared by the Republicans on the House Intelligence Committee. This memo alleges Rod Rosenstein, a Trump appointee, approved an FBI application for an extension of the surveillance warrants last spring on Page. This guy simply won't go way.

A House memo suggests the FBI abused the surveillance program. House Republicans claimed the FISA warrant was an example of the Mueller investigation's aggressive conduct. Page argued the FISA warrant and the Mueller investigation was targeting President Trump through him. In this controversy the last word came from the wisdom of Carter Page. He said: "I harbor no ill will towards anyone for past xenophobic biases and only hope that justice is eventually served."

He sought out publicity. He allegedly contacted **Rolling Stone**'s Tessa Stuart. What did **Rolling Stone** conclude? Not surprisingly, it was not a positive portrait of the nerd who would be a foreign policy adviser. Here is where it gets weird. Page believed **Rolling Stone** was one of his defenders. He didn't realize Tess Stuart is a professional journalist taking the material to its logical conclusion. He e-mailed her answers to questions.

When Stuart concluded her investigative piece on Page she wrote: "The man at the center of the #ReleasetheMemo campaign does not seem particularly concerned with the motivations of his champions in Congress or the White House. He's got other things on his mind, like the one-man war he's waging to get the original documents Nunes' memo is based on releasing…."

The Nunes memo made Carter Page the central figure in a Republican attempt to discredit the FBI securing a FISA warrant. The Nunes memo charged the FBI withheld key information from the judges who approved and renewed the bureau's application to place Page under secret surveillance. This was a Republican memo without the Democrats adding their input. The Democrats disputed the charges. The FBI suspected for a long time Page was a Russian agent. He denied it. Suddenly Page was in the middle of a political party fight to discredit the FBI. Page said the FISA warrant material should be released to protect his integrity. The FBI demurred citing his long relationship with the Kremlin.

Page told **Roiling Stone** via e-mail: "I originally hoped that DOJ and FBI would've released my illegitimate FISA application when I requested it last May, but it's been eight months since I submitted my Privacy Act/FOIA request letters to them and I haven't received any of that information…."

After e-mailing and studying the Carter Page story **Rolling Stone** theorized: "Page is so clearly hapless there is no way he could be a Russian agent-even the actual Russian spies who tried to recruit him in 2013…were caught on FBI surveillance calling him 'too much of an idiot to be useful."

Rolling Stone tried to be kind to Page concluding: "As for Carter Page-who is either the world's most skilled 3-D chess player, the idiot he's frequently characterized as, or something in between-he's just pleased the memo about him may be public shortly." That said it all as the tall scarecrow in the Wal-Mart suit looks for the spotlight.

Time reported Page bragged about being an informal adviser to the Kremlin in 2013 when he submitted a manuscript for publication. In 2016 ABC Good Morning America anchor George Stephanopoulos interviewed Page and asked him how he could have had a role advising both the Kremlin and the Trump campaign. Page didn't deny saying he was an adviser to both Russia and the U. S. Then Stephanopoulos asked him if he understood why his comments alerted the FBI to possible collusion? Page was lost for an explanation. He did respond.

Carter Page: "Look, the probable cause, based on all the evidence that keeps dripping out and now has been substantiated with the Friday, you know, first memo, is that it was based on a dodgy dossier, which was, you know, a political stunt." Stephanopoulos was momentarily lost for words. He attempted to interpret Page's strange statement. They went to a commercial. What this interchange proves is Page did more harm than help to the Trump campaign.

The Carter Page saga is an exercise of amateur auditions in foreign policy. What this means is he continues to contact the media when his name is mentioned. The irony is Republican members of the House Intelligence Committee are coming to Page's rescue suggesting he was treated unfairly as a Trump foreign policy adviser. Page never met or talked with Trump. He was named to the Trump foreign policy advisory team. He never attended a meeting nor did he talk to anyone. The House Intelligence Committee was not privy to any of this information.

In February 2018 Carter Page is a hero to Republican's who argue "misleading evidence" prompted his FISA warrant. This is simply untrue. Since 2013 the FBI followed Page around Russia. His writing, his speeches and his interviews reek of alleged cooperation with Russia. The only problem is Russian agents didn't believe he was smart enough to carry out simple tasks. So this dolt without credentials is at the center of whether or not the FBI abused its powers.

When Republican Representative Devin Nunes prepared the four-page memo stating the FBI mishandled a request for a Foreign Intelligence Surveillance Act warrant on former Trump campaign advisor Carter Page, the California Representative made a serious error in judgment. Nunes mentioned the FBI used a fact from the unverified Steele Dossier. He failed to mention the request for a FISA warrant included numerous, lengthy statements from other sources. If the FBI made a mistake does this invalidate the other facts? If you are a conservative Republican defending Trump it does. If you are thinking American you wonder when this clown show ends.

THE CARTER PAGE TIME LINE

January 2013: At an energy conference in New York, Page meets with Victor Podobnyy, according to court documents. The two exchanged contact information and have several more meetings discussing energy policy, where they also exchange documents on that subject.

January 26, 2015: Podobnyy and two other Russians are charged with working as agents for Russian intelligence in New York. Court records include a transcript of a recorded conversation in which Podobnyy talks about trying to recruit someone identified as Male-1, which BuzzFeed later reveals to be Page. "I think he is an idiot," Podobnyy says in the transcript.

December 2015: Feeling that the Trump campaign aligns with his ideas on Russia, Page asks Ed Cox, chair of the New York state Republican Party, to recommend him as an advisor. He is brought on right away. "Anyone who came to us with a pulse, a résumé and seemed legit would be welcomed," a campaign official tells the Post later.

March 21, 2016: Trump meets with the editorial board of the Washington Post. Asked about his foreign policy team, he names, among others, Page and George Papadopoulos, who later pleads guilty to lying to the FBI about contacts he had with the Russian government during the 2016 presidential campaign.

July of 2016:

- Page joins a group dinner of Trump campaign national security advisors, including then-Senator Jeff Sessions, at the Capitol Hill Club in Washington. He later testifies that he casually told Sessions about an upcoming trip to Russia during the dinner.
- Page spends three days in Moscow, where he gives a talk at the New Economic School that is critical of American policy toward Russia and favorable toward Russian President Vladimir Putin. The speech interests FBI investigators, who have kept an intermittent eye on Page since the Podobnyy case, reportedly prompting their first looks at the Trump campaign's ties to Russia.
- Former British intelligence agent Christopher Steele approaches an FBI agent with information he has uncovered about Trump's relationship with Russia while doing opposition research on behalf of the Democratic National Committee and the Hillary Clinton campaign.

Summer 2016: The FBI and the Justice Department obtain a FISA warrant to monitor Page's communications after convincing a Foreign Intelligence Surveillance Court judge that there is probable cause to believe Page is acting as an agent of a foreign power, namely Russia.

December 2016: Trump attorney Don McGahn writes Page to "immediately cease" saying he is a Trump advisor. "You were merely one of the many people named to a foreign policy advisory committee in March of 2016 — a committee that met one time," McGahn writes. "You never met Mr. Trump, nor did you ever 'advise' Mr. Trump about anything. You are thus not an 'advisor' to Mr. Trump in any sense of the word."

January 10, 2017:

- In sworn testimony at his confirmation hearing, Attorney General nominee Jeff Sessions testifies that he is "not aware of any" communication between the Trump campaign and the Russian government during the campaign.
- BuzzFeed News publishes the full-unsubstantiated dossier detailing President Trump's alleged ties to Russia and

claiming the Russian government may be blackmailing him. The dossier alleges that former campaign manager Paul Manafort used Page as an intermediary with the Russian government and that Page attended a secret meeting at the Kremlin in July of 2016.

February 12, 2017: In an eight-page letter to the Justice Department's civil rights division, Page calls the Russia investigations "frivolous" and says they are "among the most extreme examples of human rights violations during any election in U.S. history since Dr. Martin Luther King Jr. was similarly targeted for his anti-war views."

March 2, 2017: Amid concerns about his January testimony and newly revealed meetings with the Russian ambassador, Sessions announces he will recuse himself from any investigations related to the Trump campaign.

April 11, 2017: The Washington Post first reports on the existence of the FISA warrant on Page from the summer of 2016. In an interview, Page again compares the surveillance to the FBI's eavesdropping on King. "This confirms all of my suspicions about unjustified, politically motivated government surveillance," he says.

May 7, 2017: In an angry nine-page letter to the Senate Select Intelligence Committee, Carter says he had only "brief interactions" with Podobnyy in 2013 and calls requests for more information a "show trial" based on "the corrupt lies of the Clinton/Obama regime."

October 18, 2017: During five hours of testimony before the Senate Judiciary Committee, Sessions is grilled about his contacts with Russians during the campaign. When asked if any surrogates from the Trump campaign had contact with the Russians, he responds: "I did not — and I'm not aware of anyone else that did. I don't believe that it happened."

October 30, 2017: In wide-ranging interview MSNBC's Chris Hayes, Page discusses Papadopoulos's guilty plea, admitting that he was on campaign email chains with Papadopoulos about Russia. "I genuinely hope, Carter, that you are innocent of everything, because you are doing a lot of talking," Hayes says.

November 2, 2017: During six hours of closed-door testimony with the House intelligence committee, Page testifies that he told Sessions about his trip to Russia ahead of time. During the testimony, Page invokes the Fifth Amendment when asked to produce documents that could potentially be relevant to the investigation.

November 3, 2017: In an interview with CNN's Jake Tapper, Page says that the fact he told Sessions about his upcoming trip to Russia was a "nothing event" made "totally in passing." He adds that Sessions was not the only one on the campaign that he told before he took the trip. "I mentioned it to a few other people," he says.

January 29, 2018: The House Intelligence Committee votes along party lines to publicly release a classified memo overseen by Republican Rep. Devin Nunes which criticizes the FBI's handling of a FISA warrant on Page, alleging that relied too heavily on information in the Steele dossier. In a rare public statement, the FBI says it has "grave concerns" about the memo.

The Carter Page saga will continue. He has never met a camera he didn't like. Poor President Trump he has to endure this would be adviser. But Page never went away.

CARTER PAGE RE-EMERGES ONCE AGAIN: AT
THE CENTER OF THE MEMO CONTROVERSY

There were revelations that should have caused the Republican attack dogs to ignore Carter Page. "Over the past half year, I have had the privilege to serve as an informal adviser to the staff of the Kremlin in preparation for their Presidency of the G-20 Summit next month, where energy issues will be a prominent point on the agenda," Page wrote in a letter according to **Time**. Energy was a secondary issue at the G-20 proving Page's ineptness once again. He described a key role for himself that didn't exist.

Page weighed in on the issues. He told **Time** he "sat in on and contributed to a few roundtable discussions with people from around the world...." Page allegedly gave advice to Kremlin influenced sources. His statement referred to his activities between January and September 2013, as the FBI monitored this activity. Representative

Nunes and his so-called House Intelligence Committee didn't have a clue. Nunes and his House cohorts attacked the FBI without knowledge or information. They did so to defend Trump. That is the tragedy of using intelligence out of context.

There are many unanswered questions. The FBI interviewed Page concerning his contact with Russian intelligence. The U. S. Embassy in Turkmenistan sent a cable stating Page met with local government officials. Why? No one knows! The FBI investigated. The mystery remains. Was Page doing business improperly? Probably not! Is there evidence of oil, land or gas consulting? No one knows! What is known is the **New York Daily News** reported Page bragged of his connections to Russian intelligence for a decade. That is not a crime. It is an exercise in stupidity.

Much of the information on Page's activities came from his constant e-mails, phone calls and personal contacts with the media. Page displayed a virtual obsession with keeping his name in the midst of the Russian collusion investigation.

Carter Page is the nightmare that every president should avoid. Trump didn't. This lanky scarecrow is still around. If Ichabod Crane could emerge from the Legend of Sleepy Hollow he would look a lot like Page. That is a frightening thought. Then again! Carter Page is a frightening thought.

BLOOMBERG DEFENDS PAGE:
IS HIS REPUTATION RUINED?

Bloomberg News believes Carter Page's reputation is ruined as a result of the leaking of the FISA warrant. Eli Lake writes; "The current debate over Page is whether the FBI overreached by seeking a warrant to spy on him from the secret Foreign Intelligence Surveillance Court at the end of 2016." What Bloomberg concludes is word leaked to the FBI intensifying the investigation of Page. This impacted his business-professional life in a negative manner.

When Michael Isikoff was researching Page, Christopher Steele tipped him off about meetings in Moscow with Putin aides. This helped focus his book **Russian Collusion** to emphasize the nefarious side to the story. It is no more than investigative journalism. Perhaps Bloomberg should take note.

Not only does Bloomberg stand by its conclusion "the warrant placed a cloud of suspicion over a U. S. citizen without due process...." They also intimated the FBI and Mueller might have gone beyond their original mandate. This sounds like an attempt to end the Russian investigation.

Bloomberg is upset it that no one leaks to them. They seldom publish a breaking news scope. Mediocre reporting, suspect conclusions and an unwillingness to be critical about Donald J. Trump suggests why Bloomberg lacks the credibility of the **New York Times** or the **Washington Post**. In defense of the Eli Lake article it concludes: "None of this discredits the investigation of the Special Counsel Robert Mueller into Russia's influence of the 2016 election. Or does this justify the president's own attacks on the FBI. But it's a reminder that there are many guilty hands and victims in the politicization of the Trump-Russia problems one of those victims is named Carter Page."

THE NUNES MEMO HAS THE LAST WORD

After Carter Page testified before the House Intelligence Committee the senior Republican, Devin Nunes, released a document attempting to explain Page's role in the investigation. The Nunes memo concluded the FBI and the Special Counsel unfairly targeted him. Both exceeded their powers. The Democrats dissented. Nunes ran to the Oval Office like a lapdog bragging about protecting the president. He abandoned his party and his moral principles and his political integrity. Sad!

Others saw Page as an inconsequential figure. Too much was made of his role in the Trump campaign by the media. One campaign official the **New York Times** reported Page said on foreign policy "the campaign took the advice of anyone with a pulse."

The **New York Times** published a Page e-mail to J. D. Gordon and Walid Phares. Carter Page: "As discussed my strategy in order to keep in sync with the media relations guidelines of the campaign has to make my key messages as low-key and apolitical as possible. But after seeing the principal's tweet a few hours in response to the cocky 'in politics and in life, ignorance is not a virtue' quote by the same speaker at Rutgers yesterday I got another ideas. If he'd like to take my place and raise the temperature a little bit, of course, I'd be more than happy to yield this honor to him" The translation of this insipid e-mail is: Page criticized a Hillary Clinton campaign speech and he suggested Trump replace him in Moscow as a speaker. This fool told this to the House Intelligence Committee and said this validated his Russian trip. Again, this is not a crime. Stupidity cannot be prosecuted.

What is clear is the Trump campaign disassociated itself from Page. The Nunes Memo was an attempt to point out House Republican leaders were arguing Mueller and the FBI violated his rights. Not true. He was a solo flyer to Russia with limited access to the Trump campaign. Perhaps the conclusion is Carter Page is much ado about nothing.

The Nunes Memo said everyone should leave Carter Page alone. He is not important. He is not an unwitting Russian agent. He was unfairly treated. But the story plays on. It's importance? Who knows!

CARTER PAGE HAS THE LAST WORD

By June 2018 Carter Page was not a forgotten person. He said the Russian investigation destroyed his life. His fortune dwindled. His girlfriend left him. In an interview with the **New York Post**, Page lamented of his London girlfriend: "Talking with her later that evening after dinner, she told me that she didn't want me staying there anymore, and that our relationship was over." This comment tells one all they need to know about Page's life. Who does Page blame for his descent into a personal hell with loss of income, prestige and standing in the foreign policy community? The answer is a complicated one.

He blames the FBI's mole, Professor Stefan Halper, for as Page concluded spying on him. He sees a politically motivated investigation against Team Trump is what ruined his life. Page agrees with Trump's characterization of the Russian investigation as "Spygate." What is Spygate? It is the FBI placing moles within the Trump presidential campaign team to prevent his election and not accomplishing that goal destroying his presidency. Trump sees himself as protecting American democracy. He doesn't believe he is destroying it. He is trying.

Page maintains the FBI had "no basis" for spying on him or the Trump campaign. He blames people like Halper and electronic surveillance for his problems. He calls the FBI "criminal." The fourteen months that Halper stayed in touch with Page, he claims this was an orchestrated spying plan to make Page appear as a Russian agent. He has no idea it was his activity in Russia and his testimony to the House and Senate that alerted everyone to his duplicitous behavior. He takes no responsibility for what has ruined his reputation.

ELEVEN

THE G-7 2017: SETTING THE STAGE FOR EUROPE'S VIEW OF THE PRESIDENT AND AMERICA FIRST

"In order to fulfill my solemn duty to the United States and its citizens, the U. S. will withdraw from the Paris Climate Accord...."

PRESIDENT DONALD J. TRUMP, JUNE 1, 2017

"Enlightened statesmen will not always be at the helm."

JAMES MADISON, THE FEDERALIST PAPERS

"Democracies live uneasily with secrecy, and governments keep too many secrets."

MICHAEL WALZER

From May 26 to 28, 2017 in the quaint, beautiful Sicilian town of Taormina on a bucolic hill the G-7 Summit met. It was the initial foray for President Donald J. Trump into European affairs. On the surface the G-7 is little more than a friendly meeting of member nations. It is primarily an economic entity. The seven-member nations Italy, Canada, France, the United States, the United Kingdom, Germany, Japan and the European Union are a friendly group with common goals. That changed when Donald J. Trump arrived in Taormina.

The celebrities at the G-7 included Canada's Prime Minister Justin Trudeau and France's Emmanuel Macron. There were numerous photos of them walking around the Italian seaside town. "The Franco-Canadian friendship has a new face," Macron said standing

245

beside a beaming Trudeau. This set a friendly tone to discuss key issues.

Donald J. Trump, the American president, did everything in his power to distance the U. S. from this friendly G-7 atmosphere. Why? He was ill at ease and not prepared to discuss the issues. Fox TV News didn't analyze the G-7. So Trump was lost.

THE KEY ISSUES AND HELLO PRESIDENT TRUMP

On May 26, 2017 Foreign Policy and Security issues were discussed in two sessions. The day concluded with an analysis of the world economy. The emphasis was on trade, energy and climate change. World issues included food, gender equality and migration. There were long, fruitful discussions to solve serious world problems. The following day extensive discussions on African problems expanded notions of global trade, combating terrorism and providing health care too place. The concluding sessions were designed to reach out to smaller countries. There was an emphasis on the third world economy, and eradicating disease in Africa. By providing banking guarantees to fund changes the G-7 worked toward building a vibrant African economy. This opened up Africa in a new way to global trade.

African journalists complained the G-7 did little more than throw a ceremonial bone to the continent. There were six journalists from Kenya who complained that only five questions were allowed during a session with European council President Donald Tusk. There was no mention of financing projects in Africa. Since 2001 it has been traditional to discuss African economic and political problems. The Kenyan journalists charged there was a lack of urgency in funding African reforms.

TAORMINA AND THE G-7 ATMOSPHERE

The selection of the Sicily town, Taormina, was an interesting choice for its tranquil beauty. The medieval city center is beautiful with no cars allowed on a lush, hillside setting. The nearby water provides a magnificent view. By closing down all hotels from May 22 through May 28 and allowing no one but the 11,000 permanent residents of the city, as well as the world press, the Italian government guaranteed a quiet working atmosphere. The presence of 9,000 elite Italian troops, as well as U. S. secret service and other elite protection corps, made for a relaxed and tranquil, safe summit.

There were some restrictions during the G-7. The Italian government imposed a limit of one hundred guests from each country. The United States and Japan exceeded this number. The Italian government graciously accepted it. Italy also noted the Japanese delegation would remain in Italy for twenty days while other nations spent five days at the G-7.

Why did the Italian government book the entire town of Taormina for the G-7? The answer is a simple one. Taormina, one of the most beautiful Mediterranean cities, was chosen for its symbolism. It merges the concepts of "hope and hospitality," the Italian president concluded. The G-7 limited media attendance to 4000 journalists.

The Italian government remains something of a comedy show. This is thanks to the power of the Sicilian Mafia. The government announced that sixteen million dollars was spent making Taormina ready for the G-7. Maria Elena Boschi, the Italian Undersecretary, said: "The risk of corruption tainting public works contracts is a chronic problem throughout Italy. Before winning contracts in Italy, private companies must be certified that they have no ties with organized crime." Rumor has it the Mafia built many of the ramps protecting the city from tourist hordes. Mafia guides helped to direct Taormina citizens where and when they could walk for food, shopping and daily necessities. What would Sicily do without the Mafia? It would be a mess.

One of the more hilarious incidents in Taormina occurred when Mayor Eligio Giardina said a list of roads and streets had to be repaved for the G-7. This is a Mafia trick to secure government contracts. The road contracts were awarded. They are still waiting for many of these re-pavements to be finished. But, trust the Italian government, they said there is no Mafia. Another humorous incident came when the Italian government informed the Trump administration that the president's Cadillac One was too big, too unwieldy and too cumbersome for the Taormina streets. Italian authorities asked if President Barack Obama's Chevrolet could replace the Cadillac? There was no word from Trump's advisers on this request. The Italian government noted that $1.2 million seemed like lot of money for a presidential limousine. There was no response from the White House.

What do the G-7 countries represent? Plenty! When these national leaders convene they are representative of 10.3% of the world's population. In terms of GDP the G-7 brings 32.2% of the world's exports of goods and services together. In terms of goods imported to other countries 36.7% of imported world goods come from G-7 participants. It is as much an economic forum as a political marketplace. The world's most important industrial nations meet and much of future world trade is sorted out. Then there are in-depth negotiations and quietly deals are made accelerating global capitalism.

The G-7 suggested a meaningful discussion of issues was possible only if Russia and Vladimir Putin did not attend the Taormina meetings. The G-7 members invited six guest countries including Ethiopia, Guinea, Kenya, Niger, Nigeria and Tunisia.

There were many issues on the table. The dominant one was finding a solution to the Syrian crisis. The G-7 also talked of placing economic pressures on North Korea for failing to comply with U. N. resolutions. Price stability, inequality in trade and Russia's responsibility for the Ukraine conflict rounded out key talking points.

BEFORE TAORMINA: TRUMP IS ASKED FOR HIS POSITION ON RUSSIAN SANCTIONS

Before the G-7 convened there was dialogue with the United States and President Trump over Russian sanctions. This was a delicate issue. Italy and other European nations hoped for stiffer Russian sanctions. Trump wasn't predisposed to impose economic pressure. Why? Trump believed friendship with the Kremlin would benefit the American economy. This proved he knew little, if anything, about the economics of American foreign policy or Russian history.

Behind closed doors the Italian delegation talked at length with Trump and his advisers concerning Russia. Italy warned the bully in the Kremlin, Vladimir Putin, was intent upon expanding Russian influences into Europe. Putin and the Kremlin were waging war on the E. U.

The Italian government made it clear Vladimir Putin was not invited. "On the part of the Italian G-7 presidency there is no invitation to Putin to participate in the G-7 in Taormina," Gentiloni said. He was also critical of Trump remarking: "Trump has made no secret of wanting to improve the relationship between Moscow and Washington." Italy made it clear they believed the bellicose, aggressive nationalism that made Russia unpopular in European had no place at the G-7. Trump never said a word. His silence gave tacit approval to Russia's bullying countenance in European affairs. Europeans were furious.

TRUMP'S NATONALIST FOREIGN POLICY
PRIOR TO HIS FIRST EUROPEAN SUMMITS

As Trump traveled to Europe for the G-7 there was one question. How would American foreign policy change? Nationalist advisers were in charge. Trump was an outlier. He praised the right-wing Polish government. He chided the European Union's bureaucracy. He said climate change was a hoax. He derided NATO as unnecessary. He lectured NATO nations to pay their fair share of defense. The President spoke disparagingly of immigrants, Muslims and those who didn't embrace his version of democratic, capitalistic values. America was open for business. The U. S. no longer guaranteed world stability. Or for matter Trump didn't support a global economy. Trump's provincial nationalism harkened back to the 1930s isolationists.

Who crafted Trump's provincial nationalism? His chief strategist, Steve Bannon, and his senior policy adviser, Stephen Miller, appealed to Trump's raw instincts for Making America Great Again. Isolation is the key to the new foreign policy. Trade is King. Statecraft be damned. Trump believes he can bring free trade, international respect and in the process create a stronger world position. He proposes to do this by ignoring many of the world's problems. When he labeled an African country "a shithole," he added immigrants from underdeveloped countries would never want to "go back to their huts." This was a stunning remark. It bordered on pure racism.

What does a nationalist foreign policy mean? It means the rejection of past trade agreements, ignoring climate controls, renegotiating treaties, attacking the critical media and ignoring Russia's actions. These forces are the foundation stones of Trump's version of democracy. The president defines a nationalist foreign policy that is insular.

EUROPEAN LEADERS MEET PRESIDENT TRUMP

When European leaders talked with Trump at the G-7 they were curious about his program for America in world affairs. They found him aloof, pompous and unaware of the world economy. The G-7 was a chance for Trump to charm and explain his America First policy. Rather than building bridges to European leaders, Trump alienated everyone. He acted like a pompous ass when he was seen riding in a private, gold plated golf cart seven hundred yards for a picture. The other world leaders walked in tandem. They talked. They laughed. They joked with each other. Trump was alone on the golf cart. He didn't talk or joke with anyone.

The late May 2017 G-7 was a time for world leaders to relax, casually talk and enjoy the beautiful Sicilian countryside. A telling moment took place as the world leaders posed for a picture. Trump pushed another leader aside and dominated the center of the photo opportunity. German Chancellor Angela Merkel called Trump "boorish and aloof." Others observed he was "entitled."

The **Wall Street Journal** praised the changing direction of American foreign policy. The conservative **WSJ** said his Warsaw speech, prior to the G-7, emphasizing a tight border, a strong national and cultural identity and standing up to America's foes was the wave of the future. The **WSJ** reported Trump "shocked Washington" with his demands for respect and better deals. **Breitbart News** wrote: "Trump Versus The Rest" to describe the G-7 calamity. The **New York Times** and the **Washington Post** lamented the decline in America's international influence. Richard Haass observed Trump's European visit "embraced nationalism much more than internationalism." There was a contradiction to Trump's foreign policy. As he played in the press to his minions, Vice President Mike

Pence and General James Mattis were offering quiet support to the EU and NATO. Not surprisingly, Trump's policies confused Europe.

As the G-7 meeting unfolded in Taormina, the beautiful small town on a hill overlooking the sea was like a magical fairyland. The bucolic atmosphere was upset by Trump's comments.

Rather than courting diplomacy, Trump insulted, criticized and publicized his America First agenda. He announced his omnipresent importance. He criticized French President Emmanuel Macron. He told a French newspaper, Macron had a white-knuckle handshake. Trump said when they shook hands it was "a moment of truth." What did that mean? Who knows! What was obvious is that there was enough testosterone in the Taormina streets to bring Hugh Hefner back to life.

When he left the G-7, Trump told reporters: "I was elected to represent the citizens of Pittsburgh not Paris." To European diplomats he acted like a bully who didn't understand foreign policy. His foreign policy team was at odds with him on virtually every issue in the international arena.

Russia is the only country to embrace Trump's foreign policy. "He is ours," a Russian journalist wrote and Russian Television praised Trump like he lived in an apartment across the street from the Kremlin. It was as if Trump had a man crush on Putin. He loved Moscow. He was there for a beauty pageant years earlier, and his presidency was the culmination of his love affair with Russia. Trump's disdain for traditional diplomacy is making the world more dangerous. He could care less.

WHAT IS THE G-7?

The G-7 was established in 1975. The idea was to bring the U. S., West Germany, France, Italy, the United Kingdom, Japan and Canada together to discuss world economic issues. These early meetings featured finance ministers and bank representatives. The U. S. was a strong supporter of the G-7. It was a means of guaranteeing a stable European economy. After two decades Russia accepted a membership invitation making it a G-8. Then Russia was expelled for violating the sovereignty and territorial integrity of the Ukraine. There were many nations left out. In 1999 the G-20 was organized to expand the issues and the topics the G-7 would or could not discuss. China, Mexico and Argentina became key members of the G-20. The annual meetings concentrated largely upon fiscal issues. The G-20 was too unwieldy to be effective. It is important to maintaining global prosperity.

What changes took place in the beautiful hillside Sicilian town of Taormina as the G-7 leaders met? It was the first time two G-7 female leaders were principal participants. It was the first time a G-7 in Italy was not hosted by Italy's Silvio Berlusconi. Germany's Angela Merkel and Britain's Theresa May were the ladies in the spotlight. G-7 members and the European Union representatives were upstaged by the antics of the American President Donald J. Trump.

As the conference was about to begin, Simon Derrick, chief currency strategist at the Bank of New York Mellon, commented: "I continue to see this as an indication that the U. S. administration is determined to tackle what it sees as unfair trade policies."

TRUMP AT THE G-7: 2017 A FAILED EXPERIMENT IN MAKING AMERICA GREAT AGAIN

In late May 2017, as Donald J. Trump made his first significant trip in pursuit of American foreign policy, it was by all accounts a disaster. When asked about the European Union, Trump said it originated to compete with American business interests. He had no idea about the G-7 nor did he educate himself. The U. S. helped to set up the European Union. Its goal was to guarantee European prosperity. It would also act as a deterrent against Russian aggression militarily and economically. Trump was too close to Putin and Russia to advance America support of European unity.

As the G-7 Summit brought together the U. S. and six major capitalist economies to discuss the future, there was an air of optimism. After a weeklong meeting beginning in Brussels with finance ministers and others of economic important, the concluding days in the Sicilian resort Taormina set the stage for serious talks on issues surrounding Europe and U. S. relations. The stage was set for globalism. It didn't happen. Why? The G-7 introduced the new American president to the world, and he blew up concepts of global cooperation. He also visited the Pope at Vatican City and he made stops in Riyadh and Jerusalem.

Trump's image was that of a bully, an uncultured diplomat and an egomaniac. Europeans were shocked. Americans were not surprised. Trump attempted to block an Italian proposal on migrants. He also showed he had little, if any, knowledge of traditional diplomacy.

When he met the first day with Japanese Prime Minister Shinzo Abe the two talked about terrorism. They also discussed how to confront North Korea's nuclear build up. Trump basked in the glow of the Japanese leader's good manners. It didn't rub off on the Donald. He looked angry. He also looked like he didn't belong at the G-7. He had no prior knowledge of past G-7 meetings. He contributed nothing. That is unless one considers arrogance, autocracy, crass manners and diffident behavior diplomatic virtues.

Prime Minister Abe is a shrewd, brilliant diplomat. He would not allow Trump to focus on a single topic. Abe is a master at dealing with the media. He told the press of his admiration for the U. S. and Trump. He suggested the North Korea issue would not dominate their talks. Abe made it clear he would not engage in a war of words with North Korea. Trump said military action with North Korea was more than a distinct possibility.

While listening to Elton John on Air Force One, Trump heard one of his hits. He had an idea what to call Kim Jong Un. He warned "rocket man" the "full furry" of the U. S. military was "locked and loaded" and ready for a fight. There was worldwide condemnation for the president's egregious remarks. They weren't original thoughts. He stole them from listening to John's "Rocket Man."

There was another concern when Prime Minister Abe remarked the America First doctrine troubled him. He wondered! Would this new American diplomatic direction end the security guarantees America provided in the world? Trump told him it could if trade agreements were not renegotiated.

During his campaign for the presidency, he criticized Japan for taking advantage of American trade. Prime Minister Abe used his media savvy to appeal to the Donald's ego. Abe said the U. S. should continue working with Japan. "I would like to congratulate you on your successful visit to the Middle East region as well as our participation in the NATO summit, and through your visit I understand that you have demonstrated robust commitment to ensuring global security and I highly value your commitment," Abe remarked of what he called Trump's "wonderful leadership." Trump glowed. He came on board guaranteeing a continued U S. global commitment to Japan. If somewhat grudgingly! That global commitment vanished the next day.

THRASHING GERMANY AND THE SPECTRE OF RUSSIA

When the G-7 commenced Trump thrashed Germany in a Thursday meeting with European Union leaders. They stood in an awkward silence. Donald Trump: "The Germans are bad, really bad. Look at the millions of cars they sell in the U. S. We'll put a stop to that." This comment elicited shock. White House economic advisor Gary Cohn stepped in for quality control. Cohn told the press the president didn't consider one of America's oldest and closest "allies" bad. He was simply commenting on their trade policies. He emphasized first class manufacturing exports had a favored place in the American market.

Trump's comment forced German Chancellor Angela Merkel to pursue closer ties with Russia. The Russians are no longer allowed in what used to be the G-8. The Ukrainian President, Petro Poroshenko, wrote in **Political Europe**: "If the West is serious about peace and world order, it should bear in mind that restoring normal relations with Moscow still runs through Kiev."

The Italian Prime Minister Paolo Gentiloni said talks concerning Russia's bellicose and aggressive foreign policy indicated sanctions are needed. Trump ignored this comment.

Chancellor Angela Merkel also received a bill from President Trump for the money Germany owed to the U. S. for NATO defenses. Trump didn't realize Germany did not owe NATO any money. The London press ran wild with the story. In the American diplomatic community there was a sense of disbelief as career diplomats complained Trump had an "unstructured" foreign policy.

THE UNSTRUCTURED NATURE OF THE G-7

The G-7's are summits that are basically unstructured. The absence of China and Russia made for in-depth talks on the European economy and NATO. It didn't appear Trump could stumble in this setting. He did badly. Other themes in the G-7 center around the treatment of refugees, the future of climate change, protectionism in the marketplace and ideas like a web tax on the mammoth technology companies. Japan did have an agenda. They were concerned about North Korea's nuclear weapon development. No one knew what to expect from President Trump. Soon it became a G-6. Trump had nothing to offer. He also let the other six members know he wasn't interested in their thoughts, their agenda or their nations. The level of arrogance and ignorance shown by the American president was unexplainable. He remained aloof. He didn't understand the issues.

The nations comprising the G-7 were concerned about America's place in the Paris Climate Change Conference agreement. Trump did not commit to climate change. When he returned to the U. S., he opted out of the Paris agreement. The American right applauded with a vengeance. They didn't believe in climate change. They saw it as the natural evolution of the earth. It was also a means of erasing an Obama policy.

The G-7 was an opportunity for Trump to connect with our European allies. He failed. His first venture into European diplomacy was a learning experience. It didn't turn out that way. His notion of "America First" reeked of excessive white nationalism, economic self-interest and egotistical statements. As is usual with the Donald everyone he met became his next best friend. He said everything came out smelling like roses. It is the spin he gives everything that allows his egregious behavior and dangerous policies to denigrate American diplomacy.

After he labeled NATO obsolete, Trump scolded its members for not living up to their financial commitments. German Chancellor Angela Merkel looked like she had gas. Trump said maybe he would and maybe he wouldn't honor the NATO military alliance. His statements distanced the U. S. from European cooperation. As Trump praised the United Kingdom for leaving the European Union there was no doubt where the U. S. stood-on its own.

As the EU's most influential leader, German Chancellor Angela Merkel, said Trump's positions on climate change, trade, Russia and NATO meant the EU could no longer depend upon the U. S. "The time in which we could rely on others-they are somewhat over," Merkel concluded. German is now the dominant partner with France in E. U. affairs.

At the G-7 Trump said NATO should focus on terrorism and immigration. There was no mention of Trump endorsing Article 5 of the NATO treaty. This provision states an armed attack against one NATO state will be considered an attack against all and every member. Article 5 says all member nations "will assist the party or parties so attacked." Trump left the U. S. silent on that point.

TRUMP'S CLIMATE CHANGE STATEMENT TO THE WORLD AT THE G-7: HE DOESN'T UNDERSTAND IT

The notion of replacing anything and everything President Barack Obama accomplished is a mantra for Trump. When U. S. Environmental Administration Agency head, Scott Pruitt, met with his European counterparts in June 2017 to discuss President Trump's decision to end U. S. cooperation with the Paris agreement on climate change, the EPA head danced a jig and might as well have brought out the Confederate flag to celebrate the real America. He not only supported Trump's plan to eliminate U. S. participation in the 195-member climate agreement, he let it be known Christians didn't approve of tinkering with the climate. The appeal to Trump's right wing base worked.

What is the fallback from President Trump's announcement the U. S. will leave the Paris Climate Accord? He said it was in the best interest of the U.S. to leave the agreement. He proved once again he had little, if any, understanding of the issue. Trump claimed U. S. sovereignty is compromised by the climate accords. Not true!

The fallout from leaving the climate agreement is three-fold. First, it allows China to assume leadership in world climate talks. They will take advantage of business deals associated with climate change. Second, the U. S. climate withdrawal fails to generate long-term goals for reducing remissions and health hazards due to pollution. Third, the U. S. will miss out on 1.4 trillion dollars in global business opportunities connected to low carbon business agreements.

President Trump does not understand the Paris Climate Accord. It is an accord not a treaty. This means it is voluntary. The genius of the agreement's language is it requires no specific policies. There is no better deal on the environment. Trump is so intent upon renegotiating a better deal, he will hurt the U. S. economy. He bragged he destroyed another of President Obama's accomplishments.

There were some big lies from Trump as to why he ended the Paris Climate Accord. He said it hurt U. S. jobs. In reality, the opposite is true. This is why a large number of U.S. corporate leaders, including a number of CEO's on the president's advisory council, urged him to remain in the agreement. Exxon Mobil sent a letter to Trump stating the Paris Accord is an "effective framework for addressing the risk of climate change." As far as jobs are concerned Exxon said the U. S. is "well positioned to compete."

The dangers to the environment were not considered. This is due to the Christian right who view climate change as a hoax. The prevalence of severe storms over America, the big floods, the melting Arctic waters and the damage from Hurricane Sandy suggests climate change is real. It will take global action to reverse climate change. The U. S. has been a leader in climate change. That is no longer the case.

Defense Secretary James Mattis pointed out climate change will lead to an increased number of refugees flowing into developed countries. Mattis said: "Climate change is impacting stability in areas of the world where our troops are operating today." Trump refused to accept his own Secretary of Defense's assessment that global warming posits a national security risk. Mattis wants the U. S. to remain in the Climate Control Agreement as a means of policing "climate aggression." What does this mean? It means Mattis is the only Cabinet member to not support Trump's view that climate change is a hoax. "Climate change is impacting stability in areas of the world where our troops are operating today," Mattis remarked. He sees renewable energy as the best way to supply fuel to American troops. Mattis remarked by cutting reliance on fossil fuels U. S. troops would be better served.

China is filling the leadership role in world climate change. China is the largest carbon-emitting nation in the world. This provides an opportunity to continue to pollute the world without consequences. China will pretend to support climate change while taking advantage of its position.

The tensions and divisions between Trump's foreign policy and the wishes of our European allies are in flux due to changes in diplomacy. It has divided friendly nations over policies that should have brought us closer. Trump relishes his role as an outlier. Many employment opportunities in the U. S., due to the need to combat climate change, now shift to China. For Trump it is not about climate change. It is about erasing everything associated with President Barack Obama. The large cuts in the Trump budget directed at the Commerce Department's oceanic and atmospheric research is an indication Mattis's view will not prevail. Scott Pruitt, the EPA head, rejects global warming as non-scientific.

Trump's America First program made his first foreign trip to Europe a calamitous adventure. National Security Adviser H. R. McMaster and National Economic Council adviser Gary Cohn explained his policies to the **Wall Street Journal.** They wrote: "The president embarked on his first foreign trip with a clear-eyed outlook that the world is not a 'global community' but an arena where nations, nongovernmental actors, and businesses compete for advantage. We bring to its forum unmatched military, political, economic, cultural and moral strength. Rather than deny this elemental nature of international affairs we embrace it."

What does Trump fail to understand? What does he believe concerning American foreign policy? There is more to world affairs than economic advantage. The U. S. has historically sought alliances to prevent dictatorial aggression, bullying by nations like Russia under Communism and Germany under Nazi control. International peace, solving problems of hunger and education are laudable American goals. A rules based world order has been the basis of American foreign policy. Trump has thrown these concerns under the bus.

PUTIN AND TRUMP ON CLIMATE CHANGE

Why did Trump and Pruitt oppose climate change? Why did they call it a "bad deal?" The reason is they are playing to their electoral base. Coal and oil are an integral part of the Trump-Putin friendship. Trump said he would work for domestic policies, including the Clean Power Plan, to curtail emissions from power plants and regulations on methane leaks and oil and gas operations would be watched. Of course, oil and gas executives close to the Trump administration would run these programs.

Europe, China and India vowed to continue to pursue clean energy programs. Other nations can only hope the next president will alter this withdrawal from a clean energy world.

Most observers believe Trump's behavior at the G-7 was an aberration. It wasn't. He was simply warming up his views on American foreign policy. The best was yet to come. Once again the press, the other participating nations, the general American public and the world media had no idea what to expect from Trump. He was getting ready for the main show—the G-20.

Trump's performance at the G-7 was a warning about the future direction of American foreign policy. Few in Europe took Trump's pronouncements seriously. When Trump left the G-7, he said he had not made a decision on supporting the Paris Climate Control Accord. He was lukewarm on the invocation of Article 5 to militarily support NATO. He demanded increased defense spending from our allies. He argued the U. S. had too much of the financial burden of military defense.

When the G-7 concluded the member nations issued a terse, six-page summary. They stated nearly all the members agreed on climate change. There was one exception-the U. S. Gary Cohn, Trump's National Economic council adviser, stated the president's views on climate change were "evolving." Cohn said Trump arrived at the G-7 "to learn and get smarter." Then in a gratuitous closing, Cohn said: "His basis for decision ultimately will be what is best for the United States." This is not diplomacy. It is distancing the U. S. from world political affairs.

TRUMP'S MISSES AT TAORMINA

The Taormina G-7 Summit highlighted Trump's need for more training in foreign policy. When the G-7 Summit came to an end, the **New York Times** reported Trump was "at odds with the allies and back home his pro-Russian attitudes led to a firestorm."

He became the first world leader to leave the Paris Climate Accord. The leaders of Germany and France stated their disappointment. After addressing American troops at the Navel Air Station in Signella, Sicily, Trump complained about unfair trade deals. He pointed out the burdensome financing of NATO, and how it impacted the American taxpayer. Rather than discuss the issues, Trump said: "We hit a home run no matter where we are." This is, of course, utter nonsense.

WHAT TO TAKE AWAY FROM THE G-7

When the G-7 concluded the **London Guardian** observed: "Divisions between Donald Trump and other members of the G-7...in Sicily have become so broad and deep that they may be forced to issue a brief leaders statement rather than a full communiqué, dashing Italian hopes of engineering a big step forward on migration and famine." Trump refused to compromise or address key issues. The reason? He was unprepared.

The **Daily Beast** observed of Trump's initial foray into foreign affairs at Taormina. "Loud and tacky, shoving his way around the dance floor. He steps on others without realizing it. It's ineffectual." The **London Independent** said he "ripped up the diplomatic rulebook and broke precedent when he spent his first meeting with NATO allies lecturing the group on their chronic failure to pay for their own defense."

The G-7 was a training ground for the Hamburg, Germany's G-20 Summit a few weeks later. This was a chance for President Trump to meet and greet with world leaders. If he learned anything from the G-7, it was the need to polish his world image. If he did he could sell his America First program. That didn't happen.

Donald J. Trump offended European leaders at the G-7. The result is Europe's anti-American views intensified. The president destroyed alliances built since the Marshall Plan. Sigmar Gabriel, the SPD German Foreign Minister, said: "I furiously reject the way this man takes it on himself to treat the head of our country's government." This is a comment from Chancellor Merkel's rival party. Gabriel charged Trump "weakened the west" with his stand on the environment, peace and religious harmony.

The French President, Emmanuel Macron, talked of standing up to Trump. He also invited him to Paris to celebrate Bastille Day. The irony is Chancellor Angela Merkel talks regularly with ex-president Barack Obama. To the paranoid induced Trump supporters, this is a further example of the "deep state." Trump will continue to offend Europeans. It is his style.

TWELVE

TRUMP IN POLAND AND THE G-20: HIS APPEAL TO WHITE NATIONALISM

"At the G-20 Summit in Hamburg, Trump invited his daughter Ivanka to fill his chair when he exited the room. The theory of American government is that official role, not blood relationship, determines who does what."

DAVID FRUM, TRUMPOCRACY: THE CORRUPTION
OF THE AMERICAN REPUBLIC

"The G-20 Summit hadn't even officially started. Nevertheless the Schwarzer Block was up and about. While most residents in the Altona district were having breakfast, the activists were already creating carnage."

LUKE HARDING, COLLUSION: SECRET MEETINGS, DIRTY
MONEY AND HOW RUSSIA HELPED DONALD TRUMP WIN

In July 2017 Trump stopped for a short speech in Warsaw, Poland prior to attending the G-20 Summit. He was on a four-day trip to Europe. One day to speak to the Polish and the next three days to explain the future of American foreign policy to a wide range of world leaders. The G-20 was more economic than political. Trump's message was America First. It was a five-part program to end globalism. The first step was withdrawal from the Paris Climate Accord. Second, Trump demanded renegotiated trade deals fair to the U. S. Third, Europe would have to begin paying for NATO costs. Fourth, he demanded military help from NATO and other allies to defeat ISIS. Fifth, Trump would withdraw from the Iranian nuclear deal unless it was renegotiated.

PREVIEWING THE TRUMP TRIP TO
EUROPE: BUT FIRST POLAND

As Trump prepared to fly to the continent for the G-20, he told reporters he did not endorse NATO's common defense treaty. He continued to lecture world leaders for not contributing the funds to maintain NATO's armed forces.

The four-day European trip was a challenge for the president. At home he was urged to be tough on Putin and Russia hacking. There were no signs he believed this was necessary. The specter of a Trump-Putin meeting at the G-20 intrigued the press and general public.

Michael O'Hanlon, of the Brookings Institute, put it into perspective when he observed there would be an attempt at improved Russian-American cooperation. He doubted this would be successful. "I can't imagine any issue they can actually make major headway on, given the position that surrounds the relationship," O'Hanlon said.

There were nine meetings scheduled for the G-20 Summit. There were some key issues. The U.S. presence in the NATO defense treaty is one Poland needs to maintain its precarious freedom. Trump received a warm welcome in a speech at Krasinski Square the day before the G-20 commenced. It was his first major outdoor speech in a foreign country. Polish leaders embraced Trump's worldview. They applauded his foreign policy. Why? The answer is a simple one. The fear of Russia continues to dominate Poland.

As Trump prepared to fly to Europe the question on everyone's mind was: Would the U. S. commit to support NATO's Article 5? This provision states an attack on one member is an attack on all.

Once he was in Poland, Trump scolded North Korea for recent missile tests. In an abrupt shift he discussed Poland's security. He blamed Russia's hacking of the presidential election on former President Barack Obama and his rival Hillary Clinton. He answered a number of questions from the press. He intimated there was no fake news in Poland. His press conference featured softball questions from the state controlled media. A carefully selected cheering crowd buttressed the love for the American president.

The Polish speech was a turning point in Trump's foreign policy. He urged a tougher stand against Russian expansion in Eastern Europe. In his speech Trump used expressions such as "radical

Islamic terrorism" suggesting we need to protect "our civilization" and "our way of life."

The Trump speech was virtually a call to arms. He said: "The fundamental question of our time is whether the West has the will to survive?" He continued: "Do we have the confidence in your values to defend them at any cost? Do we have enough respect for our citizens to protect our borders? Do we have the desire and the courage of preserve our civilization in the face of those who would subvert and destroy it?" That was Trump's virtual call to arms.

In the Polish speech Trump complained of government bureaucracy. He emphasized "the steady creep...that drains the vitality and wealth of the people" makes it necessary to reduce the size of the bureaucracy, take way its independent powers and control its excesses. Few people realized this was the first step toward Fascism and the triumph of totalitarian rule. The Polish speech set the tone for Trump's attempt to reduce the U. S. influence in European politics. The lesson from Trump's ill-timed remarks is he was attacking the U. S. government infrastructure. The danger Donald J. Trump presents to democracy continued to develop as his over the top comments weren't challenged. The worst was yet to come.

WHAT DID TRUMP ACCOMPLISH IN POLAND?

What did Trump accomplish in a one-day visit to Poland? He told local audiences: "Polish American's came out in droves, they voted in the last election, and I was very happy with that result." What he was talking about was anyone's guess. All he said is Polish American's voted for him. The proof for that allegation remains unsubstantiated.

President Trump, while in Poland, made his earliest foreign policy suggestions regarding Europe. In two speeches in Warsaw, he presented a checklist of talking points. He explained his approach to American foreign policy. He made it clear his policies were made in secret. He attacked the American press, disrespected the U. S. judiciary and pronounced jingoistic, nationalistic white power slogans. Trump met in secrecy with Polish officials.

At the Royal Castle in Warsaw, he defined his concerns over provisions in the Three Seas Initiative and the Eastern and Western European Trade Alliance. In a public statement in Krasinski Square, he highlighted American policy; it was less about policy and more about bragging. The play to Trump's ego produced results.

While talking about how the Three Seas Initiative benefitted the Eastern European economy, Trump stated the U. S. stock market had gained "four trillion in value since his election." He couldn't resist praising his presidency. He joked: "Personally, I picked up nothing, but that's all right, everyone else is getting rich." Then he went into a sales pitch for purchasing U. S. technology. It was an embarrassing moment.

Why is the Three Seas Initiative important? It is a coalition of twelve central and Eastern Europe countries to strengthen trade, support a rebuilt infrastructure, s well as to promote new energy programs and foster political cooperation. The Three Seas Initiative involves twenty eight per cent of EU territory and twenty-two percent of its population. The problem is economics. The twelve countries have only ten percent of the gross domestic product. Trump supports the Three Seas Initiative. He sees it as an opportunity for a growing democracy while increasing trade with the U. S.

He criticized the U. S. media stating news outlets: "have been fake news for a long time." Trump continued: "They've been covering us in a very dishonest way."

WHY WAS TRUMP SUCCESSFUL IN POLAND?

His one-day trip to Poland was a success. The Polish government helped to turn out adoring crowds. The president's speech at the Warsaw Uprising Monument in Krasinski Square, before a strongly pro-Catholic right wing government, ignited the chant "Donald Trump." It was a festive pro-American rally.

The cheers were deafening for Trump. He talked of a thousand years of Polish suffering; he praised local nationalism and Polish pride. "You stood in solidarity against oppression, against a lawless secret police, against a cruel and wicked system that impoverished your cities and your souls. And you won." The cheering was deafening for Trump's speech.

Trump's speeches reaffirmed Democratic values, chiding Russia for interfering with the democratic process. He stood by the U. S. commitment to NATO. He did this while praising Poland for paying its fair share of NATO defense costs. It was Trump's first major foreign policy triumph.

The four days in Europe for the Polish visit and the G-20 Summit indicated a changing direction in American foreign policy. There were some strange aspects to the Polish speech. Trump contradicted American intelligence reports. He stated that perhaps nations other than Russia hacked into the recent presidential election. This wasn't true. He refused to criticize Putin.

After he completed the Poland trip, the Wall Street Journal observed he was inordinately successful. "Mr. Trump finally offered the core what could become a governing philosophy." On its editorial page the WSJ concluded: "Trump's Warsaw speech was a demand for tight borders, as well as a strong national and cultural identity." Not surprisingly, Steve Bannon was on this trip. Rex Tillerson sat quietly in the background. The WSJ said the Polish trip was a success because the president presented a "determined and affirmative defense of the Western tradition."

The Polish Law and Justice Party organized a campaign for a pro-Trump audience. The free busses brought in hundreds to attend the American president's speech. Paul Jones, the U. S. ambassador to Poland, appeared on various local media outlets. He invited all who were interested to attend the Trump event. A patriotic picnic at Warsaw's National Stadium added to the festivities. This is not uncommon in Poland. In 1972 when Richard M. Nixon visited, as the first president since Franklin D. Roosevelt, there was a huge turnout. George H. W. Bush's trip in 1989 included a speech to the Polish National Assembly. CNN made the point Trump gave two speeches to canned audiences.

POLAND AND THE TRUMP OF
BANNON-MILLER NATIONALISM

No one agrees about the impact of the Poland trip. One thing is certain. Trump's nationalist advisors, Steve Bannon and Stephen Miller, achieved an ideological victory. When Trump spoke to the Polish people his message praised the right wing Polish government for "defending civilization." This was a code word for downgrading press freedoms, not recognizing ideological differences and promoting racism to empower racial Polish nationalists.

The trip to Poland, where he spoke in Warsaw, was an attempt to mainstream Trump's message to European conservatives. Richard Haass, president of the Council on Foreign Relations, remarked: "Overall the trip embraced nationalism much more than internationalism." What does this portend for the world? The same thing it means domestically for Americans. Trump displayed his disdain for and disrespect for a free media. He denied Russian interference in our electoral system. He disrespected traditional diplomacy. H. R. McMaster, the National Security Adviser and Gray Cohn, the chief economic advisor, attempted to steer Trump into conventional waters. It didn't work. He was speaking to his base. That base is a bigoted white nationalism. The Polish speech was praised by the Wall Street Journal: "Mr. Trump finally offered the core of what could become a governing philosophy." The conservative WSJ praised the Warsaw speech for defending tight borders, strong nationalism and cultural identity. The Journal editorialized: "It is a determined and affirmative defense of the Western Tradition." The Warsaw speech was one of many examples where Trump told the world the U. S. would go it alone in world affairs.

Trump tells the big lie, he misuses the facts, and he fails to understand history. He derides the media. He proposes a strong economy over individual civil liberties. He talks despairingly about immigrants and people of color. It appears white nationalists advised him. There is no sugar coating the racial divide emanating from the White House. When General John Kelly defended the Confederacy and the South in discussing the Civil War, he ignored the fact the South went to war to preserve slavery. Kelly praised General Robert E. Lee. He may have been a good general, but after the war Lee advised Southerners not to hire African Americans. During press briefings Sarah Huckabee Sanders informed the press the Civil War was a failure to compromise. Everyone in the White House could use a history lesson. Especially Sanders.

While in Poland Trump made it clear he opposed multiculturalism. He believes reverse discrimination is a problem. He is a smart man. He plays this racial card close to the vest. He brings it out to white audiences often in subtle ways.

Trump, Kelly and Sanders could use a few lessons in American history. But, then again, as Trump would say, he knows things the professors don't know. It is a sad time. Our history is disrespected. The White House continues to exploit racist myths. This is one reason for the Warsaw audience-embracing Trump. He disguises his reprehensible behavior in a literary coat of nationalism. Racially divisive policies remain the core of Trump's politics. The Polish trip simply highlighted it.

Breitbart News headlined: "Trump Versus The Rest." Bannon's news service represents the conservative, pro-nationalist racism pervasive in parts of our democracy. Trump is isolating the U. S. from the world and weakening our international positions while empowering China. He is positioning Russia in Europe to play a more prominent economic role.

How times change! In May 2018 Trump signed a Holocaust property law that angered Poland. This law allows Jewish groups to attempt to reclaim property in Poland, which was seized during World War II by Nazi Germany and Russian Communist troops. Poland is the only country in Europe that has not passed legislation allowing seized assets to be challenged. Trump signed the bill. He was not happy about it. His friend, Vladimir Putin, had no comment.

THE G-20 HAMBURG SUMMIT

Trump was on his way to the two-day July 7 and 8, 2017 at the G-20 Summit and speech in Warsaw made it a good time to exit America. His leadership was called into question. His integrity was challenged. He made it worse at the G-20 Summit. This excursion provided the president with a forum to explain his foreign policy. He had a nationalistic-militaristic tinge in his remarks. It was full of contradictions. No unanimous agreements on major issues were reached. President Trump was the reason.

German Chancellor Angela Merkel was responsible for a disastrous international summit. Donald J. Trump stole the show with his pronouncements. One wonders how the G-20 even took place considering the obstacles it faced due to poor German planning and

Chancellor Angela Merkel's hostility to Trump. It was the 12th G-20 and the first time Germany hosted the event. As the delegates arrived German protesters showed up dressed as zombies in what they labeled the "Welcome to Hell" demonstration. The protesters became increasingly violent. The police showed up to fire water cannons at demonstrators. In return rocks were hurled at the police.

What did the German students want? They called for social justice. German students are noted for anti-capitalist sentiments. Combine this feeling with a long established right to protests and the result was one hundred sixty separate organizations stormed into Hamburg proclaiming "Welcome To Hell." The well planned acts of civil disobedience kept the German police busy.

A Thursday night "Welcome To Hell" demonstration set the tone for police-demonstrator clashes. Greenpeace activists. built a statue of Trump tearing up the Paris Climate Accord and they loaded it on board a small ship sailing around the Liverpool port. The attempts to infiltrate meetings and sumptuous dinners failed as the well-trained German riot police kept control.

German Chancellor Angela Merkel announced climate change, free trade and migration would be key themes of the summit. Violence erupted in the streets.

What is the purpose of the G-20? The quest for global trade, military stability and international cooperation was the broad overall theme. The press pointed out the G-20 looked like global leaders colliding with Trump's unapologetic "America First" agenda. Trump's policies at times obscured the G-20's purpose.

WHAT IS THE PURPOSE OF THE G-20?

When he left for the G-20 Trump was asked: "What is the purpose of the G-20?" He looked quizzical. He had no idea. Never at a loss for words, Trump screamed: "America First." Had he taken the time to educate himself on past summits, he would have seen a golden opportunity to Make America Great Again in world affairs.

The G-20 is a cooperative conference organized by Germany and the U. S. The initial thrust behind the G-20 was to combat the financial tsunami that periodically engulfed the world. The Asian Debt Crisis of 1997, the financial woes of Russia and the subsequent

U. S. banking and real estate crisis from 2007 to 2011 made the G-20 an important forum in maintaining a workable world economy. The G-20 provided a means of guaranteeing world fiscal stability. Trump had no idea how and why the conference originated. Initially, the G-20 meetings included only the finance ministers and central banking governors of member nations. This changed over the years. Heads of state and financial advisers are now a part of the mix.

When Trump arrived for the G-20 one member nation official remarked he was "standoffish." They said he lacked "a concept of world reality." Since the G-20 represents 67% of the world's population and 85% of the GDP, it is a major event in maintaining world prosperity. To hell with world prosperity, Trump intimated, the U. S. was open for business.

How does the G-20 differ from the G-7? The G-20 concentrates upon the issues of global economic equality. Or the search for a living standard that is comparable for all nations. The G-7 is an elite meeting focusing upon the major industrial powers. The G-20 looks to Africa and underdeveloped countries around the world as a means to improve global commerce.

WHAT DOES HAMBURG LOOK LIKE ON THE EVE OF THE G-20?

On the surface the G-20 Summit in Hamburg, Germany appeared to be little more than another dull meeting of international politicians along with a coterie of businessmen and financiers looking to line their pockets. But violence was in the air. Hamburg is a sophisticated city. It is also an urban area of contradictions. The Hamburg port is one of the world's most diverse and profitable shipping centers. The docks are alive with commerce, sailors who want to beat the hell out of you, and there is enough foreign commerce to make Germany the most prosperous EU state. The nearby Reeperbahn is an area of sleazy bars, hookers, drugs and rock and roll music. The Beatles played seven nights a week in the Reeperbahn in the early 1960s. It is a rough and tumble area with violence a nightly feature along with rock music. The university is the focal point of one of Europe's most pronounced student radical centers. When there is a political demonstration you are safer at the docks or on the Reeperbahn.

The Schwarzer Block is a militant, student oriented protest group. They began to organize throughout Hamburg before the G-20 dignitaries arrived. In the student infested Altona district, the Schwarzer Block marched through the sleepy streets early one morning destroying everything in sight. The protesters wore black, screaming their left wing message often with faces covered by bandanas. The reason for this violent protest was the arrival of the representatives of global capitalism. As the protesters smashed in car windows, then overturned coffee tables on the street, they shouted threats and dragged potted plants into the middle of a pedestrian shopping area. The police arrived. One protester called out: "Welcome to hell."

When the media interviewed members of the Schwarzer Block they remarked that Vladimir Putin, Donald Trump and Turkish President Recep Tayyip Erdogan were coming to Hamburg to address the G-20. The Schwarzer Block said they were enemies of the people. The Schwarzer Block said they were German patriots. Why did Prime Minister Angela Merkel select Hamburg for the G-20? It was a disastrous decision.

GERMANY PREPARING FOR THE G-20: WHY MERKEL AND HAMBURG FAILED

Germany spent a year preparing for the G-20. The ambitious agenda included discussions on trade, migrants, climate change, programs to help private enterprise invest in the African market, and there were forums designed to bring leaders together to build a world economic order detrimental to radical Islam. The issues were lost in anticipation of President Donald J. Trump's discussions with Vladimir Putin.

The presence of Secretary of State Rex Tillerson was anticipated and then lost in the swirl of publicity surrounding President Trump's dramatic landing on Air Force One. The European media followed Trump around religiously. It was time for Trump to stand tough against the Russian leaders who hacked the 2016 presidential election. He didn't. Putin sold Trump the story of plausibility denial. Trump accepted Putin's explanation. He never said a word about Russian interference in the 2016 election.

GERMAN CHANCELLOR ANGELA MERKEL ON TRUMP

German Chancellor Angela Merkel criticized Trump's trade policies before he arrived in Hamburg. "While we are looking at the possibilities of cooperation to benefit everyone, globalization is seen by the American administration more as a process that is not about a win-win situation but about winners and losers," Merkel remarked to Die Zeit. She vehemently disagreed with Trump's assertion the U. S. trade deficit with China, German and Mexico hurt the American economy. She said the president did not understand simple economics.

She complained Trump didn't view the world as a friendly global trading community. Merkel charged the American president wanted only a few nations to prosper. She was angry. Trump didn't want to shake her hand. She was upset. Trump criticized Germany for welcoming Syrian rebels. The president said she was "ruining Germany" with her economic policies. Her final angry pre-G-20 remarks didn't bode well for the meeting. Merkel said "anyone who believes they can solve the problems of this world with isolationism and protectionism is making a big mistake."

The sense of chaos that ensued at the Hamburg G-20 did little, if anything, to help Trump make a case for his new American diplomacy. Protesters and the presence of more than 5000 media figures brought out differences that festered before and after the G-20.

The German police were not just heavy-handed with protesters, they mistreated the press. As cars burned in the streets and businesses were set on fire, Hamburg city government was overwhelmed.

The lack of hotels was another problem. Trump was housed in a nineteenth century neoclassical villa in a suburb. When a London Guardian reporter, Philip Oltermann, attempted to interview Trump, he found the road blocked. He couldn't drive near the president's villa. German riot police were everywhere. It wasn't just chaos. Local residents said it looked like the end of the world.

The violence in the streets in front of an event at a concert hall led to an invasion by a sea of ecology protesters. The constant prodding of the press drove Hamburg's police to use excessive force. It was like a war zone. The 12,000 protesters who showed up the week before the G-20 commenced were a constant distraction. Once the conference began there were 100,000 protesters. Not surprisingly, the police cordoned them off from the main meeting place.

The protesters were kept away from the political venues. They couldn't get near the G-20 participants. They attacked the local concert hall, the Elbphilharmonic, where there were some G-20 musical events. A special dinner celebration with music featured Putin and Trump as honored guests with Ivanka Trump and her husband Jared Kushner included on the guest list.

As the world's most powerful politicians and assorted fiscal types dined on canapés and a seven-course dinner listening to Beethoven, the protesters battled the police outside the elegant concert hall. The concert venue was near a river and Greenpeace advocates using speedboats attempted to enter the back of the concert hall. They were stopped. Then other activists jumped into the water and they swim to the concert venue. A rock broke a U. S. delegates' car window. It was difficult for German police to control the violence.

Inside the concert hall Trump and his party dined, discussed and talked at length with the French President Emmanuel Macron and his wife Brigitte Trogneux. During the dinner the German hosts separated couples. Melania Trump said next to Vladimir Putin. Trump sat alongside Juliana Awada, the wife of Argentina's president. Then Trump abruptly got up and sat down next to Putin. They talked at length. They ignored the other diners. This was the dinner from hell.

Macron watched Trump. He realized ego, and a manic search for power obscured the president's lack of preparation. He was leading an unprepared American delegation. Macron would solve that problem. He invited Trump to be France's honored guest at the festive Bastille Day celebration. It was a smart move. France quickly became Europe's closest American ally. Macron became Trump's best friend.

What did Trump and Putin talk about? No one knows. The president left his interpreter behind. When questioned about the meeting, Trump replied: "No comment." The press was rife with speculation. The politicians who attended the meeting remarked Trump seemed to be disinterested in everyone but Putin.

Trump was determined to make Putin's acquaintance. He said he had a "very good" conversation with the Russian president. The White House press secretary reported they discussed a diplomatic resolution to the Syrian civil war, and the creation of safe zones to prevent indiscriminate killings, via bombings, of innocent civilians.

WAS THE WARSAW SPEECH AND G-20 BANNON'S END?

The European trips to the G-7 and G-20, as well as the Warsaw speeches, spelled the end of Steve Bannon. Ivanka Trump and Jared Kushner informed the president that Bannon was leaking material to Breitbart. As the Russian investigation heated up leaks from the White House were increasingly traced to Bannon. He also began using the derogatory term "Jarvanka" to describe Trump's daughter and son-in-law. Michael Wolff's Fire And Fury not only had a chapter on the Jarvanka couple, he wrote of Ivanka: "She's dumb as a brick." (p. 235) Bannon was the source for this comment. That singular comment began Bannon's road to oblivion. When Bannon attacked Ivanka in front of the president he said of her: "You are a fucking liar." (Michael Wolff, p. 237) This was another nail in Bannon's egotistical coffin.

As crazy as it sounds, Wolff reports Ivanka believed Bannon was blackmailing the president. How? She never said. Bannon pushed her for an answer. He complained to Wolff. Rather than being a political genius, Bannon was a petty little man who had exceeded his value to Trump. He was shown the door.

The real reason for Bannon's exile was his demand he have a greater role in decision-making. Trump, if anything, is smart organizationally. He realized Bannon was politically delusional, personally reprehensible and officially odorous. The brain fizzled. It was time for him to go. The list of people previously fired by Trump was a long one. Corey Lewandowski was gone as Chief of Staff. Long-time aide Sam Nunberg left long before the campaign heated up. There were countless others as Trump demanded servile loyalty. He was like a King in his fiefdom.

Of the many circumstances dooming Bannon the most significant one was his attempts to downgrade Jared Kushner's influence. Bannon thought he was a genius. He missed the president's connection to and loyalty for his son in law's advice. The Russian connection percolated. President Trump brought in high priced lawyers. They served as a conduit to shut Bannon down as well as the critics suggesting Russian collusion.

Ivanka Trump and Jared Kushner remained Trump's most loyal advisers. Bannon's attempts to isolate them from the president and exile them from the administration led to his banishment. Trump and Bannon made nice for the media. The president would not allow anyone to disrespect his family. Bannon excelled in this area.

By October 2017 Bannon was gone. The European trip and his advice on foreign policy was the catalyst to his exile back to Breitbart. He also spoke daily with Michael Wolff, the chameleon collecting tales without facts, for his million selling Fire And Fury: Inside The Trump White House. Bannon's ego! Poor advise! Bad decisions! These were the factors ending his time in the White House. Ironically, it all goes back to the Warsaw speech, the G-7 and G-20 and Trump's staff pointing out Bannon was dangerous. The Wolff book and the subsequent Mueller investigation would further destroy Bannon's so-called intellectual superiority and self-importance. Soon he was just another unemployed political hack looking for a vehicle to spew his ideas. Trump showed he was presidential by getting rid of Bannon.

What were the lessons from the G-20? The obvious one is Trump and Putin met, discussed various subjects and came to an agreement. On what no one knows. The wide range of issues included Syria and Russian interference in the 2016 election. Trump said after the meeting "it was time to move forward." No one knew what that meant.

The Kremlin's crime of hacking into the presidential election led Mueller to indict thirteen Russian nationals and three businesses. They were all safe from arrest as they were in Russia. Whether or not the Mueller investigation will turn up hard evidence of Trump's collusion with Russian leaders is unknown. Trump speaks positively about Putin. The Russian leader calls him "Mr. President." That is all one needs to do to become the Donald's best friend. This is a sad commentary on American diplomacy. Mueller, Congress and the American people need to right this wrong.

At the conclusion of the G-20 Trump did not hold a press conference. Why is this important? Every other major world leader held an end of G-20 press conference. Trump was not prepared to speak because he had little, if any, knowledge of diplomacy. Or for matter he didn't understand the G-20's purpose. His defenders remarked he looked at primarily bilateral agreements, and he is suspicious of the global economy. This pattern of not holding press conferences is one he pursued at home. He held only one U. S. press conference in the first six months in office. For a sitting U. S. president not to take questions on a foreign excursion is a break with precedent.

THIRTEEN

THE G-20: THE TRUMP-PUTIN 30-MINUTE MEETING TURNS INTO TWO AND A HALF HOURS AND HOW THE RUSSIAN'S OUTWITTED THE DONALD

"The lack of a U.S. translator or other support meant
the U.S. would be without a scrupulous translation
of a record of what was discussed."

JOHN KIRBY, CNN, COMMENTING ON A TRUMP-PUTIN MEETING.

Trump, who never got to meet Putin, when he was
in Moscow for the Miss Universe pageant in 2013,
finally had the chance now that he was the president.

MICHAEL ISIKOFF AND DAVID CORN

"The past and present tell us, too, that
demagogues can only thrive when a substantial
portion of the demos-the people-want him to."

JON MEACHAM, THE SOUL OF AMERICA,
THE BATTLE FOR BETTER ANGELS

The highpoint of the G-20 was the meeting between Trump and Putin. The back-story sounds like a John LeCarre novel. Russia hacked the Democratic National Committee. They may have also hacked into voting records. Their cyber crimes have never been explained. The CIA had moles within the Russian government. Only five days after Trump's inauguration a Russian business newspaper, **Kommersant**, reported Sergei Mikhailov, the Deputy Director of the

FSB's centre to investigate cyber crimes, was arrested and charged with being a CIA informant. There was a roundup of other Russian media agents who were accused of being U. S. informants.

Seth Hettena's book **Trump/Russia: A Definitive History** identifies Mikhailov as one of the "biggest names in Russian organized crime." (p. 58) He was an informant for the CIA and the operative wisdom is that Mikhailov was arrested and a black bag was placed over his head. He was charged with state crimes. In Russia that charge is treason. What does this have to do with Trump? Plenty!

It was alleged Mikhailov alerted the FBI and eventually the FBI that Kremlin insiders had a concerted plan to collect compromising material on Trump. Mikhailov vanished from Russian life. The reason? He was instrumental in helping put the Steele dossier together.

Then former FSB General Oleg Erovinkin was found dead in his car. It was alleged he helped to compile the Steele Dossier. The top Putin critic, Vladimir Kara-Murza, was poisoned but survived. It was the second attempt on his life. These events originated with or had the blessing of Vladimir Putin. This is whom Trump would meet at the G-20. The Donald would believe Putin's every bare faced lie. Sad!

THE DEVIL AND TRUMP: GENERAL FLYNN'S INFLUENCE

After Trump was inaugurated he made a deal with the devil. General Michael Flynn worked to re-establish ties with Russia. It is not uncommon for a presidential transition team to meet with foreign leaders. Flynn and Jared Kushner met with key Russian officials in Trump Tower prior to the election. This raised the possibility of collusion. The FBI's concern was there were too many Russians around Trump's inner circle.

The FBI believed Putin was working Trump's political naïve son-in-law. Those in Kushner's entourage were equally susceptible to Russian intrigue. After the FBI reviewed the Steele Dossier, their concerns increased. The explosive comment in the dossier was Russian intelligence had a potentially compromising Trump file. In other words the president would be blackmailed. Russian intelligence was rumored to have embarrassing personal data on Trump. The Steele document claimed Russia had for years collected materials on

Trump. The purpose was to compromise him. When it became obvious he had a chance to win the American presidency, the FSB began working with Trump campaign insiders. No crimes have been reported. There is scant evidence to validate these claims. Meetings took place. Crimes! The Mueller investigation will tell us.

The rumors concerning Trump's private life, according to those providing Steele with information, centered upon the quirky sexual preferences of the new American president. When FBI Director James Comey briefed Trump on rumors of hookers, golden showers and alleged assorted sexual peccadilloes, he silently decided to fire Comey. None of the charges were verified. Trump had reason to be angry. He believed this was the first step in the "deep state" taking him down. He began a program of nasty remarks on twitter, character assassinating during interviews and his goal was to cut into the FBI director's credibility. It backfired. In mid-April, 2018 Comey's book, **A Higher Loyalty: Truth, Lies, And Leadership** addressed the question of Donald J. Trump's fitness for office. Comey didn't mince his words. He believes the 45th president is morally unfit for the Executive Office. The president lies. The president engages in character assassination. The president threatens to jail his political opponents. As Comey concludes Trump is "unethical and untethered to truth and institutional values." (p. 275) Comey sees the truth and institutional values being destroyed in the Trump presidency. Like most other observers Comey is bewildered by Trump's love affair with Putin and Russia. This is what led to the Mueller investigation. So far there is no evidence of Trump's collusion or any other acts related to Russia. Yet, he continues to spin Russian tales in variance with the truth.

TRUMP AND THE RUSSIAN QUESTION

Trump repeatedly said he had no business deals in Russia. This wasn't true. What was true is that he hadn't built a Trump Tower in Moscow. He had numerous Russian business connections. The Russians were gathering information on him for the future. According to Isikoff and Corn's book, Trump's alleged weird sexual indiscretions, the data collector said, "was an open secret" (p. 146) This prompted the president to repeatedly deny Russian collusion while planning to fire Comey and destroy his reputation. Former FBI Director Comey told Trump the Steele Dossier claimed he was with prostitutes in Moscow in 2013. He said Russian agents filmed these trysts. Trump denied the dossier's claims. No evidence has proven it. "I didn't mention one particular allegation in the dossier," Comey wrote that "he was having prostitutes urinating on him." (p. 224). The president-elect was enraged when he found out Comey hadn't mentioned this in the Steel Dossier briefing two weeks before his inauguration.

The data collector told Steele the compromising material on President Trump was explosive. Comey privately presented it to the president-elect because he feared the press would blindside him. The president-elect viewed Comey's message as a threat as well as a challenge. He believed Comey was attempting to co-opt him. If Comey swore his allegiance to Trump there would not be a problem. If not, he would be fired. It would take time. Trump would build a case in the press.

It was complicated for Trump. The Steele Dossier's charge that the president-elect consorted with Russian prostitutes was all over the press. It became in time a sensational story. But Trump survived it. When Comey briefed Trump about the "gold showers" incident two weeks before the inauguration, the president-elect had fits of rage. He didn't fire Comey for briefing him on the Steele Dossier. Trump feared Comey would intensify the Russian collusion investigation. There was no thought of appointing a Special Counsel and Trump believed he ended the FBI's investigation into his inner-circle colluding with Russia by firing Comey. He became obsessed with the Russian investigation hollering "no collusion" continually.

What was Comey's initial reaction to the Steele Dossier? He deduced Russia spent five years collecting data on Trump. Why? They had no idea he would become the president. The Russian's collected this data for business reasons. When Trump was elected president, a Russian Television reporter said: "He's ours!"

According to Isikoff and Corn, "Trump has declined various sweetener real estate deals offered him in Russia...." (p. 146) The Steele Dossier alleged Trump's campaign advisers theorized they would receive damaging materials on Hillary Clinton. Trump and his campaign staff soft-pedaled criticism of Putin. A superior Kremlin intelligence machine in the political arena played them all. Amateurs without training and arrogant, entitled billionaires were no matches for season's foreign policy professionals. The point was Vladimir Putin sold Donald J. Trump the big lie. Russia did not collude, said Putin, and the inept, unsophisticated American president bought the lie. Elect a clown. Expect a circus.

MEETING PUTIN: WHAT DID IT MEAN?

The anticipated meeting at the G-20 between American President Donald J. Trump and his Russian counterpart, Vladimir Putin, was a civilized affair. There were many things discussed, nothing was accomplished. No one is sure what was said. From all accounts it appeared a positive meeting. Perhaps it was nothing more than casual conversation. No one knows. The media spent an inordinate amount of time covering a non-event.

The free press is an investigative body. They raised a number of questions. A U. S. representative did not accompany the President from the State Department or a National Security Adviser to take notes. The Russian translator had the only record of the conversation. Conspiracies were in the air.

If there was collusion there is no written or verbal evidence. Trump tweeted: "Fake News story of secret dinner with Putin is sick. The Chancellor of Germany invited all G-20 leaders, and spouses. The Press knew." This July 18, 2017 tweet was followed at 5:59 PM by another Trump tweet: "The Fake News is becoming more and more dishonest!" He continued: "Even a dinner arranged for top 20 leaders in Germany is made to look sinister." It wasn't. The press reported it accurately.

Trump was upset. His attempt to find a common ground with Russia was ignored. In the sweltering early July Hamburg heat, Trump vowed to have a one-on-one conversation with his Russian counterpart. Why did Trump feel this way? He saw it as building a bridge to Russia.

The best description of the Trump-Putin G-20 meeting is in Steven Rosenfeld's **Democracy Betrayed: How Superdelegates, Redistricting, party Insiders, And The Electoral College Rigged The 2016 Election**.

He argues Trump and Putin conspired to downplay the Russian collusion story. It would cut into both their power base if it were true that collusion was a factor. Professor Timothy Snyder of Yale University also weighed in on the argument pointed out hacking voting machines didn't matter. What the Russians did was to hack into social media organizing anti-Hillary rallies, castigating her on social media and providing a Kremlin based campaign to bring Trump to the presidency. There was more information as fake e-mails were sent to election vendors and local election offices

By targeting Clinton on Facebook and twitter Russian operatives further damaged his candidacy. Joshua Green and Sasha Issenberg, writing in **Bloomberg** in late October 2016 reported negative messages urging Democrats and independents not to vote. They said Hillary would win the election. Political ads and fake news from the Trump camp, the Kremlin and Russians assuming an American identity ruined Clinton's chances for an electoral victory.

THE TRUMP CAMPAIGN VISA VIA RUSSIA: MEETING AT THE G-20 AND JOURNALISTIC TALES OF BLACKMAIL

When he campaigned for the presidency, Trump anticipated a rapprochement with Russia. His administration has been beset with investigations claiming Russian election interferences helped him win the presidency. This outraged Trump. During the 2016 campaign Trump praised Putin. Why? No one knows!

Trump said Putin was "very smart." The Trump-Putin meetings would not take place until the July 2017 G-20 Summit. The notion of a budding Trump-Putin friendship obscured the similarities between the two world leaders. They were ideologically similar. They disliked the role of the UN. They had no respect for the European Union. They supported a bellicose, often bigoted, white nationalism. They were hard line authoritarians.

The London media was enthralled with the Trump-Putin story. Luke Harding, a **Guardian** reporter in his book **Collusion: Secret Meetings, Dirty Money, And How Russia Helped Donald Trump Win** observed of Trump's campaign: "Had Putin somehow been blackmailing the candidate?" (p. 8) Harding continued: "If Trump had indeed conspired with Russia, not only publicly but perhaps covertly too, via undisclosed back channels, that looked like treachery. It was Watergate all over again." (p. 9) There is no evidence Trump engaged in obstruction of justice, but this is the direction of Harding's book.

Harding observed, in the **London Guardian**, Trump's constant praise for Putin raised red flags. As Trump blasted other world leaders, he maintained a loyalty to Putin. The Steele Dossier and Harding's reporting made three key points: 1.) Moscow, Harding maintained, has three decades of information on Trump's finances, and his behavior. 2.) There were rumors of Russian cash from private individuals and from government sources that were a part of Trump real estate deals. There is no evidence for this, only anecdotal information. The groundwork for a lucrative arrangement in Moscow to build a business building and a Trump Tower is a project that was being negotiated for years without success. This allowed Trump to say he had not built anything in Russia. He was in the negotiating process. He had plausible deniability. There were loans in 2008 that rescued Trump financially that allegedly may have resulted from someone laundering billions of dollars of Russian oligarch's money. Again, this is rumor. There is no verification. 3.) Harding speculates the president had unknown or previously undisclosed financial windows into the Moscow banking world. Once again there is no corroboration.

The Trump-Putin talks focused upon the return of Russian diplomatic compounds seized in New York and Maryland. President Barack Obama ordered the intelligence gathering properties confiscated, as they were Kremlin fronts for spying in violation of American law. When Trump told the State Department he was in favor of returning the Russian properties, he met with heavy dissent. The president couldn't understand why the properties were seized from the Russian government. When the law was read to him, he said maybe the Kremlin was spying and maybe there were not. State Department officials couldn't believe it. There was evidence of spying and cyber attacks.

The Russian's also wanted Konstantin Yaroshenok returned to his country. He was sentenced to twenty years in prison for smuggling one hundred million dollars of cocaine into the United States.

Trump wanted to talk to Putin about the increasingly probable arms race and the return of the properties. He withheld for a time the return of these expensive properties. The State Department was beside itself with a president who had no idea about past history and Russian policy.

FINALLY, THE FACE TO FACE: TRUMP AND PUTIN

The first Trump-Putin meeting took place on a Friday July 7, 2017. It was much ballyhooed. There was little accomplished. Trump remarked the six-minute private talk, before the press came in resulted in, as Trump reflected on, "a lot of very positive things happening for Russia, for the United States and for everybody concerned. It's an honor to be with you." Putin responded: "I am delighted to be able to meet you personally, Mr. President."

The Trump-Putin meeting ignored the sharp retorts the President made in Poland. He called out Russia's "destabilizing activities." He charged Kremlin support for Syria and Iran was the wrong direction. He didn't say he believed Russia interfered in the 2016 presidential election. "I think it was Russia but I think it was probably other people and/or countries, and I see nothing wrong with that statement. Nobody really knows for sure," Trump concluded.

The press had a field day with the Trump-Putin meeting. The critics labeled it "disastrous." Why? The answer is a simple one. Trump bragged: "I strongly pressed President Putin twice about Russian meddling in our election." Then Trump backtracked stating: "It's an honor to meet President Putin." Republican Senator Lindsey Graham of South Carolina, responded: "It's not the dumbest thing I've ever heard, but it's pretty close."

WHY TRUMP DOESN'T UNDERSTAND
RUSSIA AND NEVER WILL

The ensuing Trump scandal with Russia highlights Donald J. Trump's initial failure in foreign policy. He doesn't understand Russian history. The course of diplomacy since World War I is not a subject Trump mastered. His grasp of Russian history is minimal. He has little, if any, knowledge of Vladimir Putin. The differences between the two countries are broad and varied. The constant war between our democracy and the Kremlin's Communism didn't end with the collapse of the Soviet government. It endures. Once the Cold War ended, President Ronald Reagan uttered his famous statement to "tear down the wall," a new Russia emerged.

Vladimir Putin is the unrequited leader of that new Russia. He will do and say anything to preserve, maintain and extend Russian power. The expansion into former Russian satellite nations, the increasing meddling in Syrian affairs, the friendly relations with Iran, calling out the U. S. for being hostile to North Korea and the attempts to disrupt German and European Union politics are examples of Putin's political skill. This suggests Russia's strength. There is no discernible U. S. policy toward Russia. Trump wants to be friends. He hopes to improve relations. This in itself is not a bad thing. It hasn't resulted in diplomatic gains. If anything, it is Russia that has increased its world prestige. Trump and his amateur diplomats go from one muddle to the next.

At the G-20 Summit, President Trump spent so much time shaking hands with Putin, smiling at the cameras, talking about new trade agreements that he didn't realize how shrewd Putin was in international affairs. What does the Donald not recognize about Putin and the Russians? First and foremost, Putin hopes to weaken NATO, subvert democratic institutions and weaken the U. S.'s trans-Atlantic alliance. As Trump shakes hands with Putin, America's world leadership declines. The Russian leader smiles approvingly. Another foreign policy fool, Putin thinks, to add to Russia's charm.

The question of sanctions continued as Trump told a **New York Times** reporter that he left the door open to ease sanctions. What Trump didn't tell the press is negotiations were underway to return the two diplomatic compounds that were seized under President Barack Obama. The Donald will do anything to wipe out Obama's legacy.

When the U. S. Senate voted 98 to 2 to impose tough new sanctions on Russia, Trump didn't respond. He quietly disapproved. The U. S. sent a clear message they would block any future lifting of sanctions. The U. S. Senate made a statement. Trump wasn't strong enough challenging Russian expansion into the Ukraine. The old sanctions remained. Trump in time refused a later request for increased Russian sanctions. Then he angrily capitulated. Then in a second phase U. N. Ambassador Nikki Haley announced sanctions and then two days later Trump reversed this decision. Lack of a coherent foreign policy was a problem sixteen months into his presidency. It was a mess.

Russia's oil dependent economy stagnated. Putin wants the sanctions lifted. He also wants the Russian compounds in Maryland and New York returned. That is quietly taking place. The agreement Trump has with Putin is troublesome. He said the two nations would work on a cyber security program. He ignored Russia's meddling in the 2016 election.

THE HAMBURG G-20 SUMMIT: WHAT HAPPENED?

When the G-20 Summit convened, it was looked upon as a place where the richest nations debated the global economy. In the past breaking the rules drew a swift rebuke from G-20 members. In 2014 Putin was lectured for Russia's aggressive moves into the Ukraine.

In 2017 President Trump and Putin stole the show with their meetings. The seemingly endless handshakes were daily press staples. The Donald's defense of all things Russian and the American president did everything he could to downplay Russia's dirty tricks in international politics. On July 7 and 8, 2017 there was less than a cordial atmosphere at the G-20. This is what President Trump brings to the table. He is an attack dog oblivious to the facts. He is unconcerned about feelings. His views are one-dimensional.

German Chancellor Angela Merkel said securing agreement on issues of free speech, democracy and fair trade was impossible. The U. S. refused to support these issues. Barbara Unmussig, a German political activist, commented Trump subverted democracy. What is it that bothered those who attended the G-20 Summit? President Trump's refusal to talk global issues mystified the other G-20 members. He was primarily concerned with U. S. nationalism. He demanded fairness for American products. He remarked employment for American workers was his motivation. He made it clear world agreements, like the Paris Climate Accord, would have no place in American foreign policy.

GERMANY FEARS TRUMP WILL DIVIDE EUROPE

The question of what happened at the G-20 has many answers. One stands out! Germany is convinced the U. S. is out to divide the European Union. This will increase the power of Russia and alter standing international agreements. When Trump and Putin casually chatted, Chancellor Merkel pointed out this compromised her plan to challenge Russia in the Ukraine. A German foreign minister wrote of the G-20: "The summit went very well for Russia….As long as the U. S. breaks rank, Russia can swim in the mainstream."

In Angela Merkel's political circles criticism of Trump's visit to Poland, prior to the G-20, was vocal with subtle charges of Russian collusion. His critics claimed he supported Russian policies in Eastern Europe. Germany charged Trump's unwillingness to condemn Russia's aggressive actions in Eastern Europe. This did not bode well for future international relations.

There were other concerns for Germany. The Chinese were arriving to fund European businesses. The Russians will have more input into Germany when the "Nord Stream," a gas pipeline from Russian to Germany makes Europe more dependent on Russian oil. There is no longer a cohesive view of Germany and the EU. Trump's visit, his policies, and his over the top rhetoric brought a new vision to the G-20. It was a U. S. slap in the face to European nations.

THE SECOND TRUMP-PUTIN MEETING
INTRIGUES THE PRESS

The unresolved question from the G-20 is what did Trump and Putin talked about on July 7, 2017 in their second meeting? It was a private affair. The press wasn't invited. Putin showed up with a translator. Trump came alone. There was no script. There was no record of the meeting. It was as Ian Bremmer, a political scientist and president of the Eurasia Group, told Charlie Rose, the two leaders met at Hamburg's global summit after a state dinner. The sit down with Putin lasted more than two hours.

Ian Bremmer: "Never in my life as a political scientist have I seen major countries with a constellation of national interests that are as dissonant, while the two leaders seem to be doing everything possible to make nice and be close to each other." **The New York Times** argued: "It is rare for American presidents to meet other leaders, especially adversaries, one-on-one, with little evident preparation." **The New York Times** suggested Trump doesn't believe Russia is an adversary.

When H. R. McMaster, Trump's National Security Adviser, warned him about Russia, the president ignored the message. McMaster didn't believe Putin was trustworthy. Trump probably acted on impulse in the second meeting with Putin.

Sean Spicer compounded the second Trump-Putin meeting by continually changing the story. He couldn't explain why and how it took place. Spicer's various explanations made no sense. He said it was a friendly meeting. He said it was an off the cuff discussion. He said it was about pleasantries. He said it was nothing more than small talk. Take your pick! Spicer used each of these moronic statements to defend the meeting. What took place? No one knows. Only Trump, Putin and the Russian interpreter know what was discussed. They aren't talking. According to the president any other description fits in the fake news category.

RECAPPING THE G-20: THE PUTIN-TRUMP CONNECTION
When the G-20 concluded, the major topic was Trump and Putin's second conversation. The press reported the two countries agreed informally not to meddle in each other's political affairs. "They had a very robust and healthy exchange on the subject," Secretary Tillerson said of the Russian hacking scandal. The problem was President Trump would not blame Russia for hacking. He did say the two sides came together to study how to prevent future cyber hacking.

The last Trump-Putin meeting lasted two hours and sixteen minutes with Tillerson and Sergey Lavrov in attendance with a translator. The result? It appears nothing of substance was decided. That is exactly how Putin wanted it. He can share the international spotlight and he can agree to little, if anything, of substance. Conducting an aggressive and successful foreign policy is not Trump's mantra.

When Sergey Lavrov talked with American and British reporters, seven months after this meeting, his presence was explained at the Trump-Putin meeting. Foreign Minister Lavrov was the chief apologist for Russian meddling in the 2016 election. He said time and time again Russia "could not and did not" interfere with the election. He said there is no evidence to prove this contention. He also alleged Trump would not have met with Putin and remained friendly to Russia if election meddling was a problem. The disingenuous nature of Lavrov told America all it needed to know about Russian meddling in the 2016 election. Did it go further? Robert Mueller's investigation will tell us just how far.

FOURTEEN

TRUMP'S DEAL WITH THE DEVIL: PUTIN'S SHADOW AND PREPARING FOR BASTILLE DAY

"The news is real. The president is fake."

STEPHEN KING

"If Islam is not political it is nothing."

AYATOLLAH KHOMEINI

The picture and image of Donald J. Trump in foreign affairs was established in 2017 from May 26-28 at the G-7 and from July 7-8 at the G-20. What did Europeans perceive about the American president? They concluded he had Russian friendly advisers, notably the fired General Michael Flynn, and he refused to criticize Vladimir Putin.

The first indication of Trump's pro-Russian bromance with Putin took place a year earlier on April 27, 2016 when he gave his first major foreign policy speech to the Center For The National Interest. Many attendees were intrigued that Sergey Kislyak, the Russian Ambassador, sat in the front row. This is a conservative Washington think tank. Many observers were surprised with Trump's pro-Russian remarks.

This speech provided an insight into Russia's influence. At the reception, prior to Trump's speech, Jeff Sessions and Jared Kushner talked at length with Kislyak. The NSA monitored Kislyak and the agency reported he discussed Trump's speech with his Russian superiors. That is certainly not a crime. It is an indication of Russian interest. The intriguing aspect in NSA documents is Kislyak discussed how Trump's campaign and policies would benefit Russia economically.

American observers, according to Isikoff and Corn, were concerned with a "honey pot." What is a honey pot? It is the planting of false information to hurt a candidate. At this point a Democratic strategist and Hillary Clinton's campaign manager, Robby Mook, realized the Democratic National Headquarters had been hacked. He went to campaign officials, and he suggested Russian cyber criminals were supporting Trump's campaign. No one believed him.

No one envisioned the degree of bullying, lack of knowledge and disdain for Europe that Trump would display when he became president. He was truly a foreign policy bully. Democracy was in peril. It was Trump against the world.

THE BULLY EMERGES: EUROPE AND
THE TRUMP SUMMER OF 2017

In matters of foreign policy, President Trump does not inspire confidence. He is the only American president to have neither served in the military nor in the government before settling into the Oval Office.

After bullying, insulting, intimidating, lying and ignoring the major world leaders at the G-20 in Hamburg Germany, Trump stood alone on the world stage. He was a difficult American president. He made the statement the U. S. would no longer cooperate with Europe. It was now every country for itself. The young French President, Emmanuel Macron, had a Trump moment. They shook hands so vigorously there was a testosterone melt down. President Macron recognized Trump's ego triumphed his good sense. He invited his American counterpart to Paris to celebrate Bastille Day.

Trump spent four days at home preparing to travel to Paris for the July 14, 2017 Bastille Day Parade. The French pulled out all stops. Trump was magnificent on the international stage.

Why was Trump invited to Bastille Day? The answer is the French hoped for a rapprochement with the U. S. The magic of France's Bastille Day celebration was the parade Trump witnessed down the Champs-Elysees and around to the nearby Place de la Concorde. The French military in all its pomp and circumstance is on display. It is an impressive outburst of local nationalism. "The United States is our friend-nothing will ever separate us," Macron said. What was Macron after? He talked at length with Trump about global warming. The result is the president said the U. S. would work to protect the environment despite withdrawing from the Paris Climate Agreement.

TRUMP PREPARES FOR BASTILLE DAY: PUTIN'S SHADOW

The July 14 Bastille Day holiday was celebrated in Paris with French President Emmanuel Macron inviting Trump to join him in the festive incursion into European affairs. The French trip should have given Trump the chance to explain U.S. goals in Europe. He didn't discuss in depth American foreign policy. The reason? He didn't have one. He talked about himself. He used the word "I" hundreds of times. The French wondered what he believed the U. S. role was in Western Europe.

The irony of the French trip was apparent in daily rapid-fire press questions about Putin and Russia. There was also disapproval for a speech Trump made in Warsaw the day before the G-20. He made more enemies spewing disinformation and confused explanations than any previous president.

There is no unity or cohesion to Trump's foreign policy. In the case of Poland, he played one nation off against another. This is classic Trump. Fire and fury. Confuse the issues. Never talk about policy. Trump threatens and cajoles without understanding Poland's role in the American international defense system. With 5,000 American troops in Poland the country is a strong U. S. ally. The Polish president stated the U. S. is an important player in a region dedicated to making sure Russia does not interfere in local politics. Trump had no idea.

Jeff Rathke, a Senior Fellow and Deputy Director For The European Program at the Center For Strategic And International Studies, pointed out Poland is nervous sharing a border with Russia. Although President Trump is determined to make friends with Vladimir Putin, to negotiate trade treaties and to pursue renegotiated defense agreements, much of the rest of the United States is nervous about Russia and Putin.

The question of Russian interference in the 2016 election remains a major issue. That is with everyone except Trump. At the G-20, he said perhaps it was Russia who interfered in our election, but perhaps it was someone else. The smile on Putin's face told it all. The sanctions imposed on three-dozen Russian business people and diplomats tells one all they need to know about the Kremlin's nefarious goals. Trump counters this with hope for improved relations. Sanctions? He ignores them. Or he blatantly refuses to impose Congressional mandated sanctions.

AFTER THE FACT THOUGHTS ON TRUMP-PUTIN AND RUSSIAN MONEY: IS THIS ACCIDENTAL COLLUSION OR BUSINESS?

When he met for two plus hours with Putin, Trump did not have an agenda. His aides said he was experimenting in diplomacy. What is known is Putin and Trump have talked three times on the telephone since he took office.

There is ample evidence Trump had serious contacts, if minimal ones, in Russian since 2013. Luke Harding's Collusion: Secret Meetings, Dirty Money And How Russia Helped Donald Trump Win devotes forty pages to Trump's Russian business ties. This is not to suggest he has broken the law. It suggests Trump has not been forthcoming concerning his Russian business endeavors.

Harding said Trump traveled to Russia for the first time in 1986 to attend a luncheon sponsored by Estee Lauder. In The Art of The Deal, Trump said: "One thing led to another, and now I'm talking about building a large luxury hotel, across the street from the Kremlin, in partnership with the Soviet government." Ronald Lauder has known Trump for fifty years and the Estee Lauder Company introduced Trump to Russian business insiders.

Another Harding observation is Russian agents were currying favor with the future president from the mid-1980s. In March 1986 Russian General Vladimir Alexandrovich Kruchkov arrived in the U.S. and Luke Harding claims this was part of a five-year plan to provide Kremlin friendship to Trump. Again, no collusion is proven. What is evident is Trump from the 1980s had a soft spot for Russia.

The KGB had a file on Trump. When it was opened no one knows. What we do know is the file contains business deals, personal-social life experiences, and the file stated of Trump: "His attitude toward women is also of interest."

293

When Trump traveled to Moscow in the autumn of 1986, he sat next to Soviet Ambassador Yuri Dubinin whose daughter, Natalia, told reporters she recalled Trump talked of building a Moscow hotel. By the time the G-7 and G-20 concluded Trump had a thirty year history with Russian businessmen, politicians, interested citizens and this invalidates his claims he had nothing to do with Russia. Whether or not Trump and Putin had a relationship prior to his successful presidential rum remains an unanswered question.

In the aftermath of the G-20, people wondered about the two world leaders. Again, there is no proof of collusion. There remains the mysterious and unexplainable close friendship. Putin and Trump acted like old friends in Hamburg. They also angered members of the G-20 when they didn't attend the talks on climate change. Luke Harding argues Trump "signed off on Putin's big lie." That lie is Russia was not involved in hacking or interfering in the 2016 election.

THE AFTERMATH OF THE G-7 AND G-20:
TRUMP'S POLICIES ISOLATE THE U. S.

In the aftermath of the G-7 and G-20 Summits, German Chancellor Angela Merkel made her distaste for Trump's policies a key issue. She said: "Europe must fight for its own future and destiny." President Trump accused Germany of having too favorable a trade arrangement with the U. S. He argued Germany's trade surplus takes advantage of American interests. He also points to a lack of spending by the German government on national defense.

On this point Trump is correct as NATO depends on U. S. technology, troops and monetary support. Europe does not pay fairly for its defense. Germany, Belgium, France and the Netherlands counter they are spending defense money at home fighting jihadists. The level of terrorist attacks, and the influx of immigrants are problems. The European Union has an open border and difficulty in combating ISIS. In France the right wing conservative, Marine Le Pen, a former candidate of a fringe party, came in second in France's presidential election. Her issue was domestic safety. This is the same issue that helped Trump hijack the presidency.

Another issue is defense spending. The U. S. spends more than three times the amount on national defense compared to Germany. France spends a little more than half of the U. S. expenditure as does the U. K.

TRUMP WEIGHS IN ON NATO PROVING
HE DOESN'T UNDERSTAND IT

In late May 2017, President Trump weighed in on matters of European defense. In a blistering criticism of NATO he suggested European nations "owe massive amounts of money" to the alliance. He continually charged twenty-three of the twenty-eight member nations are not paying their fair share of defense costs. He stated the U. S. pays twenty-two percent of the NATO budget. Trump has never taken the time to familiarize himself with European politics, the EU or the alliances between the U.S. and Europe. He was like a bull in a China shop, as he attended the G-7, the G-20, spoke in Warsaw and celebrated Bastille Day. It was good for the Donald's ego. It was disastrous for American Foreign Policy.

Why is Europe unable to fund national defense? The answer is a simple one! The European welfare state is funded via taxes. There is little left over for military purposes. Western Europe's extensive and elaborate welfare system relies heavily on not having to implement major defense costs.

Whether it is socialized medicine, hefty unemployment stipends, or guaranteed housing, the European Union's budget simply can't afford to pay for defense. The European welfare state is in trouble. When Britain exited the European Union in the Brexit vote, it was due to a number of factors. The English welfare state was threatening bankruptcy. Britain's National Health Service requested U. K. patients pay a special fee to see a doctor. Otherwise a nurse will take over the doctor's duties. The British reacted to their financial woes leaving the EU.

The influx of immigrants reduced native taxpayers. This added to the financial nightmares plaguing everyone. Some European Union countries were granting vacation time to married couples to have more children to produce more taxpayers.

President Trump believes the days of subsidizing Europe are over. He left the Paris Climate Accord for this reason. He believes Europe needs to spend more money on national defense. Trump and many Americans view climate change as nothing more than a hoax. There are few ways to quantify climate change. They claim it is a policy that may not lead to a better environment. There is little accountability for climate change. The policies are one's government's hope will work. The Trump administration left the Paris Climate Agreement for one reason-money. The U. S. financial contribution and scientific findings were monetarily huge.

Diplomatic experts argue America's commitment and backing of Europe since World War II is the key reason the continent grew economically and politically. It never experienced chaos. The Trump administration appears to be bringing an end to that policy.

The cost of backing away from traditional European allies is disastrous. Radical Islamic militants endanger the European Union's border policies. This is compounded by the EU's budget crisis. The massive cost of inflation for Europe's domestic welfare state threatens the comfortable middle class life style Europeans enjoy.

President Trump is not the first U.S. president who is willing to tell Europe that America can't keep financing the EU. Europe adds to its costs by refusing to budge on its open border policies. President's George W. Bush and Barack Obama pressured NATO to increase its military spending. They didn't. When Trump arrived in Europe, in the summer of 2017, his NATO policies were not markedly different from the two previous presidents'. The difference is Trump is a truculent critic demanding Europe spend more for NATO defenses.

"Many of these nations owe massive amounts of money from past years and not paying in those past years," Trump said. This statement is not true. Ivo Daalder, a former NATO Ambassador under President Obama, said: "Europe may owe itself; it certainly owes nothing to the U. S." What Trump doesn't understand is money is paid into a central bank not to the U. S.

MACRON AND TRUMP: THE FRIGHTENING SIMILARITES

At first glance French President Emmanuel Macron and his American counterpart had nothing in common. Macron is a short, stylish, well-dressed; articulate spokesperson with a sophisticated French presence. Trump is a billionaire representing guys with beer stained t-shirts with the logo "I'm A Proud Wife Beater." The Donald represents an alt-white nationalism and those who want to drain the swamp.

Macron and Trump have a great deal in common. They are legendary ladies men. Macron is married to his former teacher who is twenty years older. Trump is married to a super model twenty plus years younger. They both hate disagreement. That is agree with them, and their policies, or else prepare for a personal attack. They favor stylish clothes and hair. One has his own hair and the other is a master of hair disguise.

They both appeal to a redefined nationalism. For Macron he is intent upon making France the European leader in world affairs. He is also a symbol of vibrant local nationalism celebrating culture, fashion, food and diplomacy. The style and substance of what it means to be French is on display daily in Macron's Paris. The novelist, Michel Houellebecq, labeled Macron the leader of "a reinvigorated national pride." The novelist called the French presidency "group therapy" for a nation seeking to reenter the world arena. Macron's speeches suggest he will make France great again. The similarities to Trump are eerie and poignant.

They both practice personal and political narcissism. Sophie Pedder, Paris editor for the Economist, observed Macron lifted France into a position of international strength and fiscal credibility. The French President views the United States in the same manner. It is for this reason he invited President Trump to stand by his side at the Bastille Day parade. One narcissist to another makes sense. "Macron's invitation served no purpose other than to glorify Macron himself, who reveled in every moment of the celebrations," Pedder concluded.

Like Trump, Macron vilifies those who oppose or criticize him. Macron humiliated Pierre de Villiers, the head of the French army, when he expressed his concern at army budget cuts. Macron told

Villiers: "Je suis votre chef." Which means he is the head of the army. Like Trump, Macron never served a day in the service of his country.

In southern France, Macron challenged the parliamentary victory of the conservative opposition when they elected Deputy Emmanuelle Menard. Just like the Donald, Macron screamed fake news, fraudulent voters and erratic voting counts.

Macron may even be worse than Trump attacking the press. He summoned the editor of Paris Match to the presidential palace complaining of photographs published from the Nice massacre. Like the United States, the French courts refuse to invalidate this egregious behavior. The authoritarian smell to Macron's France is as frightening as Trump's attempt to destroy the FBI, end the investigative arm of the federal government, shut down parts of the NSA and systematically reduce the State Department.

Like Macron, Trump is incapable of manners, restraint, good sense and humility. It is a match made in heaven. The young authoritarian invites the master authoritarian to the Bastille Day parade. Then eight months later Trump is talking of a Washington D. C. parade even bigger than the annual Bastille Day celebration. You can't let those damn frogs one up you. Uber nationalism knows no bounds.

The Macron emphasis upon French national pride echoes Trump's "Making America Great Again." It is a testosterone-based nationalism based on bigotry, racism and fears of immigrants. Macron caused a controversy cancelling the annual Bastille Day press conference. Trump bans the press at times from covering his daily activity. Le Monde, Paris's premier daily newspaper, said of Macron: "His complex thought process lends itself badly." That is a polite way of remarking, like the Donald, he hasn't mastered daily government activity. Le Monde has at times suggested Macron has a battle with the truth. The Paris daily-observed Macron's ego is "the size of an eponymous planet." As he flew into Paris on Air Force One, Trump was the master of subterfuge.

TRUMP AS THE MASTER OF SUBTERFUGE:
BASTILLE DAY IS NEXT

Before he flew to Paris Trump had some explaining to do. In the 1990s, Trump repeatedly attacked France for trade reasons calling them: "the worst team player I have ever seen in my life." On March 21, 2003 he appeared on the Fox TV News show "Your World With Neil Cavuto," a day after the Iraq invasion. Trump remarked the French "never liked" the U. S. "except when we were bailing them out." The comments on France and the French were noted in the Paris press.

Since 1980 Trump has criticized French trade policies. He accused them of taking advantage of the U. S. The only problem is there is little free trade between the countries. What set the French media against Trump? It was his support for the right wing presidential candidate Marine Le Pen.

What has Trump missed in French history? Plenty! By backing Le Pen, Trump let it be known he was not a fan of democratic liberalism. What else did Trump miss? French politics always had a socialist-communist tinge. By the early 1990s, French Socialism was on the rise. The Communist Party was in decline and a new feeling was growing for a socialist government.

A large minority of French voters supported Marine Le Pen's National Front. Her right wing bigoted politics, echoed Donald Trump's anti-Muslim, anti-immigrant nationalism. This French party complained of "swarms of North African children invading Paris." Le Pen wanted all foreigners out of France. She screamed at rallies the National Front would rid France of foreign elements. The left was attacked. The press was vilified. Other political parties were disparaged. A white France was her clarion call. Like Trump's message, Le Pen fooled the electorate. By voting for the National Front some French voters envisioned a new system of equality. The French were intent on wiping out class differences. Just the opposite has taken place. Le Pen argued intellectuals abandoned the interests of working people. Le Pen's bigotry, her appeal to a motivated, highly defined French nationalism, her outrageous charges of government malfeasance, and her lamenting immigrants made her candidacy a clarion call for future white supremacists. She is France's female Trump. Macron was elected.

EMMANUEL MACRON AND TRUMP'S VISIT

As Emmanuel Macron assumed the French Presidency many American reporters had little knowledge or concern with his policies. This quickly changed. He became a major player in international politics. He quickly established ties with Germany. He also realized Trump was not interested in leading NATO. The U. S. is no longer a force in European politics. Macron saw a chance to enhance France's friendship with the U. S. That led to wining, dining and appealing to Trump's ego during Bastille Day. It worked. France is now our closest European ally.

When he was invited to Paris a dinner was planned on the second floor restaurant of the Eiffel Tower. For once the Donald checked his ego at the door. He became presidential. Trump later recalled it was the biggest crowd ever to welcome him in French history outside this famous landmark. That statement is true as it was Trump's first Paris visit. There are still peals of laughter all over Paris over this comment. What did Macron hope to accomplish in this appeal to Trump's ego?

Macron realized increased trade with the U. S. benefitted France. As German Chancellor Merkel bashed U. S. foreign policy, Macron praised Trump's leadership. Clearly, he saw the president as a political-economic partner. Now it was just a matter of convincing Trump there was a bright future with a close French alliance. Not once did Macron mention America's narrow self-interest.

How brilliant is Emmanuel Macron? Very! He told the Sunday Paris Journal Du Dimanche the famous knuckle busting handshake with Trump was important to show France's independence. He said he was no pushover. He was a European leader. When this comment was mentioned to Trump weeks later, he smiled. He liked Macron. The testosterone brothers were in business.

While in Paris, Trump realized the importance of his visit. It was the 100th anniversary of the U. S. entry into World War I. U. S. troops marched alongside their French counterparts down the Champs Elysses. When Macron was asked why Trump was invited, the

French President pointed to ties going back to the American Revolution. He was working Trump.

The military display put on by the French made an indelible impression upon Trump. He couldn't wait for his own parade. Trump's thirty-hour visit to Paris made a lasting impression. When French President Macron talked of preserving a strong military to achieve continued personal liberties, Trump cheered this statement. He would expand the American military. He would talk tough to America's enemies. He would be the next president to declare war. Did he do this with strategic information? No! He thought it was a good idea because of the pomp and ceremony of the French military during the Bastille Day parade. This is the type of shallow leadership, lack of judgment and impulsive behavior making Trump the worst president in American history.

FIFTEEN

RUSSIAN TELEVISION: EXPLAINS DONALD J. TRUMP AND LOVES HIM

"Their mission now is not to report on Russia
but to tell everyone how bad America is."

ALEXEY KOVALEV ON RT.

"Now might be a politically sensible time for Russia
to move away from the idea of a closer relationship
between the top capitals. Russia is not used to this
level of chaos in Washington. Putin may not have
liked Obama, but at least he knew where he stood."

MATTHEW CHANCE

"There was no collusion (it is a hoax) and there is
no obstruction of justice (that is a setup & trap)."

DONALD J. TRUMP TWEET

When you enter the London newsrooms of RT, the television channel formerly known as Russia Today, you are in an ultramodern and spacious 16th floor office overlooking the Thames and the London Eye. The RT London bureau chief, Nikolay A. Bogachikhin, laughs observing: "We overlook MI5 and we're near MI6." These are Britain's domestic and foreign intelligence agencies. No one in London is laughing. RT is nothing more than an official Kremlin propaganda arm. It is the instrument of Russia meddling in other countries politics. The English figured this out. Trump and his minions are denying it. Why? RT had a small role in helping Trump march to the presidency.

Those who fail to see RT's impact suggest the TV channel is unimportant as its ratings are miniscule. This conversation fails to recognize that the cumulative financial, political and media influence, while small, helped to form pro-Trump and anti-Hillary feelings in places like Wisconsin, Ohio and a host of smaller states. RT didn't elect Trump. It certainly did hurt Clinton's campaign. RT is a sophisticated modern propaganda machine that has taken the BBC model and converted it to a KGB type tool. While there is no longer a Russian KGB, there is a sophisticated, technologically sound, hacking society well and alive within the walls of Russian government. RT is sophisticated alternative news with a mainstream media bent.

The RT slogan is "Question More." Its public relations and slogans are written by a London ad agency. RT defended its support for Trump's candidacy. Anna Belkina, head of RT communications in Moscow, said the channel supported Trump because of the negative American press. "Nearly all the mainstream media came out against Mr. Trump during the campaign and much of the news coverage about him was negative," Belkina concluded. This was a defense of how and why RT supported Trump's candidacy.

The sophisticated propaganda machine that is RT should not be overlooked. They appear credible. RT programs are interesting, well produced and they spin fake news better than Fox TV News. RT is Donald J. Trump's official channel at least in Russia. One can only hope Sean Hannity and Fox TV News don't sue. Then again!

RT claims to have many foreign followers. They claim General Michael Flynn, Julian Assange and George Papadopoulos are fans. That tells one all they need to know about RT's influence. In case you wonder about RT's American presence. On November 13, 2017 the channel registered in the U. S. as a foreign agent. That was a week after Trump's presidential victory.

RT AND THE TRUMP CANDIDACY

During the year and a half prior to the presidential election of 2016 Donald J. Trump was featured prominently on the Russian government controlled television channel RT. The news from RT was excessively pro-Trump. There is no evidence he sought RT's support. He had it from the day he announced his quest for the Republican nomination. When he won the presidency, RT virtually crowned him the new American King.

What makes RT's support important? The network is a favorite cable channel outside of Russia with wide audiences in the U. K., Europe, the Middle East and North America. RT was the first legitimate news outlet to trumpet Trump's version of Making America Great Again. RT provided credibility in the media with a world audience watching the billionaire real estate mogul winning what CNN called "an unprecedented victory."

RT is the hidden factor in legitimizing Trump's presidential candidacy. Russian propagandists wanted to influence the presidential election. They did. Along the way American political amateurs were entangled with Russian government officials, looking to turn American citizens into spies. RT's coverage of American politics is little more than low-level propaganda. The RT story is an example of how fragile our democracy is in an age of cyber warfare.

WHY DOES RT LOVE TRUMP?

RT is Russian Television. They love Donald J. Trump. If Fox TV News has a bastard stepchild, it is RT. It is a professional, a polished and an effective propaganda arm of Vladimir Putin's nefarious Russian government. In July 2017, when the G-20 Summit took place, RT spent much of its coverage condemning CNN and MSNBC. The reason? They criticized Trump. RT attacks CNN and MSNBC continually in Europe. They have a unique credibility due to top-level London based journalists and a few Americans from Fox TV News. RT is a subtle propaganda machine. It is broadcast all over the world. In Europe they argue the U. S. is an imperialist nation with no regard for the common person. That is until Trump became president. They see him as America's savior. They also see him as a dedicated Russian defender.

There is no evidence RT colludes with Trump. Or for that matter he colludes with them. There is one unanswerable question. Why does RT have a romance with the Donald? The answer is complicated. RT wants sanctions lifted. They see trade with Trump's America as a lifeline to a nation in economic turmoil. RT is also making a lot of money spewing out Russian tinged propaganda disguised as news for audiences all over the world.

CNN noted in February 2017 RT's "obsession" with Trump. Matthew Chance wrote: "When President Donald Trump and President Vladimir Putin shared a phone call the weekend after Trump's inauguration, Russian news media delighted in covering every detail in near wall-to-wall coverage." The Russian hierarchy is hoping for a thaw in relations since President Barack Obama criticized the annexation of Crimea and military activity in the Eastern Ukraine. Putin was criticized for supporting Syrian President Bashar al-Assad as he gassed his people and violated U. N. sanctions. Obama led the way for Russian sanctions while Trump and Putin continue their bromance. In Moscow the word is a Trump presidency will thaw the anti-Russian sentiment simmering in America.

It is not just RT that loves Trump. The Russian news agency Interfax reported, shortly after Trump's inaugural, there was more mention of Trump than Putin in local Russian news. The Russian media noted a change in Trump's demeanor after his phone call to Putin. Konstantin Kosachev, the chair of the Foreign Affairs Committee of the Russian Federal Council, wrote Trump "is being backed into a corner, or Russophobia has already infected the new administration from top to bottom." Kosachev lamented the anti-Russian influences.

WHAT IS RT TV AND WHY IS IT SO EFFECTIVE?

RT is a multi-lingual news network concentrating on English, Arabic, French and Spanish audiences. It is known for spreading disinformation. It lacks impartiality. It breaches common rules of broadcast etiquette. It is easy to see why RT sees Trump as a savior. It has a minimal American audience. It came on American TV screens in 2010.

RT is intent on promoting Putin's point of view. The Russian government not only funds RT America, they hire high profile names like Larry King to smile and tell American audiences the political truth. Trump is right. There is fake news. It is RT America. It is a state run propaganda machine. Maybe this is why Trump loves it.

Why was RT so effective? The reason is their anchors. Ed Schultz "The News With Ed" is the brainchild of Putin friendly Russians. They hired a major MSNBC host who became a factotum for electing Donald Trump. When he was the face of The Ed Show on MSNBC, he was a talking head criticizing Trump and lambasting Vladimir Putin. How times change! Schultz called Trump "a racist lout" on MSNBC. This was soon forgotten when he became the English speaking face of RT. Larry King is another RT host who has credibility with American and British audiences.

RT has grown dramatically. It is viewed in one hundred countries with a potential audience of seven hundred million. In the U. S., RT is the fifth most watched international TV channel. The weekly U. S audience is eight million viewers. To appeal to American viewers, RT hired former Minnesota governor Jesse Ventura to host a weekly debate and interview show.

The Columbia School of Journalism studied RT concluding the propaganda channel fails to adequately check sources, it lacks honest coverage and it is at a low level professional level. Many of RT journalists are poorly trained. Many have no training. The operative wisdom is RT white washes Vladimir Putin's policies. This is not journalism. It is propaganda.

WHY IS RT IMPORTANT TO TRUMP'S POWER ABUSES?

RT, or Russian Television, is a network most Americans have never heard about. The Russian government in English, Spanish, Arabic and French funds this international TV network. RT is the best of all media sources spreading disinformation. Their favorite politician is not Vladimir Putin. It is Donald J. Trump. It is surprising with all the investigations into the Trump administration's ties to Russia; no one has looked at RT. The network provides a roadmap to Russian interference in American politics

The main purpose of RT is to improve Russia's image in the world. They have done this with excellent, if twisted, reporting. They have taken most of their cues from Fox TV News. RT screams "fair and balanced." This is of course utter nonsense.

When RT went on the air on December 10, 2005 in Europe they hired three hundred journalists with seventy reporting outside of

Russia. The high level of professionalism resulted from a BBC corporate structure. It was twenty five year old Margarita Simonyan, as editor in chief, who set up the format appealing to western audiences. Simonyan said RT offered "a different vision and news content" from that of the Western media particularly CNN, MSNBC and the BBC. Make no mistake RT is highly professional, interesting and subtle in deploying the propaganda machine. It is not friendly to interests outside Russia. In 2009, they launched RT-America and an RT Documentary channel premiered in 2011. The Russian government has done everything in its power to hide its control of content.

HOW RT INFLUENCES AMERICAN POLITICS

How does RT influence American politics? The channel attempts to hide its affiliation with the Russian government. It also uses disinformation. An ad on RT showed President Barack Obama slowly evolving into a picture of Iranian leader Mahmoud Ahmadinejd. Then a question came on the screen: "Who poses the greatest nuclear threat?" The answer was obviously as RT said: "Obama." The RT ad was banned in America's airports. It was shown throughout the world and influenced international opinion.

PRESIDENT TRUMP AND RT: THE INFLUENCE
OF THE RUSSIAN PROPAGANDA TV NETWORK

Does RT influence Donald J. Trump? There is no evidence it does. In September 2016, while campaigning for the presidency, he appeared on RT. The day prior to his RT appearance, Trump praised Vladimir Putin. In this appearance on RT Trump not only, as the Wall Street Journal observed: "bashed American foreign policy, he seemed to take the Kremlin's side on every single foreign policy issue." No one was alarmed. After all it was September 2016. Trump had no chance as CNN and other news outlets told us Trump would not be elected president. Then he was elected. RT was with him.

The Los Angeles Times remarked Trump's interview on RT was "the crowning glory" of the network. Trump said: "The media has been unbelievably dishonest." This should have shocked CNN and other news outlets. It didn't. Trump revealed his campaign kept a "blacklist" of news organizations, which included The Washington Post, The New York Times, MSNBC and CNN. No one was alarmed. They should have been as the campaign frontally assaulted the First Amendment.

The Trump campaign realized the RT interview was a mistake. They began damage control. During the interview Trump criticized what he called decades long mistakes of U. S. foreign policy during a ten minute interview that premiered on RT America to a dwindling and disinterested American audience.

ED SCHULTZ: RT'S VOICE FOR TRUMP
PRIOR TO THE 2O16 VOTE

Ed Schultz is a radio and TV media bully who will tell a story for the right price. He looks like an NFL linebacker after five concussions and no protocol to right the brain's function. He is meaty looking journalist with an ill-fitting suit that went out of style with wing tips and his hair swirls in many directions. He looks like a beaming jack-o-lantern. He made his reputation as a loud mouthed jerk, a Hillary Clinton apologist and a card carrying liberal. The Ed Show on MSNBC was designed to appeal to an aggressive liberalism by a man who needed a paycheck. Then he morphed into a Putin supporting Kremlin style apologist.

In 2011 when Trump announced he might run for president, Schultz wrote in the Huffington Post: "When it comes down to the devil in the detail of dealing with the issues…and masking real change, Trump, you don't have it." Ed would eat those words joining Russian Television. He performed a one hundred eighty degree turnaround like a trained media seal.

The loud, bellowing bully Schultz portrays on TV is perfect for Russian TV. He calls himself a "lunch pail populist." He has gone from mocking Vladimir Putin to praising him. Schultz is the face of Russia Today's American channel. It is the global propaganda machine for Russia's interference in world affairs. Instead of praising Hillary Clinton, Schultz now condemns her as he eats caviar off the RT set.

Of Trump, who he disparaged on MSNBC, Schultz now says: "Trump is a great and decisive decision-maker." One wonders what happened to Schultz's integrity. But a paycheck is a paycheck.

How did Schultz get to his present position? In 2015 MSNBC gave Schultz his last paycheck. After six years on the air the ratings for his daily program, The Ed Show, were dismal and the previous year his radio show was cancelled. He was loud mouthed, arrogant and not up to date on the news.

In a studio three blocks from the White House, Schultz spews out Russian propaganda with the disclaimer he is "fair and balanced." Not true! He is still a prairie populist but with a Putin bent. He now defends Russia against hacking in the 2016 election. One Kremlin spokesperson after another comes on RT, and Schultz legitimizes their nonsense. But Schultz is not alone. A former New York Times reporter, Chris Hedges, hosts "On Contact," which is a weekly show of "dissident voices." Tyrel Ventura, Jesse's son, hosts "Watching The Hawks," where recently he discussed World War III. RT features in depth portraits that often border on the bizarre. A recent program had Steve Malzberg discussing the news of the week with the three top stories featuring Paul Ryan, James Comey and Colin Kaepernick. Maybe some at RT need to practice their English when putting together these disparate shows. Another RT show on April 10, 2018 linked the attack on Syria to Facebook. RT is not a comedy channel. The stories make it appear that way.

MIKE CERNOVICH: ORANGE COUNTY, BANNON ALT RIGHT TRUMP SUPPORTER ON RT DURING FIRST SIX MONTHS OF TRUMP'S PRESIDENCY

Mike Cernovich is a forty-year old alt-right political spokesperson. His website "Danger and Play" is the work of a self-described despondent American nationalist. He is a regular supporter of conspiracy theories. He believed Pizzagate. This was the conspiracy notion that high-ranking Democratic Party officials were involved in a child-porn ring. Cernovich regularly hosts The Alex Jones Show. He attended the Pepperdine Law School and during the 2016 campaign effectively attacked Hillary Clinton. Cernovich popularized the false story that

Hillary had seizures. He regularly gave interviews on her Parkinson's disease. Neither story was true.

Other policies he supports are IQ testing for immigrants. He proposes ending funding to universities. Anyone who criticizes him is branded a child molester. He is so over the top that Cernovich was banned from Fox TV News.

The minute he was banned from Fox TV, Russian Television showed up to provide him with a forum. On twitter, Cernovich praised RT for its coverage. Cernovich went on RT defending Trump's Muslin ban.

When General Flynn was investigated, Cernovich appeared on RT to add his conspiracy theories. He explained why Flynn was innocent. He told RT Flynn's dismissal was a "U. S. establishment coup." The New Yorker described Cernovich as one of the "trolls for Trump." This description resulted from Cernovich's casual relationship with the truth and his mind numbing appearances on RT.

"Conflict is attention." This phrase suggests why America is divided, unable to reach any level of compromise and Cernovich's name-calling ignores rules of civility. "Attention is influence," writes Cernovich on his blog. This suggests his veracity is in question. He also self- publishes books for men who want to be real men. His first wife, a Silicon Valley lawyer, paid a seven-figure settlement to end their marriage. When he appears on RT, he gives the impression he is a serious political critic. He is a self-promoter with the mentality of Trump's other trolls-George Papadopoulos, Michael Flynn, Paul Manafort, Paul Gates, Carter Page and Anthony Scaramucci. This is not distinguished company.

He advertises his work as that of a "Pulitzer-worthy journalist." He launched his first blog "Danger and Play" in 2011 after his first wife filed for divorce. By that time a rape charge from 2003 was dropped due to community service. The media ignored it. Then Cernovich became a big time alt right media voice. Cernovich is not a household name. Thank God!

PAUL MANAFORT'S PLOT AGAINST AMERICA:
HIS RUSSIAN CONNECTION IN THE UKRAINE

When Special Counsel Robert Mueller indicted Paul Manafort for money laundering, avoiding taxes and failing to properly disclose his business-political connections there wasn't universal surprise. The rumor mill swirled around Manafort as he snuck around the periphery of political power. He was like a poisonous political snake with a venomous future. No one knew much about Trump's former campaign manager. Now the seventy-year-old Manafort allegedly faces more time in jail than he has left on earth. He was a political insider who staked his wealth, his future and his career on working for the president of the Ukraine Viktor Yanukovych. Manafort made a deal with the devil. It came back to haunt him.

Rick Gates, Manafort's close associate, bragged to a group of Washington politicians Manafort had "a shadow government in the Ukraine." Manafort's connection to President Yanukovych ended in 2014. Manafort found himself broke. He had made millions. He had spent more than he made. He sought out new deals. There were none. There was a revolution in the Ukraine and a new president emerged. Manafort was in financial trouble. The Russian oligarchs who invested with him wanted their money back. He didn't have it.

Then Manafort's personal life turned sour. After a hacker released six million of his words the suspicion Manafort broke the law became a reality. He had other problems. He invested millions in his daughters fledgling film business and more in his son-in-law's real estate schemes. None of these business ventures worked out.

His daughters discovered their dad had a relationship with a woman thirty years younger. Manafort's alleged affair was an expensive one. His mistress rented a $9,000 a month apartment in Manhattan. There were alleged rumors she lived in a sumptuous place near his home in the Hampton's. His wife and family addressed the affair. He flew to Scottsdale, Arizona and entered a rehab clinic. He was allowed one ten-minute phone call each day. He called his wife sobbing about his plight. He told his daughter, Jessica, he contemplated suicide. What had happened to Paul Manafort?

Franklin Foer, writing in The Atlantic, charged Manafort "helped corrupt Washington and laid the ground work for the subversion of

American politics." Does this sound harsh? It does! Is it true. Probably!

Manafort was a lobbyist and political consultant who changed the way Washington insiders operated. His firm combined political consultants and lobbyists. Why is this revolutionary? It allowed Manafort's company to elect someone and influence legislative bills. The agenda of corporate clients, not the well-being of America, was the direction of Manafort's business.

The Atlantic wrote: "Manafort is alleged to have laundered cash for his own benefit, his long history of laundering reputations is what truly sets him apart." Franklin Foer also observed: "Helping elect Donald Trump...represents the culmination of Paul Manafort's work. His close relationship to the Trump campaign allowed for shady business deals to erupt into multiple federal indictments." The Atlantic believes he allegedly colluded with a foreign power to subvert the American democratic process. This hasn't been proven. The word is still out on Manafort. He has declared his innocence. He will fight the charges.

In a second set of charges Mueller filed in Virginia, there was another bail hearing. Manafort was broke. He continued to charge he was the victim of a witch-hunt. The new charges in Virginia came as Manafort found out his partner, Rick Gates, accepted a plea deal. Gates would testify against him. Manafort instructed his legal team to sue Mueller. They did! The case was dismissed.

What is Manafort accused of in federal court? Mueller's team charged he acted as an unregistered foreign agent. He planned and orchestrated an alleged international laundering conspiracy hiding millions of dollars he earned from foreign political work in the Ukraine. Manafort and his attorneys complained of "piled up charges." They attacked the prosecution. This angered the judge. Justice Department prosecutor David Weinstein said: "If you continue to thumb your nose at the system itself that's going to have a negative effect on the way the judge treats the statements you make."

Manafort's attorney screamed: "There is no evidence." This was the last straw for the Judge. He turned to Manafort's lawyer, Kevin Downing, to discuss bail. The bail package included Manafort's real estate. There was a dispute over the value of Manafort's property.

The prosecution claimed he failed to meet the ten million dollar litmus test. The bail hearing prompted federal prosecutors to charge that a document from zillow did not establish the home's value. Even dealing with federal charges, Manafort allegedly was working the system. Like many of those inside the Trump inner circle he is contemptuous of governmental institutions.

MATTHEW ALFORD: AUTHOR THAT CHARGES AMERICAN FILM REWRITES HISTORY

Matthew Alford, a British author, claims the CIA is in control of a portion of the American film industry. He argues American's have a history bearing little resemblance to reality. His book National Security Cinema: The Shocking New Evidence of Government Control In Hollywood argues secrecy, militarism, manipulation and censorship are the components of modern democracy. He charges the U. S. government changes movie scripts for political reasons. He is a conspiracy advocate who believes the U.S. government conspired to allow 9/11.

He is also Dr. Alford and he is a part-time Teaching Fellow at England's University of Bath. He is an academic, and a propagandist claiming the Pentagon and other U. S. intelligence agencies infuse Hollywood films with a pro-military and anti-corporate message. He also argues the CIA and the National Security Council influence movies to paint a picture of radical Islam and other threats to the Democratic process. He believes these threats do not exist.

As an apologist for Russian aggression the professor is a brilliant mind. He describes the trailer to the movie "Grand Theft Auto: The Doomsday Heist" as a U. S. TV series attempting to create hostility to Russia. Alford also believes "House of Cards," with its fictional Russian president Viktor Petrov, is a means of vilifying Putin. The professor might watch fewer movies and less of his television set. This is complete nonsense, but RT broadcasts it daily.

Let's look at the professor through his own words. "Collectively our mainstream entertainment provides considerable support for the national security state," Alford remarked. What does this mean in plain English? He is alleging Hollywood is the factotum of President Trump, the State Department, the CIA, the FBI and the National

Security Agency. This is academic hocus pocus at the highest level. But there are other Alford comments that bring laughter. "The cliché of the Russian baddy has been around so long that it's perhaps no surprise that recent political allegations against the nation have been so easy to swallow." Again, the professor needs a translator. He is arguing that Russia did not collude in the 2016 U. S. presidential election. Thank goodness for tenure. Otherwise Professor Alford might have to get a day job.

RT: HOW DOES ONE SUM IT UP?

During the investigation into the Russian disruption of the 2016 presidential election, the evidence was clear. The U. S. intelligence community documented Russian influences. One of the ironies of the investigations is RT had a much greater impact upon the electoral process than previously recognized.

The "Never Hillary" crowd often took RT stories at face value. They had no idea it was Russian sponsored governmental propaganda. In March 2016, RT began a concerted campaign producing pro-Trump, anti-Clinton content. That was exactly the moment Russian hackers broke into the Democratic campaign. RT pictured Hillary as corrupt as they said Trump fought an electoral system rigged to defeat his presidential bid.

The Russian government and RT began a cover up report to deny RT's support for the Trump candidacy. They contacted Paul Sonne of the Wall Street Journal and they attempted to work him into denying Kremlin influences upon either RT or Trump's campaign. Sonne is a respected and brilliant journalist. He didn't buy the RT argument. The first bit of deception for the Kremlin backed television network was when RT was required to file a statement with the U. S. Department of Justice to show who owns the network. The Russian government wouldn't admit to it. They claimed T & R Productions LLC were the owners, as they filed the required Foreign Agents Registration act form. RT flouted American laws and regulation with no impunity. The Kremlin claimed to the WSJ reporter they had no idea who owned RT.

In their filing with the U S. Department of Justice, RT said it wasn't "engaging in political activities or attempting to influence U.

314

S. policy." This is the problem with a democracy. You can have any delusional opinion you like. But thank goodness for democracy. This is what Trump and his minions are attempting to destroy. RT is campaigning for a new America that looks more like the Kremlin

WHAT IS U. S. STATE DEPARTMENT FEELINGS ABOUT RT?

To the average citizen RT may not seem to be important. In American governmental circles it is taken seriously. State Department analysts argue RT is credible with viewers, as it sells propaganda. Not surprisingly, RT is more influential altering political attitudes in Europe.

A key to RT's popularity is the story it spins which is different from Western news sources. The American intelligence community argues credible journalists, like Larry King, are able to spin a tall tale into reality. RT appeals to people with less education. It is a black and white news source praising Trump.

Once American intelligence declassified material on RT and Russian hacking emerged during Trump's successful presidential run, the obvious conclusion was Kremlin interests supported the Donald and demeaned Hillary. Whether or not collusion took place is immaterial. Russia had a hand in electing Trump.

The U.S. Office of the Director of National Intelligence concluded: "Strategic messaging for the Russian government" had an impact on the election. The amount of disinformation from Kremlin sources through RT may never be fully known. The evidence is clear American democracy was compromised. The degree? We have no idea.

RT corrupts American politics. It spreads the prevalence of "fake news," blames the drug epidemic on President Obama's policies and the manner in which Trump is fixing past political-economic-social problems. RT says Trump is doing all this despite the Obama legacy.

SIXTEEN

TILLERSON'S WAR ON THE STATE DEPARTMENT: WILL IT RUN EFFICIENTLY IN THE FUTURE OR BE DESTROYED?

"President Trump is seeking to radically remodel the State Department in an unprecedented way...which includes a proposed budget cut of nearly 30 percent, a hiring freeze and a potential reshuffling of offices within the State Department...."

MORGAN CHALFANT

"They also don't see much use, frankly, in diplomacy."

STEWART PATRICK, POLICY PLANNING STAFF STATE DEPARTMENT ON TRUMP'S APPOINTEES.

When you are a CEO of a major corporation your word is law! No one disagrees with your decisions. Rex Tillerson discovered as Secretary of State, he was out of his league. He knew Russian oil and gas. That was it. This is one reason he will go down as the worst Secretary of State in American history. Surprisingly, Tillerson had some good people working for him. The best was his Chief of Staff Margaret Peterlin who helped him through the confirmation process. Peterlin is a U. S. Navy veteran, a former congressional staffer, and she was instrumental in drafts of the Patriot Act. Not even her governmental expertise could prevent Tillerson from failure.

In the early days of Tillerson's State Department tenure, Ronan Farrow arrived for an interview for his April 2018 book War On Peace: The End Of Diplomacy And the Decline of American Influence. The first thing Farrow noticed was open tension in Tillerson's office. Half of Tillerson's staff stared angrily at Farrow.

They looked like they wanted to beat him up. The other half slipped him confidential notes containing tales of incompetence. Farrow couldn't believe it. Some staffers wondered what in the hell was this kid in the nice sport coat and tie doing in the Secretary of State's inner circle?

Ronan Farrow: "The squabbling barely qualified as drama, but it was unusual behavior to display so openly in front of a reporter, and at odds with the kind of tightly organized messaging prized by most of Tillerson's predecessors. It provided a small window into a State Department that appeared to be plunged into chaos at every level." (p. 258)

THE REASONS FOR TILLERSON'S FAILURES

Tillerson's failures resulted from his Exxon CEO successes. He attempted to tell Trump how to run the State Department. Their first battle was over appointing a press secretary. Tillerson preferred the right wing zealot from the conservative Heritage Foundation, Genevieve Wood. Fox & Friends, Heather Nauert, was Trump's choice. When Nauert was appointed Tillerson acted like a first grader doing everything he could to degrade, demean, diminish and demote Nauert.

There were many reasons for Tillerson's lack of success. He had inane rules. One was that only one communications officer was allowed in his office when he sat with a reporter. When he was forced to hire Fox TV News talking head, Heather Nauert, as his spokesperson, he disrespected her, excluded her and complained about her work. This was a big mistake. Nauert was his strongest press spokesperson. She is a bright, media friendly face. She remains in the Trump foreign policy inner circle after Tillerson's firing. Her star has risen due to her over the top defense of Trump's diplomacy.

The press secretary found it difficult to work for Tillerson. He treated her as a second-class citizen. She was denied the access to Tillerson. This didn't prevent her from explaining and defending Trump's foreign policy with a verve unknown to previous press secretaries. She understood the major news outlets and worked with them smoothly. This helped to hide Tillerson's lack of success at the State Department. Trump recognized her expertise after firing

Tillerson. He promoted Nauert to a newly vacant Undersecretary of State position.

She has shown toughness towards Russia. When Vladimir Putin's RT Television featured an animated film clip of a missile headed toward the U. S., she sent a cease and desist response. She is a strong voice against Russia. She is also an avid supporter of women's rights. On International Women's Day, she organized a program to recognize State Department employees. Tillerson was nowhere in sight.

Nauert now oversees two hundred and seventy-five U. S. embassies, consulates and other posts. She is in charge of the State Department's public relations. In what only can be described as Texas sexism, Tillerson limited her actions and held her back. Why? Who knows! She is a Columbia University graduate. She had a career as a foreign policy specialist for Fox where she was well regarded. When Tillerson attempted to exclude journalists from his travels, she protested. They were included. The irony is Tillerson's foreign policy coverage was better than his performance. This was due to Nauert's independence. After Tillerson shunted her to the sidelines, she began traveling around the world visiting Bangladesh and Myanmar to see the plight of Rohingya Muslim's. She also visited Israel and Syria. The irony is she receives a much better reception than Secretary Tillerson. Nauert is a team player and an asset to Trump's foreign policy. She is one of many people doing a job that the big people on top are missing. That is the sad commentary on American foreign policy.

When Mike Pompeo arrived to head the State Department, Nauert was the spokeswoman for the North Korea planning stage of the conference between King Jong Un and President Trump. She was a key member of the planning team setting up the conference. Tillerson didn't survive. Nauert thrived. She continues to be a State Department asset.

TILLERSON COULD DO LITTLE MORE THAN READ A MAP

It was obvious to State Department employees Tillerson could do little more than read a map. He came into State in late January, and he didn't hold a round table meeting with State employees until May

2017. That didn't inspire trust in the State Department. Tillerson was inaccessible to the staff. When a new Secretary of State is appointed there are more than sixty countries that recognize the new Secretary. They wish to discuss foreign policy. Tillerson answered three of these calls a day. No more. Previous appointees finished this task in less than a week. It took six months for Tillerson to complete the job. He wasn't lazy. He was simply out of his depth.

State Department employees leaked to President Trump that Nikki Haley or Mike Pompeo would make a great head of State. Over the fourteen months he directed State, Tillerson seldom was consulted. He was treated with disdain by the president. When Ronan Farrow interviewed Tillerson for The New Yorker, one staffer said: "it's shocking" in reference to the president's treatment. Another staffer described Tillerson as "a swaggering alpha male." In the Farrow interview, Tillerson blamed Jared Kushner for his problems. He wouldn't talk to Kushner. He considered him a rank amateur.

When Tillerson formulated a policy, Trump overruled it. The downsized State Department did little to help Tillerson's cause. The hundreds of senior positions that went unfilled created instability and a lack of reliable information.

In conversation with White House officials, Tillerson told Farrell: "It was frustrating, at times, because you couldn't get a sense of 'What's the issue?'" But Tillerson acted like a bullheaded cowboy. Congress did not want to dismantle the State Department. When Congress attempted to provide eighty million dollars in funding for State, Tillerson refused it. Former Secretary of State Madeleine Albright said: "I've never heard about anything like that." Tillerson told Farrow he lacked the experience for the job. Once again an amateur in politics couldn't operate with any degree of skill or efficiency. Other Secretaries of State, notably George P. Shultz, remarked the swift downsizing was "astonishing." Amateurs destroying government was Tillerson's goal. Perhaps Trump should be thanked for firing him.

WHY IS TILLERSON HOSTILE TO
THE STATE DEPARTMENT?

Why is Donald J. Trump reducing the U. S. State Department? The answer is a simple one. He doesn't trust their advice. He is wary of specialists. He considers them elitists. They have a different version of America's international mission. They counter or disagree with his thoughts and policies. His initial budget proposed a State fiscal cut of thirty percent. The Trump administration either ignores or counters Congress when they pass legislation to improve State Department efficiency. There is a war on the State Department. It is demoralizing, depleting and destroying a key component of American foreign policy.

Prior to his inauguration three top members of the U. S. State Department resigned. They saw the coming war with the Trump administration. Stewart Patrick, a member of the policy planning staff at the State Department during the George W. Bush presidency, said: "My suspicion is that within the White House…that this seems to actually be a concerted effort to diminish the role of the State Department in U.S. foreign policy and hamper its abilities to pursue policies that would be considered overtly globalist." Trump has his own diplomacy, his own team, his own direction and his own thoughts. He is the "I" foreign policy president. He doesn't need the State Department. Trump doesn't like what he views as pacifists, or diplomacy minded career employees. Whether they are Republicans or Democrats the people Trump dismissed were long-term professionals. They were intent upon maintaining American security. Trump's lack of knowledge as to how foreign policy is structured and operates places America in harms way. His demand for unfettered loyalty creates a muddled, disingenuous foreign policy. The president dismissed those he could who did not swear complete fealty to the new King.

DISMANTLING THE STATE DEPARTMENT A WEEK
INTO HIS PRESIDENCY: THOMAS COUNTRYMAN

After he was in office for only a week Trump began the dismantling process. The president removed high-level officials for no reason. Thomas Countryman was traveling to Rome for an international conference on nuclear weapons. He was a thirty-five year career State Department employee. Countryman was sitting in Jordan's expensive Abdoun neighborhood. He was in the American Embassy, which was much like a fortress. The Director General of the Foreign Service had been trying to contact him for some time. He wanted to speak at once with Countryman. He was instructed to take the next flight to Washington.

It was January 25, 2017, Countryman was the senior U. S. diplomat concerning arms control. He oversaw the State Department's Iranian nuclear deal. He was an old school diplomat. He was assigned the serious problem of preventing the proliferation of nuclear weapons through diplomacy.

As Countryman looked back on a State Department career beginning in 1982 he had a fondness for traditional diplomacy. He had been stationed in Yugoslavia and Cairo. He was a multi-linguist with a fine reputation. A Russian spy described Countryman as: "One of those faceless bureaucrats in the State Department."

When the Trump administration arrived he was unceremoniously fired. For the four months before Trump was inaugurated, he was acting undersecretary for arms control and international security. He was dismissed without cause. There were no charges of dereliction of duty, no signs of malfeasance, no corruption, no mismanagement and there were no complaints of poor job performance. Countryman was fired because one of Trump's appointees believed he might not be loyal to the Donald. Unbelievable!

Why was Countryman dismissed? Trump's transition team allegedly believed he was a Hillary Clinton supporter. He was also a Democrat. Trump insiders didn't understand Countryman was a top-level professional providing information essential to the conduct of foreign policy. He was fired for not swearing loyalty to the president. There was a purge of bright, well-trained State Department professionals. Why? Fear! Paranoia! Delusional conclusions! A lack of understanding concerning State's role was what prompted Trump's decision.

The irony is less experienced appointees, not as well educated or experienced, replaced Countryman. When Trump's transition team met Countryman he was shocked. They had no knowledge of foreign affairs.

"The transition was a joke," Countryman remarked to Ronan Farrow. "In any other administration changeover, there were people who were knowledgeable about foreign affairs, there were people who had experience in government....In this case none of those things were true."

Tom Countryman had an impeccable record serving in Democratic and Republican administrations. Countryman and others said the firings had a ring of vindictiveness. Trump insiders didn't hide their disdain for career civil servants.

For those left behind in the State Department, there were no new bosses. There were no in-depth work orders for information on other nations. Trump ignored the intelligence community and the information that allows presidents to meet the needs of diplomacy. The State Department's most experienced career specialists were fired in mass. Those who weren't resigned or transferred to other agencies went to work in the private sector.

Erin Clancy, who came to the State Department in 2005, was fired from her $91,000 a year job. She was a model employee who remained at State despite more lucrative job offers. She was a Pickering Fellow who would not have continued to pay for her undergraduate education without the fellowship. "The Pickering program changed my life," Clancy said.

She had a perfect work record. "I am a big believer in the importance of visibility. Queer women in foreign policy can and must do more publicly and be visible as members of the foreign affairs community." Did her "queer woman" statement accelerate her firing? She complained and appealed. She survived. Trump brought her back to work some say he displayed no homophobia. Despite the initial Trump administration firing, Clancy was given a reprieve and remains in the State Department. She did so due to her expertise.

Why did Clancy survive? Her boss, Acting Deputy Secretary Tom Shannon, lobbied for Clancy and the team she headed. Trump listened to tales of their expertise and the need to remain in the nuclear proliferation area. He kept Clancy in the State Department.

Erin Clancy: "The culture of the State Department is so eroded." When Ronan Farrow interviewed Rex Tillerson about Countryman's firing, Tillerson replied: "I'm not familiar with that one."

THE STATE DEPARTMENT PURGE BEGINS

The State Department purge left a hole in U. S. diplomatic efforts. Secretary of State Rex Tillerson had no interest in hiring new employees. On the seventh floor of State's offices, it is known as "Mahogany Row" for the shiny desks. Now it had a line of empty shiny desks. The wood paneled seventh floor had no assignments and no future.

"As a career diplomat, I experienced many transitions and never saw anything like this dangerous purge of public servants now underway at State," a former ambassador Laura Kennedy tweeted.

When Theresa May visited the U.S. the British Prime Minister found the State Department had little, if anything, to do with her visit. This was not customary. She was puzzled. Trump appointed his son-in-law, Jared Kushner, to handle the British PM's visit. Steve Bannon and Michael Flynn helped him. Amateurs were in charge. Joseph Cirincione, president of the Ploughshares Fund, a global security advocacy group, said: "There is an entire global arms regime to maintain. The machinery is still there in the State Department, but there is no one in the cockpit."

After six more high ranking State officials were fired, Republican Nicholas Burns, who served as George W. Bush's undersecretary for political affairs, said: "This is no way to treat people who have served under Democrats and Republicans, who have been loyal to their country and their government."

Trump's State Department transition team didn't appear interested in issues. They made it clear the Donald would be his own Secretary of State. He told State to skip the daily security briefings. He said he knew things they didn't know. He is running the State Department into the ground. He gloats and preens. He calls himself "a quiet genius."

Conservative Republicans were harsh in mixed reviews of fiscal cuts in the State Department. Anita McBride, who worked for Reagan and Bush, observed: "We have never before seen a third of their budget potentially being eliminated." She said this would cause other countries to see little, if any, reason to invest in America. McBride hinted Trump might not fully understand the broader reach of American foreign policy.

THE FRIGHTENING MARCH 13 TRUMP EXECUTIVE ORDER

On March 13, 2017 Trump signed an executive order setting up a State Department review and reorganization. The idea was to eliminate offices and agencies. A number of State Department offices, including the Bureau of Consular Affairs and Population, Refugees and Migration would move to the Office of Homeland Security. This deprived State of a key research resource. This is how the Trump administration crippled the State Department. They no longer had the same resources.

When asked about the March 13, 2017 Executive Order, Stewart Patrick, observed Trump's advisers believe much of foreign aid spending was like "pouring money down a rat hole." The State Department responded that a portion of its work goes beyond foreign affairs. It is charged with global health and education particularly in Third World countries. Trump officials showed little interest in the problems of Third World countries.

When Steve Bannon talked of the "deconstruction of the administrative state," the State Department witnessed a bleak future. It is the career civil servant the Trump administration looks to relieve of their duties. There is no longer decision making in the State Department. Who has replaced the diplomatic professionals? Jared Kushner! It is hard to believe. This entitled rank amateur is conducting high-level diplomacy with Mexico, Israel, Russia and Saudi Arabia among others. Kushner's counsel led to Paul Manafort, Reince Priebus, Steve Bannon, Sean Spicer and General Michael Flynn being fired. Not surprisingly, Kushner is treated with great reverence in the Oval Office.

When Rex Tillerson addressed State Department employees, at his first briefing, he talked of reform and being accountable. He said nothing about the role the State would play in future American foreign policy. The new political appointments by Trump had little, if any, experience in foreign affairs. Tillerson did not have his own people in State. It is those who Trump appointed that make key decisions.

From January to May 2017 there were no major State Department press conferences. This indicated the lack of a role for State Department professionals. A constant complaint is Secretary Tillerson appears cut off, aloof and entitled by State employees. His attitude is, according to one staffer, "the less paper the better." This is due to the Trump administration's belief the State Department is bloated, inefficient and redundant. It is an indication of how Trump is systematically destabilizing the department. He is acting as a foreign policy bully. He believes intelligence reports compromise his Neanderthal notions of world affairs.

THE DESPERATION OF AMERICAN
DIPLOMATS UNDER TRUMP

How did the State Department change under Trump? The earliest complaints centered upon the lack of respect for career employees. The level of intelligence was ignored as was the nonpartisan tone of career civil servants. Trump demanded loyalty. He really asked for fealty.

There are many examples of disrespect for those in the State Department. The most egregious one took place the first Friday in May 2017 when the State Department held a staff meeting to honor the two hundred forty-eight employees who lost their lives in the line of duty. The event, organized by Barbara Stephenson, was to bring cohesion to the State Department and give the employees a chance to know Secretary of State Rex Tillerson. It didn't turn out that way.

As the event unfolded the future of the 8,000 Foreign Service officers and the department's 75,000 employees was uncertain. They, of course, were not all present at the celebration. The tone was one where reorganization, downsizing and shifting of employees and duties into other agencies streamlined the U. S. State Department. Rather than buoy State employees confidence, this celebration was much like a funeral. Tillerson made it clear State had little relevance to the Trump administration.

When he arrived in the Oval Office, Trump stated military might, not diplomacy, was the hallmark of his administration. There was a radical militarization of American foreign policy taking place. Then in April 2018 war hawk John Bolton was appointed the National Security Adviser. It appeared as though Trump was looking to declare war.

WHY THE CHANGES IN THE STATE DEPARTMENT?

Why the changes in the State Department? There are no conclusive answers. Is it due to Hillary Clinton's role as Secretary of State? Is it due to Steve Bannon's desire to deconstruct the State Department? Does it play to Trump's love of the generals? Does it reflect his refusal to accept advice from State Department professionals? The answer to these questions is: "Yes."

Rex Tillerson is clearing out the State Department. Under presidential orders he saw no reason to maintain the large number of research functionaries. After Tillerson was fired, he never stated an opinion about downsizing the State Department. One can only assume he agreed with Trump. Less State advice is more.

KILLING THE FUTURE OF THE STATE DEPARTMENT: ENDING THE RANGEL-PICKERING FELLOWSHIPS

Since the 1950s the observation Yale hires dominates the U. S. State Department is a constant complaint. To remedy this situation a State Department program, the Rangel and Pickering Fellows, was created to encourage highly qualified applicants from diverse economic, social and racial backgrounds to pursue positions in the Foreign Service. The program set up beginning with a two-year Master's degree, following by internships in the State Department. Then a rigorous selection, hiring and background vetting took place. If a candidate passed this rigorous program, they would serve as a foreign services officer for at least five years.

This was a program designed to attract scholars from a wide range of American disciplines and cultures. It was open to women without restriction, and those selected often gave up six figure jobs outside government. The Rangel-Pickering Fellows guaranteed a much-needed State Department diversity.

What is the purpose of the Rangel-Pickering Fellowships? It is to offer not only the traditional Yale, Princeton, University of Chicago and Harvard graduates jobs, but to broaden the selection process to other major universities. The desired impact would create State Department positions for African American, Latino, Asian, female, blue collar, and non-Ivy league applicants like J. D. Vance who wrote Hillbilly Elegy.

What is the purpose of the program? The Rangel-Pickering Fellow would add a new sophistication to the State Department. Someone in the Trump administration had a fit over the program. They vowed to quash it. There was racist opposition to Rangel-Pickering as an internal memo from a Trump insider commented it was administered by Howard University. This is America's top African American college.

When Secretary Tillerson testified before the United State Senate on June 13, 2017 concerning the 2018 State Department budget he was asked by Democratic Senator Christopher Coons of Delaware about the status of the Rangel-Pickering Fellows. Tillerson didn't have an answer. He had no idea about the program. His lack of competence was there in full view of the American public. The Washington Post observed of the Coons-Tillerson interchange was one where the "State Department just broke a promise to minority and female recruits." Josh Rogin, a Washington Post columnist, observed: "Dozens of young minority and female State Department recruits received startling and unwelcome news last week. They would not be able to soon join the Foreign Service despite having been promised that opportunity." The article pointed out letters went out to fellows that had already completed two years of graduate level education, as well as an internship in a foreign country. They had signed a deal with the U. S. government for a position in the State Department requiring five years of training. The Trump administration reneged on the agreement. Racism and sexism comes in many forms. It seldom takes an official government direction.

Secretary Tillerson, according to Senator Coons, knew little, if anything, about the program. If the head of State doesn't have the facts at his fingertips concerning Rangel-Pickering, he is not in charge. "This is no way to treat our next generation," a State official mentioned to Senator Coons.

As soon as Trump's minions realized the intent of the fellowship program, they systematically downsized it. This was done without Congressional consultation. The Trumpsters had no idea what the program intended. The quiet, but pervasive, racism caused State Department morale to sink even lower. What Trump insiders offered these young scholar-diplomats was disingenuous, insulting and racially insensitive.

The Trump administration offered 2017 Rangel-Pickering graduates positions stamping visas and providing information at a counter to Americans abroad. In other words, there is no job. If you did accept the position you would work next to a local from that country making minimum wage. The Rangel-Pickering Fellows left six-figure employment. They spent at least two more years in school. They have worked for at least three years at low-level State Department training positions. The Rangel Pickering Fellows are among the best-educated young people entering the State Department. Trump and Tillerson said: "No" to the advancement of well-qualified young applicants. That tells one all they need to know about the administration's approach to diversity in Trump's foreign policy.

When Trump came into office he instituted a State Department hiring freeze. The cuts in foreign aid made the Rangel-Pickering Fellows much like a person stranded on a desert island. Secretary of State Rex Tillerson refused to answer questions about why the program was stalled. When asked if it was due to budget constraints? Tillerson said: "Our budget will never determine our ability to be effective. Our people will."

Representative Joaquin Castro, a Texas Democrat, displayed the frustration of those who supported the program. He said: "As the Trump Administration's extreme proposed cuts to the State Department's budget threaten to hinder our diplomatic efforts around the world, exempting these young people from the agency's hiring freeze would be a positive and practical decision...." The freeze continued. Then the Trump administration, abruptly and without explanation, changed its mind offering a promise of one more year for the program. They allowed the 2017 trainees to be hired. This was due to The Pickering And Rangel Fellows Association known as PRFA that lobbied for their jobs and won a reprieve.

Much to President Trump's credit he recognized the Pickering and Rangel Fellows had something to offer. He directed the State Department to place the 2017 graduates into foreign service positions. The prestigious scholarship program for minority students will limp along. It is unlikely to survive. Former Senator Bob Graham said the makeup of the State Department will likely remain "white, male and Yale for years to come."

TILLERSON'S MANAGEMENT SKILLS

His management skill was the reason Tillerson was brought into the State Department. The 75,000 State Department bureaucracy is cumbersome. It was in need of reorganization and streamlining. Those inside State argue he has not reformed the State Department. He is downsizing career employees. He has also taken away management functions from the thirty-eight department heads. The result is State is without direction. Its employees are often without assignments. President Trump is suspicious of their data. He views them as part of the enemy. Trump believes they are the "deep state."

"The Secretary of State has to focus on the president, his policies and the other heads of government that he deals with, which means he cannot possibly run the department himself," R. Nicholas Burns, a retired career diplomat and Under Secretary of State in the George W. Bush administration, concluded. Tillerson has not been a good fit for State. He cannot delegate power or authority.

Tillerson's defenders say he is the captive of an unwieldy bureaucracy. He has complained there is a lack of discipline. The Secretary of State argues he is streamlining a bloated bureaucracy. His critics point to the thirty percent budget reduction, the hiring freeze, a lack of budget for proper office functions and a disregard for research as reasons for State's decline.

Those in the European Union and other countries, with close diplomatic ties to the U. S., remarked State is a dysfunctional organization. There is a logjam of paperwork crying out for decisions. Tillerson and his minions argue there is too much independent decision making in State. There are now fewer decision makers. That in itself paralyzes the department. Tillerson is a micromanager. He reviews everything. This brings State on the road to being unable to operate in world affairs. He will sign off on every piece of paperwork. This is not a recipe for success. His firing was a blessing. Trump did recognize he wasn't suitable for the position.

The U. S. State Department continues its daily activity interacting with one hundred ninety countries, writing reports sent directly to Congress, issuing visas and turning out research papers on world affairs. Tillerson said the State Department reorganization: "will end waste and duplication." He was asked about the morale of many employees. Tillerson responded: "We have given them permission to go do something else." That says it all.

Foreign service officers complain there is a "parallel department" of Tillerson people. The career employees are being shut out. Much of the daily activity is secretly carried out by a small coterie of Trump appointees. One person told me this is "an assault on the State Department."

Even more bizarre are Tillerson's close advisers. The Chief of Staff, Margaret Peterlin, and the Director of Planning, Brian Hook, a former State official under President George W. Bush, are isolated from the rest of the staff.

TRUMP SHAKES UP THE STATE DEPARTMENT

The president was elected to shake up Washington. The promise of spending more at home and less abroad brought Trump a groundswell of public support. As the Chief Diplomat, Tillerson was seldom seen and heard. He doesn't like to hold press conferences, conduct large meetings, talk to people or explain his policies. Tillerson is not a typical Washington insider. He had no previous government service. Combine this with a difficult personality and a penchant for authoritarianism and you have a lack of leadership.

When he was fired Tillerson had a litany of complaints. He kept his concerns private. Trump's son-in-law saw himself as the quasi Secretary of State. Jared Kushner conducts U. S. foreign policy with very little or no supervision. He is like a shadow Secretary of State. He does his best to minimize those around him. Tillerson finally reacted to Kushner's imperious attitude and haughty manner.

"Who is the Secretary of State" Tillerson blurted out at a staff meeting. What concerned Tillerson? He was incensed Kushner held a freelance meeting with the President of Mexico. Kushner has a close relationship with Saudi Arabia's Crown Prince Mohammed bin Salman preventing Tillerson from effective diplomacy. Kushner was continually looking to help Israel. This was Tillerson's job. When Tillerson was fired, Kushner was the reason.

As Tillerson left State in late March 2018, President Trump was acting as his Secretary of State. Of course, when Tillerson emerged as the Secretary of State in early 2017, Trump was the acting as the Secretary of State. Nothing had changed.

WHY IS TRUMP DESTROYING THE STATE DEPARTMENT?
The first sign of President Trump's war on the State Department was a decision to cut promotions by fifty percent. By blocking promotions, the most capable State Department employees left for greener pastures. By not filling entry-level positions, the State Department became a ghost town. Why the wholesale decimation of the "striped pants brigade?" Trump's appointments are older billionaire businessmen suspicious of government regulation and hostile to long serving bureaucrats. They believe the deep state is well and alive. There is no place in government that has more long serving career employees than State. Trump's appointees are determined to root out those twenty to thirty year career civil servants. Purging what Trump appointees believe to be the dangerous deep state, they are destroying our diplomatic capabilities.

The problem is President Trump. His comments on foreign affairs suggest his delusional psyche. When asked about foreign policy, Trump remarked: "I want my vision, but my vision is my vision." The reporter for Mother Jones, Kevin Drum, was flummoxed. He had no idea what Trump meant. When he asked a follow up question on Secretary Tillerson, Trump said: "He's doing the best he can." Clearly, Trump was running the State Department. The war on State is not a mystery. It is part of the Trump administration's larger strategy of weakening government regulations and institutions. Firing Rex Tillerson was the right choice. Selecting Tillerson to head State was among Trump's worst decisions. He got one of them right.

TILLERSON'S FIRING: DID JARED KUSHNER DO IT?

Rex Tillerson was fired for not being able to effectively carry out the duties of the Secretary of State. He was entitled. He was ill at ease with the press. He seldom talked to the president, and his co-workers. His policies were never challenged. Tillerson believed he was doing a superb job. His one-year tenure was a damning indictment of an arrogant, ill-suited amateur heading the State Department.

What were his failures? He didn't notify NATO when President Trump ordered missile strikes on Syria. He failed to return calls from hundreds of foreign diplomats. He was not available for office meetings. He had no concept of key foreign policy matters. The list goes on and on. It is surprising he lasted a year.

Among the most telling failures in Tillerson's regime at State took place in early May 2017 when he held a well publicized forum for State Department employees where he explained America First. It was a strange gathering. State employees showed up with enthusiasm and hopes for the agency progressing under new leadership. The meeting turned into a cold, somber description of future American foreign policy. This explanation brought a stunned silence.

Tillerson explained why 2300 employees would be terminated and thirty percent of State's budget eliminated. Acting on Trump's order to explain America First, Tillerson said long serving alliances were no longer "serving America's interest." It was time to move on from these archaic agreements. He said national security interests were really "economic interests."

In an attempt to show he disagreed with President Trump, Tillerson said the President had to be tougher on Russia. He said: "There's almost no trust." On Syria, Tillerson talked of a ceasefire. He continued his worldview of diplomacy suggesting Mexico and Canada are "ready to engage in a good faith effort" to renegotiate their trade deals. This was a reference to the North America Free Trade Agreement. He finished his remarks with a view of Asia demonstrating he knew little, if anything, about the region. He seemed possessed with punishing North Korea and negotiating new deals with China. Rex Tillerson clearly demonstrated in his address to State employees that he didn't have a worldview. He also didn't know how to be the Secretary of State.

In what may be the most disingenuous ending to a speech to State Department employees, Tillerson concluded: "I can promise you that when this is all done, you're going to have a much more satisfying, fulfilling career. Because you're going to feel better about what you are doing." There was a stunned silence in the auditorium.

KUSHNER DIDN'T FIRE TILLERSON:
THE SECRETARY FIRED HIMSELF

Jared Kushner did not fire Tillerson. This story circulated in books, articles and among TV's talking heads. Tillerson was fired for being incompetent. When asked about being fired, Tillerson's answer had everyone scratching their head. "People that matter, people that might have an interest in whether I stay or leave, there is about one hundred and sixty of them," Tillerson continued speaking to Newsweek's' Greg Price, "I know who it is.....And they know I know." This suggests he blamed President Trump for his failures. He might have looked in the mirror.

In his farewell address, Tillerson acted like a kindergarten drop out as he referred to the president's son-in-law in subtle tones blaming him for State's failures. The tenuous relationship between Tillerson and Kushner made for a soap opera year. The crux of their differences came when Tillerson charged Kushner with having a close relationship with Arabian Crown Price Mohammed bin Salman. Was this about diplomacy? No! It was a testosterone driven argument by two amateurs casting American foreign policy into an international abyss.

The State Department failed to do its job in Trump's first year. Was it Tillerson's fault? Was it Trump's fault? Was it State's fault? The answers are waiting for a solution. The future of American foreign policy requires a well-planned program.

In mid-April 2018 the Huffington Post wrote: "Trump's latest foreign policy chaos further diminishes U.S. standing, critics worry." The S. V. Date article speculated Trump has "flipped and flopped on major foreign policy issues...." The orange-hued man in the White House has everyone in the world scratching their head. Where is America headed in world diplomacy?

What does American foreign policy lack? Credibility! Consistency! Intelligence! Ethics! Trust! Until these factors are integrated into the diplomatic process the United States will act alone in the world arena. That is the way President Trump and his minions want it.

The danger of Trump's foreign policy is not just its unorthodox nature, but it is the lack of a coherent alternative. The president's fervent desire for free trade and his continual threat to make war leads to world instability. He does not show coherent leadership. Threats! Intimidation! These are the bywords of Making America Great Again. It is Trump against the world. A foreign policy bully is in the White House and democracy is in peril.

WHY TRUMP DIFFERED WITH TILLERSON: THE FIRING

When Trump fired Tillerson he did so for policy reasons. Trump tweeted to the world Tillerson was done. Then three hours later from Air Force One, the president made the phone call to his Secretary of State. Trump humiliated Tillerson with this strange firing process. That is not the issue. Tillerson and Trump differed on most issues.

Their primary difference was on the Iran Nuclear deal. Tillerson believed it was in place to prevent a nuclear build up and Israel was safer for the future. They also disagreed on the role of NATO and how to handle China. In the Middle East, Tillerson wanted a flexible but firm policy with all nations treated equally. Trump wanted those like Saudi Arabia treated better due to trade agreements. Tillerson vociferously negotiated with Trump to remain in the Paris Climate Accord. The negotiations with North Korea, Tillerson said, should be lengthy and filled with a great deal of paperwork and fewer military threats. Trump wanted a simple negotiation with Kim Jong Un. Stop the nuclear build up and restrictions will be lifted. Tillerson said it was not that easy.

Trump and Tillerson had a shouting match in the Oval Office in early 2018 where the president told him he was "too establishment" in his thinking. In foreign policy meetings Tillerson repeatedly challenged the president. It turned uncomfortable. Trump stormed out of the room screaming.

The sign that Tillerson was gone began when Trump personally contacted North Korean leader Kim Jong Un and accepted the dictator's invitation for a face-to-face meeting. Trump did something no other president could accomplish. He opened a diplomatic channel between the U. S. and North Korea. It was a momentous time. Trump deserves credit. Trump said of Tillerson he was "wasting his time trying to negotiate with Little Rocket Man....Save your energy, Rex," Trump tweeted. The lack of results in North Korea from Secretary Tillerson prompted Trump to appoint Mike Pompeo.

There were other issues. Tillerson was too strong in his condemnation of Russian agents attempting to poison former Soviet citizens turned British spies. "Much work remains to respond to the troubling behavior and actions on the part of the Russian government," Tillerson remarked of the poisoning incidents.

The comments on the British poisonings sent Trump into a shouting tirade. He told close aides Tillerson was "arrogant" and "condescending." The fighting continued in the Oval Office. Tillerson said hundreds of times "it's your thing," when Trump overruled him.

By early 2018 Trump made fun of Tillerson's Texas drawl and even called his cowboy art in the Secretary of State's office inappropriate. An aide remarked: "Trump told Tillerson there was more to the world than Texas." The Secretary of State walked away furious.

The petty nature of Tillerson's time at State was manifested in many ways. He would not return Jared Kushner's phone calls. He ignored National Security Adviser H. R. McMaster who frequently asked Tillerson to observe State Department protocol. This was a nice way of telling him to do his job. Nikki Haley, the U. N. ambassador, was opposed at every turn by Tillerson. She was viewed as a rival for his job.

Tillerson's aides leaked to the press tales of Trump's alleged mercurial behavior, and the Secretary of State's frustration dealing with him. Tillerson said he had to travel to the Middle East to clean up Trump's mess after the president agreed to isolate Qatar. This comment infuriated Trump. When Trump spoke before the Boy Scouts of America, Tillerson told scout leaders the president was "vulgar." The leaks to reporters from State were often directly linked to Tillerson insiders. This was the last straw as Trump prepared for

Secretary of State Mike Pompeo and a new regime. On his first day formally in office, Pompeo met with every member of the State Department in a show of support for their work. All indications are State is back on track with Pompeo. He also lifted the hiring freeze.

As he left State, Tillerson would not hold a farewell press conference with questions. He gave a terse farewell statement. He never mentioned the president as he slinked back to Texas. One of Tillerson's supporters the Secretary of State for Public Affairs, Steve Goldstein, was also fired as Trump vowed to reorganize and revitalize State. Time will tell if Mike Pompeo can succeed.

Richard Haass, the president of the Council of Foreign Relations, who served many Republican presidents, had for almost a year ago urged Tillerson to resign. "Rex Tillerson has been dealt a bad hand by the potus & has played it badly," Haass commented. The reason? Tillerson couldn't define America First. He wouldn't carry out Trump's policies. He was not able to make State more efficient. He opposed Congress when they told him there would be more funding for State.

The turning point was when he called the president "a moron." Trump can take bad work habits, lack of knowledge, haughty behavior but when you call him a derogatory name you are in trouble.

The degree of pettiness between Trump and Tillerson was incredible. Tillerson built three special phone lines into North Korea. Trump took them out. On Russia's increasingly muscular foreign policy, Trump called Tillerson's critiques of Kremlin militarism a figment of the Texan's imagination.

After leaving the White House, Tillerson delivered a college commencement address lamenting the lack of honesty, transparency and ethics in government. He criticized Trump without naming him. That in itself tells one why he failed. He would never directly confront the president. He would never defend his viewpoint. He would never stand up for what he believed. He never told us what he believed. He said his word was his bond. He was a good man who didn't understand how government functions. He had no idea how the presidency worked. He couldn't deal with people. These are the reasons for his abject failures. Tillerson said America is facing "A

Crisis of Ethics." That is what is going on. He failed raise his voice until he left the Trump administration. That is the tragedy of Rex Tillerson.

SEVENTEEN

THE GLOBAL CONSEQUENCES OF TRUMP'S APPROACH TO FOREIGN POLICY AND HIS QUESTIONABLE CLAIMS AT HOME WITH SUCCESS ABROAD

"Tillerson needs to acknowledge that his first months in office have cast doubt on America's fundamental mission…"

ROGER COHEN, THE NEW YORK TIMES

"What's been happening is not that the administration is undoing President Obama's legacy; it's undoing American leadership on the international stage."

SUSAN RICE

"We are mortgaging our future."

COLIN POWELL, FORMER SECRETARY OF STATE
ON TRUMP'S STATE DEPARTMENT

There are successes and failures in Trump's foreign policy. When his son-in-law Jared Kushner came up with the idea of flying to Riyadh for a meeting with Saudi Arabia's ruling family, it was to show the president was not anti-Muslim. Reince Priebus labeled Kushner's idea "brilliant." He suggested Jared had a bright future in foreign policy. This was Priebus's way of currying favor with Trump. The problem was the president would not consult with Middle East experts. This is what led to the Qatar fiasco in which the U.S.

appeared to be taking sides unnecessarily in a Qatar-Saudi Arabia dispute.

No one took the time to read about the Middle East. This caused problems. Shortly after all this took place there was the presidential trip to the G-7 and G-20. These events, combined with a speech in Warsaw, provide a window into the slippery slope of Trump's thoughts on international affairs.

STEPHEN M. WALT OF HARVARD WEIGHS IN ON TRUMP'S FOREIGN POLICY

Stephen M. Walt returned from a European vacation. He looked at what had transpired at the G-7 and the G-20. He was frustrated. Hapless naive amateurs were erasing American foreign policy since World War II. He analyzed Donald Trump's vision for Europe. He was frightened. He wrote an article for Foreign Policy. He wondered why did Donald J. Trump was changing the direction of American foreign policy?

When it comes to geopolitics, Walt wrote: "The Donald's view is fantasy and folly." Walt, the Robert and Renee Belfer Professor of International Relations at Harvard University, criticized Trump's inability to understand or even attempt to comprehend the vision necessary for a successful foreign policy.

As the president-elect Trump said that he had a low opinion of government bureaucrats. Career civil servants provide an easy target for Trump's insidious tweets. He displayed a blatant disregard for intelligence briefings by career foreign policy specialists. He vowed to downgrade, replace or ignore the federal bureaucracy. In foreign affairs this was a problem.

Once Trump was inaugurated, the State Department management team resigned in mass. Those who didn't resign were fired. Who makes up State's team? They consist of career professionals who are not policy people. They are educated specialists who provide the information necessary to effective policy making. This is why they are not political. Trump didn't understand. He views them as competition.

Professor Walt argues Trump's foreign policy was "a train wreck." What does he mean? The president is not interested in diplomacy.

He is prone to insults. A proposed meeting with Iran was cancelled due to Trump tweets. His daily public statements insult the Iranian regime, its leaders and its direction. If diplomacy is to take place there needs to be a forum for it. Trump does not recognize the formality and structure of diplomacy. He is a bully in foreign policy. His followers cheer the bully as he alienates the world. When Secretary of State Rex Tillerson talked of bringing North Korea to the negotiating table, Trump told his secretary not to waste his time. There is no vision, continuity or identifiable policy in Trump's foreign policy.

Stephen M. Walt: "If the United States is giving up its self-appointed role as the 'indispensable nation' and opting instead for 'America First,' a lot of other countries will have to rethink their policies."

THE CRACKS IN THE TRUMP SUPPORT
SYSTEM AND WORLD DAMAGE

The first sign of cracks in the Trump support system came when Fox TV news commentator Shepard Smith complained: "lie after lie after lie." He was discussing Trump's relationship with Russia. Europeans praised and missed the dignified leadership of President Barack Obama. What had happened to the U. S.? How could this arrogant bully become president?

Trump perpetuates his power mongering by misstating the facts. He continually holds up a pen, signs a bill, smiles for the camera and hands the pen off to an admirer. This beaming presidential person looks into a TV camera with a beaming smile like he has just won the lottery. Trump stated time and time again his first 100 Days he provided more new legislative bills than any president since Franklin Delano Roosevelt. Trump's claim is contrary to the facts. He signed Executive Orders to erase President Obama's legacy. Those are presidential decrees not bills. His legislative record is quite slim.

Walt's essay in Foreign Affairs "America Can't Be Trusted Anymore" sums up his belief the U. S. has international problems because, as Walt concludes: "It's hard to be powerful when nobody believes a word you say." Trump lacks flexibility. You need to combine this trait with toughness for a successful foreign policy. The world is dealing with a U. S. president without a firm policy, a limited attention span and a penchant for creating foreign policy from watching Fox and Friends. This is not a recipe for success. But there are some commentators who view Trump's incoherence as brilliant.

TRUMP'S BRILLIANT INCOHERENCE IN FOREIGN POLICY

In April 2017 Stephen Sestanovich, writing in The Atlantic, had a moment of praise for Trump. Then, later in the article, he addresses Trump's failures. He suggested Donald J. Trump's foreign policy displayed "a brilliant incoherence." What did Sestanovich mean? He suggested we fought the Korean War spending too much money, coming to a stalemate, and then the Vietnam War was more than a decade long with large sums of money failing to bring regime changes. Sestanovich concluded these failures meant we should reduce our military commitments. Trump's advisers point out Afghanistan and Iraq also failed in nation building. The costs were prohibitive.

Sestanovich argues Trump embraces a scaled down foreign policy to avoid over commitment. The president is determined to end the post-Cold War era of international cooperation. By defining America First he is changing the historic direction of American foreign policy.

The cost of foreign policy is a concern. Trump is scaling down the amount of money spent overseas. What is the impact? According to Sestanovich, the U. S. economy cannot sustain the money previously allocated for foreign policy. Sestanovich sees minor victories in Trump's foreign policy. The cost of diplomacy needs to be addressed. Trump is accomplishing that goal while destroying America's world influence.

Sestanovich does not see a silver lining to the new foreign policy. "The new president has made one wrong move after another...." Sestanovich concluded. Serious discussions of America's role in world affairs are not a part of the Trump administration. It is about spending less money, opening up more business opportunities and remaining disengaged from traditional allies.

Trump sees his electoral victory as a mandate for decreasing foreign funding. His America First policy is a popular one among those opposing internationalism. Public opinion wants the money spent at home. As Sestanovich points out, the president has a grasp of the issues, some limited background in world business affairs and a different personality. He predicted Trump could have success under the right circumstances. The courts blocked the president's Muslim ban. He had a mixed reception at the G-7 and G-20. He withdrew the U. S. from the Paris Climate Accord. He withdrew from the TPP. He talks of building a wall isolating us from Mexico. No one is paying for it.

The Pew Research Center in a May 2016 poll reported seventy percent of voters wanted the next Chief Executive to focus on domestic affairs. Trump took heed. He was elected. But the problem he had was in working out a series of compromises with Congress on domestic issues. His only major piece of legislation was the tax cut. Everything else failed in his first eighteen months due to an inability to reach agreements with Congress on legislation.

He is in the process of recasting American diplomacy while accelerating an economy wave not entirely of his own making. But he takes credit for any and all accomplishments.

TRUMP'S FOREIGN POLICY: HIS BIGGEST FAILURE YET OR NOT?

In mid-July 2017, the Washington Post headlined: "Trump's Foreign Policy: His Biggest Failure Yet?" Jennifer Rubin concluded: "Trump is willfully placing Russian interests in having him in power so as to deal leniently with their international aggression." The controversy over Donald Trump Jr.'s meeting with a Russian lawyer, Natalia Veselnitskaya, and her colleagues continue to suggest alleged collusion. Trump's critics roast him for daily lies. He has a lack of transparency. The Washington Post reported they chronicled 3001 presidential lies or distortions of the truth by mid-May 2018. He offers lame excuses and denials so that no one is sure if Russia meddled in our election. When H. R. McMaster said there was no question of collusion, he used the term "incontrovertible evidence." He said Russia created chaos and discord in the 2016 U. S. election. Trump went off on a twitter tirade remarking his National Security Adviser forgot to say that Trump wasn't involved in Russian collusion. He eventually replaced him with war hawk John Bolton. He also criticized his advisers for not following the Trump line. Blind loyalty is demanded. The lack of discussion prevents a thoughtful, rational foreign policy. Trump lies with facility and frequency. He has not paid the price for his deception.

As the Veselnitskaya incident received extensive media attention, Trump raged in the White House. He complained his family was attacked. With pressing world problems, he was like a child who had a toy taken away. Trump screamed the Russian connected lawyer, Natalia Veselnitskaya, was undermining his presidency. It was all Hillary Clinton's fault. He wanted to lock her up. Rather than governing the country, he engaged in petty attacks, nasty tweets and untruthful comments. He displayed a venality not previously seen in American politics.

Donald J. Trump: "General McMaster forgot to say that the results of the 2016 election were not impacted or changed by the Russians and that the only Collusion was between Russia and Crooked H, the DNC and the Dems. Remember the Dirty Dossier, Uranium, Speeches, Emails and the Podesta Company!" This tweet on February 17, 2018 is neither presidential nor thoughtful. What is it about?

It was all about the Donald. He displays no presidential leadership. Trump's minions continue to suggest, Russia didn't impact his presidential victory. The CIA, the FBI, and cyber security specialists have proven Russian interference. How could fifteen million dollars of Russian money illegally directed toward defeating the Clinton campaign not influence the election? In February 2018 Mueller's indictments of thirteen Russian nationals demonstrated Kremlin meddling, and these indictments came as the president threatened to shut down the Mueller investigation. Trump said there was nothing more to prove. Mueller quickly answered this charge with three Russian business indictments. The Donald is the president. He says "No" to collusion. Maybe not by him! How about his minions? Mueller's indictment of thirteen Russian citizens and three Kremlin controlled businesses detailed the fake news they peddled to defeat Clinton.

For the first time in American history voters wonder if the President is on our side. Republican Senator Lindsey Graham labeled some of Trump's Russian statements "stupid." This seems harsh. The cease-fire in Syria benefitted Putin more than Trump. The negotiations to return pricey American properties owned by Russia seized for violating espionage laws for spying is a major Trump goal. RT, the Russian television propaganda network, praised Trump for his actions. RT charged President Obama caused world problems. They gush Trump is bringing the world together. The Russian press said the two Trump-Putin meetings at the G-20 placed Putin in charge of world affairs. This is another victory for Putin.

WHY IS THERE A CONTROVERSY OVER QATAR?

Why is there a controversy over Qatar? Saudi Arabia is determined to challenge Qatar's Middle East influence. This country does not behead or execute people publicly. The last public execution in 2003 was before a firing squad for a convicted murderer. In sharp contrast, Saudi Arabia continues beheadings, public stonings and other brutal forms of capital punishment. But it is the Qatar news network, al Jazeera that bothers other Middle Eastern countries. Freedom of expression is not guaranteed in Saudi Arabia. It is in Qatar. It is not government propaganda like RT. Al Jazeera offers a sane and rational view of the Middle East.

The 11,000 American military people who operate the twenty square mile Al Udeid Air Base south of Doha, the capital of Qatar, are responsible for American bombers and jet fighters attacking ISIL, the Taliban in Afghanistan and the Houthi rebels in Yemen. The use of drones from this air base is an asset in surveillance of terrorist groups. The Qatar base is integral to the American defense system.

Will Bunch, in the Philadelphia Inquirer, wrote Trump sold out the Gulf state of Qatar, a long time U. S. ally, because they allegedly supported terrorism. In a June 6, 2017 tweet Trump said: "During my recent trip to the Middle East I stated that there can no longer be funding of Radical Ideology. Leaders point to Qatar-look." The level of sheer ignorance from this tweet caused Secretary of Defense James Mattis to point out to Trump that U. S. military forays were launched from our Qatar base. Trump said: "Oh."

What makes the Qatar story even more puzzling is the New York Times reported representatives from Saudi Arabia and the UAE met with Trump campaign insiders offering financial assistance for

Trump's presidential candidacy. When Trump won, Will Bunch wrote in a headlined op-ed piece: "How The Trump Family Sold U. S. Foreign Policy To The Highest Bidder." This explosive May 20, 2018 article in the Philadelphia Inquirer, coupled with a piece in the New York Times, alleged financial impropriety. The argument is the executives running the Trump financial empire benefit financially from the president's erratic and often unexplainable shifts in foreign policy. Why? These shifts prompt foreign government to invest in Trump properties. It is not open bribery but it is a suspect business decision. These shifts also benefitted Trump businesses. Saudi Arabia sold Trump a story of Qatar's support for terrorism to benefit their own diplomatic ends. He bought it. He didn't listen to his advisers. Ironically, despite his lack of knowledge, there were trade successes in the trip to Saudi Arabia.

TRUMP'S FOREIGN POLICY: THE SAUDIS AND THE QATAR CONTROVERSEY

After four months in office, Trump flew to Saudi Arabia for a foray into foreign affairs. He proved to be woefully inept. Yet, to his followers, he appeared successful. He was a tough guy standing up to the world. What did Trump miss or not know about the Saudis. It is a country governed by an extended family in power for almost a century. The Saudi government has complete, totalitarian control over its people. All media outlets are state controlled. Public demonstrations are illegal. Beheadings remain a way of daily governmental life. Fear! Repression! These are the Saudi tools.

Saudi control of thought, political dissent and freedoms is threatened by Qatar's al Jazeera's fair and even television coverage. This small, but very rich, nation is the home to one of the U. S.'s most important military bases. We would not want to insult them. Guess what! Trump did.

When Trump and his entourage visited Saudi Arabia, they had no notion of the repressive Saudi regime. Wilbur Ross, the richest member of Trump's cabinet, was a guest on CNBC business stating there were no demonstrations and no press complaints about U. S. foreign policy. Wilbur Ross: "The other thing that was fascinating to me was there was not a single hint of a protester anywhere during the whole time that we were there. Not one guy with a bad placard." This highlights Ross's naïve view.

The blatant ignorance of a high level White House official brought negative world headlines. All Ross could talk about was the economy. Trump was making deals with the Saudis. He told everyone "how about that economy." His statement to CNBC business was an incredible demonstration of his unfitness for office.

The Trump White House stepped in to defend Ross. They only made it worse. They defended his inane statement. CNBC commentator Becky Quick challenged Ross's knowledge of the Middle East stating: "They control people and do not let them express their feelings." Ross looked at her like she was a moron. He responded: "In theory, that could be true." This is the nature of the Trump White House. Trump's foreign policy makes him a promoter of U. S. business in the world. He is not following the traditional path of promoting liberty and freedom in world affairs.

TRUMP IS HAVING MIDDLE EAST
SUCCESS DESPITE HIS CABINET

Is there an area where Trump is successful in foreign affairs? Surprisingly, "Yes." He changed the diplomatic direction in the Middle East. The Trump trip to visit the Saudis was one of his first foreign forays. It was an unmitigated success in terms of economic reward. It was a disaster in terms of the diplomatic accomplishments. Before he left for Saudi Arabia, Trump remarked they would help finance a stronger military presence against terrorism. The idea, Trump said, was to replace the American military presence. With what someone asked? He had no idea. What the president didn't realize is the Saudis were attempting to isolate Qatar. Why? Qatar is liberal in the Middle East but moderate among Western observers. It is home to the fair and balanced al Jazeera TV network.

The successes Trump had with Saudi Arabia were reflected in their agreement to purchase $110 billion worth of American arms and to continue to purchase $350 billion arms over the next decade. "Hundreds of billions of dollars of investments into the United States and jobs, jobs, jobs," Trump bragged.

As Trump's presidential motorcade rolled into Riyadh, the president looked out the limousine window and saw a huge billboard with his picture on it. He smiled. The Saudis gave him ultimate respect. This billboard had a huge picture of President Trump next to the Saudi King with the caption: "Together We Prevail."

When United Arab Emirates Foreign Minister Anwar Gargash analyzed Trump's Middle Eastern trip, he took a phrase from the Donald's speeches. Gargash called Trump's foray "very, very successful." Saudi Arabia, Egypt and Bahrain began a political move to isolate Qatar through economic sanctions. The other issue is Saudi Arabia would like to shut down al Jazeeri news. Qatar based al Jazeeri is a professional, highly thought of TV outlet. It is also a partial voice for a segment of the moderate Muslim world. This is al Jazeeri's contradiction they are liberal on social issues but conservative on political-military concerns.

In 2013 al Jazeera announced its support for the radical Muslim Brotherhood. As a result, twenty-two journalists resigned in protest over the support for this Muslim political organization. Al Jazeeri's sin is reporting on the Muslim Brotherhood, an organization that has torn Egypt and Turkey apart. One al Jazeera journalist, Abdullah Al-Arian, argued Trump fails to understand the historical complexity of the group's evolution. Why does the Muslim Brotherhood receive favorable comment from al Jazeera? That is a good question. It appears there is genuine sympathy in Qatar for the Muslim Brotherhood. But they did not support terrorism.

That said the Qatar TV network is generally fair and balanced. The UAE wants it off the air. Trump is working to aid this goal. The Saudis played Trump. They praised him. He supported the demand to shut down Qatar's al Jazeera news network.

Secretary of State Rex Tillerson said the UAE made charges against Qatar without proof. Tillerson was still waiting for the proof when he was fired. He said he was mystified at the failure of the Gulf allies to back up their claims. Tillerson wondered if the dispute was really about terrorism? It wasn't! The UAE wants the press, partisan criticism and free speech controlled. Trump was furious with Tillerson. He brought him into the Oval Office complaining he had to realize his place on the foreign policy team. Tillerson said: "It's your show." They had a shouting match, according to the New York Times, which reported their differences in copious detail.

On June 5, 2017 Trump supported a plan to cut trade, diplomatic and transportation ties with Qatar. The New York Times reported President Trump "takes credit for Saudi move against Qatar." Saudi Arabia's move to isolate Qatar brought a swift thumbs up from the president. He said Qatar has been linked to funds moved to the Muslim Brotherhood. It was more complicated than the president realized. He changed his view backing away from his previous incredulous remarks concerning Qatar.

The day after praising the isolation of Qatar, the president called King Salman of Saudi Arabia and they talked for some time. The result Trump said was to bring unity in the region. He backed off supporting Saudi Arabia attempts to isolate Qatar. This was confusing to everyone. The Saudis were perplexed by Trump changing his mind. They had no idea that the flips and the flops were an integral part of American foreign policy. The American Ambassador to Qatar, Dana Shell Smith, tweeted "Qatar has made real progress in curbing financial support for terrorists." Qatar's financial support for extremist groups has long been an America concern. To his credit, President Trump may have influenced a decline in Qatar's cozy relationship with terrorism. His flip-flops ironically helped to defuse regional tensions.

The three Sunni Gulf countries—Saudi Arabia, Bahrain and the UAE, along with Egypt, said Qatar supports terrorism and destabilizing the region. Qatar said it has a relationship with Hamas and the Muslim Brotherhood. Qatar has said repeatedly there are no terrorist ties.

Trump's advisers pointed out the Qatar based U. S. military base at Doha is necessary to the American fight against terrorism. This placed Trump in a quandary. He had to have Qatar in the American fold to ensure the U. S. military fight against ISIS. Suddenly, Trump called for Gulf unity. Had he understood Gulf politics, he wouldn't initially have agreed to isolating Qatar only to change his mind the next day. The change in Trump's demeanor came upon advice from the Secretaries of State and Defense who said the Al Udeid base in

Qatar was the main regional center for air missions against ISIS. Suddenly Trump talked of regional unity and defeating ISIS.

The visit to Saudi Arabia was an unqualified business success. The Saudis threw a party for the president costing in excess of seventy-five million dollars. During the visit gold plated golf carts were spotted with Jared Kushner and Ivanka Trump enjoying Saudi hospitality. A special throne, also gold plated, was built for Trump. He sat in a regal presence as the sumptuous party honoring the American president.

There were fifty Arab and Muslim nations welcoming Trump as Saudi hospitality led to improved relations. Not surprisingly, Trump said Obama created a mess. He was cleaning it up.

The President of Bahrain, Hamad bin Isa Al Khalifa, met with Trump for serious discussions. The result was an agreement that the U. S. would cooperate to assist Bahrain's foreign policy goals. The Egyptian strongman, Abdel Fattah el-Sisi, told Trump: "You are a unique personality that is capable of doing the impossible." Trump didn't know what to say. He remarked: "Love your shoes." The Donald had some catching up to do on Middle Eastern affairs. He needed more knowledge of local customs and politics.

Maybe Trump had some knowledge of local customs as a Middle Eastern reporter a decade earlier threw a shoe at President George W. Bush as a sign of disrespect. Trump's defenders might have pounced on this illicit fact to demonstrate his advanced historical grasp of all things Middle Eastern.

It was incredulous in late May 2017 when el-Sisi met trump at the hotel in Riyadh when the American president suddenly called el-Sisi: "My friend." Then in the most unbelievable explanation in diplomatic history, Trump said: "boy, those shoes. Man!" There was dead silence in the room. This cozying up to Egypt's strong man prompted long time Trump acolyte, Roger Stone, to remark to the London Daily Mail: "Candidly, this makes me want to puke." Stone was referring to the medal Saudi Arabia presented to the American president.

When Trump was awarded the Order of Abdulaziz al Saud medal from the Saudi King, he beamed like an overweight Panda. Then completely changing course Trump attacked former President

Barack Obama tweeting: "Do we still want a president who bows to the Saudis and lets Opec rip us off?" Trump said he was in Saudi Arabia to offer a partnership based on shared interests and values.... This comment in a May 2017 speech to Muslim leaders in Riyadh indicted Trump approved of authoritarian behavior and supported militaristic leaders.

What the trip to Riyadh showed was in the Persian Gulf the U. S. is firmly aligned with Saudi Arabia and the smaller Gulf States against Iran. The new Saudi crown prince, Mohammed bin Salman, is Trump's latest ally. The president believes he will control the region.

The Washington Post labeled the Saudi Arabia visit "bizarre." Anne Applebaum wrote Trump's visit was "unseemly, unethical and un-American." She concluded that the four previous presidents visited countries that were "trade partners." Saudi Arabia was a strange place to speak out against Islamist extremists. Osama bin Laden was a Saudi citizen as were fifteen of the nineteen 9/11 hijackers. There were other curious incidents. Secretary of State Rex Tillerson held a press conference only for foreign journalists. Ivanka Trump made an appeal to women entrepreneurs. This was a puzzling move as Saudi women could drive cars, but they cannot travel without the permission of male guardians and they have few legal and educational rights. Ivanka made numerous public relations statements. She didn't realize female entrepreneurs are not part of Saudi society.

THE TRUMP DOCTRINE IN FOREIGN POLICY

Those who disparage Trump's foreign policy are making a mistake. There is a misunderstanding about his America First policy. It is not a recreation of the pre-World War II isolationists where California's Senator Hiram W. Johnson and Idaho's William E. Borah predicted doom for America's future if allied with European interests. It is not the America First policy that Harry Truman proclaimed with the Marshall Plan. It is a policy with ugly racial-nationalistic echoes from past U. S. history.

Donald J. Trump: "My foreign policy will always put the interests of the American people, and American security, above all else." The president believes in peace through strength. He will renegotiate

350

trade deals he feels are one sided. He prefers nation-to-nation deals. He also wants "old enemies" to become friends. He believes friends will remain allies.

When Russia dominated a portion of post World War II Europe, the U. S. had an adversary, an enemy and a focus for our foreign policy. The U. S. began the Cold War fighting Russia's advances all over the world. In the process the global economy emerged. The U. S. did very well economically. We remained the military bulwark against Communism and other foes of democracy. In other words, the U. S. was the free world's leader. This is a policy Trump is undoing.

When Ronald Reagan became the U. S. president and the Iron Lady Margaret Thatcher took over as the English prime minister, the Berlin Wall collapsed and Communism ended its reign of terror. The Soviet Union gave way to what some called a democracy. It didn't turn out that way. The Russian oligarchs, the KGB turned into a Mafia, and the result was the election of Vladimir Putin as the president of the new Russia. It is the old Russia. But that is another story.

The end of Communism was not a good thing for American politicians. They had no one to blame for world economic problems, unpopular political change, global violence and unforeseen social-economic-political circumstances. The old Kremlin bogeyman was forgotten. Without an adversary to define its goals, its place in the world and its future U. S. foreign policy shifted into a foggy morass without a direction. Now the Kremlin bogeyman is back as a cyber criminal.

MADELEINE ALBRIGHT ON AMERICA FIRST

"He is a president that has anti-democratic instincts. That bothers me." Madeleine Albright remarked. She wrote a book about the rise of worldwide fascism. Like many she sees Trump's presidency as the advanced agent of fascism. She doesn't believe Trump is a fascist. She believes the ideology is being revived throughout the world. He benefits from it.

After fifteen months of the Trump presidency, Madeleine Albright's "Fascism: A Warning" interprets America First. Albright's message is if the U. S. allows fascism to go unchecked, it is too late to undo the damage. She labels America First "as the most unbelievable step backwards, because I do believe that the United States is strong when we have friends and allies to deal with the various issues," Albright concluded.

With Trump's ascension to the presidency fascism rears its ugly head. Everyone thought it was dead with Hitler and Mussolini. Albright doesn't label Trump a fascist. She says he has instincts promoting fascist ideas. Albright's book is a historical look at fascism. She sees the dangers in Trump's leadership. Trump, like past fascist leaders, sees someone to blame. Trump labels immigrants a danger. He has coalesced his followers around Fox News. He charges "fake news" and his tweets destroy those who oppose him.

Trump does not believe the world is a "global community," Madeleine Albright argues. Trump is Darwinian. This means the strongest nation survives. The weakest country falls by the wayside. This is why Trump has built the military into the number one world-killing machine. Albright argues this is a policy of retreat from the world stage. America by withdrawing from world affairs gives a pass to dictators to do as they please. The political and military power of NATO helps maintain the world order. Trump doesn't understand how and why NATO emerged after World War II. He has trouble supporting it.

Madeleine Albright did see some positive points in America First. She pointed out it made leaders from other nations nervous. They didn't know what to expect. "Maybe Trump does have the answer, as he has claimed to forge better trade agreements…." (p. 219)

How does a nation slowly drift into tyranny? That is the question Madeleine Albright asks and answers. When people are fearful, angry and confused, Albright suggests, "They follow an authoritarian leader. They will temporarily give up some freedoms for prosperity and stability. A fascist is a person who claims to speak for the majority while ending free speech, oppositional research, a free press and compensate for taking away these freedoms with pensions, a strong military and employment opportunities. This president is anti-democracies," she concluded. Albright defines Trump as the first president to threaten democracy.

TRUMP APPOINTS THREE WHO DEFINE AMERICAN
FOREIGN POLICY: THEN TWO ARE GONE

From the outset Trump was criticized, disparaged and disrespected for his frequent historical mistakes. He is not an avid student of history. When he learns something new, he will say most people don't know this happened. It makes him look ill-informed when he explains it incorrectly.

The Secretary of Defense, "Mad Dog" James Mattis, is a brilliant appointment. As an undergraduate at the small and not particularly prestigious Central Washington State University, he majored in history. Or should I say he consumed history books. What was his favorite area of history? It was military history. Whether it was Sun Tzu on the art of war or Klauswitz on military strategy, he consumed their books. He can literally recite their major themes from memory. Somewhere along the line he began collecting military books. He is much like Tillerson. He has a calm, no nonsense demeanor. He shuns the spotlight. He is careful while talking with the press. He doesn't like dealing with the media. If there is such a thing as an intellectual in government it is Mad Dog Mattis. The only negative in his career is his nickname "Mad Dog." He is anything but unless of course you are on the battlefield. He has thoughtful defense policies. Trump listens to him.

The National Security Adviser, H. R. McMaster, is the best of the Trump appointees. Why? He understands how national security operates. After General Flynn left in a cloud of disgrace, McMaster took over on February 20, 2017 and his job was difficult from day one. Steve Bannon did not care for McMaster. He did everything he could to derail his advice. But for a time, McMaster connected with Trump while more conservative Trump insiders attacked the NSC adviser for alleged anti-Semitism and streaks of liberal thought. McMaster was fired.

The Trump inner circle is filled with right wing conspiracy-oriented fanatics. McMaster showed up at briefings well prepared with a great deal of knowledge. The whackos inside the Trump foreign policy team view him as not tough enough on Muslim radicalism.

Frank Gaffney, the president of the Center For Security Policy, was McMaster's most vocal critic. Gaffney believes former President Barack Obama is a Muslim. He said the NSC adviser was weak on radicalism. The attempts to discredit McMaster come in venal, daily criticism that borders on character assassination. For a time, Trump had confidence in his well-prepared and articulate thoughts on foreign policy. Then the Gaffney criticism hit home and Trump fired McMaster.

When McMaster left the White House, his replacement John Bolton brought in the fire and fury Trump loves. When Trump replaced McMaster he treated him with respect. This was not the case when he fired Tillerson. The president had McMaster and his family into the Oval Office for a lavish farewell ceremony. The one hundred fifty career staff members in the NSC were happy when the president implied to McMaster to keep up the good work in the private sector.

In his last week in office, McMaster delivered a speech criticizing Vladimir Putin. He remarked: "We have failed to impose sufficient costs." This was clearly a criticism of Trump's refusal to place full sanctions on Russia. He also criticized President Xi Jinping for China's unwillingness to support American foreign policy.

As McMaster left the Oval Office, it had been months since Trump listened to him. McMaster wanted to add more troops in Afghanistan. Trump was opposed to the notion. Why was McMaster fired? Insiders say it was due to his precise briefings. Trump believed he was phony, trite and unable to connect with the staff. This was Jared Kushner's view. He may have been a co-conspirator getting rid of McMaster. The number of times Trump ignored NSC recommendations tells one all they need to know. McMaster didn't criticize Trump. He was a team player. His strong views may have been the reason for his ouster.

During his tenure as NSC adviser, McMaster praised Trump for speaking out against oppression in visits to Poland, Saudi Arabia and South Korea. The expulsion of sixty Russian diplomats was another high point for McMaster. It was retaliation for Russia's role in the British nerve gas poisonings.

With a doctoral degree from the University of North Carolina, Chapel Hill, McMaster's knowledge threatened other Trump appointees. His doctoral dissertation was turned into the widely acclaimed book Dereliction of Duty, which is a staple for United States military training. His book was critical of military planning during the Vietnam war. That didn't always sit well with the Generals in and around the White House. He was also a history professor at the United States Military Academy for 1994 to 1996. This was training for precise, detailed briefings on national security. From day one this did not go down well with President Trump. He respected McMaster. But no one could tell the Donald anything. He knew more than the generals. He is after all a self-proclaimed "quiet genius."

Why did McMaster fail as the National Security Adviser? The operative wisdom is Steve Bannon with Mike Cernovich criticized him daily, radio host Alex Jones, Jared Kushner and the Breitbart News staff second-guessing his every move. There was one statement that prompted Trump to fire him. When McMaster remarked Russian interference in the 2016 election was "incontrovertible," he was on his way to civilian life. The New York Times reported Trump ranted and raved screaming "incontrovertible." One wonders! Did he know the meaning of the word? McMaster wasn't a warmonger. Neither was Secretary Tillerson. Trump believed they hampered his "fire and fury" foreign policy. Then Tillerson gave the interview that sealed his fate. He talked to 60 Minutes. He said the wrong things. He failed to properly praise Trump.

On February 18, 2018 Secretary Tillerson sat down with 60 Minutes to discuss Trump's foreign policy. In a chilling interview the Secretary of State talked with hesitation about dropping a bomb on North Korea. Tillerson was confident diplomacy would triumph. There was no need for war. He appeared to criticize Trump's bombastic military threats.

Tillerson talked about the "code of the west" in the 60 Minutes segment. He made it clear. He was a person of his word. He said in the State Department the American people were his brand. He would make sure world diplomacy made America a safe place. Then he was pressed on the State Department hiring freeze. He looked uncomfortable.

"There's been no dismantling at all of the State Department," Tillerson said in the interview with "CBS 60 Minutes." "Our foreign policy objectives continue to be met." He also remarked: "My word is my bond, that's why I am here," Tillerson said closing the 60 Minutes interview. He didn't look happy. Things would change dramatically in Trump's foreign policy as John Bolton arrived in what was increasingly becoming a War Cabinet.

TRUMP'S ANTI-RESTRAINT FOREIGN POLICY

When the new National Security Adviser, John Bolton, and the new Secretary of State, Mike Pompeo assumed their duties Secretary of Defense James Mattis was the only non-War Hawk meeting with President Trump.

The danger is real. Bolton has poor judgment. He is impulsive. He lacks diplomatic skills. If being a jackass is a crime, Bolton would be serving a life sentence. Pompeo is skilled with the media but no less combative.

The lack of restraint in Trump's first sixteen months in the presidency led to a lack of control, a dismantling of previous agreements and a playbook on foreign policy no one can figure out.

There is confusion to Trump's foreign policy. That will not end soon. When he ended American participation in the Iran Nuclear deal there was not a lot of surprise. This places France, Russia, China, Germany, Britain and the European Union in the position of attempting to maintain the Iranian deal for purposes of international security.

As the EU and its member nations talk about how Iran is living up to the terms of the deal, President Trump ignores them. When French President Emmanuel Macron arrived in Washington to discuss the Iranian situation, there was concern that the deal would implode. It hasn't. It won't.

President Hassan Rouhani of Iran said his country would live up to the deal. Now the EU and its allies need to maintain it. Israel does not believe the deal blocks Iran's path to a nuclear bomb. The EU hopes to maintain the deal with the prospect of maintaining a precarious peace with Iran as they funnel troops into Syria, lob missiles at Syria and taunt the United States with egomaniacal threats. Trump believes he is right. He maintains the Iranian deal is difficult to defend. It doesn't allow for full disclosure. The EU and its allies can maintain the Iranian deal and the U. S. sanctions will help fulfill the agreement. At home and abroad everyone disagrees with Trump.

The U. S. withdrawal, former President Barack Obama remarked, was "a losing choice between a nuclear armed Iran and another war in the Middle East." The feeling was it took five years for the Obama administration to solidify a deal for world peace and as former Secretary of State John Kerry remarked: "Instead of building on unprecedented nonproliferation verification measures, this decision risks throwing them away and dragging the world back to the brink we faced a few years ago." The reaction to U. S. withdrawal promoted one critic to suggest "ego not policy" led to the end of the Iranian nuclear agreement.

Paul Krugman: "It's pretty clear that he had no idea what was actually in the Iran agreement he just repudiated." This comment in the New York Times prompted Krugman to conclude, "when petty cruelty becomes a principle of government democracy is in peril."

JOHN FEELEY: THE AMERICAN AMBASSADOR TO PANAMA: TRUMP'S BULLYING ACT IS RUINING DIPLOMACY

John Feeley was appointed in December 2015 as the American ambassador to Panama. He was a former Marine helicopter pilot who was a three-decade career diplomat. He wasn't political. He wasn't registered to vote. When he did vote it was for both Republican and Democratic candidates. He took his career State Department oath to serve either party in an apolitical fashion with high integrity. He did!

John Feeley resigned in January 2018 as the American ambassador to Panama. When he was asked why, Feeley said of Trump: "He's like a velociraptor. He has to be boss, and if you don't show him deference he kills you." This may seem harsh. Why did Feeley resign? Were there other reasons?

His discontent with Trump began when he was called to the Oval Office for a briefing. As he entered the West Wing reception area, he heard Trump say, behind a closed door, "Fuck him! Tell him to sue the government." Then he entered the Oval Office with Trump sitting behind a large desk devoid of papers. As they talked Trump said: "So what do we get from Panama? What's in it for us?" Feeley explained the Panamanians helped with drug trafficking. He pointed out the Panama Canal's commercial efforts were important to the American economy. Before he could say another word, Trump spoke. He asked Feeley if Trump International Hotel and Tower in Panama City was "the tallest building in the skyline down there." This made Feeley uncomfortable. Trump had no knowledge of Panama. He had no interest in learning what President Juan Carlos Varela thought about American politics.

After twenty-seven years as a career diplomat, Feeley saw American foreign policy being destroyed. He decided President Trump was a danger to the future of diplomacy. He submitted a resignation letter. Then he did the unthinkable. He wrote an op-ed piece for the Washington Post "Why I Could No Longer Serve This President." He concluded: "Trump had warped and betrayed...the traditional core values of the United States."

John Feeley: "America is undoubtedly less welcome in the world today." As the second ranking diplomat for Western Hemispheric Affairs, Feeley had the opportunity to observe the strengths and weaknesses of American diplomacy. Feeley did his best to end the belief the U.S. operated in Panama only to protect its assets. When Panama was founded in 1903 it was largely due to the U. S. and our desire to control the shipping lanes in the Panama Canal. As the U. S. began building the Panama Canal the country realized U. S. governmental interests were controlling them. That didn't change until 1968 when General Omar Torrijos seized power. The level of anti-American feeling was always high in Panama. Feeley overcame that feeling and developed a connection to the locals.

The Secretary of State Rex Tillerson arrived and he informed the Panamanian government the old policy of imbalanced trade was back. Feeley pointed out Jared Kushner began meddling in Latin American politics. He made deals with Mexican officials while ignoring Panama. Feeley had trouble understanding why Kushner was a foreign policy emissary. The Panamanian ambassador received no instructions, no updates and no questions from the Trump administration. It was like they couldn't find Panama on the map.

The history of the U.S. intervening in Latin American affairs using the Monroe Doctrine as the excuse was finally over. Secretary of State John Kerry told Latin American nations the Obama administration was not interested in meddling in their affairs. That changed when Trump came to the White House.

The Donald was the foreign policy bully who let everyone know it was Trump against the world. Rather than meddle in Panama's affairs, Trump ignored the country. There wasn't enough commerce to interest him. The result is China is now Panama's chief trading partner. As the U. S. has retreated from Latin America, China's influence has grown. Banks linked to Beijing lent one hundred and fifty billion to Latin American nations. As a result, trade between China and Latin America increased twenty-seven times.

`When Feeley attempted to alert the Trump administration to China's growing influence in Panama and throughout Latin America, he was told to mind his own business. Feeley said that the change in attitude was reflected when the newly appointed Chinese ambassador to Panama had the most lavish welcome party in Panama's history.

As Feeley sent his resignation letter to Trump, there was an exodus from the State Department. Roberta Jacobson, the ambassador to Mexico, resigned after three decades in the State Department. She pointed out Mexico's hostility to the Trump administration resulted from continual racial insults and demeaning the country. The irony is in Panama and Mexico democratic leaders and movements were strong. The moral high ground in government was on the rise in Latin America. Trump was systematically dismantling it.

ANTHONY SCARAMUCCI

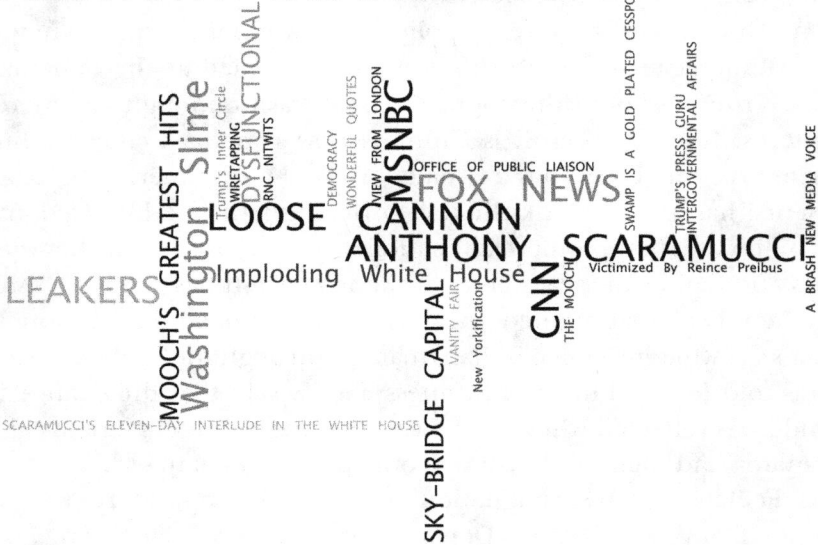

MOOCH'S GREATEST HITS
Washington Slime
Trump's Inner Circle
WIRETAPPING
DYSFUNCTIONAL
RNC NITWITS
DEMOCRACY
WONDERFUL QUOTES
VIEW FROM LONDON
MSNBC
OFFICE OF PUBLIC LIAISON
FOX NEWS
SWAMP IS A GOLD PLATED CESSPOOL
TRUMP'S PRESS GURU
INTERGOVERNMENTAL AFFAIRS
A BRASH NEW MEDIA VOICE
LOOSE CANNON
ANTHONY SCARAMUCCI
LEAKERS Imploding White House
CNN
THE MOOCH
Victimized By Reince Preibus
SKY-BRIDGE CAPITAL
VANITY FAIR
New Yorkifications
SCARAMUCCI'S ELEVEN-DAY INTERLUDE IN THE WHITE HOUSE

EIGHTEEN

THE ANTHONY SCARAMUCCI SCARE: HOW THE MOOCH EXPLAINS EVERYTHING TRUMP, DOES DEMOCRACY SURVIVE?

"Drain the swamp should be changed to drain the sewer-it's actually much worse than anyone thought, and it begins with Fake News."

DONALD J. TRUMP, JULY 24, 2017

"Our main task is to make ourselves more human."

JOSE SARAMANGO, 1999

"I predict General Kelly will go down as one of the greatest
ever."

Donald Trump On Kelly's Appointment As Chief Of Staff

"Democracy is never a thing done. Democracy is
always something that a nation must be doing."

Archibald Macleish

"The mooch and the mogul is a tender love story with
dramatic implications for the imploding White House."

Maureen Dowd, The New York Times

On July 21, 2017 an unknown Italian-American hedge fund
founder Anthony Scaramucci was selected as an Assistant to President
Trump. He was named the director of the White House Office of
Public Liaison and Intergovernmental Affairs. He was the new
communications director for the Trump administration. What was
strange about Scaramucci's selection? He didn't have public relations
or press experience. How did Scaramucci react to the appointment?
He began to bluster about the press. He said he would clear up past
communication problems.

WHO IS SCARAMUCCI?

Who is Anthony Scaramucci? He grew up in Port Washington N. Y.
He attended public school, and he graduated from Tufts and
Harvard Law. The road to Harvard Law was an improbable one. His
father was a construction worker helping to dig the foundation for
New York skyscrapers. He cashed in a $10,000 life insurance policy so
his son could study at Tufts. When he was admitted to Harvard Law,
his mother had never heard of it. She thought he was going to school
in Hartford. His Italian, blue-collar working-class background made
Scaramucci a diligent student and eventual Wall Street impresario.
His road to becoming a millionaire went through Wall Street hedge
funds. The press made fun of him. He is shrewd judge of people. He
is also one hell of a bright observer of the political scene.

There is no doubt Scaramucci is well educated. His employment
history is spotty. He has never practiced law. He began his career at

Goldman Sachs where he was let go with an $11,000 severance. He was rehired at the sales division of Goldman Sachs two months later. He left that position to co-found Oscar Capital Management where he was very successful selling the company to Berman in 2001. Then he founded SkyBridge Capital, a fund of funds, which did not do well. "That was a real bottom for me," Scaramucci told The New York Times. He rebounded in 2010 purchasing Citigroup's Fund-of-Fund Business. It was about this time he became involved in national politics.

By 2011, Scaramucci was in the midst of the SALT Conference, which was a hedge fund industry mega, company bringing together America's most prosperous hedge funds. In the midst of the American financial crisis, Scaramucci was a fiscal star as well as a multi-millionaire. He was also critical of Donald Trump. He supported Wisconsin's Paul Ryan for president.

One of the conditions of working in government is to divest yourself of conflicting business interests. After he founded SkyBridge Capital, Scaramucci attempted to sell it to a Chinese company. It was a network of hedge funds that Scaramucci founded in 2005, but federal regulators would not sign off on the deal. Trump took note. The sale was potentially a brilliant business move at least in terms of profit. Scaramucci invested ninety million in SkyBridge and sold it for one hundred and eighty million. If you fool the Chinese you have Trump's attention.

Scaramucci resigned from SkyBridge in January 2017 and more than fifteen months later the Committee on Foreign Investment in the United States, which evaluates sales of U. S. businesses to foreign entities, had not approved the sale. This opened a window for Scaramucci to return to his former business.

Since 2012 Trump shrewdly and quietly watched Scaramucci. Then, as Trump assumed the presidency in January 2017, he saw Scaramucci's intelligent analysis on Fox Business News, CNN and CNBC. He was a business friendly version of Trump as the Donald ran for the presidency. In May 2014, SkyBridge Capital acquired the licensing rights to "Wall Street Week", formerly known as "Wall Street Week With Louis Rukeyser." In April 2015, Anthony Scaramucci was featured as a co-host during the shows first few episodes. Clearly,

Trump saw Scaramucci as a media attack dog. Every indication is the president was correct.

There is more substance to Scaramucci than the press has recognized. The president's executive director of the transition team, Rick Dearborn, was told by Trump to offer him the position of assistant to the president and Director of the Office of Public Liaison. He accepted the offer. He had to sell his business to avoid charges of conflict of interest. It took some time. Those close to Trump feared Scaramucci. He is bright. He is honest. He is a strong Trump advocate. Trump's close advisers detested the mooch's middle of the road conservative approach to issues. He isn't a dedicated, fanatical right wing conservative. He is thoughtful, but mercurial, on matters of politics. He wasn't a non-thinking, ideologically driven right-winger. Bannon, Priebus, Miller and a host of lesser lights detested the mooch's reasonable political personality. That was the sin ending Scaramucci's White House career. But in eleven days he provided a window into the most dysfunctional White House since Warren G. Harding slipped his girlfriends into the Oval Office through a secret door.

Anthony Scaramucci: "The thing I have learned about these people in Washington is they have no money. So, what happens when they have no fucking money is they write about what seat they are in and what the title is. Fucking Congressmen act like that. They are fucking jackasses." Harvard Law School left something to be desired along Scaramucci's communication lines. He did make his point.

Who was responsible for convincing President Trump to appoint Scaramucci? Ivanka Trump and her husband Jared Kushner loved the way the mooch promoted Jared's foreign policy forays. The appointment caused friction in the White House. Sean Spicer was more experienced. He was insulted. He left the White House. Reince Priebus informed Trump his decision was a disastrous one. He was soon gone.

Jared and Ivanka caused the mooch mess. They pushed for Scaramucci. Why? Not because of his expertise. It was due to his support for Kushner. He had a media plan to make Jared a household word. The mooch is brilliant. He realized two things. Jared and Ivanka were a direct link to the president. Praising and supporting the president had its rewards. The slick speech, the Armani suits and the Harvard pedigree fooled Jared and Ivanka. They believed that as Communications Director he would replace the Humpty Dumpty Spicer providing the White House with positive press coverage.

After Ivanka spent time alone with her father praising Scaramucci's talents, the president announced his appointment. The media frenzy was unprecedented. No one could believe this rank amateur was running the White House Communications Office.

The question everyone asked concerned not just Scaramucci's qualifications but his over the top comments defending Trump. The mooch made it clear there were to be dire consequences for those who didn't believe in Trump's vision or support his policies.

AFTER SIX MONTHS OF TRUMP WHERE DOES DEMOCRACY STAND?

After six months of the Trump presidency the question of democracy surviving was an important one. The self-interest, the criticism of basic democratic institutions, the incoherent and contradictory statements and the self-congratulatory remarks with the word "I" in every sentence was appalling. Trump has the lowest ratings of any president after six months in office.

The Donald believes he is transparent by tweeting daily. He sees this as a direct link to the people. It is his means of combating fake news. But he is the source of fake news. He charged the Clinton campaign and later President Obama with wiretapping his campaign. He had no evidence to support these outrageous claims. He has no idea the essential role journalism performs in a democracy. Nor did he realize the eleven day Scaramucci disaster garnered more headlines for his communications staff than in the previous six months.

What are the reasons the Trump administration is a danger to American democracy? His close advisers met with Russian diplomats, suspect businessmen and those close to the Kremlin without disclosing when, where or why. The White House under Trump no longer maintains careful records of visitors, personnel or those who enter the president's lair. Security is a concern. Record keeping is faulty. There is no accountability.

He believes "fake news" controls the media. He doesn't hold regular press conferences. He has refused to release his tax returns. The Trump appointees have generally not made full disclosures for top security clearances. General Flynn's failure to disclose funds paid to him for working for a foreign government eventually led to his dismissal.

There was not always transparency from Trump's family. Donald Trump Jr's refusal to admit to a meeting with a Russian lawyer provided rumors of collusion. For a time, Donald Jr. denied meeting with Russian operatives. The press investigated. The New York Times told Donald Jr. they would break a story on his meeting the following day. He decided to come clean. After the New York Times broke the story, forcing Donald Jr. to recall the meeting there was plausible denial. The day before the Times' story a visible angry Donald Jr. detailed his meeting with the Russian lawyer. Sort of! The New York Times and Washington Post pointed out there were eight people at the meeting. Robert Mueller is investigating Russia's influence and this meeting. The result was the rumor of Trump insiders colluding with the Kremlin, there was evidence of cyber tampering in elections, the use of bots hurt Clinton's candidacy and there were other events and devices influencing the 2016 election. Donald Jr. was not implicated.

It is a small, but significant, point. When Trump arrived at the White House he clashed with the Office of Government Ethics. He demanded secret waivers for many of his appointees. The Ethics Director, Walter Shaub, resigned in protest. Why? He said the new White House Ethics Policy was "hollow." The Trump administration has made a joke of government ethics. Much of this is due to unanswered questions surrounding Russia's role in the 2016 election and what those close to Trump knew.

THE MOOCH: A BRASH NEW MEDIA
VOICE AGAINST DEMOCRACY

In late July 2017, Trump revamped the presidency. He sent the Howdy Dowdy impersonator, Sean Spicer, packing while telling the press he had great expectations for Spicer's future. During press briefings, Spicer was ill at ease, nervous and unable to explain the Trump presidency. This led to Scaramucci's appointment.

When he appointed Wall Street financier Anthony Scaramucci as a communications adviser, the handsome, articulate, well-dressed Scaramucci sounded like he was giving the press a deal they couldn't refuse. On Fox TV News, he told Chris Wallace he would press a "reset button" on press opinions. He said there was to be "an era of good feelings." He hoped to "create a more positive mojo." What this meant isn't clear. Maybe if the press didn't treat the Donald right, Don Vito Corleone might come talk to you.

How and why Scaramucci arrived at the White House is an interesting story. Priebus resigned. Scaramucci called him "Rancid Penis." He told the Chief of Staff he would report directly to the president.

Then a few days after Scaramucci was appointed, in a shocking interview, he labeled Priebus mentally ill. So Trump has a man with two specialties, the media and psychology, in the increasingly dysfunctional White House.

When Scaramucci called Priebus a "paranoid schizophrenic" everyone was shocked. Then "the mooch" charged the Chief of Staff was a leaker. To his credit Priebus is a smart politician. He is well versed in how politics works in Washington. No wonder he resigned. Some have charged that Scaramucci had puppet strings on him. The Donald was pulling them. This is nonsense.

Scaramucci is nothing if not career minded. He comes from a blue-collar background. He likes to point out he grew up in Long Island. To "the mooch" it is a badge of honor. He also had it in for Sean Spicer who resigned immediately. Priebus left a week later. The mooch is one of the smartest politicos in Washington who lasted eleven days. He began his relationship with the president working on the financial end of the 2016 campaign.

Scaramucci is an interesting pitchman. He said: "The entire world has changed; we need to rethink the way we're delivering our information." Scaramucci became the new face of the Trump administration. His job was press strategy. After the bungling amateur Sean Spicer, he was a breath of fresh air. He is a brilliant negotiator.

Ultimately, his controversial comments prompted Trump to fire him after eleven days.

If there is a person who can explain the Donald and those around him it is Scaramucci. When asked about the Russian probe, he said: "In some ways we want to deescalate things and have there be a level of diplomacy. In other ways, we want it to be very hard hitting and war-like." The moderator Chris Wallace looked on with a smile. He loved double meanings. I am not sure what this means. But it is a great answer.

On Trump's tweets, Scaramucci said: "That's the crystal essence of the president. And so some of you guys in the media think it's not helpful. But if he thinks it's helpful to him, let him do it." As he finished talking with Fox TV's Chris Wallace, Scaramucci observed the old tweets were "a total distraction."

Scaramucci is brilliant on television and often over the top in newspaper interviews. Maureen Dowd, writing in The New York Times International Edition on May 24 2017, labeled the relationship between Trump and Scaramucci: "The Story of the Mooch And A Mogul." In a hilarious piece of uber critical journalism Dowd described Scaramucci as an apologist for the Donald. Dowd said besides an affinity for hair products, Trump and Scaramucci form a mutual love society. She points out the financier from Wall Street is a master at manipulating the news. When CNN reported ties he had to a Russian business cartel, the story was incorrect. Scaramucci castigated the reporters proving inaccurate reporting. The three reporters lost their jobs. Scaramucci is tough as nails. He is ruthless dealing with the press. He appeared to be an excellent choice to run White House communications. This turned out not to be the case. Scaramucci was too boisterous in his opinions and incoming Chief of Staff John Kelly quickly established a strategy to undermine the mooch.

CNN was unhappy not being able to beat up the Pillsbury Dough Boy, Sean Spicer, they had their hands full with Scaramucci. Fortunately, for the press the mooch only lasted eleven days in the Oval Office. The incoming Chief of Staff General John Kelly accepted the position with the condition the mooch was fired. He was!

The real reason, says Dowd, for Scaramucci's appointment is his love of all things the Donald. As well as his love for Jared Kushner. Ivanka was convinced her husband was one step away from being a foreign policy media star. She envisioned Scaramucci bringing him to international prominence. Here are some quotes from Scaramucci. "I love the president. I'm very loyal to the president. And I love the mission that the president has." This could go on forever. He is a Goldman Sachs, New York executive, a wealthy man and Maureen Dowd has the nerve to call him "the mooch." Dowd writes: "The arrival of the Mooch was a win for New Yorkification of the White House, another Goldman Sachs veteran and a power shift toward those who pushed for the gregarious Scaramucci, including Jared, Ivanka and Wilbur Ross, against the players from the Republican establishment Reince Priebus and Sean Spicer." Dowd continued. "He doesn't understand that Robert Mueller is not a contractor he's in a civil litigation dispute with, someone he can intimidate and wear down and threaten and bleed out." The mooch was the new bully in the White House detracting from the Russian probe. Dowd believes there is much more to the Russia charges.

Maureen Dowd took Scaramucci to the wood shed for being a mini-Donald. She called him the "mooch" and Andrew Ross Sorkin carried on the criticism of the "mooch." In mean spirited prose Sorkin made no apologies for his opinions. He argues there is no credible employment history for the new Press Communications Director. Sorkin argues the fifty-three-year-old financier is "a consummate salesman like his boss." The Donald took note. He saw Scaramucci as a tough guy.

WHAT THE MOOCH ATTEMPTED AS TRUMP'S PRESS GURU

If you look at Scaramucci's rants about the Republican establishment you wonder about his fitness for the job. The mooch, though he lasted only eleven days, had a handle on the White House's continual dysfunction. The mooch saw a problem with the three L's: leaks, loyalty and ludicrous behavior. He said this hurt the White House. Trump envisioned Scaramucci as the savior. Everyone has written what he or she thinks of "the mooch." It is not positive. What did he envision as his White House role? He hoped for a normal press. It didn't work out that way. Why? The president blew up any signs of normalcy. He wanted confusion in the Oval Office. It was Trump's mantra. Destroy the institutions that make America a democratic icon in world affairs.

In his less theatrical moments, Scaramucci perpetually sounds like a pitchman for Trump. But, like the Donald, don't sell him short. He is savvy. He is smart. He is ruthless. When asked by Andrew Ross Sorkin of the New York Times how he envisioned his role, Scaramucci replied: "It is a client service business." Sorkin had trouble processing this comment. The New York Times reporter concluded: "The mooch would either become a star launching a potential political career or he would settle into the media dustbin."

After eleven days he left the White House, Scaramucci had some cogent comments. On March 4, 2018 the mooch tweeted: "I know General Kelly is trying to bring order to the White House but he's actually creating chaos." Scaramucci continued accusing Kelly of lying about his actions on the day he fired Scaramucci.

The mooch's insights were brilliant. Kelly didn't serve Trump. It was all about Kelly and the military. The general had personal vendettas. This prompted him to fire the mooch. When he left the Oval Office, Scaramucci alleged Kelly couldn't manage a 7-11 let alone the White House.

Anthony Scaramucci: "He doesn't like me." The mooch went on to say that Kelly covered up White House staffer Rob Porter's alleged abuse of two ex-wives and his difficulty obtaining a full security clearance. In the process the mooch's criticism alerted the media to the fact most Trump insiders had not received full security clearances.

THE MOOCH: THE VIEW FROM LONDON

If "the mooch" was a media star in the U. S., he had a rock star personality in London. The BBC, the Sun, the Guardian, the Independent, the popular magazines, and even the respectable London Times and Financial Times featured the mooch. They analyzed Anthony Scaramucci's impact upon the press, the presidency and popular culture.

Courtney Weaver, writing in the July 29-30 weekend edition of the Financial Times, labeled "the mooch" as "the disrupter in chief." She detailed how he called Chris Cuomo at CNN and said: "Can you tell two fish that don't stink? It's me and the president." This was right out of Mario Puzo's The Godfather. Maybe it is just "the mooch" is Italian. Then Scaramucci telephoned the New Yorker's Ryan Lizza, and he called Chief of Staff Reince Priebus "a fucking paranoid schizophrenic, a paranoiac." The London press was horrified when Scaramucci said: "I want to fucking kill all the leakers." Then I got the idea Scaramucci was shadowing William Shakespeare's Henry VI when the English bard wrote: "The first thing we do-let's kill all the lawyers." I guess all of them except those in the White House.

WHAT DOES SCARAMUCCI'S ELEVEN-DAY INTERLUDE TELL US?

After eleven days of setting the Washington press establishment on its ear, Anthony Scaramucci was sacked. The press noted it was difficult to pin down information on "the mooch's" finances. If the SkyBridge deal goes through Scaramucci will find one hundred million in his bank account. His time in the White House seemed to assure the deal.

As the seventh senior White House official to leave abruptly, Scaramucci was the most controversial and least experienced. He was the most outrageous. He had little, if any, lasting impact. He was an amateur shown the door. Thank you President Trump. You made a great decision. The seven firings are only half as many as the Donald averaged on "The Apprentice." I guess he realizes running the country is not a reality TV show. Or does he?

The London press had a field day with Scaramucci's removal. The Independent reported he was escorted from the White House grounds within hours of his removal. "The unceremonious removal of Mr. Scaramucci from 1600 Pennsylvania Avenue was a moment of exquisite humiliation that came in the wake of an astonishing display of hubris from a man who was brought into the White House to shake up its communications operations...." The Independent observed.

THE MOOCH'S GREATEST HITS: WONDERFUL QUOTES

Anthony Scaramucci's greatest hits are his wonderful quotes. They must be preserved to illustrate how tasteless, and how articulately inarticulate the Oval Office became under Trump. The infighting turned nasty and for pure entertainment purposes "the mooch" was an Academy Award performer. Like a rock star, he had a series of greatest hits. Let's review and rate them.

1. I know I am repeating myself. I like to do that. But here is my favorite: "I am not Steve Bannon, I'm not trying so suck my own _____" speaking to Barney Henderson, London Telegraph, July 27, 2017.

2. There is a suggestion among some of Scaramucci's friends that he has an inflated ego. Proof! Here is my favorite quote. "I'm not trying to build my own brand off the _____strength of the president. I'm here to serve the president." Speaking to Barney Henderson, London Telegraph, July 27, 2017.

3. On the question of the press, a Scaramucci tweet suggested how he felt. "I made a mistake in taunting a reporter. It won't happen again." Tweet 5:50 PM July 27, 2017.

4. In his infamous New Yorker interview, Scaramucci said: "What I'm going to do is, I will eliminate everyone in the communications team and we'll start over. What I want to do is I want to kill all the leakers." Ok. I think I understand.

5. The day before he was fired Scaramucci praised himself on twitter. "Had great call w/@GOPChairwoman. @GOP doing fantastic work to support@POT #MAGA looking forward to building even stronger relationship." He was fired the next day.

6. Someone told me Scaramucci had a level of narcissism that was extraordinary. Really! The following tweet from "the mooch" sums it up. "Killing it from the podium! Hair and make-up is on me going forward as long as you don't take all my hairspray." I am still scratching my head over this quotation.

7. Scaramucci is a communications director who believes you get rid of past communication employees. No, I am not being redundant. Here is a tweet from "the mooch" about how to guarantee full transparency. After you read it, explain it to me. "Full transparency: I'm deleting old tweets. Past views evolved & shouldn't

be distraction. I serve @POTUS agenda & that's all that matters."
Tweet on July 22, 2017.

8. "Leakers would have been hanged one hundred fifty years ago."
Scaramucci reported by Rob Crilly, July 28, 2017.

9. "The fish stinks from the head down. But I can tell you two fish
that don't stink, and that's me and the president." I think he
dreamed up this quote after watching the Godfather. He doesn't
have time to read the book. Scaramucci reported by Rob Crilly, July
28, 2017. Scaramucci needs to read Sicily's Secrets: The Mafia, Pizza
and Hating Rome. He will learn a lot. A great book!

10. Listen on-line to the actual phone call from Anthony
Scaramucci to the New Yorker's Ryan Lizza or read the piece in the
magazine. This is the only way to understand how goddamned scary
those who serve Trump are in the present battle to preserve
democracy.

THE MOOCH DAY BY DAY: A LESSON FOR ALL OF US

As Lord John Dalberg-Acton famously said: "Power tends to corrupt,
and absolute power corrupts absolutely." Well just guess. A day-by-day
examination of Scaramucci's brief, but interesting, time in the White
House offers a window into "democracy." It tells us why we cherish
"freedom." Here is the day-to-day behavior of Anthony Scaramucci.
You judge its impact on the American political system.

Day 1: On July 21, 2017. He made his debut at the White House.
Sean Spicer resigned. Melissa McCarthy's income sagged. That
afternoon, "the mooch" appeared with the newly crowned press
secretary, Sarah Huckabee Sanders, at a White House briefing.
Scaramucci professed his love for the president. It had been a long
time since dead silence occupied a White House briefing.

Day 2: On July 22, 2017. Scaramucci announces he is deleting old
tweets because they contain left leaning views on climate change and
gun control. The old tweets he said would be deleted so he could
have "full transparency." I hope Harvard Law School is re-evaluating
their admission policies.

Day 3: On July 23, 2017. "The mooch" was interviewed by CNN's
Jake Tapper. He began by praising Sarah Huckabee Sanders stating
she is an "incredibly warm person." Then he complimented her

makeup people. He used the same make up people. He sounded like a fool. He isn't. The mooch is brilliant. He is crafty as a Fox TV anchor attempting to disguise fiction as fact.

Day 4: On July 24, 2017. He criticized those who kept him out of the White House for months. These folks included Chief Strategist Steve Bannon and then Chief of Staff Reince Priebus. Scaramucci may be the only media person who could instantly elicit support for firing Bannon and Priebus. No one else had the balls to make that recommendation. Trump eventually fired all of them. In puzzling comments to the New York Times, Scaramucci said: "I was left for dead on the street, and now I'm headed for Air Force One." Translation please! The "mooch" convinced the Donald he would be the Chief defender of Trump's policies. His twitter account showed the welcome aboard package the staff receives on Air Force One.

Day 5: On July 25, 2017. The only clear news is "the mooch" says he will "fire everybody." This is a slow news day.

Day 6: On July 26, 2017. Politico publishes a financial disclosure form that upsets "the mooch." He accuses the leaker of committing a felony. The truth is financial disclosure forms eventually fall into the public domain.

Day 7: On July 27, 2017. The New Yorker publishes a foul-mouthed interview where Scaramucci labels Priebus "a fucking paranoid schizophrenic." Trump knows he has hired both a Harvard lawyer and a New York street psychologist. I guess it is a two for one. He recognized he hired a loose cannon.

Day 8: On June 28 2017. The war against Priebus prompts the Chief of Staff to resign. A former U. S. Marine General John Kelly is named as the new Chief of Staff. The door is open to throw "the mooch" out.

Day 9: On July 29 2017. Scaramucci's wife files for divorce. She is nine months pregnant and one of his buddies said she was no longer "arm candy." He allegedly didn't show up for the birth of his child. He was with the Donald and the Boy Scouts. A man certainly can't be too patriotic. He repaired his marital differences. He and his wife appear happily married.

Day 10: On July 30, 2017. We all got a vacation from "the mooch." Hallelujah!

Day 11: Trump fires Scaramucci proving he is not only a competent president but also a thoughtful one with great leadership skills. For two days there are no tweets.

Scaramucci called The New Yorker believing he could plant a story. He also contacted other media sources to tell his story. He talked to reporter Ryan Lizza and TV talking head-journalist, Chris Cuomo, to tell his version of the new Washington. I have printed the exchange verbatim or you would think I am making it up. Here is the phone call.

ALISYN CAMEROTA: Ryan [Lizza, "The New Yorker" Washington Correspondent], so sorry to interrupt you right now. If you would stand by for a second that would be great because we actually have Anthony Scaramucci on the phone.

CHRIS CUOMO: Right, so, let's get him. White House Communications Director Anthony Scaramucci joins us this morning. Anthony Scaramucci, can you hear us?

SCARAMUCCI: Yes. So, when I was speaking to you last night Ryan, I said it was unpatriotic that you would weren't telling me who the leakers were. I was on a plane landing in New York, I have to go visit my mom, and so you may have caught it the wrong way. I was teasing you and it was sarcastic. It was one Italian to another, it wasn't me trying to get you to say, if you could give me some sense for where they are, because I have a responsibility to the President of the United States –

CUOMO: Anthony –

SCARAMUCCI: when you said you didn't, I totally respect your journalism and your integrity.

CUOMO: Anthony, hold on Anthony, I just want to make sure – I don't know if Ryan can hear you.

RYAN LIZZA: I can.

CUOMO: But just in case, it did go out over the air so he heard what you meant when you were talking to him about being unpatriotic. Let's just reset us at zero here. What's going on in your perspective?

SCARAMUCCI: I want to reset at zero, but I also want you to know I just spent about 15 minutes on the phone talking with the President

374

of the United States who has given me his full support and his full blessing, and I'm going to read you something, Chris, and you bear with me. And the President also told me, if you're nice to me in this segment, he'll let me come back on the show, is that cool? So why don't you let me talk for a little bit and then you can ask me questions. But this is super, super important to the country, now, whether you agree with the President or you disagree with the President, you have to love the institution of the presidency. You have to love the office and you have to love our country and what is going on right now, I've done a major amount of work over the last five days. I've interviewed most of the assistants to the President. I've interviewed most of the people in the communications team in the White House and what the President and I would like to tell everybody, we have a very, very good idea of who the leakers are, who the senior leakers are in the White House. We'll get to that in a second. What I also want to say is that we are working together, the President and myself and other members of his team and law enforcement to undercut and undercover – or out, if you will – the leakers in the entire country. As the President would say in his own words, the White House leakers are small potatoes. I'll talk to you about a few leaks that happened last night that I find reprehensible. But the White House leaks are small potatoes relative to things that are going on with leaking things about Syria or North Korea or leaking things about Iraq. Those are the types of leaks that are so treasonous that 150 years ago people would have actually been hung for those types of leaks. So, the President brought me in, he knows I'm his friend first, Chris. You're from New York, I'm from New York, and the President is from New York. We had dinner last night. I sat next to the First Lady. I love the President. I've said that. I know the press wants to ridicule me for saying it six times from the podium. But we started out as friends. I am not a politician. I'm an American businessman and entrepreneur that have built two businesses and I try to play it straight with people. The President is trying to play it straight with people, which is why he has 140 or 125 social media followers because they want to hear it straight from the President. And I said to the President this morning, I can't afford to be a sycophant to you, sir. I have to talk to you straight as a friend so I can help you with this problem. And so, what I want to say to you is I understand the law. I know that there was a public disclosure mechanism in my financial forms. What I'm upset about is the process and the junk pool, the dirty pool, Chris, in terms of the way this stuff is being done, and the leaking won't stop. I can't have a couple of friends up from "Fox & Friends" and Sean Hannity, who is one of my closest friends, to dinner with the President and his First Lady without it being leaked in seven minutes. It's absolutely completely and totally reprehensible. As you know from the Italian expression, the fish stinks from the head down. What I can tell you two fish that doesn't stink, okay, and that's the President and me. I don't like the activity that's going on in the White House. I don't like what they're doing to my friend. I don't like what they're doing to the President of the United States or their fellow colleagues in the West Wing. If you want to talk about the Chief of Staff, we have had odds. We have had differences. When I said we were brothers from the podium, that's because we're rough on each other, some brothers are like Cain and Abel, other brothers can fight with each other and get along. I don't know if this is repairable or not, that will be up to the President, but he's the Chief of Staff. He's responsible for understanding and uncovering and helping me do that inside the White House, which is why I put that tweet out last night. When the journalists who actually know who the leakers are – like Ryan Lizza – they know the leakers. Jonathan Swan at Axios – these guys know who the leakers are. I respect them for not telling me because I understand and respect journalistic integrity. However, when I put out a tweet and I put Reince's name in a tweet, they're all making the assumption that it's him because journalists know whom the leakers are. So, if Reince wants to explain that he's not a leaker, let him do that. Let me tell you something about myself. I am a straight shooter and I'll go right to the heart of the matter. Okay, so I'm done talking. You can ask me questions. But be nice on this segment, Chris, because this is a very serious matter of interest to all of America.

IS SCARAMUCCI REALLY GONE?

This was Scaramucci's end. The press made fun of him. They missed the point he was the forerunner of the Trump administration's plan to destroy the free press, or at least to curtail its effectiveness. That plan is still in place. It is working.

What about Scaramucci? What happened to him? He resurfaced in late December 2017 telling anyone who would listen he would be back in the White House. The press eagerly picked up his comments. Scaramucci said people would be surprised about how Trump altered his views of climate change. He suggested there was an evolving opinion from the Donald. In a preposterous statement, Scaramucci implied the president wasn't opposed to climate change. He just wanted to make a better deal. There were no follow up questions. Scaramucci continued stating he talks to the president regularly. No one in the Trump inner circle verified this ridiculous comment. The mooch loves the camera, he knows how to tell a tall tale in front of it. The press is in danger as is the presidency.

By May 2018 he was back working at SkyBridge. He was all over CNN, MSNBC and Fox News discussing and defending Trump. The mooch is brilliant on television. He is a reasoned, articulate commentator. He could sell ice to Eskimos. He is the only CNN guest who can hold his own with Chris Cuomo.

THE MOOCH IS BACK IN 2018: WILL HE EVER GO AWAY?

As the New Year dawned the mooch was back. He was all over the press. He explained the greatness of President Trump. He defined the treason of those who oppose him.

He returned for round two of beating up Steve Bannon. It wasn't a fair fight. In the summer of 2016 Scaramucci went into a foul-mouthed critique of Bannon that seemed to have Trump's approval. By 2018 the mooch won the battle as Bannon faded into a well-deserved abyss. CNN welcomed Scaramucci as a guest on "New Day." He didn't disappoint. "Certainly, we all had great uncertainty in the campaign and the tightness of polling but nobody wanted to win more than the President of the United States, and frankly, nobody worked harder," Scaramucci said. Then on Fox TV News the mooch did everything but shine Trump's shoes. He also praised Donald Jr. as a full-time patriot. "Donald J. Trump Jr. is a very honest person," Scaramucci concluded.

The mooch fueled rumors he was headed back to the White House. Is he? Who knows! What is known is Scaramucci loves the spotlight. He is a bright person who is believable during interviews. He is more believable than anyone in the White House. That is a scary thought. Hang on the mooch is back.

SCARAMUCCI TELLS ALL TO VANITY FAIR

The mooch sat down with Vanity Fair as Trump's first year came to an end with a revealing interview that tells one why he was accepted at Harvard Law School. The press may make fun of the mooch, but he is an intelligent observer. He can spot an asshole from a normal guy. The White House is filled with assholes. So Scaramucci had plenty to say.

"I was in Trump Tower….We were celebrating, congratulating him on his victory. He says Trump came to him remarking: 'You got to come help me. You've got to drop that stupid business." This established Trump and Scaramucci were longtime friends. That led to the mooch eventually being appointed White House Communications Director. The truth, according to the mooch, is that those working for Trump were incompetent, stupid, self-serving, loathsome and pursuing personal political agendas. The White House was staffed with first graders running the country into the ground.

Why did the mooch last only last eleven days in the White House? The answer is a simple one. He was victimized by Reince Priebus, the Chief of Staff, who convinced Trump the mooch was an amateur in politics and perhaps a closet liberal. Scaramucci called him a "Rancid Penis" to his face. That did little to ensure a lengthy White House tenure. Priebus was so angry with Scaramucci, he withdrew the invitation for his parents to attend the ceremony-swearing Trump in as president.

Then Steve Bannon turned on Scaramucci. Bannon feared the mooch was too close to Trump. Of Bannon, Scaramucci observed: "He is the creature from the Black Lagoon."

Prior to Trump's election, Scaramucci was friends with him. To Trump's credit, he told the mooch not to call him Mr. President. He wanted the straight story, as Scaramucci saw it. This frightened everyone in the White House. The always Trumpsters hated the mooch. The RNC nitwits, like Priebus, believed he was a dangerous truth teller. Bannon and Priebus were leaking to the press. Scaramucci told Trump he would fix the leaks. That sealed his fate. Bannon and Priebus convinced the president Scaramucci was not up to the job. He was gone.

The press treated Anthony Scaramucci like he was a joke. He wasn't. In retrospect he had it right. Reince Priebus was a snake in the grass. He did nothing for Trump. He did everything for the Republican Party. "The president knew Bannon and Priebus are horrific leakers. He's not a stupid guy," Scaramucci said. He believes Bannon and Priebus joined forces to make sure his White House days were numbered. They did. Even though Priebus was fired, he continued to text, call and leave messages for President Trump. He had an agenda. He would get rid of the mooch. This added another dysfunctional feature to the White House. There was fighting from outside the inner circle There was fighting from inside the Oval Office. It couldn't get more dysfunctional.

On Bannon's duplicity, Scaramucci said: "This is a guy I wrote a 10-point memo for when he joined the campaign. And I was working alongside of him during the campaign," Scaramucci said with chagrin. Bannon lobbied the mooch not to go to work for Trump. He declined Bannon's suggestion. He lasted eleven days thanks to General John Kelly convincing Trump to oust him. They all said the mooch was a loose cannon. The reality is he was a sane voice who had ideas how to fix the press coverage. Scaramucci was the only adult in Trump's inner circle. That is why he was fired. The irony is Kelly fired the mooch five minutes after he was sworn in as Chief of Staff. It was his first act in the office. The mooch was too smart, too honest, too committed to Trump and too analytical for those around the president. Trump lost a good man when the "new swamp" sent the mooch packing back to the Hampton's. The mooch could have smoothed over some of the press differences. He didn't! Why? He has integrity.

"I learned that the swamp is a gold-plated cesspool with no drain," Scaramucci continued. "You got cesspool operators in there that know how to slow down disruptors like Donald Trump." That said it all, the mooch exited Washington with his integrity and continued support for President Trump intact. Kelly, Bannon and Priebus can't make this claim. The mooch is a real patriot amongst the Washington slime. Thank you mooch for your service.

When President Trump invited the Philadelphia Eagles to the White House the fact that only ten players were rumored to show up, Trump cancelled the event. Scaramucci appeared on CNN arguing the president had the right to disinvite the Eagles. Why did Trump disinvite the Eagles? He did so to appeal to his conservative base, Scaramucci continued. "He is not trying to divide the country," Scaramucci said of Trump. He paused and continued. "All the president is saying we have to have love for the flag."

As Scaramucci appears on television news shows, particularly CNN, Scaramucci is an intelligent Trump defender. Since leaving his eleven days in the White House, Anthony Scaramucci continues to be Trump's most intelligent defender. That is a strange occurrence. Then again Trump's presidency is even stranger.

EPILOGUE

"He's not a war hero because he was captured.
I like people who weren't captured."

TRUMP ON JOHN MCCAIN AT A FAMILY LEADERSHIP
SUMMIT IN AMES, IOWA IN JULY 2015.

"We are not the president's subordinates. We are his equals."

SENATOR JOHN MCCAIN OF ARIZONA AFTER CASTING
A VOTE DEFEATING CHANGES IN HEALTHCARE.

"The world has never built a multiethnic democracy
in which no particular ethnic group is the majority
and where political equality, social equality and
economics that empower all have been achieved."

DANIELLE ALLEN

"Trump isn't the only one having trouble
believing he is the president."

PROFESSOR ALAN KIRSHNER, OHLONE COLLEGE

"They have an excuse-they're stupid and crazy. What's yours?"

MATT TAIBBI, ON THE DRIFT TO WAR.

This book demonstrates Donald J. Trump is psychologically, educationally and temperamentally unsuited to hold public office. That he is the president of the United States is unfathomable. He is assaulting the institutions that give structure to American democracy. Why? He lacks emotional maturity, good judgment, he has few critical thinking skills, and he is in constant need of validation. Slights, which are real or imagined, find him ridiculing or perhaps destroying an opponent. This is the work of an Emperor not the President of the United States.

His personality is that of a petulant child. He is appallingly ignorant of history. He doesn't know a Shia from a Sunni Muslim. Or why these groups represent divisions within the Islam world. Since Trump is the poster boy for international relations he should spend some time with history. He praised Saudi Arabia for not having one protester on the streets. He was unaware this repressive nation executes protesters. Trump spews bigotry at Muslims while failing to recognize the small degrees of liberalism and real news concerning the region comes from Qatar through Al Jazeera. Trump sided with Saudi Arabia in attempting to limit Qatar's free press.

Those in his campaign close to Russia, notably campaign manager Paul Manafort, suggest financial ties if not political collusion. His son in law, Jared Kushner and Donald Trump Jr. are also unwitting pawns in the Russian game. As Robert Mueller investigates and attempts to unravel this complex subject Trump screams: "fake news." It is a circus. It is a mess.

The lack of decency, decorum and manners makes Trump repugnant. By asking James Comey to pledge personal loyalty, Trump shows he doesn't understand the basic elements of government. The FBI is independent of the presidency. Trump refuses to accept this commonly held constitutional principle. He ridicules anyone who criticizes him. Not just in the citizenry but also in the political arena, the business world, and he projects fear to gain support from those minimizing democracy.

His personal delusions are frightening. He knows more about war than the generals. He makes up fake facts, introduces lies and when he is caught in a faux pas he covers it up with verbal tricks. It is through his faux television show, The Apprentice that Trump trained for the presidency.

ASSUMING OFFICE AND TRUMP'S PRESIDENCY

A week after assuming the presidency, Donald J. Trump was consistent in his message. "I really don't change my position very much," he said. This statement made at a January 27, 2017 press conference was a portent of things to come. No one seemed to take the new president seriously. That was a mistake.

Donald J. Trump: "Go back and look, my position on trade has been solid for many, many years, since I was a very young person talking about how we were getting ripped off by the rest of the world."

Since very few people paid attention to what Trump thought there was no consensus of what he would do or how he would act concerning the North Atlantic Treaty Organization (NATO) or the various East Asian alliances. There is a section in the NATO agreement concerning mutual defense responsibilities of all nations. He purposely was vague on how the U. S. stood on this section. Why? Trump is a negotiator.

This led to Trump's tough foreign policy language. Public opinion polls showed his popularity in the low to mid forty per cent range when he talked foreign affairs and it was in the mid to high thirty percent range when he discussed domestic affairs. Foreign policy was a win for the new president. After fifteen months in office he ramped up a tough foreign policy. It appeared to have some successes. Perhaps this was due to changes he made the previous summer.

TRUMP REVAMPS HIS PRESIDENCY: IT WORKS

In late July 2017 Trump reorganized the presidency. He sent the Howdy Dowdy impersonator, Sean Spicer, packing while telling the press he had great expectations for Spicer's future. The new Press Secretary Sarah Huckabee Sanders was a better choice. It was in the media's image of the Donald that Sanders moved to revamp. She did an excellent job of attempting to defend his statements and the administration's policies. She couldn't overcome division, constant flip flopping on issues and indefensible statements.

The present crisis in American politics is not going away. We attempt to explain parts of our history as an aberration, a one-time occurrence, but this is not the proper way to interpret what is happening in the U. S.

What is happening? We are a society increasingly bent on name calling, casting aspersions at certain groups and disparaging others while talking of draining the swamp. This type of behavior divides us. The liberal left is in trouble. Since the 1970s blue-collar workers have moved to the Republican Party. The Christian right, the alt-right conservatives, the old people drooling in their oatmeal watching fox TV News, the blue collar worker, the high school dropout, the neglected rural voter form a frightening coalition for Trump. They are often physically menacing in public meetings. They are angrily in the face of the liberal media.

As more jobs are outsourced, as technology replaces the worker, as work becomes piecemeal and part-time, the working-class person finds it more difficult to make a living. The number of people on the wrong side of the economy voted Trump. The notion of a manipulative billionaire helping the working person became a mantra for the 2016 presidential election. There is a distrust of government and a growing hatred between people of different political opinions. Can democracy survive? It can! It will!

Trump and his acolytes are the biggest threat to democracy's future. Why! It is simple! If you oppose the Donald and his followers they will grind you into the ground. Witness his comments about the special prosecutor, Robert Mueller, and those who work for him, as Trump repeatedly charges, have something to hide. This is dangerous in a democracy. Or when Trump screams: "fake news." When a president refuses to accept criticism, attacks his critics and attempts to destroy the press the U. S. is headed toward a constitutional crisis.

How is Trump destroying democracy? After claiming on the campaign trail, he would end Wall Street fiscal abuses, Trump's administration is now proposing tax cuts guaranteeing the one percent pay less tax. By loosening regulations and ending any effective policing of American business excesses there is an economy without restrictions and regulations. Wall Street greed is now in the White House. The idea that profits will trickle down to the common person is the mantra for these folks.

AFTER A YEAR IN OFFICE: FOREIGN POLICY PROS AND CONS

After a year in office American foreign policy was diminished. As the Economist observed in the November 11-17, 2017 issue: "American influence has dwindled under Donald Trump. It will not be easy to restore." Why? He has disrespected allies. He has pulled out of trade deals. He refuses to operate by the rules of international diplomacy. When he leaves on a foreign trip there are more corporate CEO's than State Department professionals.

But not everything is a disaster. Trump has increased America's presence in Afghanistan. Unlike President Barack Obama he talks tough. He has helped Iraq recapture cities from ISIS. His main advisers are career military. They are a calming force on Trump's make war statements. He has cajoled China to exert pressure on North Korea. The fear is war is a distinct possibility.

Critics of Trump argue he is a man without principles. This is not the truth. He is a president who wants no part of a rules-oriented world order. He wants America to show what he labels "backbone." There is a consistency to Trump's message. In 1987, when President Ronald Reagan urged Russia to tear down the Berlin Wall, Trump took out full-page advertisements in major newspapers urging politicians to show more "backbone." When he campaigned for the presidency, he said "Make America Great Again" was about the nation's backbone. Recently, Trump said: "Let's not let our great country be laughed at any more." This mania for strength, power and respect is a full-blown part of his personality.

On December 18, 2017, Trump unveiled his National Security Strategy (NSS), which described his "America First" strategy. What does Trump mean by "America First." He views diplomacy as a road map to make money. "We know that American success is not a foregone conclusion. It must be earned, and it must be won," Trump said. This is an interesting comment. What does he mean? Trump continued arguing political and economic competition is the key to the future. Then in this December 2017 speech he turned his criticism on President Barack Obama. Trump remarked past presidents "negotiated disastrous trade deals" he singled out the military problems with North Korea, the power of ISIS ad the growing issue of Syria's use of chemical weapons with Obama's foreign policy failures.

When the National Security Strategy (NSS) was released The New York Times observed: "Mr. Trump's tweets, statements and actions...present the unpredictable public face of his policies...." The annual strategy report is required by an act of Congress. Since 1986 Congress has mandated the report to provide clarity in American foreign policy. The Times noted the document was at odds with Trump's public statement. The newspaper alluded to the fact that he didn't write it and perhaps he didn't understand his own NSS statement. The president is like a cannon going off in the White House while others govern. He is the face of government but the brains lie elsewhere.

When Trump described Russia as a "rival power" his speech contradicted everything he has said about how Putin and Russia have not interfered with the 2016 election. "After nearly a year in office, Mr. Trump is still refusing to accept the intelligence community's conclusions that Russia launched an attack on American democracy by interfering in the 2016 election on his behalf." This widely held view in the intelligence community caused Trump to disparage and downgrade the CIA, the NSA and the FBI. He views these agencies as an arm of Hillary Clinton and the Democratic Party. He would like nothing more than to be rid of these independent minded government agencies. Trump's supporters fail to recognize this is the first step toward authoritarian rule.

There are some puzzling comments in Trump's speeches defining foreign policy. The New York Times describes America First as a policy statement on paper only, and it is one the president ignores. Trump remarked Russia would employ "information tools in an attempt to undermine the legitimacy of democracies." Few disagree with that statement. One person who does is Donald J. Trump the president who read it off the teleprompter without understanding what it meant. Then Trump in his foreign policy speech observed the United States if threatened would carry out "swift and costly consequences on foreign governments. Criminals and other actors who undertake significant malicious cyber activities." Most Americans applauded this statement. But if you analyze it what Trump is suggesting is an Orwellian police surveillance that means 1984 has arrived. The police state will validate your thoughts is what Trump is suggesting. Welcome to George Orwell's world and the loss of contentious free speech.

Trump's foreign policy is an embarrassment to the diplomatic community. He talks of winning in the world with a boastful attitude dismissing other nations. This is not the way to international cooperation. It is the way of a bully who has minimal knowledge of the world. He talks of global stability and our allies. His actions are those of a person who wants to make personal deals to enrich the U. S. His minions support this notion as hatred to the U. S. grows and flourishes around the world. His arrogant boasts are popular among the Trumpites. He ignores the level of global cooperation that is essential to a free world. Trump just doesn't get the idea of a free world.

HOW EUROPE SEES TRUMP'S FOREIGN POLICY

Europeans were quick to react to Trump's foreign policy statement. France's Foreign Minister, Jean-Yves Le Drian, remarked Trump spoke with the demeanor of an isolationist and one who is leading the U. S. in a retreat from its world responsibilities. Le Drian told reporters the retreat from the Paris Climate Accord was the first step in isolating the U.S. from Europe and the world. He said the next step would be to end the Iran nuclear deal. Rather than making policy, Le Drian observed, Trump is retreating from the world stage. On the question of military intervention, Le Drian said; "There is no appetite for military intervention."

How does one summarize Trump's foreign policy after eighteen months in office? One thing is certain. He is unpredictable. He refuses to accept past protocol, he behaves in a manner surprising everyone and the world cannot predict his next move. He will generally do the opposite of what is expected from a U. S. president.

But there is a surprising understanding of foreign policy from Trump. He talks tough about war with North Korea while his Secretary of State pursues diplomacy. He mentions he will "blow up the Iran deal." He did! There is a tactical and shrewd side to Trump that the media often misses.

By Christmas 2017 Donald J. Trump was the most unpopular president in American history. His ratings fell into the mid-thirties as he screamed "fake news." When Trump lost the popular vote by almost three million people to Hillary Clinton, he began an attack on the media, the pollsters and denied Russian interference. He would not be the president if 80,000 voters in three states-Wisconsin, Pennsylvania and Michigan-had voted differently.

HOW TO RIG AN ELECTION USING FOREIGN POLICY: DOES RUSSIA HELP OR HURT?

This is a book on how Trump has failed to establish American foreign policy as a viable world force. But foreign affairs have another purpose. The events around the world can rig an election at home. Fears of Muslim radicals! When the president charges an influx of immigrants run to the polls to vote for the Democratic Party there is panic in Trump's inner circle. A belief Sharia law is coming. These are just a few of the crackpot theories Trump and his Republican cohorts used to win U. S. elections.

These are minor questions. The real concern is Russia. Did Vladimir Putin and his tech crazy cohorts skew the U. S. election? That is what interests the American public. To date there is evidence Russian's hacked into thirty-nine states. There is no evidence this changed the voting or the results. The evidence is Russia interfered. The success of that interference is open to speculation.

What is not open to question is Trump's refusal to criticize Putin or Russia. To be fair Trump did sign the new sanctions against Russia. Putin responded by expelling more than seven hundred American diplomats form the Embassy in Moscow. Trump thanked him for saving the taxpayers a great deal of money. This is strange behavior.

TRUMP'S FAILED ATTEMPTS TO BUOY DEMOCRACY

President Trump has the responsibility to create a secure election system and a democratic atmosphere rather than one of fear and intimidation. It appears he favors fear and intimidation. That has worked for him in business. Why shouldn't it work in government? America is resilient. We will survive Trump's bullying, his sense of personal entitlement, and his appointees are nasty amateurs destroying Those in the Republican Party willing to follow an outlier who is systematically destroying government infrastructure is unforgiveable. Fox TV News, Breitbart and other conservative media outlets tout his accomplishments. Trump screams "fake news." Not about the fake news like Fox but about anyone who disagrees with him.

The Republican Party and Trump control the direction of government. America is in danger. With his authoritarian personality Trump is a dictator in training. Congress refuses to limit his actions. He is packing the courts with appointments of unqualified justices. His attempts to purge the Justice Department and the FBI are warning signs. Constitutional checks and balances will not prevent Trump from abusing his power, as long as Congress is Republican controlled. America needs two competing party organizations. Not ones who are toadies for the president.

The resistance to Trump is real and organized. When the Women's March took place on January 21, 2017 it dwarfed Trump's inaugural crowd. Yet, to this day, he maintains he had the largest inaugural in history. It is this ego driven, maniacal personality that drives the competition. He is every bit as terrible in office as those close to him predicted.

Politics is only one of Trump's areas of destruction. He has systematically ignored the arts, failed to fund traditional federal institutions, and this is a president who doesn't read. The bipartisan events like the White House Correspondents' Dinner or the Kennedy Center Honors, which bestow awards on those who contribute to American culture, are ignored by Trump. He has no interest in culture. President Obama was seen with his wife Michelle on Broadway at Hamilton and the cast was feted at the White House. American culture is a unique phenomenon and presidents have celebrated it. Ronald Reagan, who was hostile to the National Endowment for the Humanities, said when he honored Lena Horne: "Today our nation has crowned her greatness with grace." This comment from a president who was not keen on federal support for the arts suggests Reagan's appreciation for America's cultural growth. Trump and his fellow barbarians at the gates are doing everything to destroy American culture.

THE QUESTION OF COLLUSION: TRUMP DIDN'T COLLUDE, HE IMPEDED

The question of Russian collusion dominated the first year of Trump's presidency. The Mueller investigation indicted four key members of the Trump campaign. As the second year of his presidency unfolded, a campaign insider and Paul Manafort's business partner, Paul Gates, was indicted for lying to the FBI. Russia ran an electoral campaign attacking Hillary Clinton inside the United States as Mueller indicted thirteen Russians and three companies for meddling in the 2016 election. These are incontrovertible facts. The Republican's responded attacking alleged corruption in the FBI an issue demanding the Attorney General appoint a special counsel, talking about a deep state conspiracy and muddling Mueller's investigation suspect among those in the right wing nut house. Russia interfered in the 2016 presidential election. That is an incontrovertible fact.

Did this help get Trump elected? His minions say: "No." Clinton's supporters say: "Yes." Who knows! One thing is clear Russian espionage operations influenced the election. Whether or not this altered the electoral vote is open to question. There is clear evidence Russian interests spent millions of dollars setting up pro-Trump campaign rallies, they spent large sums on Facebook, Twitter and newspaper advertisements.

The FBI, the CIA and the key officials in NSA, as well as several allied intelligence agencies, spoke out concerning Russian interference. After FBI Director James Comey alerted America to the Russian menace, Trump fired him. The president and his minions went after the FBI impugning its leadership, its integrity and its findings. When Trump fired Comey he did so because of the Russian investigation. The president labeled it "a witch hunt." Since when is the truth a witch hunt?

The notion is Russian collusion tainted Trump's victory from the day he stepped into the White House. The phrase "witch hunt" allowed him to survive the taunts, the innuendos, those charging him with collusion, and he could explain the press conspiracy that he said attempted to oust him from the Oval Office. He never acknowledged his erratic behavior. He wouldn't admit to his lack of historical knowledge. His vicious tweets and his petulant, childish behavior slowly destroyed his credibility and impeded his presidency. But there was contact from members of his campaign with Russia.

The Trump campaign made multiple attempts to set up cover back channel communications between the Kremlin and Trump Tower. While the president is not involved allegedly Paul Manafort and Carter Page were instrumental in this endeavor. Luke Harding's book Collusion: Secret Meetings, Dirty Money, and How Russia Helped Donald Trump Win isn't the definitive answer, but it raises and discusses key questions. As the London Guardian's Moscow bureau chief, Harding developed sources and insights convincing him Russia meddled, overly influenced the election results and led to Trump's presidency. Harding was expelled from Russia for his reporting.

What did Harding find? He makes a powerful case for Russia's ability to manipulate the American governmental system. Special Counsel Mueller has confirmed Harding's findings. Trump's connections to Russia go back twenty or more years as he has had close business and personal ties. This is not necessarily a recipe for collusion. Or is it?

Trump's claim he had no ties to Russia is untrue. Why has he gone to great lengths to obscure his Russian ties? That is a question only he can answer? The president's political positions align with Moscow's. His refusal to implement sanctions approved by Congress is a mystery. Harding says there is much that we don't know. Mueller will continue to investigate in Trump's second year in the White House.

Luke Harding: "I think it's bigger than Watergate because this is one set of Americans doing dirty tricks to another set of Americans, as was the case in the '70s."

The repeated cries that there was "no collusion" is wearisome. Trump is obsessed with the Russian investigation. He wants it concluded as early as possible. When Mueller indicted the thirteen Russian citizens and three companies this didn't' take the wind out of Trump's constant demands to end the investigation. He just doesn't get it. Then he never will.

When the press reports there is no evidence of collusion from the Trump camp, California Democratic Congressman Adam Schiff told radio station WNYC "witting participation" was still a possibility. Schiff said of Trump, he used Russian "information on a daily basis to denigrate Hillary Clinton...and we know there were conversations about getting dirt on Hillary Clinton between very high levels of the campaign, including the president's own son, son-in-law and campaign manager...."

WHAT DID MUELLER'S INVESTIGATION SHOW US?

By late February 2018 the Mueller investigation indicted nineteen people with four of them having close associations with the Trump campaign or the early presidency. No matter what the White House says General Flynn, Paul Manafort, Rick Gates, George Papadopoulos had intimate connections to the White House. Manafort was campaign chairman and Gates was deputy campaign chairman and a member of the transition team.

The White House counsel has done a great deal to delay, impede and cast doubt on the Mueller investigation. This may be true to the amateur nature of those involved in foreign policy. When Jared Kushner completed his application for a high security clearance, MSNBC reported he made more than one hundred mistakes on the security application. It is totally unprecedented for an array of amateurs to be involved in international diplomacy.

There was no evidence Trump colluded but those close to him were in bed financially with Kremlin connected businessmen.

THINGS HEAT UP IN MARCH 2018

The Mueller investigation heated up in March 2018 as the Steele Dossier increasingly was judged to be a credible document. As stories of Russia's influence on the selection of Rex Tillerson, Trump's supporters doubled down ion their support for the president. Jane Mayer writing in the New Yorker reported Christopher Steele met with Mueller's investigative team where he alleged Russia blocked the appointment of Mitt Romney as Secretary of State. The reason? The Kremlin wanted someone friendly to Russia. When the story broke partisan criticism from Republican's labeled the story fiction. Democrats said it was factual.

Matt Taibbi, writing in Roiling Stone, wrote: "Putin loves you; therefore you love Putin." This strange, but effective, barb aimed at Trump highlights the continued inability of the president to identify, admit and attack Russian interference in the American political system. Taibbi calls it "Russiagate." Trump's minions are attempting to ignore it.

TRUMP'S SHADOW MONEY TRAIL

As this book was winding down the New York Times editorialized: "Before there was a hint of collusion with Russia, there were questions about Donald Trump's finances. In those more innocent days, the questions were mainly about propriety-why wouldn't he release his tax returns like other presidential candidates had?" The Times continued

The revelations that Trump's personal fixer, attorney Gary Cohen paid $130,000 to Stormy Daniels without the president's knowledge quickly vanished when the Donald's new legal adviser, Rudy Giuliani, said the president reimbursed Cohen. Just weeks earlier on Air Force One, Trump denied knowing anything about where the money came from and his admission that he paid Cohen to make Daniels go away was another lie in the Trump portfolio.

To combat allegations of a shadowy money trial Trump has argued: "If the FBI implanted officials in my campaign, it would be the biggest political scandal in history." There is not a scintilla of evidence supporting this absurd claim. But distraction, disrespect and destroying any investigation into Trump's finances is the direction the president takes rather than releasing his personal financial information as required by law. Only the Mueller investigation can solve the shadowy money trail.

The sad part is Donald J. Trump convinced enough voters in the rights states he was a forceful personality with blunt truths. He said he is a masterful negotiator and a champion of the American people. He was elected president. We are now living a nightmare of the first anti-democratic president in modern American history.

BIBLIOGRAPHICAL SOURCES

The divisions in America and their historical roots are discussed in James Taranto, "Divided America Stands-Then And Now, The Weekend Interview With Allen Guelzo," **The Wall Street Journal**, July 1-2, 2017, A-11. This an interview with Professor Allen Guelzo, director of the Civil War Studies Program at Gettysburg College, who attempts to place the divisions in U.S. politics in a historical perspective. In his lengthy interview, Guelzo argues the nation is at its most divided state since the Civil War. One of Professor Guelzo's main points is the Whig Party in the 1840s and 1850s promoted an economically diverse society that attempted to create cultural uniformity. This is the mantra for the Trump administration suggesting that "business is King" and any form of criticism is demeaning. On the role of the Whig Party in early American history see, for example, Daniel Walker Howe, **The Political Culture Of The American Whigs** (New York, 1979). Also, see James Traub, "The United States Of America Is Decadent and Deprived," **Foreign Affairs**, December 19, 2017 http://foreignpolicy.com/2017/12/19/the-united-states-of-america-is-decadent-and-depraved/ for the argument it is not Trump that is confusing government, it is, in fact, most of the American's that vote. Traub, a fellow at the Center On International Cooperation, and his essay brought a heated debate about the direction of American society and foreign policy.

For background on isolationist thought see Howard A. DeWitt, **Hiram W. Johnson And American Foreign Policy, 1917-1941** (unpublished doctoral dissertation, University Of Arizona, 1972), passim. Also see Howard A. DeWitt, "Hiram W. Johnson And Early New Deal Diplomacy, 1933-1934," **California History**, (Winter, 1974, volume 53), pp. 377-386 and Howard A. DeWitt, "The New Harding and American Foreign Policy: Warren G. Harding, Hiram W. Johnson and Pragmatic Diplomacy," **Ohio History**, (Spring, 1977, volume 86), pp. 96-114. Also see Howard A. DeWitt, "Hiram Johnson And World War I: A Progressive In Transition," **Southern California Quarterly** (Fall 1974, volume 56) pp. 295-305 and Howard A. DeWitt, "Hiram W. Johnson And Economic Opposition To Wilsonian

Diplomacy: A Note," **Pacific Historian**, (Spring, 1975, volume 19), pp. 15-23. Also see Howard A. DeWitt, **A Blow To America's Heart: England Reacts To 9-11** (Dubuque, 2002) and Howard A. DeWitt, **The Road to Baghdad** (Dubuque, 2003) for background material.

The Cold War ended by the time Trump became president. A body of literature has grown up concerning what some critics see as the new Cold War. See, for example, Peter Beinart, "Trump Is Preparing For A New Cold War," **The Atlantic**, February, 2018 https://www.theatlantic.com/international/archive/2018/02/trump-is-preparing-for-a-new-cold-war/554384/ An excellent study of why Trump won the presidency is Steven Rosenfeld, **Democracy Betrayed: How Super Delegates, Redistricting, Party Insiders, And the Electoral College Rigged The 2016 Election** New York, 2018). The Rosenfeld book argues Republican lawmakers concentrated on redistricting thereby dividing Democratic voters, often minority voters, allowing the Republican Party to win GOP electoral success, and he argues state Republican lawmakers pass laws making it more difficult to vote for low income, less educated and minority voters.

RUSSIA, COLLUSION, COMEY, MUELLER
AND TRUMP'S PARANOIA

The continual ranting and raving from President Trump concerning the FBI has a lengthy literature. The CIA, the Mueller investigation and what he perceives as an attack upon this presidency is covered in many books. For materials relating to foreign policy see James Comey's account of his meeting at Trump Tower before the Senate Select Intelligence Committee on June 8, 2017. This testimony is covered in numerous publications see "Comey Testimony: Highlights of the Hearing," **The New York Times**, June 8, 2017. Also see "Full Text: James Comey Testimony Transcript On Trump and Russia," **Politico.com**, June 8, 2017 https://www.politico.com/story /2017/06/08/full-text-james-comey-trump-russia-testimony-239295.

Also, see, Clint Watts, **Messing With The Enemy: Surviving In A Social Media World of Hackers, Terrorists, Russians and Fake News** (New York, 2018). Watts testified before the Senate Select Committee regarding Russian interference in the 2016 election. His book explains terrorists and cyber criminals. He is a specialist on ISIS and Osama bin Laden.

See Eugenia Pismennaya, Stepan Kravchenko and Stephanie Baker, "The Day Trump Came To Moscow: Oligarchs, Miss Universe, Nobu," **Bloomberg**, December 21, 2016 https://www.bloomberg.com/news/articles/2016-12-21/the-day-trump-came-to-moscow-oligarchs-miss-universe-and-nobu. This article points out in 2013 Trump met with Herman Geref, the chief executive officer of Russia's largest bank and while no collusion was mentioned or proven, there was allegedly some business conducted. For concerns about Russia infiltrating Trump's business interests and how this might influence his subsequent presidency concerning Russia, see, for example, David Corn and Hannah Levintova, "How Did An Alleged Russian Mobster End Up On Trump's Red Carpet?" **Mother Jones**, September 14, 2016 https://www.motherjones.com/politics/2016/09/trump-russian-mobster-tokhtakhounov-miss-universe-moscow/.

Also see Ariel Zilber, "Miss Hungary Claims Married Donald Trump Invited Her To His Moscow Hotel Suite After the 2013 Miss Universe Pageant," **London Daily Mail**, January 14, 2017 http://www.dailymail.co.uk/news/article-4120044/Donald-Trump-invited-ex-Miss-Hungary-Moscow-hotel-room-2013-Miss-Universe-pageant-married-Melania.html.

Also see Jon Swaine and Shaun Walker, "Trump In Moscow: What Happened At Miss Universe In 2013," **London Guardian**, September 18, 2017 https://www.theguardian.com/us-news/2017/sep/18/trump-in-moscow-what-happened-at-miss-universe-in-2013.

For an article quoting mental health professionals on Trump's lack of fitness for office and how and why this is a danger, see, Emma Stefansky, "Trump Calls Himself 'Very Stable Genius' Amid Mental Health Concerns," **Vanity Fair**, January 6, 2018 https://www.vanityfair.com/news/2018/01/trump-very-stable-genius-tweets.

For Fiona Hill's Russian expertise and her view of Vladimir Putin see, for example, Fiona Hill, "3 Reasons Russia's Vladimir Putin Might Want To Interfere in the U. S. Presidential Elections," **Vox.com**, July 27, 2016 https://www.vox.com/2016/7/27/12304448/putin-elections-dnc-hack and Geoff Earle, "Trump Taps Leading Putin Critic For Senior White House Position As Administration Continues To Take Fire For Russian Contacts," **London Daily Mail**, March 2, 2017 and Gabrielle Levy, "Former Intelligence Officer And Putin Critic Tapped For

White House Role," **U.S. News And World Report**, March 3, 2017 https://www.usnews.com/news/politics/articles/2017-03-03/donald-trump-to-appoint-fiona-hill-former-intelligence-officer-and-putin-critic-to-white-house-role.

For an article clearing Trump of Russian collusion, see, "GOP-Led House Panel Officially Clears Trump In Russia Probe," **Staten Island Real-Time News**, April 27, 2018 http://www.silive.com/news/2018/04/gop-led_house_panel_officially.html and Akbar Shahid Ahmed and Ryan J. Reilly, "GOP-Led House panel Ends Its Russia Probe By Claiming To Clear Trump," **The Huffington Post**, April 27, 2017 https://www.huffingtonpost.com/entry/final-house-intelligence-committee-report-on-russia-defends-trump_us_5ae33257e4b04aa23f22a7ca.

Seth Hettena, **Trump/Russia: A Definitive History** (Brooklyn, 2018) is brilliant examination of what may or may not have taken place within Trump's inner circle and with the president. His chapter on the Steele Dossier is brilliant and the Carter Page-George Papadopoulos roles are explained briefly but with great insight and clarity. Also see the reasons for Mikhailov's arrest and why he was a CIA informant, Andrew E. Kramer, "Top Russian Cybercrimes Agent Arrested On Charges Of Treason," **The New York Times**, January 25, 2017 http://foreignpolicy.com/2011/05/03/my-three-must-read-u-s-foreign-policy-books-for-aspring-politicians

Jack Holmes, "Team Trump's Official Line: We Tried To Collude But She Didn't Have The Goods," **Esquire**, May, 2018 and Rebecca Ballhaus, Byron Tau and Erica Orden, "Senate Panel Releases Testimony On Trump Tower Meeting With Russians," **The Wall Street Journal**, May 16, 2018 are articles shedding light on the Russian collusion investigation.

See Christiano Lima, "Trump: If FBI 'Implanted' Officials In My Campaign, It Would Be Biggest Political Scandal In History," **Politico.com**, May 18, 2018 for Trump's continual charge the FBI is biased and attempting to destroy his presidency. At the one year anniversary of the Mueller investigation Trump insiders are attempting to discredit the probe, which shows no signs of abating.

For the controversy of the FBI imbedding an agent in the Trump campaign see, for example, Tom McCarthy, "Trump Claims FBI Planted Agent In His 2016 Campaign For Political Purposes," **London Guardian**, May 18, 2018 https://www.theguardian.com/us-news/2018/may/18/trump-latest-news-fbi-spying-agent-campaign-tweet-claim.

Alexander Smith, "Putin On U. S. Election Interference: I Could Care Less," **NBC News**, March 10, 2018 https://www.nbcnews.co/news/world/putin-u-s-election-interference-i-could-care-less-n855151. This is an interesting explanation from Putin concerning Russian influences on the 2016 election. Also see Rosalind S. Helderman and Tom Hamburger, "Guns And Religion: How American Conservatives Grew Closer to Putin's Russian," **The Washington Post**. April 30, 2017.

TRUMP IN EUROPE, THE G-7, G-20, POLAND AND ANGELA MERKEL

For Trump's Polish support see Philip Bump, "In Poland, Trump Offers A Questionable Credential: Polish Americans Preferred Me To Clinton," **The Washington Post**, July 6, 2017 https://www.washingtonpost.com/news/politics/wp/2017/07/06/in-poland-trump-offers-a-questionable-credential-polish-americans-preferred-me-to-clinton/?utm_term=.1842cca99c81. Also see Glenn Thrush and Julie Hirschfeld Davis, "Trump, In Poland, Asks If West Has The Will to Survive," **The New York Times**, July 6, 2017 https://www.nytimes.com/2017/07/06/world/europe/donald-trump-poland-speech.html.

For an introduction to Trump's G-7 policies see, Tara Palmeri and Nicholas Vinocur, "Trump Policy Haze Wrong-Foots Allies Ahead of G-7 Summit," **Politico.com** May 24, 2017 https://www.politico.eu/article/donald-trump-hazy-views-confuse-allies-g7-summit-nato/ and David Goodman and Alessandra Migliaccio, "Trump Doctrine Confounds G-7 As Ministers Kick Can To Sicily," **Bloomerg.com**, May 14, https://www.bloomberg.com/news/articles/2017-05-15/trump-doctrine-confounds-g-7-as-ministers-kick-can-to-sicily.

For the harsh Australian criticism of Trump at the G-20 see, Maya Oppenheim, "Australian Reporter Takes Apart Donald Trump's G-20 Performance in Scathing Monologue," **The London Independent**, July 10, 2017 https://uk.news.yahoo.com/australian-reporter-takes-apart-donald-114700812.html. The image that President Trump has for the West is one where he attacks liberalism, German trade policies, immigrants and NATO nations for not paying their way. He also said the fundamental question of our time is: "Will The West Survive?" Trump alienated the European Union, the member nations of the G-7 and G-20 Summits and isolated the U. S. from world affairs. It is all about making money, there are few environmental and humanitarian concerns. For this viewpoint see Ivan Krastev, "Reimagining The

Meaning of The West," **The New York Times International Edition**, July 12, 2017, pp. 1,13.

For Angela Merkel's anti-Trump statements prior to the G-20, see Ivana Kottasova, "Merkel Criticizes trump Trade Policy Before G-20," **Money.CNN.com**, July 5, 2017 http://money.cnn.com/2017/07/05/news/economy/merkel-trump-trade-warning/index.html. For a critique of how Trump fit into the politics of the G-7 see, Sonam Sheth, "G-7 Leaders Took A Stroll In Sicily-And Trump Followed Them In A Golf Cart," **Business Insider**, May 27, 2017 and Patrick Wintour, "Hopes For Refugee Crisis Plan Fall Into Chasm Between G-7 and Trump," **London Guardian**, May 26, 2017 https://www.theguardian.com/world/2017/may/26/trump-set-to-clash-with-other-g7-leaders-over-refugees-and-climate. Also see Patrick Wintour, "Trump At G-7: President's Last World Tour Stop Brings Uncertainty And Risk," **London Guardian**, May 25, 2017 https://www.theguardian.com/us-news/2017/may/25/trump-g7-visit-climate-refugees-japan-north-korea.

See David Smith and Alec Luhn, "Trump and Putin Had Good Talk About Ending Syria War, White House Says," **London Guardian**, May 2, 2017 https://www.theguardian.com/us-news/2017/may/02/donald-trump-vladimir-putin-conversation-syria-civil-war. Also see Karen DeYoung and Philip Rucker, "Trump Had Undisclosed Hour-Long Meeting With Putin At G-20 Summit," **The Washington Post**, July 18, 2017 https://www.washingtonpost.com/world/national-security/trump-had-undisclosed-hour-long-meeting-with-putin-at-g20-summit/2017/07/18/39c18dd4-6bd0-11e7-96ab-5f38140b38cc_story.html?utm_term=.ce0cbc3ba50d.

For successes from Trump's G-20 policies see Balazs Koranyi and Gernot Heller, "G-20 Financial Leaders Acquiesce To U. S., Drop Free Trade Pledge," **Reuters**, March 18, 2017 https://www.reuters.com/article/us-g20-germany-trade/g20-financial-leaders-acquiesce-to-u-s-drop-free-trade-pledge-idUSKBN16P0FN.

For a critical appraisal of Trump's Warsaw speech, see David Frum, "The Falsehood At The Core Of Trump's Warsaw Speech," **The Atlantic**, July 7, 2017 https://www.theatlantic.com/international/archive/2017/07/trump-warsaw-speech/532917/.

For the role of Trump in Davos and the American economy, see Daniel W. Drezner, "How Will Trump Play At Davos?" **The Washington Post**, January 10, 2018 https://www.washingtonpost.com/news/posteverything/wp/2018/01/10/how-will-trump-play-at-davos/?utm_term=.a7bcf8d2e1d3. and John F. Harris and Ben White, "Coming Soon To Davos: A Trump Stink Bomb," **Politico.com**, January 9, 2018 https://www.politico.com/story/2018/01/09/

trump-davos-switzerland-economic-forum-331063. Both of the Davos articles conclude that Trump will present a message contrary to the World Economic Forum. That is not a surprising conclusion.

For Trump's accomplishments at the G-20 see Greg Price, "What Did Donald Trump Do And Not Do At The G-20 Summit," **Newsweek**, July 8, 2017 http://www.newsweek.com/what-trump-did-g20-633890.

The hotel fiasco where Germany did not have a Hamburg hotel for Trump and Chancellor Merkel did little to alleviate this insult in covered in a story at the G-20 see Mythili Sampathkumar, "Donald Trump 'Has Trouble Finding Hotel At G-20 Summit," **London Independent**, July 6, 2017 https://www.independent.co.uk/news/world-0/us-politics/donald-trump-g20-summit-hamburg-hotel-room-germany-us-president-meetings-a7827166.html.

For violence at the G-20 see Melissa Eddy, "G-20 Protests Grip Hamburg, And Dozens Are Hurt," **The New York Times**, July 7, 2017 https://www.nytimes.com/2017/07/07/world/europe/group-of-20-hamburg-protests.html?module=ArrowsNav&contentCollection=Europe&action=keypress&region=FixedLeft&pgtype=article. Also see Justin Huggler, "G-20 Welcome To Hell Protest: German Police Fire Water Cannon After Being Attacked With Bottles and Rocks," **London Telegraph**, July 7, 2017 https://www.telegraph.co.uk/news/2017/07/06/german-police-fire-water-cannon-g20-demonstration/.

On the second Trump-Putin meeting see, Julie Hirschfeld Davis, "Trump And Putin Held A Second Undisclosed, Private Conversation," **The New York Times**, July 18, 2017 https://www.nytimes.com/2017/07/18/world/europe/trump-putin-undisclosed-meeting.html.

See an interesting take on Comey's firing in Howard Blum, "Exclusive: What Trump Really Told Kislyak After Comey Was Canned," **Vanity Fair**, November 22, 2017 https://www.vanity.fair.com/news/2017/11/trump-intel-slip.

The confusion in the Trump camp over Special Prosecutor Robert M. Mueller III was shown when the president considering firing him and then recanted in what is still an unexplainable move. See Michael S. Schmidt and Maggie Haberman, "Trump Ordered Mueller Fired, But Backed Off When White House Counsel Threatened to Quit," **The New York Times**, January 25, 2018 https://www.nytimes,com/2018/01/25/us/politics/trump-mueller-special-counsel-russia.html. This is an important article as Trump impulsively was going to fire Mueller and his lawyers allegedly told him he would be impeached. He changed his mind suggesting he had little if any understanding of presidential power or impeachment.

THE DONALD JR. AND RUSSIAN COLLUSION

On the meeting that Donald Jr. took with the female Russian attorney see, for example, Matt Apuzzo, Jo Becker, Adam Goldman and Maggie Haberman, "Trump Jr. Was Told In Email Of Russian Effort to Aid Campaign," **The York Times, International Edition**, July 12, 2017, p. 4. For later criticism suggesting Donald Jr was naïve and used by Russian intelligence see, Daniel Hoffman, "It Wasn't About Collusion," **The New York Times International Edition**, July 31, 2017, p. 10. Hoffman, a former CIA station chief, argues it was Russia's KGB mentality that entrapped young Donald. He broke no laws. It was simply Russia's attempt to influence the election. They did! For a defense of Donald Jr. see, Rosalind S. Helderman, "Newly Disclosed Email Sheds Light on Trump Jr. Meeting With Russian Lawyer," **The Washington Post**, October 9, 2017 https://www.washingtonpost.com/politics/newly-disclosed-email-sheds-light-on-trump-jr-meeting-with-russian-lawyer/2017/10/09/2d0fecb0-a9e3-11e7-92d1-58c702d2d975_story.html?utm_term=.eae708863745. This is an important article detailing an e-mail from an American lawyer arguing Donald Jr. was interested in helping his father's campaign and if that is a crime he is guilty. There was no evidence of collusion. Also see Elias Groll, "Here's The Memo The Kremlin Linked Lawyer took To The Meeting With Donald Trump Jr.," **Foreign Affairs**, October 16, 2017 http://foreignpolicy.com/2017/10/16/heres-memo-kremlin-lawyer-took-to-meeting-donald-trump-jr/. Also see, Alexandra Wilts, "Russia And Trump Campaign May Still Have Colluded, Suggests Top Democrat," **The Independent**, February 19, 2018 https://www.independent.co.uk/news/world/americas/us-politics/russia-trump-campaign-kremlin-allegations-collusion-schiff-intelligence-democrat-a8218501.html. This article is an excellent view of Congressman Adam Schiff's collusion beliefs.

For an insight into why Donald Jr. spends so much time in Russia, see Michael Crowley, "Trump Jr.'s Love Affair With Moscow," **Politico.com**. July 12, 2017 https://www.politico.com/story/2017/07/12/trump-junior-russia-connection-240436.

The June 2016 meeting Donald Jr. attended is rife with media speculation. The Senate Judiciary Committee in mid-May 2017 released more than 230 pages of testimony on the meeting. The

Senate documents showed a clear and persistent pattern of interaction with Kremlin insiders, see, Sharon LaFraniere, "Thousands of Pages of Documents On Trump Tower Meeting Are Released," **The New York Times**, May 16, 2018. Donald Jr. couldn't recall discussing the Russia probe with his father. He made this statement at the 140th annual Easter Egg hunt on the South Lawn of the White House on April 2, 2018. He told this to the Senate Judiciary Committee when he testified. The committee released more than 1800 pages of transcripts of interviews. These documents show that the Senate Committee was not able to interview Paul Manafort or Jared Kushner. No reason was stated for their inability to testify. One assumes Republican control of the committee honored Trump's request they not testify.

On the continual question of Russia favoring Trump in the 2016 election the Senate Select Intelligence Committee released documents stating this was the case. See, "Russia Favored Trump In 2016 Election, Senate Select Intelligence Committee Says, Breaking With House GOP," **Washington Post**, May 16, 2018. This story written by the **Post** staff clearly shows Russia backing Trump's candidacy. The Senate agreed with the Mueller investigation that Kremlin insiders pushed Trump's candidacy.

JARED KUSHNER'S FOREIGN POLICY
INFLUENCES AND RUSSIA

On Jared Kushner and foreign policy influences and attempts at compromising him, see, for example, Shane Harris, Carol D. Leonnig, Greg Jaffe and Josh Dawsey, "Jared Kushner's Overseas Contacts Raises Concerns As Foreign Officials Seek Leverage," **The Denver Post**, February 28, 2018 https://www.denverpost.com/2018/02/28/jared-kushner-contacts-overseas/. and Adam Smith, "Jared Kushner Still Has A Job Because The Trump Administration Doesn't Believe The Rules Apply To It," **London Independent**, February 28, 2018 https://uk.news.yahoo.com/jared-kushner-still-job-because-175100810.html. Also see Michael Kranish and Jonathan O'Connell, "Jared Kushner's Troubles Include An Impending $1.2 Billion Company Debt," **The Washington Post**, March 1, 2018 https://www.washingtonpost.com/politics/jared-kushners-troubles-include-an-impending-12-billion-company-debt/ 2018/03/01/3f248014-1cbb-11e8-b2d9-08e748f892c0_story.html?utm_term=.6cb4ab536b6e and

403

Philip Rucker, Ashley Parker and Josh Dawsey, "Jared Has Faded: Inside The 28 Days of Tumult That Left Kushner Badly Diminished," **The Washington Post**, March 2, 2018 https://www.washingtonpost.com/politics/jared-has-faded-inside-the-28-days-of-tumult-that-left-kushner-badly-diminished/2018/03/02/62acb9ce-1ca8-11e8-9de1-147dd2df3829_story.html?utm_term=.c21405a143cc.

See Bret Stephens, "The Real Russia Scandal" **The New York Times**, December 16, 2017, p. A-21 for an indictment of Flynn and questions of Trump's motives. Also see, Philip Bump, "Trump And The White House Have Denied Russian Collusion More Than 140 Times," **The Washington Post**, January 11, 2018 https://www.washingtonpost.com/news/politics/wp/2018/01/11/trump-and-the-white-house-have-denied-russian-collusion-more-than-140-times/?utm_term=.49c10b18e619

GEORGE PAPADOPOULOS AND RUSSIA

On Russia and an analysis a member of Trump's foreign policy team, George Papadopoulos, see Scott Patterson, "Witness European Road To Trump," **The Wall Street Journal**, November 4-5, 2017, A-8. Denis Slattery, "George Papadopoulos Told Greek Reporters Trump Promised Him Foreign Policy Gig, Met Him Several Times," **New York Daily News**, November 17, 2017, http://www.nydailynews.com/news/politics/papadopolous-trump-promised-foreign-policy-adviser-gig-article-1.3639946?utm_source=feedburner&utm_medium=feed&utm_campaign=Feed%3A+NydnRss+%28Top+Stories+-+NY+Daily+News%29. Also see Greg Price, "Trump-Russia Investigation: Republicans Aggressively Trying To Shutdown Mueller Probe, Schiff Says," **Newsweek**, December 15, 2017 https://uk.news.yahoo.com/trump-russia-investigation-republicans-apos-201445638.html For a court document view, see Rosalind S. Heiderman, "Who's Who In The George Papadopoulos Court Documents," **The Washington Post**, November 2, 2017 https://www.washingtonpost.com/politics/whos-who-in-the-george-papadopoulos-court-documents/2017/10/30/e131158c-bdb3-11e7-97d9-bdab5a0ab381_story.html?utm_term=.8c10b3ab3b46.

Why and how Papadopoulos became a link to Russia through an Australian diplomat is detailed in Sharon LaFraniere, Mark Mazzetti and Matt Apuzzo, "How the Russia Inquiry Began: A Campaign Aide, Drinks and Talks Dirty Politics," **The New York Times**, December 30, 2017 https://www.nytimes.com/2017/12/30/us/politics/how-fbi-russia-investigation-began-george-papadopoulos.html.

Also on Papadopoulos see, Jeff Stein, "Mueller Vs. Trump: Papadopoulos Is 'The Big One,' Not Manafort, Ex CIA Director Michael Hayden Says," **Newsweek**, November 4 2017 http://www.newsweek.com/michael-hayden-donald-trump-russia-vladamir-putin-paul-manafort-george-702085 and Aaron Blake, "Tantalizing Questions About The Russia Probe From Trump Aide George Papadopoulos's Plea Deal," **The Washington Post**, https://www.msn.com/en-us/news/politics/7-tantalizing-questions-about-the-russia-probe-from-trump-aide-george-papadoupoulos's-plea-deal/ar-AAufiqU?li=BBnb7Kz. See Harry Litman, "Why George Papadopoulos Is More Dangerous Than Paul Manafort," **The New York Times**, October 30, 2017 https://www.nytimes.com/2017/10/30/opinion/george-papadopoulos-manafort-Qlindictment.html For the danger Manafort presents see Franklin Foer, "American Hustler: Oligarchs, Shady Deals, Foreign Money-How Paul Manafort Helped Corrupt Washington And Laid The Groundwork For The Subversion of American Politics," **The Atlantic**, March, 2018, pp. 62-69. Also see Terence Cullen, "The Walls Are Closing in On Paul Manafort's Options," **New York Daily News**, February 26, 2018 http://www.nydailynews.com/news/national/walls-closing-paul-manafort-options-article-1.3843068?utm_source=feedburner&utm_medium=feed&utm_campaign=Feed%3A+NydnRss+%28Top+Stories+-+NY+Daily+News%29&utm_content=Yahoo+Search+Results.

For Manafort's second alleged attempt to illegally meddle with his trial by contacting witnesses see, Gillian Edevane, "Former Trump Campaign Chair Paul Manafort To Be Jailed For 'Stupidest' Case of Witness Tampering: Ex-Doj Official," **Newsweek**, June 6, 2018 http://www.newsweek.com/trump-campaign-paul-manafort-jail-mueller-investigation-doj-official-961500 Also see Matt Apuzzo, "Mueller Accuses Paul Manafort Of Attempted Witness Tampering," **The New York Times**, June 4, 2018 https://www.nytimes.com/2018/06/04/us/politics/paul-manafort-mueller-witness-tampering.html and David Corn and Hannah Levintova, "Manafort's Dumbest Move Yet: Using a Former Russian Intelligence Officer For Witness-Tampering," **Mother Jones**, June 5, 2018 https://www.motherjones.com/politics/2018/06/paul-manafort-mueller-witness-tampering/.

Also see Jason Meisner and Patrick M. O'Connell, "Week After Bombshell, George Papadopoulos Largely Remains A Mystery Man," **Chicago Tribune**, November 7, 2017 http://www.chicagotribune.com/news/local/breaking/ct-met-george-papadopoulos-russian-investigation-20171102-story.html.

405

The Papadopoulos story continued with a discovery of new e-mails illustrating his helpful nature to Trump. See Rosalind S. Helderman and Tom Hamburger, "Papadopoulos More Than 'Coffee Boy' In Trump Campaign, E-Mails Show," **The Minneapolis Star Tribune**, March 23, 2016 http://www.startribune.com/papadopoulos-more-than-coffee-boy-in-trump-campaign-e-mails-show/477799883/

For material on the mysterious professor see, Karla Adam, Jonathan Krohn and Griff Witte, "Professor At Center of Russia Disclosures Claimed To Have Met With Putin," **The Washington Post**, October 31, 2017 https://www.washingtonpost.com/world/professor-named-in-russia-disclosures-says-he-has-clean-conscious/2017/10/31/41a7a08e-be3b-11e7-959c-fe2b598d8c00_story.html?utm_term=.225b63f4c02e

The FBI's indictment against Papadopoulos is published in **The London Guardian**, October 30, 2017 and it contains the relevant e-mails and all the charges against him, https://www.theguardian.com/us-news/2017/oct/30/trump-russia-indictment-george-papadopoulos.

On Papadopoulos's interaction with Russia in London, see, Stephanie Kirchgaessner, Claire Phipps and Kevin Rawlinson, "Joseph Mifsud: More Questions Than Answers About Mystery Professor Linked To Russia," **London Guardian**, October 31, 2017 https://www.theguardian.com/us-news/2017/oct/31/joseph-mifsud-professor-trump-russia-inquiry-kremlin

Also see Jon Worth, "Is Joseph Mifsud Even A Legitimate Professor?" (1995) **Jon Worth blog,** November 14, 2017 https://jonworth.eu/joseph-mifsud-even-legitimate-professor/ The question of whether or not Mifsud is a legitimate professor is an interesting one. He does hold a PhD and his doctoral dissertation "Managing Education Reform: A Comparative Approach From Malta (and Northern Ireland), A Head Teacher's Perspective" is found in the Queen's College library. There is no evidence he is anything more than a lecturer with ties to the Kremlin. Also see an in-depth article on Mifsud, David D. Kirkpatrick, "The Professor Behind The Trump Campaign Adviser Charges," **The New York Times**, November 5, 2016 https://www.nytimes.com/2017/10/31/world/europe/russia-us-election-joseph-mifsud.html.

GENERAL FLYNN AND RUSSIA

For General Flynn's guilty plea and the Russian investigation, see Jonathan Martin, Maggie Haberman and Alexander Burns, "Trump Urged Republicans To End Russia Inquiry," **The New York Times**, November 1, 2017, pp. A-1-A-13.

For Russian's who met with Trump and the rollercoaster ride of cooperation, name calling and critical incidents with Kremlin insiders from a foreign minister see, for example, Emma Burrows, Angela Dewan and Lindsay Isaac, "Russian Foreign Minister Berates U. S. For 'Destabilizing' World," **CNN.com**, January 15, 2018 https://www.cnn.com/2018/01/15/world/russia-us-lavrov-trump-foreign-policy-intl/index.html Also see, Tom Schad, "Russian Foreign Minister Sergey Lavrov Claims U. S. Helped Orchestrate Olympic Ban," **US Today**, February 12, 2018 https://www.usatoday.com/story/sports/winter-olympics-2018/2018/02/12/russian-foreign-minister-sergey-lavrov-u-s-orchestrated-winter-olympics-doping-ban/328460002/

See an op-ed editorial criticizing the Mueller team for its handling of the Flynn case and suggesting the FBI was derelict in its duties and how this information was used by the Mueller investigation, "The Mystery of Michael Flynn's Plea," **Wall Street Journal**, May 7, 2018, p. A-16.

For background on Flynn see, for example, Michael Kranish, Tom Hamburger and Carol D. Leonnig, "Michael Flynn's Role In Mideast Nuclear Project Could Compound Legal Issues," **Washington Post**, November 7, 2017. Ben Collins and Kevin Poulsen, "Michael Flynn Followed Russian Troll Accounts, Pushed Their Messages In Days Before Election," **Daily Beast**, November 1 2017, Greg Miller, "Trump's Pick For National Security Adviser Brings Experience And Controversy," **Washington Post**, November 17, 2016. Also see, Bryan Bender and Andrew Hanna, "Flynn Under Fire," **Politico**, December 5, 2016. Michael S. Schmidt, Sharon LaFraniere and Scott Shane, "Emails Dispute White House Claims That Flynn Acted Independently On Russia," **New York Times**, December 2, 2017 is an excellent analysis of how and why Flynn acted on his own volition. Adam Goldman, "Flynn Pleads Guilty To Lying To The FBI And Will Cooperate," **New York Times**, **New York Times**, December 1, 2017.

TRUMP IN EUROPE 2017: FOREIGN POLICY CRITIQUES

The critics of the July European Trump foray into German politics are many and varied in tone. For the best article on the historical relationship between Germany and the U. S. and how Trump's presidency threatens our historical alliance with Germany, see the lengthy and often incisive article by David Frum, "Trump's Trip Was A Catastrophe For U.S. -Europe Relations," **The Atlantic**, May 28, 2017 https://www.theatlantic.com/international/archive/2017/05/trump-nato-germany/528429/

President's Trump and Obama arrived in Europe at the same time in May 2017. For the comparison see, Jon Henley, Kate Connolly and Julian Borger, "Trump Debuts In Europe As Obama Returns To Stir Nostalgia For The Old Days," **London Guardian**, May 24, 2017 https://www.theguardian.com/us-news/2017/may/24/trump-international-trip-barack-obama-europe-return
For the State Department see Julian Borger, "Trump's State Department Purge Sparks Worries Of 'Know –Nothing Approach' To Foreign Policy," **London Guardian**, January 29, 2017 https://www.theguardian.com/us-news/2017/jan/29/state-department-purge-trump-foreign-policy

For a view of Trump's foreign policy suggesting he was an untrained amateur see Stephen M. Walt, "The Global Consequences of Trump's Incompetence," **Foreign Policy** (July 2017) and Walt's, "America Can't Be Trusted Anymore," **Foreign Policy**, April 10, 2018 http://foreignpolicy.com/2018/04/10/america-cant-be-trusted-anymore/.

Also see Jennifer Rubin, "Trump's Foreign Policy: His Biggest Failure Yet?" **The Washington Post**, July 18, 2017 https://www.washingtonpost.com/blogs/right-turn/wp/2017/07/18/trumps-foreign-policy-his-biggest-failure-yet/?utm_term=.1ff3ab1256ce. For a view of how Trump's foreign policy changes other parts of the world see, Marc Champion and Marek Strzelecki, "The Real Impact of Trump's Foreign Trips Happens After He Leaves," **Bloomberg Politics**, July 19, 2017 https://www.bloomberg.com/news/articles/2017-07-18/when-trump-goes-abroad-radical-change-follows-in-his-footstep. Also see Elizabeth N. Saunders, "Is Trump A Normal Foreign Policy President?" **Foreign Affairs**, January 18, 2018 https://www.foreignaffairs.com/articles/united-states/2018-01-18/trump-normal-foreign-policy-president

Thomas Wright, "Trump's 19th Century Foreign Policy," **Vanity Fair**, January 20, 2016 https://www.politico.com/magazine/story/2016/01/donald-trump-foreign-policy-213546 is a reasoned explanation of what Trump lacks in foreign policy leadership and why the U. S. is taking a step backward in diplomacy. The article was completed almost a year before Trump's surprising election to the presidency. It rings true to the present day.

For an assessment of the president at the G-7 see Maya Oppenheim, "Donald Trump's Drunken Tourist Trip, U. S. President's Biggest Gaffes And Oddest Moments On Foreign Tour," **The London Independent**, May 30, 2017 https://www.independent.co.uk/news/world /americas/donald-trump-big-foreign-trip-us-president-emmanuel-macron-handshake-montenegro-shove-g7-summit-nato-a7762881.html.

AFTER SIXTEEN MONTHS IN OFFICE:
FOREIGN POLICY CRITIQUES

After a year in office there was a general consensus that America's position in the world was increasingly isolated and there was concern about his tweets causing international problems, for this view see, Steven Erlanger, "Countries See Executive Disorder In Foreign Policy Tweets," **The New York Times**, January 8,2018, p. A-1, A-8. Also se Sahar Khan, "Trump's Foreign Policy, One Year In: Ideology, Nepotism, And Above All, Unpredictability," **The Huffington Post**, November 11, 2017 https://www.huffingtonpost.com/entry/trumps-foreign-policy-one-year-in_us_5a12ea01e4b045cf4372ef7f.

There is a growing segment of the foreign press pointing to Trump's successes in foreign policy. A respected British historian Stephen Wertheim, argues there is now a Trump Doctrine. He gives the president high marks for understanding past policies, forging a new and successful path for American foreign policy and seeking to reshape the world, see Stephen Wertheim, "A Trump Doctrine Is Born," **The New York Times International Edition**, July 25, 2017, p. 10. Also see Andrew Exum, "What Trump Got Right In Foreign Policy in 2017," **The Atlantic**, January 4, 2018 https://www.theatlantic.com/international/archive/2018/01/trump-foreign-policy/549671/.

For a strong critique of his foreign policy, see Fareed Zakaria, "Trump Is Abusing America's Foreign Policy Power," **The Washington Post**, March 29, 2018 https://www.washingtonpost.com/opinions/trumps-is-abusing-americas-foreign-policy-power/2018/03/29/c5172a06-338f-11e8-8abc-22a366b72f2d_story.html?utm_term=.384741756412.

For childish nature of Trump's foreign policy, see Daniel Drezner, "The Stranger Things About Polarization And Foreign Policy," **The Washington Post**, April 12, 2018 https://www.washingtonpost.com/news/posteverything/wp/2018/04/12/the-stranger-things-about-polarization-and-foreign-policy/?utm_term=.19cb93db2ac1.

The problems Mike Pompeo faced coming into State are analyzed in Jessica Kwong, "Mike Pompeo Inherits State Department In Chaos: 4 Things To Know," **Newsweek**, April 26, 2018 http://www.newsweek.com/mike-pompeo-state-department-chaos-903104.

For the view there is less constraint in foreign policy after a year in office, see Peter Baker, "No Longer Held Back By His Advisers, Trump Puts His Imprint On Foreign Policy," **The New York Times**, May 9, 2018 https://www.nytimes.com/2018/05/09/us/politics/trump-america-first-foreign-policy.html?target=comments.

See T. A. Frank, "The Real Horror Of The Trump Doctrine: There is No Method To The Madness," **Vanity Fair**, May 15, 2018 is a critique suggesting he has set the bar too low for success. Also see Bess Levin, "Is China Straight-Up Bribing Donald Trump?" **Vanity Fair**, May 15, 2018 for a critique of the president softening a deal on a Chinese electronics maker ZTE as they are concluding a deal with Trump interests for a hotel in an area outside of Jakarta.

CAMPAIGN CLAIMS, RT PROPAGANDA, TRUMP'S PRESS CORPS

For another side of Trump's legislative claims see Michael D. Shear and Karen Yourish, "The No. 1 President In Bills Signed? Not Quite!" **The New York Times International Edition**, July 20 2017, p. 4.

For Trump's campaign appearance on Russian Television, see Damian Paletta, "Donald Trump, On Russian TV Network Criticizes U. S. Foreign Policy," **The Wall Street Journal**, September 9, 2016 https://www.wsj.com/articles/trump-on-russian-tv-network-criticizes-u-s-foreign-policy-1473394136

On why RT considered Trump a positive for Russia see, Matthew Chance, "Is Russia's Obsession With Donald Trump Waning?" **CNN.com**, February 17, 2017 https://www.cnn.com/2017/02/17/politics/russia-trump-relationship-analysis-chance/index.html For RT's denial of influence on the 2016 election and the ownership controversy, see, Paul Sonne, "Russia Backed Network RT Denis Kremlin Influence, Demurs on Ownership," **The Wall Street Journal**, November 13, 2017, https://www.wsj.com/articles/russia-backed-network-rt-denies-kremlin-influence-demurs-on-ownership-1510626159

See RT's denial of meddling in the U. S. election in Russell Goldman, "Russia's RT: The Network Implicated In U. S. Election Meddling," **The New York Times**, January 7, 2017 https://www.nytimes.com/2017/01/07/world/europe/russias-rt-the-network-implicated-in-us-election-meddling.html?module=ArrowsNav&contentCollection=Europe&action=keypress&region=FixedLeft&pgtype=article.

For the changes in Trump's press corp after Sean Spicer resigned, see Jason Schwartz, "The Puzzle of Sarah Huckabee Sanders," **Politico.com**, May/June, 2018 https://www.politico.com/magazine/story/2018/04/27/sarah-huckabee-sanders-profile-feature-2018-218014.

A scathing criticism of how and why Trump sold out to Saudi Arabia isolating Qatar and impacting foreign policy in the region is Will Bunch, "How The Trump Family Sold U. S. Foreign Policy To The Highest Bidder," **Philadelphia Inquirer**, May 20, 2018 http://www.philly.com/philly/news/politics/trump-tower-kushner-saudis-uae-qatar-nader-20180520.html

Also see, Mary Kekatos, "This Makes Me Want To Puke: Trump Loyalist Roger Stone Slams President For Accepting Highest Civilian Honor From Enemy After They Financed 9/11," **The London Daily Mail**, May 20, 2017 http://www.dailymail.co.uk/news/article-4526092/Roger-Stone-Trump-s-Saudi-award-makes-want-puke.html

The negative reaction to RT was shown in Washington D. C. when a local provider MHz ended RT broadcasts. See, Hadas Gold, "Russia's RT Television Network Will Go Dark in Washington D. C;" **Money.CNN.com**. March 30, 2018 http://money.cnn.com/2018/03/29/media/russia-rt-washington-dc/index.html Also see Simon Shuster, "The Global News Network RT Is The Russian Government Weapon In An Intensifying Information War With The West...." **Time.com**. March 5, 2015 http://time.com/rt-putin/ The Shuster article is brilliant on how RT spins news inside and out of Russia. In the U. K. there are dozens of lawsuits against RT and there is serious concern about the level of professionalism, see, for example, Jim Waterson, "Russian Broadcaster RT Faces Three New Ofcom Investigations," **The London Guardian**, May 21, 2018 https://www.theguardian.com/media/2018/may/21/russian-broadcaster-rt-three-new-ofcom-investigations

For the BBC model influencing RT see, Steven Erlanger, "Russia's RT Network: Is It More BBC or K.G.B?" **The New York Times**, March

8, 2017 https://www.nytimes.com/2017/03/08/world/europe/russias-rt-network-is-it-more-bbc-or-kgb.html The Erlanger article is a thoughtful analysis of how the Kremlin uses the BBC, the London based professional journalists and the model of the BBC, to influence a KGB style TV network with a world wide audience.

TRUMP'S AUTOCRACY, THE DEEP STATE AND IMPEACHMENT

The malevolent autocracy that is a part and parcel of Donald J. Trump's political make up is deduced from many books and articles. See, for example, Mike Lofgren, **The Deep State: The Fall of The Constitution And the Deep State** (New York, 2016); Edward Luce, **The Retreat Form Western Liberalism** (London, 2017), David Remnick, "There Is No Deep State," **The New Yorker**, March 20, 2017 and Max Fisher "What Happens When You Fight A Deep State That Doesn't Exist?" **The New York Times**, March 10, 2017. Also see Gary Grandin, "What Is The Deep State?" **The Nation**, February 17, 2017 https://www.thenation.com/article/what-is-the-deep-state/

The notion of a deep state is nonsense amongst academics and most journalists place it within the realm of conspiracy theory. Shadi Hamid, "The American 'Deep State' As A Trump Voter Might See It," **The Atlantic**, March 7, 2017 https://www.theatlantic.com/international/archive/2017/03/deep-state- democracy/518817/. This is an excellent description of how Trump supporters view criticism of the president and they see a deep, dark conspiracy to force him from office.

For studies of the deep state and other alleged plots, see, for example, David Talbot, **The Devil's Chessboard: Allen Dulles, The CIA And The Rise of America's Secret Government** (New York, 2016), Jane Mayer, **Dark Money: The Hidden History of The Billionaires Behind the Radical Right** (New York, 2017 reprint) and Tom Engelhardt, **Shadow Government: Surveillance, Secret Wars, And A Global Security State In A Single-Superpower world** (Chicago, 2014).

Tom Porter, "Deep State: How A Conspiracy Theory Went From Political Fringe To Mainstream," **Newsweek**, August 2, 2017 http://www.newsweek.com/deep-state-conspiracy-theory-trump-645376 This article shows the evolution of a crackpot theory into mainstream political discussion.

See Sam Stein and Dana Liebelson, "Donald Trump Encourages Violence At His Rallies. His Fans Are Listening." **The Huffington Post**. December 19, 2016.

On impeachment see, for example, Laurence Tribe and Joshua Matz, **To End A Presidency: The Power of Impeachment** (New York, 2018) Tribe, a well known Harvard law professor, and Matz, a recent Harvard law graduate, make the case for why and how impeachment is necessary at times in a democratic state. Not surprisingly, Trump does not come off well in this brilliant book. The authors believe support from white supremacists, bigotry, racism, anti-Semitism neo-Nazism will eventually doom Trump.

THE SPECIAL PROSECUTOR AND LACK OF TRANSPARENCY

For those who hope to discredit the Special Prosecutor see Niall Stanage, "Memo: Trump Allies Turn Fire On Mueller," **MSn.com**, June 12, 2017 https://www.msn.com/en-us/news/politics/the-memo-trump-allies-turn-fire-on-mueller/ar-BBCA9Kq and Darren Samuelsohn, "The Real Reason Trump Allies Are Attacking Mueller," **Politico.com**, December 19, 2017 https://www.politico.com/story/2017/12/19/trump-russia-mueller-pardons-investigation-304125 For a summary of Mueller's investigation see Amy Davidson Sorkin, "Robert Mueller's Distinctly American Indictments," **The New Yorker**, March 5, 2018 https://www.newyorker.com/magazine/2018/03/05/robert-muellers-distinctly-american-indictments.

For the lack of transparency in the Trump administration and why and how he has attempted to manipulate the democratic process, see Alex Howard, "Congressional Oversight Needed To Bring Secret Ethics Waivers To Light," **Sunlight Foundation**, May 1, 2017 https://sunlightfoundation.com/2017/05/01/congressional-oversight-transparency-secret-ethics-waivers/ and "On Trump, Transparency And Democracy," July 20, 2017 https://sunlightfoundation.com/2017/07/20/trump-administration-open-government-record/.

The constant tweeting and criticism by the President is testing America's political tolerance, for this subject, see, for example, Peter Baker, "Trump Tests America's Capacity For Outrage," **The New York Times International Edition**, July 26, 2917, pp. 1, 4. For Trump's threat to democracy, see, Fred Hiatt, "We're In A Battle To Defend Democracy-And Trump Is On The Wrong Side," **The Washington Post**, April 8, 2018 https://www.washingtonpost.com/opinions/were-in-a-battle-to-defend-democracy-

and-trump-is-on-the-wrong-side/2018/04/08/0ba0abfc-39b0-11e8-9c0a-85d477d9a226_story.html?utm_term=.73a23391e1b9.

See Ronald Inglehart, "The Age of Insecurity: Can Democracy Save Itself?" **Foreign Affairs**, May/June 2108, pp. 20-28 for a scholarly examination of the changes in democracy in the last decade. The good news is democracy has retreated and recovered and it will recover again, says Professor Inglehart, if the rich countries address the question of economic inequality.

TRUMP INSIDERS: SESSIONS, THE MOOCH, BANNON. ETC.

For the Jeff Sessions controversy, see, for example, Ross Douthat, "A Trump Tower Of Absolute Folly," **The New York Times International Edition**, July 28, 2017, p. 10 and Peter Baker and Jennifer Steinhauer, "Republican Outcry Shields Attorney General," **The New York Times International Edition**, July 289, 2017, p. 5

The press covers the appointment of a new White House Communications Director, Anthony Scaramucci and his disruptive influence extensively, see, for example, Maureen Dowd, "The Mooch And The Mogul," **New York Times**, July 22, 2017, Barney Henderson, "Anthony Scaramucci In Eye-Watering Foul Mouthed Rant At Steve Bannon As He Says He Wants To Kill Leakers," **London Telegraph**, July 27, 2017, Renae Merle, Damian Paletta and Heather Long, "Scaramucci Took Winding Path But Finally Landed A Top Job With Trump," **The Washington Post**, July 21, 2017, Heidi N. Moore, "Scaramucci Learned His Press Tactics From Wall Street-They'll Only Get Uglier," **The Washington Post**, July 28, 2017 and Andrew Ross Sorkin, "As Brash As His White House Boss," **The New York Times International Edition**, July 26, 2017, p. 8. The strangest of all the Scaramucci interviews came when the called the **New Yorker**. For this self-serving interview that backfired see, Ryan Lizza, "Anthony Scaramucci Called Me To Unload about White House Leaks, Reince Priebus, And Steve Bannon," **The New Yorker**, July 27, 21017 http://www.newyorker.com/news/ryan-lizza/anthony-scaramucci-called-me-to-unload-about-white-house-leakers-reince-priebus-and-steve-bannon. This is the most extraordinary interview as Scaramucci rants and raves while threatening people. He is obsessed with leaks and loyalty. The European view of Scaramucci and what he provides to the White House is detailed in Courtney Weaver,

"Trump's New Disruptor In Chief: Anthony Scaramucci," **Financial Times**, July 29-30, 2017, p. 7.

After eleven days of Scaramucci he was sacked by Trump. The press coverage was extensive, uneven and full of vitriolic comments, see, Ronald Orol, "Scaramucci Out of White House And Isn't Likely To Get His Firm Back Anytime Soon Either," **The Street.com**, July 31, 2017 https://www.thestreet.com/story/14249880/1/scaramucci-out-of-white-house-and-likely-isn-t-getting-his-firm-back-anytime-soon-either.html?puc=yahoo&cm_ven=YAHOO&yptr=yahoo.

For mainstream press comments on Scaramucci's strange eleven day White House Journey see, Zeke J. Miller and Alex Altman, "Trump's Attacks Sow Chaos In Washington," **Time**, August 7, 2017, p. 7. In this article there is a reference to Scaramucci firing Michael Short, the assistant press secretary, thereby giving credence to the notion of utter chaos in the Trump administration.

For Scaramucci's brief comeback in January 2018 see "Scaramucci: Author's Claim Trump Didn't Want to Win 'Nonsense'," **Fox News Insider**, January 4, 2018 http://insider.foxnews.com/2018/01/04/scaramucci-trump-bannon-war-breitbart-will-break-bannon Also see, Maegan Vazquez, "Scaramucci On Bannon: 'I Said The Truth Six Months Ago of What He Was Like'," **ABC, Seven News, WZVN, Fort Myers Naples Port Charlotte**, January 4, 2018 http://www.abc-7.com/story/37190253/scaramucci-on-bannon-i-said-the-truth-six-months-ago-of-what-he-was-like

The London press recognized early on that Sessions and Trump would not be a good fit, see, for example, Jamiles Lartey, "Why Is Jeff Sessions Such A Controversial Pick For U. S. Attorney General?" **London Guardian**, February 8, 2017 https://www.theguardian.com/us-news/2017/feb/08/jeff-sessions-controversy-explainer-attorney-general and Chris Graham, "Donald Trump And The Russian Connections: From Jeff Sessions' Contacts With Ambassador to Campaign's Intercepted Calls With Moscow Spies," **London Telegraph**, March 3, 2017 http://www.telegraph.co.uk/news/0/donald-trump-russia-connections-presidents-bromance-putin-campaigns/

For Bannon's successor Michael Anton, see, Samuel Chamberlain, "Trump National Security Spokesman Michael Anton To Leave White House," **Fox News**, April 8, 2018 https://www.msn.com/en-gb/news/politics/trump-national-security-spokesman-michael-anton-to-leave-white-house/ar-AAvEr7g.

For an influential Trump National Security Council adviser see, Michael Warren, "Michael Anton, Trump's Chief Intellectual, Will

Leave The White House," **Weekly Standard**, April 9, 2018 https://www.weeklystandard.com/michael-warren/white-house-watch-michael-anton-leaves-trump-administration and for an in-depth view of Anton see, for example, Rosie Gray, "The Populist Nationalist On Trump's National Security Council," **The Atlantic**, March 24, 2017 https://www.theatlantic.com/politics/archive/2017/03/does-trumps-resident-intellectual-speak-for-his-boss/520683/

For Dina H. Powell, see Gabriel Sherman. "When Should I Leave? Dina Powell's Graceful Exit Follows Months Of Quiet Concerns," **Vanity Fair**, December 8, 2017 https://www.vanityfair.com/news/2017/12/dina-powell-graceful-exit-follows-months-of-quiet-concern.

TRUMP CUTTING THE STATE DEPARTMENT AND TILLERSON

Tillerson's CEO days at Exxon are analyzed in Steve Coll, **Private Empire: Exxon Mobil And American Power** (New York, 2012). Coll lays out the grounds for failure that were implicit in his CEO days at Exxon and why he was unsuited for government service. He was a benevolent tyrant.

For Trump's cuts to the U. S. State Department, see, for example, Felicia Schwartz, "Trump Proposes Cutting State Department Budget By 37%," **The Wall Street Journal**, February 28, 2017, Glenn Thrush and Coral Davenport, "Donald Trump Budget Slashes Funds For E. P. A. And State Department," **The New York Times**, March 15, 2017 https://www.nytimes.com/2017/03/15/us/politics/budget-epa-state-department-cuts.html, Morgan Cahlfant, "Trump's War On The State Department," **The Hill**, July 14, 2017 http://thehill.com/homenews/administration/341923-trumps-war-on-the-state-department and Julia Ioffe, "The State of Trump's State Department," **The Atlantic**, March 1, 2017 https://www.theatlantic.com/international/archive/2017/03/state-department-trump/517965/ Also see Jason Zengrle, "Rex Tillerson And The Unraveling Of The State Department," **The New York Times, October 17, 2017** https://www.nytimes.com/2017/10/17/magazine/rex-tillerson-and-the-unraveling-of-the-state-department.html.

On the dismantling or reorganization of the State Department, see Gardiner Harris, "Details Are Bedeviling Tillerson In Overhaul, Diplomats Assert," **The New York Times**, August 7, 2017, p. A1, A12 and Robbie Gramer, Dan DeLuce and Colum Lynch, "How The Trump Administration Broke The State Department," **Foreign Policy**, July 31, 2017 http://foreignpolicy.com/2017/07/31/how-the-trump-administration-broke-the-state-

416

department/ and Colum Lynch, "Tillerson To Shutter State Department War Crimes Office," **Foreign Policy**, July 17, 2017 http://foreignpolicy.com/2017 /07/17/tillerson-to-shutter-state-department-war-crimes-office/. and Kevin Drum, "Why Is Donald Trump Destroying The State Department?" **Mother Jones**, November 8, 2017 https://www.motherjones.com/kevin-drum/2017/11/why-is-donald-trump-destroying-the-state-department/

For criticism of Exxon Mobil when Tillerson was a key executive see Allan Rappeport, "Exxon Is Find for Violating UI. S. Sanctions," **The New York Times**, July 21, 2017. For staff firings see Noah Daponte-Smith, "The State Department In Crisis," **National Review Online**, July 6, 2017. Also see Amber Phillips, "Even If Trump Is Blatantly Ignoring The Russian Sanctions Law, There's Not A Lot Congress Can Do About It," **The Washington Post**, January 30, 2018 https://www.washingtonpost.com/news/the-fix/wp/2018/01/30/even-if-trump-is-blatantly-ignoring-the-russia-sanctions-law-theres-not-a-lot-congress-can-do-about-it/?utm_term=.d90bcafae520. Also on sanctions see, "How The Trump Administration's Efforts To Ease Russian Sanctions Fell Short," **Yahoonews.com**, June 1, 2017.

Also see, Stephen M. Walt, "Rex Tillerson Is Underrated," **Foreign Policy**, November 20, 2017 http://foreignpolicy.com/2017/11/20/rex-tillerson-is-underrated/. Professor Walt of the International Relations Department at Harvard University argues that it is impossible for Tillerson to succeed because he is working for an egomaniacal president with limited knowledge of foreign affairs. Also see Stephen M. Walt, "Has Trump Become A Realist?" **Foreign Policy**, April 17, 2018. The Walt article suggests Trump is in the process of creating a coherent foreign policy. He claims the president is pursuing policies that brought the United States to the peak of world poser from 1945 to 1992.

For the Trump administration's objections to the Rangel-Pickering Fellows, see, Emily Shugerman, "Trump's State Department Denies Jobs To Winners of Prestigious Scholarship For Disadvantaged And Minority Students," **London Independent**, June 20, 2017 http://www.independent.co.uk/news/world/americas/us-politics/trump-state-department-scholarship-rangel-pickering-fellowship-jobs-harvard-minority-poor-students-a7798261.html. Also see, Josh Rogin, "How The State Department Just Broke A Promise to Minority And Female Recruits," **The Washington Post**, June 18, 2017 https://www.washingtonpost.com/opinions/global-opinions/the-state-department-just-broke-a-promise-to-minority-

417

and-female-recruits/2017/06/18/cd1f9d44-52b9-11e7-b064-828ba60fbb98_story.html?utm_term=.9646b9878461.

For Tillerson on Russia and how one reporter saw the **NYT** op-ed piece, see Eli Watkins, "Tillerson: US Has 'Poor Relationship With Russia," **Yourerie.com**, December 28, 2017 http://www.yourerie.com/news/politics/tillerson-us-has-poor-relationship-with-russia/890033691.

The idea that the Trump administration is completely reshaping or perhaps almost eliminating State is examined in Roger Cohen, "The Desperation of The Diplomats," **The New York Times International Edition**, July 29-30, 2107, p.11.

Tillerson's firing and the timing behind it as well as the reputed influence of the Kremlin are analyzed in David Frum's, "Why Did Trump Fire Tillerson Now?" **The Atlantic**, March, 2018 https://www.theatlantic.com/politics/archive/2018/03/exodus-rex/555473/ and for an articles labeling Tillerson the most incompetent Secretary of State, see Daniel Drezner, "Five Thoughts About The Firing of Rex Tillerson," **The Washington Post**, March 13, 2018 https://www.washingtonpost.com/news/posteverything/wp/2018/03/13/five-thoughts-about-the-firing-of-rex-tillerson/?utm_term=.27e0d2e630e2. Also see, Marc A.Thiessen, "Tillerson's Insubordination Meant He Had To Go," **The Washington Post**, March 13, 2018 https://www.washingtonpost.com/opinions/tillersons-insubordination-meant-he-had-to-go/2018/03/13/35aaf386-26e0-11e8-874b-d517e912f125_story.html?utm_term=.c337cdb771ef.

The influence of Jared Kushner and his role in Tillerson's dismissal is discussed in Jessica Kwong, "Jared Kushner Conducted Foreign Policy, Via Private Unrecorded Conversations With Leaders, Angering Tillerson: Report," **Newsweek**, March 20, 2018 https://www.yahoo.com/news/jared-kushner-conducted-foreign-policy-153608472.html.

On Tillerson's last diplomatic mission to Africa see, Gardiner Harris, "From Jokes To Near Tears, Tillerson's Final Brush With Diplomacy," **The New York Times**, March 15, 2018, p. A-10. Also see the editorial, "Reasons To Fear On National Security: Rex Tillerson Leaves With Worse To Come," **The New York Times**, March 15, 2018, p. A-26.

On Tillerson's legacy and firing see, Heather Hurlburt, "The Mess Rex Tillerson Is Leaving Behind," **New York Magazine**, March 13 2018 http://nymag.com/daily/intelligencer/2018/03/the-mess-rex-tillerson-is-leaving-behind.html. For unwisely sums of money Tillerson spent in his attempt to downsize the State Department, see Anna Palmer, Jake Sherman and Daniel Lippman, "Tillerson's Legacy: 12 Million Dollars in Private Consulting Fees At State," **Politico.com**, April 5, 2018 https://www.politico.com/newsletters/playbook/2018/04/05/rex-tillerson-state-department-262292.

For Jared Kushner's role in undermining Tillerson, see, Nick Wadhams and Erik Schatzker, "Kushner Is Leaving Tillerson In The Dark On Middle East Talks, Source Say," **Bloomberg Politics**, December 1, 2017 https://www.bloomberg.com/news/articles/2017-12-01/kushner-is-said-to-leave-tillerson-in-dark-on-middle-east-talks

On Heather Nauert, see, for example, Matthew Lee and Josh Lederman, "Heather Nauert's Meteoric Rise Takes State Department By Storm," **Washington Times**, March 18, 2018 https://www.washingtontimes.com/news/2018/mar/18/heather-nauert-rise-takes-state-department-surpris/. and "At State Department, Heather Nauert's Star Is Ascendant," **New York Daily News**, March 18, 2018 http://www.nydailynews.com/newswires/entertainment/state-department-heather-nauert-star-ascendant-article-1.3882058

Also for the strange tale of Tillerson talking to State employees and why it was a disastrous move on his part damning morale, see, Josh Lederman, "Tillerson Calls For Balancing U. S. Security Interests, Values," **AP News.com**, May 3, 2017 https://www.apnews.com/7afff2131d7b4b10b2c84b89c721b6c9.

For reasons why Tillerson was fired, see Ashley Parker, Philip Rucker, Josh Dawsey and Carol D. Leonnig, "It Was A Mind-Set': How Trump Soured on Tillerson As His Top Diplomat," **The Washington Post**, March 13, 2018 https://www.washingtonpost.com/politics/it-was-a-different-mind-set-how-trump-soured-on-tillerson-as-his-top-diplomat/2018/03/13/899b1fba-26d7-11e8-b79d-f3d931db7f68_story.html?noredirect=on&utm_term=.77f5bbc449b0. Also see, Peter Baker, Gardiner Harris and Mark Landler, "Trump Fires Rex Tillerson and Will Replace Him With CIA Chief Pompeo," **The New York Times**, March 13, 2018 https://www.nytimes.com/2018/03/13/us/politics/trump-tillerson-pompeo.html

For China and Tillerson see, Jane Perlez, "Rex Tillerson And Xi Jinping Meet In China And Emphasize Cooperation," **The New York Times**, March 19, 2017 https://www.nytimes.com/2017/03/19/world/asia/rex-tillerson-xi-jinping-north-korea.html On Tillerson's departure see Robbie Gramer, Colum Lunch, Emily Tamkin, "Tillerson Out, Mike Pompeo To State," **Foreign Policy**, March 13, 2018 http://foreignpolicy.com/2018/03/13/secretary-of-state-rex-tillerson-out-mike-pompeo-c-i-a-director-new-diplomat-trump-diplomacy-state-department/

An article on a career employee reflecting on Tillerson's firing is Elizabeth Shackelford, "Rex Tillerson Neuters The State Department. Don't Mourn his Firing," **Los Angeles Times**, March 18, 2018. She resigned from the State Department in a mass exodus of experienced career professionals. In 2017 the State Department lost sixty percent of its career ambassadors. Most state employees outside the country had two full jobs as consular officer and political officer and they worked eighty to ninety hour weeks. Trump had no idea.

TRUMP BULLYING, DYSFUNCTION AND A PRIVATE LIFE

For Trump as a bully see, for example, Maureen Dowd, "Trump's Really Weak Week," **The New York Times International Edition**, July 31, 2107, p. 11.

On why the Republican Party could not legislate see, Ross Douthat, "The Empty Majority," **The New York Times International Edition**, July 31,2017, p. 11.

The dysfunction in the Oval Office after six months and the appointment of General John Kelly to clean up the mess is cogently analyzed in Jonathan Stevenson, "The Generals Can't Save Us From Trump," **The New York Times International Edition**, July 31, 2107, p. 9. Also see, Peter Baker, "Trump Tries To Regroup His Battered Government," **The New York Times International Edition**, July 31, 2017, pp. 1, 6. On Trump's authoritarian behavior see, Yascha Mounk, "Trump Is Destroying U. S. Democracy," **The New York Times International Edition**, August 2, 2017, p. 2. Also see W. Robert Connor, "A Vacuum At The Center," **The American Scholar**, Spring, 2018, pp. 20-31 for an article on Trump as a demagogue and what impact his behavior has potentially upon American democracy. Connor is a professor of classics emeritus at Princeton University. Professor Connor's conclusion is one in which he laughs at a demagogue and remember he is not only fooling the public, he is deluding himself.

For General John Kelly's complaints about Trump and why he called him an idiot see Jennifer Rubin, "If President Trump Is An Idiot, What does That Make John Kelly?" **The Washington Post**, May 1, 2018 https://www.washingtonpost.com/blogs/right-turn/wp/2018/05/01/if-president-trump-is-an-idiot-what-does-that-make-john-kelly/?utm_term=.992a29af98ac.

For his Palm Beach life see Mary Jordan and Rosalind S. Heiderman, "Inside Mar-a-Lago, Trump's Palm Beach Castle, And His 30-Year Fight To Win Over The Locals," **The Tampa Bay Times**, November 16, 2015 http://www.tampabay.com/news/politics/stateroundup/inside-mar-a-lago-trumps-palm-beach-castle-and-his-30-year-fight-to-win/2254128.

Trump claims he promotes equality and jobs for the blue-collar worker. But the academics, as well as the popular press, disagree claiming he is not telling the truth. This is the myth of meritocracy. For how and why he uses it see, Jo Littler, "Meritocracy: The Great Delusion That Ingrains Inequality," **London Guardian**, May 20, 2017 https://www.theguardian.com/commentisfree/2017/mar/20/meritocracy-inequality-theresa-may-donald-trump.

BOOKS AND ARTICLES ON FOREIGN POLICY AND DONALD J. TRUMP

An excellent analysis of Trump's foreign policy ideas employing his interview is the work of two brilliant English historians. For their conclusions, see Charles Laderman and Brendan Simms, **Donald Trump: The Making Of A World View** (London, 2017). For a right wing, pro-Trump, see John Bolton, **Surrender Is Not An Option: Defending America At The United Nations And Abroad** (New York, 2008). This is the view of an American lawyer and diplomat who served in several Republican administrations. He was the U.S. ambassador to the United Nations from August 2005 until December 2006. He is a neoconservative who personally rejects any view but his own. He would have difficulty even with Republican's winning any further political appointments. Bolton is the NSC adviser.

Richard Haass, **A World In Disarray: American Foreign Policy And The Crisis Of The Old Order** (New York, 2017), and Edward Luce, **Time To Start Thinking: America In the Age of Descent** (London, 2012) are important to understanding how and why Trump's foreign policy moved in certain directions.

See Graham Allison, **Destined For War: Can America And China Escape Thucydides's Trap?** (New York, 2017) for the argument by a Harvard professor that the rise of China economically will lead to war.

For the conspiratorial tone of Trump's followers see, Richard Hofstadter, **The Paranoid Style In American Politics** (New York,

1964) and Thomas B. Edsall, "The Paranoid Style In American Politics Is Back," **New York /times**, September 8, 2016 http://www.nytimes.com/2016/09/08/opinion/campaign-stops/the-paranoid-style-in-american-politics-is-back.html

For Trump's paranoid politics as he worked toward the Republican Party nomination see, Connor Lynch, "Paranoid Politics: Donald Trump's Style Perfectly Embodies The Theories Of Renowned Historian," **Salon**, July 7, 2016 http://www.salon.com/2016/07/07/paranoid_politics_donald_trumps_style_perfectly_embodies_the_theories_of_renowned_historian/. On America's acceptance of Trump's authoritarianism see, for example, M. J. Hetherington and J. D. Weiler, **Authoritarianism And Polarization In American Politics** (London, 2009) and M. C. MacWilliams, "Who Decides When The Party Doesn't? Authoritarian Voters And the Rise of Donald Trump," **PS: Political Science And Politics**, volume 49, number 4, Cambridge, pp.716-721. Also see, David Cole, "Could It Happen Here? Donald Trump, Tony Judt, And The Future of American Democracy," **The Nation**, March 6, 2018 https://www.thenation.com/article/could-it-happen-here-donald-trump-tony-judt-and-the-future-of-american-democracy/.

A selection of academic essays on the rise of authoritarianism political types and voters threatening traditional civil liberties is the focus of many books. For a collection of lucid and insightful essays see, Cass R. Sunstein, **Can It Happen Here? Authoritarianism In America** (Cambridge, 2018).

For Trump clinching the Republican nomination and its impact upon Ted Cruz and John Kasich see, John Martin and Patrick Healy, "Donald Trump All but Clinches G. O. P. Race With Indiana Win; Ted Cruz Quits," **The New York Times**, May 3, 2016 http://www.nytimes.com/2016/05/04/us/politics/indiana-republican-democratic.html?_r=0

For the view of an American newsperson with a wide ranging view of the world see, Fareed Zakaria, **The Post American World: And The Rise Of The Rest** (New York, 2009). Also see Henry Kissinger, **World Order** (New York, 2014).

The changes in the economic atmosphere and the sophistication prompted by technology and new ways of doing business is the subject of a growing number of academic books, see, for example,

Richard Baldwin, **The Great Convergence: Information Technology And The New Globalization** (Cambridge, 2016).

The general Asia policy is covered in John Pomfret, **The Beautiful Country and the Middle Kingdom** (New York, 2016). For the TPP see David Mobert, "8 Terrible things About The Trans-Pacific Partnership," **In These Times.com**. December 16, 2015, http://inthesetimes.com/article/18695/TPP_Free-Trade_Globalization_Obama and Stan Sorscher, "How To Tell TPP Is A Bad Deal," **The Huffington Post** January 5, 2016   http://www.huffingtonpost.com/stan-sorscher/how-to-tell-tpp-is-a-bad_b_8914388.html.   A spirited defense of the TPP treaty is Eduardo Porter, "Why Dropping The Trans-Pacific Partnership May Be A Bad Idea," **The New York Times**, July 26, 2016 http://www.nytimes.com/2016/07/27/business/economy/why-dropping-the-trans-pacific-partnership-may-be-a-bad-idea.html?_r=0.

For an article suggesting how America's worldwide influence has declined and what it means for Trump's foreign policy, see, for example, Christopher A. Preble, "Adapt To American Decline," **The New York Times**, April 21, 2018 https://www.nytimes.com/2018/04/21/opinion/sunday/adapting-to-american-decline.html. Also see Preble's, **The Power Problem: How American Military Dominance Makes Us Less Safe, Less Prosperous And Less Free** (Ithaca, 2009).

TRUMP AND THE RACIAL QUANDRY

For a strong reaction to Trump's racial policies from a distinguished African American Professor at Emory University, see Carol Anderson, "The Policies of White Resentment," **The New York Times**, August 6, 2017, pp. SR 1, 3. Also see Carol Anderson, **White Rage: The Unspoken Truth Of Our Racial Divide** (New York, 2016) and Ibram X. Kendi, **Stamped From The Beginning: The Definitive History of Racist Ideas In America** (New York, 2016). For residential segregation in America and how it influences race policies and attitudes see Richard Rothstein, **The Color of Law: A Forgotten History of Our Government Segregated America** (New York, 2017). Also see Ta-Nehisi Coates, "The First White President," **The Atlantic**, October 2017 https://www.theatlantic.com/magazine/archive/2017/10/the-first-white-president-ta-nehisi-coates/537909/. This article deals with how Trump negates President Barack Obama's legacy is a manner destroying or altering many government practices and institutions.

See Michael Tesler, "Views About Race Mattered More In Electing Trump than In Electing Obama," **The Washington Post**, November 22, 2016 https://www.washingtonpost.com/news/monkey-cage/wp/2016/11/22/peoples-views-about-race-mattered-more-in-electing-trump-than-in-electing-obama/?utm_term=.a3f421f18dbb. For an analysis of white racism and the 2016 election, see Michael Tesler, **Post-Racial or Most-Racial? Race And Politics In The Obama Era** (Chicago, 2016). For an argument that racial resentment led to Trump's victory see, German Lopez, "The Past Year of Research Has Made It Very Clear: Trump Won Because of Racial Resentment," **Vox.com**, December 15, 2017 https://www.vox.com/identities/2017/12/15/16781222/trump-racism-economic-anxiety-study.

BOOKS AND ARTICLES IMPORTANT
TO UNDERSTANDING TRUMP

The background to Trump running for the presidency is discussed in Michael D'Antonio, **The Truth About Trump** (New York, 2015) and David Cay Johnston, **The Making of Donald Trump** (New York, 2016). Johnston is a Pulitzer Prize winning reporter who covered Trump's career for thirty-eight years. After Trump was elected president, Johnston's book was re-published with a new introduction and epilogue. Johnson says of Trump "dishonesty" is a pattern in his life. He proves it throughout a book ending before Trump's successful presidential run.

For the role of Trump's lies in national politics and how they impacted the 2016 election, see, for example, Paul Krugman, "The 'Big Liar' Technique," **New York Times**, September 9, 2015, p. A23. On Arkansas Attorney General Leslie Rutledge see, Lindsey Millar, "Leslie Rutledge Is Not Fit To Be Attorney General," **Arkansas Times**, http://www.arktimes.com/arkansas/leslie-rutledge-is-not-fit-to-be-attorney-general/Content?oid=3522505.

For an early Trump biography by two experienced **Washington Post** writers see, Michael Kranish and Mark Fisher, **Trump Revealed: An American Journey of Ambition, Ego, Money and Power** (New York, 2016). For a hit piece biography on Trump see John R. O'Donnell and James Rutherford, **Trumped!: The Inside Story of The Real Donald Trump-His Rise and Spectacular Fall** (New York, 2016). There was no definitive Trump biography during the 2016 election.

Tim O'Brien, **Trump Nation: The Art Of Being The Donald** (New York, 2005) is a book challenging what Trump said was a net worth of $5 billion dollars. O'Brien stated Trump was worth between $150 million and $250 million dollars. Trump sued filing a 2.5 billion dollar lawsuit in compensatory damages and another 2.5 billion in punitive damages. After the lawsuit sales of O'Brien's book skyrocketed. The lawsuit was dismissed. Trump concluded: "That was total fiction."

For the argument against a businessman as president see, for example, Ben Adler, "This Is What a Businessman In The White House Looks Like," **The Nation**, June 21, 2012 https://www.thenation.com/article/what-businessman-white-house-looks/. Also see, Timothy Egan, "The Wrong Resume," **The New York Times**, May 31, 2012 and Robert J. Shiller, "Businessmen As Presidents: A Historical Circle," **The New York Times**, November 3, 2012. For an anti-business president who was excellent for bailing out Wall Street, see John Micklethwait's interview with President Barack Obama. Micklethwait was editor-in-chief of **Bloomberg Business Week**, see "The 'Anti-Business' President Who's Been Good For Business," **Business Week**, interview June 13, 2016 http://www.bloomberg.com/features/2016-obama-anti-business-president/. Also see observations of key members of the business community in James Fallows, "Businessmen Against Trump," **The Atlantic**, July 13, 2015 http://www.theatlantic.com/politics/archive/2015/07/are-we-all-part-of-trump-nation-some-readers-say-no/398462/.

For a survey of American foreign policy essential to placing Trump in world affairs, see Bruce W. Jentleson, **American Foreign Policy: The Dynamics Of Choice In The 21st Century** (New York, 2015, 5th edition).

For the manner in which Trump has used the presidency to enrich his company, see, for example, Peter Schweizer, **Secret Empires: How The American Political Class Hides Corruption And Enriches Family And Friends** (New York, 2018).

The changes in presidential behavior are discussed in Ronald Kessler, **The Trump White House: Changing The Rules of The Game** (New York, 2018). The Kessler volume argues Trump will go down in history as important as Ronald Reagan for changing the rules of the Chief Executives behavior and ability to govern. His book is based on extensive interviews with Trump and those close to him. Kessler is a veteran journalist with numerous awards. He is the best-selling author of four best sellers dealing with the FBI, the CIA and the First Family. The Kessler book lacks in-depth reporting, critical comments and it is hostile to the media. To be fair he does say nasty things about Anthony Scaramucci. Not surprisingly, Kessler writes of Michael Wolff's book it "is riddled with false clams...." (p. 234) That said Kessler writes like he hopes to be the administration's voice on the new order.

For an academic explanation of Trump's rise, see, for example, John Sides and Michael Tesler, "How Political Science Helps Explain The Rise of Trump: Most Voters Aren't Ideologues," **The Washington Post**, March 2, 2016 https://www.washingtonpost.com/news/monkey-cage/wp/2016/03/02/how-political-science-helps-explain-the-rise-of-trump-most-voters-arent-ideologues/?utm_term=.0979fcf0d421.

Madeleine Albright **Fascism: A Warning** (New York, 2018) is a brilliant analysis of Trump and others using the barometer of fascism.

There were many interviews from 1980 to 2014 demonstrating Trump had consistent views on foreign policy for almost thirty-five years. For the best of these numerous interviews see the British journalist who went to Trump Tower for a talk, Gaby Wood, "Donald Trump: The Interview," **London Guardian**, January 7, 2007 https://www.theguardian.com/business/2007/jan/07/media.citynews.

For the early years and the friendship in New York with Roy Cohn, see, Frank Rich, "The Original Donald Trump," **New York**, April 30-May 13, 2018, pp. 20-265, 85-86. Rich argues Trump's behavior is so appalling to sophisticated New Yorkers that early in life his friend, Roy Cohn, taught the Donald deportment, good manners and the art of the con. The author attributes Trump ruthless bullying and profane braggadocio to Cohn's mentoring.

The amateur nature of Trump's politics are evident in Michael Tomasky, "We Are Truly Living Through The Amateur Hour Presidency," **The Daily Beast**, May 24, 2018 https://www.thedailybeast.com/we-are-truly-living-through-the-amateur-hour-presidency?ref=author.

See Wayne Barrett, **Trump: The Deals And The Downfall** (New York, 1992) for an excellent book by a **Village Voice** columnist who is critical of New York real estate moguls. Barrett's book chronicles the rise and fall of Trump's real estate empire. His articles concentrate on the 1970s through the 1980s giving insights into Trump's business and political personality.

See an article Trump wrote that tells one all they need to know about how and why he formulated America First, see Donald J. Trump, "There's Nothing Wrong With American Foreign Policy That A Little Backbone Can't Cure," **The New York Times**, September 2, 1987. This article was ignored, as Trump was not thought of as a key figure in future American politics.

On how and why Trump has taken over the Republican Party see the op-ed piece "The Cult of Personality," **The New York Times**, June 8, 2018, p. A-24.

HANNITY AND TRUMP: FOX TV NEWS AS AN ADVISER

For Sean Hannity's too close and too non-critical relationship with Donald Trump, see, for example, Jennifer Bendery, "Sean Hannity Ducks Questions About Trump Support For Iraq War," **Huffington Post**, October 10, 2016 http://www.huffingtonpost.com/entry/sean-hannity-trump-iraq-war_us_57fb1b96e4b068ecb5dfc649.

For a criticism of Hannity's pro Trump support and lack of journalistic ethics, see, for example, Amanda Hoover, "Has Sean Hannity's Trump Support Crossed the Line?" **The Christian Science Monitor**, September 21, 2016. http://www.csmonitor.com/USA/Politics/2016/0921/Has-Sean-Hannity-s-Trump-support-crossed-the-line-video. Also see Dylan Byers, "Sean Hannity Participates In Trump Promotional Video," **CNN Money**, September 21, 2016 http://money.cnn.com/2016/09/20/media/hannity-trump/index.html.

The strangest part of Sean Hannity's support for Trump came when he criticized Glenn Beck for his early views on Trump's candidacy, see, Nick Gass, "Hannity Defends Trump From Glenn Beck," **Politico.com**, August 17, 2015 http://www.politico.com/story/2015/08/sean-hannity-defends-donald-trump-from-glenn-beck-121421.

See a strange article on Fox News, "Sean Hannity Defends Trump Grabbing P*ssy: King David Had 500 Concubines," **Raw History.com**, October 9, 2016 http://www.rawstory.com/2016/10/sean-hannity-defends-trump-grabbing-pssy-king-david-had-500-concubines/ and Laura Clawson, "Sean Hannity Won't Reveal His Pillow Talk With Trump About Iraq War," **The Daily Kos**, October 10, 2016 http://www.dailykos.com/story/2016/10/10/1580378/-Sean-Hannity-won-t-reveal-his-pillow-talk-with-Trump-about-Iraq-war.

TRUMP'S LACK OF QUALIFICATIONS, POWER AND RESTRAINT

On Trump's lack of qualifications for the presidency see Chris Edelson, "Opinion: Donald Trump's Worldview, Rules Apply to Other People Not Me," **Market Watch.com**, October 20, 2016 http://www.marketwatch.com/story/donald-trumps-worldview-rules-apply-to-other-people-not-me-2016-10-20?siteid=rss&rss=1 Also see Chris Edelson, **Power Without Constraint: The Post 9-11 Presidency And National Security** (Madison, 2016) for changes in the nature of presidential power in the aftermath of 9-11 and Chris Edelson, **Emergency Presidential Power: From The Drafting of The Constitution To The War on Terror** (Madison, 2013).

For a U. S. Senator who from day one has opposed Trump, see Aaron Blake, "Kirsten Gillibrand Has Voted Against Almost All of Donald Trump's Nominees. 2020 Anyone?" **The Washington Post**, January 25, 2017 https://www.washingtonpost.com/news/the-fix/wp/2017/01/25/kirsten-gillibrand-has-voted-against-almost-all-of-donald-trumps-nominees-2020-anyone/?utm_term=.0fc8a0b5f22b.

See Robert D. Kaplan, **The Return Of Marco Polo's World: War, Strategy And American Interests In The Twenty-First Century** (New York, 2018) for a geo-political look at present day foreign policy.

TRUMP'S OVERSTATEMENT, PSYCHOLOGY

The literature surrounding Trump's penchant for overstatement suggests his mercurial personality and behavior, see, for example, David Sable and Will Johnson, "Trump's New Problem: He's, Becoming A Bore," **CNN.com, October** 19th, **2016** http://www.cnn.com/2016/10/18/opinions/trump-brand-becoming-boring-sable-johnson/index.html.

The psychological side of Trump is revealed in Michael Barbaro, "What Drives Trump? A Fear of Fading Away," **The New York Times**, October 26, 2016 pp. A-1, 20. There are two excellent articles on Trump, Ryne A. Sherman, "The Personality Of Donald Trump," **Psychology Today**, https://www.psychologytoday.com/blog/the-situ Ghaation-lab/201509/the-personality-donald-trump and Nassar Ghaemi, "Not Narcissistic, But Not Normal," **Psychology Today** October 23, 2016 https://www.psychologytoday.com/comment/878136. Also see Henry Alford, "Is Donald Trump Actually A Narcissist? Therapists Weigh In!" **Vanity Fair**, November 11, 2015 http://www.vanityfair.com/news/2015/11/donald-trump-narcissism-therapists.

On Trump's bullying see, for example, Greg Sargent, "In the End, Trump's Bullying And Misogyny May Seal His Doom," **The Washington Post**. November 3, 2016 https://www.washingtonpost.com/blogs/plumline/wp/2016/11/03/in-the-end-trumps-bullying-and-misogyny-may-seal-his-doom/ and "In Campaign Appearance, Melania Trump Vows to Take on Cyberbullying As First Lady," http://www.sun-sentinel.com/news/politics/ct-melania-trump-cyberbullying-20161103-story.html

The best stories on Trump's National Security Adviser and his controversial background and firing by President Obama are Richard Wolffe, "Michael Flynn Will Be A Disaster As National Security Adviser," **The London Guardian**, November 19, 2016 https://www.theguardian.com/commentisfree/2016/nov/19/michael-flynn-will-be-a-disaster-as-national-security-adviser and Matthew Rosenbert, Julie Hirschfeld Davis and Maggie Haberman, "Trump Is Said To Pick General As Security Aide," **The New York Times**, November 18, 2016, p. A-1, A-17.

TRUMP THE FAILURES OF LIBERALISM AND POST 9-11 U. S.
The rejection of liberalism is examined in Mark Lilla, "The End of Identity Liberalism," **The New York Times**, September 20, 2016, pp. SR-1, SR-6. Also see two books by, Mark Lilla, **The Shipwrecked Mind: On Political Reaction** (New York, 2016) and **The Reckless Mind: Intellectuals In Politics** (New York, 2001, revised edition 2016).

On the decline, failures and redefined liberalism see, for example, Roger Cohen, "The Death of Liberalism," **The New York Times**, April 14, 2016 http://www.nytimes.com/2016/04/14/opinion/the-death-of-liberalism.html?_r=0.

A controversy over the failures and future of liberalism emerged after the Trump victory. For this debate see, for example, Nick Bryant, "Was The Summer of Liberalism Really The Dawn of Trump," **BBC News**, November 16, 2016 http://www.bbc.com/news/world-us-canada-37994898. Also see, Ross Douthat, "Can Trumpism Survive A Trump Administration?" **The New York Times**, November 16, 2016 http://www.nytimes.com/2016/11/16/opinion/can-trumpism-survive-a-trump-administration.html?rref =collection%2Fcolumn%2Fross-douthat&action=click&contentCollection=opinion&region=stream&module=stream_unit&version=latest&contentPlacement=2&pgtype=collection.

The failure of liberalism is a theme many see as the reason for Trump's election, for this view see, for example, Preteek Sibal, "Why Trump's Election Is A Failure of Liberalism," **The Huffington Post**,

November 11, 2016 http://www.huffingtonpost.in/prateek-sibal/why-trumps-election-is-a-failure-of-liberalism/. The most brilliant book on the failures of liberalism is Richard Rorty, **Achieving Our Country: Leftist Thought In Twentieth-Century America** (Cambridge, 1999, reprint 2016).

Contributing to the failures of liberalism were those in the Tea Party, as well as the voter who was shunned or forgotten. For a look at Tea Party voters who felt alone see, Arlie Russell Hochschild, **Strangers In Their Own Land: Anger And Mourning On The American Right** (New York, 2016). Hochschild spent five years researching the Tea Party and the book was a finalist in the nonfiction category for the National Book Award. As a Sociology Professor at the University of California, Berkeley, Hochschild spent years studying the human emotions which lead to political shifts and changes in attitudes. Her work is important in drawing a link between private thoughts and troubles and social-political issues in the political arena.

For the post-Trump political world see, E. J. Dionne Jr, Norman J. Ornstein and Thomas E. Mann, **One Nation after Trump: A Guide For The Perplexed, The Disillusioned, The Desperate, And The Not Yet Deported** (New York, 2017). This book has a list of suggestions for those attempting to change the Trump phenomenon but the authors point out he is not going away. As eighty percent of his base still supported him, the Dionne volume went to press. Also see Hillary Rodham Clinton, **What Happened?** (New York, 2017) for her clear explanation why she lost the 2016 election. Katy Tur, **Unbelievable** (New York, 2017) is the work of a journalist who covered the Trump campaign and was frequently singled out and personally attacked by the candidate. Tur, an NBC news correspondent, points out how difficult it is to be objective when you are drawn in the vortex of the campaign. Her book is a hidden gem written in a popular style but Tur has depth and critical observations.

ASPECTS OF A TROUBLING FOREIGN POLICY

For the August 2017 Phoenix speech see Matt Taibbi, "The Madness of Donald Trump," **Rolling Stone**, October 5, 2017, issue 1297, pp. 32-39. The Taibbi article highlights the violent nature of Trump campaign rallies.

The new foreign policy and the direction it is taking in the present day is covered in Reuben Fischer-Baum and Julie Vitkovskaya, "How Trump Is Changing American Foreign Policy," **The Washington Post**, October 27, 2017 https://www.washingtonpost.com/graphics/2017/world/trump-shifting-alliances/?utm_term=.5117eb785ed1. This is an excellent article covering the successes, the failures and the partial achievements of Trump's foreign policy. The authors provide a time line for successful events and concomitant failures.

Also see problems on Trump's leadership or lack of it in Amy Zegart, "Trump Isn't The Only Problem With Trump's Foreign Policy," **The Atlantic**, October 25, 2017 https://www.theatlantic.com/international/archive/2017/10/the-complexities-of-foreign-policy/543891/.

For a view of how Steve Bannon and Stephen Miller gained new prominence after Trump's Poland trip see, for example, Michael Crowley, "Trump Nationalists Triumph After Poland Trip." **Politico**, July 8, 2017 https://www.politico.com/story/2017/07/08/trump-nationalists-bannon-europe-g20-240325. For a brutal critique of Bannon's influence see Martin Amis, "Pax Americana," **Esquire**, November, 2017, pp. 110-115, 122-123. Also see the in-depth analysis on the insiders' book on Trump, Aaron Blake, "What In The World Was Bannon Thinking, 3 Theories," **The Washington Post**, January 4, 2018 https://www.washingtonpost.com/news/the-fix/wp/2018/01/04/what-in-the-world-was-steve-bannon-thinking-3-theories/?utm_term=.978a7a80032f. This article is a reaction to Michael Wolff's book.

For praise of Wolff's book by Trump's most perceptive biographer see, Michael D'Antonio, "A Trump Biographer Reviews 'Fire And Fury," **CNN Opinion**, January 7, 2018 http://www.cnn.com/2018/01/05/opinions/much-of-wolffs-trump-book-rings-true-opinion-dantonio/index.html.

For problems of staffing fourteen months into Trump's presidency, see, for example, Debra J. Saunders, "Trump, Democrats Create Logjam In Confirmation of Diplomats-Confirmation," **Las Vegas Review Journal**, April 1, 2018 https://www.reviewjournal.com/news/news-columns/debra-saunders/trump-democrats-create-logjam-in-confirmation-of-diplomats-analysis/.

For Trump's danger to the future of democracy, see, Timothy Snyder, **The Road To Unfreedom: Russia, Europe, America** (New York, 2018). Snyder, the Levin Professor of History at Yale University, places Trump's presidency in the worldwide rise of anti-democratic, authoritarian leaders. For a discussion with Professor Timothy Snyder where he discusses how Trump is systematically downgrading civil liberties and is taking the U. S. down the road to authoritarian rule, see, Chauncey Devega, "Historian Timothy Snyder On Trump's War On Democracy: He Is Deliberately 'Hurting White People," **Salon.com**. May 9, 2018 https://www.salon.com/2018/05/09/timothy-snyder-on-trumps-campaign-against-democracy-he-is-deliberately-hurting-white-people/.

To understand the Cold War and the role of American diplomacy in a memoir by a former American ambassador see Michael McFaul, **From Cold War To Hot Peace: An American Ambassador In Putin's Russia** (New York, 2018). This is a thoughtful and broad analysis of the shift in U. S. foreign policy since Trump took over the presidency.

TRUMP'S CABINET AND ADVISORY WHACKOS: CARTER PAGE

For Rick Perry's strange fossil fuel story and his strange remarks in Africa, see Gail Collins, "Rick Perry's Strange Sex Story," **The New York Times**, November 4, 2017, p. A-22.

On Carter Page's strange foreign policy interaction see, Alan Nehauser, "Page: Trump Campaign Knew About Russia Contacts," **U. S. News & World Report**, November 7, 2017 https://www.usnews.com/news/national-news/articles/2017-11-07/page-top-trump-campaign-officials-knew-about-russia-contacts. Also see Jason Zengerle, "What (If Anything) Does Carter Page Know?" **The New York Times Magazine**, December 24, 2017, pp. 24-27. Also see Zola Ray, "Former Trump Adviser Failed Ph. D. Exam Twice, Blamed Anti-Russian Bias Report," **Newsweek**, December 26, 2017 http://www.newsweek.com/trump-carter-page-russian-phd-757793?yptr=yahoo.

See Todd Gitlin and Steven E. Halliwell, "Carter Page's Multimillion-Dollar Dream," **The Daily Beast.com**, March 26, 2018 https://www.thedailybeast.com/carter-pages-multimillion-dollar-dream.

For an early article on the mystery of Carter Page, see Mirren Gidda, "Who Is Carter Page And Why Is the FBI Surveilling Him?" **Newsweek**, April 12 2017 http://www.newsweek.com/carter-page-fbi-surveillance-us-presidential-election-russia-donald-trump-583066. For a Fox News defense of Page see, Kaitlyn Schallhorn, "Carter Page: Who Is He And How Is He Linked To Trump?" **Fox News**, February 6, 2018 www.foxnews.com/politics/2018/02/06/carter-page-who-is-and-how-is-linked-to-trump.html.

For a Republican insiders who allegedly approved Page's Russia trips, see, Andrew Prokop, "Carter Page's Bizarre Testimony To The House Intelligence Committee, Explained," **Vox.com**, November 7, 2017 https://www.vox.com/policy-and-politics/2017/11/7/16616912/carter-page-testimony-trump-russia.

Also see the in-depth analysis by Ken Dilanian and Mike Memoli, "Who Is Carter Page And What Does He Have To Do With The Russia Probe?" **Nbcnews.com**, February 5, 2018 https://www.nbcnews.com/politics/donald-trump/who-carter-page-what-does-he-have-do-russia-probe-n844821.

The inability to figure out Page's role in the Trump campaign is analyzed in Julia Ioffe, "The Mystery of Trump's Man In Moscow," **Politico.com**, September 23, 2016. For the alleged charge Page might be a spy see, Christina Maza, "Trump Campaign Aide Carter Page May Have Been Russian Agent, Justice Department Believed, According To Nunes Memo," **Newsweek**, January 29, 2018 http://www.newsweek.com/trump-campaign-aide-carter-page-may-have-been-russian-agent-justice-department-793554.

An allegation the FBI misuses the FISA warrants and how this applies to Carter Page is "The House Memo, The FBI And FISA," **The Wall Street Journal**, January 31, 2018, p. A-14. For a spirited and in-depth defense of the FBI securing the FISA warrant, see Philip Bump, "What We Know About The Warrant To Surveil Carter Page," **The Washington Post**, January 3,1 2018, https://www.washingtonpost.com/news/politics/wp/2018/01/31/what-we-know-about-the-warrant-to-surveil-carter-page/?utm_term=.073fcc84a731.

For the total ineptness of Page, see Tessa Stuart, "Carter Page, Man At The Center Of #ReleasetheMemo, Speaks," **Rolling Stone**, January 31, 2018 https://www.rollingstone.com/politics/features/carter-page-man-at-the-center-of-releasethememo-speaks-w516062. Also see, Terence Cullen, "Carter Page Reportedly Boasted About Ties To Moscow In 2013 Letter," **New York Daily News**, February 4, 2018 http://www.nydailynews.com/news/politics/carter-page-reportedly-boasted-ties-moscow-2013-letter-article-1.3798398?utm_source=feedburner&utm_medium=feed&utm_campaign=Feed%3A+nydnrss%2Fnews%2Fnational+%28News%2FNational%29&utm_content=Yahoo+Search+Results.

For Carter Page's anonymity, see David Corn, "Republican Congressman Leading Russia Probe Says He Never Heard Of Key Figure In The Scandal," **Mother Jones**, March 20, 2017 https://www.motherjones.com/politics/2017/03/devin-nunes-intel-committee-says-never-heard-of-roger-stone-carter-page/.

The Russian bank branch in New York, VEB, has long been a front for Kremlin espionage, see, Alec Luhn, "Moscow Condemns Arrest of 'Spy' Yevgeny Buryakov As 'Anti-Russian Move," **London Guardian**, January 27, 2015 https://www.theguardian.com/world/2015/jan/27/moscow-condemns-arrest-yevgeny-buryakov-spy.

In the aftermath of his appearances before Congressional committees and his notoriety see, for example, Paul Sperry, "Carter Page: The FBI Ruined My Life," **New York Post**, May 26, 2018 https://nypost.com/2018/05/26/carter-page-the-fbi-ruined-my-life/. Also see, Katie Leach, "Carter Page Blames FBI For Problems In His Life," **Washington Examiner**, May 26, 2018 https://www.washingtonexaminer.com/news/carter-page-blames-fbi-for-problems-in-his-life.

For corruption in the Trump Cabinet see, Paul Krugman, "Corruption Hits The Small Time," **The New York Times**, June 8, 2018, p. -25.

CLIMATE CHANGE, FAILURES AND CRITIQUES OF TRUMP

On climate change and its dangers politically see, Daniel B. Baer et. al, "Why Abandoning Paris Is A Disaster For America," **Foreign Policy**, June 1, 2017 http://foreignpolicy.com/2017/06/01/why-abandoning-paris-climate-agreement-is-bad-for-america-trump/. For Trump's advisers statement on climate change see, H. R. McMaster and Gary Cohn, "America First Doesn't Mean America Alone," **The Wall Street Journal**, May 30, 2017 https://www.wsj.com/articles/america-first-doesnt-mean-america-alone-1496187426.

For the end of the G-20 and Trump on climate change see, for example, Nicola Slawson, "G-20 Summit: 'G-19' Leaves Trump Alone In Joint Statement on Climate Change-As It Happened," **The London Guardian**, July 8, 2017 https://www.theguardian.com/world/live/2017/jul/08/g20-summit-may-meets-world-leaders-in-bid-to-boost-brexit-trade-prospects.

The lobbying in the U. S. prior to Trump withdrawing from the Paris Climate Accord is analyzed in Ben Wolfgang, "Conservatives Pressure Trump To Dismiss Moderate Voices, Scrap Paris Climate Accord," **The Washington Post**, April 18, 2017 https://www.washingtontimes.com/news/2017/apr/18/future-paris-climate-deal-hangs-balance-white-hous/?cache.

For Secretary Mattis's support for climate change and why he is the only Cabinet member supporting it, see, Andrew Revkin, "Defense Secretary James Mattis Breaks With Other Cabinet Members

On Climate Change," **Huffington Post**, March 15, 2017 https://www. huffingtonpost.com/entry/james-mattis-climate-change_us_58c92f8ae4b01c029d77a713.

A year after Trump threatened withdrawal from the Paris Climate Accord **The New York Times** op-ed editorial "The Silver Lining of Leaving Paris," June 2 2018 argued cities and states increased efforts at climate control, thereby making the U. S. environment a safer one.

DIVERSE CRITICS OF TRUMP'S FOREIGN POLICY

After a year in office many have weighed in on Trump's foreign policy and the reaction is uniformly negative but with grudging admissions of fleeting successes. For the best article with this direction, see, for example, Stephen Sestanovich, "The Brilliant Incoherence of Trump's Foreign Policy," **The Atlantic**, May 2017 https://www.theatlantic.com/magazine/archive/2017/05/the-brilliant-incoherence-of-trumps-foreign-policy/521430/.

For a strong critique of the forces threatening American intelligence see Michael V. Hayden, **The Assault On Intelligence: American National Security In An Age of Lies** (New York, 2018). General Hayden after retiring from the U. S. Air Force was a former Director of the National Security Agency, and he continued to teach and write about foreign policy. He is able to take the issues of cyber intrusion, information warfare and Trump's comments to illustrate the danger to American national security. Hayden's comments on Sheriff Joe's pardon suggested his feeling Trump had little concern with the "rule of law." Also see James R. Clapper, **Facts And Fears: Hard Truths From A Life In Intelligence** (New York, 2018) for a look inside the intelligence community from the fourth U. S. Director Of National Intelligence.

See CNN sometimes contributor Amanda Carpenter's. **Gaslighting America: Why We Love It When Trump Lies To Us** (New York, 2018) for an in-depth look by a veteran of GOP politics who has some doubts about the veracity of the present political situation. Gaslighting, according to John Dean, is deviant political behavior. That is the charm of this well written and wonderfully argued book.

For an excellent and in depth academic critique arguing the contradictions of Trump's foreign policy and why they are dangerous to the future of U S. diplomatic relations see, Daniel W. Drezner,

"Why Donald Trump's Foreign Policy Ambitions Will Always Collapse," **The Washington Post**, November 13, 2017 https://www.washingtonpost.com/news/posteverything/wp/2017/11/13/why-donald-trumps-foreign-policy-ambitions-will-always collapse/?utm term=.5eadfa392b79.

For Trump's pre-election scandals, see, David A. Graham, "The Many Scandals of Donald J. Trump A Cheat Sheet," **The Atlantic**, January 23, 2017 https://www.theatlantic.com/politics/archive/2017/01/donald-trump-scandals/474726/.

The professionals, both academic and in the U S. State Department, offer a dim view of Trump's foreign policy, see, for example, Max Boot, "Trump's Worst Trip Ever. Until His Next One," **Foreign Policy**, November 14, 2017 https://foreignpolicy.com/2017/11/14/trumps-worst-trip-ever-until-his-next-one/. Max Boot is a conservative writer, a lifelong Republican and his articles on Trump's foreign policy are outstanding. Also see Max Boot, "Time Is Up For Tillerson," **Foreign Policy**, August 23, 2017 http://foreignpolicy.com/2017/08/23/time-is-up-on-rex-tillerson/.

For the lack of historical knowledge in foreign affairs by the president see Robin Wright, "Why Is Donald Trump Still So Horribly Witless About The World?" **The New Yorker**, August 4, 2017 https://www.newyorker.com/news/news-desk/why-is-donald-trump-still-so-horribly-witless-about-the-world/. Also see Stephen Mewl, "The Worst Mistake of Trump's First 100 Days," **Foreign Policy**, April 26, 2017 http://foreignpolicy.com/2017/04/26/the-worst-mistake-of-trumps-first-100-days/.

Brian Klaas, **The Despot's Apprentice: Donald Trump's Attack On Democracy** (New York, 2017) is a defense of the democratic process and a look at the demons driving Trump's presidency. For Trump's anger at the press for reporting his incendiary comments see, James Risen and Sheri Fink, "Trump Said, 'Torture Works,' An Echo Is Feared Worldwide," **The New York Times**, January 5, 2017. Also see Hadas Gold, "Donald Trump: We're Going To Open Up Libel Laws," **Politico**, February 26, 2016. The attack on the press is unprecedented. It will not end soon.

On General Flynn's duplicity in the Russian investigation and his plea deal see, Paul Waldman, "Michael Flynn May Have Just Flipped On Trump. And Evidence That The President May Have Obstructed Justice Is Mounting," **The Washington Post**, December 1, 2017 https://www.washingtonpost.com/amphtml/blogs/plum-line/wp/2017/12/01/michael-flynn-has-flipped-on-trump-and-evidence-that-the-president-may-have-obstructed-justice-is-mounting/. Also see the in-depth article raising key questions about Russia, Adam Serwer, "Flynn's Plea Rises New Questions About Whether Trump Obstructed Justice," **The Atlantic**, December 1, 2017 https://www.theatlantic.com/politics/archive/2017/12/flynns-plea-raises-new-questions-about-whether-trump-obstructed-justice/547328/. Chris Megerian, "Michael Flynn Grew Up Breaking The Rules. It Caught Up To Him As Trump's National Security Advisor," **The Virginia Gazette**, December 1, 2017 http://www.vagazette.com/la-na-pol-flynn-profile-20171201-story.html. On the Russian investigation see Jeffrey Toobin, "The Russian Portfolio," **The New Yorker**, December 11, 2017, pp. 26-32 and Andrew S. Weiss, "What Was Trump's Russia Plan?" **The Wall Street Journal**, December 9-19, 2017, p. C-3.

The influence of Russian Television is shown in Jack Coleman, "Shocker From Ed Schultz: Trump Would Function Very Well As President," **Mrc News Busters**, January 20, 2016 https://www.newsbusters.org/blogs/nb/jack-coleman/2016/01/20/shocker-ed-schultz-trump-would-function-very-well-president/.

To understand presidential power, see, for example, Theodore J. Lowi, **The Personal President: Power Invested, Promise Unfulfilled** (Ithaca, 1985), and Richard Neustadt, **Presidential Power And The Modern Presidents: The Politics of Leadership, Roosevelt To Reagan** (New York, 1990),

On the Berlusconi comparison to Trump, also see, James B. Stewart, "Berlusconi A Precedent For Trump," **New York Times**, December 2, 2016 and Fedja Buric, "Trump's Not Hitler, He's Mussolini: How GOP Anti-Intellectualism Created A Modern Fascist Movement In America," **Salon**, November 3, 2016 https://www.salon.com/2016/03/11/trumps_not_hitler_hes_mussolini_how_gop_anti_intellectualism_created_a_modern_fascist_movement_in_america/. For a harsh view of Trump see, Isaac Chotiner, "Is Donald Trump A Fascist? Yes and No," **Slate**, number 10, February 2016.

On the F agency in the State Department see, Gordon Adams and Robert Goldberg, "Rex Tillerson Is About To Make A Terrible Mistake," **Foreign Policy**, December 14, 2017 and the F Agency home page "Office of U. S. Foreign Assistance Resources," https://www.state.gov/f/.

On Tillerson-Trump differences see John Dawsey and Anne Gearan, "Trump Allies Say Tillerson Has Not Learned His Lesson And Cannot Continue In Job For Long," **The Washington Post**,

December 14, 2017, and Krishnadev Calamur, "Tillerson Acknowledges Differences With Trump On Iran Deal," **The Atlantic**, August 1, 2017 https://www.theatlantic.com/news/archive/2017/08/tillerson-iran-jcpoa/535602/. and Krhishnadev Calamur, "Their Final Disagreement: How Trump Fired Tillerson," **The Atlantic**, March 13, 2018 https://www.theatlantic.com/international/archive/2018/03/rex-tillerson-firing-timeline/555464/.

For Trump's humiliation at the 2011 White House Correspondents' Dinner see, Adam Gopnik, "Trump And Obama: A Night To Remember," **The New Yorker**, September 12, 2015 https://www.newyorker.com/news/daily-comment/trump-and-obama-a-night-to-remember. For a different view of the 2011 dinner see, Roxanne Roberts, "I Sat Next To Donald Trump At The Infamous 2011 White House Correspondents' Dinner," **The Washington Post**, April 28, 2016 https://www.washingtonpost.com/lifestyle/style/i-sat-next-to-donald-trump-at-the-infamous-2011-white-house-correspondents-dinner/2016/04/27/5cf46b74-0bea-11e6-8ab8-9ad050f76d7d_story.html?utm_term=.13ced75c3f88. Roberts is critical of the Gopnik piece suggesting that the 2011 dinner had little, if anything, to do with his campaign for the presidency. Also see Emma Lake, "Donald's Revenge: Barack Obama's Searing 2011 Public Humiliation of Donald Trump Was The Moment He Decided To Run For President," November 20, 2016 https://www.thesun.co.uk/news/2150292/barack-obamas-searing-2011-public-humiliation-of-donald-trump-was-the-moment-he-decided-to-run-for-president/.

The **Sun** is one of London's sensationalist newspapers with little basis in fact. Also see Nikki Schwab, "Did Trump Decide To Run When Obama Mocked Him As A Birther Conspiracy Theorist At White House Dinner?" **London Daily Mail**, September 22, 2016 http://www.dailymail.co.uk/news/article-3802949/Did-Trump-decide-run-Obama-mocked-birther-conspiracy-theorist-White-House-dinner.html. Also see Amy B.Wang, "It was Fantastic: Trump Denies 2011 White House Correspondents' Dinner Spurred Presidential Bid," **The Washington Post**, February 28, 2017 https://www.washingtonpost.com/news/arts-and-entertainment/wp/2017/02/26/did-the-2011-white-house-correspondents-dinner-spur-trump-to-run-for-president/?utm_term=.c0076dc61d69.

Philip Klinkner a Professor at Hamilton College, has a number of papers and publications suggesting how race, conspiracy theories, a rethinking of the civil rights movement and a demagogue can erase or at least slow down racial progress. Klinkner holds an endowed chair at Hamilton college and for his views see, for example, **The**

Unsteady March: The Rise And Decline Of Racial Equality In America (Chicago, 2002). This pioneering book suggests the difficulty of achieving racial equality and virtually predicts the rise of a demagogue like Trump. For a view of Klinkner's brilliant scholarship see, for example, see the interview by Michael Knigge, November 18 2011, "Trump's Election Is Evidence Of The Retrenchment of Liberal Values," http://www.dw.com/en/trumps-election-is-evidence-of-the-retrenchment-of-liberal-values/a-36444812. and German Lopez, "Trump Is Still Reportedly Pushing His Racist 'Birther' Conspiracy Theory About Obama," **Vox**, November 29, 2017 https://www.vox.com/policy-and-politics/2017/11/29/16713664/trump-obama-birth-certificate. Klinkner concludes racial resentment is the key to the birther controversy.

For the failure of Trump's diplomacy regarding Syria see, Simon Tisdall, "Trump's Disdain For Diplomacy Is Making The World More Dangerous," **London Guardian**, June 27, 2107 https://www.theguardian.com/us-news/2017/jun/27/donald-trumps-disdain-for-diplomacy-is-making-the-world-more-dangerous. The notion that Trump's advisers are running an alternate foreign policy is hinted at in a **New York Times** editorial. See "A Foreign Policy On Paper Only," **The New York Times**, December 22, 2017. In foreign policy Trump defined his actions as ones that either ignore or skirt around constitutional issues. This is what is known as "an illiberal democracy." In 1997 Fareed Zakaria warned of the potential danger of this impulse and the ironies of this notion in the democratic process. See Zakaria's "The Rise of Illiberal Democracy," **Foreign Affairs**, November/December, 1997 https://fareedzakaria.com/1997/11/01/the-rise-of-illiberal-democracy/. Timothy Snyder goes a step further warning about the dangers of the rise of authoritarianism in the world and the potential future of Trump's authoritarian personality in the American political process. See Timothy Snyder, "The Reichstag Warning," **The New York Review of Books**, March 26, 2017. It is Snyder's view that government must promote both freedom and safety. This explains why Trump is a dangerous president. He values safety over freedom. That attitude is the death knell of democracy. For the dangers of Trump's economic nationalism see Scott Horsley, "Trump's 'America First' Agenda Marks Sharp Break In U. S. Economic Policy," **National Public Radio**, February 28, 2017 https://www.npr.org/2017/02/28/517565701/trumps-america-first-agenda-marks-sharp-break-in-u-s-economic-policy. Also see David Rothkopf,

"Trump Keeps Making Bad American Foreign Policy Worse," **Los Angeles Times**, January 3, 2018 http://www.latimes.com/opinion/op-ed/la-oe-rothkopf-iran-protests-20180103-story.html. This op-ed piece calls out Trump's tweets, his zig zagging on issues and his failure to establish sound international diplomacy.

To understand how Trump's campaign team was able to disenfranchise African American, Latino and low income voters see, Brian Klaas, **The Despot's Apprentice: Donald Trump's Attack On Democracy** (New York, 2017), pp. 108-118 for how the Trump campaign employed voter suppression in the 2016 election. The key to suppressing votes came in the career of Kris Kobach. For material on how voter suppression influenced the 2016 election, see, Ari Berman, "The Man Behind Trump's Voter Fraud Obsession," **The New York Times Magazine**, June 13, 2017.

For a list of Trump lies see Jane C. Timm, "Trump's Biggest Whoppers of 2017," **NBC New**, December 24, 2017 https://www.nbcnews.com/politics/donald-trump/trump-s-biggest-whoppers-2017-n830746. For Greg Phillips see, Vann R. Newkirt II, "Trump's Favorite Voter-Fraud Activist Hedges His Claims," **The Atlantic**, January 31, 2017 https://www.nbcnews.com/politics/donald-trump/trump-s-biggest-whoppers-2017-n830746https://www.nbcnews.com/politics/donald-trump/trump-s-biggest-whoppers-2017-n830746.

For perspective on Trump's lies, see, the op-ed editorial, "Mr. Trump's War On The Truth," **The New York Times**, April 6, 2018, p. A-22.

ASPECTS OF TRUMP'S FOREIGN POLICY AND THE STEELE DOSSIER

For a book looking to the future of American foreign policy, see Paul B. Stares, **Preventive Engagement: How America Can Avoid War, Stay Strong And Keep The Peace** (New York, 2017). Paul Krugman, "America Is Not Yet Lost," **The New York Times**, December 26, 2017, p. A-24, analyzes the future of America and Trump's danger to it in an editorial. Also see another editorial "Donald Trump's Dangerous Plan To Destabilize Democracy," **The Washington Post**, October 14, 2016 https://www.washingtonpost.com/opinions/donald-trumps-dangerous-ploy-to-destabilize-democracy/2016/10/14/105ca4f4-9225-11e6-9c52-0b10449e33c4_story.html?utm_term=.7508cd9a9c22.

On Trump and mercantilism, see, for example, Hernando de Soto, "The Real Enemy For Trump Is Mercantilism, Not Globalism," **The Wall Street Journal**, November 2, 2016 https://www.wsj.com/articles/the-real-enemy-for-trump-is-mercantilism-not-globalism-1480279192. There is extensive literature on Trump pursuing a mercantile course of action in foreign policy.

Also see, Daniel Hoffman, "The Steele Dossier Fits The Kremlin Playbook," **The Wall Street Journal**, January 29, 2018, p A-17 for the conservative view of how damaging Russian intelligence was to the American political process.

See Natasha Bertrand, "Carter Page's Testimony Is Filled With Bombshells-And Supports Key Portions of The Steele Dossier," **Business Insider**, November 6, 2017 http://www.businessinsider.com/carter-page-congressional-testimony-transcript-Steelee-dossier-2017-11.

After almost fifteen moments in office a career diplomat looks at Trump's foreign policy, see, Ken Borsuk, "Former Ambassador Blasts Trump's Foreign policy In Greenwich Talk," **New Canaan News**, April 4, 2018 https://m.newcanaannewsonline.com/local/article/Former-ambassador-blasts-Trump's-foreign-policy-12806151.php.

For an argument that Fusion was an unwitting accomplice to the problems of the Steele Dossier, see Rowan Scarborough, "Fusion GPS C0-Founer 'Framed' In Production of Anti-Trump Dossier, Russian Lawyer Says," **The Washington Post**, pril 23 2018 https://m.washingtontimes.com/news/2018/apr/23/natalia-veselnitskaya-says-fusion-gps-co-founder-g/.

For Glenn Simpson's testimony see the House Permanent Select Committee on Intelligence, U. S. House of Representatives, November 14, 2017. Also see Jane Mayer, "Christopher Steele: The Man Behind The Dossier," **The New Yorker**, March 12, 2018 and Tom Hamburger and Rosalind Helderman, "Hero Or Hired Gun? How A British Former Spy Became A Flash Point In The Russian Investigation," **The Washington Post**, February 6, 2018. Also see David Corn, "A Veteran Spy Has Given The FBI Information Alleging A Russian Operation To Cultivate Donald Trump," **Mother Jones**, October 31, 2016.

Also see in the Steele Dossier, "Russia/U. S. Presidential Election: Further Indications of Extensive Conspiracy Between Trump Campaign Team And The Kremlin," Company Intelligence Report 2016/095, BuzzFeed posting. Also see, Massimo Calabresi and Alana

Abramson, "Carter Page Touted Kremlin Contacts in 2016 Letter," **Time,** February 4, 2018 and David Corn, "A Veteran Spy Has Given The FBI Information Alleging A Russian Operation To Cultivate Donald Trump," **Mother Jones**, October 31, 2016.

See the material from Pages House testimony, "The Testimony of Carter Page, The Permanent Select Committee on Intelligence," U. S. House, November 14, 2017 https://intelligence.house.gov/uploadedfiles/carter_pae_hpsci_hearing_transcipt_nov_2_2017.

For the Iranian nuclear deal see the liberal pro-Obama article by Steven Simon and Jonathan Stevenson, "Europe Should Stand Up To Trump," **The New York Times**, May 11, 2018, p. A-27. Also see, Mark Landler, "Trump Abandons Iran Nuclear Deal He Long Scorned," **The New York Times**, May 8, 2018 https://www.nytimes.com/2018/05/08/world/middleeast/trump-iran-nuclear-deal.html. and Saeed Kamali Dehghan, "What Is the Iran Deal And Why Does Trump Want To Scrap It?" **London Guardian**, May 9, 2018 https://www.theguardian.com/world/2018/may/08/iran-nuclear-deal-what-is-it-why-does-trump-want-to-scrap-it.

For Senator John McCain's role in securing a copy of the Steele Dossier and sharing it with the FBI see, John McCain and Mark Salter, **The Restless Wave: Good Times, Just Causes, Great Fights And Other Considerations** (New York, 2018) Like Comey's memoir, McCain sees little of value in the Trump presidency.

As Trump met Vladimir Putin at the G-20 there was a great deal of reporting on his top Russian insiders with ties to the Kremlin would place their intelligence agency, the FSB, in a compromising position due to help from key insiders with the Steele Dossier. For this complicated story see, Amy Knight, "Putin's Intelligence Crisis," **The New York Review of Books**, February 3, 2017, http://www.nybooks.com/daily/2017/02/03/putin-intelligence-crisis-trump-dossier-fsb/.

See the revealing information of how Russia twisted support away from the Clinton candidacy and swung the election to Trump in Timothy Snyder, "On Tyranny: Lessons From The Twentieth Century," June 17, 2017 lecture at the International Festival Of Arts And Ideas, New Haven, Connecticut, You Tube, June 17, 2017 https://www.youtubme.com/watch?v=_4T9aGYoONU. Also see the intriguing ideas in David Becker, "What We Know And Don't Know About Election Hacks In 2016," Center For Election Innovation and Research, June

6, 2016 https://www.electioninnovation.org/news/2017/6/6/what-we-know-and-doon't-know-abut-electio n-hacks-in-20165.

BASHING WOLFF, DEFENDED BY THE WSJ

Trump bashing reached a high point with the publication of Michael Wolff's **Fire And Fury: Inside The Trump White House** (New York, 2018). The Wolff volume claims to have interviewed 200 sources. Most of the material is difficult to verify and many top level Trump people disavowed the book. Despite the criticism, it is well done, and there are elements of truth in the prose. Trump's behavior and the inherent dysfunction in the White House are documented. An excellent book but read it with caution. See Summer Meza, "Top 20 Revelations From Trump 'Fire and Fury' Book About Golden Showers, Ivanka, Bannon and More," **Newsweek**, January 3, 2018 http://www.newsweek.com/top-20-revelations-trump-fire-and-fury-book-about-golden-showers-ivanka-bannon- 769899?utm_source=yahoo&utm_medium=yahoo_news&utm_campaign=rss-related&utm_content=/rss/ yahoous/news.

An analytical piece suggesting the quick publication of Wolff's book may have not been vetted is Callum Borchers, "How Did Michael Wolff's 'Fire and Fury' Get Past A Fact Checker? It's Not Clear That The Book Was Vetted," **The Washington Post**, January 9, 2018 https://www.washingtonpost.com/news/the-fix/wp/2018/01/09/how-did-michael-wolffs-fire-and-fury -get-past-a-fact-checker-its-not-clear-that-the-book-was-vetted/?utm_term=.928b56be65cf.

Also see, Angie Drobnic Holan, "A Fact-Checker's Guide To Michael Wolff's 'Fire And Fury: Inside The Trump White House'," **Politfact.com**, January 9, 2018 http://www.politifact.com/truth-o-meter/article/2018/jan/ 09/fact-checking-read-fire-and-fury-michael-wolff/.

For the **Wall Street Journal's** defense of Trump see the op-ed piece "Fusion's Russia Fog" **Wall Street Journal**, January 4, 2018, p. A-16. This op-ed piece attacks the research firm for its role in the Steele Dossier. This is part of a conservative, right wing mantra to question the credibility of the Mueller investigation. Also see the editorial "Fusion's Russian Dirty Work," **Wall Street Journal**, January 29, 2018, p. A-16. https://www.washingtonpost.com/news/the-fix/wp/2018/01/09/how-did-michael-wolffs-fire- and-fury-get-past-a-fact-checker-its-not-clear-that-the-book-was-vetted/?utm_term=.e546c21c9427.

On the people in his Cabinet and the idea that he would hire the best, for an article refuting this idea, see, Debra J. Saunders, "New

Book Shows Trump Falling Short On Vow To Hire Best People," **Las Vegas Review Journal**, January 5, 2018, https://www.reviewjournal.com/news/news-columns/debra-saunders/new-book-shows-trump-falling-short-on-vow-to-hire-best-people-analysis/.

The Saunders article is a review of the Michael Wolff book, and she agrees the best people were not appointed to key positions. For background material on Michael Wolff see, for example, Katie Reilly, "Who Is Michael Wolff? What To Know About The Author Of The Explosive New Trump Book," **Time**, January 5, 2018 https://www.yahoo.com/news/michael-wolff-know-author-explosive-195028765.html. The notion of money laundering is a key point in Wolff's book. For an analysis of this question see, Timothy O'Brien, "Bannon's Big Reveal In New Trump Books Is All About Money Laundering," **Chicago Tribune**, January 5, 2018.

See James Warren, "How Michel Wolff Stuck A Shiv In Donald Trump," **Vanity Fair**, January 4 2018 https://www.vanityfair.com/news/2018/01/how-michael-wolff-stuck-a-shiv-in-donald-trump. The Warren article is a hilarious one comparing Trump and Wolff's ego as well as stating how and why the book emerged. The sensational quotes and some far-fetched claims suggest Wolff and Trump deserved each other.

NORTH KOREA, MENTAL HEALTH AND TRUMP'S SUCCESSES
The explosive North Korea situation and the taunts between Trump and Kim Jong Un are analyzed in Peggy Noonan, "Button It, Mr. President," **The Wall Street Journal**, January 6-7, 2018, p. A-11. Noonan makes the point there is not an adult in the exchanges between the American and North Korean leaders.

On Trump's mental health see Jason Silverstein, "Trump Might Have Dementia, ADHD or Learning Disabilities, 'Fire And Fury' Author Michael Wolff Says," **Newsweek**, January 7, 2018 https://uk.news.yahoo.com/trump-might-dementia-adhd-learning-134022590.html. Also see, Bandy Lee's, **The Dangerous Case of Donald Trump: 27 Psychiatrists and Mental Health Experts Assess A President** (New York, 2017).

For Trump's successes in foreign policy and hope for the future see, for example, David Gordon and Michael O'Hanlon, "President Trump's Twitter-Fueled Foreign Policy: Not As Bad As You Might Think," **VC Star**, January 5, 2018 http://www.vcstar.com/story/opinion/2018/01/05/president-trumps-report-card-foreign-policy-not-bad-might-think-michael-ohanlon-david-gordon-column/1004880001.

Also see General John Allen and Michael O'Hanlon, "Donald Trump Makes Right Move In Afghanistan: General John Allen and Michael O'Hanlon," **VC Star**, August 22, 2017 http://www.vcstar.com/story/opinion/2017/08/22/trumps-afghanistan-moves-will-prevent-new-terror-safe-haven-column/588142001/.

See David Brooks, "The Decline of Anti-Trumpism," **The New York Times**, January 8, 2018 https://mobile.nytimes.com/2018/01/08/opinion/anti-trump-opposition.html. for an interesting analysis of his tweets, the operations of the Oval Office and how this impacts government.

Some of the nations surrounding Russia approve of Trump's foreign policy. Estonia is one of these nations, see Michael Kelemen, "Estonian President Says She Is More Confident About Trump Administration's Foreign Policy," **National Public Radio**, April 4, 2018 https://www.npr.org/2018/04/04/599579239/estonian-president-says-she-is-more-confident-about-trump-administrations- (START)foreig?ft=nprml&f.

AUTOCRACY AND IMMIGRATION
Masha Gessen, "One Year After Trump's Election, Revisiting 'Autocracy': Rules For Survival," **The New Yorker**, November 8, 2017 https://www.newyorker.com/news/our-columnists/one-year-after-trumps-election-revisiting-autocracy-rules-for-survival. This article presents a quirky set of rules to survive an autocrat in office. The Gessen piece makes a case for Trump's autocratic behavior, and he brilliantly suggests how to cope with it. Also see Keren Yarhi-Milo, "After Credibility: American Foreign Policy In The Trump Era," **Foreign Affairs**, January-February, 2018, pp. 68-77.

See David Leonhardt, "Trump Tries To Destroy The West," **The New York Times**, June 11, 2018, p. A-19 for the manner in which Trump's autocratic behavior destroys relations with our close allies.

For Trump's immigration "shithole" comment see Ed O'Keefe, Erica Werner and Josh Dawsey, "Immigration Talks Founder After White House Rejects Deal and Trump Insults Foreign Countries," **The Washington Post**, January 12, 2018 https://www.washingtonpost.com/politics/talks-on-a-potential-immigration-deal-continue-with-deep-skepticism-on-both-sides/2018/01/11/d9f53ae8-f6cd-11e7-a9e3-ab18ce41436a_story.html?tidr=a_breakingnews&utm_term=.0e4cfed3201b.

For more on Trump's "shithole" comment see, Julie Hirschfeld and Sheryl Gay Stolberg, "In Vulgar Terms, Trump Disparages Some Immigrants," **The New York Times**, January 12, 2018, p. A-1, A-13 and Zach Schonfeld, "Trump's 'Shithole' Comment And The New

Era of Newspapers Publishing Profanity," **Newsweek**, January 11, 2018 http://www.newsweek.com/shithole-donald-trump-new-york-times-african-immigation-779041. The **Newsweek** article is interesting for analyzing how the media will use a word to focus a story. "Shithole," said **Newsweek** replaced last week's word, which was Trump's description of himself as "a stable genius." American newspapers are now deciding what is and what is not proper in publishing to illustrate a story. The operative word is that more profanity is in the major newspapers. "We've reached out to a **New York Times** spokesperson," **Newsweek** remarked "regarding the decision to use the term 'shithole' in the article on Thursday." They decided to use the term. Dean Baquet, **Newsweek's** executive editor, said that the term "shithole" gave "full credence" to the president's remarks. They were outrageous.

For the authoritarian voter see Marc J. Hetherington and Jonathan D. Weiler, **Authoritarianism And Polarization in American Politics** (Cambridge, 2009). This is a study identifying the authoritarian voter. Long before Trump appeared on the political landscape these two distinguished political scientists discovered that rather than issues there was a voter who voted due to personality. If this voter had a choice between issued and such appeals as "a strong candidate," a politician who talked in "simple language" and approached issues in a "black and white moralistic tone." he or she would ignore the issues. Trump appeals to this authoritarian voter. The result is the polarization of American politics. See Steven Levitsky and Daniel Ziblatt, **How Democracies Die** (New York, 2018) for a study by two Harvard political scientists on how Trump and his minions are altering the course of American democracy. David Cay Johnston, **It's Even Worse Than You Think: What The Trump Administration Is Doing To America** (New York, 2018) is a brilliant analysis of the manner in which Trump is taking advantage of the presidency for personal gain while systematically altering the state of government. Some say he is dismantling the basic structure of American government. The chapter on Trump's August 2017 Phoenix rally in which the message was the president is above the law demonstrates the danger to the future of American democracy.

RACE, APOLOGISTS AND THE DEMAGOGUE

For Trump's racial attitudes see Marc Fisher, "Trump And Race: Decades of Fueling Divisions," **The Washington Post**, August 16, 2017 https://www.washingtonpost.com/politics/trump-and-race-decades-of-fueling-divisions/2017/08/16/5fb3cd7c-8296-11e7-b359-15a3617c767b_story.html?utm_term=.f3832c7bf4ca.

For Trump's comments to the **Washington Post** editorial board, see Eugene Robinson, "Donald Trump's Shocking Ignorance, Laid Bare," **The Washington Post**, March 24, 2016 https://www.washingtonpost.com/opinions/donald-trumps-shocking-ignorance-laid-bare/2016/03/24/b66d2b6c-f1f7-11e5-89c3-a647fcce95e0_story.html?utm_term=.4d7f6483cb06. For a scathing review of Trump's demagoguery see Michael Gerson, "Trump Is The Demagogue That our Founding Fathers Feared," **The Washington Post**, March 10, 2016 https://www.washingtonpost.com/opinions/trump-is-the-demagogue-that-our-founding-fathers-feared/2016/03/10/58584278-e6df-11e5-b0fd-073d5930a7b7_story.html?utm_term=.1e95638f93f0.

For a leading Trump apologist's view of the presidency, see, Corey R. Lewandowski and David N. Bossie, **Let Trump Be Trump: The Inside Story of His Rise To The Presidency** (New York, 2017). Lewandowski is a particularly arrogant and name-calling individual who testified to Congress that they could basically kiss his ass. His book reflects that lack of intellectual viewpoint. Lewandowski is typical of the amateur in politics who has risen to the top.

On Trump's lack of historical knowledge, his unwillingness to read, and his misuse of Andrew Jackson's legacy as well as other blatant historical mistakes, see, James Johnson and Karen Tumulty, "Trump Cites Andrew Jackson As His Hero-And A Reflection of Himself," **The Washington Post**, March 15, 2017 https://www.washingtonpost.com/politics/trump-cites-andrew-jackson-as-his-hero--and-a-reflection-of-himself/2017/03/15/4da8dc8c-0995-11e7-a15f-a58d4a988474_story.html?utm_term=.81d8570316a4. and Adam Edelman, "President Trump Questions Why Civil War Happened, Thinks Andrew Jackson Would have Prevented It-Why Was There The Civil War?" **New York Daily News**, May 2, 2017 http://www.nydailynews.com/news/politics/trump-thinks-andrew-jackson-prevented-civil-war-article-1.3122527.

See Vegas Tenold, **Everything You Love Will Burn: Inside The Rebirth of White Nationalism In America** (New York, 2018). This book is an interesting look at how and why white nationalists brought Trump to the presidency. For an academic look at the problems of violent extremism for youth, see the academic study by Michael

447

Kimmel, **Healing From Hate: How Young Men Get Into-And Out Of-Violent Extremism** (Berkeley, 2018) Also see, Charles J. Sykes, **How The Right Lost Its Mind** (New York, 2017) for a mid-western conservative talk show host who laments the rise of Trump.

Masha Gessen, "In The Trump Era, We Are Losing The Ability To Distinguish Reality From Vacuum," **The New Yorker**, May 25 2018 https://www.newyorker.com/news/our-columnists/in-the-trump-era-we-are-losing-the-ability-to-distinguish-reality-from-vacuum?mbid=nl_Daily%20052618&CNDID=52975370&spMailingID=13586914&spUserID=MjU3MjMyMjI3NTIxS0&spJobID=1402348413&spReportId=MTQwMjM0ODQxMwS2. The Gessen article is a tour de force in pointing out how to survive and protect the U. S. from Trump's machinations and willingness to blow up American democracy. Also see, Dahlia Lithwick, "How To Survive Trump's Presidency Without Losing Your Mind," **Slate.com**. May 14, 2018 https://slate.com/news-and-politics/2018/05/how-to-survive-trumps-presidency-without-losing-your-mind.html.

THE 1990 PLAYBOY INTERVIEW, PARIS AND STABILITY

For Trump's 1990 Playboy interview see, Elena Holodny, "Trump's 1990 Playboy Interview Perfectly Lays Out His View Of the World." **Business Insider**, February 11, 2017 https://finance.yahoo.com/news/trumps-1990-playboy-interview-perfectly-134400506.html and see how this interview laid out his plans to win the presidency in Michael Barbaro, "Between Playboy's Pages, A Peek At How A Future Donald Trump Would Campaign," **The New York Times**, March 31, 2016 https://www.nytimes.com/2016/04/01/us/politics/donald-trump-playboy-interview.html.

The **Playboy** interview had a second life; see, for example, Adam Chandler, "Why Foreign Leaders Read Trump's 1990 Playboy Interview," **The Atlantic**, March 18, 2017 https://www.theatlantic.com/international/archive/2017/03/trump-playboy-merkel/520014/. Also see, Cleve R. Wootson Jr., "Donald Trump Was Proud of His 1990 Playboy Cover. Hugh Hefner, Not So Much," **The Washington Post**, September 28, 2017 https://www.washingtonpost.com/news/arts-and-entertainment/wp/2017/09/28/donald-trump-was-proud-of-his-1990-playboy-cover-hugh-hefner-not-so-much/?utm_term=.6faa41e160c6.

For Trump's description of himself as a "very stable genius" see David Nakamura, "Trump Boasts That He's 'Like, Really Smart' And A 'Very Stable Genius' Amid Questions Over Mental Fitness," **The**

Washington Post, January 6, 2018 https://bangordailynews.com/2018/01/06/news/nation/trump-boasts-that-hes-like-really-smart-and-a-very-stable-genius-amid-questions-over-mental-fitness/.

For Trump's visit to Paris for Bastille Day, see, for example, Jonathan Miller, "Donald Trump and Emmanuel Macron Are Alike In Their Narcissism," **The Spectator**, July 15, 2017 https://blogs.spectator.co.uk/2017/07/donald-trump-and-emmanuel-macron-are-alike-in-their-narcissism/. Also see, Jonathan Miller, **France: A Nation On The Verge Of A Nervous Breakdown** (Gibson Square, 2015). For an in-depth analysis of Bastille day, see, Angelique Chrisafis, "Donald Trump To Visit Paris For Bastille Day Ceremonies," **London Guardian**, June 28, 2017 https://www.theguardian.com/world/2017/jun/28/donald-trump-to-visit-paris-for-bastille-day-ceremonies. Also, see, Angelique Chrisafis, "Donald Trump to Visit Paris For Bastille Day Ceremonies," **London Guardian**, June 28, 2017 https://www.theguardian.com/world/2017/jun/28/donald-trump-to-visit-paris-for-bastille-day-ceremonies and Angelique Chrisafis, "Trump Downplays Differences With France On Climate Change," **London Guardian**, July 13, 2017 https://www.theguardian.com/world/2017/jul/13/donald-trump-greeted-with-military-fanfare-in-paris. See Rachel Lewis, "President Trump Is Visiting Paris on Bastille Day. Here's Why That Matters," **Time**, July 12, 2017 http://time.com/4854413/bastille-day-2017-donald-trump-macron-france-paris/.

RUSSIA, COLLUSION AND DEFENDING TRUMP

For Donald Trump Jr. see, for example, Michelle Ye Hee Lee, "Timeline: Donald Trump Jr.'s Contradictory Statements About Russia Meeting," **The Washington Post**, July 21, 2017 https://www.washingtonpost.com/news/fact-checker/wp/2017/07/21/timeline-donald-trump-jr-s-contradictory-statements-about-the-russia-meeting/?utm_term=.629bf1b3c995 and Chris Baynes, "British Publicist Who Arranged Donald Trump, Jr.'s Meeting With Russian Lawyer Breaks Silence on Collusion," **The Independent**, November 19, 2017 http://www.independent.co.uk/news/world/americas/us-politics/british-publicist-arranged-donald-trump-jr-meeting-russian-lawyer-breaks-silence-rob-goldstone-a8063371.html.

An interesting analysis of why Trump is not involved in Russian collusion is Jonah Goldberg, "Let's Get Real: Trump Is No Mastermind. Secretly colluding Isn't In His Skill Set," **Los Angeles Times**, February 20, 2018 http://www.latimes.com/opinion/op-ed/la-oe-goldberg-russia-theories-20180220-story.html.

Also see Mythili Sampathkumar, "Russian Lawyer Who Met With Trump Jr. 'Shared Talking Points With Kremlin Beforehand',"

London Independent, October 27, 2017 http://www.independent.co.uk/news/world/americas/us-politics/trump-jr-russia-meeting-lawyer-kremlin-links-natalia-veselnitskaya-reports-a8024151.html.

Mark Moore, "Bannon: Trump Jr. Meeting With Russians Was 'Treasonous'," **New York Post**, January 3, 2018 https://nypost.com/2018/01/03/bannon-trump-jr-meeting-with-russians-was-treasonous/.

Luke Harding, **Collusion: Secret Meetings, Dirty Money And How Russia Helped Donald Trump Win** (New York, 2017) is a brilliant book forecasting much of what happened after its publication. Also see, Joshua Holland, "Luke Harding on Trump, Russia And Collusion," **The Nation**, December 11, 2017 https://www.thenation.com/article/luke-harding-on-trump-russia-and-collusion/. Also see, Michael Isikoff and David Corn, **Russian Roulette: The Inside Story of Putin's War On America and the Election of Donald Trump** (New York, 2018). The Isikoff-Corn argument points to collusion from those close to Trump with key Russian businessmen and people close to Putin and the Kremlin. Also see Timothy Snyder, **The Road To Unfreedom: Russia, Europe, America** (New York, 2018) for a study of how Vladimir Putin's strategy of attacking democracy, rivals like the European Union and extending Russia's influence in Ukraine and other satellite nations. The end result is fascism. Snyder argues Donald J. Trump and Marine Le Pen are part and parcel of Putin's strategy.

On Trump and Qatar see, Mark Landler, "Trump Take Credit For Saudi Move Against Qatar, a U. S. Military Partner," **The New York Times**, June 6, 2017 and Nicole Gaouette and Ryan Browne, "Trump Reverses Course in Qatar Call," **CNN.com**, June 8, 2017 https://www.cnn.com/2017/06/07/politics/trump-qatar-call/index.html Also see Anne Applebaum, "Trump's Bizarre And Un-American Visit To Saudi Arabia," **The Washington Post**, May 21, 2017 https://www.washingtonpost.com/news/global-opinions/wp/2017/05/21/trumps-bizarre-and-un-american-visit-to-saudi-arabia/?utm_term=.0a214b99c2fc.

Robert Kagan, **The World America Made** (New York, 2013) is the work of a conservative writer working in a liberal political think tank. It is a brilliant examination of the importance of the U. S.'s global leadership in maintaining the ideals of unbridled capitalism and responsible democracy. For support of Trump's withdrawal from world affairs by two well respected conservative academics see, Daniel Quinn Mills and Steven Rosenfelt, **The Trump Phenomenon And The**

Future of U. S. Foreign Policy (London, 2016). The Mills-Rosenfelt book labels Obama's foreign policy "feckless" and labels Secretary of State John Kerry, "a bully." Daniel Quinn Mills is a Professor Emeritus at the Harvard Business School and his assessment of Trump is an interesting defense of Trump's foreign policy.

Steven Rosenfeld, **Democracy Betrayed: How Superdelegates, Redistricting, Party Insiders, And The Electoral College Rigged The 2016 Election** (New York, 2017) for a veteran journalists view of the present political situation. For the alt-right see David Neiwert, **Alt America: The Rise of The Radical Right In The Age of Trump** (New York, 2017). For a conservative columnists view of Trump's first year see Eliot A. Cohen, "Trump's Lucky Year: Why The Chaos Can't Last," **Foreign Affairs**, March-April, 2018, pp. 2-9. Also see Adam S. Posen, "the Post-American World Economy: Globalization In The Trump Era," **Foreign Affairs**, March-April 2018, pp. 10-19.

For defenses of Trump's foreign policy see, for example, Aaron Blake, "Trump's Madman Approach To North Korea Is Getting Real Credit," **The Washington Post**, March 6, 2018 https://www.washingtonpost.com/news/the-fix/wp/2018/03/06/trumps-madman-approach-to-north-korea-is-getting-real-credit/?utm_term=.91eb84447129 and Daniel Drezner, "Is President Trump's Foreign Policy Better Than We Think?" **The Washington Post**, January 9, 2018 https://www.washingtonpost.com/news/posteverything/wp/2018/01/09/is-president-trumps-foreign-policy-not-as-bad-as-we-think/?utm_term=.c23ceb1ac425.

See Thomas Frank, "Four More Years: The Trump Reelection Nightmare And How We Can Stop It," **Harper's**, April, 2018, pp. 23-32 for an essay pointing out how and why Trump was elected. Frank's does a brilliant job showing how liberals have failed and how they restructure their political approach for the 2020 election.

Tessa Stuart, "Adam Schiff's Russia Crusade," **Rolling Stone**, June 14-28, 2018, pp. 35-37 is an excellent piece on how Schiff is the ranking Democrat on the House Permanent Select Committee on Intelligence working to convince the Republicans to investigate Trump. "The Republicans on the Intel Committee viewed their jobs differently than I did," Schiff continued. "They viewed their job as defending the president."

TRUMP'S ATTEMPTS TO CENSOR
BIOGRAPHIES AND STORMY DANIELS

The number of law suits, threats, intimidation and outright agreements to limit biographies, studies of his finances and those who write about him politically are many and varied. For the best examples of how he attempts to censor Trump studies when Ivana accused him of violence during their divorce, see, for example, Brady Zadrozny and Tim Mak, "Ex-Wife: Donald Trump Made Me Feel 'Violated' During Sex," **The Daily Beast**, July 27, 2017 https://www.thedailybeast.com/ex-wife-donald-trump-made-me-feel-violated-during-sex and the story where Trump's lawyer unsuccessfully attempted to bully Ivana Tanya Basu, "Donald Trump Lawyer Sorry For 'Saying You Can't Rape Your Wife," **Time**, July 28, 2015 http://time.com/3974560/donald-trump-rape-ivana-michael-cohen/. The best biography of Trump is by Pulitzer Prize winning journalist David Cay Johnson, **The Making of Donald Trump** which is 288 pages of things you didn't want to know about Trump and his business tactics.

For bulling by Trump's lawyers see the op-ed editorial "All The President's Thugs," **The New York Times**, March 28, 2018, p. A-22. For Stormy Daniels see, Maria Perez, "Trump And Stormy Daniels Had Sex Four Months After Melania Gave Birth, Adult Film Star Claims," **Newsweek**, January 17, 2018 http://www.newsweek.com/president-donald-trump-stormy-daniels-affair-melania-trump-783790.

Elise Viebeck, "Stormy Daniels Attorney Predicts Michael Cohen Will 'Flip,' Cooperate With Federal Prosecutors," **The Washington Post**, April 30, 2018 https://www.msn.com/en-us/news/politics/stormy-daniels-attorney-predicts-michael-cohen-will-'flip'-cooperate-with-federal-prosecutors/ar-AAwv8nW?li=BBnbcA1. Also see Maria Solis, "Michael Avenatti Says It's 'Outrageous' To Suggest Stormy Daniels Can't Be Defamed Because She's An Adult Film Actress," **Newsweek**, May 1, 2018 https://uk.news.yahoo.com/michael-avenatti-says-apos-apos-140214367.html.

For an early attempt to understand the Russia issue see Angela Dewan and Kara Fox, "Trump And Russia: What The Fallout Could Be," **CNN.com**. March 22, 2017. This article early on examines what the authors call the "murky web of ties and contacts to Russia."

THOSE FIRED BY TRUMP

For the changes in the Veteran's Administration see, "Fired VA Secretary Blasts 'Toxic' DC in Op-Ed," **Cumberland Times-News**, March 29, 2018 http://www.times-news.com/cnhi_network/david-shulkin-out-as-secretary-of-veterans-affairs/article_6ec9efb5-48be-594b-9d80-f942ea05206e.html.

See David J. Shulkin, "A Move That Will Hurt Veterans," **The New York Times**, March 30, 2018, p. A-21. On Tom Price's resignation and the curious circumstances behind hit, see, Juliet Eilperin, Amy Goldstein and John Wagner, "HHS Secretary Tom Price Resigns Amid Criticism For Taking Charter Flights At Taxpayer Expense," **The Washington Post**, September 29, 2017 https://www.washingtonpost.com/news/post-politics/wp/2017/09/29/trump-to-decide-friday-night-whether-to-fire-hhs-secretary-price/?utm_term=.d9a5d6d034e0.

BOOKS AND ARTICLES FROM TRUMP'S DEFENDERS AND FOX TV BASED AUTHORS

There is a genre of books that are Fox TV News based apologies for and defenses of Trump. For the media and how it treats Trump see, Howard Kurtz, **Media Madness: Donald Trump, The Press, And The War Over The Truth** (Washington, 2018). See Newt Gingrich, **Understanding Trump** (New York, 2018) for the former Speaker's well-written comments on how to deal with the unexpected president.

Jerome Corsi, **Killing The Deep State: The Fight To Save President Trump** (West Palm Beach, 2018) is a defense of Trump and an indictment of the deep state short on facts, devoid of responsible research and writing in the style of a PhD carving a manuscript from stone tables. Tim Scott and Trey Gowdy, **Unified: How Our Unlikely Friendship Gives Us Hope For A Divided Country** (Carol Stream, 2018) is a surprisingly solid piece of work on our current political malaise. It is the only intelligent look at the conservative, pro-Trump view. In chapter 3 there is an attempt to place the shootings in Charleston in perspective, and to analyze it. This is the books highpoint.

See Victor Davis Hanson, "Donald Trump: Tragic Hero" **National Review**, April 30, 2018, pp. 13-15 for an article arguing his flaws may actually be strengths. The author defends authoritarian and violent means of implementing governmental reform. The movie **The Magnificent Seven** is a used as a metaphor for change. He sees Trump as a tragic hero who can't operate in "a polite society." This is, of course, an excuse for his roughish behavior.

For an over the top right wing argument against the media from a Trumpster using history in a convoluted and precarious manner see Rodney Howard-Browne, **The Killing of Uncle Sam: The Demise of the United States of America** (River Publishing, 2018). The author holds a Phd in philosophical theology and he is the author of fifteen books all of which have a religious, contrarian bent. He is an excellent writer with the message that Muslims, the Mafia, the CIA and a host of other wackadoodle influences are taking the United States down to road to hell. He is a founder of Revival Ministries International and a voice for conservative Christianity in the world. His views on politics are extreme and Trumpian. His book is well written.

Andrew F. Puzder, **The Capitalist Comeback: The Trump Boom And The Left's Plot To Stop It** (New York, 2018) is by a Trump appointee and former CEO of CKE Restaurants. It is a hit piece on Hillary Clinton, liberalism, any form of government regulations and a paean to private enterprise capitalism.

For the conspiracy minded see Theodore Roosevelt Malloch, **The Plot To Destroy Trump: How The Deep State Fabricated The Russian Dossier To Subvert The President** (New York, 2018) Roger Stone wrote the forward and this book is well written. The conclusions, however, are what one would suspect as the author presents pages of documents purported to prove those inside our government systematically attempted to destroy Trump's presidency. One of the supreme ironies of this book is Malloch discusses American meddling in other countries election.

Salena Zito and Brad Todd, **The Great Revolt: Inside The Populist Coalition Reshaping American Politics** (New York, 2018) is an attempt to "delve into the minds and hearts" of those who voted for Trump. It is a well-researched, well-written and thoughtful look at why the Donald became the 45th president. The authors believe Trump's victory is only the beginning of populist reforms.

HILLARY CLINTON AND THE 2016 ELECTION
AND ASSORTED LIBERAL BOOKS

See Lanny J. Davis, **The Unmaking of The President 2016: How FBI Director James Comey Cost Hillary Clinton The Presidency** (New York, 2018) for a slanted Democrats view of the election. Amy Chozick, **Chasing Hillary: Ten Years, Two Presidential Campaigns And One Intact Glass Ceiling** (New York, 2018) for the definitive account of how and why Clinton lost the presidency. The Chozick book is a delightful one as the author battles her feminist side with the elector process and this creates one of the best books on Clinton. It is an inside look into Hillary Clinton that allows one to understand the candidate and the journalist chasing her in the light of the women's movement.

In order to understand Hillary Clinton's thinking and her relationship and interaction with Vladimir Putin, see, Hillary Clinton, **Hard Choices** (New York, 2014). For a wonderful liberal, hilarious book on those who attacks liberals by a veteran reporter see, Amanda Marcotte, **Troll Nation: How the Right Became Trump-Worshipping Mobsters Set On Ratf8cking Liberals, America, And Truth Itself** (New York, 2018). Also see Alexander Zaitchik, **The Gilded Rage: A Wild Ride Through Donald Trump's America** (New York, 2018). The blind resentment of conservatism runs rampant through Marcotte and Zaitchik's look at the horror of recent American politics.

See Bernie Sanders, **Our Revolution: A Future To Believe In** (New York, 2016) for key issues important to understanding the 2016 election. For the view of Sanders' campaign manager see, Jeff Weaver, **How Bernie Won: Inside The Revolution That's Taking Back Country-And Where We Go From Here** (New York, 2018).

Is the U. S. headed toward tyranny? That is the question posed by Professor Timothy Snyder. The Yale University Professor in a short book **On Tyranny: Twenty Lessons From The Twentieth Century** (New York, 2017). The answer to Professor Snyder's timely book is that liberal democracy is in peril. The threats daily from President Trump to jail Hillary Clinton, to have a U. S. Senator from Montana resign because he criticized a poor choice for appointive office or that Amazon should be taxed more for using the U. S. postal service—

these threats are contrary to a civilized, liberal democracy. Things have gone wrong. They need to be fixed.

See Jon Meacham, **The Soul of America: The Battle for Our Better Angels** (New York, 2018) for a brilliant analysis by a Pulitzer Prize winning historian on how and why character, integrity and leadership matter in American history. By looking back at how presidents and citizens combine to "defeat the forces of anger, intolerance and extremism."

The background necessary to understanding the evolution of Trump's foreign policy see, for example, Steven W. Hook and John W. Spanier, **American Foreign Policy Since World War II** (Los Angeles, 2018, 21st edition). This is the standard textbook on American foreign policy providing the material necessary to placing Trump's foreign policy in the context of diplomacy since 1945. Also see Daniel W. Drezner, "My Three Must Read U. S. Foreign Policy Books For Aspiring Politicians," **Foreign Policy**, May 3, 2011 http://foreignpolicy.com/2011/05/03/my-three-must-read-u-s-foreign-policy-books-for-aspring-politicians/.

The Drezner article is brilliant. He suggests why and how politicians fail in foreign policy. The three books he suggests all politicos read tell one a great deal about how American foreign policy should operate but often doesn't because of ignorance, lazy politicians and a disregard for the world. See Walter Russell Mead, **Special Providence** (Milton Park, Abingdon, 2002) for an examination of American foreign policy in the aftermath of 9/11. He links the sweep of American history to foreign affairs suggesting there were four areas of world affairs. First, the Hamiltonian period in which the goals were to further American commercial interests. Second, the Wilsonian area in which the goal was the creation of international organizations such as the League of Nations, the United Nations and the World Court would create an international order. Third, the Jeffersonian school which attempted to minimize foreign entanglements and to avoid potential foreign conflicts. Fourth, the Jacksonian school which emphasizes little in the way of policy and more in the way of patriotism. Jackson believed that war should not be limited and the U. S. would fight to a clear victory using all of its resources. He also believes in a different set of rules and standards in the diplomatic area.

Drezner offers David Halberstam's **The Best And The Brightest** (New York, 1993, Anniversary edition) for Democrats and James Mann, **Rise Of the Vulcans** (New York, 2004) for Republicans. Both sides, says Drezner, can benefit from past party mistakes by reading these books. Finally, Drezner concludes Richard Neustadt and Ernest R. May, **thinking In Time: The Uses of History For Decision-Makers** (New York, 1988) provides a roadmap for proper diplomatic decisions.

ACKNOWLEDGEMENTS

A book on a developing scandal, a mysterious story of collusion with Russia, an election won by a candidate who received almost three million votes more than the winner and a terrifying, lying bully who went beyond good taste and established political norms to create an American government high jacked by old, white, billionaires. The story sounds like a piece of fiction. Unfortunately, it is reality. American democracy is strong and resilient. This is why this book is necessary. It is a reflection, hopefully with some scholarly analysis with a pop writing direction, and the hope is years later historians will see a few grains of truth in this book.

The genesis of this book was a 2017 European trip where I happened to be when President Trump arrived, spoke and made his pitch for America First. I watched first hand as the locals shuddered at this duplicity and lack of transparency. I read the local press and I was horrified by the reaction to the Trump agenda. Then the question of Russian collusion and the decline in personal rights indicated there was more to the story than foreign policy. While diplomacy and Trump's notion of foreign affairs is central to the book, equally important is the threat to institutions, the rise of fascism and the egregious manner in which Trump has changed the political landscape.

The daily changes in the news, real and imagined, the continued investigation of the Special Counsel Mueller, the war between the press and President Trump the changes in the Democratic party and the division in the electorate make this book my most difficult. There is no formula for perfect writing. As a forty year veteran as a history and political science professor I have come to realize a writer is only as good his the material. That said, I have quoted sources that run more than fifty pages in the selected bibliography. The attempt is to foster as many different opinions, theories, and in the process to be fair to all sides. That said it is difficult to defend Donald J. Trump. This lays out the facts and they are interpreted to let the reader know Trump is the most ill-suited, most ill prepared and most ill-tempered president in American history.

Trump Against The World: Foreign Policy Bully, Russian Collusion does three things. First, it shows the degree of inexperience, lack of training, amateur moves in diplomacy and the isolation from world affairs during Trump's first sixteen months in the Oval Office. Second, there are many people under the radar of mainstream players in the Trump presidency and they make up a significant portion of this book. Third, the systematic dismantling of the federal government infrastructure, the attack on the media and First Amendment and the disregard for the rule of law makes trump and his followers a threat to democracy. This book addresses that issue and suggests why in accordance with select Russian influences trump marched into the Oval Office.

The writing of dedicated, professional journalists, the reporting of major television outlets, the flood of books and the biographies and academic studies form the core of this book. I have also spent hundreds of hours in coffee shops in America talking politics. I was in Paris for Bastille Day witnessing the majesty of Trump's trip and I used Freedom of Information requests to fill in key points. The release of House and Senate investigations and **Buzzfeed** publishing the Steele Dossier helped a great deal. My PhD in American Foreign Policy from the University of Arizona provided tools to analyze the disparate points of view in recent American foreign policy.

Writers have a tendency to describe their craft as a solitary pursuit. In reality, it takes many people to create a political book. I am indebted to quite a few individuals, and I would like to express my deep appreciation and gratitude to all of the people who aided me in this process. They include many people who responded to questions and I wish to thank all of them. The writings of Daniel W. Drezner, Peter Schweizer, Luke Harding, Laurence Tribe, Dan Pfeiffer, David Cay Johnston, Howard Kurtz, David Frum, Robert Kagan, Michael Wolff, Steven Pinker. Max Boot, Michael Isikoff, David Corn, Jeffrey Toobin, Robert Kagan, Steven Levitsky and David Cole helped to fill out key points.

The problem writing about contemporary politics is one handicapped by a lack of interviews. Most people will not talk about key points in government. As a result TV journalists provide a window into Trump and his administration. Among the best of these sources are Brian Williams, Katy Tur, Don Lemon, Anderson Cooper, Fareed Zakaria, Jake Tapper, Major Garrett, Chris Cuomo and Lester Holt.

Reports from the House Intelligence Committee were an important source. Buzzfeed published the Steele Dossier and the salacious document when fact checked has an eighty percent validity.

There were a number of important investigative journalists who were kind to answer my questions. They requested anonymity as did House and Senate staffers.

The words of those not interviewed provide insights through their writings and articles-books and interviews, while appearing as talking heads on CNN, MSNBC, Bloomberg, ABC, NBC, CBS, Fox News, Fox Business and even at times Congressional testimony. They include Glenn Simpson, Jeanine Pirro, Sean Hannity, Chris Matthews, Fareed Zakaria, Chris Wallace, Jake Tapper, and a host of others.

The confidential or anonymous sources run over one hundred since this book took shape in the early months of 2016. To write a book about a dysfunctional, unqualified president and a potential Russian scandal while the investigation continues is a difficult task. All facts, opinions and conclusions were buttressed with two sources and most of the time five or six sources were embedded in the story.

Buzzfeed released the Steele Dossier and former FBI chief James Comey's testimony before the Senate Select Intelligence Committee on June 8, 2017 helped to straighten out the narrative.

Finally, I would like to recognize Scott A. (Copy Editor, Illustrator and Cover Designer), for his invaluable contribution in producing the finished product and for all of his technical assistance in the final stages of preparation. I appreciate it and you have made the book much better. Thank you Scott! *All other errors and content mistakes are the product of the author.*

About The Author

Howard A. DeWitt is Professor Emeritus of History at Ohlone College, Fremont, California. He received his B. A. from Western Washington State University, the M. A. from the University of Oregon and a PhD from the University of Arizona. He also studied at the University of Paris, Sorbonne and the City University in Rome. Professor DeWitt is the author of twenty-five books and has published over 200 articles and more than 200 reviews in a wide variety of popular and scholarly magazines.

DeWitt has also been a member of a number of organizations to promote the study of history. The most prestigious is the Organization of American Historians where he was a reviewer for a decade.

For more forty-five years he has taught full and part time at a number of U. S. colleges' is best known for teaching two college level courses in the History of Rock n Roll music. He continued to teach the History of Rock and Roll music on the Internet until 2011. In a distinguished academic career, he has also taught at the University of California, Davis, the University of Arizona, Cochise College and Chabot College. In addition to these teaching assignments, Professor DeWitt was a regular speaker at the Popular Culture Association annual convention and at the National Social Science Association meetings. He has delivered a number of addresses to the Organization of American Historians.

DeWitt is an award nominated writer. His 2017 book **Searching or Sugar Man II: Coming From Reality, Heroes and Villains** was a finalist for the best pop music book by the Association for Recorded Sound Collections. This was DeWitt's eleventh book on rock music.

He wrote the first book on Chuck Berry, which was published by Pierian Press under the title **Chuck Berry: Rock N Roll Music** in 1985. DeWitt's earlier brief biography, **Van Morrison: The Mystic's Music**, published in 1983, received universally excellent reviews. On the English side of the music business DeWitt's, **The Beatles: Untold Tales**, originally published in 1985, was picked up by the Kendall Hunt Publishing Company in the 1990s and is used regularly in a wide variety of college courses on the history of rock music. Kendall Hunt also published **Stranger in Town: The Musical Life of Del Shannon** with co-author Dennis M. DeWitt in 2001. In 1993's **Paul McCartney: From Liverpool To Let It Be** concentrated on the Beatle years. He also co-authored **Jailhouse Rock: The Bootleg Records of Elvis Presley** with Lee Cotten in 1983. His two books on Sixto Rodriguez are benchmark studies of the record business and how it is difficult for obscure performers from collecting their royalties.

DeWitt is working with Ken Burke on a study of Gary S. Paxton, Kim Fowley and how they had success despite the music industry.

Professor DeWitt's many awards in the field of history include founding the Cochise County Historical Society and his scholarship has been recognized by a number of state and local government organizations. DeWitt's book, **Sun Elvis: Presley In The 1950s**, published by Popular Culture Ink was a finalist for the Deems-ASCAP Award for the best academic rock and roll book. His first book on Sixto Rodriguez was] a finalist for a Michigan Notable Book Award.

In his research for any and all of his books, Professor DeWitt employs the Gay Talese method interviewed everyone around and connected to his project

Professor DeWitt is a renaissance scholar who publishes in a wide variety of outlets that are both academic and popular. He is one of the few college professors who bridge the gap between scholarly and popular publications. His articles and reviews have appeared in **Blue Suede News, DISCoveries, Rock 'N' Blues News**, the **Journal of Popular Culture**, the **Journal of American History, California History**, the **Southern California Quarterly**, the **Pacific Historian, Amerasia**, the **Western Pennsylvania Historical Magazine**, the **Annals of Iowa**, the **Journal of the West, Arizona and the West,** the **North Beach Review, Ohio History**, the **Oregon Historical Quarterly**, the

Community College Social Science Quarterly, **Montana: The Magazine of the West**, **Record Profile Magazine**, **Audio Trader**, the **Seattle Post-Intelligencer** and **Juke Box Digest**.

For forty plus years DeWitt has combined popular and academic writing. He has been nominated for numerous writing awards. His reviews are combined with articles to form a body of scholarship and popular writing that is frequently footnoted in major works. As a political scientist, Professor DeWitt authored three books that questioned American foreign policy and its direction. In the Philippines, DeWitt is recognized as one of the foremost biographers of their political leader Jose Rizal. His three books on Filipino farm workers remain the standard in the field.

During his high school and college years, DeWitt promoted dances in and around Seattle, Washington. Such groups as Little Bill and the Bluenotes, Ron Holden and the Playboys, the Frantics, the Wailers and George Palmerton and the Night People among others played at such Seattle venues as the Eagle's Auditorium and Dick Parker's Ballroom.

Howard and his wife Carolyn have two grown children. Darin is a Professor of Political Science at California State University, Long Beach and Melanie is a Special Education teacher with two children Natalia and Katarina. They both live in Los Angeles. Howard's wife of forty-seven plus years, Carolyn, is an educator, an artist and she continues to raise Howard. She is presently retired and vacationing around the world. The DeWitt's live in Scottsdale, Arizona. That is when they are not in Paris looking for art, books and music. Howard is working on a book on Portugal's Secrets. That is a year or two away.

His book on the president **Obama's Detractor's: In The Right Wing Nut House** is a marvelous look at the radical right and the tragedy of Fox TV News, right wing book authors and political kooks like Laura Ingraham and Ann Coulter. His novels **Stone Murder** and **Salvador Dali Murder** feature a San Francisco P.I. Trevor Blake III and a gay mobster Don Gino Landry, and much of the story line will evolve around crimes that DeWitt witnessed while working four years and two days as an agent with the Bureau of Alcohol, Tobacco and Firearms. He was a street agent for the BATF and his tales of those years are in manuscript waiting for publication. He was also a key figure in the BATF Union.

Meeting Hitler: A Tragicomedy, published in 2016 was a best seller with excellent reviews. In 2017 **Sicily's Secrets: The Mafia, Pizza and Hating Rome** was a number one best seller for travel books on Amazon. DeWitt is working on a like-minded book on Portugal.

Any corrections or additions to this or the subsequent volumes that will follow this study can be sent to Horizon Books, P. O. Box 4342, Scottsdale, Arizona 85258. DeWitt can be reached via e-mail at Howard217@aol.com.